Building After Auschwitz

Jewish Architecture and the Memory of the Holocaust

Gavriel D. Rosenfeld

Yale University Press New Haven and London

Published with assistance from the Alisa and Peter Savitz Foundation; the College of Arts and Sciences, Fairfield University; the Lucius N. Littauer Foundation; and the foundation established in memory of Amasa Stone Mather of the Class of 1907, Yale College.

Copyright © 2011 by Gavriel D. Rosenfeld.
All rights reserved.
This book may not be reproduced, in whole or in part, including illustrations, in any form (beyond that copying permitted by Sections 107 and 108 of the U.S. Copyright Law and except by reviewers for the public press), without written permission from the publishers.

yalebooks.com

Designed by Jena Sher
Set in type by Amy Storm
Printed in China by Regent Publishing Services Limited

Library of Congress Cataloging-in-Publication Data
Rosenfeld, Gavriel David, 1967–
 Building after Auschwitz : Jewish architecture and the memory of the Holocaust / Gavriel D. Rosenfeld.
   p. cm.
 Includes bibliographical references and index.
 ISBN 978-0-300-16914-0 (cloth : alk. paper) 1. Architecture, Modern—20th century. 2. Architecture, Modern—21st century. 3. Holocaust, Jewish (1939–1945), and architecture. 4. Judaism and architecture. 5. Jews—Identity. I. Title. II. Title: Jewish architecture and the memory of the Holocaust.
 NA680.R655 2011
 724'.6089924—dc22   2011009738

A catalogue record for this book is available from the British Library.

This paper meets the requirements of ANSI/NISO Z 39.48 – 1992 (Permanence of Paper).

10 9 8 7 6 5 4 3 2 1

Jacket illustrations: *(front)* Manuel Herz, Synagogue and Jewish Community Center, Mainz, Germany, 1999–2010. Photo by Stefan Nink; *(back)* Max Abramovitz, United Nations Headquarters, New York (fig. 48).

Building After Auschwitz

Contents

vi   Preface

1   Introduction
13   **Part One. Jewish Architecture Before the Holocaust**
15   1. From the Wilderness to World War II: A Brief History of Jewish Architecture

41   **Part Two. After the Holocaust: Jewish Architecture in the Era of Modernism**
45   2. Adorno's Echoes: The Holocaust's Cultural Legacy at Mid-Century
53   3. American Synagogue Architecture and the Missing Holocaust
78   4. Synagogues in Germany: Between Forgetting and Remembrance
93   5. Jewish Architects and Secular Jewish Architecture
115   6. Toward a More Jewish Modernism: The Architecture of Louis I. Kahn

137   **Part Three. Jewish Architecture in the Postmodern Era**
142   7. Postmodernism, Post-Holocaust Culture, and Architectural Discourse
157   8. The Deconstructivists: Eisenman, Libeskind, and Gehry
219   9. Jewish Architects Between Alienation and Assimilation
258   10. Holocaust Museums: A New Form of Jewish Architecture?
296   11. Jewish Architecture Between Nightmare, Nostalgia, and Normalcy
336   Conclusion

357   Notes
417   Acknowledgments
421   Index
438   Illustration Credits

Preface

Not far from where I live in Greenwich, Connecticut, stands one of the town's best-known architectural icons, the Second Congregational Church (fig. 1). Built during the years 1856–58 for a congregation that traces its founding back to the year 1705, the church is a towering presence in the surrounding environment. Its location on the crest of a large hill — reputed to be the highest shoreline point between New York City and Boston — makes it visible from near and far, even from Long Island Sound, where boaters have long used the landmark as a point of orientation. When I first moved with my family from Los Angeles to Greenwich in December of 1999, we lived in a small fifth-floor apartment with a direct view of the church. During my first weeks in town, I often gazed out at the structure, which reminded me of the many neogothic churches I had seen during my years living in Germany. I felt especially drawn to the building as a symbol of my return to New England, the place where I was born and went to college, but had not lived in for a decade. For weeks, I enjoyed my privileged view of the church. But as the months passed and I acclimated to life on the East Coast, its symbolic resonance began to fade. By the time my family moved across town in the spring of 2000, it had become just another familiar landmark in a historically rich suburban landscape.

It may seem odd to begin a book on Jewish architecture by reflecting on the significance of a church. But the Second Congregational Church is no ordinary Christian religious edifice. As I came to learn in the course of researching this book, it was one of the first churches in American history to be designed by a Jew. I had never heard of the architect, a German-speaking immigrant from Bohemia named Leopold Eidlitz (1823–1908). But as I learned more about his illustrious career as the first Jewish architect in the history of the United States, I began to reassess some of my views on the subject of Jewish architecture. At the most obvious level, Eidlitz's success undermined the longstanding notion — one that I confess having originally accepted — of Jewish architectural underachievement. But it also complicated my understanding of how Jewish architecture should be defined. If Jewish architecture traditionally referred to synagogues and other buildings serving Jewish communal needs, I now wondered whether the concept should be expanded to encompass any building designed by a Jewish architect — even a Christian church. Could the Second Congregational Church, I asked myself, be an example of Jewish architecture?

A related question soon emerged with respect to another building located several hundred yards down the Boston Post Road from the church: Greenwich's Conservative synagogue, Temple Sholom (fig. 2). My family and I had joined the synagogue not long after moving to town. For years thereafter, I had found little remarkable about the structure, a faintly postmodern, stone-clad building designed by the firm of Perkins Eastman in 1988–91. In researching this book, however, I learned

Figure 1. Leopold Eidlitz, Second Congregational Church, Greenwich, Connecticut, 1856–58. The church was designed by America's first Jewish architect.

that Temple Sholom *could* have been one of the Jewish architectural wonders of the postwar period. In 1953, the synagogue leadership was planning to build a new sanctuary and had the opportunity to accept—but ultimately rejected—famed architect Philip Johnson's design for what became one of the most important modernist synagogues in early postwar America, Kneses Tifereth Israel in nearby Port Chester, New York (1953–56). Whether or not this decision was wise, it raised another interesting theoretical question: Had Temple Sholom's building committee accepted Johnson's design, would the resulting edifice—conceived by a Christian architect—have been more or less Jewish than the church designed by the Jewish architect, Leopold Eidlitz?

As the above questions make clear, it is no easy task to define Jewish architecture, yet doing so is a precondition for examining a number of important questions about its postwar evolution. The question that originally inspired this study was a simple one: why have Jews become increasingly accomplished within the field of western architecture in the years since 1945? My interest in this question dates back over a decade to the mid-1990s when I was living in Los Angeles and completing my first book on the reconstruction of Munich after the Second World War. That study, which examined the city's postwar development as a reflection of the Germans' struggle to deal with their Nazi past, had been influenced by the two years—1989–90 and 1993–94—that I had lived in Germany. During this period, as well as in the years that followed, I closely followed the German architectural press and noticed that many of the high-profile architectural projects that were being proposed for, or were under way in, the country either revolved around Jewish themes or had been designed by Jewish architects. Daniel Libeskind's Felix Nussbaum Museum in Osnabrück, Peter

Figure 2. Perkins Eastman, Temple Sholom, Greenwich, Connecticut, 1988–91. In the 1950s, the congregation declined Philip Johnson's design for a new sanctuary, which was later used by Congregation Kneses Tifereth Israel for its new home in Port Chester, New York (see figs. 23, 36).

Eisenman's Max Reinhardt House in Berlin, Frank Gehry's DZ Bank headquarters in Berlin, and Zvi Hecker's synagogue and Jewish community center in Duisburg, among others, confirmed that Jewish architects were more visible than ever before. This trend was further borne out, it seemed to me, by the fact that three of the world's most celebrated architectural projects in the 1990s — Richard Meier's Getty Center in Los Angeles, Frank Gehry's Guggenheim Museum in Bilbao, Spain, and Daniel Libeskind's Jewish Museum in Berlin — were designed by Jews. By the end of the decade, I found my hunch about Jewish architectural achievement validated by the growing number of references to the phenomenon in the mass media. At the same time, however, I was surprised by the absence of scholarly efforts to explain it in systematic fashion. I thus resolved to pursue my curiosity about the new prominence of Jewish architects by writing a comprehensive history of postwar Jewish architecture in all of its dimensions.

Soon after beginning my research, I added a second focus to my study by drawing on my interest in the memory of the Third Reich and the Holocaust. Ever since researching the reconstruction of Munich in the early 1990s, I had become keenly aware of the deep connections between architecture and the memory of the Nazi period. I therefore came to notice that many of the Jewish-related architectural projects under way in Germany were linked to the country's Nazi past. As I reflected on these links, it struck me that it was worth examining how Jewish architects (and the architectural profession more broadly) had responded to the Holocaust after 1945. The topic was virtually unexplored. While scholars in the 1990s had begun to examine the representation of the Holocaust in various branches of culture, there were no major studies on how the discipline of architecture had responded to Theodor Adorno's famous demand for postwar western culture to rethink its underlying principles "after Auschwitz."

This book is thus an attempt to examine the ties between Jewish architectural achievement and the memory of the Holocaust. It seeks to understand how Jewish memory has influenced the postwar evolution of Jewish architecture. And it examines how Jewish architecture sheds light upon the evolution of Jewish memory. In so doing, it seeks to clarify an understudied dimension of contemporary Jewish identity in the Diaspora.

Writing this book has been challenging. As I proceeded with my research, my study expanded far beyond my original expectations. Although I first came to the topic through my work on postwar German history, I soon recognized that I had to delve into the fields of American history, Jewish history, Holocaust history, comparative history, architectural history, and memory studies. Embracing an interdisciplinary approach has immeasurably enriched the book. But it has also forced me to alter my original plans for it. I had initially hoped to supplement my analysis of postwar Jewish architecture with a discussion of Jewish historic preservation in the United States and Europe. I had also intended to examine architectural trends in Israel. Needless to say, had I kept to my original plan, I would still be writing. I have, therefore, reluctantly chosen to exclude these topics from this study. Nevertheless, I hope that by leaving certain questions open about the postwar development of Jewish architecture, my book may inspire others to investigate its unexplored dimensions and broaden our understanding of what is arguably one of the more intriguing dimensions of contemporary Jewish culture.

Introduction

Figure 3. Daniel Libeskind, "Memory Foundations" proposal, 2003. Among the crystalline towers proposed by Libeskind to replace the vanished World Trade Center, the tallest of them, the Freedom Tower, echoed the outstretched arm of the Statue of Liberty.

For a long time after the terrorist attacks of September 11, 2001, I refused to visit Ground Zero in lower Manhattan. Three months passed before I was willing to venture into any part of New York. It took a year before I went anywhere near the location of the vanished twin towers. I cannot explain what prevented me from going there. I was engaged intellectually with the fate of the World Trade Center site in the aftermath of 9/11, writing several newspaper opinion pieces about how the event might be commemorated.[1] But fear of the recent past's immediacy, fear of future attacks, fear of the unknown all conspired to keep me away from the spot where the towers once stood. Only in December 2002 — fifteen months after 9/11 — did I visit Ground Zero. It was a bitterly cold, windswept day, the kind that sharpened the site's aura of desolation. As I gazed into the void, I was sure that nothing would ever be able to fill it.

Then on February 26, 2003, everything changed, for on that day, Daniel Libeskind was named the master planner in charge of redeveloping the World Trade Center site.[2] Several months earlier, Libeskind had submitted a visionary scheme for the future of Ground Zero. Entitled "Memory Foundations," it called for preserving portions of the massive pit that was left by the towers' collapse and ringing it with five crystalline skyscrapers, the tallest of which — the so-called Freedom Tower — was to rise 1,776 feet into the air as a beacon of American resilience in the face of catastrophe (fig. 3). The plan's combination of sober commemoration and ambitious reconstruction spoke to the public's desire to move forward without losing sight of the recent past, and it justifiably earned widespread acclaim. For weeks thereafter, Libeskind was a media darling, celebrated by journalists and critics for his evocative design. For many observers, his triumph at Ground Zero confirmed his status as one of the world's most acclaimed architects.

I shared in the excitement, but for a different reason. As I noted in a short newspaper article just before Libeskind's triumph, his status as a finalist in the World Trade Center competition underscored the increasing prominence of Jews in the western architectural profession.[3] This development, I argued, represented a new phenomenon in modern Jewish cultural history. For years, the achievements of Jews in architecture had paled in comparison with their accomplishments in other cultural fields, such as literature, film, theater, music, and painting. Yet in the decades since 1945, and especially since the late 1970s, Jewish architects began to attain unprecedented international visibility. Libeskind was the most obvious representative in the year 2003, but he was hardly alone. Any survey of postwar architecture was incomplete, I pointed out, without also mentioning Louis I. Kahn, Frank Gehry, Peter Eisenman, Richard Meier, James Ingo Freed, Eric Owen Moss, Moshe Safdie, James Stewart Polshek, Allan Greenberg, Robert A. M. Stern, and Stanley Tigerman, among others. It was not just that these architects came from Jewish backgrounds, however; many of them, I noted, consciously drew on Jewish sources of inspiration in their work, so much so that their architecture was arguably more "Jewish" in orientation than that of earlier Jewish architects. Thanks to their creative efforts, I concluded, Jewish architects during the postwar period had registered achievements heretofore unknown in modern Jewish history.

Since 2003, I have come to recognize that my claims about Jewish architectural achievement are far from uncontroversial. In speaking about my research in front of scholarly and lay audiences, I have seen more than a few people bristle at the phrase "Jewish architecture." This reaction is largely rooted in the widespread belief that Jewish architecture is a contradiction in terms. Like the

Loch Ness Monster, Jewish architecture has long been famous for (allegedly) not existing. Indeed, to paraphrase Harold Rosenberg's paradoxical observation about Jewish art, Jewish architecture has long been viewed as existing *only* in the frequent claims of its nonexistence.[4]

The very idea of Jewish architecture raises many conceptual problems, most of which derive from the fact that no single style of architecture has ever existed across the vast temporal and spatial parameters of Jewish history. In the absence of a unifying style, it is unclear what the concept of Jewish architecture might mean. Does it refer only to Jewish religious structures? Or also to secular buildings used by Jews? Does Jewish architecture have to be designed by Jewish architects to qualify as Jewish? Or do synagogues created by non-Jewish architects qualify as well? What, moreover, are we to make of Jewish-designed buildings that have no specific Jewish functions? And what about structures erected due to Jewish patronage? These questions underscore the difficulty of defining Jewish architecture.

The Problem of Jewish Culture

This difficulty is compounded by the larger problem of defining "Jewish culture."[5] While it sounds simple enough, the idea of Jewish culture has come under increasing scholarly scrutiny in recent years. Because Jews have lived as a dispersed people, scattered across the world, for much of Jewish history, many scholars have concluded that there is simply no such thing as Jewish culture — at least in any monolithic sense. As David Biale has observed, Jewish culture should not be seen as "immutable [in the sense of being] the fixed product of . . . ancient ethnic or religious origins," but rather as a body of traditions, practices, and behaviors that has "changed as the cultural context changed." This claim makes it tempting to abandon the concept of Jewish culture altogether in favor of Jewish "cultures" in the plural. Yet the fact that Jews have historically seen themselves as possessing a common cultural heritage reminds us that the desire for unity has long coexisted with the reality of diversity. For this reason, Biale is right to conclude that the "defining characteristic of modern Jewish culture is precisely the question of how to define it."[6]

This difficulty of definition is highlighted by the subjective ways in which "Jewishness" has often been employed as a category of cultural analysis. Few would be surprised to see Saul Bellow's novels or Marc Chagall's paintings classified as "Jewish" in one way or another. But what should we make of comedian Lenny Bruce's famous declaration from the 1960s that Count Basie, Dylan Thomas, and "all Italians" were "Jewish"? Or Norman Podhoretz's description of Johann Sebastian Bach's music as "Jewish"? Or the idea that the twentieth century was a "Jewish century"? Or the notion that modernity itself has "Jewish roots"? The subjectivity of these definitions raises the question of whether any objective method exists for determining the "Jewishness" of individual cultural artifacts. We readily speak of Jewish literature, Jewish music, Jewish art, and Jewish humor; yet, what is it that makes a novel, a song, a painting, or a joke "Jewish"?[7]

There are no easy answers to these questions. One method of defining Jewishness might be to focus on a given work's theme or its creator's identity; yet the fact that non-Jews can easily focus on similar themes (and the fact that certain Jews may avoid them entirely), exposes the problem of relying on content and identity as factors for defining Jewishness. It is equally problematic to seek

Jewishness in the formal or aesthetic properties of cultural artifacts. Even if a predisposition toward certain ways of writing and painting could be identified among Jewish novelists and artists, they would not automatically become inherently "Jewish," since the same techniques could easily be identified in the works of non-Jews. In light of these realities, it is best to set aside the essentialist idea that Jewishness can be defined in a transcendent sense in favor of the constructionist notion that culture and identity are forged under specific historical circumstances and evolve with the passage of time.[8] Given that Jewishness is always in flux, that it is subjective, and that each era has its own definition of Jewishness rooted in the particular realities of Jewish life, Jewish culture must be studied with great precision.

This is especially the case given the tendentious ways in which Jewish culture has often been assessed. Among its proponents, Jewish culture has long been viewed from a self-congratulatory, "contributionist" perspective devoted to emphasizing the important role that Jews have played in the cultural and intellectual life of the west.[9] Jewish culture, however, has just as often been condemned, mostly by antisemites who, from the nineteenth century through the first half of the twentieth, accused it of being degenerate, subversive, and pernicious.[10] Of late, finally, Jewish culture has become trendy, with Jewish themes being packaged, marketed, and consumed as part of the western culture industry.[11] All these approaches have elicited consternation among scholars, many of whom have come to regard the concept of Jewish culture with considerable wariness.[12]

The Problem of Jewish Architecture

The problems associated with Jewish culture are magnified in the realm of architecture. Surprisingly, there has been comparatively little attention to Jewish architecture among scholars. Most general surveys on the topic, such as those by Karl Schwarz, Ernst Cohn-Wiener, Franz Landsberger, Cecil Roth, and Gabrielle Sed-Rajna, have treated Jewish architecture as a subfield of Jewish art instead of an independent area of inquiry.[13] More architecturally focused studies, meanwhile, have focused on the design of synagogues. To be sure, the works of Rachel Wischnitzer, Harold Hammer-Schenk, Carol Krinsky, Dominique Jarrassé, H. A. Meek, and Samuel Gruber have enriched our understanding of Jewish architecture immeasurably.[14] But we still lack general studies of Jewish architecture from a broader theoretical and empirical perspective.

This absence reflects the prevailing skepticism about the very existence of Jewish architecture. For years, scholars cast doubt on the possibility of a distinctive style of architecture belonging to the Jews. This negative consensus largely reflected the skepticism toward the broader idea of Jewish artistic creativity.[15] The belief that the Jews were a "people without art" dates back to the late eighteenth century and the birth of the larger western discourse on Jewish "aniconism," or hostility to images. As articulated by a wide range of philosophers, art historians, and intellectuals, this discourse held that the biblical Second Commandment against the creation and worship of graven images had contributed to the Jewish people's artistic impoverishment. In contrast to the more artistically gifted Greeks, whose "Hellenic" brand of thought was oriented toward matters of space, the "Hebraic" thought of the ancient Jews was considered to be more oriented to concepts of time and thus unable to foster genuine artistic expression. Shackled by their restrictive religious laws and lacking the freedom to develop their artistic potential, the Jews had little choice, it was widely believed, but to live up to their reputation as the "people of the book" and favor the verbal over the visual, ethics over aesthetics.[16]

A corollary of the belief that the Jews were a people without art was the idea that they lacked a coherent tradition of architecture. Scholars throughout the west embraced this view beginning in the nineteenth century and continued to support it throughout much of the twentieth century. According to the prevailing consensus, the absence of Jewish architecture dated back to antiquity and was epitomized by the fact that the most famous buildings associated with the Jewish religion—the succession of Temples erected in Jerusalem during the first millennium B.C.E.—were designed by non-Jewish architects and displayed no discernible Jewish traits. As the *Jewish Encyclopedia* of 1902 put it, "Roman architecture was invoked in the building of Herod's Temple just as Phoenician architecture was in the construction of those of Solomon and Zerubabel." This tendency to copy the architectural styles of other nations was widely seen as persisting after the Jews' expulsion from their homeland and the onset of the Diaspora. Scholarly analyses of medieval, early modern, and modern synagogue architecture revealed a clear Jewish pattern of architectural imitation—so much so that most scholars concluded, as the *Architectural Record* did in 1906, that "there is no distinctly Jewish architecture."[17]

The reasons for this imitative impulse were frequently traced back to the anti-Hellenic tradition of Jewish aniconism. In 1874, the eminent Jewish historian Heinrich Graetz attributed the ancient Israelites' failure "to leave behind any gigantic . . . architectural wonders" to a basic "lack . . . [of] architectural skill," rooted in the Jews' disregard of aesthetics in favor of ethics. The German Jewish rabbi Joseph Carlebach observed in 1928 that the Jews' belief in the temporary nature of life in the Diaspora discouraged architectural "displays of grandeur" and instead fostered a gravitation to spirituality. These comments reveal that the absence of a Jewish style of architecture was not only accepted among Jews but viewed as a badge of distinction. Like the Jews' aversion to art, their lack of a national architectural style highlighted their moral uprightness. Moreover, the absence of such a style proved the Jews' commitment to assimilation. At a time when Jewish national loyalties were being challenged by antisemites throughout Europe, the assertion that there was "no national architecture of the Jews," as the Jewish art historian Karl Schwarz put it in 1928, signaled Jewish loyalty to their European homelands.[18]

These assurances were timely, as the alleged absence of Jewish architecture was an idea that easily lent itself to anti-Jewish exploitation. European antisemites cited the absence of a Jewish architectural style to deny that Jews possessed the skills necessary for architectural creativity. In the mid-nineteenth century, Richard Wagner sniffed that he knew "nothing of a single Jewish architect . . . in our own times," while over a half-century later Adolf Hitler declared in *Mein Kampf* that "architecture . . . owe[s] nothing original to the Jews." Most antisemites attributed the Jews' lack of architectural achievement to their alleged rootlessness as a race. Believing, as the Nazi architect and racial theorist Paul Schultze-Naumburg put it in 1935, that a nation's art and architecture had "to grow from the blood and soil if it wants to live," antisemites affirmed that the Jews' historic penchant for wandering and their resulting lack of ties to the land prevented them from developing an authentic architectural tradition. Fittingly, if paradoxically, the only architectural movement that displayed Jewish traits, according to antisemitic critics, was modern architecture, whose universal aspirations and international scope evoked the same rootlessness of Jewish culture. In 1932 the Nazi newspaper *Völkischer Beobachter* made this clear by derisively declaring that Walter Gropius's Bauhaus building in Dessau "damned well looked like a synagogue."[19]

In the years since the end of World War II, claims of Jewish architectural underachievement have lost their antisemitic associations but have nonetheless persisted among scholars. In his book *Aesthetics and History* (1948), Bernard Berenson declared that nothing produced by the Jews in the realm of architecture had "proved . . . either original . . . or in the least Jewish." Not long thereafter, Aharon Kashtan denied the existence of a "specific Jewish art of building," while the American architect Percival Goodman bluntly observed: "If we look for a 'Jewish architecture,' . . . with characteristic themes, spirit, and function, we shall not find it; it is not there to be found." Recent scholars have affirmed this assessment. Carol Krinsky has written that a "Jewish feeling for architecture or a common Jewish architectural style is impossible to define." Similarly, the second edition of the *Encyclopedia Judaica* (2006) has authoritatively concluded, "In modern times there is an abundance of Jewish architects but . . . no Jewish architecture to speak of."[20]

In denying the existence of Jewish architecture, postwar scholars have advanced a combination of explanations. Some have adhered to the theory of Jewish aniconism, pointing to the Second Commandment as the reason the Jews, in the words of Max Dimont, had historically "turned away from . . . architecture." The most influential promoter of this theory was the Norwegian theologian Thorleif Boman, who lent it unprecedented authority in his 1952 book *Hebrew Thought Compared with Greek*. Boman's study was primarily a linguistic analysis of the differences between the "static, peaceful, moderate, and harmonious" thought of the Greeks and the "dynamic, vigorous, passionate, and . . . explosive" thought of the Hebrews. But his analysis had architectural implications by reinforcing the notion that Jewish culture was disinterested in architectural space. In showing how the Hebrew Bible paid greater attention to architectural function than form (especially in its description of how structures were used in time instead of how they appeared in space), Boman upheld preexisting explanations of Jewish architectural underachievement.[21]

By contrast, other postwar scholars abandoned the theory of aniconism for other explanations of Jewish architectural underachievement. Already in 1946, the German Jewish emigré scholar Franz Landsberger cautioned against exaggerating the Second Commandment's impact on Jewish architectural history, noting that it referred "only to representational art — painting and sculpture — [and] . . . not to architecture."[22] More recently, Kalman Bland and Margaret Olin have shown how the idea of aniconism obscured the diversity of pre-modern Jewish artistic accomplishments.[23] Today, scholars mostly gravitate to historical and sociological explanations for Jewish artistic underachievement. Most point to the Diaspora as the reason Jewish architecture has lacked one of the key ingredients for architectural creativity: sovereignty over space.[24] Without being able to dwell in spatial security, Jews were denied what Martin Heidegger claimed was a precondition for genuine building.[25] The fact that Jewish history was furthermore defined by dispersion meant that Jews never enjoyed the spatial contiguity necessary for developing a unified form of architectural expression.[26] In short, the basic diversity of the Jewish historical experience is now seen as the chief impediment to the emergence of a genuine form of Jewish architecture.

Lately, however, perceptions of Jewish architecture have begun to change. Rather than seeking explanations for Jewish underachievement, scholars, journalists, and critics since the mid-1990s have tried to explain the recent surge in Jewish architectural creativity. A series of exhibitions and conferences in Europe and the United States, such as the Amsterdam Jewish Historical Museum's 2004 traveling exhibition "Jewish Identity in Contemporary Architecture," have testified to the desire to revise older views on Jewish architecture.[27] The increasing attention to the subject in major architectural journals and the mainstream press provides further indication of this trend.[28] Scholars have also begun to follow suit. Some architectural historians, such as Fredric Bedoire, Klemens Klemmer, and Franklin Toker, have explored the contributions that Jews have made to modern architecture, while others, such as Kathleen James, Renato Rizzi, and Charles Jencks, have considered the ethnic and religious identities of Jewish architects in analyzing their work.[29] Finally, Jewish architects themselves have begun to comment on the phenomenon. Peter Eisenman has highlighted the rise of Jewish architects in recent years, remarking, "If you look at the hegemony of Jewish architects, Frank Gehry, Richard Meier, Stanley Tigerman . . . there was no such thing fifty years before this."[30] To be sure, certain observers have spoofed the phenomenon, referring sardonically to a "Jewish conspiracy in architecture."[31] Others, meanwhile, have perceived a surfeit of attention to the subject and declared "enough."[32]

Methodological Reflections on Studying Jewish Architecture

It is far too early for a backlash, however. While the reality of postwar Jewish architectural achievement has been identified, it has yet to be sufficiently explained. This study aims to fill this gap by accounting for the remarkable achievements of Jewish architects in the postwar era. In undertaking this project I have proceeded with caution, aware of scholars' caveats about Jewish architecture. Before introducing the contours of my argument, therefore, I would like to clarify my own approach to the topic.

To begin with, I do not believe that doubts about Jewish architecture's existence justify discounting it as a topic of scholarly analysis. While it is true that there is no such thing as a unified Jewish architectural style, the same can be said about the stylistically diverse architectural traditions of other religions, whether Christianity, Islam, or Buddhism. Plenty of studies exist on these architectural traditions, a fact that, to my mind, shows that Jewish architecture should be treated no differently.[33] That said, I am uninterested in discussing whether Jewish architecture exists as a distinctly identifiable style and see little point in typologizing the ideal typical traits of Jewish buildings. I prefer to focus on the ways in which buildings built by and for Jews since 1945 have been imbued with Jewish significance by their creators and users. I am particularly interested in the ways in which such buildings have been shaped by Jewish historical memory and reveal the shifting nature of Jewish identity in the postwar era.

I would also like to stress the timeliness of studying Jewish architecture, especially the ways in which it reflects the broader multicultural turn in world architecture. Jews are but one of many groups that have recently become interested in examining their identities in architectural form.[34] Native Americans in the United States, for example, have attempted to fashion an architecture appropriate to their own historical experiences, as seen in Douglas Joseph Cardinal's National Museum of the American Indian in Washington, D.C. (2004), and James Stewart Polshek's Mashantucket Pequot Museum in Connecticut (1998).[35] African Americans have begun to explore the concept of "Blackness" in architecture and have drawn on their cultural heritage in such buildings as David Lee's John D. O'Bryant African-American Institute at Northeastern University in Boston (2007), Robert A. M. Stern's Museum for African Art in New York City (2011), and David Adjaye's National Museum of African American History and Culture on the National Mall in Washington, D.C. (projected for completion in 2015).[36] When one considers comparable discussions about "Dutchness," "Scottishness," and homosexual identity in architecture, it becomes clear that the topic of architectural Jewishness is fully within the mainstream of current architectural thought.[37]

Of course, focusing on the Jewish dimensions of architecture entails certain methodological risks, particularly those of essentialism and reductionism. In examining works of Jewish architecture it is tempting to identify specific traits and patterns as embodying an essential sense of Jewishness. Yet doing so, Anthony Julius reminds us, can fetishize them and limit our ability to appreciate other factors that shape a building's significance.[38] I have therefore paid attention to all the factors — whether economic, technological, or aesthetic — that influence how buildings come into being.[39] At the same time, I admit that I focus less on the material than the psychological, cultural, and religious forces that determine how buildings are made. I am intrigued by the ways in which architects assign meaning to their work and how they use larger theoretical arguments to justify their design strategies. I am equally interested in how their buildings resonate within society at large and how they have been assigned significance by ordinary people. To put it simply, I place special weight on the subjective forces that have shaped the production and reception of Jewish architecture.

In pursuing these interests I have been inspired by scholars who have embraced notions of authorial intention and reception theory in interpreting works of literature.[40] Applying these insights to architecture, I argue that architects have consistently played a central role in determining the Jewishness of their work. The extent to which they have consciously drawn on Jewish sources of inspiration or cited Jewish justifications for their designs has directly shaped their buildings' Jewish character. At the same time, I reject the idea that architects are solely responsible for their works' ultimate meaning. Just as readers help construct the meaning of texts apart from the authors' intentions, ordinary people's responses to buildings help determine their overall significance. With these observations in mind, I examine both the intentions behind and the responses to works of Jewish architecture through a wide range of sources. I utilize project descriptions, manifestoes, and interviews to understand how architects have approached their work. And I use architectural publications and mainstream press accounts to shed light on how buildings have been viewed by critics and society at large.

Utilizing this kind of empirical approach is indispensable for tackling certain interpretive problems that arise in the process of determining the Jewishness of Jewish architecture. Although the intentions of architects are important for ascertaining a building's Jewish character, Jewish architects have themselves frequently drawn on problematic conceptions of Jewishness in their work. As I discuss in Part Two, one of them is the idea, derived from the work of Thorleif Boman, that Jewishness in architecture is manifested in a "Hebraic" penchant for dynamism instead of a "Hellenic" penchant for stability. Another is the sociological notion of the Jew as the prototypical modern/

postmodern outsider who is alienated from, and ultimately rebels against, architectural tradition. Still other examples equate Jewishness with a penchant for Talmudic questioning or a Kabbalistic orientation toward healing the world. To the extent that architects have explicitly cited these notions as influences on their buildings, I willingly acknowledge them as important sources of their architecture's Jewish character. But I am less open to architecture critics and historians who read such Jewish traits into works of architecture in the absence of empirical support.

The same empirical approach can also help resolve the question of whether buildings designed by Jewish architects can be seen as Jewish simply by virtue of their creators' backgrounds. Many Jewish architects have been disinterested in assigning Jewish significance to their work and have tried to avoid being viewed as "Jewish architects." This was especially true of Jewish modernists in the early postwar era, but present-day architects have displayed the same kind of aversion. Some of the architects that I discuss in this study were reluctant to speak with me about their work in a Jewish context, and some flatly refused to be interviewed. Even architects who have credited the influence of Jewish ideas on their designs have expressed reservations about making too much of the links between architecture and Jewishness. A good example is Peter Eisenman, who declined to be included in the 2004 "Jewish Identity in Contemporary Architecture Exhibit" and recently remarked: "I do not think that there is any such thing as Jewish architecture or Jewish identity in architecture."[41] This resistance raises the question of how the backgrounds of Jewish architects should be considered in evaluating their work. If authorial intention is the standard of measure, the silence of many architects about their work's Jewish dimensions would seem to prohibit interpreting them from such a perspective. Yet it would be mistaken to remove their identity from consideration altogether. For, to paraphrase Harold Rosenberg, while Jewish architects "may not have been creating as Jews, they have not been working as non-Jews either. Their [work is] . . . the closest expression of themselves as they are, including the fact that they are Jews, each in his individual degree."[42] Whether they were religious or secular, affiliated or assimilated, identifying or self-denying, Jewish architects have invariably disclosed their views of themselves in their work. For this reason I have integrated considerable biographical information into my discussion of the architects who are featured in the pages that follow.

In thinking about these and other methodological issues, I have aimed for a new level of interdisciplinarity in writing this book. I have, first of all, tried to integrate two fields that, according to David Engel, have often been treated separately from one another: Jewish history and Holocaust history.[43] I have simultaneously attempted to integrate them with architectural history, a discipline whose insights have seldom been applied to either field. I have also utilized methodological approaches from the field of memory studies. I have drawn on the insights of all these scholarly fields in order to address questions that have remained unanswered within them. I hope to contribute to the field of Jewish history, for example, by showing how works of Jewish architecture help us understand patterns of assimilation and identity-formation among postwar Jews in the United States and Europe; how they point to areas of divergence and convergence in postwar American and European Jewish history; and how they highlight the increasingly central place of architecture in modern Jewish life. I also hope that my study helps to clarify questions that linger in the field of Holocaust history, among others: the nature of the Holocaust's impact on postwar western culture, the extent to which the Holocaust inspired new forms of artistic expression after 1945, and the degree to which the Holocaust was openly discussed or avoided during the postwar period. Finally, for the field of memory studies, I hope that my book serves to deepen our appreciation of how the forces of remembrance and forgetting have shaped the built environment.

Assessing Postwar Jewish Architecture

No question looms larger in this study, however, than the one that originally inspired it—Why have Jewish architects registered such unprecedented accomplishments in the years since 1945? To be sure, the claim that postwar Jewish architects *have* registered such accomplishments should not be accepted uncritically, for it is tied to the controversial contention that Jews before 1945 were architectural underachievers. Skeptics might be tempted to dismiss this contention as based on myth and bias; yet the fact that important Jewish architectural historians, such as Bruno Zevi, have described the field of architecture as one "where, historically, the Jews have been few and far between" obliges us to take claims of Jewish architectural underachievement seriously and assess them as objectively as possible.[44] The accomplishments of Jewish architects must therefore be compared with those of Jews in other realms of culture. I pursue this line of inquiry throughout the book, but even here in the introduction, a few preliminary observations are worth making.

Historically, Jews were undeniably present in the field of architecture, but their accomplishments did not match those of Jews in other areas of culture. Perhaps the most striking example is in literature. The many Nobel Prizes won by Jewish writers clearly testify to Jewish literary achievement, as does the long list of celebrated Jewish novelists and poets.[45] A similar case can be made for music, which boasts an equally impressive list of major composers and performers.[46] Theater, film, and television are arguably just as defined by pioneering Jewish contributions.[47] Even in the visual arts, where Jewish creativity should have theoretically been hampered by the Second Commandment, Jews registered notable achievements.[48] By way of comparison, far fewer Jews attained equivalent international renown in architecture in the decades before 1914—the period in which Jews had already begun to achieve considerable success in literature, music, theater, and painting.[49] In the interwar years, meanwhile, the few Jewish architects who made names for themselves did not rank among their profession's top leaders.

Since the end of the Second World War, however, much has changed. If Jews were comparative underachievers in the field of architecture, they have now become overachievers. The reasons for this dramatic development are numerous and form a major part of this book's focus. I begin to investigate it in Chapter 1, by surveying the history of Jewish architecture from antiquity to the outbreak of the Second World War. In this chapter I discuss Jewish religious architecture, secular Jewish architecture, and Jewish architectural patronage; I acknowledge that, in all three areas, Jews demonstrated undeniable achievements. At the same time, I show how their achievements were limited relative to other realms of Jewish culture and how they were ultimately cut short by the outbreak of war and the onset of genocide.

After 1945, the development of Jewish architecture reflected the altered circumstances of the postwar world. In Part Two of the book, I begin to probe the roots of postwar Jewish architectural achievement by introducing a second major area of focus: the impact of the Holocaust. What role did the Holocaust play in shaping the work of Jewish architects after 1945? To what extent was it involved in laying the foundation for postwar Jewish architectural achievements? Chapter 2 begins to address these questions by surveying the theoretical challenges that the Nazi genocide posed to western culture in the immediate postwar years. During this period, a wide range of Jewish intellectual and cultural figures — writers, painters, and filmmakers, among others — wrestled with Theodor Adorno's admonition to rethink their principles in the wake of Auschwitz. Most architects, however, declined to follow suit. Instead, they embraced the forward-looking mindset of the modernist movement and acted as if the recent past had few consequences for their work. Chapters 3 and 4 describe this evasive impulse by examining how Jewish synagogue architecture in the United States and the Federal Republic of Germany avoided contending with the Holocaust's legacy in attempting to realize the promise of modernism. Jewish architects also neglected to confront the Holocaust in their secular work during the early postwar years. Chapter 5 examines this trend by discussing how the modernist buildings of Richard Neutra, Marcel Breuer, Gordon Bunshaft, Max Abramovitz, Morris Lapidus, and others exhibited an ahistorical sensibility that resisted seeking inspiration in the Jewish past. This resistance did not prevent these architects from registering unprecedented achievements. Indeed, their work proved that Jewish architects could achieve greatness without drawing inspiration on their Jewishness. By contrast, the career of Louis I. Kahn, which is the subject of Chapter 6, shows how the most important Jewish architect of the era rose to the top of the American architectural profession by rejecting the amnesiac aspects of modernism and seeking inspiration in the Jewish past. By drawing on Jewish mysticism, Jewish architectural history, and even the legacy of the Holocaust, Kahn showed how Jewish architects could enrich their work by consciously making it more Jewish. In so doing, he helped pave the way for the explosion of Jewish architectural creativity in the postmodern era.

In the 1970s, a revolution occurred within Jewish architecture. Not only did more Jewish architects gain prominence in this period than ever before, but their work was more markedly "Jewish" as well. Numerous factors played into this development. In Chapter 7, I discuss how the rise of postmodernism, multiculturalism, and Holocaust consciousness helped to set the stage for the unprecedented achievements of Jewish architects after the late 1970s. Chapter 8 examines the important movement of deconstructivism and profiles three of the world's best known contemporary architects: Peter Eisenman, Daniel Libeskind, and Frank Gehry. It shows how all three hit their architectural stride by finding inspiration in their Jewish backgrounds and exploring Jewish themes, ideas, and imagery in their innovative work. Significantly, all of them reflected to varying degrees on the architectural implications of the Holocaust, which they saw as necessitating an architecture of rupture and instability. Not all Jewish architects, however, drew on their Jewishness in forging their reputations. Chapter 9 discusses how diverse architects, such as the postmodern classicist Robert A. M. Stern and the stalwart modernist Richard Meier, achieved renown by working in an assimilationist fashion. Yet even they had to contend with the Holocaust's legacy, being forced to minimize its magnitude in order to justify their decision to embrace an architecture of harmony instead of rupture. The most vivid legacy of the Holocaust for postwar architecture is the subject of Chapter 10, in which I discuss the rise of a brand-new category of Jewish architecture — Holocaust museums.

Finally, Chapter 11 examines the Holocaust's impact on Jewish synagogue architecture in Germany and the United States while also showing how other Jewish buildings have asserted a more positive sense of Jewish identity.

In outlining these trends, my primary aim is to analyze postwar Jewish architecture, not praise it. In my conclusion I highlight some of the criticisms that have been indirectly leveled at the new Jewish architecture, such as its connections to the "starchitecture" phenomenon of recent years and its complicity with the intensifying pace of Jewish assimilation. These qualifying remarks notwithstanding, the story of postwar Jewish architecture is a compelling one that warrants careful study. Now that the "people of the book" have begun to build, their architecture serves as an important means of understanding contemporary Jewish life.

Part One

Jewish Architecture Before the Holocaust

Figure 4. The late thirteenth-century Altneuschul, or Old New Synagogue, in Prague is the oldest synagogue in continued use in Europe.

Chapter 1
From the Wilderness to World War II
A Brief History of Jewish Architecture

When I first visited Prague's medieval Altneuschul (Old New Synagogue) as a recent college graduate in May of 1990, the last thing on my mind was Jewish architecture. The turbulent events of the Velvet Revolution were foremost in my thoughts, and I was eager to soak up the politically charged atmosphere in the streets around Wenceslas Square. After chancing upon a massive outdoor political rally one afternoon and hearing an explanation of its significance from a local bystander, I became preoccupied with experiencing history as it was unfolding in the present and gave little thought to the city's past. Only at the end of my trip did I seek out Prague's old Jewish quarter. I was drawn there by its famous cemetery, with its thousands of tilting gravestones, not by the thirteenth-century Altneuschul, which I stumbled upon more or less by accident (fig. 4). I do not recall whether I noted the building's status as Europe's oldest functioning synagogue, but its historic atmosphere made an impression on me. Once inside the synagogue's subterranean sanctuary, I took note of its cool stone interior, wrought iron and wood bima, and flickering chandeliers dangling from the vaulted ceiling. Here was a building, I felt, that radiated an authentic sense of Jewishness.

It is hard to say what it was about the Altneuschul that epitomized its Jewish character to me. This difficulty partly reflects the fact that there is no such thing as Jewish architecture in a monolithic sense. The heterogeneity of three thousand years of Jewish history has made sure of this. Although Jews have built similar kinds of structures wherever they have lived — synagogues, schools, community centers, museums, private homes, and cemeteries — the diverse spatial and temporal circumstances of their erection have made them extraordinarily diverse in appearance. This is why when we think of the world's most famous Jewish structures — the Western Wall in Jerusalem, the Scuola Grande Tedesca in Venice, the Jewish Museum in Berlin — it is so difficult to say what makes them Jewish.

Architectural Meaning and Jewishness in Architecture

The difficulty in determining the Jewishness of Jewish architecture is partly due to the difficulty in defining architectural meaning. Architectural historians have embraced multiple strategies for assessing meaning in architecture.[1] In this study, I follow the lead of William Whyte, whose holistic method of examining all aspects of a building's conception, creation, and reception convincingly demonstrates that architectural meaning is always in flux.[2] The initial factor shaping a building's meaning is its intended function, which is typically determined by the client's program. Also playing a crucial role is the architect's creative vision, which is expressed through building technologies, materials, and aesthetic traditions. Unlike these objective factors, a third and more subjective one — how groups in society come to view buildings — underscores how architectural meaning is inherently unstable. As social, economic, and political circumstances change, so do the original meanings of buildings. The violent fate of Catholic churches during the Protestant Reformation, gothic cathedrals during the French Revolution, and Nazi-era buildings in postwar Germany clearly shows how the forces of history — and historical memory — can dramatically alter the symbolism of architecture.[3] In short, from their initial conception to their eventual destruction, buildings are malleable in meaning.

There is thus no such thing as architectural "Jewishness" in any immutable sense. Rather, the buildings built by and for Jews over the centuries have exhibited Jewish traits in the myriad ways that they reflect the historical forces that have shaped Jewish life. The experiences of national consolidation and exile during antiquity, of anti-Jewish persecution during the Middle Ages, and of emancipation, assimilation, and national reawakening during the modern period, have all left their mark on the Jewish built environment.[4] These diverse experiences are mirrored in the different categories of buildings that constitute Jewish architecture. Buildings associated with Jewish religious life, whether designed by Jewish or non-Jewish architects, represent the most obvious examples of Jewish architecture. Secular buildings designed by Jewish architects also deserve inclusion, as do those secular buildings commissioned by Jewish clients but designed by non-Jewish architects. The Jewishness of all of these buildings, in turn, is directly influenced by the ways that their designers tried to infuse them with Jewish meaning and the ways that society at large has responded to them. These facts clearly emerge from a brief historical survey of Jewish religious architecture, secular Jewish architecture, and Jewish architectural patronage prior to the Holocaust.

Jewish Religious Architecture

The roots of Jewish architecture date to the biblical period with the birth of the Jewish people. There are few references in the Hebrew Bible to structures serving religious functions, but the first is the famous Tabernacle, or "tent of meeting" (fig. 5). According to the book of Exodus, this structure was constructed by the craftsman Bezalel at Moses's request to serve as the Israelites' main religious sanctuary during their desert wanderings after the escape from Egypt. The Tabernacle was a medium-sized tented structure constructed of acacia wood and cloth that was situated within a large rectangular enclosure and divided into two interior spaces, one of which, the "holy of holies," housed the ark of the covenant, containing the tablets of the law brought down by Moses from Mount Sinai. Architecturally the Tabernacle was undistinguished, yet its flexibility and mobility made it perfect for a nomadic people that had not yet found a permanent homeland.[5]

With the conquest of Canaan and the creation of a unified Kingdom of Israel under King David around the year 1000 BCE, Jewish architecture became more substantial. Of the many buildings erected during the next millennium, the most distinctive was the central building of Jewish religious life, the Temple (*Beit HaMikdash*). Following David's decision to replace the temporary Tabernacle with a more permanent structure, the first of several temples was completed under the rule of his son, King Solomon. As is described in the book of Kings, the first Temple closely followed the rectangular, longitudinal plan of the Tabernacle and again featured a holy space containing the ark of the covenant.[6] The Temple was much larger than the Tabernacle, however, and the materials used in its construction were sturdier and more opulent: hewn stone, cedar beams, and abundant gold overlay. The Bible tells us little about the building's architecture, and modern archaeologists have turned up no physical traces that might help clarify it.[7] It is probable, however, that the Temple was built according to the construction traditions of its Phoenician architect, Hiram of Tyre, whom King Solomon commissioned to design the edifice. One of the few details that the Bible mentions is the presence of two freestanding, thirty-foot-high bronze columns, named Jachin and Boaz, that stood immediately in front of the Temple's entryway (fig. 6).[8] These pillars, along with the Temple's layout, would prove highly influential for the subsequent history of Jewish architecture, for they were among the edifice's few architectural features to retain a place in Jewish memory after the Temple was destroyed by the Babylonians in 586 BCE.

After the Jews' return from Babylonian exile to the land of Israel in the late sixth century BCE, a replacement Temple was built on the ruins of Solomon's original structure.[9] Little is known about this building, due to its modest form and eventual replacement by King Herod's expanded Temple in 19 BCE. This so-called Second Temple was far larger than the first and was built with even more costly materials, such as brilliant white marble. Yet, Herod's Temple adhered to the plan of Solomon's and exhibited no new principles of spatial organization. Of course, the Temple displayed one highly influential feature, rough-hewn Jerusalem limestone, which was used in the complex's retaining walls. With the Temple's destruction by the Romans in the year 70 C.E., this surviving remnant, the so-called Western Wall, became not only one of Judaism's most sacred religious symbols, but one of its iconic architectural symbols as well (fig. 7).[10]

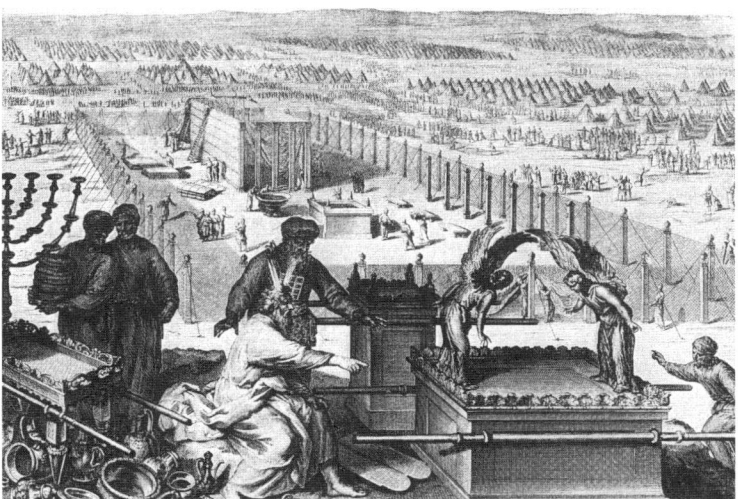 

Figure 5. Biblical Tabernacle, illustration by Gerard Hoet, *Figures de la Bible,* 1728. The Tabernacle is the tented structure in the background, surrounded by the rectangular enclosure. In the foreground are the ark of the covenant (right) and the menorah (left), which were housed in two separate rooms within the Tabernacle.

Figure 6. Solomon's Temple, featuring the twin columns Jachin and Boaz, woodcut by François Vatable, 1540.

The destruction of the Temple and ensuing dispersion of the Jewish people brought about a return to the model of the Tabernacle by giving rise to a more versatile religious structure, the synagogue. While there were precedents for localized prayer sites in the Kingdom of Israel itself, it was only after the Babylonian exile and the destruction of the Second Temple that the synagogue became the primary physical locus of Judaism. As it developed over the centuries, the synagogue's basic function remained fixed, serving as a house of assembly, prayer, and study. Yet, as Salo Baron has noted, "the Jews of Palestine developed no specific architectural style" for their synagogues as they prioritized the liturgical and educational activities that went on inside them over their structure and appearance. This indifference to architecture was further reflected in the Talmud, which largely neglected the issue of synagogue design.[11]

Without strict liturgical requirements, synagogue architecture developed in many directions in the centuries that followed. While all synagogues had the same basic functional requirements — an ark (*aron kodesh*) for housing the Torah scrolls and a pulpit (*bimah*) from which to read them — the spatial relationship between the ark and pulpit varied considerably, with longitudinal and centralized plans being embraced at different times and in different places.[12] Moreover, since both plans were compatible with multiple architectural solutions, synagogue interiors and exteriors ended up being shaped largely by local circumstances. One of the most important was the Jews' level of integration into the societies in which they lived. Where Jews suffered persecution, their anxieties led them to avoid overt expressions of religious particularism and build inconspicuously according to local traditions. Where they enjoyed greater security, by contrast, Jews felt more confident about articulating a distinct sense of religious identity in architectural form. As a result, the Jewishness of synagogue architecture varied considerably from the Middle Ages into the modern period.

In medieval Europe, the discrimination faced by Jews inhibited the expression of Jewishness in synagogue design. Because Jews were excluded from medieval craft guilds and could not become architects, most synagogues were built by non-Jews and consequently echoed the dominant architectural styles of the countries and eras in which they were built. Examples include the Synagogue of El Transito in Toledo (ca. 1350), which was influenced by the Moorish architecture of Muslim Spain, and the gothic-influenced synagogue of Regensburg (ca. 1250) in Germany. Residency restrictions (most famously in the form of ghettos) and limitations on property ownership further limited the expressiveness of synagogue architecture. Never knowing when they would lose their residency rights and be expelled, Jews built quite modestly. They also built unobtrusively, constructing their houses of worship inside interior courtyards and behind profane structures. During this period, synagogue architecture avoided exterior display and favored interiority, a trend that was epitomized by such externally anonymous but internally grand synagogues as the Scuola Grande Tedesca (1528) and the Scuola Spagnola (1655) in the Jewish ghetto of Venice (fig. 8).[13]

While this interiority reflected the influence of persecution, a more affirmative Jewish sensibility was also visible in the era's religious architecture. According to Jewish law, synagogues were supposed to be the tallest structures in town, yet Christian prohibitions prevented them from exceeding the height of church steeples. One way of evading this regulation entailed placing the main floor of the synagogue sanctuary below street level in order to raise the height of the interior space. The subterranean character of many synagogues, such as the Altneuschul in Prague and the

Heidereutergasse synagogue (1712–14) in Berlin, signaled this more assertive Jewish sensibility. The synagogues of the Venice ghetto reflected a different approach to honoring this traditional injunction to strive for height by being built on the top floors of high-rise buildings. A more subtle form of asserting a sense of Jewishness architecturally was the practice of adding an extra rib to the cross vaults in synagogue ceilings in order to mute any suspicion of Christian religious symbolism. Finally, Jews preserved the memory of the twin columns in front of Solomon's Temple, Jachin and Boaz, in synagogues such as the one in Worms (ca. 1150), which featured two columns at the center of its double-naved interior.[14]

If Jewish anxieties shaped the development of synagogue architecture in Western Europe, the comparative security enjoyed by Jews in Eastern Europe allowed synagogue design to evolve in a more creative direction. During the sixteenth and seventeenth centuries, half of world Jewry lived in the Polish-Lithuanian Kingdom, a fact that gave Polish Jews the spatial sovereignty necessary to achieve important innovations in their religious architecture. The first major development was the advent of the four-pillared stone synagogue, which integrated the bimah into the building's very structure by placing it in a central bay framed by four columns supporting a vaulted ceiling.[15] A second and more famous development was the emergence of wooden synagogues. Designed most likely by Christian craftsmen with Jewish communal input, these structures exhibited multitiered and dramatically sloping exterior roofs that framed soaring and richly decorated interior spaces (fig. 9). So distinctive were these synagogues that historians, such as Salo Baron, have defined them as a "genuinely Jewish style" of architecture. Even though recent scholarship suggests that this architectural type was influenced by Polish vernacular tradition, the view remains common that "the use that the Jews made of it [was] . . . profoundly original."[16] In the end, though, early modern Poland was exceptional. Only in the modern era would Jews widely come to enjoy the freedom and security necessary for genuine architectural innovation.

Figure 7. The Western Wall of Herod's Temple complex is the most famous work of Jewish architecture from antiquity.

Figure 8. Scuolo Grande Tedesca, Venice, 1528. The structure's exterior is relatively inconspicuous, but its interior is ornate.

Figure 9. Synagogue, Wolpa, Poland, eighteenth century. The building is an important example of Polish wooden synagogue architecture, widely seen as the most authentic form of Jewish architectural expression in the early modern period.

Figure 10. Eduard Knoblauch, Oranienburgerstrasse synagogue, Berlin, 1859–66. The building was designed in the Moorish or neo-Islamic style, which was widely popular in the mid-nineteenth century.

Beginning in the late eighteenth century, Jewish architecture began to evolve in dramatically new ways. In the wake of the French Revolution, Jews were granted civil equality in many parts of Western and Central Europe and were freed from previous restrictions. As ghettos and guilds were eliminated, Jews were no longer limited by where they could build and could finally become architects.[17] It took several generations before European Jews entered the field of architecture in significant numbers, but in principle they were now free to decide how they wanted to represent themselves communally in their houses of worship.

This freedom of choice, however, presented Jews with as many dilemmas as opportunities, for it coincided with an unprecedented era of aesthetic freedom in European architecture. The nineteenth century witnessed the rise of architectural historicism, which elevated stylistic eclecticism over uniformity and confronted architects with the question, "In what style should we build?" Architects answered this question in diverse ways throughout Europe, but most were strongly influenced by the era's nationalistic spirit and sought to build according to what they saw as their own national architectural traditions.[18] For obvious reasons, Jews found it difficult to embrace historicism since their status as a Diasporic people prevented them from laying claim to a national architectural tradition of their own. Jews were furthermore divided about the advisability of working to develop one. In some parts of Europe where Jews felt confident about their integration into Christian society, they supported a form of architecture that asserted a clear sense of Jewish particularity. Where Jews remained insecure, by contrast, they rejected this particularistic strategy as reinforcing an image of foreignness and instead embraced local building traditions in the effort to win social acceptance.

The conflicting desires for self-assertion and adaptation shaped the development of Jewish architecture throughout the western world, nowhere more powerfully than in the German-speaking lands of Central Europe. German Jews expressed both tendencies at different times during the nineteenth century due to the turbulent course of emancipation in the Germanic Confederation and the Habsburg Empire. German Jews received equal rights from the French during the era of Napoleonic rule, but these rights were largely repealed following the French army's defeat in 1815. As a result, German Jews in the decades that followed were at pains to prove that they deserved equal rights by showing themselves to be loyal citizens who had embarked upon a path of assimilation and integration. This quest for acceptance was clearly reflected in the synagogues of the era. In the initial years after the repeal of emancipation, German Jews hesitated to intrude too visibly into European public space. Many new synagogues remained invisible to public view and were constructed in rear courtyards, as with Josef Kornhäusel's Seitenstettengasse Synagogue in Vienna (1824–26). Where synagogues were built in more public locations, they were built in the same architectural styles as adjoining buildings, as with Jean Baptiste Metivier's neoclassical Westenrieder Strasse synagogue in Munich (1826).[19]

By the 1840s and 1850s, however, German Jews' progress toward emancipation gave them the confidence to assert a distinct sense of identity in their architecture. Instead of constructing synagogues at inconspicuous locations, they built prominent, free-standing edifices in particularistic architectural styles. The most famous was the Moorish or neo-Islamic style, which was first seen in the interior of Gottfried Semper's synagogue in Dresden (1840), and which reached its apogee in Eduard Knoblauch's monumental Oranienburgerstrasse synagogue in Berlin (1859–66) (fig. 10).

For many German Jews, these synagogues' unique appearance symbolized Judaism's oriental roots, while their increasing presence in the urban environment signaled the growing acceptance of Jews within German society.[20]

This optimistic tendency toward architectural extroversion was visible in other countries as well. Monumental synagogues were built in France, such as Alfred-Philibert Aldrophe's Romanesque Great Synagogue in Paris on the Rue de la Victoire (1865–74); in Hungary, such as Ludwig von Förster's Moorish Dohány Street synagogue in Budapest (1853–58); and in Italy, where the Mole Antonelliana would have been Europe's tallest synagogue had the Jewish community of Turin not run out of money midway through construction.[21] The situation was different in the United States, where Jews already enjoyed political equality and thus had fewer concerns about the symbolism of synagogue architecture. American Jews' comparatively carefree approach was illustrated by their tendency to follow the era's architectural trends and their construction of synagogues in every style from the neoclassical to the gothic.[22] Yet even American Jews had moments of doubt when they questioned how their synagogues' appearance might make them look in the eyes of others. In 1870, following a spike in American antisemitism during the Civil War, congregants of Manhattan's Central Synagogue cautioned against "external ostentation" in building a new sanctuary for fear it would "provoke . . . envy, grudges, and hate on the part of our enemies."[23] As was shown by the congregation's eventual decision to accept Henry Fernbach's opulent and exotically foreign Moorish design (1872), however, their doubts were fleeting. On the whole, synagogue architecture in the era of emancipation was boldly optimistic.

With the rise of political antisemitism in Germany and other parts of Europe after the 1870s, however, many Jews lost their self-confidence and began to question their embrace of architectural particularism. The most obvious sign of this reassessment was the widespread abandonment of the Moorish style in synagogue architecture. This trend reflected the fear that the style played into the hands of antisemites by perpetuating a negative image of Jewish otherness, a charge that German Jews were sensitive to because of the concurrent migration of unassimilated Eastern European Jews, or *Ostjuden*, into Germany. It also reflected the desire of the first generation of German Jewish architects to wrest control of synagogue design from Christian architects (who had originally selected the Moorish style because it evoked the Jews' exotic origins). At the forefront of the campaign against the Moorish style was the German Jewish architect Edwin Oppler (1831–1880), who declared that "a German Jew in a German state must build in a German style." Convinced that German Jews needed to demonstrate their patriotic commitment to integration, Oppler embraced the Romanesque, which he believed had deep German roots without the gothic style's Christian connotations, and which influenced his synagogue designs in Hannover (1870), Danzig (1887), Munich (1887), and Cologne (1895).[24]

In the end, this new wave of architectural assimilation proved short-lived, for as the nineteenth century neared its close, the realization among German Jews that they still had failed to gain full acceptance sparked a return to architectural particularism. For the first time, German Jews began to search for a truly Jewish form of architecture. This quest grew out of a larger "dissimilationist" trend that found expression in the desire to usher in a Jewish "cultural renaissance."[25] Promoted by cultural Zionists like Martin Buber, the hope for such a renaissance was part of a broader effort to renationalize Jewish identity by demonstrating that Jews possessed a tradition of cultural achievement equal to that of other nations. In this effort, cultural Zionists were especially eager to prove the existence of Jewish art, which they believed would show that Jews deserved their own nation and would refute antisemitic claims that they were incapable of genuine artistic creativity.[26]

These efforts also generated new interest in creating a Jewish form of architecture. Zionists were at the forefront of the quest, with some, such as Theodor Herzl, calling for the creation of a "neo-Jewish style" of architecture, and others, like the Bulgarian sculptor and later founder of the Bezalel art school in Jerusalem, Boris Schatz, urging the creation of a "Jewish Palestinian style" of architecture in Ottoman-ruled Palestine. Jewish architects, meanwhile, argued that in order to "express the idea of Judaism in sensual form," synagogues needed to become less like churches. One proposal called for future synagogue plans to abandon the nineteenth-century practice — influenced by Protestant church design — of placing the bimah close to the ark in favor of reviving the Jewish tradition of locating it in the sanctuary's center. The effort to return to this older synagogue configuration was visible in the increased use of centralized domes in such early twentieth-century synagogues as Ehrenfried Hessel's Fasanenstrasse synagogue in Berlin (1912), Edmund Körner's synagogue in Essen (1913), and Fritz Landauer's synagogue of Augsburg (1914 – 17) (fig. 11). Even

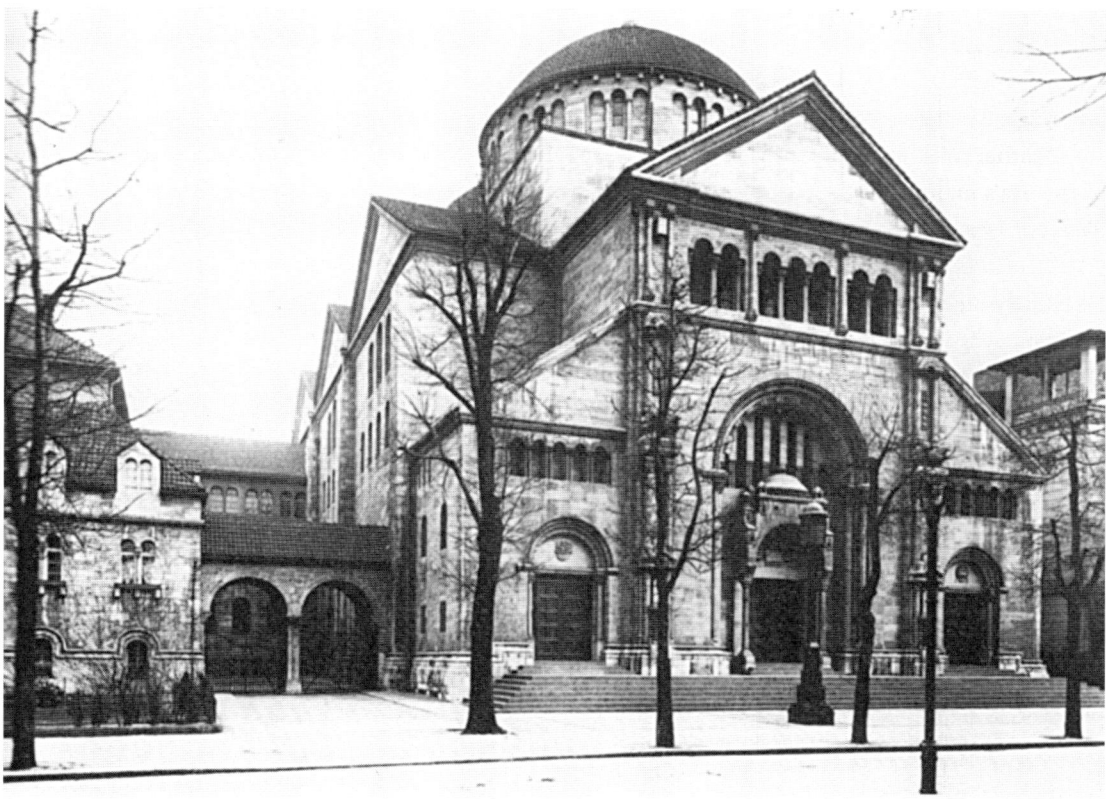

Figure 11. Ehrenfried Hessel, Fasanenstrasse synagogue, Berlin, 1912. This monumental building featured three domes and was part of the Byzantine revival of the early twentieth century.

though these buildings remained wedded to a historicist mentality, they were hailed at the time as representing hopeful signs for the creation of a Jewish architectural style.[27]

World War I interrupted this progress, but with the end of hostilities, architects and critics returned to discussing how a truly Jewish form of architecture might emerge. By this point, however, the terms of architectural discourse had radically shifted. In Europe and, to a lesser extent, the United States, historicism had come under attack by the new modernist movement, which rejected the architectural styles of the past in favor of new design principles rooted in modern materials and construction methods. This development convinced many Jewish architects that a truly Jewish style would be attainable only within the modernist movement. As the German Jewish art historian Karl Schwarz wrote in 1928, a strong chance existed that an artist would emerge from the ranks of Jews "active in the realm of modern architecture . . . whose Jewish blood would . . . lend his works a Jewish note." Jews differed on how to move beyond historicism in synagogue design, however, a fact that was illustrated by the disagreement in the 1920s between the half-Jewish American architectural historian and social critic Lewis Mumford and the Austrian Jewish art historian Max Eisler. Mumford hoped to transcend the era's "haphazard eclecticism" by embracing the dome, which he believed "would give the stamp of Judaism to a synagog as plainly as the baroque gives the stamp of the Jesuit order to a church." By contrast, Eisler crusaded against the dome and instead recommended building in such a way that "the outer form of our Temples will . . . derive from the living architectural tradition of our place of residence." For him, that meant concentrating on the synagogue's interior space—which he called the "Jewish core of the matter"—and returning to the centralized plans of earlier synagogues, but from a modernist perspective.[28]

Neither Mumford's nor Eisler's strategies carried the day during the interwar period. While some of the era's major synagogues reflected the vogue for the dome, such as Charles Greco's Temple Tifereth Israel in Cleveland (1924) and A. M. Edelman's Wilshire Boulevard Temple in Los Angeles (1929), others were more in keeping with modernism, such as Dutch Jewish architect Harry Elte's De Stijl synagogue on Jacob Obrechtplein in Amsterdam-Zuid (1928), Fritz Landauer's cubic synagogue in Plauen (1930), and Felix Ascher and Robert Friedmann's Oberstrasse Temple in Hamburg (1931) (figs. 12, 13).[29] These competing approaches symbolized the diverging status of interwar American and European Jewry. For Mumford, the domed synagogues of Cleveland and San Francisco symbolized American Jews' security, prosperity, and stability—traits that stood in contrast to the Jews' situation in Europe, where "poverty and political repression . . . made the Jew keep his religious conceptions to himself and worship in buildings which were obviously secular . . . in character." Eisler, by contrast, believed that European Jewry's bleak postwar circumstances required a more modest modernist approach. In reviewing the Austrian architect Josef Hoffmann's design for a synagogue in Sillein, Slovakia, in 1926, Eisler was reminded of the biblical Tabernacle and observed: "Since we are in the midst of wandering, far from the old holy homeland, . . . the splendid [Moorish] palaces are inappropriate. For the expelled and dispersed, . . . a more appropriate form is the temporary structure like the tent [of meeting] which can be dismantled at any minute."[30]

In the end, neither Mumford's nor Eisler's positions prevailed, as the interwar period represented a missed opportunity for the emergence of modern Jewish synagogue architecture. In the United States, where the modernist movement was less developed than in Europe, few new ideas emerged

Figure 12. A. M. Edelman, Wilshire Boulevard Temple, Los Angeles, 1929. This building expressed the interwar era's embrace of domed synagogue designs.

Figure 13. Fritz Landauer, synagogue, Plauen, Germany, 1930. This building was a rare example of interwar modernist synagogue architecture influenced by the International Style.

in the area of synagogue design. Aside from an adventurous proposal in 1929 to build a synagogue atop the roof of a skyscraper in the financial district of lower Manhattan, conservative historicist designs tended to hold sway.[31] By comparison, Europe was more advanced in generating progressive ideas but offered a less conducive climate for construction. Postwar economic difficulties, the inevitable fall-off in demand for new synagogues following the construction binge of the late nineteenth century, and the onset of the Great Depression after 1929 limited their number across the continent. By the time World War II erupted in 1939, the effort to create a modern synagogue style had come to a halt.

Secular Jewish Architecture and the Rise of Jewish Architects

As with Jewish religious architecture, the origins of secular Jewish architecture also date to antiquity. Although the Hebrew Bible says little about the architectural activity of the Jews apart from the construction of the Tabernacle and the Temple, there is ample archaeological evidence that numerous secular structures — including royal palaces, fortresses, and tombs — were erected during the millennium of Jewish existence in the land of Israel after the ninth century BCE. These structures mostly reveal the influence of Egyptian, Phoenician, Hellenistic, and Roman architectural traditions, however, and show few signs of a distinctive Jewish style.[32] As Peter Richardson has concluded, "The distinctiveness of Jewish architecture [in this period] lay more in its . . . mixing [of] diverse influences than in anything inherent in Judaism's own architectural traditions."[33]

The influence of foreign traditions upon ancient Jewish architecture provides the oldest evidence supporting the notion of Jewish architectural underachievement. The idea that Jews registered few major accomplishments as architects is first implied in the Hebrew Bible, which portrays the first Jewish architect in history, Bezalel, as merely taking orders from God, who is the chief architect in charge of coordinating construction work on the first Jewish structure, the Tabernacle.[34] The

Jews' expulsion from the land of Israel further entrenched the idea that they were undistinguished as architects. Everywhere they lived in the Diaspora, Jews rose to positions of economic, intellectual, and political prominence, but very few achieved architectural renown prior to the modern era. This was especially true in Europe, where discriminatory laws kept Jews from becoming architects. The result was that most secular Jewish buildings were designed by non-Jewish architects and consequently displayed few Jewish traits.

This is not to say that such traits were entirely lacking in secular Jewish architecture. During the High Middle Ages, the dwellings of wealthy Jewish bankers and moneylenders were frequently grander than the homes of their Christian neighbors. In late twelfth-century England, for example, Aaron of Lincoln, a Jewish banker said to be the second-richest man after the king, built an imposing mansion entirely of stone, which departed radically from the nearby wood-frame structures. According to Salo Baron, this house and others like it were unusual for the time and were regarded as "Jewish" by poorer Christian neighbors.[35] A more explicitly Jewish work of secular architecture was found in sixteenth-century Prague, where the Jewish community built a new town hall with a Renaissance-style tower that featured a clock with Hebrew letters instead of numbers (fig. 14). Like Aaron of Lincoln's mansion, this unusually extroverted building suggests that outward displays of Jewishness were most likely to appear in periods of security.[36]

Figure 14. Pancratius Roder, Jewish Town Hall, Prague, 1565–68 (subsequently rebuilt by Josef Schlesinger, 1763–65). The baroque building, which stands next to the Altneuschul, was an unusually extroverted work of secular Jewish architecture, as is shown by the Hebrew-lettered clock on the gable and the Star of David atop its tower.

26 Before the Holocaust

For most of medieval and early modern Jewish history, however, the Jews' secular buildings reflected the realities of persecution. In the same way that confinement in ghettos made the Jews' synagogues turn inward, their spatial confinement thrust their secular buildings upward. The overcrowded conditions in some ghettos left Jews little choice but to build higher in order to maximize available living space. In the famous *ghetto nuovo* and *ghetto vecchio* of Venice, for example, apartment buildings soared to eight stories in height, making the district appear as a collection of towers and lending it the reputation of being a "citadel within the city." It remains unclear to what extent verticality was seen as "Jewish" at the time, but the fact that Jews were occasionally prohibited from building tall buildings — in the early eighteenth century, the city of Frankfurt rejected as immodest the request of the Jewish banker Israel Nathan Oppenheim to build a formidable four-story stone home for himself on the *Judengasse* — suggests that verticality may have become associated with Jewishness in certain parts of Europe.[37]

The consequences of insecurity and poverty were also visible in the shtetls of Eastern Europe. As Mark Zborowski and Elizabeth Herzog documented in their book *Life Is with People: The Culture of the Shtetl* (1952), Eastern European Jews' "long history of exile and eviction strengthen[ed their] tendency to regard their dwelling place as a husk" and led them to build with an eye toward temporariness instead of permanence. The result, Zborowksi and Herzog concluded, was that there was "no 'Jewish architecture'" as such in the shtetl. In reality, of course, the indifference of many shtetl Jews toward architecture expressed a sense of "Jewishness" insofar as it contrasted sharply with how their more secure Christian neighbors treated their own homes. Precisely because "even the poorest peasant spends his spare time puttering about his home, repairing the door, the fence, and the whitewashed walls," Christian houses were defined by "better grooming," while Jewish ones were defined by "shabbiness." The uncertain circumstances of shtetl life, in short, had clear architectural consequences.[38]

With the dawn of modernity, however, secular Jewish architecture began to develop in new directions. As Jews gained emancipation in Europe and rose in socioeconomic status in the United States during the nineteenth century, they began to enter the architectural profession. It is unclear how many Jews became architects in this period; statistics are hard to find, as is reliable information about the Jewish background of individual architects. Many Jewish architects were reluctant to be identified as such, a fact suggested by the frustrated complaint of the German Jewish writer and critic Adolf Kohut, who in his two-volume encyclopedia from 1901, *Berühmte israelitische Männer und Frauen in der Kulturgeschichte der Menschheit* (Famous Israelite Men and Women in the Cultural History of Mankind), lamented that most "architects of Israelite descent" had tried to "hide their origins as much as possible." This reaction partly reflected the fact that while the architectural profession was technically open to Jewish talent, it was easier for Jews to gain admission and become successful if they converted or otherwise denied their identity. Erich Mendelsohn, the most important Jewish architect of the early twentieth century, was initially dissuaded from pursuing architecture by a German government building officer who told him he had no chance as a Jew of becoming an architect in any official capacity. Mendelsohn never tried to cover up his Jewishness, but the willingness of other Jewish architects to do so makes it hard to determine their real numbers. Still, Myra Warhaftig has been able to determine that in Germany prior to the Nazi takeover in 1933 there were some 450 Jewish architects practicing nationwide, while Frederic Bedoire has shown that in Hungary, nearly 70 percent of Budapest's architects were Jews or had Jewish backgrounds.[39]

Given these numbers, it should come as no surprise that Jewish architects designed notable buildings in both Europe and the United States in the nineteenth and early twentieth centuries. In Germany's capital of Berlin, Georg Friedrich Heinrich Hitzig (1811–1881) was responsible for the headquarters of the Stock Exchange (1859–63) and the Reichsbank (1868–77), while Alfred Messel (1853–1909) designed the celebrated Wertheim department store on the Leipziger Platz (1896–1905) (fig. 15). In the Austro-Hungarian Empire, Carl König (1841–1915), Max Fleischer (1841–1905), and Wilhelm Stiassny (1842–1910) were widely known for their neobaroque, neogothic, and Moorish revival buildings in Vienna, Prague, and other parts of the Dual Monarchy. And in England, two pupils of John Soane, George Basevi (1794–1845) and David Moccatta (1806–82), were, respectively, responsible for the Fitzwilliam Museum in Cambridge (1848) and the Brighton Train Station (1839–40). In the United States, the first Jewish architect in American history, Leopold Eidlitz, helped design the New York State Capitol Building in Albany (1875–83) and the New York County Courthouse (1861–72). And the German Jewish immigrant to America Dankmar Adler (1844–1900) collaborated with his legendary partner Louis Sullivan in the construction of such important buildings as the Wainwright Building in St. Louis (1890–91), the Guaranty Building in Buffalo, New York (1896), and the Auditorium Building in Chicago (1886–90).[40]

Yet while Jewish architects were indisputably active in this period, their work never attained major significance. None of them achieved the renown of such pioneering historicist masters as Karl Friedrich Schinkel, Leo von Klenze, and Gottfried Semper in Germany, A. W. N. Pugin in England, and Charles Garnier in France, not to mention Thomas Ustick Walter, Richard Upjohn, Frank Furness, H. H. Richardson, and the firm of McKim, Mead, and White in the United States. A variety of reasons lie behind the modest achievements of Jewish architects, but a significant factor was their conformist mindset. In the same way that they strove to assimilate in their personal lives (many of the leading Jewish architects had grown distant from Judaism, and some, such as Hitzig and Messel, had converted to Christianity), they adhered to architectural tradition in their work. Because most Jewish architects lacked the inclination toward architectural innovation, they never succeeded in producing any truly pioneering buildings. As a result, they failed to match the achievements of Jews in other branches of culture. No Jewish architect matched the status of Sholem Aleichem in literature, Heinrich Heine in poetry, or Felix Mendelssohn in music.[41]

Figure 15. Alfred Messel, Wertheim department store, Berlin, 1896–1905. This building was a pioneering work of commercial architecture, despite its historicist elements.

With the advent of modern architecture, however, Jewish architects began to register more distinct achievements. This development partly reflected the important role of European and American Jews in giving rise to the broader cultural movement of modernism.[42] Understood as a revolt against cultural tradition that aimed to identify, evoke, and artistically document the ever-shifting reality of the modern world, modernism was a cultural movement that — whether in the realm of literature, theater, art, or music — was advanced by creative individuals who largely stood outside of the cultural mainstream and possessed the proper outsider status to question and challenge its underlying values.[43] Many different people performed this creative function in European life: political dissidents, expatriates, gays and lesbians, and ethnic or national minorities being among the more prominent. But the archetypal outsiders were the Jews, who, despite striving to assimilate into European life, were continually rebuffed by the persistence of antisemitism. Their resulting feelings of exclusion led many Jews to question, challenge, and formulate alternatives to Europe's reigning cultural traditions.[44] Among the classic representatives of this destructively creative trend were such Jewish (or Jewish-descended) figures as the writers Franz Kafka, Marcel Proust, and Gertrude Stein; the poets Tristan Tzara and Else Lasker-Schüler; the composers Gustav Mahler and Arnold Schönberg; and the painters Max Liebermann, Camille Pissarro, Marc Chagall, and Chaim Soutine.

Jewish architects partly followed in this tradition by contributing to the emergence of the modern movement after the turn of the century. The first major Jewish modernist was the Dutch Jewish architect Michel de Klerk (1884–1923). His work displayed many of the hallmarks of modernism's expressionist wing, most notably a gravitation toward individualistic architectural forms created via an intuitive, rather than wholly rational, design process. A member of the so-called Amsterdam School, De Klerk is best known for his large-scale worker housing complexes: the first designed for the Eigen Haard housing association in Amsterdam in 1913–21 (fig. 16) and the second designed with Piet Kramer for De Dageraad (1918–23). Clad in brick and exhibiting dynamic forms and organically derived decorative details, the buildings — especially the nautical-looking third block of the Eigen Haard complex known as "the ship" (*Het Schip*) — have long been regarded as canonical works of architectural expressionism. To be sure, because of the expressionist movement's second-class status in the eyes of leading architectural historians, De Klerk never attained the reputation enjoyed by the architects associated with the International Style. Still, in recent decades his work has been rediscovered and his reputation rehabilitated to the point where De Klerk has been hailed as an "inimitable genius."[45] Had he not died of pneumonia in 1923 at the age of thirty-nine, De Klerk might have distinguished himself further. As it is, he can be seen as the first pathbreaking Jewish architect of the modern movement.

Another major Jewish modernist was El Lissitzky (1890–1940). A central member of the Russian constructivist movement, Lissitzky was a multitalented figure best known for his radically innovative works in painting, photography, typography, and exhibition design. He was also an architect, however, having studied architectural engineering in Darmstadt, Germany, before becoming affiliated with the architecture wing of the Soviet version of the Bauhaus, the VkhUTEMAS State Art and Technical School in Moscow. In his capacity as an architect, Lissitzky designed several visionary projects, most notably his Wolkenbügel ("cloud iron") series of cantilevered horizontal skyscrapers in 1926 (fig. 17). His famous "Proun" paintings of intersecting three-dimensional geometric

Figure 16. Michel de Klerk, Het Schip ("the ship") apartment building, Amsterdam, 1917–21. The design is an iconic example of expressionist architecture.

Figure 17. El Lissitzky, Wolkenbügel, 1926. This photomontage shows a dramatic view of Lissitzky's horizontal skyscraper concept.

Figure 18. Erich Mendelsohn, Berliner Tageblatt building (Mossehaus), Berlin, 1921–23. The headquarters of the Mosse publishing company displayed Mendelsohn's trademark streamlined forms.

shapes, his sculptural designs, such as his famous Lenin Tribune (1919–23), and his theoretical writings on urban space also displayed utopian tendencies in their striving to create new points of convergence between art and architecture. Thanks to these achievements, Lissitzky's reputation as a pioneer of modern design is widely acknowledged, though, like De Klerk he never really reached his potential as an architect. Since the turbulent early years of the Soviet Union did not provide a conducive atmosphere for realizing ambitious works of architecture, Lissitzky completed only one building before turning most of his creative energy to nonarchitectural projects. Still, he showed how Jews could take advantage of modernism's limitless design possibilities.[46]

Ultimately surpassing both De Klerk and Lissitzky was the German Jewish architect Erich Mendelsohn (1887–1953). Hailed as the "national architect of the Jews" by Frank Lloyd Wright, Mendelsohn was the most important Jewish architect of the early twentieth century. He first gained attention for his expressionistic Einstein tower in Potsdam (1921), a structure housing an observatory and scientific offices devoted to proving Einstein's theory of relativity. Mendelsohn earned further acclaim later in the decade for a series of commercial buildings in Berlin—the Berliner Tageblatt building (known as the Mossehaus, 1921–23), the Universum Cinema (1927–31), and the Columbushaus (1932)—as well as three buildings for the Schocken Department Store chain in Nuremberg (1925–26), Stuttgart (1926–28), and Chemnitz (1928–30) (fig. 18). These and other works clearly expressed Mendelsohn's belief that modern architecture should express the dynamism of the modern world—especially its love of speed—and could only do so by combining "functionalism with dynamics." As a result of his innovative designs, Mendelsohn achieved professional success, eventually presiding over the largest firm in Germany. More than a few architectural historians have honored his accomplishments, with Reyner Banham describing him as "one of the more remarkable architectural talents of the twentieth century." Yet by virtue of his work's expressionist character, Mendelsohn, like De Klerk, has never been granted the same status in the history of modern architecture as his rivals associated with the International Style.[47]

Whether or not such assessments are fair, most Jewish architects during the interwar period were not idiosyncratic expressionists but sober functionalists. The most notable ones were Jews of European origin who came to prominence after moving to the United States. Probably the best known was the American-based Austrian emigré architect Richard Neutra, whose Lovell Health House in Los Angeles (1927–29)—the first steel-framed modern house built in the United States—was described by Kenneth Frampton as the "apotheosis of the International Style" (fig. 19). Neutra's Los Angeles–based Austrian colleague Rudolf Schindler is also well known thanks to his pioneering Lovell Beach House in Newport Beach (1922–26) and his own Kings Road House in West Hollywood (1921–22), which Reyner Banham described as "one of the most original . . . and ingenious domestic designs of the . . . century." Not far behind is the Bauhaus-trained Hungarian architect and designer Marcel Breuer, who was best known before 1945 for his pioneering furniture designs, especially his tubular steel and canvas "Wassily" chair, but who also produced the pathbreaking Harnischmacher House in Wiesbaden (1932), which Henry-Russell Hitchcock called "one of the finest modern houses in the world." Beyond these three architects—all of whom remained active during the early postwar period—other lesser-known Jewish architects embraced the modern movement. The French Jewish architect Pierre Chareau (1883–1950) was known for his steel and glass Maison de Verre in Paris (1928–31). The Jewish Austrian architect Josef Frank (1885–1967) helped establish the modernist Vienna School of Architecture and contributed a two-level apartment building for the Weissenhof Settlement exhibition in Stuttgart in 1927. Other Jewish architects, such as Richard Kauffmann, Zeev Rechter, and Arieh Sharon, studied at the Bauhaus and moved to Palestine during the 1920s and 1930s, where they contributed to the construction of the modernist "White City" of Tel Aviv. Few of these men, however, are perceived today as ranking among the profession's top figures of the interwar period.[48]

The limited achievements of Jewish architects in these years was also visible in the United States, where the two most innovative American Jewish architects of the interwar era, Albert Kahn and Ely Jacques Kahn (no relation), retained strong links to historicism and never fully embraced modernism. Albert Kahn (1869–1942) was a pioneering figure in industrial architecture, designing more than two thousand buildings for the automotive and aviation industries during his long career. Yet while his buildings for the Ford Motor Company — especially its gigantic River Rouge complex, built in 1917–39 — were pathbreaking and helped the "Fordist" assembly line system reach its full potential, his nonindustrial work, such as his neoclassical General Motors world headquarters in Detroit (the largest office building in the world when it was built in 1919–22) — remained wedded to a historicist mentality (fig. 20).[49] Similarly, while Ely Jacques Kahn (1884–1972) was one of New York City's most prolific designers of Art Deco office buildings in the 1920s and 1930s, he too remained distant from the International Style and does not figure prominently in most histories of modern architecture.[50]

Still, the work of these Jewish architects during the interwar period proved their ability to achieve professional success. This development was especially welcome to Jews who had long resented the charge that they were architectural underachievers. In the summer of 1931, the leading German Jewish organization, the Central Union of German Citizens of the Jewish Faith (Central-Verein deutscher Staatsbürger jüdischen Glaubens, or C.V.) profiled the accomplishments of German Jewish

Figure 19. Richard Neutra, Lovell House, Los Angeles, 1927–29. The building was the first steel-framed home in the United States.

Figure 20. Albert Kahn, General Motors world headquarters, Detroit, 1919–22. The structure was the largest office building in the world at the time of its completion.

architects in a special issue of the *C.V.-Zeitung* devoted to the topic of "Builders and Buildings." Published during a period of rising antisemitism, the newspaper sought to publicize the "creative participation of Jewish Germans [in the field of architecture]" as a means of "refuting the anti-Jewish canard that the Jewish mind was . . . predominantly 'commercially' oriented." This point was emphasized in the issue's feature article, written by the German Jewish art critic Max Osborn, which aimed to show that "Jewish forces played a . . . meaningful role in the development of European and German architecture." Although he was prone to exaggeration in discussing German Jewish architectural accomplishments (he called Alfred Messel the "ancestor of all German modern architecture"), Osborn convincingly showed the "extent to which artistry and creative energy have emerged out of Judaism."[51]

Yet no matter how many successes were registered by Jewish architects during these years, little of their work exhibited discernible "Jewish" qualities. None of the architects—neither the expressionists nor the representatives of the International Style—drew upon their Jewishness in their designs. As is discussed at greater length in Chapter 2, this was partly due to the fact that, with a few exceptions, most Jewish architects in the interwar period possessed a weak sense of Jewish identity and seldom worked on the kinds of Jewish commissions—for synagogues, schools, or community centers—that might have inspired them to draw on it. Marcel Breuer, for instance, formally withdrew from the Jewish religion in the 1920s and devoted little attention to Jewish construction projects. Richard Neutra grew up in an agnostic family and, while he produced several unrealized designs for Jewish institutional clients early in his career while working for Erich Mendelsohn, never produced any Jewish-related structures once his career took off after the mid-1920s. The same is true of the highly secularized and bohemian Rudolf Schindler, who, apart from producing plans for an unrealized synagogue while working in a Chicago firm before 1914, produced nothing of Jewish relevance. Similarly, Ely Jacques Kahn's upbringing in a wealthy and highly assimilated German Jewish family—like his decision to join the secular humanist Society for Ethical Culture in 1912—explains his lack of interest in pursuing Jewish projects. Finally, while Albert Kahn was the son of a rabbi, his commercial view of his profession—he famously said "architecture is 90% business and 10% art"—helps explain his disinclination to draw on his religious background in his work.[52]

This disinclination was visible not just among secular-minded Jewish architects, however, but among more affiliated Jews as well. Michel de Klerk seems to have had a strong sense of Jewish identity, as shown by his traditional Jewish education and marriage to a Jewish woman. Yet, apart from designing a building in Amsterdam for a Zionist organization, there is no evidence that his Jewish background shaped his architectural work in any serious way.[53] El Lissitzky hailed from a traditional Jewish family, supported the idea of secular Jewish cultural renaissance, and actively drew on Jewish sources of inspiration in his early design work; yet Jewish ideas did not influence his thinking about architecture, which was shaped more directly by his commitment to Soviet communism.[54] The same pattern is true, albeit to a lesser extent, of Mendelsohn. On the one hand, the architect had an extremely strong sense of Jewish identity. All his clients in the 1920s were Jewish, including the advertising and media baron Hans Lachmann-Mosse and the department store magnate Salman Schocken. Mendelsohn furthermore accepted commissions for Jewish institutions in Germany, designing a Jewish cemetery in the East Prussian city of Königsberg (1927–29), a Jewish social hall (containing a small synagogue) in the East Prussian town of Tilsit (today Sovetsk) in 1924, and a Jewish youth center in the industrial city of Essen (1929–30). He was also a Zionist and worked on building projects for the Jewish Yishuv in Palestine (none of which was ever realized). These facts notwithstanding, there is little evidence that Mendelsohn's Jewishness shaped his architectural philosophy in any deep sense during the most productive phase of his career.[55]

In refraining from finding inspiration in their backgrounds, modern Jewish architects differed noticeably from Jews in other realms of modernist culture. Well-known Jewish modernists in literature, painting, and music combined Jewish themes with avant-garde methods of representation in their work. The Paris-based Russian Jewish painter Marc Chagall, for instance, embraced a cubist approach in portraying Eastern European shtetl life and episodes from the Hebrew Bible. He also affirmed the centrality of his Jewishness for his art, famously declaring, "Had I not been a Jew I never would have been a painter, or an entirely different one."[56] Other noted figures drew on their Jewish backgrounds less consciously but nevertheless owed much of their creativity to anxieties stemming from their status as Jewish outsiders in European society. Franz Kafka never explicitly tackled Jewish themes in his writing, but his conflicted sense of Jewishness (rooted in his alienation from his father's assimilated Jewish identity, his concerns about antisemitism, and his growing fascination with Hasidism, Kabbalah, and Zionism) found expression in his writings.[57] The half-Jewish French writer Marcel Proust's conflicted views towards his Jewish heritage in the wake of the Dreyfus Affair colored his portrayal of French society in his magnum opus, *Remembrance of Things Past* (1913–27).[58] The great Viennese composer Arnold Schoenberg's disillusioning experiences with antisemitism in the early 1920s motivated him to seek musical inspiration in Jewish themes, whether the Bible, as with his twelve-tone opera *Moses and Aron* (1928–32), or the Jewish liturgical tradition, as with his composition *Kol Nidre*, op. 38 (1938).[59] Finally, Camille Pissarro, Max Liebermann, and Chaim Soutine were all influenced by their sense of social marginality in producing their impressionist and expressionist paintings.[60] In all these cases, Jewish modernists channeled aspects of their identities into universalistic forms of modernist expression.

By contrast, Jewish modernists in architecture were not driven by similar impulses prior to 1945. In part, this was due to the unique features of architecture as a branch of the larger modernist movement. Many realms of modernist culture, especially literature, art, and poetry, have classically been defined by alienation, gloom, and pessimism about modernity. The novels of James Joyce, the paintings of Otto Dix, and the poems of T. S. Eliot, among many other examples, have long been seen as critical commentaries on the modern world's anomie, violence, and bleakness. By contrast, modernism in the field of architecture was underpinned by the exuberant conviction that the modern world had given rise to new technologies and materials that could be used to improve the condition of humankind. Dating back to the use of steel and reinforced concrete in the mid-nineteenth century by architects such as Joseph Paxton and Gustav Eiffel, through the embrace of factory methods of mass production for housing in the early twentieth century by architects associated with Italian Futurism and the German Bauhaus, up through the radical overhaul of city planning concepts by visionaries like Le Corbusier, modern architects fervently believed that rationally harnessing the technologies and materials of modern industry could pave the way for a utopian future. Especially after the carnage of World War I, when modernist writers and painters were bemoaning the crisis of the modern world, architects optimistically believed that it could be redeemed through architectural means.

The forward-looking character of modernism in architecture strongly conditioned the attitudes of Jewish modernists toward their Jewishness. Modern architecture's upbeat nature made it less suited than other areas of modernist culture to express the plight of the Jew as an alienated outsider in the modern world. For this reason, architecture as a career may have appealed more readily to those Jews who were more comfortable with their identities than to those who were plagued by the contradictions of the modern Jewish experience (and who consequently gravitated to fields that allowed for greater personal self-expression). To be sure, Jewish architects throughout Europe faced the same pressures of assimilation and antisemitism as Jewish writers, painters, and composers, but their range of responses was limited by the optimistic nature of their discipline. Rather than drawing inspiration from their outsider status in their work, therefore, they deemphasized it and affected the pose of the insider. This response not only reflected modern architecture's inherent optimism but also its universalism. Because modern architecture strove to create a style of absolute universal validity, it discouraged expressions of particularism, whether individual or collective. For this reason as well, Jewish modernists refrained from emphasizing their ethnic, religious, or cultural differences in their work.

The aversion to expressing a sense of Jewishness in architecture was also reinforced by the collaborative nature of architecture as a form of cultural endeavor. Erecting buildings is a collective enterprise, one in which architects have to rely on outside clients for commissions, secure the support of city authorities to obtain building permits, and pay attention to other restrictions in the design process. Compared to writers, poets, and musicians who can more readily preserve the purity of their work by living the life of a starving artist, architects rely exclusively on others for their livelihood and have thus traditionally enjoyed less independence in expressing themselves creatively. This dependence further explains why Jewish architects deemphasized their Jewishness in their professional work. Any Jewish architect who was interested in landing a commission had to attract the interest of Christian clients and be practical enough to put up with their potential anti-Jewish prejudices. Albert Kahn, for example, worked for thirty years for Henry Ford, despite the latter's overt antisemitism. Given the realities of antisemitism in the first half of the twentieth century, only Jewish architects who downplayed their identities were likely to receive commissions. This further helps explain why the work of Jewish modernist architects was less "Jewish" than the work of Jewish modernist painters, writers, or composers like Chagall, Kafka, or Schoenberg. That Jews participating in the architectural rebellion against historicism had to do so in a universal rather than particularistic code may help explain why they were less distinguished in modern architecture than in other areas of modernist culture.

This universalistic tendency may also explain why the Jewish architects who did embrace modernism were less accomplished than their Christian modernist colleagues. Comparatively speaking, few Jewish architects were at the forefront of the modernist movement. None of the major architects associated with the Art Nouveau and Arts and Crafts movements in Europe, such as Charles Rennie Mackintosh, Henry van de Velde, Victor Horta, Otto Wagner, Hermann Muthesius, August Endell, or Antoni Gaudi, were Jews. None of the architects who contributed to the rise of the

International Style—Adolf Loos, Peter Behrens, Walter Gropius, Ludwig Mies van der Rohe, Auguste Perret, Tony Garnier, Le Corbusier, or Alvar Aalto—was Jewish either. Neither were there any Jews among the American founders of modern architecture, which was pioneered by Daniel Burnham, William LeBaron Jenney, Louis Sullivan, and Frank Lloyd Wright. In short, while Jewish architects were certainly present in the modern movement, their absence from its elite ranks suggests that the movement did not allow Jewish talents to unfold in the same way as other branches of modernist culture.

Yet, no matter how much Jewish architects may have ignored their Jewishness during the interwar years, the rise of fascism and the eruption of the Second World War made them unable to avoid their identities any longer. In October 1933, Erich Mendelsohn was notified by the Federation of German Architects (*Bund Deutscher Architekten*) that only architects of "Aryan descent" would be allowed as members. Several years later, in 1941, the headline "Jewish Architects Restricted by Vichy" revealed that the French collaborationist government had followed suit. Other nations in Europe soon did the same, until Jewish architects—like Jews in all other walks of life—had lost their ability to work entirely. Prior to the Holocaust, in short, Jewish architects had been relegated to the status they held in the Middle Ages when they had not existed at all.[61]

Jewish Architectural Patronage

The history of Jewish architecture encompasses not just religious and secular buildings, but also Jewish architectural patronage. Long before they became architects, Jews in Europe and the United States commissioned works of architecture for themselves and their communities. They did so in every era and in every locale where they possessed the necessary financial means, but never as dramatically as in the modern period when they enjoyed unprecedented levels of affluence. The pivotal role of Jews in the emergence of the modern industrial capitalist economy put them in a unique position to foster the emergence of new architectural movements. Jews did not favor any one movement, commissioning buildings in a variety of styles. But they were disproportionately open to modern architecture after its emergence in the late nineteenth and early twentieth centuries.[62] The

Figure 21. Adolf Loos, Looshaus, Vienna, 1909–11. The building, built for the Jewish businessman Leopold Goldman, shocked many Viennese because of its lack of ornamentation.

support of Jewish clients was pivotal in the emergence of modern architecture, whose development would have been adversely affected without it.

The first precondition for Jewish architectural patronage was Jewish wealth. During the nineteenth century, significant numbers of Jews ascended into the European economic elite, becoming phenomenally successful in finance, commerce, and industry. Banking was one of the fields in which Jews excelled, as shown by the fortunes of such illustrious families as the Pereires in France, the Bleichröders, Warburgs, and Oppenheims in Germany, and, above all, the Rothschilds (who were represented in France, Germany, England, the Habsburg Empire, and Italy). Jews also played leading roles in the development of the railroad, chemical, and electricity industries in Europe and the United States. Despite comprising less than 1 percent of the population in many Western European countries, Jews made up over 20 percent of all the millionaires in England; 30 percent of the richest families in Germany; and over 70 percent of the richest taxpayers in Hungary.[63]

Thanks to their financial clout, Jews played an important role as patrons of European architecture in the nineteenth and early twentieth centuries. They helped develop significant sections of Europe's major cities, building apartment complexes, department stores, and railway stations, among many other structures. In France, the founders of the Credit Mobilière, Emil and Isaac Pereire, developed significant sections of Paris during the reign of Napoleon III (1852 – 70), including the city's first major hotel and train stations (Gare de l'Est and Gare St. Lazare, for example), while Jewish entrepreneurs, such as Jules Jaluzot and Alphonse Kahn, commissioned such architecturally trendsetting department stores as the Grands Magasins du Printemps and the Galeries Lafayette. In Germany, Jewish businessmen bought major chunks of real estate in Berlin, especially in the Friedrichstadt district, where they established the city's three main department stores: Wertheim, Tietz, and KaDeWe. Finally, in the Habsburg monarchy's twin capitals of Vienna and Budapest, Jews developed the major commercial and residential areas around the Ringstrasse and Andrássy Utca. These architectural projects were secular, although from time to time they betrayed hints of their patrons' Jewish backgrounds, as with Hungarian iron magnate Henryk Schossberger's decision to commission a sculptural figure of Moses for the entryway to his family's opulent house at Andrássy ut 8 in Budapest and Lionel de Rothschild's decision to leave a cornice on his house at 148 Piccadilly unfinished, in memory of the destruction of the Second Temple.[64]

Jews were also involved in promoting modern developments in architecture during this period. Some of the iconic works of early modernism were built for Jewish clients. Peter Behrens designed his AEG Turbine factory in Berlin (1908 – 9) at the request of the company's Jewish chief, Emil Rathenau, while Adolf Loos built his seminal Looshaus building on the Michaelerplatz in Vienna (1909 – 11) for the Jewish businessman Leopold Goldman, the owner of the men's clothing store Goldman and Salatsch (fig. 21). Some of the most famous private modernist homes were also built for Jewish clients. Loos built his purist Steiner Haus (1910) for the Jewish textile mill owner Hugo Steiner and his wife, Lilly. Le Corbusier designed the Villa Stein at Garches (1927) for Gertrude Stein's brother, Michael, a wealthy art collector. Ludwig Mies van der Rohe's Tugendhat House (1928 – 30) outside Brno, Czechoslovakia, was constructed for the Czech textile manufacturer Fritz Tugendhat. Rudolf Schindler built his Lovell Beach House (1922 – 26) and Richard Neutra built his steel-framed Lovell Health house (1929) for the American Jewish health and fitness guru Philip

Figure 22. Frank Lloyd Wright, Fallingwater, Bear Run, Pennsylvania, 1938. The modernist home was built for the Jewish department store owner Edgar J. Kaufmann, who commissioned it partly to express his frustration over being excluded from Pittsburgh's high society.

Lovell. In England, where modern architecture faced stiff resistance in the interwar period, the two most innovative homes of the 1930s were built for Jewish clients: Walter Gropius's 1936 house for Benjamin Levy and his wife; and Erich Mendelsohn and Serge Chermayeff's house for Levy's cousin (and immediate neighbor) Dennis Cohen. Finally, and most famously, Frank Lloyd Wright built the legendary weekend country house Fallingwater (1938) for the Pittsburgh department store owner Edgar J. Kaufmann (fig. 22).[65]

To a large degree, these Jewish patrons supported modern architecture because their outsider status encouraged them to challenge the traditions of the day. Lovell was a self-proclaimed "'radical' in health and dietary matters [who] . . . liked to associate with [other] 'radicals' in . . . politics, economics, [and] the arts."[66] Michael Stein was a bohemian art aficionado who was among the first Americans to recognize the genius of such French modernist painters as Henri Matisse. Lilly Steiner was an expressionist artist. The best representative of this trend, however, was Kaufmann. According to Franklin Toker, Kaufmann was a typical Jewish outsider, highly assimilated and removed from religious tradition but unable to gain acceptance, despite his vast wealth, into the antisemitic Pittsburgh social elite of the Mellons, Carnegies, and Fricks. Pained by his systematic exclusion from the city's better clubs and social organizations, he decided to commission Fallingwater as a means of "redress[ing] the wrongs . . . done [to him]" by the "anti-Jewish snobbery of Pittsburgh." It was Kaufmann's outsider status, in short, that made him willing to serve as a "courageous patron" to a style of architecture that more traditionally minded Americans avoided.[67] In the final analysis, of course, it would be mistaken to conclude from the examples of Kaufmann and other Jewish patrons that modern architecture owes its very existence to Jewish sponsorship. Yet without the latter, the history of the modern movement surely would have been very different.

Conclusion

The preceding survey shows that the history of Jewish architecture prior to the Holocaust was generally one of modest achievement. Beginning in antiquity, when Jewish architecture was largely influenced by foreign traditions, and continuing into the Diaspora, where Jews were unable to become architects, Jews made few notable contributions to the history of architecture. Only with the onset of modernity and emancipation did Jews finally get the chance to make a mark on architectural history. Jews ended up sponsoring important works of architecture as patrons and designed numerous secular buildings as architects. On balance, however, their works were more respectable than pathbreaking. Their buildings, moreover, displayed few Jewish traits. This absence was especially visible in religious architecture, where Jewish architects' efforts to develop a distinctly Jewish style of synagogue design faltered due to their continued reliance on historicism. The ensuing attempt to create a Jewish style of synagogue architecture with the help of modernism, meanwhile, never had a chance to succeed. With the eruption of the Second World War, all meaningful Jewish architectural activity came to an abrupt halt. Only after 1945 would Jewish architects be able to resume the quest to create a Jewish style of architecture. By this point, however, they were designing for a world that had been irrevocably altered by the rupture of the Holocaust.

Part Two

After the Holocaust
Jewish Architecture in the Era of Modernism

I am seldom taken aback by works of architecture, but when I first visited Congregation Kneses Tifereth Israel in Port Chester, New York, on a cloudy day in the fall of 2007, I was surprised that I could barely see the synagogue, surrounded as it was by a thick row of cedar trees (fig. 23). I had made an appointment with Rabbi Jaymee Alpert of KTI (as the synagogue is locally known) to see the building's modernist interior, but throughout my brief tour I could not stop thinking about the dense blanket of trees just outside. One reason for my interest was that the trees' presence reminded me of another building that was equally shrouded in greenery — Munich's notorious House of German Art (Haus der Deutschen Kunst) (fig. 24). Commissioned by Adolf Hitler and built according to the design of Paul Ludwig Troost in 1933 – 37, the monumental Nazi art temple was widely viewed as an embarrassing eyesore after 1945. In the late 1950s, therefore, Munich city authorities decided to camouflage the building by planting a thick row of trees in front of it. Being aware of this precedent, I wondered if KTI's congregation might have been motivated by similar considerations.

Figure 23. Philip Johnson, Congregation Kneses Tifereth Israel, Port Chester, New York, 1953–56. This photograph from 2007 shows the synagogue's front facade when it was still surrounded by cedar trees. The trees were removed in the summer of 2009. Compare with fig. 36.

Figure 24. Paul Ludwig Troost, Haus der Deutschen Kunst, Munich, 1933–37. The former Nazi art museum, today known as the Haus der Kunst, was partly hidden behind a row of trees in 1958 at the request of Munich's city council.

I thought this was especially possible since KTI had its own embarrassing historical legacy to hide — the unseemly past of its architect, Philip Johnson. As I discuss in Chapter 3, Johnson was an antisemitic Nazi sympathizer in the 1930s and 1940s before making a dramatic about-face after World War II. Were the congregants aware of Johnson's past, I wondered, when they accepted his generous offer in 1953 to design their new sanctuary for free? Might the trees signify a guilty conscience, a desire to hide what could be seen as a morally compromised building? I subsequently learned that the congregation planted the trees in the early 1970s for aesthetic reasons, to soften the building's harsh rectilinear lines.[1] Yet, the Nazi past was not so easily separated from KTI's history. In 2006, the congregation made headlines for its controversial decision to get rid of Johnson's original interior furnishings — including a celebrated wire sculpture by Ibram Lassaw, which some congregants reportedly thought resembled barbed wire and, by extension, Nazi concentration camps.[2] Together with Johnson's past, this example underscored for me how the Holocaust's shadows could extend far beyond Europe and disrupt the impression of normalcy at an otherwise placid suburban American synagogue.

As is shown by the example of KTI, the Holocaust provides a crucial backdrop for understanding the development of Jewish architecture after 1945. Following the end of the Second World War, Jewish architects continued to wrestle with the question of Jewish architecture, but now they did so in a radically transformed world. The wartime murder of some 6 million Jews raised massive questions for western cultural and intellectual life, notably whether any kind of cultural creativity was possible after Auschwitz. In Chapter 2, I describe how western thinkers, writers, and artists began to confront the Holocaust after 1945 and how architects largely avoided doing so. Few architects, Jewish or Christian, asked whether architecture was possible after Auschwitz. Few called their principles into question or reassessed their validity. In short, few architects directly confronted the Holocaust's legacy in their early postwar work. As a result, early postwar Jewish architecture displayed few signs of the recent past. In Chapter 3, I examine this evasion of memory in American synagogue architecture, while in Chapter 4, I discuss Jewish houses of worship in the Federal Republic of Germany.

This avoidance of the past coincided with a notable surge of Jewish architectural accomplishment. Chapter 5 shows how Jewish architects, such as Richard Neutra, Marcel Breuer, and Gordon Bunshaft, solidified their reputations in these early years as major figures in the western architectural profession. Their achievements helped refute the longstanding idea of Jewish architectural underachievement. At the same time, however, their highly assimilated identity and reluctance to draw creative inspiration from their backgrounds meant that their buildings were not particularly Jewish. These architects' disinterest in Jewish history and culture helps explain why they refrained from reflecting on the legacy of the Holocaust in their work. Although a few Jewish architects participated in competitions to design Holocaust memorials (none of which were realized), the recent tragedy did not affect their mainstream architectural practices. Yet, Chapter 6 shows how by the end of this period, signs of a new sensibility were beginning to appear, as the pioneering work of Louis I. Kahn revealed the possibility of a more Jewish form of modernism, open to the influence of the Holocaust.

Chapter 2
Adorno's Echoes
The Holocaust's Cultural Legacy at Mid-Century

Anyone strolling down Park Avenue in midtown Manhattan cannot help but be struck by its impressive array of modernist skyscrapers. Two buildings in particular, Gordon Bunshaft's Lever House (1951) and Ludwig Mies van der Rohe's Seagram Building (1958), stand on opposite sides of the avenue at 53rd Street, their facades soberly conveying the seriousness of the modernist mission (fig. 25). A few blocks away, several office buildings designed by Ely Jacques Kahn in the 1950s loom over the street as simplified versions of his interwar Art Deco skyscrapers. And at Park Avenue and 44th Street, the fifty-eight-story MetLife Building designed in 1963 by Emery Roth and Sons looms over the ornate Helmsley Building. Most pedestrians rushing to work probably pay little heed to these and Park Avenue's other towering edifices. But those who stop to contemplate their unornamented facades may sense their essential reticence. I was recently reminded of this after seeing the 1961 film *Breakfast at Tiffany's,* which features a scene in which Audrey Hepburn's character, Holly Golightly, stands in front of the Seagram Building, her existential emptiness echoed in the building's ahistorical blankness. Yet there is a deeper meaning to this architectural silence: the blankness of Park Avenue's modernist monoliths also symbolizes the failure of early postwar western architecture to confront the Holocaust.

It may seem presumptuous to expect to see the Holocaust's legacy reflected in the commercial architecture of midtown Manhattan. After all, why should buildings erected for functional purposes refer to the tragic events of the war years in the first place? The answer is that they have no such obligation. And yet, their silence is nevertheless significant. The meaning we find in buildings — even when absent — is determined subjectively by the differing expectations we bring to them. These expectations are largely informed by our social class, education, and aesthetic taste, but they are also shaped by the historical eras in which we live. Since the end of the Second World War in 1945, western society has been living in what is commonly called the postwar era. But we have also been living in what some have described as a "post-Holocaust" era.[1] This concept reflects the belief that the Nazi genocide irrevocably altered the course of western civilization and cast doubt on its intellectual and cultural traditions. The concept further implies the obligation of postwar western society to identify the extent to which its traditions — its philosophy, theology, literature, poetry, music, art, and architecture — were implicated in the Holocaust; finally, the concept implies the obligation to determine how these traditions should be refashioned to suit the realities of the post-Holocaust

Figure 25. Ludwig Mies van der Rohe, Seagram Building, New York, 1958. This iconic work of postwar modernism displays no signs of having been built in the post-Holocaust world.

world. To be sure, most people have not been preoccupied by this demanding task in their daily lives. But for those who believe that the Nazi genocide permanently changed western life, the silence of Park Avenue's buildings is telling.

The concept of a post-Holocaust world traces its origins to the influential writings of the German Jewish cultural critic Theodor Adorno. In 1949, Adorno famously offered a provocative injunction when he declared that "to write poetry after Auschwitz is barbaric."[2] Scholars have long struggled to determine whether Adorno meant his remark as an admonition, a directive, or a diagnosis.[3] At the descriptive level, his remark suggested that the Holocaust represented an unprecedented rupture in the culture of the west, yet at the prescriptive level, its implications were less clear.[4] Although Adorno initially seemed to suggest the impossibility of all cultural expression in the wake of the Holocaust, he later accepted the necessity of preserving the memory of suffering through artistic means.[5] He remained concerned, however, that the Holocaust could easily be exploited for aesthetic enjoyment, especially in realistic and mimetic modes of representation.[6] For this reason, Adorno concluded that any form of cultural expression after 1945 needed to be fundamentally rethought and reformulated. "After Auschwitz," he declared, "no word . . . has any right unless it underwent a transformation."[7] In keeping with this stance, Adorno's own tastes gravitated toward modernism, which avoided realism in favor of abstraction.[8] But his main concern lay less in the realm of artistic style than in artistic responsiveness. Disturbed by western society's attempt after 1945 to resume life as if the war never happened, Adorno believed that postwar culture could preserve its validity only to the degree it registered the impact of the Nazi genocide and embraced new modes of representation.

Assessing the extent to which postwar western culture has fulfilled Adorno's mandate is difficult. Scholars have long disagreed about the Holocaust's status in western memory during the early postwar period; while some have claimed its status was minimal, others have insisted it was prominent.[9] There is a rough consensus, however, that in Europe, the United States, and Israel the confrontation with the Holocaust during the first several postwar decades was comparatively tentative.[10] Jews in this period largely preferred to deal with their traumatic experiences in private and focused less on past traumas than present-day needs.[11] This tendency to downplay the Holocaust explains why the murder of approximately 6 million Jews was not initially seen as an event ontologically distinct from the Nazis' other war crimes.[12] Indeed, it took a decade and a half before the term "Holocaust" even came into existence as a signifier for the Nazi genocide.[13] Only in the wake of such headline-grabbing events as the vandalism of synagogues in Germany by neo-Nazis in 1959–60 and the capture and ensuing trial of Nazi war criminal Adolf Eichmann in 1960–61 did a wider awareness of a specifically Jewish Holocaust begin to take root in western consciousness.

This dawning awareness was reflected in early postwar western intellectual and cultural life. Although individual thinkers and artists began to confront the Nazi genocide immediately after 1945, their efforts were relatively exceptional and not widely acknowledged until the late 1950s and early 1960s. Academic studies of the Holocaust, for example, were slow to emerge after 1945, with the first major work of synthesis, Raul Hilberg's *Destruction of the European Jews*, appearing only in 1961.[14] Similarly, works of philosophy and theology that grappled with the Holocaust, such as Emmanuel Levinas's *Totality and Infinity* (1961) and Richard Rubenstein's *After Auschwitz* (1966), also took time to appear.[15] Early postwar memoirs by Holocaust survivors such as Primo Levi and Elie Wiesel initially attracted little interest but were increasingly hailed by the late 1950s and soon were followed by the memoirs of other writers, such as Charlotte Delbo and Jean Améry.[16] Works of Holocaust fiction also increased during this period, with the early postwar writings of Yehiel De-Nur and Tadeuz Borowski being followed a decade later by the novels of André Schwarz-Bart, Piotr Rawicz, Jerzy Kosinki, and others.[17] The poems of Paul Celan and Nelly Sachs, like the plays of Erwin Sylvanus, Rolf Hochhuth, and Peter Weiss, further testified to the growing literary exploration of the Holocaust.[18] Musical compositions dealing with the Holocaust by figures such as Dmitri Shostakovich and Mikis Theodorakis also increased in the early 1960s.[19] And films and television programs became more focused on the Nazi genocide's Jewish dimensions.[20] Finally, in the visual arts, painters like Marc Chagall, Barnett Newman, Mark Rothko, Morris Louis, Friedensreich Hundertwasser, and Samuel Bak directly drew inspiration from the Holocaust in their work, as did sculptors Alberto Giacometti, Jacques Lipschitz, and Nathan Rapaport.[21]

Beyond their sheer number, these works were often distinguished by their creators' willingness, in the wake of Auschwitz, to heed Adorno's call and abandon old methods of representation for new approaches. Writers of Holocaust fiction, such as Rawicz and Kosinski, abandoned realism in favor of expressionism and surrealism.[22] Playwrights Sylvanus, Hochhuth, and Weiss adopted new experimental methods of probing the Holocaust's moral and theological lessons.[23] Celan's poetry was noted for its novel use of imaginative metaphors ("black milk") and neologisms ("no-one's-rose"), while Sachs also strove for poetic innovation, declaring in 1948 that "our time, as horrible as it is, does have to find its expression in art; it must be attempted with all new means, for the old means are no longer sufficient."[24] Certain European films undertook experiments in representing the Holocaust.[25] And in art, Newman destroyed all his prewar work and developed his abstract expressionist "zip paintings," an experimental path followed by his colleagues Rothko and Louis.[26] In short, more than a few distinguished figures in western cultural life rethought their principles in light of Auschwitz and transformed their work for the post-Holocaust era.

Architecture and the Holocaust

By contrast, European and American architects after 1945 largely refrained from reflecting on the Holocaust's legacy. The Nazi genocide posed particular challenges for postwar architecture. Since antiquity, architecture has been a profession largely devoted to the Vitruvian goals of beauty and aesthetic delight.[27] After the ugliness of Auschwitz, however, architects could not pursue these ideals as innocently as before. Like writers, poets, and painters, architects faced the challenge of wrestling with the Nazi genocide's implications for their discipline. Yet few stopped to think whether it was possible or permissible—let alone "barbaric"—to build after Auschwitz. Most went on designing and building as they always had.

The missing architectural confrontation with the Holocaust was largely a function of architecture's unique features as a form of cultural expression. Since architecture is fundamentally an affirmative, humanistic art, there was little precedent for an architectural response to the Holocaust after 1945 that did not reaffirm the act of building. Throughout history, the architectural response to destruction — whether by war or natural disaster — has been reconstruction.[28] Only in rare cases where destroyed cities were simply left as ruins and abandoned — as with Carthage after the Punic Wars or Oradour-sur-Glane after World War II — have architects, representing the wishes of society at large, refrained from rebuilding (fig. 26). Architects thus lacked a model for responding to the Holocaust in a way that acknowledged its unprecedented magnitude.

The early postwar failure of architects to acknowledge the Holocaust was also due to the fact that architecture is arguably the least individualistic of the arts. Architects have traditionally enjoyed less independence than writers, poets, or painters in translating their visions into reality because of their dependence on clients for commissions (not to mention their need to adhere to building regulations, zoning laws, and, at times, popular aesthetic taste). After 1945, most architects in the United States and Europe felt that their freedom of architectural expression was especially limited. Having gone without significant work since the lean years of the Depression, most architects were desperate after 1945 to participate in what one architectural journal predicted would be the "greatest building campaign in history."[29] Most were thus disinclined to explore the kinds of experimental and impractical architectural visions that would have resulted from wrestling with the Holocaust's legacy.

Figure 26. Ruins of Oradour-sur-Glane. A rare instance when architects were not called on to pursue reconstruction after destruction.

Finally, even had certain architects been motivated to express the legacy of the Holocaust in their work, it is unclear how they would have done so in architectural form. In the early years after 1945, western architecture was in the final stage of its long transition from historicism to modernism. By embracing modernist abstraction, architects surrendered most of the representational tools that they might have used to confront the Holocaust.[30] In any case, most architects were not inclined to do so in the first place, and so the question of how to build after Auschwitz largely went unasked.

This is not to say that architects ignored the recent past entirely. In Europe after 1945, the Second World War's legacy was unavoidable. Especially in Germany, the postwar debate about how to reconstruct the nation's ravaged cities was accompanied by intense disagreement about the Nazi era, with modern architects and their traditionalist opponents each invoking the recent past to justify their respective reconstruction philosophies. German modernists, for example, argued that the Nazi regime's preference for traditional over modern building styles during the Third Reich vindicated the use of modern architecture in reconstruction.[31] By contrast, German traditionalists lobbied for a conservative reconstruction strategy by claiming that the Nazis had pursued radically modern architectural and city planning policies.[32] In truth, each groups' invocation of the past was tendentious and ignored the ways that each was complicit in the Nazi regime's policies. Moreover, in invoking the "lessons" of the Third Reich, both groups focused exclusively on the regime's cultural policies and ignored its crimes against the Jews and other innocents.

If early postwar architectural discussions in Germany tendentiously exploited the Nazi past, discussions in the United States largely ignored it. Immediately following World War II, the country's major architectural journals ran editorials about the need for architects to design suitable housing for returning veterans and ensure that their skills were used for construction rather than destruction in the new atomic age.[33] But no attention was paid toward the Nazis' atrocities and their possible architectural implications. Unlike their European colleagues, American architects did not exploit the Nazi experience for partisan purposes. Since the continental United States had escaped wartime bombings and did not face the same magnitude of postwar construction as European cities, there was less at stake in the architectural debates. Moreover, the architectural culture in the United States was far less politicized than that of Europe. Since modernism in America was never subjected to the same polemical attacks that it experienced in Europe in the 1920s and 1930s, there was little animosity between American modernists and traditionalists after 1945.[34] Finally, the fact that most American architects quickly embraced the modern movement after the war meant that modernists had less reason to invoke historical rationales to justify their postwar construction philosophies. The result was that many of the leading figures of the postwar American architectural profession, such as Philip Johnson, Ludwig Mies van der Rohe, and Walter Gropius, adhered to their prewar principles rather than question them in light of the recent past. Of course, Johnson, Mies, and Gropius all had personal reasons for not wanting to gaze backward. Johnson's involvement in fascist politics during the 1930s and 1940s, and Mies's and Gropius's early collaboration with the Nazi regime helps explain their reluctance to use historical arguments to promote modern architecture after 1945.

There were few exceptions to the avoidance of the Holocaust in early postwar architecture. A relatively unknown example was Polish architect Bohdan Lachert's 1948 design for a massive modernist apartment complex on the site of the former Warsaw Ghetto, whose Jewish inhabitants were killed (and whose homes were razed) during the Nazis' crushing of the uprising of 1943. Lachert strove to commemorate the "great barbarity of Nazism and the heroism of the Ghetto fighters" in his design by cladding his buildings with rubble taken from the ghetto's ruins and using dark red bricks to symbolize the "blood of the Jewish nation." Lachert's apartment complex was never completed as envisioned, however, as Communist Party officials found the building "monotonous [and] sad" and ordered its red walls covered with whitewashed stucco and cheerful historicizing elements.[35]

Another partial exception was Le Corbusier's celebrated modernist chapel Notre Dame du Haut, in Ronchamp, France (fig. 27). Completed in 1954, this monumental and expressive edifice represented a radical departure from his purist prewar work and signified, according to Bruno Zevi, the architect's reaction to the Second World War. "Faced with . . . catastrophe," Zevi wrote, "Le Corbusier refused to close his eyes and . . . resist history by continuing to entrench [himself] . . . in rationality. . . . [At] Ronchamp, he exploded."[36] Le Corbusier's shift in approach, however, was not a response to the Holocaust as such. Because the chapel was meant to replace a chapel destroyed by the Germans in 1944, it largely symbolized French suffering under German occupation.[37] Moreover, the idiosyncratic design was highly exceptional for the era. Most architects refused to gaze back at the past and instead looked optimistically to the future.

It was only from outside the architectural profession that scattered pronouncements were expressed about architecture's future in the post-Holocaust world. In the initial aftermath of the war, when most architects were pursuing ambitious reconstruction projects, a few isolated Jewish voices pointed to the Holocaust as grounds for renouncing architecture altogether. This radical position was powerfully articulated in 1946 by the Jewish Holocaust survivor and later head of the Central Committee of Liberated Jews in Germany, Samuel Gringauz. In a discussion with the histo-

Figure 27. Le Corbusier, Chapel of Notre Dame du Haut, Ronchamp, France, 1954. The chapel was built on the site of a chapel destroyed by German bombs in the Second World War.

rian and director of the Joint Distribution Committee in Germany's Education Department, Koppel Pinson, Gringauz indicted the west's entire architectural heritage, observing: "We [Jews] do not believe in progress . . . [or] in the 2,000-year-old Christian culture of the West, the culture that, *for them,* created . . . Westminster Abbey on the Thames, the wonder gardens of Versailles, . . . the Uffizi and Pitti palaces in Florence, the Strassbourg Münster, and the Cologne cathedral . . . , but [that], *for us,* [led to] the . . . gas chambers of Auschwitz."[38]

Such expressions of skepticism toward architecture appeared not only in postwar Europe but also in the United States. In *The Sabbath* (1951), Rabbi Abraham Joshua Heschel drew on the lessons of the Nazi genocide to reaffirm the wisdom of what he took to be Judaism's traditional deemphasis of space in favor of time. Like Gringauz, Heschel was skeptical about western civilization's alleged virtues and criticized what he called "technical civilization" for enslaving people to the fragile "things" of the material world. "Things of space," he declared, "are at the mercy of mankind [and] are not fireproof. . . . Monuments of stone are destined to disappear." Significantly, Heschel's comments were influenced by the Nazis' wartime destruction of the Jews' architectural heritage, a connection that he made clear in explaining why it was necessary for the postwar world to devalue space — and, by extension, architecture — in favor of time. As he put it, "Judaism teaches us to be attached to holiness in time, to be attached to sacred events. . . . The Sabbaths are our great cathedrals; and our Holy of Holies is a shrine that neither the Romans nor the Germans were able to burn." The Nazi experience confirmed, in other words, the virtues of Judaism's historic elevation of time over space — a tradition that, by ensuring the Jewish religion's mobility, ensured its survival. For this reason, Heschel's appeal for postwar Jews to recognize religious ritual as an "architecture of time" can be seen as representing a bold effort in the wake of the Holocaust to reconceptualize architecture in nonspatial terms.[39]

Gringauz's and Heschel's conclusions were among the most uncompromising reflections on the significance of the Holocaust for postwar architecture. But they were ultimately nihilistic — architectural equivalents of Elie Wiesel's and George Steiner's later calls to respond to the Holocaust with silence rather than words. Rather than respond to destruction by pursuing reconstruction, Gringauz and Heschel indicted all architecture as contrary to a proper Jewish sensibility after Auschwitz. Predictably, the absolutist character of their position prevented it from shaping postwar architectural trends in any meaningful way. Because they came from outside the architectural profession, Gringauz's and Heschel's radical appeals for architectural silence went unheeded.

Conclusion

On the whole, apart from a few isolated voices, few people in western society paid attention to the Holocaust's architectural implications in the early years after 1945. Compared with the broader intellectual and cultural confrontation with the Nazi genocide that defined the same period, the architectural confrontation was negligible. No major architects reflected on the import of the Nazi genocide for their profession. None posed the question of how or whether to build after Auschwitz. Given the Holocaust's irrelevance for western architecture on the whole in this period, it is unsurprising that the specific evolution of Jewish architecture largely followed suit.

Chapter 3
American Synagogue Architecture and the Missing Holocaust

Walking into Congregation B'nai Israel in Bridgeport, Connecticut, is a reassuringly familiar experience to anyone accustomed to attending religious services in a suburban American synagogue. That was my first thought, anyway, as I entered B'nai Israel's sanctuary in the early spring of 2007 to give a lecture on Jewish architecture and the memory of the Holocaust. The sanctuary was a dark, rectilinear space featuring a high wooden ceiling with exposed structural supports (fig. 28). Wide windows running the length of the walls just below the roofline allowed light to filter in. An enormous metal candelabrum with cylindrical lanterns hung from the ceiling, and a wall of multicolored stained glass panels flanked the ark. Aside from these decorative features, the interior was spare and sober. Its simplicity, moreover, was matched by its functionality. As I looked to the rear, I saw several removable wooden partitions for expanding the sanctuary into the social hall behind it, a design element meant to accommodate extra congregants on the High Holidays.

In identifying these features, I recognized that B'nai Israel was typical of early postwar modernist synagogue architecture. And no wonder, for it was one of the many designed by the most prolific designer of modernist synagogues in postwar America, Percival Goodman. I had never been inside one of Goodman's synagogues, but I was eager to visit one, since I was intrigued by the architect's claim that his postwar commitment to synagogue design had been partly inspired by Hitler's crimes against the Jews. If this were so, I wondered, why were there no visible signs of the Holocaust's legacy in the building's architecture?[1]

The absence of references to the Holocaust in early postwar synagogues such as B'nai Israel was one visible manifestation of the reluctance to confront the Nazi genocide in Jewish architecture after 1945. In the early years after the end of the Second World War, American Jewish architects, rabbis, intellectuals, and lay leaders resumed the interwar discussion about the possibility of creating a specifically Jewish form of synagogue architecture. Yet in doing so they largely ignored the altered circumstances of the post-Holocaust world. This aversion was visible not just in architectural discourse, but in the actual buildings built in this period, the designs of which displayed few signs of the Holocaust's legacy. This absence was due to a variety of factors, but an important one was American Jews' enthusiastic embrace of modern architecture for their postwar houses of worship. Modernism's hostility toward the past and its focus on the future meant that the early postwar

Figure 28. Percival Goodman, Congregation B'nai Israel, Bridgeport, Connecticut, 1958. Although Goodman attributed his postwar interest in building synagogues to Hitler's war against the Jews, no references to the Holocaust were visible in his design for the Bridgeport congregation.

synagogues built by Jewish congregations across the United States were ahistorical in appearance and kept the Holocaust at arm's length. As was confirmed by B'nai Israel and countless other synagogues like it after 1945, modernism and memory were fundamentally at odds with one another in early postwar American synagogue design.

Jewish Religious Architecture: The Early Postwar Discussion

Between the end of the Second World War and the early 1960s, many American Jews optimistically believed that an authentically Jewish style of synagogue architecture would finally be attainable through the embrace of modernist architectural principles. Convinced that the prior failure to develop such a style was attributable to the reliance on historicism, Jewish architects, intellectuals, rabbis, and lay leaders believed that modernism would provide a liberating effect on synagogue design. What had previously been a liability for Jewish architects — a lack of their own architectural tradition — now became an asset. Without any specific tradition to defend, Jewish architects were free to adapt modern architecture to postwar synagogues as they saw fit.

In thinking along these lines, however, Jewish architects largely ignored the Holocaust. Nowhere was this clearer than in a discussion on synagogue architecture sponsored by *Commentary* magazine in 1947. The discussion commenced in the March issue with a long essay by the Russian Jewish émigré art historian (and trained architect) Rachel Wischnitzer-Bernstein entitled, "The Problem of Synagogue Architecture." After surveying the evolution of synagogue styles in Europe and the United States from the early modern period up through the early twentieth century, Wischnitzer-Bernstein concluded that "it is impossible . . . to put your finger on anything in the plastic arts that constitutes an authentically Jewish style." The reason for this absence, she noted, was the long tradition of designing synagogues in "historicizing styles" that were "artificially established . . . by Christian architects" and lacked authentic Jewish roots. There was hope for genuine architectural Jewish creativity in the future, however, as long as Jewish architects broke with the past and built in modern form. As she put it, "The present and future demand something new, expressive of the aspirations of a more self-conscious Jewishness, at home in America."[2]

Given the upbeat nature of Wischnitzer-Bernstein's conclusion, it was no surprise that she left the Holocaust unmentioned. Although she fleetingly cited the "bitter lessons of the war" as a reason for showing "respect for . . . what is unpretentious and human in scale" in postwar synagogue design, she left unclear what specific implications, if any, the Nazi genocide had for postwar Jewish architectural practice.[3] Her comment's terseness may have reflected her own difficulty in articulating a response to the Holocaust. Born in Minsk in 1885, Wischnitzer-Bernstein had worked in Berlin beginning in 1922 as the editor of the art journal *Rimon* and as the curator of the Jewish Museum until fleeing for France in 1938 and for the United States in 1940. During this period she experienced multiple tragedies: her mother committed suicide in 1939, and her elderly father was killed by the Nazis after being deported from Paris on the last convoy out of the city in the spring of 1944. Her method of coping was to throw herself into research and writing, which she later credited with saving her from "utter depression."[4] Since dwelling on the recent Jewish catastrophe was too painful, Wischnitzer-Bernstein adopted a typically American strategy in choosing optimism over despair.

Even if European Jews had been murdered, Jews in the United States were secure enough to believe that they were "at home in America."

Several months after the appearance of Wischnitzer-Bernstein's essay, *Commentary* published several replies from prominent Jewish art historians and architects. The German Jewish emigré art historian Franz Landsberger expressed support for modernist synagogues, declaring that the "new modern style commends itself ... to us as Jews ... [since] it parallels our striving toward clarity and truth in our religious thinking." Ely Jacques Kahn agreed, though he cautioned that, since "there is no modern style" as such, the "final goal" should not be fixed in appearance but merely a "workable and sensible structure." Similarly, Percival Goodman and his brother, the social theorist Paul Goodman, argued that the traditions of "the service and the congregation" should primarily inform synagogue architecture. Taken together, the essays focused on the practical aspects of synagogue design, a fact epitomized by Kahn's emphasis on "good lighting and ventilation." But they were entirely divorced from their historical context.[5]

Only the German Jewish emigré architect Eric Mendelsohn, in his essay "In the Spirit of Our Age," invoked the recent past's relevance for the new wave of synagogue construction. In declaring that the "experience of two world wars ... will of necessity translate the ideals upon which our country was built into the terms of a new age," Mendelsohn acknowledged that recent historical events would leave a mark upon the postwar world. Yet the age he had in mind was not one that meditated upon the past's horrors but one that optimistically sought to transcend them. Mendelsohn foresaw a new American age, emphatically positive and forward-looking. Describing America as a "promised land," he confidently affirmed it was for the "generations of our children" that the new synagogues were to be built. As he concluded, "If contemporary building methods [are] boldly and surely employed, the result is bound to be stimulating and sincere — visual proof that we Jews are full participants in this momentous period of America's history."[6]

The upbeat discourse on early postwar synagogue architecture was further illustrated several years later in 1954 by the appearance of the influential book *An American Synagogue for Today and Tomorrow*. Edited by the German Jewish emigré architect Peter Blake and published by the Reform-oriented Union of American Hebrew Congregations (UAHC) following several important conferences on the subject in 1947, the book was meant to guide American congregations looking to build new synagogues. Echoing the discussion in *Commentary* several years earlier, most of the volume's contributors repudiated historicism and supported modernism. Rabbi Alexander Kline, for example, condemned the "architectural mishmash [called] ... 'meshugothic,'" while Ely Jacques Kahn declared that "[if] we respect ourselves as artists or Jews we will evolve [architectural] solutions that are worthy of our time." The book furthermore displayed the same sense of expectation as the *Commentary* essays. As Rabbi Kline concluded: "If there was ever a hope for developing a distinctly Jewish style of synagogue architecture it is now."[7]

It was easy for the volume's contributors to offer buoyant predictions, of course, so long as they did not reflect on the Holocaust's implications for postwar architectural practice. Like the essays in *Commentary*, those in Blake's volume were silent about the Nazi genocide. Indeed, their silence was a precondition for their optimism. Had the authors stopped to meditate upon the questions posed by Theodor Adorno — and had they recognized how certain writers, poets, and playwrights were already starting to wrestle with the Holocaust—they might not have been able to maintain such a confident outlook.

On balance, it was only on rare occasions that the Holocaust was invoked in early postwar discussions on synagogue design. In 1949, for example, Percival and Paul Goodman's *Commentary* article "Modern Artist as Synagogue Builder" linked the surge in postwar synagogue construction to the Nazi genocide, arguing that the slaughter of "six million Jews . . . in three or four years just because they were Jews . . . has had the . . . effect . . . [of making them] aware of themselves as a physical community, a congregation." Similarly, in 1950 the writer and social philosopher Will Herberg argued in *Commentary* that the nascent boom in synagogue building was a result of the "shattering experience of demonic anti-Semitism . . . [which] helped reverse the trend toward assimilation . . . among American Jews" and stimulate a "new urge to Jewish self-affirmation." And in 1955, Rachel Wischnitzer (now writing under her husband's surname), observed that while synagogues prior to the Second World War had difficulty attracting and keeping members, the "traumatic experience inflicted on the Jewish people by the Nazis. . . . [was one of the] major factors in the growth of the spiritual influence of the synagogue" and the attendant increase in synagogue construction after 1945.[8]

Such assertions have led certain scholars to hypothesize that the postwar rush to build synagogues was part of a broader affirmative response to the Holocaust. In the mid-1960s, Avram Kampf wrote that the "experience of World War [II and] the destruction of European Jewry" promoted a "deeper feeling of group consciousness . . . within American-Jewish society" that found expression in the sanctuaries, social halls, and educational facilities of postwar American synagogue centers. More recently, Henry and Daniel Stolzman have observed that "American Jews sought catharsis, a way to process the horror inflicted upon their relatives and fellow Jews and to create something new in response. By establishing new houses of worship, they reaffirmed . . . their Jewish identity . . . as a people." Supporting such claims is the broader contention of Meredith Clausen, that after 1945, "many Americans, disillusioned by the horrors of war . . . turned back to . . . churches and synagogues [which] provided comfort, a sense of rootedness, and continuity with the past . . . in the wake of Auschwitz and Hiroshima."[9]

At first glance, these arguments seem plausible. After all, in the same way that many Jewish Holocaust survivors in Europe responded to mass death after 1945 by choosing life—by quickly marrying and having babies—Jews in America could arguably be seen as responding to destruction by pursuing synagogue construction. Rachel Wischnitzer's observation in 1955 that "it is typical of times of war . . . [and] destruction to dream of building" supports the proposition that postwar synagogue construction was part of a larger psychological coping strategy. The argument also dovetails with the tendency of American Jews after 1945 to view the Holocaust from a redemptive perspective. If early postwar essays in *Commentary* are any indication, American Jews widely believed that the Holocaust had made the American Jewish community "the largest and strongest in the world" and opened up the possibility of a "great Jewish culture . . . flower[ing] in the United States" that would rival the "Golden Age of Spain."[10]

Yet there is little hard evidence that synagogue construction was a direct reaction to the Holocaust. The wave of postwar synagogue building in the United States mainly resulted from the mass migration of Jews from America's inner cities to its suburbs and the resulting need to establish new institutional homes for Jewish communities. This migratory trend was the result of numerous practical factors — including American Jews' economic success during the war years, their desire to leave cramped inner-city housing for roomier suburban quarters, and the Federal Highway Act — all of which would have promoted Jewish suburbanization even if the Holocaust had never happened. No causal link can thus be established between the Nazi genocide and the postwar push to build Jewish houses of worship. Had the construction of synagogues truly been a response to the Holocaust, the early postwar discussion about Jewish religious architecture should have been accompanied by frequent references to its legacy. But such references were few and far between.[11]

Doubt can also be cast on the related assertion of scholars that American Jews' embrace of modernism in synagogue design was a reaction to the Nazi genocide. Carol Krinsky has claimed that the emphasis on "rationality" in modernist synagogue design "was particularly appealing to counteract the terrifying madness of the Holocaust." Philip Nobel has observed that, after 1945, "modernism became the de facto vehicle of a 'Jewish style' [of architecture]" because it was most "suitable for a religion [that was] seeking, after the Holocaust, to break clearly with tainted European models" of synagogue design. Samuel Gruber has also echoed this point, writing that, after the war, many "congregations were eager to break with the historicism of the past — especially in light of the Holocaust."[12]

These assertions remain speculative, however. There is little evidence that Jewish architects ever cited the irrationality of the Holocaust as a reason for embracing the ostensibly more rational modernist movement after 1945. Neither is there much proof that they viewed the Nazi genocide as a reason for rejecting "tainted" (read: historicist) European models of synagogue design. For that matter, the premise that the postwar embrace of modernism was a reaction against "tainted" prewar designs is undermined by the fact that some synagogues before World War II were already being designed according to modernist principles (which theoretically should have been equally discredited after 1945). In truth, the absence of references to the Holocaust in postwar discussions of synagogue architecture suggests that American Jews in general and Jewish architects in particular simply did not think about the Nazi genocide's architectural implications in any meaningful way.

This absence partly reflected the American Jewish community's broader social ambitions. After 1945, most American Jews were focused on the self-affirming mission of establishing a new place for themselves in the postwar world. American Jews had much to be upbeat about after 1945. Having just arrived in the suburbs, they wanted to establish synagogues that would be comfortable institutional homes for their families. American Jews joined synagogues in unprecedented numbers after 1945; whereas only 20 percent belonged to synagogues in the 1930s, over 60 percent had joined one by the 1960s. In their rush to affiliate, however, most Jews were driven by social rather than religious goals. It was not the case, as certain observers claimed at the time, that the new wave of synagogue construction reflected something of a "religious revival" among postwar American Jews. Already in the mid-1950s, Nathan Glazer pointed out that most suburban Jews' needs were oriented toward Sunday school, teenage dances, and sisterhood events rather than religious services. Jews were also eager to measure up to their Christian neighbors, who were experiencing their own surge in religious institutional affiliation during the early postwar decades. As most Jews were primarily focused on the immediate needs of the present, they were disinclined to think deeply about the recent past.[13]

If the forward-looking mindset of postwar American Jews inhibited a discussion of the Holocaust in synagogue design, so did the forward-looking modernist principles of most Jewish architects. From the inception of the modern movement in the early twentieth century, modern architects had supported the Nietzschean notion that new creation was possible only by breaking with the past and escaping the stranglehold of history and memory. Needless to say, the embrace of this anti-mnemonic stance after 1945 inhibited any serious reflection on the Holocaust. So did modern architecture's underlying optimism as a discipline. From the beginning of the modernist movement, modern architects possessed great faith in modernity and the ability of technology to bring about progressive, if not utopian, change. After 1945, most modernists saw themselves as called upon to apply their mastery of technology to the myriad challenges left by the war. Few modernists were inclined to address the sobering implications of Auschwitz's gas chambers and crematoria for the emancipatory potential of modern technology. Finally, modernism's inherent universalism promoted silence toward the Holocaust. Jewish architects knew that if they strayed from the movement's universalistic mission and reflected upon the ramifications of their people's suffering, they ran the risk of being branded parochial and irrelevant.[14] As art critic Clement Greenberg cautioned in 1950: "No matter how necessary it may be to indulge our feelings about Auschwitz, we can do so only temporarily and privately. . . . Jewishness, insofar as it has to be asserted in a predominantly Gentile world, should be a personal rather than a mass demonstration."[15] Jewish architects who wanted to remain in the modernist architectural mainstream, in short, needed to remain silent about the past and keep their Jewish feelings to themselves.

Jewish Architects and Early Postwar Synagogues

The tendency to evade the full implications of the Nazi genocide was clearly visible in the physical form of many early postwar synagogues.[16] Hundreds of Jewish houses of worship were built in the United States in the first two decades after 1945.[17] Designed by a wide range of Jewish and Christian architects, they were diverse in appearance but were linked by their aversion to historical reference. The irrelevance of the past in these buildings reflected their designers' reluctance to view the Holocaust as a historic rupture that required them to rethink their architectural principles. Convinced that modern architecture could meet the challenges of the postwar era, most architects preserved their prewar architectural philosophies intact.

This trend was particularly visible in the work of the two most prominent Jewish architects involved in early postwar synagogue construction: Eric Mendelsohn and Percival Goodman. Their synagogue designs betrayed few signs of the Holocaust's impact. They also did not display many discernible Jewish traits. Built in the new American suburbs, where there was no prior Jewish presence, Mendelsohn's and Goodman's synagogues differed little in appearance from secular modernist buildings being erected at the same time. As a result, the most important Jewish houses of worship built in early postwar America were largely indifferent to Jewish history, memory, and identity.

Eric Mendelsohn

From 1945 until his death in 1953, Eric Mendelsohn designed more than a half-dozen pathbreaking synagogues in the United States. His intense engagement with postwar synagogue design reflected his personal experience of the Nazis' rise to power in Germany and the years of the Second World War. Yet, despite his closeness to the recent past, little of it found overt expression in his postwar architectural work.

Unlike many other Jewish architects after 1945, Mendelsohn's lack of engagement with the Holocaust did not reflect any personal ambivalence about his Jewishness. Born in 1887, Mendelsohn was brought up in a traditional Jewish family in Allenstein, East Prussia, a medium-sized town with a visible Jewish population. He received a traditional Jewish education and developed what his wife, Louise, termed a "close relationship with his Jewishness." For this reason, Mendelsohn understandably became "enraged" when he saw "Jews [being treated] differently from other Germans" and eventually joined the Zionist movement. As early as the early 1920s he was undertaking the first of what would be many visits to Palestine and seriously considering moving there.[18]

Soon after Hitler's seizure of power in 1933, Mendelsohn and his wife left Germany and embarked upon a peripatetic existence, moving first to England, then to Palestine in 1939, and finally to the United States in 1941.[19] Throughout these difficult years Mendelsohn personified the stereotype of the wandering Jew. He learned new languages, became accustomed to new systems of measurement, acquired new citizenship, and, once in the United States, even Anglicized his first name (dropping the letter "h" from Erich). But he had difficulty adapting his expressionist architectural philosophy to the built environment of the Middle East and North America. His designs after 1933 have thus mostly been regarded as less distinguished than his earlier work. What Mendelsohn would have achieved had Hitler never come to power will never be known, but the year 1933 represented a rupture from which the architect never entirely recovered.

During his years of exile, Mendelsohn nursed bitter resentments against the Germans. Already in 1933 he saw the German people as responsible for the Nazi catastrophe, writing that the Nazis' "degradation of . . . the Jewish nation" would forever stand as a "mark of shame for Germany." During the war, he contributed to the U.S. Air Force's aerial bombing campaign against Nazi Germany by designing scale replicas of German apartment buildings at the Dugway Proving Grounds in Utah. After 1945, Mendelsohn expressed his determination to hold the Germans accountable for their wartime misdeeds. In 1947, he told the German architect Richard Döcker that "Germany's desire that the world quickly forget [its crimes] is a utopia. . . . . It is Germany's fate to experience this pernicious stigma, after . . . murdering its Jews." And in 1951 he explained his decision not to attend an architectural exhibition in the Federal Republic by noting, "As long as Germany lacks the courage . . . to publicly extirpate the anticultural things that . . . occurred in its name, . . . I as a Jew cannot contribute to the cultural significance of your country."[20]

Despite his strong commitment to remembrance, however, Mendelsohn made little effort to acknowledge the Holocaust directly in his postwar architectural work. Instead of dwelling on past horrors, he preferred to look optimistically to the future. Mendelsohn expressed this view on several occasions; for example, in his wartime lecture "Architecture in a Rebuilt World" (1942) he confidently spoke of his postwar plan — despite the "great fire of this war" — to construct "homes for heroes." This upbeat stance also reflected his longstanding modernist belief that creating the new could take place only by forgetting the past. As far back as 1925, Mendelsohn had praised amnesia in a poetic manifesto entitled "Why This Architecture?" in which he declared: "Only he who cannot forget has no free mind." This attitude may further explain why Mendelsohn, despite being personally committed to remembering the Nazis' crimes, believed that memory had little place in architecture.[21]

This belief was visible in his postwar American synagogue designs. Before arriving in the U.S., Mendelsohn had never completed a synagogue.[22] After 1945, however, he built four: the B'nai Amoona Synagogue and Community Center in St. Louis (1945–50); the Park Synagogue in Cleveland (1946–52); the Emanu-El Synagogue and Community Center in Grand Rapids, Michigan (1948–52); and the Mount Zion Synagogue and Community Center in St. Paul, Minnesota (1952–54) (fig. 29).[23] These buildings were all pioneering, especially in their embrace of the new architectural paradigm of the "synagogue center," which included not merely the sanctuary but also wings dedicated to social and educational functions.[24] Aesthetically, Mendelsohn's synagogues were defined by a modernist aversion to historical reference and an embrace of formal experimentation, especially B'nai Amoona, which featured a sweeping parabolic roof that harkened back to his 1920s work in Germany. It is true that Mendelsohn tried to lend his designs some degree of Jewish symbolism: he reemployed the standby of 1920s synagogue design — the dome — in his hemispherically domed Park Synagogue; he subtly evoked the Mosaic tablets of the law in an unrealized design for the Beth-El Synagogue in Baltimore (1947); and he obliquely referred to tefillin in his Mount Zion synagogue in St. Paul.[25] But these gestures were subordinated to functional considerations. In none of his projects, moreover, did anything evoke recent cataclysmic events. As Bruno Zevi has written, Mendelsohn felt no "need to celebrate the gangrene and horrors" in his work and instead retained his commitment to the "absolute and the eternal."[26]

Indeed, Mendelsohn believed that Jewish architects' chief postwar task was to provide consolation after destruction. In 1947 he described B'nai Amoona as a "house of joy, light, and serene festivity. No more persecution and Jewish misery, no pessimism, but the affirmation of the age of man." That same year he noted that it was a "welcome task" for an architect like himself "to lift the mind of our people [by designing] . . . fine synagogues and community centers." In 1946, finally,

Figure 29. Eric Mendelsohn, Park Synagogue, Cleveland, 1946–52. The building's domed design represented a throwback to the interwar era.

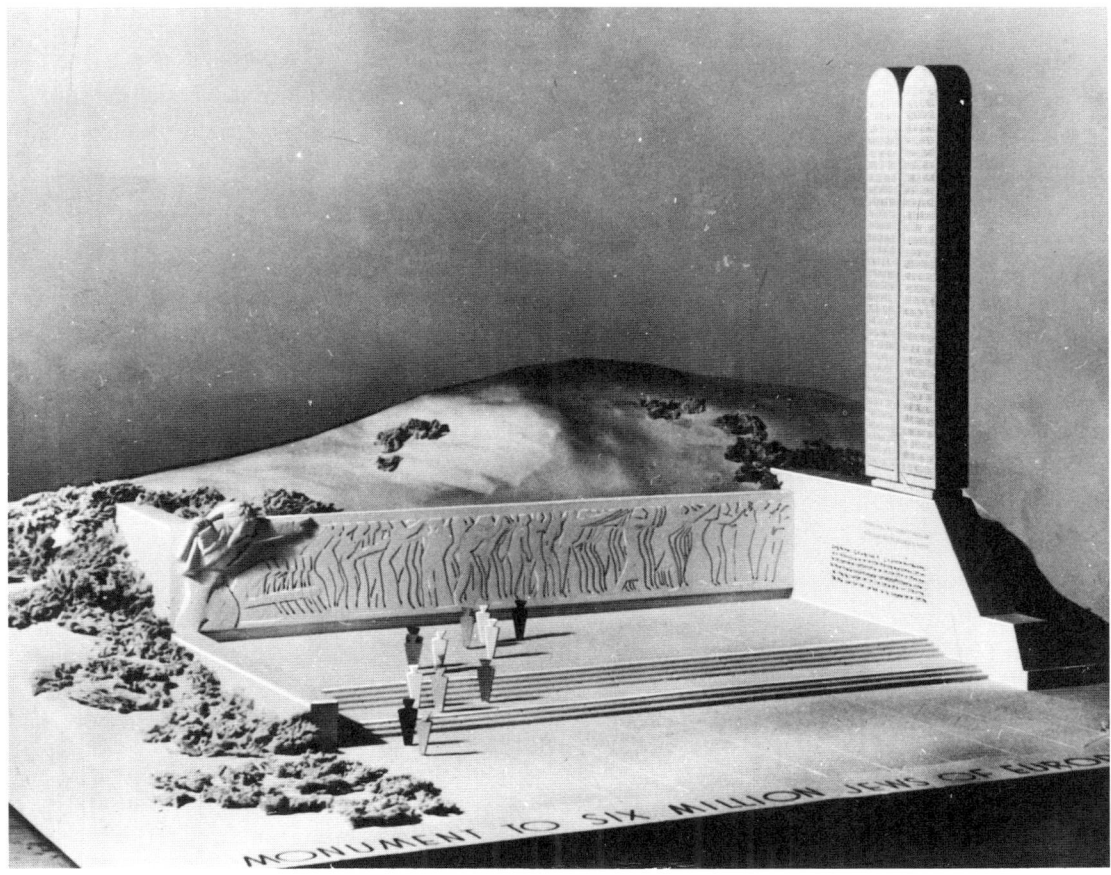

Figure 30. Eric Mendelsohn, Holocaust memorial proposal, New York, 1949. The design featured an oversized sculpture of the Ten Commandments and communicated a clear message of German guilt for the Holocaust.

Mendelsohn declared: "To . . . educate [congregants about] the age-of-man we are . . . entering, our temples must be built to human scale. . . . [Their interiors] should reject . . . the mystifying darkness of an illiterate time and should place their faith in the light of day which its principles should rule." In short, Mendelsohn believed that avoiding the past could herald a better future. At the dedication ceremony for B'nai Amoona, Mendelsohn praised the congregation as the "first in the country . . . to accept a design for a Synagogue which does not try to imitate the past" and concluded that if the building symbolized anything, it was the realities of the present, where "new physical forces" and "technical inventions[s]" were heralding "the beginning of a new age of man."[27]

Yet while Mendelsohn shied away from confronting the Holocaust in his architecture, he did not neglect it entirely. In 1949 he entered the competition for the American Memorial to Six Million Jews of Europe in New York City's Riverside Park. Mendelsohn proposed an eighty-foot-high granite sculpture of the Ten Commandments (carved by the Yugoslav sculptor Ivan Mestrovic) flanked by a one-hundred-foot-long wall featuring bas-reliefs of humankind's struggle to live up to the decalogue's mandate (fig. 30). The inscriptions proposed for the memorial — including an unsparing reference to the "Six million Jewish martyrs . . . annihilated by the barbarian Nazi leaders of Germany" — were significant for constituting a more direct commentary on the Holocaust than any of Mendelsohn's other postwar architectural commissions. Yet its specificity was undercut by the architect's declaration in 1952 that the memorial was "not Jewish . . . but . . . American" and his claim that its inclusion of the Ten Commandments was intended to make it a "universal monument . . . whose meaning will be apparent to people of all nationalities and creeds." As is shown by these remarks, Mendelsohn vacillated between particularistic and universalistic approaches to representing the Holocaust. In the end, however, his commemorative effort came to naught. Although the architect's project received formal approval from the New York Art Commission in 1951, the reluctance of the Jewish community to contribute funds to the project, combined with Mendelsohn's death in 1953, doomed it to failure.[28]

This result notwithstanding, the architect's involvement in the Holocaust memorial project was significant for underscoring his avoidance of the Nazi genocide in his broader architectural practice. The best explanation for this inconsistency of approach is that Mendelsohn embraced a division of labor in his work after 1945, preferring to focus his mainstream architectural efforts on the forward-looking task of restoring hope to the postwar Jewish community while commenting upon the past only in more specialized commemorative projects. For Mendelsohn, the past was not to be forgotten, but it was not to overwhelm the present. In embracing this approach, moreover, he was not alone.

Percival Goodman

After Eric Mendelsohn, the most important figure in postwar American synagogue design was Percival Goodman (1904–1989). Goodman never attained the same international reputation as Mendelsohn, but he had a major impact on Jewish architecture since he was the most prolific designer of synagogues in postwar America, producing more than fifty buildings in nearly thirty years.[29] All his designs were rigorously modern, combining a strong focus on function with a boldly experimental approach to form. In this respect they symbolized the era's break with the past and optimistic embrace of the future. One consequence of their ahistorical character, however, was their general neglect of the Holocaust. As was also true of Mendelsohn's work, the recent Jewish catastrophe left no visible mark on Goodman's postwar synagogue designs. That said, it would be a mistake to view Goodman as uninterested in the Nazi genocide, for even if it did not find overt expression in his synagogues, it informed his commitment to building them.

Nothing in Goodman's early career foreshadowed his later interest in synagogue design. Born in New York City into an assimilated German Jewish family, Goodman was brought up in a nonreligious home and displayed minimal interest in traditional Jewish life. When he first went to work in the partnership of Whitman and Goodman in the late 1920s, Goodman worked exclusively on secular projects, designing apartments and department store interiors for companies like Saks and Company and Bonwit Teller. In this early phase of his career, Goodman worked in the Art Deco style, but during the Great Depression he developed into a committed modernist, designing public housing projects and drafting progressive city planning schemes. He also began to embrace socialist politics, submitting an ambitious modernist design to the Palace of the Soviets competition in the

Soviet Union in 1930 and collaborating with his brother, Paul Goodman, on a utopian city planning project known as Communitas.[30]

After 1945, the architect made yet another change in his career and became committed to Jewish architectural projects. This shift did not reflect a newfound commitment to religion, which Goodman scorned as the "most poisonous thing that humans ever thought of," but resulted from his social connections to wealthy Jewish clients, such as the Warburg family, who hired Goodman in 1944 to transform the Felix Warburg mansion on Fifth Avenue into the Jewish Museum of Manhattan. Thanks to this connection, Goodman was able to secure an invitation to deliver a lecture at the Union of American Hebrew Congregations' important 1947 conference "An American Synagogue for Today and Tomorrow." His lecture made such a positive impression that, by the time the conference was over, he had landed three synagogue commissions.[31]

At a deeper level, however, the most important factor shaping Goodman's postwar commitment to synagogue design was the Holocaust. Later in life Goodman often said that he had been converted by Hitler to a greater sense of Jewishness.[32] As he put it, "Hitler led me, like many other Jews, to wonder: 'Where do I belong?' And 'Who the hell am I?'"[33] Goodman's answer was to affirm Jewish group cohesion. In a 1949 *Commentary* essay, "Modern Artist as Synagogue Builder," he had written that Hitler's assault against the Jews had reinforced their sense of themselves as a community, and in 1963 he reiterated that the "Nazi atrocity" had led Jews to express a "need for a concrete expression of kinship."[34] As Goodman's wife, Naomi, recalled, "religion had previously not been important to him. [But after the war] he . . . [believed] that the world had changed because of the Holocaust [and] he no longer wanted to spend his time and talents on commercial work or on living arrangements for the rich. Percy decided that he should design for the Jewish community, both as an expression of his Judaism and because of the losses suffered by Jews."[35]

Yet while the Holocaust strongly influenced Goodman's decision to concentrate on synagogue construction after 1945, its legacy left few visible traces on his buildings. This absence partly reflected the fact that the Nazi genocide was not the only factor behind Goodman's embrace of synagogue architecture. In his writings of the 1950s and 1960s, Goodman linked his synagogue designs to concerns about other postwar problems. In the early 1950s, for example, he railed against "machine-made thought, mass-produced feeling, and the destruction of the human personality," while in the 1960s he expressed fears of nuclear war and the "danger of annihilation."[36] In the face of such dangers, Goodman viewed the synagogue as a "community asset" thanks to its ability to bring Jews together socially while also enabling the "highest form of personal experience," namely, prayer.[37] Goodman believed that synagogues existed to reassure people. As he noted in 1952, "'In a Jewish house of worship . . . you want to convey to . . . people that they [belong] . . . to an essentially good world that God has made, and that any future world is but an extension and beautification of this world as we know it.'"[38]

The absence of allusions to the Holocaust in Goodman's synagogues also reflected his modernist architectural principles. Like many modern architects, Goodman deemphasized architectural representation in favor of function. In describing his approach to synagogue design in a 1947 *Commentary* article, "Tradition from Function," he wrote that the "architect must look for his design to the service and congregation, employing whatever means most simply and directly serve their functions." Goodman believed that the increasingly secular functions of modern synagogues and the declining relevance of religious observance required architects to cease focusing on the sanctuary and give equal attention to the synagogue center's other spaces. The architect, he noted, "will find no need for making the worship hall more elaborate than the social hall, the social hall more elaborate than the school. All will be treated as well arranged space, as beautiful as honest material and good design permit."[39]

The minimal impact of the Holocaust on Goodman's synagogue designs further reflected his disinterest in expressing an architectural sense of Jewishness. Goodman made little effort to imbue his synagogues with Jewish symbolism, whether historical or aesthetic. He was emphatically opposed to incorporating "banal symbol[s] of Judaism," such as the Star of David, in his designs.[40] It is true that Goodman enlisted prominent Jewish and Christian artists to produce works of Jewish applied art — especially sculptures, murals, tapestries, and ceremonial objects — for his buildings' interiors and facades. But he never bothered to develop a distinctly "Jewish" philosophy of architecture. Although his guiding motto was a proto-modernist excerpt from Psalm 96, "O Sing unto the Lord a new song," he did not ground his architectural philosophy in any deeper Jewish context.[41] This failure to develop a systematic Jewish philosophy of architecture meant that Goodman's synagogues displayed few Jewish traits apart from exterior ornamentation and never exhibited a signature style.

Indeed, his synagogues were highly eclectic in appearance. Goodman's Temple Beth El in Gary, Indiana (1954), was a low-slung glass and steel box that strongly resembled Mies van der Rohe's early postwar buildings at the Illinois Institute of Technology (IIT), especially his Alumni Hall Building of 1945–46 (fig. 31). At the other end of the spectrum was Goodman's comparatively conservative Baltimore Hebrew Congregation (1952), whose austere neoclassical facade recalled the conservative stylistic trends of the 1930s. His design for Beth Sholom in Miami (1956), with its bulbous concrete dome and parabolic stained-glass windows, was an example of "googie" architecture (fig. 32).[42] Temple Beth El in Providence, Rhode Island (1954), with its curving barrel vault, looked like a Quonset hut. Temple Beth El in Rochester, New York (1960–63), was a curvilinear brutalist structure executed in brick. And Goodman's Fifth Avenue Synagogue in Manhattan (1957–58) had a minimalist stone facade punctured by rows of vertical cat's eye windows anticipating the op art movement of the 1960s. The closest Goodman came to drawing inspiration from Jewish sources was in such vertically oriented synagogues as Temple Beth-El in Springfield, Massachusetts (1953), Congregation B'nai Israel in Bridgeport, Connecticut (1958), and Congregation Shaarey Zedek in

Figure 31. Percival Goodman, Temple Beth El, Gary, Indiana, 1954. The building resembled Mies's glass and steel buildings at the Illinois Institute of Technology.

Southfield, Michigan (1963), which scholars have seen as inspired by the biblical tent of meeting; there is little evidence, however, that Goodman drew consciously on this ancient precedent.[43]

Goodman's general disinterest in using architecture to express a sense of Jewishness further explains why his synagogues hardly ever alluded to the Holocaust. The only one that partly did was his first completed synagogue, Congregation B'nai Israel in Millburn, New Jersey (1949–51) (fig. 33). Goodman did not draw on the recent past in designing the form of the building, which was a low-slung rectilinear structure composed of brick, glass, and steel. But in planning its interior he designed special memorial niches for displaying stones that had been salvaged from two synagogues destroyed in Mannheim, Germany, on Kristallnacht in 1938.[44] The decision to include this commemorative feature stemmed from B'nai Israel's rabbi, Max Gruenewald, formerly the head

Figure 32. Percival Goodman, Beth Sholom, Miami, 1956. The synagogue's bulbous design displayed the influence of "googie" architecture.

Figure 33. Percival Goodman, Congregation B'nai Israel, Millburn, New Jersey, 1949–51. The building's form displayed no signs of the Nazi experience, but its interior included special niches for stones salvaged from synagogues destroyed on Kristallnacht.

of the Mannheim Jewish community, who emigrated to the United States in 1948 and later arranged for American military officials in Germany to send the stones to the United States.[45] Gruenewald was also responsible for another design feature that indirectly related to the Holocaust — the twelve-foot-tall, lead-coated copper sculpture of the biblical burning bush on the synagogue's main exterior facade. Designed by the artist Herbert Ferber and entitled . . . *and the Bush Was Not Consumed,* the sculpture was created to satisfy Gruenewald's desire to communicate a message of Jewish survival after Auschwitz.[46] Goodman's acceptance of these measures reflected his willingness to acknowledge the Holocaust, yet his failure to refer to it in his speech at the synagogue's dedication suggests that the event possessed little importance for his architectural philosophy.[47]

The exception that proves the rule was Goodman's participation in the New York City Holocaust memorial competition of 1949. Although Eric Mendelsohn ultimately won the competition, Goodman submitted a proposal that enjoyed early support from the memorial committee. His proposal featured a long stone plaza that led, via a large stone stairway, to a massive memorial wall bearing quotations and figurative sculpture. Adjacent to the memorial wall was a monumental bronze menorah perched atop a forty-foot-high stone pylon (fig. 34). These figurative features notwithstanding, Goodman remained true to his modernist principles, noting, "In developing the . . . memorial . . . foremost in my mind was function. . . . Jews memorialize not with stones and bronze, but with a service. Thus, my prime consideration was to create a fitting milieu for such a service." Goodman hoped that, just as other ethnic groups in New York City had their own parades, once a year there could be a "Jewish Day," in which Jews and others would march uptown and gather, up to five thousand strong, at his site, where they would listen to sermons by rabbis about the "sorrows of the world, peace, and redemption."[48]

Compared with Mendelsohn's subsequent proposal, Goodman's was far less accusatory. Instead of focusing on the responsibility of the German perpetrators, he emphasized consolation and reconciliation. In his explanatory statement for the memorial, Goodman wrote, "Six million human beings were killed because they were Jews. It is this simple and awful fact that we must recall to mind and mourn, and find what solace we can for it. There is no satisfaction to be got from hatred or resentment, but by the labor of mourning the hard knot of pain in the breast is loosed and one can breathe again. This is a memorial of mourning, of forgiveness, and there is the hope of resurrection."[49] The message of rebirth was visible in Goodman's choice of quotations for the memorial wall's north side, the famous biblical quotation from Ezekiel 37: 4–5: "Thus saith the Lord God unto these bones: 'O ye dry bones, hear the word of the Lord. Behold, I will cause breath to enter you and ye shall live.'" The resurrectionist message was also visible in the engraving of the Hebrew words "Etz Hayyim," or "tree of life," on the pylon bearing the menorah — words that Goodman believed heralded a "cheerful message" of life triumphing over death.[50] By taking inspiration in the words of Ezekiel, Goodman, like others at the time, turned away from the atrocities of the past and toward a more hopeful vision of the future.[51]

In February 1950, Goodman's proposal was displayed at the Museum of Modern Art and praised by Philip Johnson and other major figures in the New York art world. But it could not overcome the opposition of the New York City Parks Commission's legendary director Robert Moses, who feared that the memorial would claim too much of Riverside Park and distract motorists driving on the

Figure 34. Percival Goodman, Holocaust memorial proposal, New York, 1949. The design featured an oversized menorah and strove to communicate a redemptive message of resurrection and reconciliation.

West Side Highway. Goodman was predictably frustrated by Moses's decision and angrily noted that he was interested only "in a design that will stir no comment, awaken no feeling, . . . [and] arouse no interest." Goodman further believed that Moses's ambivalence about his Jewish heritage doomed the project.[52] Finally, meager fund-raising contributed to the memorial committee's failure to defend Goodman's design.[53] The result was that even a comparatively upbeat message about the Holocaust was unable to find architectural expression in the early postwar period.

Goodman's involvement in the memorial competition cast a revealing light on the Nazi genocide's place in his design philosophy. The architect's decision to enter the competition showed that he was open to remembering the Holocaust. Yet, like Mendelsohn, Goodman allowed the event to inform only a minor portion of his practice. While he was willing to commemorate the Jewish tragedy in memorials, he was reluctant to do so in buildings. For him, architecture was not about dwelling on the past but solving the problems of the present. In the end, Goodman's prodigious output during the 1950s and 1960s suggests that he succeeded in realizing his goal. That said, scholars have been careful to distinguish between the quantity and quality of his work. Samuel Gruber has described some of Goodman's designs as "exceptional" but concedes that "many of them are quite mundane" from the vantage point of today. Similarly, one of Goodman's former students, Peter Eisenman, has honored him for his capable teaching but has been less complimentary about his work, noting that "history may not be kind to Percival Goodman, Architect." Whatever scholars may conclude in

American Synagogue Architecture and the Missing Holocaust 67 the future, Goodman's synagogues perfectly embodied the priorities of most American Jews in the early postwar era. Ambivalent about extroverted expressions of Jewishness and averse to reflecting on the Holocaust, Goodman's religious architecture epitomized the era's assimilationist mindset.[54]

The Jewishness of Modernist Synagogues

It was not just the modernist synagogues of Eric Mendelsohn and Percival Goodman that displayed few Jewish traits but those of other architects as well. While it is impossible to survey the hundreds of synagogues that were built in the early postwar years, those that were profiled in the era's architectural journals and monographs avoided overt displays of Jewishness. Examples of this trend include Cecil Moore's Anshei Israel in Tucson, Arizona (1946), Braverman and Helperin's Temple Beth El in Akron, Ohio (1951), Louis Gordon Redstone's Temple Beth El in Flint, Michigan (1950), and Fritz Nathan's Congregation Sons of Israel in Woodmere, Long Island (1948–50).[55] Little distinguished these buildings as synagogues apart from their external ornamentation. It is telling, moreover, that the description of them in journals like the *Architectural Record* and *Progressive Architecture* avoided discussing their Jewish traits and concentrated instead on their technical features.[56]

The era's disinterest in architectural expressions of Jewishess was underscored by Max Abramovitz's ensemble of Jewish, Catholic, and Protestant chapels at Brandeis University in the mid-1950s, all of which were nearly indistinguishable from one another in their abstract modernist forms (fig. 35). Abramovitz's goal of "reflecting the similarity of all faiths while respecting their doctrinal differences" partly expressed the ecumenical spirit of the war years. But his universalistic vision ultimately reflected a larger assimilationist impulse. Rabbi Maurice N. Eisendrath, the president of the Reform United Association of Hebrew Congregations, spoke for many American Jews in 1954 when he expressed the desire for "Jewish houses of worship" that "would be American in form and spirit."[57]

The limited Jewish character of modernist synagogues was epitomized by the fact that the era's most critically celebrated works were designed by non-Jews. Philip Johnson's Kneses Tifereth Israel (KTI) in Port Chester, New York (1953–56), Frank Lloyd Wright's Beth Sholom in Elkins Park, Pennsylvania (1954–59), Walter Gropius's Temple Oheb Shalom in Baltimore (1954–60), Pietro Belluschi's Temple B'rith Kodesh in Rochester, New York (1959–63), and Minoru Yamasaki's North Shore Congregation Synagogue in Chicago (1959–64) have been hailed as important synagogues of the early postwar years.[58] Nearly all of them lacked overt Jewish traits. Johnson's spare, whitewashed structure featured an elliptical entry foyer connected to a rectangular, steel-framed sanctuary punctured by a series of thin vertical stained-glass windows (fig. 36). Apart from an interior ceiling canopy made of plaster, which some scholars have interpreted as a reference to the biblical tent of meeting (a reference denied by Johnson), there were no allusions to Jewishness in the building.[59] And no wonder, for the synagogue was based on an unrealized design for a church in Greenwich, Connecticut.[60] Oheb Shalom, which Gropius's postwar firm, the Architects' Collaborative (TAC), codesigned with the firm of Leavitt Associates, was a largely rectilinear, steel-framed complex, clad in brick, that combined a sanctuary, social hall, and classroom wing. The latter structures were purely functional and of modest appearance, but they were enlivened by the sanctuary, whose main feature

Figure 35. Max Abramovitz, Bethlehem and Berlin chapels, Brandeis University, Waltham, Massachusetts, 1953–55. The Bethlehem chapel (left) serves Catholic worshippers, while the Berlin chapel (right) serves Jewish worshippers.

Figure 36. Philip Johnson, Congregation Kneses Tifereth Israel synagogue, Port Chester, New York, 1953–56. This photograph from the 1950s shows the synagogue before it was hidden behind a row of cedar trees in the 1970s. Compare with fig. 23.

was a series of four arched towers, vaguely evoking the Mosaic tablets of the law, which supported its interior barrel-vaulted ceiling (fig. 37). The towers' Jewish associations were diluted, however, by being four in number, rather than two. There was also little Jewish character in Belluschi's Temple B'rith Kodesh, whose central twelve-sided cupola strongly resembled his earlier octagonal design for the Portsmouth Abbey church in Portsmouth, Rhode Island (1957 – 61).[61] Belluschi, indeed, never intended the synagogue to radiate a sense of Jewishness in the first place, observing that since "there is no architectural tradition to match the Jewish faith," synagogue architecture should express the "spirit of man."[62] Finally, Yamasaki's design for the North Shore Congregation was hailed for its structural inventiveness, especially its interlocking, reinforced concrete fan vault shells, which formed the basis of the synagogue's structure and allowed light to pour in from skylights. Yet neither these forms, nor Yamasaki's use of small, quasi-gothic pointed arches in the synagogue's side walls, had any Jewish significance.[63]

The exception to this trend was Frank Lloyd Wright's design for Beth Sholom, which displayed abundant Jewish symbolism (fig. 38). The synagogue's symbolic richness, however, did not stem as much from Wright as from its rabbi, Mortimer J. Cohen, who worked closely with the architect on the project. Like Wright, Cohen was committed to building a modern synagogue that owed nothing to bygone architectural styles; yet he also wanted it to possess a deeper sense of Jewish symbolism. Cohen wanted the synagogue to evoke Mount Sinai, the place where, according to Jewish tradition, God had told the Israelites to build a portable tentlike tabernacle for their desert wanderings. In accordance with Cohen's wishes, Wright designed Beth Sholom as a towering pyramidal structure of steel, aluminum, and glass that evoked a mountain or a tent. Along the synagogue's sloping ridges Wright included seven abstract menorahs. He also included a fountain at the entrance, in memory of the traditional laver that once stood in the Temple in Jerusalem. Yet while these features lent Beth Sholom a clear sense of Jewishness, the synagogue nevertheless reflected the era's assimilationist tendencies. Despite wanting Beth Sholom to possess Jewish meaning, Rabbi Cohen never intended it to be overly particularistic, preferring instead to have it symbolize "a 'new thing' — the American spirit wedded to the ancient spirit of Israel." And, while he never admitted as much, Wright obliged by basing his design for Beth Sholom on an earlier design for a church, specifically his

Figure 37. Walter Gropius, Oheb Shalom, Baltimore, 1954–60. The synagogue's dominant feature is its barrel vaults, which allude to the tablets of the Ten Commandments.

Figure 38. Frank Lloyd Wright, Beth Sholom, Elkins Park, Pennsylvania, 1954–59. The synagogue's design was partly inspired by Mount Sinai.

pyramidal Steel Cathedral project for New York from 1926. Few recognized this connection at the time, and Beth Sholom went on to garner immense fame, eventually being designated a National Historic Landmark.[64]

The case of Beth Sholom points to ironies that underscore the limited Jewishness of early postwar modernist synagogues in the United States. It is ironic, for one thing, that the synagogue with the most vivid Jewish symbolism after 1945 was designed by a Unitarian, while many Jewish-designed synagogues were far less Jewish in orientation. It is also ironic that some of the most celebrated synagogue designs of the early postwar period — by Wright, Belluschi, and Johnson — were either based on or closely resembled previous church designs. These facts, together with the interchangeable appearance of the Jewish, Catholic, and Protestant chapels at Brandeis University, make clear that Jewish architects were mistaken in believing that modernism could help emancipate synagogues from their reliance on historicist Christian architectural precedents.

Still, even if many of the early postwar era's most celebrated synagogues lacked overt Jewish qualities, they were not completely unaffected by recent Jewish history. Indeed, a case can be made that three of the most important early postwar synagogues—those of Johnson, Wright, and Gropius—were subtly influenced by the legacy of the Holocaust. It is striking that three of America's best-known architects accepted synagogue commissions after World War II, despite never having worked on such Jewish projects before. Was it merely a coincidence? Or is it possible that Johnson, Wright, and Gropius became involved with synagogue projects after 1945 to atone for their anti-Jewish attitudes and behavior in the years leading up to the Holocaust? It is well known that all three had exhibited varying degrees of antisemitism before the war. All three had either actively supported Hitler, collaborated with his regime, or opposed going to war against it. Johnson, Wright, and Gropius bore no personal guilt for the Holocaust, but might they have believed that designing a synagogue after 1945 could enhance their compromised reputations?

The best evidence for this supposition is provided by the case of Johnson. During the 1930s the architect had supported the racist and antisemitic political agenda of domestic fascist groups in the United States, such as Father Charles Coughlin's National Union for Social Justice, going so far as to write racist and antisemitic articles for the organization's newspaper, *Social Justice*. Johnson also declared his support for Hitler and the Nazi regime, a decision that led the FBI to suspect him of being a German-paid spy. Although Johnson began to distance himself from his fascist political leanings following the United States' entry into the war, his reputation as an "American Fascist," as *Harper's Magazine* put it in 1940, persisted, and he was put on trial for sedition in 1944. Despite being found innocent, Johnson sensed the need after 1945 to rehabilitate himself and took steps to gain forgiveness. After the war he visited the New York office of the Anti-Defamation League, where he apparently apologized for his prewar sins. He went out of his way to support the Holocaust memorial project of 1949 in New York and behaved magnanimously toward his Jewish architectural colleagues Percival Goodman and Louis I. Kahn, whose careers he promoted through his position at the Museum of Modern Art.[65]

The most famous example of Johnson's postwar efforts at rehabilitation, however, involved his design for KTI. After the architect learned in 1953 that the Port Chester congregation was seeking to build a new sanctuary, he made the unusual gesture of forgoing his normal fee and offering his design at no charge. It is unclear whether Johnson was motivated by genuine contrition or merely by the hope of rehabilitating himself in the eyes of potential Jewish clients.[66] At the time, Johnson had built no large-scale projects and had become discouraged by his failure to secure a client for the design. Not only had it been rejected by the Greenwich church, it had been turned down by another local house of worship as well. It is a little known fact that before Johnson offered the design to KTI he had offered it to the Conservative synagogue of Greenwich, Temple Sholom. He had been encouraged to do so by two influential congregants with whom he was friendly, Albert and Vera List. Despite the Lists' energetic lobbying, the Temple Sholom building committee rejected the design because it was more expensive than one drafted at no charge by an architect who belonged to the congregation.[67] Since Johnson did not initially offer his design to Temple Sholom for free, it is likely that his later decision to do so for KTI was animated less by altruism than desperation. Indeed, only after Johnson met KTI's Rabbi Joseph Speiser at a party hosted by the Lists and learned that the congregation was looking to build a new sanctuary did the architect offer his design at no cost. In doing so, moreover, he may have been pressured by the Lists, who had both lost family members in the Holocaust and reportedly required him to make a gesture of contrition before they would financially support the project.[68] Johnson's precise motives will probably never be known, but in the end, his work on behalf of the project was inseparable from the Holocaust's legacy.

The case of Wright is more complex. The architect expressed deep anti-Jewish prejudices on countless occasions during his career, frequently using antisemitic slurs against apprentices and employees. Wright's antisemitism was rooted both in social prejudices and political convictions. Like Johnson, he supported the antisemitic ideas of Henry Ford and the isolationist politics of Charles Lindbergh. During the 1930s he alleged that plutocratic American Jews were leading the country into war against Nazi Germany and instead urged neutrality — a stance that cost him his friendship with the architecture critic and staunch interventionist Lewis Mumford. Wright was also investigated by the FBI during the war for suspected sedition. Some scholars have contended that Wright used antisemitism only when he felt threatened — as when he pointed out the Jewish identity of competitors Richard Neutra and Rudolf Schindler — and pragmatically abandoned it when he needed the technical expertise of Jewish engineers or the patronage of Jewish clients. Indeed, many of Wright's clients were Jews, such as Edgar Kaufmann and Solomon Guggenheim, for whom Wright designed two of his most renowned works, Fallingwater and the Guggenheim museum.[69]

In view of Wright's contradictory behavior toward Jews, it is impossible to know how he viewed the Holocaust after 1945 and whether he felt compelled to reassess his prewar antisemitism. On the one hand, he must have recognized that his views of Hitler and his stance on the war had been mistaken. Yet Wright was famously unapologetic by temperament, and there is anecdotal evidence that he defended his wartime isolationism even after 1945.[70] It is improbable, therefore, that Wright saw the Beth Sholom commission as a personal means of atonement, as Johnson did at KTI. Yet the fact that Beth Sholom was Wright's only synagogue remains significant. After 1945, most American congregations that were planning new synagogues passed Wright over in selecting an architect — a fact that may have reflected Jewish disapproval of his stance on the war.[71] Whether or not that was the reason, Wright's typical reaction to feeling snubbed was to redouble his work ethic and prove himself to his detractors. He may have had extra motivation, therefore, to land a synagogue commission. This may explain why the normally dictatorial architect took the unusual step of accepting creative input from Rabbi Cohen on the synagogue's final plans — to the point where he actually named him codesigner.[72] Whatever the case may be, the fact that a former antisemite designed a major synagogue after 1945 reflected the altered circumstances of the post-Holocaust world.

The same can be said of Walter Gropius and his design for Oheb Shalom. Gropius's past was also defined by a hostile attitude toward Jews and an opportunistic relationship with the Nazi regime. The architect had frequently expressed antisemitic feelings during the years of the Kaiserreich and the Weimar Republic. During World War I he lashed out against Jews for allegedly undermining the German war effort, describing them as a "poison which I begin to hate more and more" and blaming them for "social democracy, materialism, capitalism, and [war] profiteering." After his break with Alma Mahler in 1919, he accused his ex-wife of having fallen victim to the "Jewish persuasion" of her new lover, the novelist Franz Werfel, and predicted that she would eventually return to her "Aryan origin." Following Hitler's seizure of power, Gropius joined Josef Goebbels's Reich Chamber of Culture and entered Nazi-sponsored architectural competitions for the Reichsbank complex and a *Kraft durch Freude* education and recreational building in 1933. He also tried to convince Hitler's officials that the modern movement was compatible with German values. Only after Gropius failed in this effort and determined that he would never achieve the recognition he desired did he leave Nazi Germany, first for England in 1934, and then America in 1937. It is true that Gropius experienced harassment by the Nazi regime and expressed considerable distaste for it. He also went out of his way to help Jewish Bauhaus colleagues Marcel Breuer and László Moholy-Nagy emigrate to England. But his postwar reputation as a victim of the Nazi regime masked a more ambiguous reality.[73]

It is unclear whether Gropius's past shaped his decision to design the Oheb Shalom synagogue. In 1958, when he was first contacted by codesigner Sheldon Leavitt to participate in planning for the congregation's new suburban complex, his controversial behavior lay far in the past.[74] Gropius had long since made a new life for himself in the United States, having built up a successful practice with his Boston-based firm TAC and worked on a wide range of institutional and commercial projects. It is unlikely, therefore, that Gropius saw himself as implicated in the destruction caused by the Nazis or felt any personal responsibility to mend it. Still, he may have viewed the synagogue commission as a small opportunity to create a better postwar world. After 1945, Gropius displayed idealistic impulses, advising the American military government on reconstruction efforts in the American occupation zone of Germany and sending CARE packages to former friends and colleagues in Germany, both Jewish and Christian.[75] Gropius never regarded the war—let alone the Holocaust, about which he was silent—as a rupture that required him to reconsider his architectural principles. But it is hard to imagine that his sole synagogue commission did not have resonance for him. His remark on the occasion of Oheb Shalom's dedication that the synagogue should promote a "contemplative state of mind" may have been directed not only at the congregants but at himself as well.[76]

That some of the postwar period's most famous synagogues were designed by men with antisemitic pasts bears contemplating. It is impossible to know whether Johnson, Wright, and Gropius ever completely let go of their prejudices. They need not have done so, of course, in order to have accepted synagogue commissions. Most Christian architects who built synagogues over the centuries probably harbored certain anti-Jewish beliefs. Philip Johnson's famous quip from the early 1970s about being a "whore" who would "work for the devil himself" probably applies to more than a few architects.[77] Yet the fact that architects who had formerly expressed antisemitic opinions designed major synagogues after 1945 testifies to the Holocaust's role in decisively discrediting antisemitism in American society. For architects who may have been self-conscious about their antisemitic pasts, designing synagogues after the war provided a useful, if unspoken, alibi that implicitly testified to their upstanding character. Finally, the Holocaust may have also increased the prestige of synagogue commissions after the war. Before 1939, few major non-Jewish modern architects had designed Jewish houses of worship. That they began to do so after 1945 may reflect the fact that synagogues had now become forward-looking symbols of Jewish survival and renewal. They had now become appealing projects for architects looking to create a new postwar world.

Synagogue Architecture at the End of the Early Postwar Years

The early postwar optimism about the possibility of creating a Jewish and modern form of synagogue architecture continued throughout the 1950s and into the early 1960s. Already in the mid-1950s, Jewish observers felt confident enough to declare that modernism had won over the Jewish masses. Rachel Wischnitzer noted in 1955 that while Jews had initially compared early postwar synagogue designs to "'airplane hangars' and 'ranch cottages' . . . ten years of building have converted the most conservative-minded to the modern style." Nearly a decade later, in 1963, the New York City Jewish Museum's exhibition "Recent American Synagogue Architecture" seemed to confirm Wischnitzer's upbeat assessment. Organized by architect Richard Meier, the exhibition surveyed some of the more impressive synagogue designs of the preceding decade, such as Wright's Beth Sholom, Johnson's KTI, and Goodman's Shaarey Zedek, and concluded that they testified to the "emergence in contemporary America of a new spirit in religious architecture." To be sure, the exhibition's organizers did not believe that any single method of modern synagogue design had yet been identified and conceded that the "final definition [of the modern synagogue] lies somewhere in the future." But at this point, few doubted that synagogue design was heading in the right direction.[78]

As it turned out, this confidence was not destined to last. By the mid-1960s the great hopes that many American Jews held for modern synagogue design were increasingly being questioned. Even though modernist synagogues had successfully broken with the styles of the past and embraced a new functionalist aesthetic, their lack of Jewishness gradually came to be seen as a deficiency. Assessing the situation in his 1966 book *Contemporary Synagogue Art,* Avram Kampf wrote, "Architects have sacrificed expression to function. . . . The synagogues they have erected are well built; they have . . . soft-cushioned seating facilities, perfect acoustics, . . . ample ventilation, good lighting and fine plumbing. But we often hear that these buildings 'do not feel like a synagogue'; nor do they convey any sense of the cultural and religious meaning of Judaism." Kampf acknowledged individual works of merit, but he concluded that "none of these designs has been convincing enough in its expressiveness to be generally adopted and further developed by others."[79]

Not even a notable shift in synagogue design in the 1960s was able to change this perception. During this decade, a sculptural turn in western architecture, partly associated with the New Brutalism movement, led to the appearance of more expressive synagogues. Among the more significant examples were Max Abramovitz's Beth Zion in Buffalo, New York (1967), whose oval arrangement of ten tilted, scalloped walls clad in limestone resembled "arms raised in prayer" (fig. 39); William N. Breger's Civic Center Synagogue in lower Manhattan (1967), whose bulbously curving white marble facade resembled a scroll or eternal flame; and Minoru Yamasaki's monumental Temple Beth El in Bloomfield Hills, Michigan (1974), which resembled a high-tech version of the tabernacle.[80] Yet even these daring designs were unable to connote a clear sense of Jewishness. On the occasion of the 1976 exhibition "Two Hundred Years of American Synagogue Architecture," at Brandeis University, art historian Gary Tinterow surveyed these and other synagogues and declared that, despite "engaging the most talented and respected architects in America . . . synagogue architecture often lacks one major component; expression of the specifically Jewish activity within." None of the synagogue designs of the postwar period, he concluded, was "expressive of a Jewish architecture."[81]

What is more, the failure of modernist synagogues to grapple with the legacy of the Holocaust was becoming noticed as well. In 1966, Kampf pointed out this failure with reference to modern synagogue interiors. As he put it, "The tragedy of World War II, the concentration camps and the death trains, . . . have had, with notable exceptions, a surprisingly small influence on the artworks placed on or designed for synagogues up to now." The reasons for this avoidance of the Holocaust were unclear: "It is difficult to tell," he wrote, "whether the congregants do not wish to be reminded of the horrors of those days or whether the artist finds it difficult to grapple with themes of such magnitude."[82] Kampf was one of the period's few commentators to note the absent confrontation with the Holocaust in synagogue design. The lack of similar comments from other observers suggests that few American Jews had any expectation in the first place that the Holocaust should be acknowledged in the setting of the synagogue. Kampf's observations, however, displayed their own shortcomings. By restricting his analysis to the question of why the interior artworks of postwar synagogues had been minimally influenced by the Holocaust, Kampf neglected to ask why the event had influenced synagogue architecture even less. The failure to pose this related question suggests that few Jews at this time could even conceive of an architectural—as opposed to an artistic—confrontation with the Holocaust.

Figure 39. Max Abramovitz, Beth Zion, Buffalo, New York, 1967. The scalloped concrete walls embodied the shift toward a more sculptural form of synagogue design.

Conclusion

On balance, the development of synagogue architecture in the United States in the first decades after 1945 can be described as a mixed success. American Jews began the postwar period with the goal of creating an authentically Jewish form of synagogue architecture with the help of modernist design principles. By liberating synagogues from the slavish imitation of historical styles, modernism was supposed to aid in the creation of a more genuine Jewish style of architectural expression. In the years immediately following World War II, hundreds of Jewish communities across America enthusiastically committed themselves to building modernist synagogues. They produced many daring and innovative designs that functioned well and satisfied the needs of their suburban communities. Yet without the trappings associated with prewar synagogues, those built after 1945 eventually came to be seen as insufficiently "Jewish." By the late 1960s it was clear that the early postwar hopes for creating an authentically Jewish form of synagogue architecture had not been realized.

The main reason for this failure was the fact that modernism's hostility to history and memory had severed postwar Jewish architecture from the Jewish past. When American Jews embraced modernism after 1945 they effectively committed themselves to a path of historical amnesia. An obvious effect of this decision was the refusal to acknowledge the legacy of the Holocaust in postwar synagogue architecture. To be sure, the evasion of the Holocaust may not have been merely an effect but also a cause of the Jewish embrace of modernism. Both reinforced one another—the desire not to be reminded of a painful past dovetailed perfectly with the embrace of a style of architecture that enabled that past to be ignored. Jewish architects (as well as their Christian colleagues) played a crucial role in this process of forgetting. For reasons both professional and cultural, American Jewish architects during the early postwar years refrained from reflecting on the implications of Auschwitz for their profession and refused to reconsider their principles in its aftermath. Even if some, such as Mendelsohn and Goodman, believed that synagogue architecture could provide consolation to their coreligionists, this view constituted more of an evasion of than a confrontation with past horrors. Significantly, their approach would be echoed by architects in early postwar Germany as well.

Chapter 4
Synagogues in Germany
Between Forgetting and Remembrance

Tucked away on the Fasanenstrasse in the Berlin neighborhood of Charlottenburg stands the Jüdisches Gemeindehaus. Built in 1957–59 according to the design of the German architects Dieter Knoblauch and Heinz Heise, it was the first major Jewish community center and synagogue complex erected in Berlin after the end of the Second World War. When I first saw it as a college student in 1987, my initial impression was of a nondescript glass and steel edifice built according to modernist principles. Set back from the street, the building's facade appeared to be dominated by two bands of repetitious windows that radiated anonymity. Upon closer inspection, however, I noticed a historic-looking stone portico flanking the building's entrance and a solitary stone pillar at its opposite end to the north (fig. 40). I later learned that the two stone structures were fragments of the prewar synagogue that had once occupied the site. Built in 1912 according to the design of Ehrenfried Hessel, the triple-domed Fasanenstrasse synagogue had once been one of Berlin's largest; but like so many other Jewish houses of worship, it was vandalized on Kristallnacht and heavily damaged in wartime bombings (see fig. 11). For over a decade after 1945, the building stood as a hulking ruin until Jewish community leaders decided, in the mid-1950s, to replace it with a new synagogue and community center complex. The new building, which was completed at the end of the decade, closely resembled comparable structures in the United States by virtue of its modernist design. Yet it differed in one significant respect. By incorporating fragments of the original synagogue, it embraced a form of modernism open to remembrance.

The case of the Berlin Jewish Community Center highlights some of the ambiguities of synagogue architecture in early postwar Germany. Unlike the situation in the United States, where hundreds of synagogues were built in the decades after World War II, there were relatively few synagogues built in the Federal Republic.[1] Most that were built, however, resembled their American counterparts in their modernist aversion to historical reference. Early postwar synagogues in Germany were thus largely silent about the events of the recent past. As German Jewish architect Salomon Korn has written, they "showed no signs in their architecture of the historical context in which they were created—the period following the wave of synagogue destruction and genocide."[2] As is shown by the historically evocative architecture of the Berlin Jewish Community Center, however, the silence toward the past was not total. In contrast to the case in the United States, where the Holocaust's legacy was successfully kept at arm's length, it was less easily evaded in Germany and influenced synagogue design in subtle ways.

The Path to Modernism

Synagogue architecture in early postwar Germany was inescapably defined by rupture. Following the destruction of more than one thousand synagogues on Kristallnacht and the decimation of German Jewry in the Holocaust, it initially appeared that synagogues had no future in Germany at all.[3] But a small Jewish community of twenty-five thousand persons remained, and synagogues were soon built in the country once again. These new buildings differed considerably from those erected before the rise of the Nazis. While late nineteenth- and early twentieth-century German synagogues had been powerful urban presences, those built after 1945 were relatively inconspicuous. This shift reflected the diminished size and relative poverty of German Jewish congregations, as well as their downcast mood.[4] Unlike in the United States, where there was a buoyant discussion about the possibility of creating an authentically Jewish form of synagogue architecture, the difficult circumstances of life in postwar Germany made an equivalent discussion inconceivable. Most Jews were unsure whether they would stay in the country and saw themselves as "sitting on packed suitcases." For this reason they saw little point in striving for architectural grandeur and preferred the modesty of modernism.

Figure 40. Dieter Knoblauch and Heinz Heise, Jewish Community Center, Berlin, 1957–59. The architects incorporated portions of the demolished Fasanenstrasse synagogue in their building. The most prominent element was a stone portico at the building's entrance (far right), which can be seen in its original state in fig. 11.

Jews in Germany also embraced modernism for its ahistorical abstraction, a trait that aided their desire to forget the painful past. One of the most explicit expressions of this desire was Rabbi Leo Baeck's remark in a 1945 sermon — delivered on the subject of Germany's and Austria's destroyed synagogues — that Jews "should be allowed to forget certain things. We will not be able to endure our lives . . . if the hardship and horror remain with us indefinitely. . . . It is a gift from God that we are capable of forgetting."[5] More broadly, Salomon Korn has observed that, in the early postwar period, the "memories and fears of the victims may have been too severe to find public expression in architectural form." Especially as many German Jews felt the "shame" of survival, the imperatives of "self-protection" understandably led the "deeply humiliated" survivors to embrace an "architecture of . . . neutrality and silence instead of [an architecture of] . . . admonition."[6] Only this kind of architecture could help German Jews reestablish a sense of security, comfort, and consolation in the wake of catastrophe. Focused as they were on rebuilding their lives in the present, German Jews generally did not want overt reminders of the past impeding their hopes for a better future. And yet, German Jews were hardly advocates of amnesia. Even as their synagogues reflected their desire to move forward, they did not do so without an occasional look backward.

The Modernist Synagogues of Hermann Zvi Guttmann and Helmut Goldschmidt

This backward-looking impulse was especially apparent in the work of the two main German Jewish architects responsible for designing synagogues in the early postwar period, Hermann Zvi Guttmann and Helmut Goldschmidt. Like Eric Meṇdelsohn and Percival Goodman in the United States, Guttmann and Goldschmidt were Germany's most prolific synagogue architects, designing nearly half of the synagogues that were built in the early postwar years.[7] Both were committed modernists whose buildings abjured historical reference. Yet, as Jewish architects living in Germany after the Holocaust, they could not entirely avoid addressing the recent past in their work.

The challenge of balancing the ahistorical principles of modernism with a commitment to remembrance was clearly visible in the architectural work of Hermann Zvi Guttmann. Biographical details about Guttmann's early life are sketchy, but he was born into a traditional family in the town of Bielitz in Austrian-ruled Silesia in 1917 and had just begun to study architecture in Lemberg (now L'viv) when the Second World War erupted. It is unclear how Guttmann experienced the war years, but the editors of his posthumously published book *Vom Tempel zum Gemeindezentrum* note that he fled German troops and suffered severe "privations" for the duration of the conflict.[8] After 1945, Guttmann resumed his studies in Munich and then established his architectural practice in Frankfurt, where he became a pillar of the local Jewish community.

Guttmann soon turned his attention to designing synagogues, producing plans for nearly a dozen of them throughout the Federal Republic between 1956 and 1972. The most important of his completed works were in Offenbach, Düsseldorf, Hannover, Osnabrück, Würzburg, and Frankfurt. Guttmann's synagogues were diverse in appearance, but they were distinguished by their curvilinear and parabolic forms. His first postwar design was a complex of buildings for the Jewish community of Offenbach near Frankfurt in 1955 – 56. The synagogue was a stucco-clad rectangular building with subtly rounded corners that gave it a smooth and graceful appearance (fig. 41). A Star of David set inside a circular window clearly revealed the structure's identity as a synagogue. Yet its location in a tree-lined garden tucked behind the attached Jewish community center suggested a desire for privacy and symbolized its function as a place to provide the community shelter from outside forces.[9] By way of comparison, Guttmann's next synagogue, built in Düsseldorf in 1956–58, was more assertive. Prominently situated on the corner of a public street, it was dramatically curvilinear, assuming the form of a travertine-clad oval topped with a squat domed roof. Along its sides were long vertical windows, and a menorah set inside a circular window stood over its entrance. The synagogue's interior was equally curvilinear and, for the first time, featured parabolic shapes behind the ark and in second-story balconies. These forms assumed further prominence in Guttmann's next synagogue for Hannover in 1961–63. There, parabolic shapes provided the basis for the synagogue's ground plan and determined the shape of its concave exterior facade and its interior space (fig. 42). Similar parabolic and curvilinear shapes recurred in his Jewish cemetery reception hall in Hannover (1958–60), his synagogue for Würzburg (1966–70), and his small synagogue in the city of Frankfurt's Jewish old age home (1973–77).[10]

In their outward appearance, Guttmann's synagogues seemed completely divorced from the recent past, even though nearly all of them replaced synagogues that had been destroyed during the Nazi era. In keeping with his modernist principles, Guttmann concentrated on his buildings' structural form and avoided historical references. His use of curvilinear and parabolic shapes fulfilled both of these goals. Not only were they structurally innovative, they also reflected a focus on the present rather than the past. Indeed, his sweeping curves betrayed the influence of the period's "kidney table" (*Nierentisch*) aesthetic, which dominated early postwar interior design in both the Federal Republic and other parts of the western world.[11] They also reflected the era's fascination

 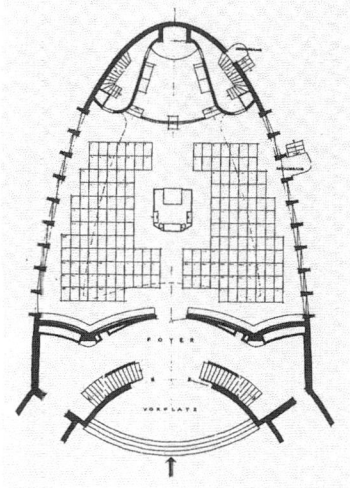

Figure 41. Hermann Zvi Guttmann, synagogue, Offenbach, Germany, 1955–56. The synagogue, which is set back from the street behind the attached community center, reflected the postwar German Jewish community's desire for privacy.

Figure 42. Hermann Zvi Guttmann, synagogue plan, Hannover, 1961–63. Guttmann's synagogue designs were known for their parabolic forms, which symbolized the virtue of modesty in the wake of war.

with parabolic forms, seen in Eero Saarinen's Gateway Arch in St. Louis (1948 – 66), William Pereira and Charles Luckman's Theme Building at Los Angeles International Airport (1961), and even McDonald's Restaurants' trademark golden arches (introduced in 1953).[12]

Yet while Guttmann's curvilinear style echoed the era's optimism about the future, it possessed deeper symbolic meaning related to recent historical events. In *Vom Tempel zum Gemeindezentrum*, Guttmann made clear that parabolic forms possessed more than mere formal significance. As he put it, "Despite their greatness and grandeur, buildings ultimately remain the products of human spirit and labor; no matter how far upward . . . they aspire, they remain limited. It was a mistaken belief in limitlessness that led to the Tower of Babel and its many consequences. I see the parabola as a symbol of this . . . vertical striving, which at its peak reveals a resistance to the futile human striving towards divine infinity." The precise meaning of this poetic passage is elusive, but Guttmann's citation of the biblical story of Babel may have been meant to refer allegorically to the disasters that resulted from the hubris of the Nazi regime. Just as the effort to reach God by building a vertical tower had led to disaster in the Bible, so too had the Nazis' monumental building plans and their grandiose geopolitical schemes led to catastrophe. Guttmann seemed to suggest that the antidote for such boundless striving was the parabola. Unlike vertical architectural forms, which soared toward the infinite, the parabola was a form that rose skyward only to curve gently back toward the ground, thus remaining a mere "expression of potential." In short, Guttmann implied that by investing synagogue architecture with a sense of restraint and modesty, parabolic forms could help in the larger task of improving the world by counteracting the destructive excesses of human ambition.[13]

Indeed, parabolic forms reflected Guttmann's broader belief that synagogue architecture could offer sanctuary from both past and present dangers. Like Eric Mendelsohn and Percival Goodman in the United States, Guttmann strove to have his synagogues satisfy "the security that our era demands" by making them "life-affirming" in nature. One way of accomplishing this task was by bringing light into his sanctuary spaces. This strategy was especially important, Guttmann believed, for "in our era, in which extermination is present on a nearly daily basis," it was necessary "to keep fear away from a house of God and [instead] to allow . . . hope to enter it." In making this comment, Guttmann, like Goodman around the same time, was expressing his apprehension about what he referred to elsewhere as the "dangers of the atomic era." And yet the Holocaust also lurked in the background. In commenting on the parabolic shapes of his Jewish cemetery hall in Hannover, Guttmann noted that they were intended to suggest the "gate to the afterlife," a concept that he said Jews had to believe in, for "how could Jews not believe in the afterlife after all that [has] happened? [Without this belief], the catastrophe that unfolded before God's visage could not be humanly comprehended."[14]

Yet, however much Guttmann's synagogues were inspired by the past, they were ultimately meant to affirm the present. As was revealed by the press coverage of the dedication ceremonies for many of his synagogues, both German Jews and their Christian German neighbors optimistically viewed Guttmann's religious buildings as symbols of reconciliation. For their part, Jewish congregations strove to reassure Germans that they bore them no ill will. At the dedication of the Offenbach synagogue, for example, the head of the local Jewish community, Siegfried Guggenheim, reminded gathered guests that "despite everything that has happened to us, Jewish teaching [requires us] not to carry grudges, not to hate, [but] to love God with all [of our] hearts . . . and love your neighbor as yourself." Germans, meanwhile, aimed to reassure Jews about their nation's newfound commitment to religious tolerance. When Guttmann's Düsseldorf synagogue was dedicated, West German chancellor Konrad Adenauer praised it as a "visible sign of the success of [the Federal Government's] reparations policy," while the *Rheinischer Post* opined that the synagogue's dedication had succeeded in "atoning, at least externally, for the evil deed of Kristallnacht in 1938." Similarly, at the dedication of the Hannover synagogue, the press described it as a "house of reconciliation" and noted with satisfaction that "no bitterness remains among our Jewish fellow citizens."[15]

For his part, Guttmann resembled most German Jews in wanting to remember recent history without blocking the way to the future. At the dedication of his Düsseldorf synagogue in 1958, he said that "the new house of worship is at once a component of the present and a warning about the past." Overall, Guttmann's optimism as a Jewish modernist tended to prevail over any competing impulses. When asked how Jews such as himself could summon the strength to build synagogues again after all that had happened in Germany, he attributed it to the Jewish people's "deep religious belief and the nearly boundless optimism that derived from it."[16]

Despite his generally upbeat response to the Holocaust, Guttmann was not averse to alluding to its darker dimensions in his work. Between 1964 and 1967, Guttmann designed what is probably his best-known building: the Jewish memorial chapel on the grounds of the Dachau concentration camp outside Munich (fig. 43). Anticipating the later postmodern revival of historical reference,

Figure 43. Hermann Zvi Guttmann, Dachau Memorial Chapel, 1964–67. The parabolic chapel was one of the first postwar buildings to make use of Holocaust iconography, seen most clearly in the allusion to barbed wire in its wrought-iron railings.

Synagogues in Germany 83

his design was one of the first to incorporate concentration camp iconography into its very form. The building was a stone-clad structure, half-buried in the ground, which featured a parabolic roof topped with a white marble menorah. Despite its heavy exterior appearance, the building expressed a sense of movement thanks to the sharp tilt of its roof, which descended some twenty feet from its peak to ground level. A similar tilt was visible in the long ramp that descended from ground level to the building's subterranean entrance. Along this passageway, explicit allusions to concentration camps were visible, especially twin black metal railings and a large iron gate that was crafted to resemble barbed wire. Inside the chapel were numerous commemorative plaques and a stone bimah for reciting the Kaddish. There was no ark, however, since Torah scrolls were prohibited from being housed there per rabbinic decree. The chapel was thus not a synagogue in the strict sense of the term.[17]

The chapel reflected Guttmann's struggle to balance his optimistic inclinations with a more somber commitment to remembering the Holocaust. Some scholars have interpreted the chapel's entrance as the entry door to a crematorium oven (and its white menorah as a wisp of smoke); others have seen it as a "death ramp" to underground gas chambers.[18] One might even interpret the tilted structure as a coffin being lowered into a waiting burial plot. Guttmann's building clearly suggested a sense of dread. As he wrote, the building was meant "to commemorate the horrible era of . . . persecution." At the same time, however, he also wanted it to remind "survivors not to lose hope." Guttmann communicated this redemptive message with the stone menorah that rose through the chapel's roof. Crafted of marble quarried from the northern Israeli town of Peki'in—where Jews have lived without interruption since the time of the Second Temple—the menorah was intended by Guttmann to "symbolize the continuity of Judaism" despite the ravages of history.[19] Thanks to this affirmative message, the chapel echoed the symbolism of Guttmann's less representational modernist synagogues. Its main architectural significance ultimately lay elsewhere, however. In explicitly evoking the Nazi genocide in the chapel's design, Guttmann was one of the first Jewish architects after 1945 to wrestle directly with the Holocaust's legacy.

Closely resembling Guttmann's approach to dealing with the recent past was that of the Cologne-based architect Helmut Goldschmidt (1918–2005). Like Guttmann, Goldschmidt suffered great hardship during the Nazi era. Born to a Jewish father and Catholic mother, Goldschmidt ranked as a *Mischling* according to the Nazis' racial laws, but because his father had sent him to a series of Jewish schools, he was viewed as a "de-facto Jew" and was therefore unable to study architecture at the university.[20] Instead, he apprenticed with local Jewish architects who provided him with training that ended up saving his life. With the outbreak of war in 1939, Goldschmidt was sent to an expropriated Jewish agricultural estate in eastern Germany, where he designed farm buildings. He returned in 1941 to Cologne to be with his parents, who, thanks to their intermarried status, were able to evade the first deportations of Jews in the fall of that year. In November 1942, however, Goldschmidt was arrested by the Gestapo for associating with politically suspicious "swing youth" and kept in a police prison for four months until being sent to Auschwitz in March 1943 as a political prisoner. After four months of hardship (during which his weight declined to seventy-seven pounds) he was sent to Buchenwald in July 1943, where he was put to work in the building department, an assignment that provided him with the life-saving privilege of working indoors. Of inestimable benefit was the German Interior Ministry's decision in September 1944 to grant Goldschmidt the more privileged status of *Mischling,* second degree.[21] These twists of fate enabled the architect to survive until being liberated by American troops in 1945.

Goldschmidt's particular experience of the Holocaust helps explain his subsequent architectural career. In a comparative sense, Goldschmidt was extremely fortunate. Both of his parents survived the war. His father evaded arrest by escaping to his in-laws' rural house in the Eiffel region, where he was protected by local villagers. And two of his uncles survived in hiding in Belgium. Goldschmidt's time in Buchenwald, moreover, was comparatively mild. As he later recalled, "No matter how grotesque it sounds, . . . Buchenwald seemed like a life-saver for me. I thought: this is not like Auschwitz, here you can survive." Compared to most other Jews, in short, Goldschmidt escaped the worst of the Holocaust. With his immediate family intact, thanks to the aid of Christian Germans, he did not lose his faith in his homeland like so many other German Jews. This may explain why he was willing to remain in Germany and help in the postwar task of reconstruction. Immediately after the war Goldschmidt settled in Mayen, his maternal grandparents' hometown, where he used his Jewish background to win permission from French military government authorities to work on local reconstruction projects. In 1948 in Cologne he established his own office (which he shared for a short time with his one-time employee and later partner, the neo-Rationalist architect Oswald Mathias Ungers) and permanently moved there in 1951. Thanks to the prominence of Goldschmidt's father, who was named the head of the tiny Jewish community, he worked on the first modest synagogue on the Ottostrasse in 1949. This paved the way for later commissions.[22]

Like Guttmann, Goldschmidt distinguished himself by designing a variety of early postwar modernist synagogues. The most important were in Dortmund (1956), Bonn (1959), and Münster (1960), while smaller prayer rooms were built in other cities.[23] Goldschmidt's synagogues were generally smaller than Guttmann's, being intended to hold fewer than two hundred congregants.[24] They were also less architecturally noteworthy. While Guttmann's synagogues were defined by gracefully sweeping curvilinear forms, Goldschmidt's were more rigidly rectilinear in their plans and exterior appearance. Like Guttmann, however, Goldschmidt also avoided historical reference in his work. His synagogues were recognizable as religious edifices only by their exterior symbols, such as the menorah and Hebrew lettering gracing the street facade of his synagogue in Münster (fig. 44).

Figure 44. Helmut Goldschmidt, synagogue, Münster, 1960. Compared to the prewar synagogue on the same site, the postwar building was less open to the street and strove for a "sense of inner seclusion."

His synagogue in Dortmund, by contrast, was so integrated into the adjacent community center that it resembled an apartment complex.

Goldschmidt's reasons for embracing modernist forms are unknown, but his scattered writings suggest that he agreed with Guttmann that a modern form of synagogue architecture could provide security and comfort for Jews after the Holocaust. Goldschmidt commonly referred to his designs as "up to date" and "fitting for the contemporary era."[25] His remark at the dedication of his Bonn synagogue that he wanted his buildings to exude a "bright modernity" suggests that he shared the optimistic mindset of the modern movement. He clearly embraced the modernist goal of breaking with the past, noting in 1959 that while many of his fellow Jews in Germany continued to "adhere . . . to the model of the destroyed turn-of-the-century synagogues and their 'demonstrative' architecture," he believed that "every new building . . . should be an expression of its era."[26]

In spite of their modern features, Goldschmidt's synagogues exhibited signs of German Jewish uneasiness after the Holocaust. Goldschmidt himself remained haunted by the experiences of the Nazi genocide. As he recalled in a 1990 interview: "Even though it was forty-five years ago, a week does not go by that I do not dream of Auschwitz at least three times. . . . Such feelings . . . simply do not go away. It is like a sickness." Goldschmidt's feelings of insecurity were subtly visible in his Münster synagogue. In 1961 he publicly declared that the local Jewish community could be "justifiably proud" of its "worthy and contemporary house of worship." Yet aspects of the building's design revealed an underlying desire for anonymity, privacy, and security. Instead of trying to lend the synagogue a Jewish appearance, Goldschmidt laconically observed that its form "adhered to the contemporary mode of building that is typical of the area." This assimilationist desire to remain unnoticed was further visible in the synagogue's orientation to its site. Although it was built at the same location on the Klosterstrasse as the prewar Moorish synagogue (which was destroyed on Kristallnacht), it was less publicly accessible. Whereas the prewar sanctuary had an entrance that

Figure 45. Bernhard Below and Wilhelm Emil Schreiterer, Roonstrasse synagogue, Cologne, 1895–99, restored by Helmut Goldschmidt, 1956–59.

opened directly onto the street, Goldschmidt's displayed a solid brick wall to the street and could be entered only after passing through a small courtyard and antechamber, creating a "sense of inner seclusion." This design feature revealed how even an abstract and relatively ahistorical building could be subtly influenced by the past.[27]

Goldschmidt confronted the Nazi experience more directly with his reconstruction of the Roonstrasse synagogue in Cologne. Originally erected in 1895–99 according to the design of Bernhard Below and Wilhelm Emil Schreiterer, the Roonstrasse synagogue was a massive neo-Romanesque edifice that was severely damaged on Kristallnacht and later hit by Allied bombs. It stood as a hulking ruin after 1945. Initially the tiny Jewish community had no plan to reconstruct the building and considered selling it to a theater company for performance space. Goldschmidt himself favored tearing the ruin down and building a "modern community center and . . . synagogue." Yet as the Jewish community slowly grew during the early 1950s, its leadership "overcame its doubts" and reconsidered the building's fate. Helping in this task was German chancellor and former mayor of Cologne Konrad Adenauer, who wanted the building restored to the city's heavily damaged urban landscape and helped secure funding. In 1956 the Jewish community resolved to rebuild the ruined building and commissioned Goldschmidt to produce plans for the project. The architect responded by accommodating the community's desire to transform the nineteenth-century synagogue into a mid-twentieth-century synagogue center.[28]

This was no easy task for a modernist, yet Goldschmidt strove to "adapt [the new center] to the era."[29] To do this, he inserted a new ceiling above the ground floor, turning the resulting lower level into a massive social hall. This elevated the sanctuary one floor higher, reducing the height of its vaulted spaces. Goldschmidt also simplified the interior, refraining from reproducing the original ceiling decorations in favor of simple whitewashed surfaces. Goldschmidt also simplified the building's monumental exterior, refusing to reproduce the ornate stone gables and dormers on the building's front and replacing them with unornamented rectilinear forms (fig. 45). The synagogue's resulting appearance was thus less grand than before. Yet in undertaking the restoration project, which was completed in September 1959, Goldschmidt counteracted the widespread demolition and profanation of damaged prewar synagogues in West German cities after 1945.[30] In so doing, he preserved a clear sign of the German Jewish community's once monumental presence in the German urban landscape. The restored Roonstrasse synagogue thus functioned as both a testament to the past and an admonition for the future. Small wonder, then, a mere three months after its completion, it attracted the ire of neo-Nazis who defaced it with swastikas and other antisemitic graffiti in December 1959. With this infamous deed, which made headlines the world over, the synagogue's commemorative power was dramatically underscored.

The Call of the Past: Other German Synagogues

Guttmann's and Goldschmidt's synagogues were not the only ones that confronted the dilemmas of memory in early postwar Germany. Other synagogues, designed by an array of mostly Christian architects, did so as well. These buildings were stylistically diverse. Some, such as Franz May and Karl-Heinz Wrongel's modernist synagogue in Hamburg (1960), made no effort to communicate the building's religious function as a Jewish house of worship. Others, such as Karl Gerle's domed synagogue in Bremen (1961) and Alfons Leitl's fortress-like, domed synagogue in Trier (1956–57) exuded a whiff of prewar historicism. Historians have been right to see these structures as indifferent toward Germany's recent history. But just as Guttmann's and Goldschmidt's synagogues could not entirely avoid the challenges posed by the Holocaust, those built by other architects could not help doing so either.[31] Two in particular—the new synagogue of Stuttgart and the new Jewish community center of Berlin—declined to break with the past and instead emphasized continuity with it.

Stuttgart's new synagogue was the first one to be rebuilt in postwar Germany. Designed by the German Jewish architect Ernst Guggenheimer (1880–1973) in the late 1940s and built in 1951–52, the synagogue was defined by its clear links to the past, most obviously in its conservative design (fig. 46). It was built on the stone foundations of the prewar synagogue on the Hospitalstrasse, a mid-nineteenth-century Moorish structure destroyed on Kristallnacht. Like the original, the new building was set back from the street and featured a small forecourt surrounded by an iron fence. It was also built of stone but designed in a simplified style. Guggenheimer was a progressive architect who approved of the antihistoricist direction of synagogue architecture during the interwar period.[32] Yet, being nearly forty years older than Guttmann and Goldschmidt, he did not embrace their assertive postwar modernism. His design for the Stuttgart synagogue was more classical, as was seen in its symmetrical plan, rectilinear form, stone exterior, and traditional features, such as casement windows surrounded by robust moldings. The synagogue's interior was equally traditional, featuring a coffered ceiling and formal chandeliers.

Figure 46. Ernst Guggenheimer, synagogue, Stuttgart, 1951–52. The synagogue's interior displayed conservative features, such as a coffered ceiling and traditional chandeliers.

Guggenheimer's most poignant nod to history, however, was his incorporation of salvaged remnants of the original synagogue in the new building's interior. These included a stone sculpture of the Ten Commandments that had once graced the prewar synagogue's roof and a World War I memorial that had been damaged on Kristallnacht. For him and other community members, these remnants were important symbols of Jewish survival. While Guggenheimer described them as a "bridge from then to now," the state rabbi of Württemberg-Hohenzollern, S. J. Neufeld, observed that they were a "visible sign of the eternal . . . strength of the Jewish people that can be destroyed neither by fire nor floodwaters." This symbolic message probably had great personal significance for Guggenheimer. Having spent most of the war in hiding outside Stuttgart, he was captured early in 1945 and sent to Billroda, a satellite camp of Buchenwald. He survived, and after returning to Stuttgart contributed to the revival of the Jewish community to which he had belonged for over sixty years by volunteering to design its new synagogue — a task that he described as the "capstone of his life's work."[33] By reestablishing architectural continuity with the congregation's past, Guggenheimer strove to give its members hope for the future.

A similar effort to reestablish continuity with the past was visible in the Jewish Community Center of Berlin. Like the Jews of Cologne, who around the same time were discussing the future of the Roonstrasse synagogue ruin, the Jews of Berlin had to decide what to do with the ruin of the Fasanenstrasse synagogue. Guiding their decision was the realization of communal leaders, most notably Heinz Galinski, that the community's growing size (caused by the return of former emigrés and the birth of children) required a new central institution to cater to its social and educational needs.[34] In 1956, therefore, the Berlin Jewish community forged an agreement with local political leaders to raze the Fasanenstrasse synagogue's ruin and use the space to build a new community center and synagogue.

Shortly thereafter, the Bochum-based architectural firm of Dieter Knoblauch and Heinz Heise was commissioned to design the community center. Knoblauch and Heise won the competition partly thanks to their successful postwar design for the new domed synagogue of Essen, which they completed in 1957.[35] In Berlin they designed a more rectilinear structure that was dominated by two rows of windows interrupted by a stark, stone-clad rectangular form housing the social hall and synagogue. Only inside this multipurpose hall did the architects lend the building a more Jewish feel, inserting three domed skylights into the ceiling. This feature acknowledged the three domes of the historic Fasanenstrasse synagogue and represented a subtle memorial to the bygone edifice.

Yet the community center's most explicit reference to the past had little to do with the architects. Before any architectural competition was held, Jewish community leaders made the remarkable decision to incorporate salvaged portions of the original synagogue into its main facade. The Fasanenstrasse synagogue's original portico was placed at the entrance to the new community center, while a column and two tablets of the Ten Commandments salvaged from the synagogue's front facade were placed at the facade's north end (fig. 47). The reason for this decision, which reportedly originated within "local rabbinical circles," differed substantially from the case of Stuttgart.[36] While Guggenheimer's incorporation of remnants from the prewar synagogue was restricted to the postwar synagogue's interior (and thus was inwardly directed toward the Stuttgart Jewish community), the inclusion of remnants from the Fasanenstrasse synagogue in Berlin was meant to serve as a "warning column" (*Mahnsäule*) that would remind the German people of the "great guilt of the past." As the community center's commemorative brochure (*Festschrift*) declared, "Everyone who

Figure 47. "Warning Column," Jewish Community Center, Berlin. This fragment, which is located on the north side of the building, was part of the Fasanenstrasse synagogue's main facade (see fig. 11).

passes by this house should gaze upon the warning column. Jews [should do so], in the awareness that the past obligates [them] to be wary of the future. . . . Non-Jews should remain . . . constantly aware of the guilt of the past, since what has happened cannot be completely undone through reparations." This message was blunter than the anodyne statements of reconciliation that accompanied the dedication of Guttmann's and Goldschmidt's synagogues and probably came closer to articulating the sentiments of most German Jews after 1945. Whether or not this bluntness was due to the Berlin Jewish community's special status as the largest in Germany, local Jewish leaders clearly looked to the Holocaust in conceiving the new community center's design. As a commemorative text inserted into the building's cornerstone concluded: "The past lives on. The hurts and hardships have been symbolically integrated into this new building."[37]

Conclusion

In the end, the Berlin Jewish Community Center's design was exceptional. Most synagogues and community centers in early postwar Germany shared the building's modernist elements but rejected its historical references. Yet even if German synagogues resembled their American counterparts in emphasizing the modernist promise of a bright future, they never fully escaped the reminders of the recent past. In so doing, they hinted at the Holocaust's untapped potential to influence postwar architecture. It would be some time, however, before that potential was realized. In the early decades of the postwar period, both German and American synagogues strove to be free of history. Significantly, this trend within Jewish religious architecture defined the realm of secular architecture as well.

Chapter 5
Jewish Architects and Secular Jewish Architecture

On the far east side of midtown Manhattan, along the East River, stands one of the most famous works of mid-century modern architecture in the United States, the headquarters of the United Nations (1947–52). Soaring thirty-nine stories into the air, its glass and steel tower, known as the U.N. Secretariat Building, symbolizes the International Style's rise to prominence in early postwar America (fig. 48). When it was completed in 1950, the U.N.'s modern design was hailed for its technological advancement (it featured the first glass curtain wall in Manhattan) and for idealistically symbolizing postwar hopes for international cooperation.[1] What few observers bothered to point out at the time, however, is that a Jewish architect had a major role in designing it. Max Abramovitz, together with his partner Wallace Harrison and an international team of architectural consultants, is today acknowledged as one of the guiding forces behind one of New York's most recognizable edifices.[2] Looking at the U.N., of course, one cannot discern any signs of a "Jewish" sensibility. Indeed, the building was intended to symbolize the universal modern style, a point made by Abramovitz himself in 1947 when he declared: "The United Nations must have a look all its own.... We are not interested in a replica of a past style. We are a different, new, strong generation, and we feel that it is up to the architects to express the age."[3] Nevertheless, the fact that a Jewish architect helped design a building of such international significance points to a noteworthy trend.

Indeed, it highlights the fact that after the Second World War, Jewish architects in the United States achieved success as never before. Not only did they make their presence felt in the architectural profession in unprecedented numbers, they also developed world-class reputations and secured for themselves a lasting place in the annals of modern architectural history. During the first two decades of the postwar period, architects such as Eric Mendelsohn, Richard Neutra, Marcel Breuer, Gordon Bunshaft, Morris Lapidus, and Max Abramovitz either solidified or established their reputations as architects of international stature.[4] That said, the success of Jewish architects was highly paradoxical, for the very work that earned them their fame exhibited few Jewish characteristics. Partly due to the universalistic principles of the modernist movement and partly due to their ambivalent Jewish identities, most Jewish architects in the early postwar period registered their achievements while ignoring their Jewishness. Small wonder, therefore, that the Holocaust also had little impact on secular Jewish architecture in the years after 1945.

Figure 48. Max Abramovitz, United Nations Headquarters, New York, 1947–52. This building epitomized the idealism of early postwar modernism.

The Postwar Prominence of Jewish Architects

In the immediate aftermath of the Holocaust, there were few indications that the postwar era would witness unprecedented Jewish architectural productivity. Many European Jewish architects from the prewar period had seen their careers interrupted by the rise of the Nazis and the onset of the war. Among those who were forced to flee Europe and reestablish themselves abroad were the German Jewish architects Erich Mendelsohn, Fritz Nathan, and Fritz Landauer; the Hungarian Jewish architect Marcel Breuer; the Austrian Jewish architect Josef Frank; and the French Jewish architect Pierre Chareau. They were lucky to have escaped with their lives. The Dutch Jewish architect Harry Elte, who designed the modernist Jacob Obrechtplein synagogue in Amsterdam-Zuid (1928), was murdered in Theresienstadt. And a young Austrian Jewish architect by the name of Simon Wiesenthal was so traumatized by his internment in multiple concentration camps that he abandoned architecture and devoted himself to hunting fugitive Nazi war criminals.[5]

Soon after the war, however, Jewish architects began to register new achievements that brought them widespread attention. A good example of this dawning awareness was provided by an article published in *Commentary* in July 1957 by Paul and Percival Goodman entitled "Jews in Modern Architecture." Subtitled "After a Late Start," the essay explained why Jews had suddenly ceased being architectural underachievers. The primary explanation for the "bewilderingly large number of Jews active in every form and function of building," the Goodmans argued, was that architecture had, over the course of the modern era, become particularly "congenial to [the] abilities and needs developed . . . in Jews by historical circumstances." Jews, they affirmed, had long been absent from architecture because of feudal restrictions that had limited their entry into the craft and artisan guilds. But architecture's transformation into a "gentleman's profession" by the nineteenth century — and the resulting fact that "there . . . [was] little exclusion or quota monkeyshines in schools of architecture" — "made it easier for rich, well-connected Jews to enter [the field]." Moreover, these Jews' "friendship[s] and family connections" with wealthy Jewish patrons helped them succeed. "The mansion of a rich Jew," the Goodmans asserted, "was likely to built by a Jew who was a gentleman."[6]

But it was not just the patronage of the rich that benefited Jewish architects. The modern world's growing need for community-oriented projects — or what the Goodmans called an "architecture of general welfare" — meant that socially and politically progressive Jews found opportunities to build workers' housing settlements. Michel de Klerk's Eigen Haard complex in Amsterdam was a prime example of this trend. Thanks to "changes in the field of architecture . . . that have made it receptive to the entry of Jews," the Goodmans argued, the number of Jews who had become architects had grown considerably. A glance at the overall history of "avant-garde architecture during this century" confirmed the fact that "whether we consider . . . Expressionism or the International Style . . . there are many Jews among the disciples and [even] a few among the leaders." The Goodmans conceded that the architecture produced by such Jewish architects was not "Jewish" in any specific sense. And they cautioned that the "question remains [open] whether . . . the Jews will go on to develop a characteristic [architectural] style of their own." But they concluded that "Jews are represented on a great scale in modern architecture."[7]

More descriptive than analytical, the Goodmans' essay left unexplained the reasons for Jewish architects' postwar prominence. For one thing, it neglected to point out that it was mostly in the United States that Jewish architects had registered unprecedented achievements after 1945. One reason for this was the country's historic openness to immigrants from Europe. Already in the early twentieth century, the Austrian Jewish architects Rudolf Schindler and Richard Neutra had migrated to America, lured by the work of Frank Lloyd Wright. Somewhat later, the rise of the Nazis drove Erich Mendelsohn, Marcel Breuer, and others to the U.S. as well. Without this influx of talent from abroad, the postwar rise of American Jewish architects would not have been as dramatic as it was. Finally, the devastation of European Jewry in the Holocaust and the ensuing emergence of the United States as the most important center of world Jewry after 1945 inevitably made the country the home of the postwar Jewish architectural renaissance.

Aiding Jewish architects in their rise to postwar prominence was the comparatively open and meritocratic character of the American architectural profession. As early as the mid-nineteenth century, Jews had been able to find work as architects in the United States. Some, such as Leopold Eidlitz, were first-generation immigrants from Central Europe who came to America after having undergone architectural training abroad. Others, such as Arnold Brunner, were second-generation Jews, born in the U.S. to Central European immigrant families, whose economic success provided the wherewithal to pursue a career in the "gentleman's profession." Jews did not have to hail from upper-class backgrounds, however, to become architects in America. More than a few of the Jewish architects who developed major reputations after 1945 had either been born in Eastern Europe and moved to the United States very young (Morris Lapidus and Louis I. Kahn) or were born immediately after their parents' arrival from Eastern Europe (Gordon Bunshaft and Max Abramovitz).

To be sure, the introduction of quotas for Jews at American universities during the interwar years prevented many from entering architectural schools.[8] But unlike the situation in pre-emancipation Europe, these limitations never kept Jews out of the profession entirely. Moreover, after 1945 these hurdles gradually disappeared. In the wake of the Holocaust, and with the waning of antisemitism in American society, quotas in universities were abolished and Jews who were interested in studying architecture were able to enter the university system in greater numbers than before.[9] Of course, this shift mostly benefited the later generation of Jewish architects, who went to architecture school after the war. The Jewish architects who gained prominence in the early postwar years had already established themselves in the profession. They did profit, however, from the more ecumenical spirit of the post-Holocaust years, as they were able to secure commissions from clients who previously might not have worked with them. All of these changes were important preconditions for postwar Jewish architectural achievement in the United States.

The Jewishness of Secular Jewish Architecture

The buildings designed by Jewish architects in the early postwar era, however, displayed few discernible Jewish qualities. Needless to say, this claim raises the obvious question of how secular structures — schools, hospitals, hotels, office buildings, corporate high rises, and the like — might be able to articulate a sense of Jewishness in the first place. To address this question, it helps to recognize that Jewishness in architecture exists less in the visible attributes of buildings than in the sensibilities that Jewish architects expressed in designing them. Jewish architects are no different, after all, from Jewish artists, novelists, composers, poets, and playwrights, many of whom have drawn on their Jewish backgrounds and expressed Jewish concerns in their creative work in the modern era. The well-known commitment of Jews to progressive social and political causes, for example, was visible in the social realist paintings of Ben Shahn and Raphael Soyer, as well as in the novels of Ben Hecht, Michael Gold, and I. J. Singer. The alienation felt by Jews buffeted by the forces of assimilation and antisemitism found expression in the modernist novels, paintings, and musical compositions of Franz Kafka, Chaim Soutine, and Arnold Schönberg. And, as was discussed in Chapter 2, the shock of the Holocaust was registered by Jews in a variety of fields, ranging from poetry to painting. There is no reason why Jewish architects in this period could not have acted similarly and expressed Jewish concerns in their work. For example, some could have expressed a Jewish commitment to social justice by designing public housing developments, schools, hospitals, or other socially oriented projects. Others could have been influenced by anxieties stemming from their identities as outsiders trying to break into the American social mainstream. Still other Jewish architects could have reflected on the Holocaust's implications for their discipline.

Yet while Jewish architects could have easily drawn on their backgrounds in their secular work during the early postwar years, most chose not to. One reason for their reluctance was their attachment to the modern movement. Because modernism had rebelled against a historicist tradition that few Jews had a vested interest in preserving, and because it opened up the architectural profession to talent and innovation, many Jewish architects embraced the movement as it developed in the early decades of the twentieth century. Yet this embrace came at a price: the denial of their heritage in their work. Ever since its inception, modernism had sought a formally abstract language of universal validity and had shunned expressions of particularism.[10] References to ethnic and religious identity were frowned upon, and so Jewish architects were inhibited from seeking creative inspiration in the deep reservoir of Jewish historical experience.

Many Jewish architects also refrained from drawing on their backgrounds because of their weak sense of Jewish identity. With certain exceptions, most of the accomplished Jewish architects in the modernist era were formally unaffiliated and nonobservant in their religious life. Most lacked a broader interest in Jewish culture or Jewish history. Not even the turbulent events of the 1930s and 1940s inspired them to identify more closely with the Jewish people. Even though some had firsthand experience of the Nazi regime — having either studied in or traveled through Germany around the time of Hitler's takeover — and even though others fought the Germans while serving in the U.S. military during the Second World War, few were inspired to connect with their Jewishness in any meaningful way.

For this reason, they can be described as "non-Jewish" Jewish architects. This paradoxical designation derives from Isaac Deutscher's famous notion of the "non-Jewish Jew," a concept referring to Jews who, trapped between an unwanted religious tradition and an unwelcoming Gentile society, embraced creative rebellion as a means of escaping their outsider status on the "borderlines" of European life.[11] As seen in the careers of Baruch Spinoza, Sigmund Freud, and Karl Marx, the concept of the non-Jewish Jew refers to the tendency of rebellious Jews to pursue the universal in their thinking, transcend the limitations of their religious background, and create a utopian realm in which all human beings could meet as equals. The ultimate goal of this universalistic mission was clearly non-Jewish. And yet, in a paradoxical twist, the pursuit of universalism became a subtle marker of Jewishness in its own right, and so Jews striving for non-Jewish status could never entirely escape their heritage.[12]

Many Jewish architects followed this pattern in embracing modernism. Their quest to create a universally valid style of modern architecture dovetailed with their desire to distance themselves from their Jewishness. This connection was especially visible among European Jewish architects, such as Neutra and Breuer, who were exposed to the dual pressures of assimilation and antisemitism in Europe and who embraced modernism even before emigrating to the United States. By contrast, American Jewish architects had fewer acute anxieties, living as they did in a country that afforded them greater opportunities for professional advancement. But many nevertheless saw themselves as outsiders because of their immigrant backgrounds. Almost without exception, the American Jewish architects who rose to postwar prominence, such as Bunshaft, Abramovitz, Lapidus, and Louis I. Kahn, were either immigrants or the children of recent immigrants. They conformed to the cultural outlook of what Herbert Gans has called "second generation" Jews—Jews whose liminal status between an "inhibiting" orthodoxy and a "permissive" American culture foisted on them a marginal identity that "stimulated an inordinate need to prove themselves" in their chosen professions, usually at the cost of denying their backgrounds.[13] Jewish architects were especially eager to escape their heritage because of the fierce anti-immigrant sentiment that prevailed in the U.S. when they were beginning their careers in the 1920s and 1930s.[14] By embracing modernism, they strove to create new universal norms that would be welcoming to all, including outsiders like themselves. In the same way that other non-Jewish Jews pursued their own respective universalistic missions, Jewish architects strove to create a modern, revolutionary, and universal form of architecture as a way of becoming insiders in a society remade in their own image.

It was not just the universalistic principles of modernism and the weak Jewish identity of Jewish architects that inhibited the conscious expression of Jewishness in early postwar architecture, however, but the larger postwar crisis of American Jewish identity. After 1945, it became more difficult for American Jews to preserve their connections to Jewish life. The end of large-scale Jewish immigration to the United States by the 1920s, together with the postwar abandonment of the tight-knit Jewish inner-city neighborhoods for the more heterogeneous suburbs, brought about the demise of the Jewish urban space that had long preserved Jewish identity. Jews thus had to make greater efforts to maintain their Jewishness after 1945 than before the war. Enduring fears of antisemitism also made many Jews ambivalent about their Jewish identities. Although the Jew-baiting of the 1930s and early 1940s disappeared after the end of World War II, American Jews displayed a "cultural lag" in recognizing the dawn of a new era of tolerance. This delay partly reflected American Jews' fears that antisemitism had assumed the guise of anticommunism during the cold war. But it also reflected the traumatic legacy of the Holocaust. Writing in *Commentary* in 1948, David Bernstein asserted that the Nazi genocide made Jews feel "'separate,' homeless, [and] apart" and led them to develop an "inferiority complex from the fact that [they] . . . are Jewish." As a result of such feelings, many American Jews felt that it was safest to avoid particularistic expressions of Jewishness in public.[15]

This trend manifested itself in various ways. After 1945, many Jews preferred to stress how they were similar to, instead of how they were different from, the members of other religious traditions. The emphasis on interfaith work, which grew out of the war years, was one indication of this tendency, as was the frequent invocation of "Judeo-Christian values." Will Herberg's popular 1955 book *Protestant, Catholic, Jew* was widely embraced by Jews as proof of their religion's status as one of the three main religious faiths in the United States. The deemphasis of Jewish particularism was also visible in American culture. Growing out of the interwar years, when Jews responded to anti-immigrant sentiment by emphasizing the American aspects of their identity, the reluctance of Jews after 1945 to display signs of their Jewishness partly reflected the legacy of the Holocaust. As Henry Popkin argued in a 1952 *Commentary* essay, "The Vanishing Jew of Our Popular Culture," Americans' fears of being accused of spreading antisemitic stereotypes of Jews contributed, after 1945, to a general process of "de-Semitization in the popular arts," in which all things Jewish were reduced or eliminated. This ethnoreligious form of bowdlerization may have been a well-intentioned response to the Holocaust, but it led to the dramatic diminution of Jewish themes and characters from American mass-market novels, films, and other works of popular culture. In the early postwar period, in short, Jewishness was viewed as a liability instead of an asset.[16]

"Non-Jewish" Jewish Architects: Profiles in Evasion

Against this backdrop, Jewish architects had little incentive to draw on their backgrounds in their postwar work. Modernism's shunning of historical reference, its opposition to expressions of ethnic or religious particularism, and the negative associations surrounding post-Holocaust Jewish identity all help explain why Jewish architects preferred to transcend, rather than find inspiration in, their heritage after 1945.

Richard Neutra

One of the most important architects after World War II was Richard Neutra (1892–1970). After 1945, Neutra continued to build on his prewar successes, designing iconic modernist homes in California, such as the Kaufmann Desert House in Palm Springs (1946), the Tremaine House in Montecito (1948), and the Moore House in Ojai (1952) (fig. 49). His achievements in rethinking the layout of the private home in America earned him great fame. In 1949 he was featured on the cover of *Time* magazine in an article on the revolutionary place of modern architecture in postwar America. Ever since, architectural historians have recognized him as one of the major figures of the twentieth century.[17]

Neutra's work, however, displayed next to no Jewish traits. This is not very surprising, given the architect's indifference to his Jewish identity. In his 1962 autobiography, *Life and Shape,* Neutra made no reference at all to his Jewish background. Yet, as Thomas Hines has shown in his richly detailed biography of the architect, Neutra's Jewish identity was not completely irrelevant to him earlier in his life. Born in Vienna into an agnostic and nonreligious family, he had many encounters with antisemitism, which was rampant in the city around the turn of the century and which he experienced elsewhere as well. The first documented evidence of Neutra's encounter with anti-

Jewish prejudice appears in the aftermath of World War I, when he was embarking upon his architectural career in Switzerland. As he wrote in the early 1920s, "The prejudice against my race made me unhappy.... I could not even make a modest start in my profession.... I suffered unspeakable loneliness.... I often thought of suicide.'" He also had to put up with antisemitic comments from his non-Jewish fiancée and future in-laws in the early 1920s. At this early juncture, Neutra responded by defending his heritage, insisting to his in-laws, for example, that his religious background be explicitly noted in the wedding announcement. In November 1922 he further embraced his identity, writing, "I am a descendant of my ancestors who were massacred, burnt, and tormented in many ways."[18]

Yet Neutra mostly remained distant from his Jewish background and did not draw on it for architectural inspiration. Like other non-Jewish Jews, he preferred to transcend his heritage by finding refuge in the universal — in his case, the emerging modernist movement in Southern California. His decision to settle in Los Angeles in 1925 allowed him to overcome his status as a wandering Jewish outsider (he had moved from Vienna to Switzerland, Berlin, and New York before arriving on the West Coast) and become a consummate insider. By the early 1930s, his success with the Lovell House had made him one of the country's best-known modern architects, and from that point on he had little reason to look back.

Figure 49. Richard Neutra, Kaufmann Desert House, Palm Springs, 1946. Neutra's most famous postwar house was built for Edgar J. Kaufmann, the same client who commissioned Frank Lloyd Wright's Fallingwater.

Neutra's forward-looking mentality and his distance from his heritage was epitomized by his reluctance after 1945 to reflect on the architectural implications of the Holocaust. This reluctance is somewhat surprising, given how closely he followed events in Nazi Germany during the 1930s and early 1940s. After the Anschluss of 1938, Neutra was personally affected by the growing turmoil in Austria when his sister Josephine's house was ransacked by Nazi thugs. He and his wife, Dione, went out of their way — as did Eric Mendelsohn and his wife, Louise — to help family members and friends flee the Reich. Unlike his former employer Mendelsohn, however, Neutra was apolitical by nature and less overtly hostile to the Nazi regime. Whereas Mendelsohn actively supported the American war effort against Nazi Germany, Neutra declined to support a petition for the United States to boycott the 1936 Olympic games in Berlin, a stance that earned him the disapproval of some of his closest friends. It is unknown whether Neutra lost family or friends in the Holocaust. But his public silence on the subject both during and after the war shows that the Nazi genocide did not prompt him to reassess his architectural principles in any way.[19]

In the end, Neutra remained wedded to the optimistic goals of the modernist movement. While he may have regarded the war as a tragedy, he also viewed it as an opportunity. Professionally, the war years were busy for Neutra; like many of his fellow Jewish modernists, he found consulting and design work through the U.S. government, especially planning for postwar construction projects in Puerto Rico. He also devoted considerable time to issues of postwar reconstruction in Europe and Asia. In all of this work he took the upbeat modernist position that the war's destruction provided new opportunities for improving the design, layout, and organization of bombed-out cities. "The chance to start from scratch," he declared during the war, "is . . . a real blessing after all the misery." To be sure, it was easier for Neutra to take a redemptive view of the war from his comparatively safe American refuge. Had he lost his career, like Mendelsohn had, he may have been more embittered. But safeguarded from that fate by his earlier departure from Europe and content with his thriving career in the United States, Neutra was able to move into the postwar period unshaken in his confidence. It was little wonder, then, that he felt no inclination to meditate on the recent Jewish tragedy.[20]

Marcel Breuer

The same can be said of Marcel Breuer (1902–1981). Having become famous during the interwar period for his modern furniture designs, Breuer became one of the best-known architects in the United States in the first decades after 1945. At first in partnership with Walter Gropius in Cambridge, Massachusetts, between the years 1937 and 1941, and then after World War II in private architectural practice in New York, Breuer received numerous commissions to design buildings for a wide range of private and institutional clients, including government agencies, corporations, museums, universities, and libraries. Among his best-known works were the Exhibition House at the Museum of Modern Art in New York (1949), the UNESCO headquarters in Paris (1952–58), the Whitney Museum of American Art in New York (1964–66), and the Cleveland Trust Company skyscraper in Cleveland (1969–71) (fig. 50). Breuer's architectural work evolved considerably during the first postwar decades, shifting from his lighter International Style designs of the 1930s and 1940s to his heavier brutalist works of the 1960s. Many of these buildings initially received strong praise, even

Figure 50. Marcel Breuer, Whitney Museum of American Art, New York, 1964–66. The museum is Breuer's best-known building and a classic example of New Brutalism.

if recent critics have been less enthusiastic about them.[21] Still, by virtue of his broad-ranging work, Breuer ranks as one of the most accomplished Jewish architects of the mid-twentieth century.

And yet, like Neutra, Breuer refrained from drawing on his Jewish background for architectural inspiration. This stance was predictable given the architect's distance from his heritage. Born into a largely secular middle-class Jewish family in Pecs, Hungary, Breuer had withdrawn from the Jewish religion in the 1920s after moving to Germany. His distance from his Jewishness remains surprising, however, given his exposure to the injustices of the Third Reich. Like other German Jewish cultural luminaries, Breuer left Nazi Germany because of the oppressive political situation and bleak employment opportunities facing "non-Aryan" architects. After moving to England in 1935, he relocated to the United States in 1937, finally heeding Gropius's request to join him on the architecture faculty at Harvard.[22]

Unlike Erich Mendelsohn and Percival Goodman, Breuer did not align himself with the Jewish people's fate as a result of his experiences. He took on few Jewish-oriented commissions in the United States, working only on a single completed synagogue, the Westchester Reform Temple in Scarsdale, New York (1957–59), for which he is merely listed as the design consultant. Indeed, he designed a far greater number of churches and monasteries. Like Neutra, moreover, he made no references to Jewish subjects in his postwar writings. All of these facts lend credence to the claim of one of Breuer's most famous employees, Richard Meier, that Breuer essentially "denied that he was a Jew." Breuer's downplaying of his Jewish background may have partly reflected his desire not to run afoul of the anti-Jewish prejudices of Gropius, his Bauhaus mentor and later partner. It also probably reflected what Meier recalls as Breuer's "introverted" personality. But Breuer's reluctance to seek inspiration in his background mostly reflected his functionalist approach to architecture and resulting disinterest in architectural representation, history, and meaning. This orientation ultimately explains why the architect saw little need to acknowledge the Holocaust's significance in his postwar work. Despite his Central European Jewish background, he preferred to evade the burdens of his heritage after 1945 and instead pursue the universalistic agenda of the modern movement.[23]

Gordon Bunshaft

Neutra's and Breuer's careers echoed that of another prominent Jewish architect of the early postwar period, Gordon Bunshaft (1909–1990). Bunshaft was a partner at Skidmore, Owings, and Merrill (SOM) from 1937–79 and helped establish the firm's reputation after 1945 as one of the nation's leading partnerships in the design of commercial and corporate office buildings. He was responsible for designing some of the more significant modernist works of architecture in the early postwar United States. The most prominent was undoubtedly the Lever House office building in midtown Manhattan (1951–52), which was the first glass and steel corporate skyscraper erected in the city after World War II and is widely considered to be one of the most influential modernist buildings in early postwar America (fig. 51).[24] Bunshaft also designed the Beinecke Rare Book and Manuscript Library at Yale University (1963), the Lyndon Baines Johnson Presidential Library and Museum in Austin, Texas (1971), and the Hirshhorn Museum in Washington, D.C. (1974), as well as numerous glass and steel skyscrapers in Manhattan.[25] Thanks to these and other works, Bunshaft has long been viewed as one of America's leading postwar modernists, a fact confirmed by his receipt of the Pritzker Prize in 1988.

Yet while Bunshaft was one of the most important Jewish architects of the mid-twentieth century, his work displayed no identifiable Jewish traits. The architect did not design any synagogues and never sought creative inspiration in Jewish religious traditions or historical experiences. An important reason for this neglect was Bunshaft's lack of interest in his Jewish identity. Born in Buffalo, New York, as the first child of Ukrainian Jewish immigrants, he was not brought up with a traditional Jewish education and was personally unreligious. As he noted in an interview in the late 1980s, "I didn't live with a close relationship with fellow Jews. I made no effort. I don't believe in any religion. I think it's a crutch to avoid thinking about dying, so I never believed any of that." Bunshaft's biographer, Carol Krinsky, confirms that the "subject [of Jewishness] was ... minor in his life." Bunshaft also declined to identify with the Jewish people in an ethnic or a cultural sense. In 1935–36, he traveled to Europe on a Rotch Traveling Fellowship and visited Nazi Germany. Yet he did not feel any discomfort in the country as an American Jew. His upbeat comments in a 1936 letter about his visit to Munich—which he praised for its beer, operas, and "jolly spirit of living"— betrayed no sense that he felt out of place as a Jew in the Nazi party's ideological capital. By all indications, this calm demeanor was typical for Bunshaft, who later observed, "I've never had any sensitivity about being a Jew all my life." Not even four years of service in the U.S. Army in World War II (during which time he worked as an architect on emergency medical facilities and field hospitals) motivated Bunshaft to identify more closely with his Jewishness. No wonder then, that most architectural historians have found Bunshaft's Jewish background unworthy of comment.[26]

Bunshaft's modernist design principles also explain his work's lack of Jewish features. Like Breuer, Bunshaft was a committed functionalist who believed that modern architecture had "nothing to do with political or economic ideology" and had little business being influenced by either "philosophy . . . [or] theory." He refrained from any introspective approach to his work, believing that scholars were often guilty of subjective speculation in analyzing buildings. He abjured an intellec-

Figure 51. Gordon Bunshaft, Lever House, New York, 1951–52. The building was the first glass and steel corporate skyscraper in postwar Manhattan.

tual approach to architectural design, declaring in a 1972 interview that while "I eat and sleep architecture, I don't like to talk about it." Instead, he preferred for his "architecture to speak for itself." In short, since Bunshaft's buildings were dedicated to pure function, they alluded to little beyond it.[27]

That said, Bunshaft's Jewish background indirectly shaped his career. As was true of many Jews before him, the architect's status as a Jewish outsider motivated him to become an insider by assimilating into the non-Jewish mainstream. Bunshaft's outsider status was partly rooted in his immigrant family's inability to make sense of his architectural interests. During his adolescent years he viewed himself as an "odd duck" because he liked to "spend his . . . weekends . . . making furniture," and he recalled his father worrying about his lack of a social life and the fact that he "didn't drink." Yet Bunshaft's outsider identity also reflected his awareness of antisemitism. When he first set out to become an architect, Bunshaft realized that pursuing such a career was a "nontraditional choice for a Jewish man" and feared that his background might limit his professional opportunities. As he later explained, "I had the feeling in . . . the early 1930s, that architecture was a gentleman's profession and that they were all club members and they got work at clubs. . . . I figured [that] . . . being Jewish, . . . I wasn't geared for getting jobs." This fear explains why Bunshaft decided to work for SOM, an equal-opportunity firm whose meritocratic ethos afforded him an unusual degree of job security. As he put it, "at Skidmore, Owings and Merrill . . . there was never any question of whether you're Jewish, Chinese, black, green, purple or whatever it was. If you had something on the ball, you had a future." Bunshaft was clearly grateful to be employed where he was, but his comments suggest that he ultimately viewed his Jewishness as a professional liability that was best ignored in his work. Like Neutra and Breuer, he too embraced modernism as a means of transcending his heritage.[28]

Ely Jacques Kahn

The career of Ely Jacques Kahn is very similar. After establishing himself as one of America's best known designers of Art Deco skyscrapers in the 1920s and 1930s, Kahn reinvented himself after World War II by embracing the modern movement and designing a series of respected International Style office buildings in New York. Among them were his Universal Pictures Building at 445 Park Avenue, which was the first speculative office building erected in Manhattan after World War II (1947), his high rise at 100 Park Avenue (1950), the Astor Plaza Building at 399 Park Avenue (1961), and the Union Dime Building at 40th Street and 6th Avenue (1958) (fig. 52). Together with Bunshaft's Lever House and Mies's Seagram Building, these stripped-down versions of Kahn's interwar skyscrapers helped define the look of midtown Manhattan in the 1950s.

Little of Kahn's work was inspired by Jewish sources, however. Having abandoned traditional Judaism prior to 1914, Kahn remained distant from traditional Jewish practice for most of his life. Like Neutra, he never mentioned his religion in his memoirs. This silence may have reflected Kahn's experiences with anti-Jewish prejudice, which had impeded his initial attempts to find employment at architectural firms before 1914. It is equally true, however, that Kahn later reconnected with his heritage during the war years, when antisemitism was on the rise. He went out of his way to help German Jewish refugees during the war, most notably Eric Mendelsohn, whom he befriended and provided with free office space in New York. More significantly, he collaborated with the noted

American sculptor Jo Davidson on the first design commissioned for the ill-fated Holocaust memorial on Riverside Drive in 1948. In the end, though, Kahn remained wedded to an assimilationist vision of Judaism. The membership of his wife, Beatrice, on the executive committee of the anti-Zionist American Council for Judaism after 1945 suggests that he probably supported the group's stated mission of "[integrating] . . . Jews in the country of which they are citizens" rather than working to build a national home for them in Palestine. As a modernist and a largely unaffiliated Jew, Kahn was an unlikely candidate to reflect on the relevance of his identity for his architecture.[29]

Rudolf Schindler

Rudolf Schindler (1887–1953) exhibited a comparable profile. A major figure of the interwar years, Schindler figures less prominently in the story of postwar Jewish architectural achievement, as he was nearing the end of his distinguished career. After 1945, Schindler did not register the same level of success as his former partner, Richard Neutra, or other Jewish modernists, such as Breuer or Bunshaft. He did design expressive and structurally inventive private homes in the Los Angeles area, including the Maurice Kallis Residence and Studio (1946–48), the Ellen Janson Residence (1948–49), and the Adolph Tischler Residence (1949–50) (fig. 53). But architectural historians have

Figure 52. Ely Jacques Kahn, Universal Pictures Building, New York, 1947. This building was the first speculative high-rise erected in postwar Manhattan.

Figure 53. Rudolf Schindler, Adolph Tischler Residence, Los Angeles, 1949–50. This geometric private home was one of Schindler's best-known postwar works.

typically regarded them as less refined than his interwar works.[30] Nevertheless, at the time of his death, Schindler had secured for himself a reputation as a pathbreaking figure in the field of modern housing design.

His buildings, however, did not reflect any Jewish sensibility. Schindler had never exhibited a strong sense of Jewish identity in the first place. After moving to the United States he married a non-Jewish woman and regularly celebrated Christmas.[31] He also never sought out commissions for synagogues or other Jewish institutions. Schindler's disinterest in his heritage may have reflected his exposure to anti-Jewish prejudice in Vienna. Yet because he left Austria for Chicago in 1914 and missed the upheaval of the First World War (with its attendant spike in antisemitism), anti-Jewish experiences probably figured minimally in his identity. Indeed, unlike Neutra, Schindler decided to emigrate less because of disaffection with Europe than because of the lure of America (especially the innovative architecture of Frank Lloyd Wright, for whom he eventually worked).[32] Once in America, moreover, Schindler embraced the country with great enthusiasm, acclimating himself rapidly to the bohemian milieu that he helped to create in Los Angeles.

While Schindler's distance from his Jewish origins is understandable, it is hard to believe that he remained entirely unaffected by the Nazis' rise to power in Austria in the late the 1930s or by the fate of the country's Jews during the Second World War. It is unknown whether he, like Neutra, still had family and friends in Austria and whether any of them fell victim to the Holocaust. But there is no evidence that the tragic events shaped his work in any way. In this sense, Schindler differed little from his fellow Jewish modernists.

Bertrand Goldberg

The same can be said of Bertrand Goldberg (1913 – 1997). Over the course of his career Goldberg designed a variety of structures, including hospitals, schools, and other institutional buildings in his home city of Chicago and elsewhere. He is best known for his design of the Marina City mixed-use residential and commercial complex (1959 – 64), a pair of cylindrical, reinforced concrete residential towers near the Chicago River, which became one of the city's most recognizable modernist icons and a model for many other apartment complexes across the United States in the 1960s (fig. 54). He is particularly known for his attention to socially progressive architectural projects, such as the Raymond Hilliard Houses (1966), two sixteen-floor housing towers sponsored by the Chicago Housing Authority for low-income residents, which were added to the National Register of Historic Places in 1999. Given this focus, Goldberg's work might be seen as expressing a Jewish commitment to social justice.

Goldberg's sense of Jewish identity, however, was not particularly strong. Unlike many of his fellow Jewish modernists, he hailed from a more assimilated background, being a third-generation American. His decision to become an architect did not please his family, though not because of any Jewish bias against the profession. Goldberg denied that his Jewish background had much relevance for his architectural career, noting that it had not played any role either "adversely or supportively." He never had any problems receiving commissions because he was a Jew, and he professed ignorance about the idea that architecture might not have always been a hospitable profession to Jews. In short, Goldberg had little sense of being an outsider.[33]

Figure 54. Bertrand Goldberg, Marina City complex, Chicago, 1959–64. The twin cylindrical towers immediately became one of the Windy City's most famous landmarks.

He also showed little interest in reflecting on the Holocaust. This disinterest is surprising because Goldberg had spent time in Germany in the 1930s and witnessed the rise of the Nazis. Like Bunshaft, he had gone to Germany to study architecture as a young student, traveling there in 1932 to work with Mies at the Bauhaus. During that year, Goldberg witnessed the violent excesses of the Nazis, recalling how, while in a nightclub one evening, he saw "Nazis . . . dragging out people and beating the hell out of them . . . on the sidewalk." He not feel any discomfort with being Jewish, however, noting that he "was recognized, really, as an American rather than as a Jew, although with my name and nose I don't know how they could have mistaken me for anything else." Goldberg's failure to be shaken by the experience was probably due to his youth; he was only nineteen at the time and recalled thinking that "whatever happened was always for other people but never for myself." Not even the unsettling experience of having his landlady in Berlin calling the police to arrest him for a minor prank — a scare that prompted him to finally flee the city — brought him to a firmer sense of Jewishness.[34]

If anything, the Nazi experience reinforced his optimistic tendencies as a modern architect. As was the case for Neutra and Bunshaft, World War II provided Goldberg with new career opportunities. When he established his own practice in 1937, the American economy had not yet emerged from the Depression, but during the war Goldberg designed prefabricated housing for the federal government and worked on other experimental projects, such as a mobile delousing station and a penicillin manufacturing laboratory. He thereby developed his ability to experiment with new materials and construction techniques, which served him well in the postwar period. Like his fellow Jewish modernists, Goldberg pursued his career with his gaze directed optimistically toward the future.[35]

Morris Lapidus

A final Jewish architect who epitomized the ahistorical mindset of the early postwar period was Morris Lapidus. Lapidus is best known for his lavish resort hotels in Miami Beach, such as the Sans Souci (1949), the Fontainebleau (1954), and the Eden Roc (1955) (fig. 55). Later hotels and apartment buildings in Florida and New York City built in the late 1950s and early 1960s have also received attention. These structures represented an unusual form of modernism. While their dynamic, curvilinear forms lacked exterior ornamentation, their interiors were outfitted with highly theatrical flourishes. Some of these features, such as gilded columns, gaudy chandeliers, and antique French furniture, were blatantly historicist; others, such as Lapidus's trademark "woggles, cheeseholes, and bean poles," were more abstract. Not surprisingly, the hybrid character of Lapidus's buildings proved controversial. The American middle class flocked to his hotels, but architecture critics hated them. At an exhibition of his work at the Architectural League in New York in 1970, one observer snidely likened his hedonistic interiors to a "pornography of comfort." By the 1990s, however, assessments of Lapidus's work became more positive, and his buildings are now seen as anticipating the playfulness of postmodernism. No less a figure than Philip Johnson, widely regarded as the paterfamilias of postmodernism, magnanimously described Lapidus as the "father of us all."[36]

While Lapidus's work may have diverged stylistically from that of other Jewish modernists, he, too, refrained from allowing Jewish influences to shape it. Part of this refusal was due to his back-

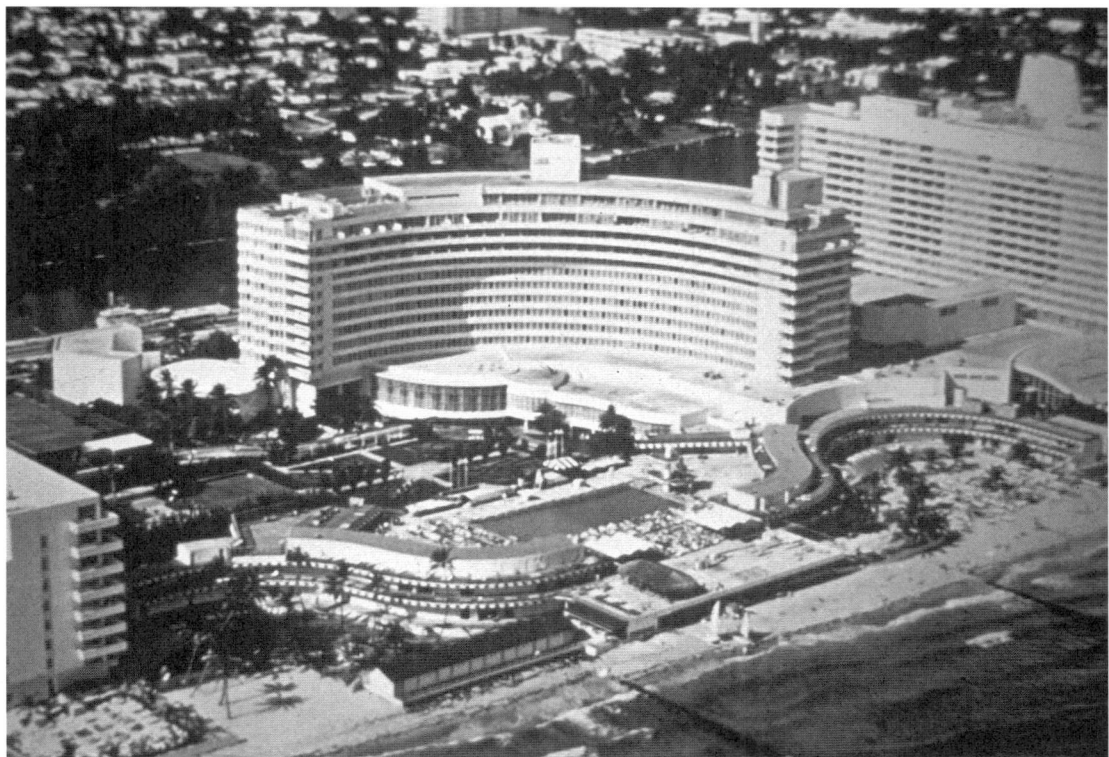

Figure 55. Morris Lapidus, Fontainebleau hotel, Miami Beach, 1954. Lapidus's best-known building was long viewed as the most luxurious hotel in Miami.

ground. Lapidus embodied the prototypical Eastern European Jewish immigrant experience in America. Born in Odessa in 1902, he came with his family to New York's Lower East Side in 1903, due to his mother's fear of pogroms. Thanks to the guidance of an older and more assimilated uncle, Lapidus embarked upon a path of assimilation from which he never strayed. He entered the field of architecture unintentionally, falling into it after failing to realize his goal of pursuing a career in designing theater sets. When he enrolled at the Columbia University School of Architecture in the early 1920s, Lapidus immediately recognized that he was out of his element. Of the twelve other students in his introductory class, the "other men were graduates of Ivy League Colleges—Princeton, Harvard, and Yale.... All of my classmates were what [my] Professor called 'gentlemen' who were entering a gentleman's profession. I was the outsider, a prisoner of my own deep-rooted sense of inferiority."[37]

Thanks to his tremendous work ethic, however, Lapidus gained the attention of his professors and eventually secured so many commercial commissions that he remained unaffected by the Great Depression. After the war his keen business sense was also reflected in his writings. His book *Architecture: A Profession and a Business* was a manual for young architects starting out in the profession and revealed his practical approach to his discipline.[38] In all of these respects, Lapidus displayed the can-do mentality typical of first-generation immigrants. The fact that Lapidus later

Jewish Architects and Secular Jewish Architecture 109

designed several synagogues and a Jewish school may be taken as evidence that he preserved a stronger sense of Jewish identity than many of his colleagues.[39] Yet his focus on commercial projects generally kept him from drawing on Jewish themes in his professional work.

There is scattered evidence, however, that some of Lapidus's Miami Beach resort hotels unintentionally exhibited Jewish features. As Alice T. Friedman has argued, the hotel developers for whom Lapidus worked were mostly Jews who built their hotels for a predominantly Jewish clientele. Miami Beach was the travel destination of choice for northeastern Jews in the 1930s and became even more popular after 1945, when the city's permanent Jewish population swelled along with the number of tourists. By the postwar period, this Jewish clientele had become more economically privileged and craved luxurious surroundings and generous, but inexpensive, cafeteria buffets. As one publicist described the area: "Miami Beach . . . is primarily a Jewish resort . . . [that] . . . Jews like . . . because . . . [it] says 'Indulge yourself, live a little.'" Lapidus catered to this impulse in his hotel designs, a fact that did not go unnoticed by certain observers. Ada Louise Huxtable's sarcastic use of Yiddishisms in criticizing his Americana Hotel (she said its lobby exhibited "tropical chutzpah") suggests that Lapidus's hotels did, in fact, radiate a certain Jewish character.[40]

In their own way, indeed, they may have been indirectly influenced by the legacy of the Holocaust. Lapidus's hotels were conceived as temples of escapism, a fact that the architect confirmed in 1979, recalling: "We were coming out of the war and the postwar period. People wanted fun, excitement, and all of it against a background that was colorful, unexpected . . . [and full of] visual excitement." These escapist urges would have been especially strong among Jewish visitors to Miami Beach, many of whom were of Eastern European descent and had lost relatives in the war. This being the case, Lapidus's flamboyant hotels may be seen as secular versions of Erich Mendelsohn's and Pervical Goodman's synagogues in the sense that they also provided a consolation to Jews after Auschwitz. That his hotels may have been partly intended to serve this function, finally, is suggested by Lapidus's later invocation of the Nazi era to justify his flamboyant style. Justifying his populist desire to give "people what they want" in his buildings, Lapidus contrasted his fun-loving approach with the authoritarian preference of elitist modern architects like Mies to dictate architectural taste to the public. As he put it in 1979, "I have always been in disagreement with Mies. To me, he represented the Germanic state of mind, . . . the kind of reasoning that gave birth to the Nazi movement." The importance of such a comment should not be exaggerated. Lapidus surely had far more pressing concerns on his mind during the early postwar years than the relevance of the Nazi era for his practice. Still, the fact that its legacy hovered in the background suggests that certain Jewish architects may have been subtly influenced by the past, even though their work bore no visible traces of it.[41]

The Exceptional Case of Max Abramovitz

This was even true of the secular work of Jewish architects who identified more closely with their heritage. A case in point is Max Abramovitz (1908–2004).[42] With his partner, Wallace K. Harrison, Abramovitz designed many major buildings for corporate, governmental, and educational institutions during the early postwar decades. These included, in addition to the U.N. (1947–53), the high-rise headquarters of the Alcoa Corporation and of U.S. Steel (built in Pittsburgh in 1952 and 1971, respectively); the central headquarters of the Central Intelligence Agency in Langley, Virginia (1961); the

Philharmonic Hall (later renamed Avery Fisher Hall) at the Lincoln Center for the Performing Arts (1962) (fig. 56); the master plan (and numerous buildings) for the campus of Brandeis University (1952–60); and numerous skyscrapers for banks and other corporate clients in American cities such as Los Angeles, Dallas, Hartford, and Milwaukee. Abramovitz made significant technological breakthroughs in his structural designs, finding multiple uses for aluminum in the Alcoa Building, for example, and devising an external steel skeleton for the U.S. Steel office building. Although he never developed an identifiable architectural style, the high quality of his work has led him to be deemed "one of twentieth-century America's foremost architects."[43]

Few of Abramovitz's buildings, however, displayed Jewish traits, a fact that is surprising given his strong Jewish identity. Born in Chicago into a Romanian immigrant family that spoke Yiddish and kept kosher at home, Abramovitz celebrated his bar mitzvah, wrote his high school thesis on American synagogue design, joined a Jewish fraternity at the University of Illinois, and traveled after college to Palestine to visit its many Jewish archaeological and architectural sites.[44] Most importantly, Abramovitz's Jewish background prompted him to join the U.S. Army and fight against the Nazis in World War II. While studying at the École des Beaux-Arts in Paris in the early 1930s, Abramovitz visited Germany and saw Hitler deliver a speech in Braunschweig. The experience stimulated Abramovitz's interest in European affairs, especially the dangers of German nationalism. Once the war erupted, Abramovitz recalled, "I was furious about the Germans . . . and what they were doing to the Jews." He concluded, "I was teed off about the French being in trouble and the Jews being in trouble, so I just changed my life."[45]

Figure 56. Max Abramovitz, Avery Fisher Hall, New York, 1962. This building, together with the New York State Theater and the Metropolitan Opera House, make up the core of the Lincoln Center for the Performing Arts.

Given his motivations for joining the Army, Abramovitz might have been expected to reflect on the Holocaust's legacy in his postwar architectural work. For a brief period after the war, he seemed to follow the lead of Percival Goodman by turning his thoughts to building synagogues. In 1948, he published an essay entitled "Trends in Synagogue Design," in which he discussed the history of synagogue architecture and its postwar prospects in the United States. Like many others who tackled the topic at the time, Abramovitz found little that was "original or creative" in the "sad past" of Jewish architecture and affirmed that "[the synagogue's] mature and wholesome expression is yet to be born."[46] Unlike Goodman, however, he never mentioned the Holocaust and restricted his architectural analysis to functional criteria. Abramovitz's concluding prediction that postwar Jews would be able to create an "architecture . . . that bears the stamp of its people and its builders" was thus unintentionally prophetic.[47] His buildings expressed the postwar Jewish community's preference to avoid the recent past.

One reason for Abramovitz's postwar inattention to the Nazi legacy may have been the fact that he was not sent to the European theater during the war, but rather to the Pacific, specifically to China, where he designed airfields as part of the Army Corps of Engineers. The expertise he developed quickly brought him a flood of construction projects after 1945. Like Bunshaft and Goldberg, who had also spent the war building for the military, Abramovitz was inclined after 1945 to build rather than to commemorate. This forward-looking mindset was also a reflection of his positive sense of Jewish identity. Unlike Neutra and Breuer, Abramovitz never experienced much antisemitism. Even his minority status as a Jew in the American architectural profession did not alienate him. In the architecture school at the University of Illinois, he recalled, there were only "three or four Jews" in an entering class of more than eighty. But the fact that "architecture had very few Jews in the profession" never intimidated him. As he later said, "I never denied my Jewishness and always maintained it." To be sure, Abramovitz was not personally religious, as was shown by his marriages to two Christian women. But this fact merely confirms his own self-description as a man who was adept at living in a "very mixed world" and dealing with people from all backgrounds. Abramovitz strove for, and achieved, a successful balance between his identity as a Jew and as an American.[48]

This balance was epitomized by a series of Jewish-themed secular architectural projects that Abramovitz undertook immediately after the war. Through his friendship with Abraham Sachar, who had been a history professor at the University of Illinois before becoming the national director of the Hillel Foundation in 1933, Abramovitz received commissions to design Hillel Houses after the war at the University of Illinois and Northwestern University, both of which were completed in 1948.[49] Both buildings were exercises in modernist functionalism without any identifiable Jewish features, but they testified to Abramovitz's openness to Jewish-related secular commissions.[50] More important, when Sachar was named president of Brandeis University in 1948, Abramovitz was entrusted with designing a series of buildings for the new campus, the most important of which was an ensemble of Jewish, Catholic, and Protestant chapels (see fig. 35). When the architect was tapped for the commission, the plan was to build a single interfaith chapel that would serve all the religions represented at the predominantly Jewish but officially nonsectarian university. Yet when one of the project's financial contributors complained about the idea—he noted that he had lost many relatives to the Nazis and was tired of Jews being "pushed around"—Abramovitz drew on his knowledge of Jewish architectural history to design a stand-alone Jewish chapel. He did not pursue the project from a narrowly particularistic perspective, however. When Sachar, citing the failure of Christian denominations to contribute funds for an interfaith chapel, controversially proposed allotting space to the Christian groups "in the basement" of the Jewish chapel, Abramovitz insisted that all three religions deserved to "have different spaces" that were equal in character. He thereupon proceeded to design three chapels, each of which had its own character: the glassy Protestant chapel was "clean-cut and without any mystery," the Catholic chapel was darker, with a sense of "mysticism," and the Jewish chapel displayed "two half-round . . . forms to emphasize a oneness . . . with the . . . direction towards the bema." In short, when presented with the opportunity to produce an explicitly Jewish building, Abramovitz instead drew on his modernist principles and affirmed an ecumenical kind of universalism. In so doing, he showed how even Jewish architects who identified with their heritage deemphasized it in their early postwar work.[51]

Conclusion

The secular buildings of Jewish architects during the early postwar period testified to the new prominence of Jews in the American architectural profession. These architects' success resulted from their own talent and will to succeed; from the comparative openness of the American architectural profession; and from the abundant opportunity for building in the prosperous postwar environment. Perhaps most important, Jewish architects were able to attain unprecedented levels of achievement by embracing modern architecture. All the architects who enjoyed postwar success had committed themselves to the modernist movement before the Second World War and were thus well positioned to profit from the movement's postwar rise to dominance. Modernism's breakthrough after 1945 had the coattail effect of enabling Jewish architects to accomplish more than ever before. Their success, however, came at the price of denying their Jewishness. By embracing modernism, Jewish architects embraced a movement whose universalistic thrust inhibited any expression of particularism. Modernism's aversion to history and memory meant that Jewish architects had to sever their links to their people's historical experience in pursuing their profession. For this reason, Jewish architects during the early postwar years refrained from reflecting on the Holocaust's significance in their secular work. Only once modernism itself came to be challenged would Jewish architects slowly begin to awaken to the creative possibilities afforded by the past.

Figure 57. Louis I. Kahn, Yale University Art Gallery extension, New Haven, 1951–53. This modernist building helped earn Kahn a national reputation.

Chapter 6
Toward a More Jewish Modernism
The Architecture of Louis I. Kahn

On the southern edge of Yale University's campus stands a building that is easy to overlook. It is a boxy structure made of glass, steel, and brick that contrasts sharply with the neogothic building adjoining it. Most pedestrians who walk past Louis I. Kahn's Yale University Art Gallery extension (1951–53) probably do not give it a second glance (fig. 57). From a present-day perspective, the building's outward appearance—especially its windowless brick wall on Chapel Street—looks banal. The fact that it recently received a lavish $44 million renovation, however, testifies to its enduring reputation as a jewel of the modernist movement.[1] The museum's formally innovative features and its status as the first modernist structure on Yale's historic campus help explain the building's exalted status, but it is equally significant as a milestone in Kahn's overall career. Before he completed the project in 1953, Kahn had been working for over twenty years without much recognition. Afterward, however, he became a force to reckon with, dominating the American architectural profession for the next two decades. The Yale Art Gallery thus stands as a pivotal work in the unfolding of Kahn's postwar success.

Little about the building, however, suggests that Kahn was about to emerge as the early postwar period's most important Jewish architect. The Yale Art Gallery displayed few signs of what soon made Kahn famous the world over—his turn toward the past. Not long after completing the project, however, he began to draw on history in his work and quickly established himself as one of the modern movement's most visionary leaders. Kahn's interest in the past spanned multiple eras and civilizations, but Jewish history was especially inspiring for him. Thanks to a trip to Israel in 1949 and a series of Jewish commissions for synagogues, community centers, and memorials after the mid-1950s, Kahn began to delve into the history of Jewish architecture, theology, and mysticism. He also confronted the Holocaust. Kahn, indeed, was one of the first Jewish modernists after 1945 to reflect, however haltingly, on the Nazi genocide's implications for postwar architectural practice. To be sure, the Holocaust never prompted Kahn to rethink or revise his architectural principles; he remained an idealistic modernist, convinced that modern architecture could help fashion a better world. But his readiness to think about the Holocaust in the context of the broader Jewish past helped him move beyond modernism's identity-denying universalism toward a more historically sensitive philosophy that allowed for a greater expression of his Jewishness. In becoming a more self-consciously Jewish architect, Kahn emerged as a pioneering figure. Even if he was not the first, he was certainly the most prominent Jewish architect of his time to seek inspiration in his ethnic and religious heritage. In so doing, he helped lay the groundwork for the more explicit architectural embrace of Jewishness that came with postmodernism. Like Moses, who approached, but never entered, the promised land, Kahn pointed Jewish architects toward the promise of a more affirmatively Jewish architecture, even if he never achieved it himself.

Louis I. Kahn: How Jewish a Jewish Architect?

Louis I. Kahn was easily the most important Jewish architect since Eric Mendelsohn and can be viewed as the most influential Jewish architect of the twentieth century. Although he hit his professional stride only after the midpoint of his career, Kahn came to be celebrated as an architectural genius in his own lifetime. The "canonization of Louis Kahn," as Philip Johnson described it, began with his one-man retrospective at the Museum of Modern Art in New York City in 1966 and culminated several years later when he was described as having inherited Frank Lloyd Wright's mantle as the "greatest living American architect of our time."[2] Although his reputation sagged with the rise of postmodernism in the 1980s, it revived dramatically during the 1990s so that, today, Kahn's historical status is unchallenged. Among some critics and historians Kahn is viewed as the "single greatest influence on world architecture during the second half of the twentieth century."[3] Public awareness of him has also grown thanks to the success of the Oscar-nominated film, *My Architect*, directed and produced by his son Nathaniel Kahn in 2003. The result of all this attention is that Kahn is now viewed, along with Walter Gropius, Ludwig Mies van der Rohe, and Le Corbusier, as a seminal figure of the modern movement.

Kahn's reputation largely rests on his pivotal role in helping to break the International Style's hold on the western architectural profession. Following its emergence in the 1920s, the International Style gradually gained acceptance among architects worldwide and eventually assumed hegemonic status following the end of the Second World War.[4] In the process, it became equated with modernism writ large. Epitomized by the open-plan, glass and steel designs of Gropius, Mies, and Le Corbusier, International Style modernism radically broke with the past in order to fashion a better future. Kahn shared the idealistic and socially conscious desire to improve the world through modern architecture, but he objected to its rejection of the past.[5] A romantic at heart, Kahn found inspiration in the architectural achievements of bygone civilizations—especially those of classical antiquity—and believed that their timeless spirit could be expressed in modern ways. Kahn strove to create a modern form of monumentality, a trait that he believed was present in the great edifices of the past but absent in the translucent glass and steel designs of the present. As his career evolved, Kahn came to utilize heavier and rougher materials, especially brick and concrete, and employed them in designs that abstractly evoked the monumental buildings of bygone eras.[6] His fondness for massive cylindrical towers and thick walls punctured by glassless voids in the form of oversized circles, half-circles, triangles, and arches evoked the timeless ruins of ancient Rome that so captured his imagination.[7]

Kahn was no mere formalist, however. At a time when the International Style was increasingly criticized for having been co-opted by the corporate establishment, Kahn remained a socially committed idealist who strove to foster a sense of community by creating symbolically resonant public buildings.[8] Finally—although the claim is hotly debated by scholars—Kahn lent a mystical aura to the practice of architecture. In contrast to the architects of the International Style, who described their building in practical terms, Kahn waxed poetic about "silence and light," spoke of his ardent quest for "volume zero," and cryptically asked "what buildings wanted to be."[9] In so doing, Kahn helped shift western architecture onto a new track. As Vincent Scully has noted, Kahn's work "effectively [brought] . . . the International Style to a close and open[ed] the way to a much solider modernism, one in which the revival of the vernacular and classical traditions of architecture . . . would eventually come to play a central role."[10] No wonder, then, that many architectural historians have viewed Kahn as a forefather of postmodernism.[11]

While Kahn's achievements are not in doubt, their relationship to his Jewish background is less clear. Since his death in 1974, scholars have become increasingly interested in Kahn's Jewishness, though they have disagreed about the extent to which it influenced his work. While some have claimed that his mystical streak was rooted in his interest in the Kabbalah, others have insisted that he was an assimilated Jew whose career was mostly influenced by practical concerns.[12] There is little doubt that some observers have overemphasized Kahn's Jewishness. Yet those who underplay its significance do him a disservice. Kahn was undeniably a spiritual man who spoke frequently about religion in his work.[13] He was also an architect who eagerly took on commissions for religious structures. Finally, he was a committed Zionist who often visited Israel and identified with the fate of the Jewish people. Kahn's Jewishness deserves to be considered, therefore, in evaluating his career.

Louis I. Kahn was born Leiser-Itze Schmuilowsky in Russian-controlled Estonia in 1901. At the age of five, he moved with his family to the United States, settling in Philadelphia in 1906. He never went to religious school and did not complete the necessary training to celebrate his bar mitzvah. Instead, Kahn's parents pursued an assimilationist strategy in rearing him. His father's decision to change the family's name from the Yiddish-sounding Schmuilowsky to the more Germanic Kahn in 1915 was an early example of this attitude (his son had already exchanged his given name, Leiser, for Louis). Because of his secular upbringing, Kahn remained an unaffiliated Jew for the rest of his life, refraining from ever joining a synagogue or associating closely with Jewish institutions. His wife, Esther, was Jewish, but she shared his assimilationist inclinations to the point that they sent out yearly Christmas cards bearing religious messages.[14]

Nevertheless, Kahn exhibited a Jewish sensibility in his spiritual and mystical tendencies. Scholars disagree whether Kahn was a genuine mystic or merely adopted the guise of one late in his career. But to the extent that he exhibited any mystical tendencies at all, he likely absorbed them from his mother. Kahn was extremely close to Bertha Mendelsohn Kahn, an educated and spiritual woman who claimed ancestral ties to the illustrious German Jewish Mendelssohn family. Like so many German Jewish families of the era, Bertha instilled in her son an appreciation for cultural and intellectual learning (*Bildung*), but her most important contribution, according to Joseph Burton, was introducing young Louis to the family tradition of "Jewish mysticism, most likely the kabbalah." Bertha's father, and Kahn's maternal grandfather, Abraham Mendelsohn, was a "well-beloved Jewish mystic and spiritual healer in Riga" who probably passed on his spiritual leanings to his daughter. Even scholars who question the depth of Kahn's mysticism, such as Susan Solomon, concede that he exhibited a "sincere" interest in Jewish texts. In short, Kahn may have been formally unobservant, but he was not entirely secular.[15]

Moreover, even if Kahn lacked a traditional Jewish religious background, he personified many of the classic qualities of the immigrant Jewish experience. Upon arriving in Philadelphia from Estonia, Kahn and his family settled in the Northern Liberties neighborhood, which was heavily populated by Eastern European Jews. Kahn grew up in poverty, his parents never being able to make more than a modest living working in the garment industry and operating a small candy store. He moved seventeen times in the span of two years due to his parents' inability to pay the rent. This peripatetic lifestyle accentuated his family's rootlessness and may have led Kahn to view himself as an outsider. This self-perception was probably compounded by his sense of physical inadequacy. Already quite short (being only 5 feet, 6 inches tall), Kahn had been severely disfigured at the age of three when he accidentally burned the lower part of his face while playing with hot coals at his home. He also suffered a childhood bout of scarlet fever, which affected his vocal pitch and delayed his enrollment in school. As a student, Kahn endured the taunts of fellow classmates, some of whom called him "scarface." His identity as a rootless Jewish outsider defined the rest of his life, both professionally and personally. "He was a nomad at heart," Kahn's former employee, architect Moshe Safdie, noted, recalling that the architect "would be in the office for two or three days intensely and then pack up and go." As his son Nathaniel observed, "Lou had a little carpet in the office that he'd roll out on the floor and sleep on when he was too tired to keep working. Maybe he never felt settled anywhere. He was a wanderer from the beginning." Certain scholars point out, however, that Kahn was a socially adept and gregarious man who loved the company of others. But there is little doubt that his personal behavior was highly unconventional. Revelations about his extended extramarital relationships with coworkers Anne Tyng and Harriet Pattison—both of whom bore his children—suggest not only a refusal to abide by traditional social norms but a more general restlessness that may have origins in his itinerant early years.[16]

Further contributing to Kahn's feelings of outsiderness was his experience of antisemitism. Although Kahn's Jewish background never caused him undue hardship in America, he felt the sting of anti-Jewish prejudice on more than one occasion. A former employee of Kahn's, William Huff, recalled that "there was always the suspicion that Lou had never got very far because of his Jewish background; he wasn't in the elite." And the film *My Architect* raised the possibility that Kahn never received a major commission in Philadelphia because of the city's latent antisemitism. Kahn himself recalled that his friend George Howe (famous for his design—together with William Lescaze—of the modernist PSFS skyscraper of 1929–32) "would take me for lunch at . . . the Union League Club . . . that would never have admitted me, a Jew, if I was the last living human in Philadelphia; and he would introduce me to all those stuffy Mainline neighbors of his, whom he really couldn't stand, and he'd tell them that I was the most talented architect in America." Kahn may also have felt that anti-Jewish prejudices contributed to the rejection in 1947 of his application to the American Academy of Rome—an institution notorious for turning away Jewish (and female) applicants. Antisemitism never prevented Kahn from succeeding in his career, but he may have believed he could have achieved even more had he not faced barriers of prejudice. In the end, the realities of antisemitism probably reinforced Kahn's sense of himself as a Jew and may have subtly shaped his architectural philosophy. As Richard Saul Wurman, the editor of Kahn's writings, surmises, "Frustration and failure are really the things that make you. Maybe [Kahn] was made by being short and ugly and Jewish."[17]

It is also likely that the Holocaust reinforced Kahn's sense of Jewish kinship and vulnerability. There is little evidence about Kahn's knowledge of the Nazi genocide during the war years, but it is hard to believe that the subject never came up within his family. By all indications, Kahn still had relatives living in Estonia who would have been affected by the outbreak of World War II. As late as 1928, he spent several weeks visiting family, including his grandmother, in his boyhood home in the town of Arensburg (today Kuressaare) on the island of Ösel (today Saaremaa). It is unknown what happened to his family during the war. Saaremaa was occupied by the Russians in 1939, and much of the male population was deported to serve in the Red Army. In 1941 the Nazis took Kuressaare and murdered most of its remaining Jewish population. It is unclear whether Kahn was aware of these events. But there is little doubt that, as the war dragged on, he would have been deeply concerned about his extended family's welfare.[18]

It is equally clear, however, that the Holocaust did not affect Kahn's architectural work in any direct way in the early years after 1945. Like most modernists, Kahn was less interested in dwelling on the war's horrors than in helping western society recover from them. This forward-looking stance was visible in his famous 1944 essay "Monumentality." In it, Kahn insisted on the possibility of fashioning a "democratic" form of monumentality, one distinct from the pompous variety used by the authoritarian regimes of the 1930s and early 1940s. Kahn's accompanying sketch of a massive, futuristic cultural center constructed of tubular steel clearly testified to his faith in the possibility of creating modern monuments that radiated "eternity." But his defense of monumentality was most notable for implicitly rejecting the claims of European modernists after 1945 that it was politically tainted by the recent past. By refusing to stigmatize monumentality in toto, Kahn refused to let the memory of dictatorship, war, and genocide influence his architectural philosophy.[19]

Yet even if Kahn exhibited little inclination to confront the Holocaust in the early years after World War II, his postwar work was shaped by Jewish influences. For one thing, Jewish clients provided him with a relatively steady stream of commissions. As far back as the 1930s, Kahn had forged contacts in the Philadelphia Jewish community that immeasurably aided his career, especially during the lean years of the Depression. Kahn's Jewish background and his low fees helped him secure his first independent commission as an architect — an urban synagogue in Philadelphia for the conservative Eastern European Congregation Ahavath Israel (1936 – 37). The building — a rectilinear, two-story brick structure defined by seven bands of glass blocks near the roof line — was not particularly distinguished, but it set the stage for further commissions (fig. 58). Around the same time, he designed visitor housing at a summer camp affiliated with the Jewish Socialist Workmen's Circle organization. Between 1935 and 1937 he worked in Washington, D.C., as an assistant to architect Alfred Kastner, designing multifamily housing units for the left-leaning Jersey Homesteads agricultural settlement for Jewish workers leaving the garment trade. Finally, during the war years, Kahn worked for several government housing agencies, such as the Federal Public Housing Agency (FPHA), where he made other Jewish contacts. One in particular, Philip Klutznick, an FPHA member and an active participant in numerous American Jewish organizations, led Kahn to be invited to join the advisory committee of the National Jewish Welfare Board's Building Bureau, an office that, after 1945, advised on the design of Jewish Community Centers. Thanks to this position, Kahn himself helped design the New Haven Jewish Community Center (built 1949 – 51) and was contacted several years later to design one for Trenton (discussed below), which proved pivotal in the evolution of his architectural philosophy.[20]

After 1945, Kahn did not lack for work, but he had not yet found his defining style. Although a committed modernist, he felt a growing frustration with the movement's inability to produce buildings that embodied larger social values and radiated a sense of monumentality. When he first saw Gordon Bunshaft's modernist Lever House in midtown Manhattan in 1953, for example, he observed that it looked "dead." In the early 1950s, Kahn tried to move away from International Style orthodoxy with his Yale University Art Gallery extension. Yet, while this building was celebrated at the time for abandoning the purist modernism of Mies, it did not prefigure the direction of Kahn's subsequent work. During the early 1950s, Kahn went through a short-lived "techno-organicist" phase, in which he utilized technological forms such as polyhedric space frames and Vierendeel trusses. By the middle of the decade, however, he began to find his voice. It was at this time that he turned away from the promise of the future and instead sought inspiration in the past.[21]

The Turn to the Past: Between Rome and Jerusalem

A wide range of factors contributed to the new direction in Kahn's career, but the most important was the epiphany that he experienced over the course of several months in late 1950 and early 1951 after finally being awarded the architect-in-residence fellowship at the American Academy in Rome. During this period Kahn's exploration of the Italian capital and his side trips to Egypt and Greece exposed him to the architectural wonders of the ancient world. Kahn was already well acquainted with

Figure 58. Louis I. Kahn, Ahavath Israel, Philadelphia, 1936–37. Kahn's first independent commission was this modest synagogue for an Eastern European congregation.

120 In the Era of Modernism

the architectural legacy of antiquity from his architectural studies at the University of Pennsylvania, whose traditional Beaux-Arts curriculum required the study and copying of ancient Greek and Roman buildings. This course of study helped him develop an appreciation for classical principles of symmetry, axiality, order, and monumentality. But his first-hand encounter with the monuments of the Mediterranean provided new sources of inspiration. Some scholars have argued that Kahn was particularly attracted to the sight of Roman ruins, which, stripped of their ornamentation, were powerfully evocative through their sheer structural mass and pure geometric volumes. Others have insisted that he was more taken by the primal forms of the Egyptian pyramids. Whatever the case may be, ancient architecture proved influential for his evolution. As Robert McCarter has written, "It led to his renewed understanding of the importance of history in contemporary design, summarized by his saying . . . 'what will be has always been.'"[22]

Most scholars, however, have overlooked an important Jewish dimension to Kahn's renewed interest in the architectural past. Kahn's trip to Italy was preceded by a trip to Israel. Thanks to his growing contacts with American Jewish institutions, Kahn was invited in 1949 to accompany an American organization called the Israel Housing Survey Committee to advise the Israeli government on the construction of low-cost immigrant housing. While in Israel, Kahn toured the country and met with such leading architects as Arieh Sharon and Ram Karmi, with whom he remained in contact for years after. Most important, however, as Susan Solomon has convincingly shown, was Kahn's appreciation for Israel's built environment. He visited not only such ancient sites as Capernaum and Caesarea, but also works of modern architecture designed by Bauhaus-trained German Jewish immigrants who had adapted the International Style to the Middle Eastern climate. Kahn thereby came to view Israel as a "new state of ancient beginnings." As Solomon writes, "In Israel, Kahn became an observant visual artist who . . . confront[ed] a mix of ancient and modern buildings as well as . . . indigenous construction techniques. . . . His experiences in Israel forced him to rethink architecture as part of the beginnings of a new society and . . . as a synthesis of past and present ideals. This happened at the same time that he began to question what constituted an appropriate type of modernism for the postwar period. The trip to Israel . . . allowed Kahn to envision modernism as a fusion of disparate traditions." Rather than privileging his Mediterranean sojourn as the chief source of Kahn's growing turn to history, therefore, his visit may be seen as part of a continuum that began in Israel one year earlier. Moreover, Kahn's experiences in Israel and Egypt reinforced his Jewish identity. According to Vincent Scully, the fact that Kahn visited the "remains of ancient Egypt [at a time when] . . . the state of war between Egypt and Israel was in one of its most bitter stages, suggested his Jewishness to him, as if he were there with Moses before the Exodus." Solomon has added that the trip to Israel "ignited a Zionist impulse in Kahn" and helped him forge relations with leading Israeli cultural and political figures, who later helped him land important commissions in the country. Finally, Kahn's trip to Israel may have further sensitized him to the magnitude of the Holocaust. It is hard to imagine that Kahn overlooked the fact that the housing he was being asked to help design in the country was intended for Jewish refugees made homeless by Hitler's war.[23]

Whatever the origins of influence, Kahn's architecture underwent important changes after his return to America. The watershed project in this transformation was his famed Trenton Bath House.

Designed in 1954 as part of larger unrealized plan for the Trenton Jewish Community Center, the bath house was a cruciform arrangement of four square pavilions, containing men's and women's changing rooms, surrounding an interior courtyard (fig. 59). The structure's most visible feature was its four pyramidal roofs, each of which featured a central oculus and rested on massive corner columns in such a way that gaps were created for natural light to filter down to the spartan spaces below. Scholars have described the bath house as a "foundational work" in Kahn's subsequent career and "critical in his personal struggle to reinvigorate modernism." Not only was it the first project that explored his famous distinction between "servant" and "served" spaces, it was also the first to translate the spirit of the architectural past into modern form. With the bath house, Solomon notes, "Kahn had forcefully responded to the ... prevailing unease with modernism by forging a new vocabulary and spatial sensibility. He had absorbed the look, feel, procession, and light of ancient buildings while retaining the rigors of modernist problem solving." Kahn himself said as much, describing the commission as the "starting point of his mature art" and the one that led to his self-discovery.[24]

It is significant that Kahn took a definitive step within the context of a Jewish architectural commission. To be sure, there was little about the bath house that was identifiably Jewish; its defining forms — a Greek cross plan and pyramidal roofs — were of non-Jewish origin. Still, Jewish connections helped Kahn receive the commission in the first place and enabled the trip to Israel that helped stoke his interest in the ancient forms that inspired his ultimate design. More importantly, the Trenton project's success brought Kahn further Jewish commissions, all of which provided him with the opportunity to delve more deeply into Jewish ideas in the years that followed.

It is true that Kahn's most famous buildings from the late 1950s to the early 1970s had no Jewish connections. These buildings include the Alfred Newton Richards Medical Research Building at the University of Pennsylvania (1957–65), the Salk Institute for Biological Studies in La Jolla, California (1959–65), the Phillips Exeter Academy Library in Exeter, New Hampshire (1965–72), the National Assembly Building in Dhaka, Bangladesh (1962–74), and the Kimbell Art Museum in Fort Worth, Texas (1967–72) (fig. 60). Kahn developed his designs for each of these projects independently,

Figure 59. Louis I. Kahn, Trenton Jewish Community Center Bath House, Trenton, New Jersey, 1954. Kahn believed he "found himself" with the design for this commission, which displayed early signs of the modern monumentality for which he later became famous.

Figure 60. Louis I. Kahn, National Assembly Building, Dhaka, Bangladesh, 1962–74. The most monumental of Kahn's buildings, the National Assembly displays his characteristic use of glassless voids.

working to satisfy the client's functional requirements and starting, as always, with the compositional aspects of the plan. At the same time, his designs were inspired by a variety of historic works of architecture with which Kahn was familiar. The Richards Medical Building's stairwells evoked the medieval towers of San Gimignano (which Kahn had visited and sketched in 1929); the National Assembly Building recalled the bulky fortified town of Carcassonne in France; and the Kimbell Art Museum drew on the numerous arched buildings in the ancient Roman city of Ostia. Kahn's development into what *Time* magazine cleverly described in 1966 as an "avant-garde anachronist" should thus be seen as having occurred largely outside a Jewish context.[25]

Kahn's Synagogues and the Specter of the Holocaust

Nevertheless, during this same period, Jewish influences also began to shape Kahn's architectural philosophy. For a decade beginning in the early 1960s, he pursued a variety of Jewish-related architectural projects, including several synagogues and a Holocaust memorial. Only one was completed, but they all displayed a pronounced Jewish character shaped by Kahn's views of the Jewish religion and Jewish history. Kahn's synagogues in this period were largely abstract in their symbolism and rejected the explicit Jewish references of the era's most famous synagogue, Frank Lloyd Wright's Beth Sholom, which he disdained. This penchant for abstraction reflected the nonparticularistic, indeed pantheistic, nature of Kahn's spirituality, which he expressed less in terms of Jewish theological doctrine than artistic creativity; as he put it: "Art is the language of God." Yet, while Kahn's synagogues may not have been profoundly shaped by Jewish religious influences, they revealed the influence of Jewish history. Indeed, his intensive work on a major Holocaust memorial in this period raises the strong possibility that his synagogue designs may have been shaped by the legacy of genocide.[26]

Kahn's growing interest in the Holocaust was clearly visible in his work on the Memorial to the Six Million Jewish Martyrs in New York City (1966–72). The architect's involvement in this project came about abruptly. He had not participated in the ill-fated competition to design a Holocaust memorial in New York in 1949. But in 1966 the newly reconstituted memorial committee, acting on the advice of member Philip Johnson, invited Kahn to submit a design for its projected new location in Battery Park. Kahn accepted the invitation and over the next two years produced several proposals, settling on a final plan in 1968 that was as striking as it was novel. The design featured six enormous piers made of glass blocks, ten feet square and eleven feet high, that surrounded a similar-sized seventh pier containing a chapel (figs. 61, 62). The ensemble stood on a raised black granite plinth sixty-six feet by sixty feet. The design's most notable feature was its use of glass. In employing this unusual material, Kahn's design set itself apart from most prior Holocaust memorials, such as those of Nathan Rapaport, which were composed of stone. Glass also emphasized the memorial's unique approach to representing the Holocaust. Up to this point, most postwar memorials had typically featured figurative representations of anguished Jewish victims and resolute Jewish resisters (not to mention familiar Jewish symbols, such as menorahs and Stars of David). Kahn's giant glass piers, by contrast, accorded with the memorial committee's preference for abstraction and communicated a sense of dispassionate sobriety.[27]

The aesthetic and compositional dimensions of Kahn's design spoke volumes about his views of the Nazi genocide. Like his modernist colleagues Mendelsohn and Goodman, Kahn did not so much want to grapple with the Holocaust's horror as heal its wounds. This optimistic attitude was most visible in the memorial's embrace of light. Natural light was central to Kahn's overall design philosophy and determined his approach to creating architectural space. During the late 1960s Kahn

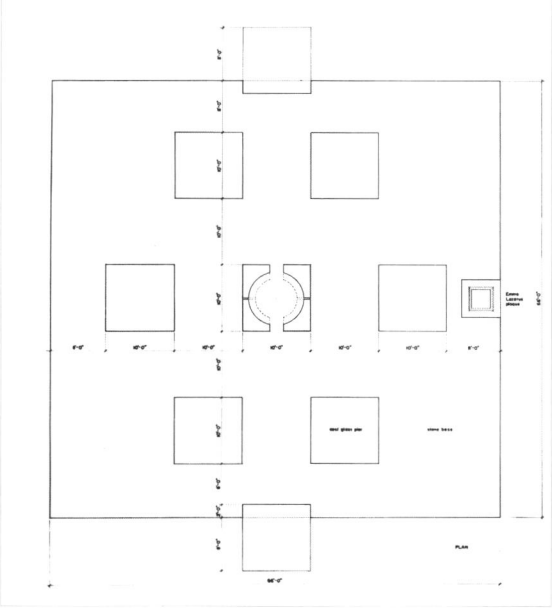

Figures 61 and 62. Louis I. Kahn, Memorial to the Six Million Jewish Martyrs in New York City, model and plan, 1966–72. The model featured six glass cubes surrounding a seventh cube (center), which was planned as a chapel. The cubes face toward the Statue of Liberty, seen in the distance. The memorial's plan displayed a total of ten squares: six in memory of the six million Jews killed by the Nazis; the seventh (center) serving as a chapel; the eighth and ninth (top and bottom) designating steps leading to the raised memorial platform; and the tenth (right) a small square designating a plaque in honor of Emma Lazarus.

increasingly spoke of his work in terms of "silence and light." First articulated in a 1968 speech at the Guggenheim Museum in New York, and in dozens of speeches thereafter, the two concepts described Kahn's view of the creative process. "Silence," for Kahn, was the "realm of ideal truth" and referred to that which did not yet exist, while light was "the giver of all presences" and designated the force that brought about creation. Scholars have long disagreed about whether these statements deserve serious consideration as part of a spiritual turn in Kahn's career or whether they were merely obscurantist window-dressing for a design philosophy whose roots lay in far more practical considerations.[28]

But there is little doubt that Kahn's notions of silence and light possessed Jewish dimensions. At the rhetorical level alone, his use of the terms resonated with biblical associations. One example was his proclamation, "Light is the source of all being.... When the world was an ooze without any kind of shape or direction, the ooze was completely infiltrated with the desire to express, which was a great congealment of Joy."[29] This statement clearly evoked the opening lines of Genesis, where the world is described as null and void (*tohu va vohu*) until God created light out of darkness. The quasi-religious coloring of Kahn's words likely stems from the conversations that he had around the time with Rabbi Murray Saltzman of Temple Beth-El in Chappaqua, New York, for whom Kahn was then designing a new synagogue (discussed below) and who, Susan Solomon argues, was pivotal in convincing Kahn that his design philosophy had Jewish roots.[30] Kahn's views on light furthermore resembled those in Kabbalistic thought. According to the cosmogony of Lurianic Kabbalah, light is the basis of creation. When God withdrew into himself to make space for the universe (a process known as *zimzum*), a stream of divine light flowed into the empty space to create primal man, who contained the light within ten vessels (*sephirot*). Unfortunately, these light-filled vessels — each of which represented an attribute of God's earthly presence — were unable to contain their divine contents and quickly shattered, giving rise to evil in the world. According to Jewish ethics, human beings ever since have been obliged to restore the damaged vessels and repair the world (an idea known as *tikkun olam*) through good deeds (*mitzvot*), which could banish evil and restore the rule of morality. It is unknown whether Kabbalistic ideas directly informed Kahn's concept of "silence and light." But his familial tradition of Jewish mysticism and contact with Rabbi Saltzman make it possible. Kahn's appropriation of Kabbalistic rhetoric can thus be seen as part of an effort to use architecture to promote the goal of tikkun olam.

This possibility is supported by the larger social and political context in which Kahn labored on the Holocaust memorial and first began to speak of "silence and light." The late 1960s, with its battles over civil rights and the Vietnam War, represented a period of turmoil in America that called out for healing. Kahn, a longtime supporter of progressive political causes, may have embraced the restorative power of light partly in response to these crises. But it was not just Americans who needed healing, but Jews as well, and for reasons having to do less with the present than the past. During the 1960s, awareness of the Holocaust began to spread throughout western culture. The Eichmann trial of 1961 revived painful memories of the Nazi genocide in the early part of the decade, while the Six Day War of 1967 — especially Arab governments' calls to drive the Jews into the sea — evoked the horrifying prospect of a second Holocaust. What Kahn thought of these events is unclear, yet the presence of news clippings on the Eichmann trial and Israel's difficult geopolitical situation in his papers at the University of Pennsylvania suggests that, like many American Jews, he had become interested in the Nazi past and its lessons for Israel's present. Kahn displayed his growing interest in the Holocaust in other ways as well. He solicited recommendations from memorial committee members about books to read on the subject. And his decision to work on a pro bono basis also showed a deep personal commitment to the project. All of these factors suggest that Kahn's light-filled Holocaust memorial was meant to provide the Jewish people with hope and healing.[31]

Indeed, the memorial ultimately represented an affirmative response to the Holocaust. Kahn implied as much in the spring of 1968, when he expressed his determination to avoid a "funereal attitude" in his design, explaining that the glass cubes would permit "sun . . . [to] come through and leave a shadow yet filled with light." He added that the memorial should have a "non-accusing character" focused less on past horrors than present-day renewal. As he explained, "The memorial is not conceived as a presentation of an event but [is] inspired by the will to live."[32] These statements confirmed Kahn's faith in the creative, life-giving power of light. But they also reflected his reluctance to probe the Holocaust's more devastating aspects. Rather than admit that darkness had often triumphed over light during the genocide, Kahn's shimmering glass cubes used light to ward off dark memories of the event's unrepresentable dimensions. On that subject, Kahn favored a stance of silence. But his decision to take it was influenced neither by Theodor Adorno's warnings about the permissibility of cultural creation after Auschwitz nor by George Steiner's ruminations in his book *Language and Silence* (1967) on the impossibility of representing the Holocaust's horror. Instead, Kahn's optimistic design strategy reflected a typically American approach to confronting the Nazi genocide.

This was clearly visible in the memorial's location, which Kahn positioned to face three iconic edifices: the Statue of Liberty, Castle Clinton, and Ellis Island. These structures were central to the American Jewish immigrant experience and were surely meaningful to Kahn, himself an immigrant. At Castle Clinton, previously known as Castle Garden, many Eastern European Jewish immigrants had been processed until 1890, when Ellis Island became the main port of entry; the Statue of Liberty was the first landmark viewed by arriving immigrants and featured the words of Emma Lazarus's famous poem "The New Colossus" engraved in its pedestal. Kahn envisioned these structures standing in dialogue with the Holocaust memorial both visually and symbolically, writing that the memorial's glass form would promote a sense of "dematerialization [which] would allow all of these symbolic structures . . . to enter the Monument." As Susan Solomon surmises, Kahn "seems to have been juxtapositioning the tragedy of the Holocaust with more positive themes of rescue and hope."[33] In so doing, he anticipated one of the primary strategies utilized nearly thirty years later by James Ingo Freed's U.S. Holocaust Memorial Museum in Washington D.C., which similarly juxtaposed its disturbing narrative with the redemptive architectural symbols of liberty on the National Mall.

The response to Kahn's design was split. On the one hand, the proposal's affirmative character resonated with many in the general public. When the design was profiled at the Museum of Modern Art in the fall of 1968, *New York Times* architecture critic Ada Louise Huxtable praised it as "a cool, abstract, poetic, powerful and absolute statement of unspeakable tragedy." At the same time, however, Kahn ran into resistance from Holocaust survivors on the committee who remained unconvinced by the memorial's abstract form. For them, Kahn's failure to adequately represent the Holocaust's horror and his omission of recognizable Jewish symbols left the memorial mute and raised questions about its ability to fulfill the task of preserving memory. Even though Kahn acceded to requests to include inscriptions in Yiddish, Hebrew, and English, as well as recognizable Jewish symbols, the committee remained uncomfortable with the memorial's aversion to representation. Ultimately, however, it was the failure to raise sufficient funds that doomed the project. Ironically, the event that helped underscore the memorial's urgency — the Six Day War — undermined its chances of success, as American Jewish fundraising efforts focused on helping Israel recover from the conflict. By 1969 the committee had ceased soliciting donations for the project. And by 1973, despite Kahn's efforts to keep it alive, the project had ground to a halt.[34]

This failure notwithstanding, Kahn's intense work on the memorial raises the possibility that his views of the Holocaust's legacy may have shaped his approach to other Jewish commissions during the 1960s. His concurrent designs for three synagogues — Mikveh Israel in Philadelphia (1961–72), the Hurva in Jerusalem (1967–74), and Beth-El in Chappaqua, New York (1966–72) — have rarely been interpreted with an eye to the Holocaust's possible influence.[35] Nevertheless, its influence can be detected at these projects' margins.

Beginning in the year 1961, Kahn started work on a new synagogue complex for the Mikveh Israel congregation in Philadelphia. Founded in 1740, Mikveh Israel was the oldest congregation in Philadelphia and one of the oldest in the United States. Kahn quickly worked up several drafts, producing his final design for the complex in the fall of 1962. The design for the sanctuary was a striking composition of ten hollow, brick-clad, cylindrical towers arranged in an octagonal plan, which stood adjacent to an adjoining chapel and school (figs. 63, 64). Kahn intended the towers, which were cut with upright and inverted arches, to bring indirect light into the central sanctuary

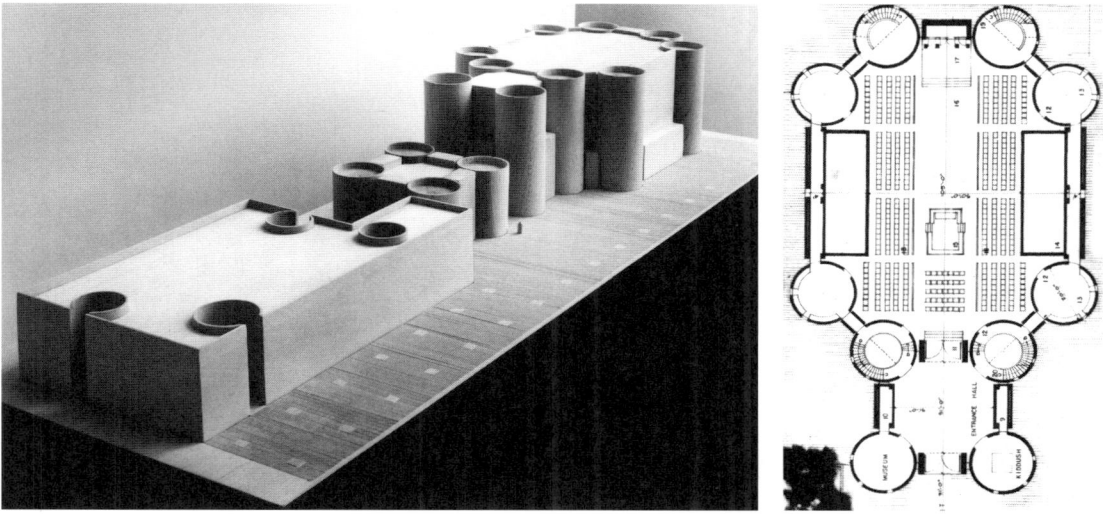

Figures 63 and 64. Louis I. Kahn, Mikveh Israel congregation, model and plan, Philadelphia, 1962. The model for the synagogue displayed ten hollow, brick-clad cylindrical towers arranged in an octagonal plan. Next to the synagogue was a small chapel (center) composed of four cylindrical towers. At left is the school wing, also featuring towers. The plan of the synagogue shows its interior layout, with the bima at the center and the ark at the top.

Toward a More Jewish Modernism **127**

and produce an aesthetic effect that would be "subtle, deep, and emotional." Ada Louise Huxtable praised the project in the *New York Times* as the standout design in the Jewish Museum's 1963 exhibition "Recent American Synagogue Architecture." The congregation's building committee was also enthusiastic. But fundraising problems surfaced in 1967, and although efforts to bring the design to completion lasted into the early 1970s, it was ultimately canceled.[36]

Kahn was disappointed by this outcome, but the project was important for his evolution into a more self-consciously Jewish architect. By the early 1960s, Kahn had firmly committed himself to finding inspiration in the architectural past, but Mikveh Israel directed him toward the more specific realm of Jewish architectural history. This gaze backward was partly inspired by the congregation, which initially requested that Kahn base his design upon the synagogue's original building, an Egyptian revival structure designed by the American architect William Strickland in 1820. Kahn, in fact, consulted old plans for the synagogue in drawing up his designs. But he also immersed himself in the larger history of synagogue architecture. He specifically aspired to recapture the Ur-form of the first synagogues of antiquity, writing, "I must rediscover that sense of beginnings through belief." Apart from his inclusion of a permanent sukkah in the plan, however, little else appeared to be Jewish in inspiration. The synagogue's most striking features, its numerous cylindrical towers, were probably influenced by the round buttresses surrounding the apse of the medieval Cathedral of St. Cecile in Albi, France, which Kahn sketched while visiting in 1959. Moreover, Kahn's subsequent use of similar tower forms in the Salk Institute and the Muslim mosque at the Dhaka government complex in Bangladesh undermines the notion that they were Jewish in any way.[37]

That said, there is intriguing evidence that Kahn's design for Mikveh Israel may have been influenced by Kabbalistic ideas. Numerous scholars, beginning with Jeffry Kieffer and Joseph Burton, have argued that Kahn's plan for the synagogue bore a remarkable resemblance to, and was possibly shaped by, an image of the Kabbalistic sephirothic tree that was on the cover of a book in his possession, Gershom Scholem's study of the Zohar (fig. 65).[38] Like Kahn's plan, the cover

Figure 65. This image of the Kabbalistic sephirot, or vessels, is taken from the cover of the book *Portae Lucis,* by Paolo Riccio, a German Jewish convert to Christianity. Published in 1516, the book is a Latin translation of the thirteenth-century Kabbalistic text *Sha'are Orah*. The arrangement of ten spheres bears a striking similarity to those of the Mikveh Israel plan and to the arrangement of squares in Kahn's plan for the Memorial to the Six Million Jewish Martyrs.

image featured an octagonal arrangement of ten circles, the so-called sephirot, or vessels, which, according to Lurianic Kabbalah, contained the earthly manifestation of God that were produced at the moment of zimzum when God retreated into himself to make space for the creation of the universe. The similarity between Kahn's plan and the image is uncanny. But their causal relation is unclear. It is true that Kahn's copy of the book was printed in 1963, after the final design for Mikveh Israel was completed, but Kahn could have seen the image, which dated to the sixteenth century, elsewhere.[39] Yet it remains unclear why Kahn would have used the Kabbalistic image in the first place.

Could it have represented an oblique attempt to confront the Holocaust? Art historians Ori Soltes, Mark Godfrey, and Matthew Baigell have invoked the idea of tikkun olam in interpreting the postwar art of Jewish abstract expressionists Barnett Newman and Mark Rothko, whose work they have seen as representing an effort to console Jews in the wake of genocide. It is possible that Kahn utilized the sephirothic tree in Mikveh Israel's design for similar reasons. As an optimistic modernist, Kahn may have embraced the motif as a symbolic method of treating the wounds of the post-Holocaust world with the healing means of architecture. There was a precedent for this approach in the work of Barnett Newman, who designed a synagogue in 1951 that was influenced by Kabbalistic symbolism. The synagogue, which was later profiled at the 1963 exhibition "Recent American Synagogue Architecture," featured a centralized sanctuary surrounded by steeply pitched walls that were folded like an accordion. Newman had written "tzim tzum" next to the walls in his plan, raising the possibility that the zigzagging folds were meant to symbolize God's contraction into himself, which, according to Kabbalistic thought, was the first step in the chain of events that marked the emergence of evil in the world and the ensuing human attempt to repair it. Given Newman's frequent use of Kabbalistic titles for his paintings and sculptures, as well as their likely connections to the Holocaust, his synagogue design may been seen as responding to the Nazi genocide by pursuing the goal of healing.[40]

It is unknown whether Kahn knew of Newman's design prior to designing Mikveh Israel, although the participation of both men in the 1963 "Recent American Synagogue Architecture" exhibition makes it tempting to hypothesize a connection. Whatever the case may be, the fact that other Jewish architects, such as Percival Goodman and Erich Mendelsohn, viewed synagogue design as a means of consoling the Jewish community in the wake of the Holocaust allows the possibility that Mikveh Israel was partly inspired by similar goals. If true, the synagogue can be seen as a precursor to Kahn's uplifting Holocaust memorial in Battery Park. Indeed, the formal similarities between the two designs' arrangements of cylindrical towers and glass piers suggest precisely such a connection (compare figs. 62, 64).[41] The reason Kahn may have been inspired to pursue this approach in the early 1960s is impossible to determine, although his interest in the Eichmann trial, which took place around the same time, cannot be discounted.

The possibility that the Nazi genocide shaped Kahn's architectural thinking is further suggested by a design that he produced a few years later for Temple Beth-El in Chappaqua, New York. The only postwar synagogue completed by Kahn, Beth-El has long been seen as one of his least successful works. But it is significant for its possible links to the Holocaust. The origins of the building date back to spring 1966, when the synagogue's rabbi, Murray Saltzman, approached Kahn to submit a design for the congregation's new suburban synagogue. The architect's early thinking about the

Figure 66. Louis I. Kahn, Temple Beth-El, Chappaqua, New York, 1966–72. The design was influenced by Polish wooden synagogue architecture (compare with fig. 9).

project focused on issues related to the synagogue's size, interior flexibility, and budget. But thanks to Kahn's frequent philosophical discussions with Rabbi Saltzman about the history of synagogue architecture and the nature of Jewish space, he became interested in the history of Polish wooden synagogue architecture. Kahn proceeded to read Maria and Kazimierz Piechotka's influential book *Wooden Synagogues* (1959) and probably drew inspiration from it for the synagogue's eventual design. During the summer of 1967, Kahn developed his initial plans for the structure; he refined them in 1968. The building, completed in 1972, clearly revealed the influence of Polish wooden synagogue architecture (fig. 66). Temple Beth-El is a strongly vertical, two-story structure, clad in wood, that features a square upper-level sanctuary, crowned with a wood-shingled hip roof positioned above an octagonal ground level base containing a social hall and classrooms. Its exterior appearance — especially its simplified pitched roof and corner gables — resembles a modernized version of Polish wooden synagogues from earlier centuries. It certainly differed substantially from Kahn's monumental brick and masonry designs of the same period.[42]

Given the likely inspiration of Kahn's design in Polish wooden synagogue architecture, the possible influence of the Holocaust is worth considering. Polish wooden synagogues were not only historically significant as the most original form of Jewish architecture in early modern Europe, they were nearly entirely obliterated during the Nazi invasion of Eastern Europe during the Second World War. Any effort to invoke their legacy after 1945 was thus a de facto confrontation with Hitler's war against the Jews. The Piechotkas' book implied as much, declaring in its introduction that it was dedicated to commemorating "martyred buildings."[43] It remains unclear whether Kahn's receptivity to Rabbi Saltzman's interests in Polish wooden synagogue architecture reflected a growing sensitivity to the Holocaust on his part. But given his work on the Holocaust memorial at the same time, the possibility is strong.

Significantly, Temple Beth-El's congregation today represents its synagogue in precisely such terms. Inside the foyer is a small memorial, composed of a large framed photograph of the wooden synagogue of the Polish town of Janów Sokólski and a commemorative text that reads: "Our Temple was designed as a modern memorial to the wooden synagogues destroyed in the Holocaust. The people Israel lives." This text is also highlighted on the synagogue's web site. This fact notwithstanding, Susan Solomon has questioned whether commemorative considerations truly figured into Kahn's design. No documentary evidence attests to such influence, and Kahn did not mention any commemorative intent in his remarks at the synagogue's dedication in 1972. Finally, the memorial was not created when the synagogue first opened, but only thirteen years later in 1985, at a time of growing Holocaust consciousness nationwide. In light of these facts, Solomon may be correct that the Beth-El congregation retroactively reinterpreted Kahn's design through the lens of the Holocaust in order to impart deeper meaning to a structure that was one of the great architect's least distinguished works. And yet, it would be wrong to dismiss the structure's links to the Holocaust altogether. Local newspapers mentioned the building's connections to Polish wooden synagogues as early as 1976, so its historical associations were not solely an invention of the 1980s. Moreover, as is discussed in Chapter 11, other architects who designed synagogues based on Polish wooden synagogues in the 1960s explicitly cited their wartime destruction by the Nazis as grounds for seeking inspiration in them. For this reason, even if the Nazi genocide hovered around the margins of the synagogue, its presence was nonetheless significant.[44]

The same can be said, finally, about Kahn's most famous unrealized work, the Hurva synagogue (1967–74). Its origins date back to Israel's conquest of the Old City of Jerusalem in the Six Day War of 1967. In the Old City's famous Jewish quarter the largest synagogue had long been the "Hurvat Rabbi Yehuda ha-Hasid" synagogue. Known as the Hurva (or ruin), the synagogue was begun in 1701 and was only partly complete two decades later when its Eastern European Hasidic congregation ran out of money and was expelled from the city by local Arabs who tore down the half-finished structure. The remnants stood for a century untouched, giving the synagogue its name, until it was rebuilt in 1836–64 by disciples of the Lithuanian religious sage known as the Vilna Gaon. For the next eighty years, the synagogue dominated the skyline of the Jewish quarter, but in 1948 the Jordanian army demolished it during the War of Independence. After the victory over Jordan in the Six Day War, however, the remains of the Hurva once more fell into Israeli hands. And in the fall of 1967, Kahn—who had maintained connections in Israel—was contacted by Israeli officials and invited to design a new version of the Hurva on its old site.[45]

The prospect of fostering rebirth in the wake of destruction appealed to Kahn's idealism, and he responded by drafting a design with unusual rapidity. The first and most famous plan of the synagogue (there were three in all) envisioned two square concentric buildings: an interior sanctuary defined by four massive concrete piers that ascended into umbrella-like, rectilinear roof supports; and an external structure, composed of sixteen enormous pylons made of Jerusalem stone, meant to house niches for smaller services and ceremonies. Kahn consciously drew on a wealth of Jewish sources, both religious and architectural, in drafting his design. In making his preparations he checked out numerous books from the library of the Jewish Theological Seminary in New York on the history of the first tabernacle in the desert, on Solomon and Herod's Temples, and early synagogue architecture. He had done similar preparatory work for Mikveh Israel, but with the Hurva, he appeared more motivated than usual to lend his design a distinctly Jewish character. He said as much to officials in Jerusalem in 1969, declaring, "I have been honored to express the history and religion of Jerusalem through my design . . . [which] came from inspirations never before felt."[46]

Scholars have uncovered striking parallels between ancient works of Jewish religious architecture and Kahn's Hurva design. Most have focused on its geometric affinities to Solomon's Temple — conjectural reconstructions of which Kahn saw in James Fergusson's nineteenth-century book *History of Architecture*. These affinities included the utilization of four central columns in the central sanctuary space, interconnected ambulatories, and miniature versions of the twin pillars, Jachin and Boaz. Kabbalistic influences have also been identified: Kahn's comparison of the Hurva's four massive interior columns to a sheltering "tree" resembled the divine symbolism imparted to trees in Kabbalistic texts; and his insertion of twelve exterior openings in the Hurva's walls satisfied the Kabbalistic mandate to acknowledge the twelve tribes of Israel. To be sure, Kahn was also inspired by the Egyptian Temple of Karnak, whose massive stone pylons were evoked in the Hurva's slanted exterior buttresses (fig. 67). This influence suggests that Kahn was less interested in evoking a particularistic "Jewish" form of architecture than in returning to the origins — or what he called "volume zero" — of the architectural prototypes devoted to the universal human activity of "assembly." Still, the project undeniably encouraged him to delve into the history of Jewish architecture and lend his own architectural thinking a more Jewish coloring.[47]

Perhaps the Hurva design's most intriguing dimension was its evocation of ruins. The two concentric parts of the synagogue's plan clearly embodied Kahn's concept of "wrapping ruins around buildings." This concept, which was first developed in the early 1960s for his unrealized American embassy in Angola and later used at the Salk Institute and the Dhaka government complex, was premised on the idea of designing "double shelled" buildings with two sets of walls: an interior set, housing the main structure, and an exterior set that shielded it from the sun's glare while still letting in filtered light through glassless voids, slits, or keyhole windows. This concept made functional sense in the hot climates where Kahn employed it, but it possessed special symbolic relevance for the Hurva project. Because the Hurva was a ruin twice over and had a long history of destruction, it was appropriate that Kahn's design employed ruin-like forms, such as his angular glassless concrete voids (fig. 68).[48]

His decision to do so may also have reflected the subtle influence of the Holocaust. In the years after 1945, ruins unavoidably connoted World War II's legacy of destruction. Kahn undoubtedly was aware of this fact, having visited Italy a mere five years after the war's end and witnessed the many scars it had left on the country's buildings. Kahn no doubt also recognized that ruins pos-

Figures 67 and 68. Louis I. Kahn, Hurva synagogue, Jerusalem, 1967–74. The model's massive buttresses lent Kahn's design a pronounced sense of monumentality. The digital reconstruction of the Hurva's interior sanctuary by Kent Larson illustrates Kahn's concept of "wrapping ruins around buildings."

sessed particularly ominous symbolism for Jews. The Nazis' attacks against Jewish synagogues on Kristallnacht in Germany and their later campaign of destruction against Eastern European synagogues during the war meant that, for most Jews after 1945, ruins signified their recent persecution. The same can be said about the symbolism of the Hurva synagogue. Both its original destruction in the eighteenth century and its destruction in 1948 stemmed from Arab anti-Jewish and anti-Zionist feeling — neither of which had subsided as threats after the 1967 military victory. Even though Israelis had averted a second Holocaust by triumphing in the Six Day War, the Hurva's remains stood as a reminder of the enduring threat to the Jewish state's existence. The fact that Kahn was working on the Holocaust Memorial project at the same time as the Hurva further raises the possibility that the painful Jewish past and the volatile Israeli present influenced his embrace of ruins in the design.

Nevertheless, Kahn ultimately viewed ruins less as symbols of tragedy than beauty. His oft-cited remark, "I thought of the beauty of ruins," and the presence of framed prints of Giovanni Battista Piranesi's eighteenth-century engravings of ancient Roman ruins on his office wall showed that he viewed ruins romantically, as picturesque reminders of bygone eras. In embracing this aestheticized view of ruins, however, Kahn disregarded the historical forces that created them. As with his Holocaust Memorial, his Mikveh Israel project, and the Beth-El synagogue, he was less interested in commemorating destruction than in mending its effects. Although the Hurva synagogue's design may have evoked ruins (and although he intended to preserve the original synagogue's surviving ruins in an adjacent garden), its massive size was clearly meant to signify the Jewish state's victory over historical adversity. As Vincent Scully has eloquently put it, the Hurva "could have evoked the ultimate image out of Ezekiel, the new city rising after the destruction of all other cities, celebrating the site of ruin, Judaism unconquerable after all the conquests and burnings." The fact that the synagogue project was linked to a larger plan of urban renewal in Jerusalem's Jewish quarter — one that was meant to compete with the city's dominant Muslim and Christian works of architecture — reveals this as well. In the end, the very grandiosity of Kahn's vision doomed it. Orthodox Jews feared that it would rival the Western Wall and suspected that it heretically aspired to be a "third" Temple. Israeli politicians, meanwhile, were anxious about its aggressive political symbolism as a sign of Jewish assertiveness. Although the project remained technically undecided by the time of Kahn's death, its fate had effectively been sealed years earlier.[49]

Conclusion

Most of Kahn's Jewish projects were never realized. Yet they played an important role in his evolution into a more self-consciously Jewish architect. Compared to his fellow Jewish modernists in the early postwar decades, Kahn exhibited a far greater willingness to draw on Jewish themes in his work. In part, this inclination reflected his background as an immigrant Jew who, while not personally religious, felt sufficiently affiliated with his people to maintain close contacts with the Jewish community both in the United States and Israel. It was partly thanks to these contacts that Kahn eventually came into his own as an architect. They enabled his visit to Israel, which helped reawaken his interest in the architectural legacy of antiquity. And they provided him with the synagogue and community center commissions that helped him synthesize his interest in classical architectural tradition with his curiosity about Jewish architectural history. Kahn's willingness to preserve and nurture his Jewishness facilitated his return to the past, which was crucial for his postwar career. It helped him transcend the limits of the International Style and develop a more historically sensitive form of modernism.

Kahn's interest in the past allowed him to confront the legacy of the Holocaust. His work on the New York City Holocaust Memorial project was the most obvious example of this shift, although the Nazi genocide also hovered in the background of his work on the Mikveh Israel, Beth-El, and Hurva synagogues. In the end, however, Kahn did not allow the Holocaust to challenge his steadfast faith in the ability of modern architecture to fashion a better world. He remained too wedded to his modernist beliefs to view the Jewish tragedy as a historical rupture requiring the embrace of radical new architectural principles. In this sense, Kahn resembled his fellow modernists Eric Mendelsohn and Percival Goodman in responding to the Holocaust with an affirmative, redemptive impulse. Nevertheless, by looking to the past, Kahn paradoxically influenced Jewish architecture's future by making it clear that it would not be nurtured solely by an ahistorical present.

Part Three

Jewish Architecture in the Postmodern Era

On the north side of Chicago, just off Lake Shore Drive, stands a building that at first glance attracts little notice. The east facade of the Pensacola Place II apartment tower, designed by the Chicago architect Stanley Tigerman in 1978 – 81, displays a stark Miesian curtain wall that resembles the blank facades of countless other multistory apartment buildings erected in the 1960s and 1970s. A close look at the building's western facade, however, reveals something quite different. Its glass and steel grid is punctuated by six vertical rows of half-rounded balconies that assume the form of abstracted pilasters as they ascend towards the roof (fig. 69). Each pilaster, in turn, is crowned with rounded windows forming Ionic capitals. A rooftop entablature, concealing mechanical equipment, caps the entire composition, completing a witty homage to the classical architecture of ancient Greece. What is important about the Pensacola Place II apartment complex, however, is less its outward appearance than the significance bestowed upon it by its designer. As Tigerman noted in the early 1980s, the apartment building's different facades symbolized the decisive moment in his career when he abandoned his modernist design philosophy and its belief in unitary architectural truth in favor of a more "dualistic [mode of] thought [typical] . . . of Post-Modernism." Tigerman went further, however, and added an unexpected Jewish gloss to his interpretation. The dualistic thought of postmodernism, he declared, could be compared to "talmudic thought," which he described as the "simultaneous study of opposites without the necessity of creating a new synthesis." Indeed, the similarities between the two dualistic modes of thinking led the architect to conclude provocatively that "Post-Modernism is a Jewish Movement."[1]

Tigerman's declaration practically begs to be misunderstood. Taken literally, of course, it makes little sense. The postmodern movement in western architecture was anything but a Jewish affair, originating in a broad range of social, economic, and cultural factors that were transcendent rather than ethnically specific in nature. Yet, if interpreted more loosely, Tigerman's observation invites readings that yield valuable insights into the relationship between postmodernism and the evolution of Jewish architecture after the 1970s. At one level, Tigerman's remark reminds us that, with the emergence of the postmodern movement, Jewish architects rose to an unprecedented level of prominence in the American architecture profession. Beginning in the 1970s, Tigerman, along with Peter Eisenman, Daniel Libeskind, Frank Gehry, Richard Meier, Allan Greenberg, Robert A. M. Stern, Eric Owen Moss, Moshe Safdie, James Stewart Polshek, and others, collectively produced a body of work that, while representing different movements, had an unprecedented impact on the western architectural profession. Through their writings, manifestoes, polemics, and actual buildings, these figures played a central role in helping to transform the profession from a relatively monolithic one, in which modernism held sway, to a pluralistic, postmodern one, in which such diverse movements as deconstructivism, revivalist classicism, and neomodernism coexisted.

It is not just the new prominence of Jewish architects, however, that lends truth to Tigerman's claim. With the advent of postmodernism, Jewish architecture arguably became

---

(previous spread) **Figure 69.** Stanley Tigerman, Pensacola Place II apartment tower, Chicago, 1978–81. The projecting balconies of this postmodern building form abstract pilasters capped with rounded windows that evoke Ionic capitals.

more "Jewish" as well. For the first three decades of the postwar period, Jewish architects had seldom found creative inspiration in their heritage; rarely had they attempted to infuse their designs with Jewish meaning — and then only if they were designing synagogues. Beginning in the 1970s, however, Jewish architects became more inclined to draw on Jewish sources of inspiration in their mainstream secular projects; they also began to assign them Jewish significance — so much so that the concept of "Jewish architecture" started to apply just as much to secular as to religious buildings.

The increasingly Jewish character of Jewish architecture after the 1970s reflected the emergence of several major trends. Two are discussed in Chapter 7: the emergence of postmodern architecture and the intensification of Holocaust consciousness. By challenging modernist taboos against historical reference, postmodernism enabled architects the world over to once more seek inspiration in the past. This development was liberating for Jewish architects, for if modernism's abstract universalism had prevented them from expressing Jewishness in architectural form, the rise of postmodernism enabled them to explore issues of Jewish history, memory, and identity in their work. The concurrent rise of Holocaust consciousness, in turn, explains why the Nazi genocide headed the list of Jewish topics in which Jewish architects became interested. This deepening interest made its initial impact on architectural theory and discourse in West Germany, as well as in the writings of the eminent Jewish architecture critic Bruno Zevi. But its impact was most visible in the subject of Chapter 8, the deconstructivist movement, whose main Jewish representatives, Eisenman, Libeskind, and Gehry, cited the Nazi genocide — along with experiences of antisemitism and feelings of being Jewish outsiders — as a major influence on their work. To be sure, not all Jewish architects sought creative inspiration in the Holocaust or in their Jewish identities during this period. In Chapter 9, I discuss how major figures such as Moss, Greenberg, Stern, and Meier exhibited an assimilated mindset in their work. Yet even they could not entirely avoid the Holocaust's legacy, which surfaced in unexpected ways in their architectural writings and designs. The genocide's most obvious architectural impact during this period is discussed in Chapter 10 with the emergence of Holocaust museums. Finally, in Chapter 11, I describe how the Holocaust has shaped the design of recent synagogues in the United States and Germany, before concluding with a brief look at the ways that a more affirmative form of Jewish architecture, unrelated to the Nazi genocide, has emerged in recent years. Taken together, these trends confirm that western architecture in general and Jewish architecture in particular have finally begun to wrestle with the Holocaust's legacy.

Chapter 7
Postmodernism, Post-Holocaust Culture, and Architectural Discourse

Among architecture aficionados, the German city of Stuttgart is well known as the home of one of the world's most famous works of postmodern architecture: James Stirling's Neue Staatsgalerie (1977–83) (fig. 70). Stirling's museum is one of Stuttgart's most popular tourist attractions, and anyone who visits it, as I first did in the spring of 1994, quickly learns why. Apart from its excellent collections, the building itself offers a wealth of aesthetic attractions and delights. The museum's exterior is a doubly coded mix of populist and elite motifs, including Renaissance arched windows, Doric columns, Egyptian gorge-cornices, and neon-pink metal handrails. Stirling even included a fake "ruin" in the building's facade, removing several stones from an exterior wall and scattering them on the ground below in order to expose, through the resulting gap, the presence of an underground parking garage. Given the building's cheerful quirkiness, most museumgoers might be surprised to learn that when its design was first publicized in 1977, it was immediately denounced by German critics as "fascist." While Stirling was not Jewish, the controversy over his building highlights the important ways in which postmodern architecture became embroiled with the legacy of the Third Reich and the Holocaust in the 1970s.

The controversy over Stirling's museum reflected the influence of two new trends in western intellectual and cultural life: the appearance of postmodernism and the full emergence of what has been called "'post-Holocaust' culture."[1] These two trends developed simultaneously and were connected in important ways. Postmodernism appeared in response to a variety of economic, social, and political forces in the 1960s and 1970s, but it was also shaped by the era's deepening interest in the Nazi genocide. The emergence of post-Holocaust culture, meanwhile, expressed the intensifying fascination (some would say obsession) with the Nazi past among writers, artists, and other creative figures, many of whom began to confront the Holocaust's legacy through new postmodern methods of representation. Significantly, both trends affected the development of western architecture in general and Jewish architecture in particular during this period.

The Rise of Postmodernism

The idea of postmodernism traces its origins to the crisis in western life that erupted several decades after the end of World War II. Up through the mid-1960s, economic prosperity, social stability, political moderation, and cultural optimism had reigned in Western Europe and the United States. By the end of the decade, however, the onset of economic recession, the emergence of generational conflict, and the eruption of political upheaval — epitomized by the violent revolutions of 1968 — produced

Figure 70. James Stirling, Neue Staatsgalerie, Stuttgart, Germany, 1977–83. This canonical work of postmodern architecture displayed a mixture of classical and modern motifs. In the museum's circular courtyard, Doric stone columns frame a bright-red, metal-clad entrance. An Egyptian gorge-cornice can be seen through the rectangular void (top left). Modernists quickly attacked the building as "fascist."

a climate of instability that only deepened after the dawn of the 1970s. In this unsettled situation, a deep sense of skepticism began to grow toward the west's prevailing cognitive, moral, and aesthetic traditions—one that, by the end of the decade, had become labeled a "postmodern condition." First diagnosed by the French philosopher Jean-François Lyotard, this skeptical condition was defined by multiple traits, but it primarily rejected what the German philosopher Jürgen Habermas described as the "project of modernity." This project was informed by the optimistic Enlightenment idea that reason and science could liberate human beings from their traditional sources of bondage—whether the strictures of religion or the tyranny of nature—and move them toward happiness. For Lyotard and other critics, however, the methods that had been used to pursue this goal in the twentieth century—whether totalizing "metanarratives," instrumental reason, or creative destruction—had succeeded merely in purging diversity from human existence. This critique of the "Enlightenment project," as it was also known, did not just have a philosophical basis but a political one as well. Many Europeans who later became proponents of postmodernism were leftists who had lost faith in socialism after the failure of the revolutions of 1968 and responded by formulating an alternative body of ideas that came to be known as postmodern thought.[2]

Influenced by a variety of disciplines, including structural and post-structuralist linguistics, literary theory, and philosophy, postmodern thought embraced a variety of ideas, but one of the most important was the opposition to metanarratives. Many intellectuals beyond Lyotard contributed to this oppositional stance by challenging a key foundation of all metanarratives, the belief in objective truth. The structuralist philosopher and historian Michel Foucault, for example, showed how knowledge was ultimately a function of language, whose embeddedness in systems of power created the subjective "discourses" that passed for reality. Similarly, the post-structuralist philosopher Jacques Derrida's idea of supplementarity revealed how meaning was linguistically produced via exclusion and gave postmodern thought a powerful weapon with which to "deconstruct" hegemonic concepts rooted in repressive binary oppositions.[3] These and other related ideas had powerful political implications, for they enabled challenges to be launched against any values, institutions, or ideas that claimed universal validity. In their place, postmodernists aimed to substitute more modest, local initiatives that respected particularism and diversity.

Postmodern thought had a profound impact on western culture, specifically on the movement of modernism. Since its inception in the nineteenth century, modernist culture had partly been defined by the pursuit of artistic autonomy, the desire that art should exist not for any external utilitarian purpose (whether moral, political, or economic) but "for its own sake." In order to achieve this autonomous realm of limitless creative possibility, modernists had attempted to separate their artistic work from life and purge anything that was alien to, or that compromised the purity of, their respective mediums. Painters, for example, eliminated the representational, three-dimensional, and narrative influences that their medium had inherited from theater and literature in order to approach the absolute flatness of the picture plane. Architects purged buildings of sculpture and painting in the effort to create pure structure. This process unleashed great creativity, but over time, it had resulted in a "great divide" between modernist high culture and the mass culture from which it tried to isolate itself. Modernists of all types had hoped that their abstract works would be incomprehensible to the masses and thereby remain free of their allegedly corrupting influence. But while this purist sensibility lasted through the war years and into the early postwar period, it began to lose credibility by the 1960s. By then, the embrace of International Style architecture and abstract expressionist art by the corporate establishment made it difficult to sustain modernism's claims to purity and eventually generated calls for reform.[4]

These calls soon sparked a rebellion within the modernist movement and prompted a postmodern turn in western culture. Like postmodern thought, the nascent movement of postmodernism in culture was highly varied in expression. On balance, however, it was characterized by a return to history. If modernism had pursued creative innovation by banishing the past, postmodernism returned to the past as a nourishing tradition. This return to history was not straightforward, however. Postmodernists were convinced skeptics who believed that the modernist dream of perpetual new creation was a flawed metanarrative; as a result, they insisted that original works were no longer possible. Everything that was worth doing had already been done. New creation thus had to take place by drawing on the past. Yet, because postmodernists were skeptical about history, they did not draw on the past naively — say, by reembracing historicism — but ironically. They recycled past images by merging them with present-day ones, creating a form of imitation known as pastiche. Postmodernists also dismantled the boundaries that modernism had erected between different cultural realms — especially between high and low — and blurred the lines between other binary oppositions, such as original/copy, fact/fiction, and so on. These trends found expression in many works of western culture, whether in Andy Warhol's paintings of Campbell's soup cans from the 1960s, Umberto Eco's detective novel-cum-philosophical-manifesto, *Foucault's Pendulum* (1988), Terry Gilliam's sci-fi film noir *Brazil* (1985), or Sherrie Levine's photographs of photographs. These and countless other examples made clear that postmodern culture preferred hybridity over purity.[5]

Postmodernism's rebellion was especially pronounced in architecture. By the late 1960s and early 1970s, many of modern architecture's shortcomings had become increasingly visible. By allowing itself to be embraced by the capitalist establishment after World War II, modernism became identified with corporate high-rises instead of worker housing. Moreover, as modern architecture spread throughout the world, its ahistorical aesthetic and elitist formal language proved challenging to mass audiences.[6] Finally, the standardized character of modernist city planning principles contributed to the eradication of local architectural traditions and transformed huge swaths of the globe into interchangeable places of anonymity. Whether employed in the reconstruction of war-ravaged European cities, such as Rotterdam and Hamburg, the urban renewal of America's inner cities, or the creation of brand-new capital cities like Brasilia and Chandigarh, modernism ended up creating uniform urban landscapes that largely ignored local history, identity, and tradition. In the process, modern architecture sacrificed the concept of meaning.

In reaction to modernism's perceived deficiencies, a variety of innovative developments emerged within the western architectural profession that, by the late 1970s, crystallized into architectural postmodernism. Linking them all was the return to history.[7] In architectural theory and discourse, this return was visible in the tendency of architects to cite historical, and not merely technical, rationales in justifying their work. In architectural practice, it was apparent in their tendency to draw inspiration from historically rooted plans, forms, and materials, as well as their interest in representation and narrative. These trends were visible in the work of diverse architects. In the United States and Europe, postmodern architects like Robert Venturi, Charles Moore, Philip Johnson, James Stirling, and Ricardo Bofill ironically quoted from the architectural past and created structures that combined modern and neohistoricist forms. Venturi's Gordon Wu Hall at Princeton University (1983), Moore's Piazza d'Italia in New Orleans (1976–79), Johnson's AT&T (today, Sony) Building in New York (1978–84), Stirling's Neue Staatsgalerie in Stuttgart (1977–83), and Bofill's Theater of the Palace of Abraxas outside of Paris (1978–82) are all examples of this trend (fig. 71). Elsewhere, a more conservative kind of postmodernism emerged. The British architect Quinlan Terry, the Luxembourg architect Leon Krier, and the architecture enthusiast Charles, the Prince of Wales, all echoed Krier's mantra, "Forward comrades, we must go backwards!" and embraced a nostalgic, classically inspired form of postmodern architecture. It was visible in several notable projects in England, including Terry's Richmond Riverside Development in Surrey (1984–87) and Krier's traditionalist buildings for Prince Charles's experimental new town of Poundbury (in construction since the early 1990s). A third variety of postmodernism applied a more abstract approach to history and was seen in the work of neorationalist architects Aldo Rossi and Oswald Mathias Ungers, both of whom reacted against modernist functionalism by embracing an "architecture of memory" based on universally recurring, "typological" urban forms. Finally, trailing behind and partly resisting these movements, was a rebellious and philosophically oriented offshoot of postmodernism that

Figure 71. Philip Johnson, AT&T Building (today, Sony Building), New York, 1978–84. The overscaled Chippendale pediment atop Johnson's iconic skyscraper epitomized postmodernism's return to the past.

sought inspiration in the early history of the modernist movement itself. Variously described as "theoretical postmodernism" and "schismatic postmodernism," it eventually came to be known as deconstructivism (and is discussed in Chapter 8).[8] All of these movements differed in formal appearance, but they were linked by their interest in history. By seeking inspiration in the past, however differently, they tried to halt modernism's anonymous universalism from further threatening local identity. In the process, they sought to rediscover architecture's capacity to generate meaning.[9]

Postmodernism for Jews

The advent of postmodernism had important implications for Jewish social and cultural life after the 1970s. For one thing, postmodern thought challenged American Jews to rethink their postwar commitment to assimilation. The ideal of assimilation had already begun to come under attack in the 1960s, with various social liberation movements — representing African Americans, women, gays and lesbians, and others — asserting racial, ethnic, gender, and sexual particularity in the face of majority bias and discrimination. This drive intensified in the 1980s with the emergence of multiculturalism and identity politics. Both of these movements were influenced by the postmodern idea that the Enlightenment metanarrative of human liberation through reason had suppressed difference by forcing groups to sacrifice their particularities on the altar of universalism. In reaction, the supporters of multiculturalism and identity politics urged previously disadvantaged groups to take pride in, rather than suppress, their "otherness" and demand redress for historical legacies of injustice. The supporters of these new movements embraced the ideal of diversity instead of assimilation.

These trends posed dilemmas for Jews. In the United States, most advocates of multiculturalism came from racial or ethnic groups that did not view Jews as a disadvantaged minority but as members of the white privileged majority. Since most Jews did not perceive themselves in this way, they viewed multiculturalism with suspicion, a reaction that was reinforced by the movement's postmodern critique of the Enlightenment as an oppressive rather than a liberating force in history.[10] Yet whatever doubts American Jews had about postmodernism and multiculturalism, both movements ultimately encouraged them to take renewed pride in their heritage. By the 1970s and 1980s, American Jews had achieved an unprecedented level of security and had become the country's most affluent ethnic group. They had also benefited from the dramatic decline in antisemitism. As a result, they became increasingly self-confident and took to heart Alan Dershowitz's recommendation, expressed in his 1991 book *Chutzpah*, that the time had come for them to "shed [their] self-imposed second-class status" and declare their right to be both "proud . . . Jew[s]" and "proud . . . American[s]."[11]

American Jews asserted themselves in a variety of ways. Some embraced their Eastern European immigrant roots, a trend that found expression in the smash Broadway musical *Fiddler on the Roof* (1964), Irving Howe's bestselling *World of Our Fathers* (1976), and popular films like *Hester Street* (1975) and *Yentl* (1983).[12] Other American Jews began to identify with Israeli culture, especially after the 1967 Arab-Israeli war, giving Israeli names to their children, learning Israeli dancing, and traveling to the Jewish state. After Israel's allure began to fade, following the Lebanon War of 1982 and the Palestinian intifada of 1987, still other Jews began to affirm Diaspora Jewish culture. This trend, which was encouraged by the rise of multiculturalism, found expression in the literary and artistic work of Philip Roth and R. B. Kitaj, the resurgent interest in Klezmer music, and renewed curiosity about the Yiddish language.[13] Around this time, affirmative expressions of Jewishness also began to proliferate in American popular culture, whether on television programs such as *Thirtysomething, Northern Exposure*, and *Seinfeld*, or in diverse musical genres such as rap, reggae, and punk.[14] By the turn of the millennium, public expressions of Jewishness had become so mainstream that a VH-1 television special in 2005 went so far as to declare, "It's never been hipper to be a Jew."[15]

The Rise of Holocaust Consciousness and Post-Holocaust Culture

Jewish identity was also influenced by the era's heightened interest in the Holocaust. Scholars have disagreed about why the Holocaust received so much attention in this period, but a combination of external events and internal social trends combined to boost awareness of the Nazi genocide beyond where it had been in the early postwar years. In the United States, fears of a "second Holocaust" during the Arab-Israeli wars of 1967 and 1973, as well as worries of accelerating Jewish assimilation, persuaded many American Jews — especially those in institutional leadership positions — to stop downplaying the Holocaust and instead invoke its legacy as a way to garner sympathy for Israel and shore up flagging Jewish group solidarity. The rise of multiculturalism and what some have called the "culture of victimization" also promoted Jewish interest in the Holocaust, for it enabled Jews to find common cause with other minorities in American society who were seeking redress for historical injustices. Most notable of all, however, was American Jews' success in fostering the Holocaust's entrance into the American cultural mainstream. Following two major milestones in 1978 — the sensational success of the NBC-TV docudrama *Holocaust* and President Jimmy Carter's commissioning of the United States Holocaust Memorial Museum in Washington D.C. — it became clear to many observers that the Holocaust had become "Americanized" and firmly integrated into popular consciousness.[16]

In Western Europe, meanwhile, the surging interest in the Holocaust reflected the growing willingness of certain nations, especially West Germany and France, to confront the full dimensions of their behavior during the Second World War. This willingness to discuss the past was encouraged by the generational conflict of the 1960s, as young people born after the war realized they could attack the existing order by directing attention to, and politicizing, the historical legacies that their parents had long tried to ignore.[17] The debates that erupted in West Germany and France during the late 1960s and early 1970s focused mostly on the reasons for the two nations' respective embrace of, and collaboration with, the Nazis and did not address the Holocaust itself.[18] But this changed during the late 1970s and early 1980s, when Jewish efforts to focus attention on the Holocaust prompted a conservative backlash in West Germany, Austria, and France and generated major controversies, such as the Historians' Debate of 1986–87, the Waldheim Affair of 1988, and the extended debate over the Vichy legacy in the 1990s.[19] As the Holocaust surged into the headlines, it assumed an increasingly central place in the Western European memory of the Second World War.[20]

The growing interest in the Holocaust found ample expression in western intellectual and cultural life, with scholars, philosophers, and various artists confronting the Nazi genocide with growing intensity after the 1970s. This flood of attention—in the form of scholarly monographs, novels, films, paintings, memorials, and other cultural works—far exceeded the more sporadic early postwar engagement with the Holocaust. Many of these works arose as part of a larger reaction against the notorious "Hitler Wave" and the concurrent spread of fascist imagery in popular culture during the early 1970s.[21] In response to the relative neglect of the Holocaust in the era's many Hitler biographies, for example, scholars in Germany, the United States, and Israel deepened their research into the Nazi genocide's origins and propelled Holocaust historiography into an unprecedented phase of productivity.[22] The worrisome fascination with the perpetrators that marked many of the Hitler Wave's cultural works similarly led filmmakers, writers, and artists to focus on the suffering of their Jewish victims. Films such as Vittorio De Sica's *Garden of the Finzi Continis* (1971) and Steven Spielberg's *Schindler's List* (1993); literary works, such as Imre Kertesz's 1975 novel *Fatelessness* and Cynthia Ozick's short story "The Shawl" (1981); musical compositions by Morton Feldman and Steve Reich; plays by George Tabori; paintings by R. B. Kitaj; and countless Holocaust memorials built after the 1980s in cities across the United States and Western Europe all testified to the Holocaust's intensifying cultural resonance.[23]

These and other works were notable not just for their quantity but for their postmodern quality. Unlike the early postwar cultural confrontation with the Holocaust, which was informed by the modernist belief that the Holocaust's truth could be conveyed only through radically new methods of representation, the postmodern works of this period were more relativistic and questioned whether it was possible to convey any truth about the past at all.[24] Convinced that representations of the past inevitably reflected the circumstances of the present—and that all artistic claims to truth were thus subjective—postmodern writers, artists, and other creative figures were more self-reflexive about the methods they used to represent the Nazi genocide. They frequently pointed to their works' constructedness, highlighting their limitations and undermining their claims to authority. In so doing, they expressed the postmodern skepticism toward metanarratives.

A wide range of intellectual and cultural works in this period exhibited these postmodern traits. In philosophy, many of the pioneering figures of postmodern thought, such as Lyotard and Derrida, developed their ideas in reflecting on the Holocaust's significance for the western philosophical tradition, insisting that Auschwitz's gas chambers exposed the terroristic logic of Enlightenment reason.[25] Postmodern ideas also shaped the work of Holocaust scholars, whether Zygmunt Bauman and Götz Aly, who proposed that the Nazi genocide was a byproduct of modernity, or Saul Friedlander and Hayden White, who explored whether the Holocaust was beholden to any "limits of representation."[26] In literature, postmodernism's blurring of cultural boundaries was visible in novels blending fact and fiction, such as William Styron's *Sophie's Choice* (1979) and D. M. Thomas's *White Hotel* (1981).[27] Postmodern doubts about truth and representation informed Claude Lanzmann's epic documentary film *Shoah* (1985), which refused to dramatize scenes from concentration camps in favor of relying on interviews with eyewitnesses.[28] Various postmodern concepts influenced the Holocaust-related art of Anselm Kiefer, Audrey Flack, and Judy Chicago.[29] Finally, the postmodern skepticism toward metanarratives found expression in a new variety of memorials known as "counter-monuments," which rebelled against the authoritarian bearing of traditional monuments by self-reflexively subverting their own claims to commemorative truth.[30]

In all areas of western intellectual and cultural life, in short, the emergence of postmodernism and the growing attention to the Holocaust reinforced one another. Having partly inspired the emergence of postmodern thought, the Holocaust's legacy found ample expression in postmodern culture. In the process, postmodern culture and post-Holocaust culture emerged as two facets of the same cultural impulse.

The Holocaust and Architectural Discourse in the Postmodern Era

The Holocaust also had a major impact on architecture in this period. As is discussed in Chapters 8–11, the Holocaust's legacy helped inspire architectural movements, such as deconstructivism, new categories of buildings, such as Holocaust museums, and new trends in the design of Jewish synagogues, community centers, and schools. But before the Holocaust's legacy found architectural expression in these ways, it made a distinct impact on architectural discourse. For a generation after 1945, discussions about architecture in the west had largely revolved around practical issues, such as technology, function, and economics. After the 1960s, however, this orientation began to change. The social and political upheaval at the end of the decade forced architects to confront their discipline's responsibility for the era's problems and challenged them to devise remedies for them. Economic recession in the early 1970s also had a major effect, as it brought a halt to the postwar building boom and prompted many newly idle architects to reflect on the state of their profession. Finally, the rise of postmodernism gave architects an alternative to modernism. What ensued was a wave of theorizing, discussion, and debate that was unprecedented in the postwar period. For the first time in decades, architects discussed issues of form, style, aesthetics, symbolism, and — most important — history. In the process, they opened up space for the Holocaust to enter into architectural discourse.

Exploiting the Holocaust: The Architects' Debate

The most public and controversial way in which the Holocaust's legacy shaped the field of architecture during this period was in the Architects' Debate. Pitting the representatives of modern and postmodern architecture against one another, this debate erupted in West Germany in 1977 when James Stirling won the competition for the Neue Staatsgalerie in Stuttgart. Stirling's design was an ironic, demonumentalized version of Karl Friedrich Schinkel's famous Altes Museum in Berlin (1824–28) that displayed a quirky mix of historicist and modernist features. As soon as it was publicized, various critics deplored Stirling's design as "brutalistic," "a kind of fortress architecture," and a "demonstration of power," while some polemically called the architect "Schultze-Stirling," a reference to the traditionalist architect and leading figure in the Nazi *Kampfbund für Deutsche Kultur*, Paul Schultze-Naumburg.[31]

Deep-seated reasons lay behind this politicized attack. Ever since the fall of the Nazi regime in 1945, most German architects had viewed historically rooted styles of architecture, such as neoclassicism, as discredited by their Nazi associations and instead valorized modernism as a superior "democratic" alternative. When postmodernists tried to rehabilitate historically rooted architectural plans, materials, and forms for present-day use, therefore, modernists feared that they were deliberately trying to forget or excuse the Nazis' exploitation of traditional architecture for political ends. The modernist assault against Stirling's Stuttgart design thus signaled a commitment to preserving a morally grounded view of recent architectural history.

Traditional architecture did not possess any inherent political tendencies, of course, but modern architects were correct in suspecting that postmodernists wanted to challenge the modernist memory of the Nazi period. While postmodernists initially focused on defending their innocence, they soon went on the offensive and accused the modernist establishment of possessing its own unsavory ties to fascism. Postmodern architectural historians showed, for example, that major modern architects, such as Mies, Gropius, Le Corbusier, and Giuseppe Terragni, had collaborated with fascist regimes in Germany, France, and Italy.[32] This collaboration, they insisted, disproved the postwar belief that modernist architecture had been victimized by Nazi intolerance. Indeed, by going on to show that many architects who helped establish modernism in the Federal Republic after 1945 previously had been employed by the Nazi regime, postmodern scholars, such as the Swiss architectural historian Vittorio Magnano Lampugnani, provocatively declared that "modern architecture could easily be National Socialist."[33] In the process, he undermined modernism's democratic credentials and supported the postmodern challenge against it.

Postmodernists also tried to implicate modern architecture in the Holocaust. The figure most responsible for advancing this argument was the architect Leon Krier. A former employee of Stirling's, Krier stridently criticized modernism in the late 1970s and early 1980s, arguing that its role in disfiguring Europe's cities after 1945 disqualified it for contemporary use. Only by returning to the eternally valid principles of neoclassical architecture, he believed, could Europe's damaged urban fabric be mended and its historic identity restored. Krier faced a major problem in rehabilitating neoclassicism, however, because of its authoritarian associations. To address this issue, Krier defended the figure whose work had indelibly stigmatized it: Hitler's court architect, Albert Speer. In 1985, Krier published a lavishly illustrated volume, *Albert Speer: Architecture, 1932–1942*, that refuted the modernist charge that neoclassicism was politically suspect. Krier pointed out that the Nazis' monumental neoclassical architecture was far less responsible than modern industry for the evils of the Third Reich. It was the factories of Volkswagen, Krupp, and Messerschmitt, he noted, that had fueled the Nazi military assault against Europe. The Nazis' "barbaric crimes" against the Jews, he added, "were not committed in a monumental environment but in demeaning industrial barracks and camps." For Krier, the Holocaust was mostly a result of modern industrial society. He wrote, "Industrial civilization is unable . . . to create meaningful and beautiful places. It erects suburbs, zones, transportation systems, . . . and concentration camps. It is always concerned with mass housing, . . . mass transport, . . . and mass extermination. Auschwitz-Birkenau and Los Angeles have the same parents."[34] This provocative comment revealed Krier's clear debt to postmodern thought. By embracing the postmodern critique of the Enlightenment, Krier was able to claim that modern architecture's roots in modern rationality, industry, and technology implicated it in the Nazi genocide. In the process, he legitimized the postmodern crusade against both modernity and architectural modernism.

Krier's invocation of the Holocaust ratcheted up the intensity of the Architects' Debate and drew the Nazi genocide even deeper into the era's architectural discourse. By 1987 the eruption of the Historians' Debate in West Germany provided a new and more politically controversial aspect to Krier's position. At a time when many conservative German politicians were trying to normalize

German national identity by minimizing the uniqueness of the Nazis' crimes, Krier's defense of Speer and his inflammatory accusations against modern architecture were viewed as part of a larger attempt of right-wing Germans to relativize the nation's guilt for the Holocaust. When Krier claimed that Speer's "neo-classical architecture was always the civilized and proper side" of the Nazi regime, modernist critics responded that the Nazis' use of the style was inseparable from their criminality and pointed to the importance of slave labor in the creation of the regime's grand architectural facades.[35]

By the end of the 1980s, the Architects' Debate had hardly ebbed when the collapse of the Berlin Wall and the subsequent reunification of Germany propelled it into yet another phase. This new phase, which is briefly discussed in Chapter 8, centered around the future architectural form of the new nation's capital, Berlin, and featured further politicized debates about democratic and authoritarian forms of architecture. Before this new discussion had even begun, however, the main legacy of the Architects' Debate had already become clear. In the same way that the Holocaust had challenged the western philosophical tradition and helped give rise to postmodern thought, the Nazi genocide's legacy had helped challenge the authority of architectural modernism and legitimized the rise of postmodern architecture.

Theorizing the Holocaust: The Writings of Bruno Zevi

The Architects' Debate may have been the most dramatic example of the Holocaust's growing relevance to postwar architecture, but it was not the first. Several years earlier, one of the world's most respected architectural historians, the Italian Jewish scholar and critic Bruno Zevi, had reflected on the Holocaust's architectural implications and concluded that it required a fundamental rethinking of western architectural practice.

Zevi's philosophy reflected his personal background as an Italian Jew who lived through the upheavals of the fascist era. Born in 1918 into a prosperous and assimilated Jewish family in Rome, he began studying architecture at the University of Rome in 1936, but he was quickly dismayed by the conservatism of its faculty, most of whom embraced the monumental neoclassicism of Benito Mussolini's favorite architect, Marcello Piacentini. Zevi rejected this state-sponsored architectural style and instead encouraged his fellow students to support modernism. Yet as the climate for Italian Jews began to worsen after Mussolini's alliance with Hitler in 1938, Zevi decided to leave the country, departing in 1940 for the United States to study with Walter Gropius at Harvard University's Graduate School of Design. Soon after arriving at Harvard, however, Zevi broke with Gropius's brand of International Style modernism, convinced that it had lost sight of its social mission and degenerated into a form of "mannerism." For the next several years Zevi pursued a vigorous form of "self criticism" in the effort to solve modernism's ills before ultimately settling on a new approach that he called "organic architecture."[36]

Influenced by the work of Zevi's hero, Frank Lloyd Wright, organic architecture was Zevi's solution to what he saw as the International Style's postwar crisis. Zevi first articulated his ideas in his famous book *Towards an Organic Architecture* (1945), which hailed Wright's open, flexible, and humanistic modernism as preferable to the International Style's rigid functionalism. In the decades that followed, Zevi expanded his diagnosis of modernism's crisis, explaining that it was due to its postwar turn toward classicism. As he pointed out in a speech in 1967, Gropius and Mies had betrayed their original principles after the war by abandoning their experimental work of the 1920s and producing "reactionary" buildings influenced by classical ideas. For Zevi, this classicizing trend ran counter to the essence of modernism because it relied on timeless, universal rules of design, such as symmetry, that "totally ... repress[ed] social ... freedom." Lamenting the situation in 1967, Zevi concluded that the "magnificent heritage [of modernism]" had moved from innovation to mannerism and back to classicism.[37]

In seeking ways to counter this trend, Zevi hit upon a novel method in the early 1970s when he lent his architectural philosophy an explicitly Jewish gloss and reconceptualized "organic architecture" as "Hebraic" architecture. In a speech entitled "Hebraism and the Concept of Space-Time in Art," which he delivered on June 9, 1974, at the Congress of the Italian Jewish Communities in Rome, Zevi expanded upon his belief that all architectural innovations are exceptions to the rules of classicism and identified "Hebraism" as the source of true architectural creativity. For Zevi, Hebraism was a concept of time as opposed to space. Other cultures and civilizations had associated their gods with "places and things," but the ancient Israelites, he noted, conceived of God as a "god of events" responsible for acting in time and achieving great deeds in history. Drawing on the thinking of Abraham Joshua Heschel, Zevi added that Jewish religious life had long been measured by time, which was sanctified in the form of the Sabbath and which effectively became the Jews' equivalent of "great cathedrals." Zevi affirmed that the Jews' historical experience of exile and dispersion had made them "anti-static" and "anti-spatial" as a people and prone, instead, to embrace "change and redemption."[38]

The effect of these trends upon the art of the Jews, in turn, was profound. As Zevi argued, "Hebraism in art emphasizes the anti-classical, the expressionistic de-structuring of forms; it rejects the ideological fetishes of golden proportions and celebrates relativity; it denies the authoritarian rules concerning what is beautiful, and opts for the illegality and disorderliness of what is true." The most frequent manifestation of this Hebraic sensibility in modern art was Expressionism, which he described as "the only movement determined to demolish all aesthetic ... tabus [sic] without immediately erecting others." The iconoclastic work of Einstein, Freud, Schönberg, Kafka, and Soutine were all powerful examples of this "Hebraic" trend.[39]

In architecture, Hebraism manifested itself in the attempt to "release space from its static constraint and make it time-conscious." By this, Zevi meant the liberation of architecture from the tyranny of classical rules. Borrowing from Thorleif Boman's 1952 study *Hebrew Thought Compared with Greek,* Zevi identified comparable differences between Hellenic and Hebraic architecture. As he put it, "Architecture taking its inspiration from Hellenic thought is based on colonnades, proportions, refined moulding, a composite vision according to which nothing may be either added or eliminated. ... An architecture taking its inspiration from Hebrew thought is ... an organic architecture, ... capable of growth and development, free of formalistic tabu, free of symmetry, alignments, fixed relationships between filled and empty areas, free from the dogmas of perspective, in short an architecture whose only rule, whose only order is change." Using this definition, Zevi affirmed that the Hebraic impulse had found its "major exponent" in the German Jewish architect Erich Mendelsohn, whose expressionist buildings "seem to spring free by telluric motion from a lava-like boiling substance rising from the earth itself."[40]

Zevi's idea of Hebraism in architecture, however, contained a fundamental paradox. Despite the fact that, in Mendelsohn, "Hebraism found a Hebrew architect," Zevi conceded that "most Jewish architects do not follow the time concept in the least."[41] As evidence of this, he pointed out that the "cities of Israel are almost all rationalist" and had been built according to the principles of the International Style. He added that the "most Hebraic of architects is a non-Jew, Frank Lloyd Wright." Here, Zevi drew on architectural historian Norris Kelly Smith's interpretation of Wright's oeuvre (an interpretation also heavily influenced by Boman's *Hebrew Thought Compared with Greek*) to conclude that Wright's hatred of neoclassicism and his completion of such dynamic, "organic" buildings as Fallingwater represented perfect "architectural incarnation[s] of Hebrew thought." This led Zevi to insist that "Hebraism . . . goes beyond the delimitation of the Jewish people" and should not be confused with Jewishness per se. Hebraic architecture, in other words, could not be equated with Jewish architecture.[42]

That said, Zevi's concept of Hebraic architecture was profoundly shaped by Jewish concerns. Although he had little formal education in either Jewish history or the history of Jewish architecture, his identity as an Italian Jew committed to antifascism directly influenced his postwar architectural ideas. Zevi had been active in antifascist resistance groups during World War II and was anxious to rid postwar Italy of fascism once and for all. He believed architecture could contribute to this political task, and in 1945 he established a new organization, the Association for Organic Architecture, which aimed to "creat[e] . . . a new democratic civilization" by fighting the "monumental architecture used to create official myths." The organization's mission reflected Zevi's belief that classical architecture was politically reactionary. He expressed this belief as early as 1945 in *Towards an Organic Architecture*, where he wrote: "Dictators . . . infallibly go back to the classic" while "people [who] love. . . . liberty . . . cannot help being modern." He never wavered from this stance in the decades that followed, declaring in 1979 that even if "all classicism is not authoritarian, . . . all authoritarian architecture is classical." The reason for this, he argued, was that classical design principles, such as symmetry, restricted creative freedom both in aesthetics and politics. It was therefore no surprise, he noted, that the "public buildings of Fascism, Nazism and Stalinist Russia are all symmetrical." These remarks show that Zevi's longstanding opposition to political authoritarianism lay at the root of his early opposition to classicism and his ensuing embrace of Hebraic architecture.[43]

Zevi did not limit his attacks to classicism in the abstract, however, but also condemned its manifestations in modernism and postmodernism, both of which he accused of having fascist leanings. In 1979 he sharpened his critique of modernism's reversion to classicism by bitterly noting that while the "modern movement was born to fight Fascism," it was not long before "Fascist elements corrupted the modern movement." This observation partly reflected Zevi's awareness that many fascist architects in Italy had opportunistically migrated from monumental classicism to modernism after the war. But Zevi ultimately located modernism's fascist leanings in its doctrinaire mentality, writing that after 1945, "the International Style tried to impose . . . [an architectural] dictatorship, and this is why I have opposed many aspects of it since the very beginning." Zevi, moreover, also perceived authoritarian tendencies in postmodernism, using the term "fascist" to criticize the work of Philip Johnson and Aldo Rossi.[44]

These politically charged accusations culminated with Zevi's invocation of the Holocaust to justify his radical architectural evolution. By the late 1970s, Zevi had arrived in a kind of architectural no-man's land, being alone in his suspicion of modernism, his opposition to postmodernism, and his idiosyncratic embrace of architectural Hebraism. In truth, Zevi had arrived at a proto-deconstructivist position, a fact suggested by his combination of post-structuralist critiques of the Enlightenment with reflections on the Holocaust's legacy. In 1979, Zevi wrote:

> I am against totalitarianism in politics, ethics, and of course architecture. When I say totalitarianism—or Fascism—I do not mean Mussolini, Hitler, and Stalin but all kinds of absolutes, the absolutes of the Enlightenment, of Marxism. All fixed rules, order, precepts, tendencies toward monumentalism are expressions of power that tend to oppress the individual, to deny what is different, to exclude the exceptions.[45]

Significantly, Zevi explained that he came to this position after reading Theodor Adorno and Max Horkheimer's influential *Dialectic of Enlightenment* and realizing how Enlightenment absolutes had failed to protect the Jews during the Nazi era. As he put it in "Hebraism and the Concept of Space-Time in Art" in 1974,

> [the Enlightenment] idea of universal equality, of liberty, of equal rights for all, was meant to give a sense of security even to Jews. And how many of them embraced this ideal, fought for it. It took the death camps for Adorno to discover how Illuminism [i.e., the Enlightenment] can logically debouch in Nazism.[46]

Zevi added in 1979 that "when I learned from . . . Adorno that from Voltaire you could jump directly to Hitler, I became opposed to the Enlightenment and all absolutes, dogmas and principles that do not admit diversity."[47] Finally, Zevi made clear that his sensitivity to diversity—to the plight of the "other"—was rooted in his own sense of Jewishness. Indeed, in 1979 he observed:

> Because I am Jewish, I belong to the "diverse," which has nothing to do with whether I am an observant Jew, liberal, orthodox, or reformed. Since the Holocaust, I consider myself orthodox as a matter of principle. As such, I must oppose the Enlightenment and its neoclassical architecture, because it spurns the diverse.[48]

Conclusion

Zevi's remarks show that by the late 1970s, issues of Jewishness, the Holocaust, and postmodern identity politics had coalesced in his architectural philosophy. Zevi's idea of Hebraism in architecture was significant for several reasons. It expressed a Jewish sensibility and represented a new method of articulating Jewishness in architectural terms. It reflected a growing awareness of the Holocaust's place in the history of western civilization and, as such, confirmed the growing influence of memory in architecture. Finally, and most significantly, it anticipated and may have helped to stimulate many of the ideas that constituted the deconstructivist movement. In short, like Louis Kahn before him, Zevi helped to usher in a new and more overtly Jewish phase in the postwar history of Jewish architecture.

Chapter 8
The Deconstructivists
Eisenman, Libeskind, and Gehry

Until recently, visitors to San Francisco's Yerba Buena Gardens cultural district were accustomed to seeing a stately brick edifice marked by neoclassical flourishes. The structure, built as the Jessie Street Pacific Gas and Electric Power substation in 1906, has long been a fixture in the district, its red-brick facade and white arched entryway testifying to the continuity of the classical architectural tradition. Since 2007, however, the building's conservative appearance has been dramatically altered. Disjointed shapes, clad in blue steel panels, appear to be exploding out of its roof and west facade. The forms belong to a new structure that has been grafted onto the old building: the Contemporary Jewish Museum of San Francisco (fig. 72). Designed by Daniel Libeskind, the new museum is a fitting symbol of the changing nature of Jewish architecture in recent years. If Jewish architecture for most of the early postwar period was defined by its embrace of modernist design principles, it has recently developed in a very different direction. Libeskind's design betrays the unmistakable influence of deconstructivism, one of the best-known and most celebrated architectural movements of the last generation. What is less known about deconstructivism, however, and what Libeskind's museum symbolically underscores, is the important role of Jewish architects in bringing the movement into existence. Indeed, deconstructivism today stands as the clearest example of how Jewish architecture in recent years has become increasingly "Jewish."

Deconstructivism's origins date back more than twenty years to the summer of 1988 when the highly publicized exhibition "Deconstructivist Architecture" opened at New York's Museum of Modern Art. Sponsored by Philip Johnson, the exhibition garnered considerable media coverage and brought immediate public attention to a nascent architectural trend that the curators touted as capturing the uncertain spirit of the era. Seven architects were profiled in the exhibition—Peter Eisenman, Daniel Libeskind, Frank Gehry, Bernard Tschumi, Zaha Hadid, Rem Koolhaas, and the Austrian firm Coop Himmelb(l)au—all of whom had produced radical designs that resisted easy categorization. Rejecting both modernist abstraction and postmodern revivalism, the work of these architects seemed nihilistically bent on subverting the most basic traditions of western architecture. Rather than pursuing the traditional architectural goals of "formal purity . . . , harmony, unity, and stability"—as the exhibition's associate curator, Mark Wigley, put it—the deconstructivists proposed buildings that appeared in danger of collapse.[1] The models on display in the MoMA exhibition were

Figure 72. Daniel Libeskind, Contemporary Jewish Museum of San Francisco, 1996–2008. The museum is a deconstructivist parabuilding composed of new forms (the blue steel-clad volumes) grafted onto a preexisting structure (the neoclassical Jessie Street Pacific Gas and Electric Power substation of 1906).

composed of bent, warped, and fragmented shapes, punctured by flying beams, pierced by sharply angled planes, and tenuously held up by reed-thin supports. Slanted and skewed, tilted and twisted, the designs left a disturbing impression of disruption and destabilization.

In attempting to make sense of this puzzling new architectural movement, architecture critics, historians, and journalists initially focused on the origins of the term "deconstructivism" itself, explaining that it was a portmanteau word influenced by the post-structuralist idea of deconstruction and the early twentieth-century Russian avant-garde movement of constructivism.[2] On the face of it, the deconstructivist designs in the MoMA exhibition bore a striking formal resemblance to the work of Russian constructivists, such as Kazimir Malevich and Yakov Chernikov, whose designs of the 1920s were characterized by dynamic planes intersecting at sharp angles. Deconstructivism also seemed to be influenced by the radical method of linguistic, philosophical, and literary analysis known as deconstruction. Its central contention, that the unstable foundations of language undermined the attempt to ground meaning in objectively valid truth claims, seemed to sanction the spirit of rebellion that was on display in the exhibition.

Interestingly, few of the architects profiled in the MoMA exhibition had been influenced by constructivist aesthetics or deconstructionist theories. Most had developed their radical architectural philosophies independently through years of innovative work.[3] Many architects bristled at being labeled "deconstructivist," and some, like Frank Gehry, rejected the term outright.[4] Compounding the confusion surrounding deconstructivism were the fervent denials of MoMA curators that such a coherent movement existed at all.[5] This curatorial ambivalence gave rise to suspicions among critics that deconstructivism was merely a convenient packaging term that exploited the contemporary intellectual fascination with deconstruction in order to legitimize an architectural movement that was unconnected to it.

Nevertheless, the term gained immediate traction in architectural circles. Deconstructivism came to dominate architecture schools and journals in the United States and Europe in the late 1980s and early 1990s and has since become accepted among scholars as a term of classification and analysis. Viewed historically, deconstructivism can be regarded as the first architectural movement since the dawn of the modern era to abandon modernity's optimistic faith in progress. Until deconstructivism, every major architectural movement of the nineteenth and twentieth centuries — from the Arts and Crafts movement to the International Style — had embraced the utopian idea that architecture could help solve the problems of the modern world. By contrast, deconstructivism endorsed Bernard Tschumi's observation from 1988 that "our time and age are not about being comfortable, but about disturbance, . . . uneasiness and stress." This bleak stance was in keeping with the broader postmodern rejection of totalizing metanarratives. Yet in criticizing modernity the deconstructivist movement did not follow other postmodern forms of cultural expression and take inspiration from the past in a nostalgic or lighthearted sense. Instead, it looked to the past only to subvert it, going so far as to nihilistically attempt to deconstruct architectural "presence" altogether. Deconstructivist architects employed different strategies in pursuing this goal, but all of their work exhibited a clear oppositional impulse. This impulse was best expressed in the deconstructivist fondness for designing what Herbert Muschamp later called "parabuildings," new buildings that, like parasites on a host, took shape through the violent grafting of additions onto existing structures. Seen in such examples as Frank Gehry's own house in Santa Monica, Peter Eisenman's Wexner Center for the Visual Arts in Columbus, Ohio, and Daniel Libeskind's Contemporary Jewish Museum in San Francisco, among many others, these works reflected Mark Wigley's claim that the movement aimed to "find new territory within old objects," "expose . . . the unfamiliar hidden within the traditional," and "subvert . . . the center." In pursuing these radical goals, deconstructivism emerged as the first movement to translate the skepticism of postmodern thought into architectural form.[6]

From today's vantage point, we can view deconstructivism as a uniquely dynamic and productive movement. Many of the most innovative works of architecture of the last half generation—Gehry's Guggenheim Museum in Bilbao, Libeskind's Jewish Museum in Berlin, Zaha Hadid's Contemporary Arts Center in Cincinnati, and Rem Koolhaas's Seattle Public Library, among others—have been designed by deconstructivist architects. The movement's success, however, has also encouraged its maturation. Over the course of this period, as its leading representatives actually began to build instead of just theorize, the deconstructivist movement gradually abandoned its fascination with radical ideas in favor of concentrating on bold formal experimentation. For this reason, even though deconstructivism originally rejected the modernist movement's universalism as an intolerant meta-narrative, it has slowly reconnected to the modernist ideal of constant innovation. Two decades after its arrival on the architecture scene, deconstructivism may be viewed less as a "third way" alternative to both modernism and postmodernism than a revisionist extension of the former.[7]

Deconstructivism as a Jewish Movement?

For all the attention that architectural historians, critics, and other writers have lavished upon deconstructivism, most observers have neglected to note the movement's significant Jewish dimensions.[8] A striking fact about the MoMA exhibition was that nearly half of the architects profiled in it— Eisenman, Libeskind, and Gehry—were Jewish. It was not just their Jewish backgrounds that were important, however, but the fact that Jewish concerns informed their broader architectural philosophies. In pursuing their mainstream work, all of them had reflected at one time or another on such topics as the Holocaust, modern antisemitism, and the nature of postmodern Jewish identity. They also exhibited an openness to the influences of historical memory, whether individual or collective. Finally, Eisenman, Libeskind, and Gehry expressed their interest in Jewish themes not merely in architectural theory but in practice. Many of their buildings exhibited a high degree of symbolism and narrativity that—while sometimes esoteric—was related to Jewish sources of inspiration. To be sure, it would be an exaggeration to label deconstructivism a Jewish movement given the non-Jewish backgrounds of the other major architects associated with it.[9] Nevertheless, even if deconstructivism cannot be viewed as primarily Jewish in character, it is undeniably the movement with the most self-consciously Jewish features in modern western architectural history.

The presence of these features can ultimately be traced back to the strong, if conflicted, sense of Jewish identity held by Eisenman, Libeskind, and Gehry. Each of the three architects had been exposed to the major forces that had shaped mid-century Jewish life—antisemitism, the Holocaust, and the pressures of assimilation—and had consequently developed Jewish "outsider" personalities that encouraged them to rebel against reigning architectural conventions. While earlier Jewish architects, such as Richard Neutra and Gordon Bunshaft, had also felt themselves to be outsiders, they had reacted by fleeing from their ethnic and religious heritage into the universalism of the modern movement. By the late 1970s and early 1980s, however, the emergence of postmodernism and multiculturalism had increased respect for ethnic diversity and enabled Jewish architects to view their backgrounds as assets instead of liabilities. The decline of antisemitism and the impressive economic success registered by American Jews also allowed them to feel more secure in affirming their Jewishness. The growth of Holocaust consciousness and its role in giving rise to postmodern thought further encouraged the injection of Jewish-related themes into architectural discourse. And the increasing number of important Jewish architectural projects — for Holocaust museums and memorials, Jewish museums, Jewish schools, and synagogues — provided new opportunities for Jewish architects to express Jewish themes in architectural form. The willingness of Eisenman, Libeskind, and Gehry to work on such projects fostered the Jewish turn in their work by compelling them to think more deeply about the relationship between architectural form and Jewish-related functions. In all of these ways, their deconstructivist architecture displayed far more Jewish characteristics than the modernist work of their Jewish architectural predecessors. More importantly, by tapping into their Jewish backgrounds, these architects exceeded their predecessors' achievements and attained unprecedented international prominence within the western architectural profession.[10]

Peter Eisenman

Deconstructivism's spiritual godfather is Peter Eisenman. Eisenman did not set out to become a deconstructivist architect, and his work has transcended the movement's boundaries. Never one to remain wedded to a single architectural philosophy, he has constantly reinvented himself over the course of his career. Indeed, in keeping with his reputation as one of the world's most cerebral architects, he has been influenced by an extremely wide range of philosophical ideas, scientific theories, and cultural trends. It would be simplistic, therefore, to brand him simply as a deconstructivist. For the same reason, it would be equally simplistic to examine his work from an exclusively Jewish perspective.[11]

That said, there are many important connections between Eisenman's Jewish identity and his career as a deconstructivist. Architectural historians have, to a certain degree, begun to examine the Jewishness of Eisenman's architecture. Renato Rizzi, for example, has analyzed it from a formalistic perspective influenced by the Jewish tradition of Kabbalah, while Charles Jencks has connected it to the legacy of the Holocaust.[12] Yet while these analyses have been suggestive, they remain incomplete. Only by comprehensively tracing the emergence and evolution of Jewish themes in Eisenman's work can we understand its deeper Jewish dimensions.

Peter Eisenman's early career exhibited few Jewish influences. Born in 1932 in Newark, New Jersey, Eisenman received a master's degree in architecture from Columbia University in 1960 and earned a Ph.D. in architecture at Cambridge University in 1963 before returning to the United States to practice. In the late 1960s and early 1970s he became widely known to the broader architectural profession as a member of the "New York Five." This group, which included Richard Meier, Michael Graves, Charles Gwathmey, and John Hejduk, was also known as the "Whites" for their revival of the purist, geometric architectural forms of Le Corbusier.[13] At this time Eisenman and his colleagues had begun to rebel against what they took to be the increasingly functionalist character of modern architecture, which throughout the United States and Europe had lost its innovative edge in becoming the official architectural style of postwar corporate capitalism. The Whites' rediscovery of early Le Corbusier — and, in Eisenman's case, the work of the Italian Rationalist Giuseppe Terragni — represented an attempt to revive modern architecture by returning to its early roots and creating a paradoxical "historicism of modernism."[14] Eisenman made important contributions to this ambitious "neomodernist" project, especially with his creation in 1967 of the theoretically oriented Institute for Architecture and Urban Studies (IAUS) in New York, which quickly became a major institution for the East Coast architectural establishment.

Both Eisenman's writings and buildings in these years revealed a preoccupation with formalism. He was particularly influenced by structural linguistics, a discipline that inspired him to seek out the "deep structure" of architecture. Eisenman hoped to develop a compositional strategy that could generate a self-referential, non-symbolic, and universally valid architectural language that was completely independent of the architect's will.[15] This architecture was to be completely autonomous and exist for its own sake; it was meant to serve neither the functional needs of the client nor the expressive ambitions of the architect. For this reason Eisenman took the unusual step of identifying his buildings in this period — mostly private houses — by numbers instead of the client's name. His first completed work was simply entitled House I (1967–68), followed by House II (1969–70) through House VI (1972–75) (fig. 73).[16] All of these buildings were defined by a formal sobriety — gridlike designs of intersecting lines, planes, and volumes — that, in typical modernist fashion, abjured all representation and denoted nothing but their structural essence. At the same time, they also exhibited unconventional features, especially House VI, which included a dead-end stairway on the kitchen ceiling and a bedroom whose marital bed was pierced in half.

Figure 73. Peter Eisenman, House VI, Cornwall, Connecticut, 1972–75. The house avoided any symbolism and strove to exist for its own sake.

Eisenman justified his formalism by citing its broader cultural relevance, notably its connection to the "death of humanism." This idea, which Eisenman took from the structuralist writings of Michel Foucault, emerged gradually after the mid-1970s and became central to his evolving architectural philosophy. In an influential 1976 essay entitled "Post-Functionalism," Eisenman historicized western culture's "shift away from . . . humanism" as a process that had begun in the late nineteenth century. It was then, he noted, that modernist culture had displaced man from the central position he had occupied in the world since the Renaissance. By promoting such pathbreaking movements as abstract painting, atonal music, and atemporal literature, modernism had led to man's diminution "as an originating agent" and had elevated "objects . . . as ideas independent of man." Unfortunately, according to Eisenman, this momentous turn away from humanism had been ignored by architecture, which maintained its "dogged adherence to . . . function" and insisted that buildings existed to serve man's needs. The only solution was for architecture to take note of humanism's demise and acknowledge mankind's newly decentered position by embracing a new kind of "post-functionalism."[17]

At this point, however, Eisenman did not know how exactly to fashion a post-functionalist kind of architecture. In a sense, his early house designs had represented an initial attempt to do so, given their focus on formalism over function. But by the mid-1970s, Eisenman lost interest in architectural autonomy and began to pursue more radical ideas.[18] This shift was apparent at the end of his essay "Post-Functionalism," where he claimed that a post-functionalist architecture could emerge through a "decompositional" method of design. This method refrained from seeing architectural form as a stable entity logically related to function and instead favored a more dynamic conception of form as the product of a dialectical clash between "pre-existing geometric . . . solid[s]" and "form[s] . . . understood as . . . fragments." Through a method of design based in "negation," Eisenman declared, the "new consciousness in architecture which . . . is potentially upon us" could be properly expressed. This method would reveal the bleak truth that post-functionalism was defined by "absence."[19] Eisenman's observations were inchoate at this point. But by proposing fragmentation, decomposition, and absence as the hallmarks of a new architecture, he embraced ideas that later became leitmotifs of deconstructivism. Eisenman would require more than a decade to fully develop these ideas before deconstructivism emerged as a coherent movement. But by the late 1970s he was prepared to undertake a radical overhaul of his previous architectural principles. It was at this point that Eisenman's architecture took a "Jewish" turn.

Eisenman's Jewish Turn and the Legacy of the Holocaust

Among the factors that shaped Eisenman's new architectural agenda was his heightened sense of Jewish identity. Up until the late 1970s, Eisenman's sense of Jewishness was not particularly strong. Having grown up in a thoroughly assimilated Jewish family in suburban South Orange, New Jersey, he received no formal religious education. As he remarked in a recent interview, "I couldn't have been raised more as a Gentile. We never lit candles. We never went to shul. I [even] went to the burlesque on Yom Kippur." His father was a "lefty intellectual" and "very much against rabbinical Judaism" — a stance that Eisenman says he greatly "admired." His mother also failed to serve as a positive Jewish role model. "I never was very close with my mother," Eisenman recalls. "She came from a lot of money" and was "spoiled." "I associated her with a Jewish princess. . . . [And] I never wanted to get near that." As a result, Eisenman grew up distant from traditional religious Judaism, and he has remained so. He has spoken repeatedly of growing up with a Christmas tree at home, never having been bar-mitzvahed, and having married two Christian women. In short, for most of his life, as he puts it, "I rarely faced up to being Jewish."[20]

Eisenman began to reconnect to his Jewish roots in the late 1970s, however, when he embarked upon what turned out to be a twenty-year course of psychoanalysis. This decision was partly precipitated by a crisis in his architectural practice. By the end of the decade, Eisenman had tired of his role as director of the IAUS and, following the loss of a major commission, feared that his practice had "started to go downhill." In 1978, therefore, he decided to consult a psychoanalyst in order to begin to "become myself." Eisenman recalls that in the ensuing discussions the question of "being Jewish" was frequently broached. Today, he openly credits these discussions with making him feel more positive about his Jewish heritage. As he recently put it, "[Even though] I've always . . . felt more comfortable in a Gentile society . . . I'm much more comfortable through my analysis . . . to be able to say . . . 'I'm Jewish. I'm different. I'm other.'"[21]

To reach this state of comfort, Eisenman first had to probe the psychological roots of his ambivalence toward his Jewish origins. To a large degree much of his ambivalence stemmed from painful boyhood encounters with antisemitism. Eisenman experienced frequent anti-Jewish hostility during his childhood in suburban New Jersey. "In the fourth grade," he recently recalled, "my best friend said to me: 'You can't come to my house any more because you're Jewish.' . . . That scarred me." He added that as a youth in South Orange, the "dancing class that I went to . . . was segregated, [with] Jews [going] one Saturday and Gentiles the next." Eisenman even encountered what he has called a "variation of antisemitism" in his own home. His Alsatian-descended grandmother "was very much against *Ostjuden* [Eastern European Jews]" and frequently expressed her prejudices within the family; on one occasion, Eisenman recalled, "my grandmother actually said to me . . . about my father: 'You don't have to listen to him, he's not one of us.' . . . meaning he was not from Western Germany but [from] . . . somewhere on the German/Polish border." "These conversations," Eisenman notes, "[practically] made me feel antisemitic [myself]."[22]

Eisenman's negative experiences were magnified during the Second World War when he sensed the dangers facing Jews in Europe. As he declared in 1996, "In this country I grew up frightened to death. I used to hear Father Coughlin on the radio . . . spewing about k---- and Jews and . . . that was scary. If you went to school in 1940 in my little school in suburban New Jersey, they'd beat you up. . . . And when you used to listen under the bed at night . . . about these reports coming out of Germany about mass extermination of Jews and things like that, you're really . . . I lived in terror." As a result of these childhood experiences Eisenman became alienated from his Jewish background and began to fear that it would prevent him from fully assimilating into American society. "I have always felt . . . as an outsider," he noted in 2006, "[as a result of] the antisemitism in the community [where] I grew up." For much of his early life, therefore, Eisenman followed the maxim that "an outsider desperately desires to be an insider" and separated himself from his Jewishness. The anxieties he felt during the Second World War — even from his safe perch in the United States — convinced him that he "would never marry a Jew, because I didn't want my kids to be subjected to [antisemitism]"; as a result, he "consciously didn't date Jewish women." In college, Eisenman tried to become an insider by taking part in student government and cheerleading. But even there he ran across antisemitism. "I didn't make head cheerleader at Cornell because I was Jewish," he recalls. "[And] I didn't make Red Key [honor] society because I was Jewish." In short, Eisenman's effort to distance himself from his roots never obscured his underlying sense of outsiderness.[23]

This fact is suggested by his increasing tendency after the early 1980s to describe himself as a Jewish "outsider." Eisenman first invoked his Jewish background to justify his emerging architectural philosophy in a 1983 debate with the conservative architect Leon Krier. Responding to Krier's affirmation of classicism, Eisenman declared: "As a Jew and an 'outsider,' I have never felt a part of that 'classical' world." This declaration revealed Eisenman's newfound willingness to fashion an identity related to his Jewish background. To be sure, his definition of Jewish identity was wholly secular and abstract. Like the American Jewish painter R. B. Kitaj, who was then beginning to create a similar kind of identity for himself, Eisenman embraced a sociological understanding of Jewishness as emblematic of the alienated, homeless, and rootless condition of human beings in the modern world. To be a Jew, Eisenman believed, was to be a modernist; as he explained to Krier, "Modernism was the product of an alienated culture with no roots.... Modernists were suddenly out of the ghettos and in the cities." Convinced that these prototypically Jewish traits defined the modern world, Eisenman insisted that architecture had to bravely confront the bleakness of the present and refrain from nostalgically looking to the past. He elaborated on this point in an interview in 1985 when he declared that, as a "cultural Jew [like] ... Walter Benjamin ... for whom Jewishness was a state of mind ... outside the reality of religion, [I believe] in an architecture which attempts to stand outside the Graeco-Christian tradition ... [and] talks about the condition of Diaspora ... [and] wandering." Later that year, Eisenman's remark to Jacques Derrida that he had "begun to consider Hebraic thought and its implications for architecture" suggested that Eisenman had also been influenced by the ideas of Thorleif Boman and Bruno Zevi. All of these comments indicate that at the very moment that his subversive architectural philosophy was beginning to take shape in the early 1980s, Eisenman recognized that being a Jewish "outsider" was something to assert rather than hide.[24]

At the same time that he was beginning to show greater comfort with his Jewish identity, Eisenman also started to display a growing interest in the Holocaust. In explaining this interest, Eisenman recalls that he first became exposed to the subject by reading the works of Theodor Adorno and George Steiner in the 1960s, but he adds that his interest deepened after he started reading the post-structuralist writings of Derrida, Blanchot, and Lyotard, all of whom made frequent reference to the Holocaust. Eisenman's immersion in postmodern thought explains why his engagement with the Holocaust was highly philosophical and not articulated from a particularistic "Jewish" perspective. Just as many postmodern thinkers saw the Nazi genocide's significance in universalistic terms as one of several historical events that exposed the bankruptcy of modern civilization (another was the dropping of the atomic bomb at Hiroshima), Eisenman viewed Auschwitz as an event of broad civilizational significance rather than one of relevance only to Jews. That said, Eisenman's Jewish background, particularly his youthful experiences with antisemitism, clearly made him more prone than other architects at the time to consider the Holocaust's architectural significance.[25]

Eisenman's engagement with the Nazi genocide was also encouraged by other architects' reflections on the Second World War's architectural legacy. It is unclear to what extent Eisenman was influenced by Bruno Zevi's ideas about the Holocaust's relevance for postwar architecture.[26] But several architects with whom he maintained close friendships prompted him to seek inspiration in the events of the war years. A particularly important figure was Philip Johnson, whose infamous postwar description of his Glass House in New Canaan, Connecticut (1950), as having been inspired by a "burnt wooden village ... [in Nazi-occupied Poland] where nothing was left but the foundations and chimneys of brick," made Eisenman aware of the Second World War's symbolic architectural legacy. In 1977 he wrote that the design was "Johnson's own monument to the horrors of war" and "prefigure[d] ... the parallel anxiety of post–World War II architecture."[27] Another influential figure was Aldo Rossi, many of whose designs in the 1960s and 1970s expressed the idea that the "continuous 'narrative' of the progress of Western civilization has been broken." In particular, Rossi's stark 1965 monument to the Italian partisans of Segrate, who fought against the German occupation in 1944, and his 1971 design for a cemetery at Modena testified to the emergence of an "architecture caught between the memory of a not forgotten past and an unwanted present that promises nothing for the future." For Eisenman, Johnson and Rossi's works revealed the possibility of fashioning an architecture that fit into a "landscape shadowed by the reality of mass death" and paved the way for him to try a similar move.[28]

As a consequence of his deepening sense of himself as a Jew, his reading of postmodern theory, and his exposure to the historically evocative work of other architects, Eisenman increasingly began to refer to the Holocaust's legacy in his writings during the 1970s. His important texts from this period make clear that his interest in the Nazi genocide evolved out of his prior concern with the "death of humanism," the concept that had originally justified his rebellion against traditional architectural practice. By the decade's end, however, and especially after the beginning of the 1980s, his understanding of the concept had changed dramatically. Instead of attributing the demise of humanism to the advent of modernism, he now explained it as a result of the Second World War's horrors. As early as the fall of 1977, Eisenman referred to the legacy of "humanism [which was] so debilitated by the events of 1945." Several years later he went further, declaring that the "mythos that sustained our culture for five hundred years" had "died [altogether] in 1945, not to be resurrected." The result of humanism's demise, Eisenman asserted in 1984, was the rise of a "new sensibility ... born in the rupture of 1945" and visible "in the stones of Hiroshima and the smoke of Auschwitz."[29]

This new sensibility represented a dramatically new form of consciousness "called post-modernism." According to Eisenman, it was defined by a "view of history" that was conscious of the "ruptures" that had recently shaken western civilization to its foundations. It was also a sensibility that recognized the dangers still faced by civilization and was thus a sensibility of fear. As he declared in 1983, "Today, we have a society of people born after 1945 who subconsciously feel there has been a fundamental change—a collective anxiety." It was urgently necessary for architects to apply the lessons of this historical rupture to their own work. As he noted in a 1982 interview with Robert Venturi, "Since the Holocaust and with the increasing potential for nuclear disaster, we live in a world of what I call memory and imminence—of what was before and what could potentially be.... It seems to me that architecture could reflect this condition symbolically."[30] Architecture, Eisenman implied, needed to be fundamentally rethought to reflect the anxious realities of the post-Holocaust, post-humanist, postmodern world.

Eisenman saw this task as especially urgent, given the tendency of existing architectural movements to ignore this new world's realities. The worst offender, in his view, was architectural postmodernism, whose neohistoricist revival of bygone architectural styles, associated with Robert Venturi, Michael Graves, and Robert A. M. Stern, effaced the ruptures of the recent past by emphasizing tradition. These postmodern architects, Eisenman argued, were psychologically incapable of admitting the post-humanist reality of a "centerless world" and kept "trying to restore those elements in architecture which are responsive to a condition of man's centric position." But, as he put it, the "estranging vector moving out from the center is not subject to man's volition, and no postmodern retreat into simulated symbols of a benign past can mask it." Eisenman also assailed classicism and modernism. Rejecting the prevailing view that modern architecture represented a break with the classical tradition, he argued that both movements had certain goals in common, most notably the anthropocentric belief that buildings should communicate meaning, attain timeless validity, and achieve formal perfection through the pursuit of "strict compositional means." These common goals, he asserted, showed that both classicism and modernism belonged to a broader five-hundred-year architectural continuum rooted in humanistic values. Yet, since these values had been rendered obsolete by the rupture of the Holocaust, it was clear that classicism and modernism—like postmodernism—were unsuited for the new era's post-humanist sensibility.[31]

To replace these outmoded architectural movements Eisenman recommended a new architecture of "decomposition." The architect had first floated this concept in the mid-1970s, but he now described it in terms borrowed from the post-structuralist thought of Derrida. In several essays in the 1980s, Eisenman defined decomposition as a third way "outside the classical/modernist definition" of architecture. It was a "transgressive" architecture that, "through the introduction of the negative of the classical," strove to create a "not-classical" form of architecture. This negation took aim at all of western architecture's time-honored traditions. One of the most important, for Eisenman, was the "strong bond between form and function." While conceding that "architecture must function," Eisenman insisted that "architecture may also function without necessarily symbolizing that function." He was especially opposed to the idea that architecture had "to symbolize . . . its function . . . [of] providing shelter and enclosure." Believing that this idea was based on the "unnoticed repression . . . [of] the truth of instability," Eisenman called for an architecture that would "struggle against . . . symbolizing [shelter]" and instead "embrace the instabilities and dislocations that are today in fact the truth." This demand was closely connected to Eisenman's rejection of architecture's traditional tendency to "operate . . . as a condition of presence," which had "always sought . . . to repress the essential aspect of absence which operates within [architecture]." Eisenman demanded that this "condition of absence" be given adequate architectural expression. A proper form of "dislocating architecture," he observed, "must be at once presence and absence." Finally, Eisenman rejected architecture's traditional aesthetic goals of purity, perfection, and representation. Instead of an architecture that pursued "objecthood" and "image" through the "simulation of reality," Eisenman called for an architecture of "traces"—of "partial and fragmentary sign[s]"—that refused to exist as a "representational object" and that conceded the nonexistence of a "representable 'reality.'" By embracing the technique of decomposition, architecture would be able to express the Holocaust's legacy and redefine itself in keeping with the spirit of the postmodern world.[32]

Eisenman's Post-Holocaust Architecture

Eisenman's interest in the Holocaust was visible not just in his architectural writings but in his building designs as well. After the early 1980s his buildings showed no single identifiable style. Nonetheless, they evoked themes — insecurity, instability, anxiety, fragmentation, absence, loss, and memory — that reflected the legacy of genocide.

These new themes first found expression in a series of unrealized designs for private homes. Beginning with House X (1978) and continuing with House 11a (1980), House El Even Odd (1981), Fin d'Ou T Hou S (1984), and the Guardiola House (1988), Eisenman abandoned the orthogonal grids that defined his work in the 1970s and instead made increasing use of what he called the L-shape (fig. 74). For him this fragmented, voided section of a cube was a highly symbolic and "ideological" form. As he noted, "The L-shape . . . is destabilised. It is an incomplete form. It is . . . topologically symmetrical, and yet unsymmetrical. It forces many issues." One of these issues was Eisenman's desire to question the traditional notion that architecture should symbolize stability and security. "What I am against," he declared, "is the habitual notion that architecture shelters and encloses." Eisenman clearly expressed this idea in the Guardiola House, whose L-shape design and partially subterranean location made it appear ready to topple over. The architect made no explicit references to the Holocaust in explaining his design, but certain scholars have seen it as informed by Jewish considerations. Mark Taylor has pointed out, for example, that Eisenman's L-shape, when spelled "EL-shape," denotes one of the Hebrew terms for God (or "Elohim," commonly shortened to "El") and symbolically illustrates the Jewish conception of the divine as dialectically positioned between presence and absence. Moreover, Eisenman himself has observed that his housing designs of this period reflected the influence of what he has called the "Jewish" field of psychoanalysis, for in deciding to partially bury many of his buildings he symbolically alluded to the psychoanalytic agenda of delving into the unconscious.[33]

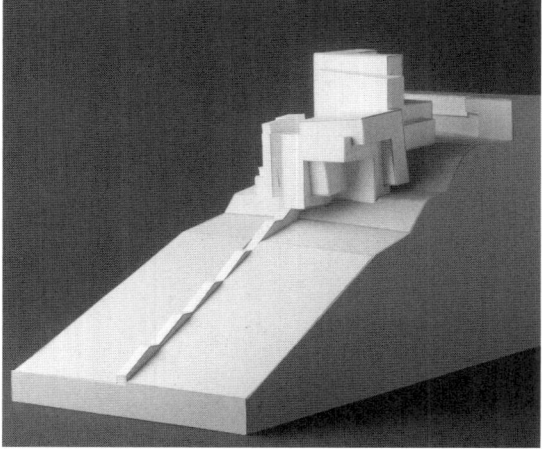

Figure 74. Peter Eisenman, Guardiola House, 1988. The house is composed of multiple L-shapes, which are meant to suggest instability.

Around the same time, Eisenman began to pursue larger projects through a new design approach that he called "artificial excavation." This approach grew out of his subterranean house designs by being archaeologically oriented to the specific history of the architectural site. Deeply influenced by the concept of memory, artificial excavation demanded that new buildings acknowledge a site's absent past without reconstructing it nostalgically, as was becoming fashionable among postmodern architects. Through this site-specific method, Eisenman designed many of the key buildings that helped establish his reputation as an innovator. These buildings also revealed subtle markers of the Holocaust's legacy.[34]

These markers were visible in Eisenman's 1980 design for an apartment complex for the 1983 Internationale Bauausstellung (IBA) in Berlin. In tackling this project Eisenman directly confronted the recent tragedies of German history. The site of the buildings was a desolate block on the corner of the Friedrichstrasse and the Kochstrasse, near Checkpoint Charlie, where all but three buildings had been destroyed by wartime Allied bombings. Keeping in mind the IBA mandate to mend the city's torn urban fabric, Eisenman produced a design that exposed the scars of the recent German past. Rather than reconstructing the nineteenth-century buildings that once stood at the site or designing comparable structures to fill in the gaps (as postmodernists might have done), Eisenman called on artificial excavation to stimulate remembrance. His complex design imposed on the site a matrix of three overlapping grids: at the lowest level, one corresponding to the city's absent eighteenth-century city walls; above that, a grid denoting its nineteenth-century street patterns; and, at the top, the Mercator grid designating the meridians of the globe (fig. 75). Along these grids, canted from one another by 3.3 degrees, Eisenman planned a series of fragmented buildings that penetrated the surviving nineteenth-century buildings, along with low-lying abstract walls and L-shaped stairwell towers that seemed to be rising out of (or sinking into) the ground. In submitting this plan, Eisenman sought to direct attention to the site's absent past and lend it significance as a "place of reflection." At the most obvious level, his plan alluded to the city's postwar division in the sense that its walls were exactly the same height as the nearby Berlin Wall, while its stairwell towers evoked the ominous guard towers alongside it. At a deeper level, Eisenman observed that the design identified

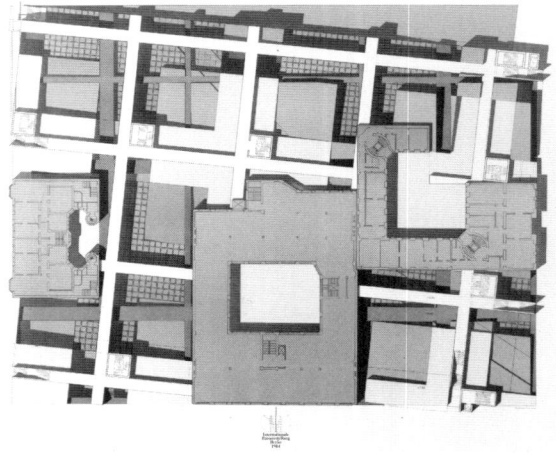

Figure 75. Peter Eisenman, IBA Apartment Building, plan, Berlin, 1981–85. An example of "artificial excavation," Eisenman's plan for a series of new buildings was dictated by three overlapping grids imposed between existing nineteenth-century structures. The only completed building was erected in the space at the lower left-hand corner.

Berlin as the location of the "end of the history of the Enlightenment," a comment that reflected a postmodern understanding of the Holocaust's metahistorical significance. Unfortunately for Eisenman, the project was only partially completed; while a ten-story apartment building arose on the corner of the Friedrichstrasse and the Kochstrasse in 1985, his intricate arrangement of intersecting walls and L-shaped stairwell towers was never realized (fig. 76). In its incomplete form, the resulting building failed to evoke the events that helped to inspire it.[35]

Figure 76. IBA Apartment Building. The building, which occupies the corner of the Friedrichstrasse and the Kochstrasse, partly assumes the form of an inverted L-shape overhanging the smaller volume below it. Note the grid patterns on its facade, which evoke the overlapping grids in the plan.

Figure 77. Peter Eisenman, Wexner Center for the Visual Arts, Columbus, Ohio, 1983–88. The museum is a "nonbuilding" composed of several volumes linked by a long white metal grid resembling scaffolding. The museum bisects Weigel Hall (left) and Mershon Auditorium (right).

Nevertheless, Eisenman profitably utilized the technique of artificial excavation several years later to ring up his first great success — the Wexner Center for the Visual Arts on the campus of the Ohio State University in Columbus (1983–88). As he did in Berlin, Eisenman took a street plan — this time, of Columbus — and superimposed it over the Mercator grid, which diverged from it by some 12 degrees, thus creating a matrix of angles that provided the basis for his main structure, a long white metal grid resembling scaffolding that bisected two existing buildings on the site, Weigel Hall and Mershon Auditorium (fig. 77). The resulting structure, according to Eisenman, was a "nonbuilding" that was designed to look "fractured and incomplete"; it was also supposed to refrain from "symbolizing its function as shelter."[36] The most striking and evocative part of Eisenman's design, however, was his inclusion of an artificial ruin — a fragmented re-creation of the crenellated tower of a nineteenth-century brick armory that once stood at the site (fig. 78). This ghost structure evoked the memory of the site's past while averting any postmodern nostalgia. Indeed, far from giving visitors a pleasing evocation of a vanished past, Eisenman hoped to instill in them a sense of unease. As he noted in a 1984 interview, "I think the general public are going to feel a very definite level of anxiety in the building."[37] This goal was promoted by various interior features, such as a heavy white beam that dangled threateningly over a central staircase. In evoking fragmentation, ruin, memory, and anxiety, the Wexner Center provided the clearest evidence yet of Eisenman's desire to have contemporary architecture acknowledge the bleak realities of the post-Holocaust world.

Figure 78. Peter Eisenman, Wexner Center for the Visual Arts, Columbus, Ohio, 1983–88. Another illustration of "artificial excavation" was an artificial ruin of the crenellated tower of a nineteenth-century brick armory that once occupied the museum's site.

By the late 1980s, Eisenman had ceased mentioning the Holocaust in his theoretical writings and abandoned artificial excavation for new design techniques, such as "scaling" and "folding," which were derived from fractal geometry, chaos theory, and other scientific fields. As a result, most of his projects from the late 1980s through the mid-1990s bore no obvious connection to the Holocaust. Still, Eisenman's designs of this period reflected its disruptive legacy by expressing what, by then, was seen as a "deconstructivist" commitment to destabilizing traditional architectural practice. Among his most important buildings of this period, some—such as the headquarters for the Nunotani corporation in Tokyo (1990–92) and the Aronoff Center at the University of Cincinnati (1995)—illustrated the theme of rupture and destabilization so vividly that they seemed on the verge of collapsing (fig. 79). Moreover, Eisenman remained engaged in projects that were symbolically related to the Holocaust. His 1992 design for the Max Reinhardt House in Berlin—an inverted skyscraper in the form of a contorted Möbius strip—evoked the Nazi past by being dedicated to the influential German Jewish theater director who was forced into exile by the Nazi regime (fig. 80).[38]

The Holocaust was not the only aspect of the modern Jewish experience that Eisenman explored at this time. Indeed, he reflected on aspects of the Jewish religion as well. This new phase in Eisenman's development as a Jewish architect was prompted by his agreement to produce a design for the Jewish Museum of San Francisco in 1996. Given Eisenman's longstanding distance from traditional Jewish life, his pursuit of this commission seems out of character, but his interest in Jewish religious themes actually dated back to the beginning of his career. As early as 1955, while an undergraduate at Cornell, he designed a synagogue for his thesis project. And in 1986 he participated in an Israeli-sponsored exhibition, "*Nerot Mitzvah:* Contemporary Ideas for Light in Jewish Ritual," for which he designed a rectilinear menorah using his technique of scaling. For the San Francisco project, Eisenman sought to create what he called a "new kind of Jewish architecture." Eisenman's ideas for San Francisco were concerned with "the Jewish situation as we approach the 21st century—post-Holocaust." As he put it, the building "should be an expression of what it means to be a Jew—morally, spiritually, culturally." Eisenman's vision was profoundly shaped by his post-structuralist—or what others might interpret as Talmudic—tendencies. He refused to define Jewish architecture according to any clear aesthetic criteria and instead insisted that it was epitomized by a rejection of epistemological certainty in favor of ceaseless questioning. As he put it in a letter to the museum committee in January 1996, "The history of cultures, other than the Jewish culture, has always been about providing . . . answers. This is particularly true of architecture, which in gentile cultures has traditionally embodied the meaning of the culture. But in the important book of Jewish thought, Pirke Avoth . . . the question is asked, Does God exist? Instead of providing the answer, the book gives no answer. Rather it is a catalogue of the debate. The answer is the debate, the argument. Therefore a Jewish Museum could be, in the sense of the Pirke Avoth, not so much about establishing the identity of Jewish artifacts, but about putting these artifacts into question without providing answers." For this reason, Eisenman concluded, it was "wrong" to ask the question: "How can a Jewish Museum express its Jewishness?" Especially "since the history of Jewish building . . . has been explicitly against any overt symbolism, any so-called graven images, . . . it would seem quite natural," he concluded, "that the architecture of this museum [would] be questioning rather than expressing."[39]

Figure 79. Peter Eisenman, Nunotani corporation headquarters, Tokyo, 1990–92. The building appears poised to collapse.

Figure 80. Peter Eisenman, Max Reinhardt House, Berlin, model, 1992. This design for an inverted skyscraper was named after the influential German Jewish theater director.

Eisenman did not specify exactly how these ideas would be translated into built form. In its original conception, the envisioned museum was to be constructed around the historic 1906 Jessie Street electric substation, whose neoclassical facade was to serve as a contrast for what Eisenman called a Hebraic facade. An early model of his design reveals that Eisenman planned on embodying his oppositional impulses by producing a parabuilding, inserting three large, jagged volumes into the substation's structure and covering the entire redesigned edifice with transparent pitched roofs of glass and steel (fig. 81). Behind the substation Eisenman placed a taller, cubic building that displayed billboard-sized, supergraphic-style Hebrew letters (including two Yuds, spelling out the name for God). Leading to the museum's main entrance was a redesigned central plaza defined by angled cuts and terracing. Due to public objections to his redesign of the plaza, however, he was dropped from the project in 1996 and eventually replaced by Daniel Libeskind.[40]

This setback notwithstanding, Eisenman remained involved in Jewish projects by showing new interest in the design of Holocaust memorials. In 1995 he entered the competition for a memorial to the Jewish victims of Nazi terror in Vienna. For this project Eisenman returned to artificial excavation, probing the history of the memorial's site — Vienna's medieval Judenplatz — as a means of arriving at its form. The basis of the design was a series of overlapping maps: two of the Vienna ghettos that were destroyed in 1421 and 1678, and one of the German Reich after the Anschluss of 1938. These maps provided the outline for a rupture in the ground some three meters deep. The rupture was enclosed by a series of slanted vertical steel plates that framed an arrangement of ground-level lights evoking the boundaries of the Auschwitz extermination camp (fig. 82). The resulting form, Eisenman asserted in postmodern fashion, represented "rationality gone mad" and suggested that "under the generally laudable reason of the Enlightenment lies the possibility of inhumane reason." Eisenman did not see this as the memorial's sole message, however, and questioned whether memorials could communicate any message about the Holocaust at all. He articulated this skeptical claim by citing the same Jewish rationale he used in his design for the San Francisco Jewish museum. Noting that the Talmud refrained from "having an answer to every question," Eisenman asserted that the tendency of "Jewish culture and thought" to encourage "debate" made it appropriate for the memorial to do so as well. As he wrote, "Instead of producing a memorial that embodies meaning, . . . the architecture of our project . . . questions . . . the conditions of . . . [the Holocaust's] horror and the means through which a cultural form may represent these conditions." His goal, therefore, was less to dictate a specific moral lesson than to create a "powerful and evocative spatial experience that will . . . precipitate . . . discussion about the past . . . [so as] to ensure that . . . [it] will never [be] repeat[ed]."[41] Eisenman, however, never got the opportunity to realize his vision, as he came in second to Rachel Whiteread, whose winning design was completed in 2000.

Nevertheless, Eisenman continued his engagement with Holocaust memorials and soon registered one of the most notable successes of his career with his victorious design for Germany's national Memorial to the Murdered Jews of Europe in Berlin. Originally conceived with the American sculptor Richard Serra in 1997, the memorial design was as much a work of sculpture as architecture (fig. 83). The memorial, in its first conception, consisted of some four thousand concrete pillars, or steles, of varying heights that were placed close to one another to create an undulating field of

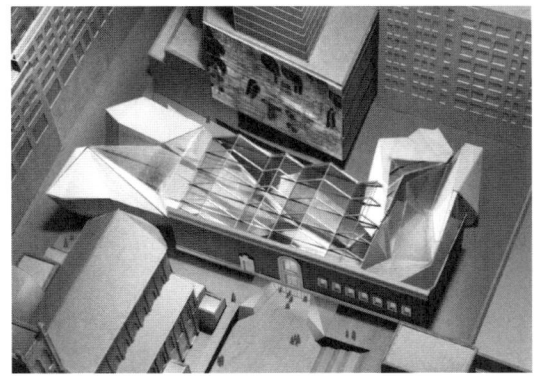

Figure 81. Peter Eisenman, Jewish Museum of San Francisco, model, 1996. Eisenman inserted three jagged volumes into the Jessie Street substation's neoclassical structure and added transparent pitched roofs made of glass and steel. He envisioned a building, erected behind the substation, displaying billboard-sized Hebrew letters spelling out the name of God.

Figure 82. Peter Eisenman, Holocaust memorial, Vienna, model, 1995. The memorial's form derived from a series of overlapping maps of Vienna's medieval and early modern ghettos and the German Reich after the Nazi Anschluss of 1938.

Figure 83. Peter Eisenman, Memorial to the Murdered Jews of Europe, Berlin, 1997–2005. Composed of 2,711 concrete steles, the memorial embodied Eisenman's deconstructivist opposition to representation and resisted any didactic message.

vertical monoliths. While hardly a traditional work of architecture, the design bore notable signs of Eisenman's deconstructivist architectural philosophy. He insisted that the memorial not be representational because the "enormity and horror of the Holocaust are such that any attempt to represent it by traditional means is inevitably inadequate." Believing that "no understanding is possible," Eisenman refused to have the memorial didactically advance any specific historical or moral message. The monument was to be a "place of no meaning," a place of "silence" that would "speak without speaking." It was supposed to prompt visitors to ask "why?" without answering it decisively.[42]

In truth, Eisenman honored this pledge in the breach. Despite rejecting any didacticism in the memorial, his comment that its size would evoke the "excess of ... reason gone mad" showed that he shared the postmodern view of the Holocaust as a byproduct, rather than a betrayal, of Enlightenment values. Moreover, while he did not want the memorial to preach a single message, Eisenman intended it to have a specific impact. As with his Wexner Center, Eisenman created a space that deliberately provoked anxiety, insisting that visitors to the field of steles have a "spatial experience ... similar to what one would have in Auschwitz ... a feeling of loneliness and being lost." The memorial space was meant to be "strange," Eisenman insisted, noting that "it should be both alluring and disturbing."[43]

In pursuing this plan, Eisenman hoped to do justice to Adorno's concerns about producing art in the wake of atrocity. Aware of the danger that his memorial, like any work of art, might "aestheticize" the Nazis' crimes, Eisenman strove to subvert its identity as a work of architecture. In good postmodern fashion, the memorial blurred the boundaries between architecture and sculpture. This was best seen in the memorial's effort to "displace ... the ground" as a basis for architecture. According to Eisenman, architecture had traditionally been "site specific" in being rooted in the ground. Yet, because ground had been essential to "the "Nazi ideology of blut und boden" (blood and soil), and because this racist idea had "made the Jew placeless, alien, and other," Eisenman undermined it by having the ground under his steles undulate, forcing visitors into a "zone of instability" in which the "ground falls away" from them. This gesture, he believed, would help counter architecture's inclination to "provide ... meaning ... in ... [an] aesthetic way" in general, and the Nazis' tendency to "aestheticize ... politics" in particular.[44]

As is well known, Eisenman's design sparked extended discussion in Germany. Due to objections about the memorial's initial conception, Eisenman had to make numerous compromises in order to secure the German government's approval. The memorial's original four thousand pillars were reduced to 2,711; their size and spacing were drastically reduced for safety reasons; and a documentation center was incorporated in a space beneath it. These changes, however, did not prevent other objections about the memorial from surfacing. For example, the president of the Central Committee of the Jews in Germany, Paul Spiegel, lamented the memorial's failure to identify the perpetrators, while non-Jewish groups complained about its exclusion of the Nazis' other victims.[45] Since the memorial's dedication in May 2005, however, its overall reception has been positive, with most observers praising its aesthetic power and open-ended symbolism.[46] That said, few commentators took note of the memorial's roots in Eisenman's deconstructivist philosophy. Contrary to the impression left by many reviews, his design did not reflect a sudden shift in his career.[47] Rather, it represented the culmination of nearly three decades of thought on the history and memory of the Nazi genocide.

Beyond its importance for enhancing Eisenman's reputation, the Berlin Holocaust memorial revealed a great deal about his evolving sense of himself as a Jew. "I initially did not regard myself as a Jew," he claimed in 1999, adding, "I have never seen myself as a Jewish-American architect. I was always an architect who was coincidentally a Jew." Nevertheless, working on the memorial allowed Eisenman to reconnect with his "neglected Jewish heritage" and helped the "Jewish aspects of my person to reemerge." To be sure, his Jewish identity remained completely secular. Insisting that he still does not attend synagogue and finds "rabbinic Judaism . . . alien," Eisenman explained that the memorial commission helped him rediscover the "repressed Jew within me—my psychological Judaism." In effect, this amounted to a generalized sense of outsiderness. As he put it, "For me as a Jew . . . I have always been strongly aware that Jews are outsiders who live in the diaspora."[48]

This observation confirmed that Eisenman's notion of Jewishness was secular and universalistic. When asked his opinion of how the Germans have dealt with their Nazi past, Eisenman responded, "I view Germany as a fascinating . . . country. I could live there. I believe that Jews should return to Germany. It is a much more interesting country than Israel, because I believe that the secular Jew always lives in the Diaspora and not in a homeland." With this comment, Eisenman indicated his opposition to a particularist and territorially based form of Jewish identity, a point he later reiterated. "My understanding of what a Jew is is spiritual. People in Israel are not Jews; they are Israelis. For me, a Jew lives in the Diaspora." Eisenman's disavowal of Jewish particularism was further evident in his original desire to have the Holocaust memorial commemorate not just the Nazis' Jewish victims. He had intended the steles to "simply symbolize otherness," which was the main reason, he believed, the Nazis persecuted the Jews. This inclusive stance proved temporary, however, for as Eisenman read more extensively about the history of the Holocaust, he changed his opinion and approached the project from a strictly Jewish perspective. Still, Eisenman ultimately remained wedded to the same abstract view of the Nazi genocide that he had first embraced in the late 1970s. Even as he regarded the Jews as the Holocaust's chief victims, he viewed the perpetrators from a clear postmodern perspective, noting that the memorial will "warn against the belief in reason, . . . [for] when reason becomes all-consuming . . . terrible things can happen." Paradoxically, then, while the memorial project led Eisenman to a stronger sense of Jewish identity, it was largely universal in nature.[49]

The idiosyncrasies of Eisenman's Jewish identity become even more apparent in considering other aspects of his architectural career. For an architect who has been committed to acknowledging the Holocaust's legacy in his built work, he has maintained a surprisingly nonmoralistic stance about controversial architectural topics related to the Nazi era. Most notable is his longtime admiration for the designers and defenders of fascist architecture. For decades Eisenman has studied the work of the Italian Rationalist architect Giuseppe Terragni, whose famous Casa del Fascio (1938), in Como, he has hailed as a masterpiece of modern architecture, despite its function as the headquarters of the local fascist party. Eisenman has also maintained a long friendship with Leon Krier, despite the latter's attempts in the 1980s to rehabilitate the architectural work of Albert Speer. Eisenman was equally close with Philip Johnson, choosing to ignore his fascist activities in the 1930s and early 1940s and working closely with him on numerous occasions, notably in planning MoMA's "Deconstructivist Architecture" exhibition of 1988.[50]

Eisenman's politically indeterminate stance has earned him many critics, especially among left-leaning architectural historians committed to architecture's social mission. In 1994 the American architectural historian Diane Ghirardo accused Eisenman of being an opportunistic "self-promoter" who had used "masterful public relations" and obscure theoretical musings to mask the fact that his formalistically adventurous architectural projects were functionally conservative. In producing such a "bogus avant-garde" kind of architecture, Eisenman, according to Ghirardo, mimicked the behavior of his idol, Terragni, and a "host of other architects in fascist Italy."[51] Eisenman did not respond to this and other attacks, preferring to keep politics and morality removed from architecture.[52] But he concedes that his resistance to being pigeonholed politically — "I don't want to be either . . . left or right" — has led him to be "attacked more readily by the left."[53]

It is difficult to explain the apparent contradiction between Eisenman's commitment to remembering the horrors of the Nazi and fascist eras and his uncritical stance toward those who have preferred to forget. In part, Eisenman's position can be traced back to his theoretical approach to architecture. Both his early structuralist commitment to architectural autonomy and his later poststructuralist opposition to architectural "presence" have inclined Eisenman to divorce architecture from its political and social contexts. His aversion to probing the deeper social and political meaning of architecture — indeed, his aversion to architecture as conveying any signification — suggests that he may not be so committed, in a deep moral sense, to an architecture of memory. Indeed, Eisenman has long opposed injecting moral issues into discussions of architecture, saying, "I haven't got a moralistic bone in my body." This position partly explains why he has chosen to engage, rather than spurn, those architects with whom he has disagreed. He insists that he and Krier are "still close" even though "he's against everything I'm for and I'm for everything he's against." Eisenman's desire to engage with opposites also explains his friendship with the German architect Albert Speer, Jr. As he has noted, "Why did Albert . . . and I become close friends? Because he needed to befriend a Jew and I needed to befriend [the son of] a Nazi." From Eisenman's perspective, engaging with difference rather than repressing it is a precondition to dialogue. "I don't want 'yes' people around me," he has said. "I want 'no' people around me." Finally, he observes that his opposition to moralism does not imply disregard for ethics. As he puts it, "I am a person that believes in doing good."[54]

Still, Eisenman's aversion to taking moral positions has gotten him into trouble on occasions when he has addressed the topic of the Third Reich. In 2004, the architect ran afoul of German Jewish communal leaders when, alerted to the fact that the graffiti-resistant coating sprayed onto his memorial steles in Berlin was manufactured by a company, Degussa, that was linked via a subsidiary to the production of Zyklon B gas during the Holocaust, he tried to dispel the memorial board's moralistic desire to dismiss the company from the project by making the lighthearted comment that his New York–based dentist had recently told him that the gold fillings in his teeth were made of the same substance — and could be yanked out if he so desired. Thinking Eisenman was relativizing Degussa's involvement in the extraction of gold fillings from concentration camp victims during the Holocaust, several members of the memorial board stormed out of the meeting and demanded that Eisenman be reprimanded.[55] Eisenman soon apologized, and the furor caused by his casual comment blew over; but the controversy highlighted the perils of Eisenman's devil-may-care aversion to moralism. It is also jarring to hear Eisenman glibly reflect on one of the more sensationalistic dimensions of his friendship with Albert Speer, Jr. As he noted in 2006, "I'm fascinated by the fact that Albert talks about sitting on Hitler's knee at Berchtesgaden and [that] he was Hitler's only godson. And I thought, gee, you know, if I . . . [made] Albert . . . my [own] son's godfather, then he could say: 'My great godfather was Adolf Hitler.' I was fascinated by this possibility."[56] Such remarks further suggest that Eisenman's relationship to the Holocaust, however significant it has been for his work, differs substantially from the more solemn form of remembrance that has come to define American and German official culture.

That said, the fact remains that Eisenman's identity as a Jew concerned with the course of modern Jewish history has been vital in shaping his architectural career. It remains an open question whether the Holocaust's legacy actually inspired Eisenman's radical turn in the late 1970s or whether it merely served as a convenient justification for it. In reality, both explanations have merit. As he began to fashion for himself the identity of a Jewish "outsider" he became more receptive to the growing awareness of the Holocaust within American cultural and intellectual life. For this reason Eisenman's increasing invocation of the Holocaust in his writings can be seen as originating in a deeply personal interest in the topic. Had Eisenman not been Jewish, it is doubtful that the growing attention toward the Holocaust would have resonated with him as it did. It is true that Eisenman in the late 1970s was searching for new ways of justifying his inner need to rebel against architectural convention, and the Holocaust provided a convenient rationale for doing so. It is equally true that had he lived in a different time and place, his rebellious instincts would have found some other articulation. And yet Eisenman's embrace of the Holocaust was more than just a matter of fortuitous timing. His need to buck architectural convention was not merely a function of his personality but also stemmed from a conflicted sense of Jewishness typical of many Jews in postwar American society. Eisenman has never resolved his inner tensions, and some may find his pronouncements on Jewish identity to be contradictory or offputting. But whatever one's perspective, the trajectory of Eisenman's career as a deconstructivist architect exhibits an undeniable Jewish provenance.

Daniel Libeskind

Besides Peter Eisenman, the Jewish architect most closely associated with deconstructivism is Daniel Libeskind. Since he first gained international attention at the "Deconstructivist Architecture" exhibition of 1988, Libeskind has continually rebelled against architectural tradition by embracing a design philosophy marked by disruption, destabilization, and fragmentation. Significantly, this rebellion resembled Eisenman's in being partly inspired by Jewish concerns, especially relating to the Holocaust, whose legacy he explored in a large number of projects devoted to its commemoration. Best seen in his Berlin Jewish Museum (1988–2001), Libeskind's reflections on the Holocaust's significance for contemporary architecture helped him develop a distinctive architectural language that was narrative without being historicist. Its defining traits — its symbolic ground plans, colliding volumes, slashed facades, and contrasting materials — were similar to Eisenman's in their site-specific orientation. Yet his architecture's overtly brooding and ominous character made its connection to the Holocaust more obvious. Further differentiating Libeskind from Eisenman is his greater willingness to consider himself a Jewish architect and lend explicitly Jewish features to his work. Libeskind has designed not only buildings that commemorate the Jewish past but that also serve Jewish needs in the present—synagogues, museums, community centers, and schools. Here, too, Libeskind has exhibited signs of a noticeably Jewish design method, deriving his plans from Hebrew letters and larger Jewish theological and moral concepts. In mediating between the tragic Jewish past and the hopeful Jewish future, in short, Libeskind has strived to develop an assertive form of Jewish architecture.

Libeskind's Jewish Identity

Libeskind's architectural engagement with Jewish subjects is largely explained by his personal history. Born in Lodz, Poland, in 1946, he did not experience the horrors of World War II himself, but its legacy surrounded him throughout his childhood. His parents eluded Hitler's grasp by fleeing into Soviet central Asia at the start of the war, but they still suffered tremendous privations. They were interned separately in forced labor camps until 1942, at which point they met in a refugee camp in Kyrgyzstan and eked out a meager existence for the remainder of the war. Libeskind's parents personally escaped the Holocaust, but they could not escape its aftermath. When they returned to Poland in 1945, they learned that eighty-five of their family members had been murdered by the Nazis.[57]

From his earliest years Libeskind was painfully aware of the Holocaust's magnitude. As a boy he often accompanied his father to the desecrated and overgrown Jewish cemetery in Lodz, where they tended the gravestones of friends and relatives. They also sought out other Jews with whom they could furtively speak Yiddish and inquire after missing friends and loved ones. Being a Jew in postwar Poland also exposed Libeskind to persistent antisemitism. At an early age he exhibited prodigious musical talents, but his parents insisted that he study the accordion rather than the piano, which some Polish neighbors viewed as a bourgeois (and thus Jewish) instrument. These burdensome dimensions of the Jewish past, moreover, did not surround Libeskind only in Poland. When he was eleven, he and his family moved to Israel. But after his arrival Libeskind felt self-conscious about his Eastern European Jewish roots, recalling how Israelis would hush him and his father on the street when speaking Yiddish—"Don't talk that loser language," he was told. After two years in Israel, Libeskind's family moved to the United States, settling in the Bronx in 1959. Only after arriving in New York—a city where "everyone . . . could be equally at home"—did he feel that the weighty aspects of his Jewish heritage had been lifted from him.[58]

As a result of this background, Libeskind developed a strong sense of Jewish identity. Today, he defines his identity in nonsectarian terms, noting: "My immediate background is rabbinical on one side, anarchist on the other. So my own sense of Jewishness has nothing to do with either fundamentalism or rebellion." He adds, "You could put me at a table with chasidim on one side and virulent atheists on the other. And I could speak to all of them." Despite this ecumenicism, Libeskind has tended, like Eisenman, to embrace the identity of the Jewish outsider. He has described himself as "always in exile, always homeless," noting that "if one is Jewish, one doesn't really have a place anywhere." He has also referred to himself as the "quintessential wandering Jew." This concept can easily be overused, but in Libeskind's case it is appropriate. Between arriving in America in 1959 and the turn of the millennium, Libeskind moved fourteen times—a pace that rivaled the peripatetic early years of Louis I. Kahn. While emphatically a Jew, Libeskind does not intend his Jewish identity to be all-encompassing. He has said that he "hated being pigeonholed as a 'Jewish architect.'" Yet unlike Eisenman, who also bristled at that description, Libeskind has been more willing to entertain it as a possibility. When asked if he considered himself a "Jewish architect," Libeskind answered: "There is a Jewish dimension to my life in general. It's in my life, [so] how can I do something foreign to that?" He has further noted, "Being a Jewish architect means that I bring to my work a way of understanding the world that has to do with humanity and how human beings are related to one another." And he concludes, "My sensibility is a Jewish sensibility, whether I'm building an apartment in Korea or building a Jewish museum in San Francisco."[59]

Libeskind's Early Career

Libeskind's early work did not exhibit overt Jewish traits. Indeed, during the first phase of his career, he shied away from building altogether in favor of writing, teaching, and theorizing. In 1965, Libeskind enrolled at the Cooper Union for the Advancement of Science and Art in New York, where he studied architecture with a variety of professors, including Peter Eisenman. Libeskind graduated in 1970 but decided not to practice immediately, preferring to study architectural theory at the University of Essex in England, where he received a master's degree in 1972. After returning to America he took several jobs in architectural firms but was unsatisfied with his options for creative expression. He returned to teaching, holding down several university positions in the mid-1970s before being appointed the head of the architecture department at the Cranbrook Academy of Art in Michigan in 1978. Libeskind stayed at Cranbrook until 1985, when he left for Italy and founded an experimental school called Architecture Intermundium in Milan. The restless and highly intellectual trajectory of Libeskind's career during this period echoed that of Peter Eisenman's in that he spent far more time theorizing than building. Yet Libeskind's work in these years was even more radical. Fourteen years Eisenman's junior, Libeskind was too young to have experienced the euphoric climate that defined modernism's early postwar heyday; instead, he began studying architecture only when its principles were coming under widespread attack during the countercultural years of the 1960s and early 1970s.

From the early 1970s to the late 1980s, Libeskind produced a wide range of architectural drawings, collages, models, and sculptures, in addition to a series of passionately written, if highly cryptic, essays. Much of this work was abstract and reflected the influence of dadaism and surrealism. Collages such as *Plegma* (1978), nonsensical wordplay poems such as "Energia Iaener," and nonfunctioning "architectural machines" were far removed from the typical work of most architects and were not intended to have real-world applications. Instead, they displayed a nihilistic quality that seemed to question the very discipline of architecture. In an essay entitled "End Space," which appeared in his 1981 book *Between Zero and Infinity,* Libeskind wrote obscurely of his desire "to recover modes of awareness quite removed from the initial hypothesis of rationality" and seemed, like Eisenman, to condemn both the shortcomings of modernism and postmodernism. Later proclamations that the "very word [architecture] has lost its reputation," that the "everyday architect is dead," and that "architecture has entered its end" testified to Libeskind's dissatisfaction with the state of the profession. Unlike Eisenman, however, Libeskind neither spelled out the basis of his complaint nor his recommendations for the future. In preferring poetry to punditry, Libeskind already was displaying some of the elusive traits that became hallmarks of his deconstructivist sensibility.[60]

Libeskind exhibited signs of this sensibility in the first work that brought him widespread attention—his architectural drawings, entitled *Micromegas*. Made in 1979, these intricate drawings displayed Libeskind's commitment to challenging the foundations of western architectural practice. His minutely detailed compositions of colliding geometric forms, angled planes, and fragmented lines abandoned conventional notions of perspective and resisted easy interpretation (fig. 84). By denying observers a fixed perspective from which to make rational sense of them, the drawings expressed the decentered, post-humanist view of the world espoused by postmodern theorists at the time. The *Micromegas'* post-humanist quality was further visible in the drawings' total disregard of architectural function. Whereas architecture traditionally served human needs, the *Micromegas* contained forms without identifiable functions. The drawings' radical separation of form and function prompted Peter Eisenman to describe them admiringly as "not-architecture" and seemed to answer his call for a "post-functionalist" approach to building. Libeskind's description of them as "deconstructive constructions" further revealed that he was sympathetic to Eisenman's theories. At this time, of course, the notion of deconstructivist architecture had not yet been conceived, and Libeskind—like Eisenman—did not see himself as part of a burgeoning movement. Yet, in displaying a suspicion of modern reason, a rejection of traditional architectural form and function, and a penchant for cryptic poetry, Libeskind's work displayed clear signs of an incipient deconstructivist mentality.[61]

Libeskind's Jewish Turn and the Legacy of the Holocaust

The clearest sign of this mentality, however, was Libeskind's growing tendency to invoke the Holocaust in his architectural writings. These references first surfaced in 1983 when he published a new set

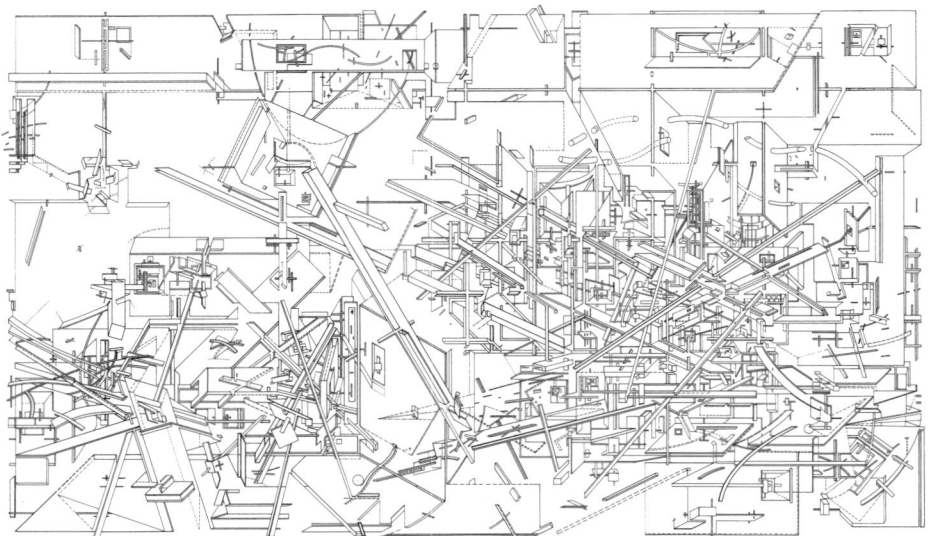

Figure 84. Daniel Libeskind, *Micromegas,* 1979. These drawings of colliding forms, planes, and lines abandoned traditional architectural notions of perspective and function.

of architectural drawings, entitled *Chamber Works*. They were similar to the *Micromegas* in their nonfigurative portrayal of colliding lines, shapes, and forms. But they were noticeably darker in tone, featuring dense masses that came to resemble black holes where they came together (fig. 85). The drawings also contained much more empty white space, which contrasted sharply with the dark masses adjacent to it. Moreover, the space of the drawings shrank as the series progressed, ending with extremely narrow, fragmented lines that resembled Alberto Giacometti's impossibly thin early postwar sculptures. Far more important than the aesthetic features of Libeskind's drawings, however, was his decision to cite the Holocaust in explaining their significance. At the text's beginning, Libeskind quoted an exchange between a Holocaust survivor and an interviewer recording her oral history:

> "What do you suppose that white line in the sky that you saw from the crack in the cattle car on your way to Stutthof really was?" the interviewer asked Elaine some thirty years later in her Brooklyn home.
> "You see, in order to survive you must believe in something, you need a source of inspiration, of courage, . . . something to overcome reality. The line was my source of inspiration, my sign from heaven.
> "Many years later, after liberation, when my children were growing up, I realized that the white line might have been fumes from a passing airplane's exhaust pipe, but does it really matter?"[62]

This introductory quotation bore little relation to the remainder of Libeskind's essay, which was a bleak meditation on architecture's lost promise. As he poetically, if opaquely, declared: "When the once potent truth of Architecture is reduced to a sign of its absence," then "the practice of Architecture becomes the case of the false pleading the cause of reconciliation." This remark, together with his reference to a "return to the Unoriginal," suggests that Libeskind, like Eisenman before him, was criticizing the derivative architectural movement of postmodernism. Yet Libeskind also seemed to

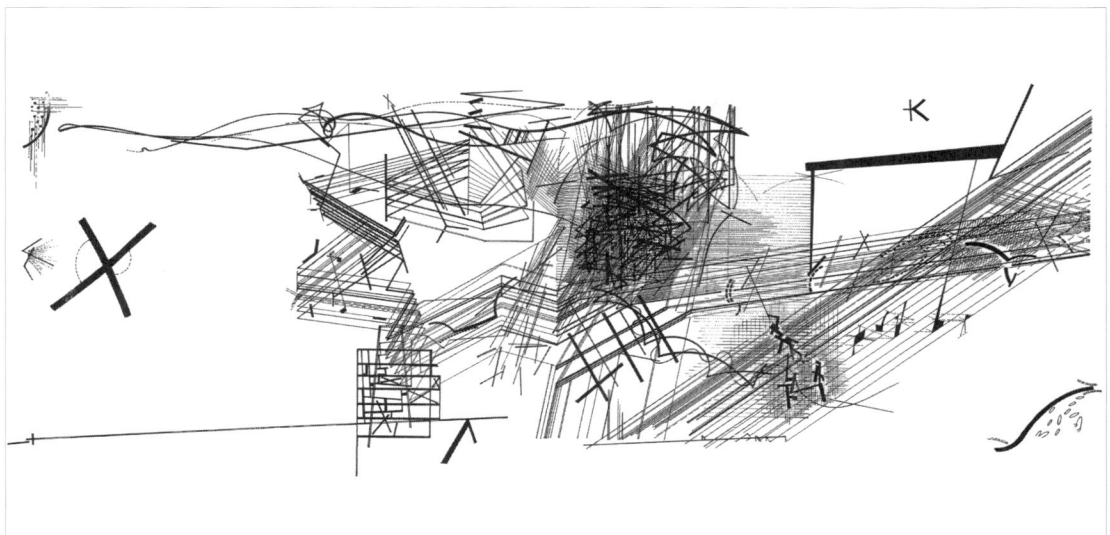

Figure 85. Daniel Libeskind, *Chamber Works,* Daniel Libeskind, 1983. These nonfigurative drawings were darker in tone than the *Micromegas*.

take aim at the bankruptcy of modernism, writing: "Night is sinking on realities that have had their Day, one can still hear some lamenting a vanishing present." For Libeskind, architecture's inability to renew itself by seeking sustenance either in the past or the present seemed to have left it a "nonexistent reality" defined by little more than a "trail of hieroglyphs in space." This, in all probability, was the intended message behind the *Chamber Works*' indecipherable forms.

Libeskind was vague in outlining the causes of architecture's present-day predicament, but, like Eisenman, he subtly attributed part of it to the traumas of the Nazi era. His description of "architecture as a practice of control" that had produced "truths . . . in space" resembling the "very ones that have been inscribed upon the flesh" — like his observation that the act of "inscription" had "[been performed] in the twentieth century . . . with all manner of precise instruments, including knives" — invoked both the Nazis' architectural policies and their tattooing of concentration camp prisoners. Similarly, his conclusion that architects had created great "disorder" by "having followed Orders" alluded to the common excuse cited by Nazi war criminals at their postwar trials.[63] Such historically inflected comments seem to have been intended to cast doubt on the prospects for traditional architectural practice in the post-Holocaust world. And yet Libeskind was unwilling to succumb to despair. By beginning his essay with the hopeful words of a Holocaust survivor he seemed to hold out the possibility of redemption. In the end, Libeskind probably meant his *Chamber Works* drawings to be read on two levels. Even if the trail of hieroglyphs symbolized a fragmenting world without meaning, they could also be seen — like the trail of white lines in the sky recalled by the Holocaust survivor — as beacons of hope to those architects who were perceptive enough to recognize their redemptive significance.

It is uncertain why Libeskind began to invoke the Holocaust in the early 1980s. His family background certainly made him more inclined than other Jewish architects to examine the Holocaust's architectural ramifications. But Libeskind has denied there was any particular catalyst for his deepening interest in the event, emphasizing that it has long "shaped how I think about things." "I did not come to [be interested in] the . . . Holocaust in any artificial way," he has noted. "I never thought about it so consciously. . . . It wasn't [as though I chose it as] my theme. It was just a part of the world I grew up in" as the "son of survivors." This claim notwithstanding, the concurrent growth of Holocaust consciousness in the U.S. likely encouraged him to express in public thoughts that he had harbored privately. Also playing a role was Libeskind's anger about Leon Krier's rehabilitation of Albert Speer during the German Architects' Debate in the early 1980s — a "reactionary" development that Libeskind has said influenced his later work in Berlin. Finally, Libeskind's invocation of the Holocaust was influenced by Eisenman's ideas about the need to rethink architectural practice in the wake of Auschwitz. In an essay published in 1984 entitled "Peter Eisenman and the Myth of Futility," Libeskind criticized Eisenman's claim that the Holocaust provided the grounds for renouncing architecture's traditional desire to base its legitimacy in myths, arguing that this claim risked becoming a new myth in and of itself. As he put it, "[Eisenman's notion of] decomposition . . . has a directionality and a goal, however unable one is to articulate this teleology in anything but a mythical form." This response clearly showed Libeskind to be in disagreement with Eisenman about Auschwitz's architectural legacy, but his willingness to engage the topic whatsoever reflected his belief that the Nazi genocide had implications worth considering.[64]

Libeskind's interest in the Holocaust became more explicit later in the decade. The precipitating factor was his move to Europe in 1985 and his ensuing entry into several architectural competitions in Germany. The challenge of building in Germany, especially in the divided city of Berlin, forced Libeskind, like Eisenman, to confront the nation's Nazi past and his own feelings about the Holocaust.[65] Libeskind addressed the Holocaust's legacy in the first competition that he won, Berlin's City Edge competition of 1987. For this unrealized design, which was part of the IBA exhibition of that same year, Libeskind took the Berlin Wall as his point of inspiration. His design featured a five-hundred-foot-long apartment complex (known as the "bar") that was horizontally hoisted on stilts and rose to a height of ten stories along the Flottwellstrasse several blocks from the Wall (fig. 86). The design, which ignored the traditional block structure of its Tiergarten neighborhood, was meant to symbolize the Berlin Wall's disruptive power.[66] By directing attention toward the city's most famous historic wound and, by extension, to its origins in Germany's defeat and division, Libeskind refused to efface the scars of German history as had been attempted by other, more revivalist postmodern works at the IBA by Charles Moore, Robert A. M. Stern, and Rob Krier.

This decision reflected Libeskind's commitment to remembering the legacy of the Holocaust. In refusing to follow the IBA's preference for reconstruction, he noted: "I suggested not rebuilding. I believe the Holocaust is not something you can get away from. The placelessness [of Berlin] should not be bemoaned."[67] Instead of trying to create the illusion of a healed world on scarred ground, Libeskind expressed his commitment to confronting Berlin's Nazi past. This was visible in his design's accompanying text, in which he wrote: "Erased Line: Historical Axis.... Edge, limit, delusion. Speer's ordered disorder. Underneath the ground, the city traces is own schizoid memory and protects it by insulating and covering the site. What is unforgotten cannot be eradicated, concealed."[68] This remark alluded to Speer's megalomaniacal plan for a North-South Axis in the heart of Berlin, which would have run along the Flottwellstrasse right past the site of Libeskind's proposal. The architect's

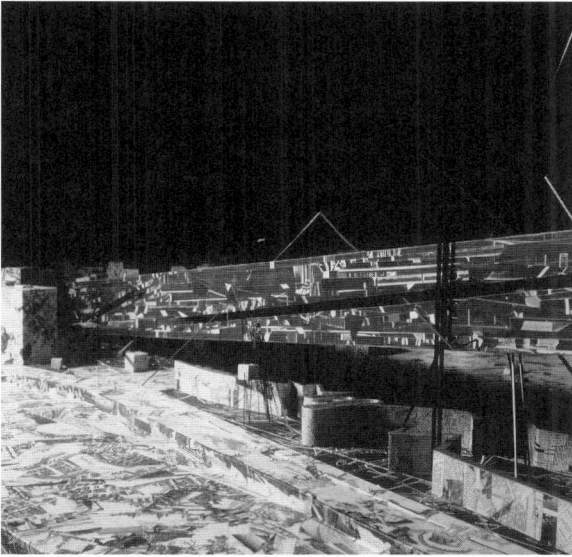

Figure 86. Daniel Libeskind, City Edge proposal, Berlin, 1987. This radical plan featured a five-hundred-foot-long apartment complex perched on stilts near Nazi architect Albert Speer's proposed North-South Axis.

decision to align his elevated bar roughly parallel to Speer's North-South Axis directed attention to the site's Nazi past and highlighted the need for remembrance. Given that German historic preservationists had recently excavated the remnants of the Gestapo Headquarters on the former Prinz-Albrecht-Strasse several blocks away (displayed prominently in the "Topography of Terror" exhibition), Libeskind's effort to direct attention to the site's underground past fit the era's mood.[69] For the first time, he embraced what would become a trademark of his work, a site-specific reference to local history through abstract rather than neohistoricist methods. In so doing he declared his commitment to an architecture of memory.

From Museums to Memorials: Libeskind's Holocaust-Related Buildings
In 1988, Libeskind seized on a career-changing opportunity to further develop his architectural philosophy by entering the competition for what was then called the Extension to the Berlin Museum with Jewish Museum Department. His proposal for what later became known as the Jewish Museum of Berlin was extremely unorthodox. Typed on music paper and entitled "Between the Lines," it contained multiple allusions to history, music, and philosophy and included symbolic justifications for its unconventional form. Libeskind's plan for the museum was based on two intersecting lines: a dominant one in the form of an unbroken zigzag, and a secondary one that was straight but broken where it intersected with the zigzag's gaps (fig. 87). The zigzag line determined the museum's external appearance, which, seen from above, resembled a disassembled Star of David or an SS-style lightning bolt. The museum's interior was determined by the relationship between the zigzag and the straight line. Where the latter intersected with the former, the two lines exposed a void, which became the building's central thematic conceit. As Libeskind explained it, "The idea is very simple:

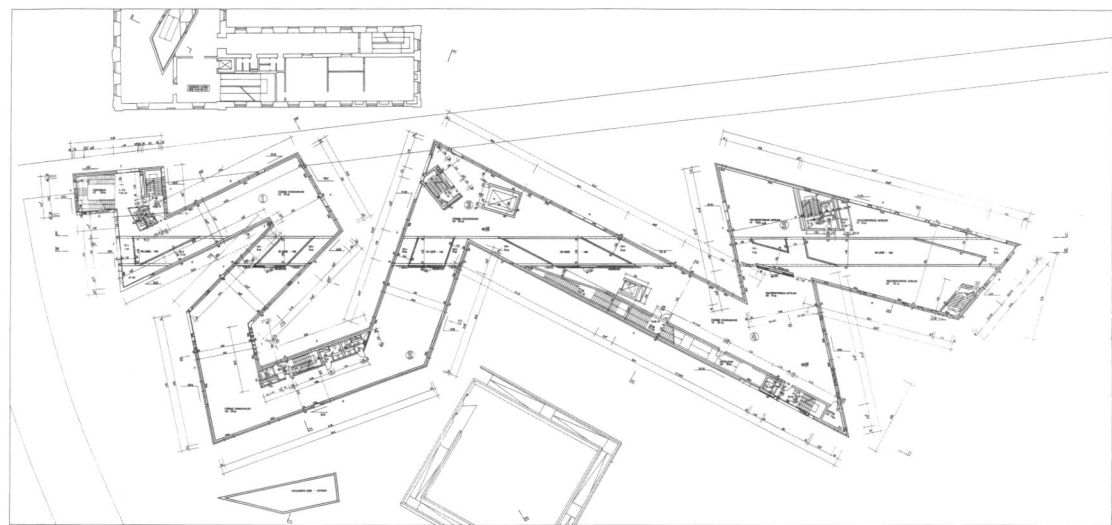

Figure 87. Daniel Libeskind, Berlin Jewish Museum, plan, 1988. Entitled "Between the Lines," the plan featured a dominant line in the form of an unbroken zigzag and a straight line that was broken where it intersected with the zigzag's gaps. The spaces formed by the latter line were part of what Libeskind called the "void" and symbolized Berlin's absent Jews.

to build the museum around a void that runs through it, a void that is to be experienced by the public. Physically, very little remains of the Jewish presence in Berlin. . . . I thought therefore that this 'void' . . . should become the structural feature that is crystallized in this particular space of the city." Libeskind added other historical and philosophical justifications for his design, including an "irrational matrix" of intersecting lines derived from the street addresses of prominent Berlin Jews; Arnold Schoenberg's unfinished opera *Moses and Aaron;* Walter Benjamin's book *One-Way Street (Einbahnstrasse)*; and the Memorial Book (*Gedenkbuch*) of Berlin Jews who were deported to die in the Nazi camps. Libeskind left vague how these sources of inspiration actually determined the building's design. But his plan clearly revealed that the edifice was profoundly shaped by the Holocaust's legacy.[70]

Libeskind's proposal also made clear that he viewed the Holocaust from a postmodern perspective. Like Eisenman, he interpreted the Nazi genocide as a specific byproduct of Enlightenment rationality. This view was evident in his claim that the "best works of the contemporary spirit come from the irrational, while what prevails in the world, what dominates and often kills, does so always in the name of reason." It was also echoed in his observation that the "Jewish history of Berlin is not separable from the history of modernity, from the destiny of this incineration of history." Libeskind agreed with Eisenman's deconstructivist idea that architecture could no longer provide comfort, centeredness, and stability in a postmodern, post-Holocaust world. Describing the Jewish museum as the "first truly decentered building," Libeskind argued that it rejected logical organization because "any sense we might try and make out of the world . . . only gives us a 'false sense of security.'" Instead, he emphasized the museum's fragmented character, noting in his proposal that "fragmentation and splintering mark the coherence of the ensemble." This design element was best seen in the voids that ran, like the "broken backbone of society," throughout the building. In a move befitting the deconstructivist desire to unearth the repressed within modernist architecture, the voids were to possess no functions and to remain empty, symbolizing nothing but themselves.[71]

Although Libeskind's proposal exhibited numerous hallmarks of a deconstructivist sensibility, it was also distinguished by its strong moral commitment to preserving memory. This stance was determined by the German context in which Libeskind began to build. When he entered the competition for the Berlin Jewish Museum in 1988, the Germans had not yet acquired their current reputation for owning up to the crimes of the Nazi era. In the late 1980s, conservative Germans—many associated with the government of Chancellor Helmut Kohl—were actively striving to create a normal sense of national identity by relativizing the crimes of the Nazi era. The international controversies sparked by the Bitburg Affair of 1985 and the Historians' Debate of 1986–87 revealed that influential Germans were not prepared to accept the full burden of the Holocaust's legacy. The intense debate about how to remember Germany's Nazi past explains why Libeskind pointedly declared that his proposal sought "to reconnect . . . Berlin to its own eradicated memory, which should not be camouflaged, disowned or forgotten." Libeskind saw many distressing signs that the Germans had already begun to forget the Third Reich's crimes. He claimed that the original name for the Jewish museum project—Jewish Department (Jüdische Abteilung)—evoked the name of Eichmann's Jewish Department in the SS and was thus a sign of the Germans' historical amnesia.

He also expressed unease about the euphoria that accompanied the collapse of the Berlin Wall and German reunification in 1989–90, saying that the "huge crowds of Germans wandering the streets brought back terrifying associations from the past." Libeskind worried how "German history [would] be regarded" and whether there would be a "further forgetting, a greater distancing" from it. He was especially fearful of this possibility after Berlin's building director, Hans Stimmann, mandated a conservative style of architecture, rooted in neoclassical principles, for new projects in Berlin. Libeskind had reason to fear Stimmann when the latter dismissed his Jewish museum plan as an "architectural fart" and declared, "I'm sick and tired of all this Jewish history. We've got too much Jewish history in Berlin as it is. We don't need any more." The Berlin senate's attempt to cancel the project in 1993 for lack of funding underscored Libeskind's conviction that the museum was crucial for didactic purposes.[72]

In the end, Libeskind triumphed. He helped his own cause by publicly challenging Stimmann and Berlin's conservative architectural establishment about their approach to rebuilding the city. In a move that intensified the second phase of the Architects' Debate, he argued that the city's reactionary architectural tendencies under Stimmann were rooted in an "authoritarian mood" and an "antidemocratic view of society," both of which were part of an overall "atmosphere that resembles the pathology of a time in which the notion of degenerate art was born." Libeskind's shrewd playing of the fascism card, like his subsequent effort to organize an international letter-writing campaign on his behalf, were important in getting the museum's funding reapproved. At a time in which rising neo-Nazi violence against Jews and foreigners had made German political elites deeply concerned about their nation's image, the Jewish museum project implicitly became a litmus test of Germany's post-unification political reliability.[73]

When the building was finished in 1999, it vividly expressed Libeskind's vision of an architecture of memory. One of the museum's defining features — and one that has become a hallmark of many of the architect's subsequent buildings — was its confrontational relationship with the building next to it. The Jewish Museum was originally conceived as an extension of the city museum, which was housed in an early eighteenth-century baroque building known as the Kollegienhaus (fig. 88). Libeskind made little effort to adapt his design to its historical context (as nostalgia-minded postmodernists would have) and instead strove for extreme contrast. The Jewish Museum was clad not in stone but in shimmering zinc. It did not stand parallel to the street line but abutted it at an acute angle. It also abandoned other architectural conventions, such as a front entrance. Libeskind forced visitors to enter the Jewish Museum by first proceeding through the existing city museum, which was connected to it via an underground passageway. This subterranean approach was part of Libeskind's strategy of highlighting the connectedness of German and Jewish history and preparing visitors for an architectural experience deeply influenced by the violent history of the Nazi era. After entering Libeskind's museum wing, visitors ascend a long staircase and walk through slanted hallways with canted walls and oddly angled windows. At various junctures they can peer into the museum's seven voids, some of which, such as the "memory void," they can physically enter (fig. 89).[74] The most dramatic void is detached from the main museum — an empty eighty-foot-high "Holocaust tower" (called a "voided void" by Libeskind) — that is entirely dark except for a shaft of

Figure 88. Berlin Jewish Museum, aerial view. The zinc-clad Jewish museum contrasts sharply with the original Berlin city museum, located in the eighteenth-century Kollegienhaus, at right. The path of the void is marked by the parallel lines on the museum's roof. The disembodied gray concrete volume at the top left is the Holocaust tower.

Figure 89. Berlin Jewish Museum, interior. The "memory void" is one of the museum's seven voids.

The Deconstructivists

light that enters through a vertical sliver near the top of the exterior wall. All these voids, like the disjointed spaces through which visitors approached them, are meant to instill a sense of disorientation analogous to that perceived by Jews in the Holocaust. The Jewish Museum's narrative drama, however, takes place in its exterior as well. The building's zinc facade is slashed with numerous black diagonal lines, suggesting violent incisions, with those on the main facade taking the form of a distorted Star of David. Multiple crosses puncturing the facade, meanwhile, raise the issue of Christianity's role in the Holocaust.[75]

The initial response to Libeskind's museum was euphoric. The building's opening in 1999 drew 350,000 people even though its permanent exhibition had not yet been installed and the interior space was entirely empty. From this point until the evening of September 9, 2001, when it was formally dedicated, the museum received nonstop attention. Leading architecture journals in the United States and Europe profiled the building on their covers, while prominent architecture critics praised it in adulatory reviews. Martin Filler described the museum as a place of "immense psychological and emotional impact" and lauded it as the "definitive statement on the Holocaust in architectural form." Herbert Muschamp called it "as vital a cultural expression of this time as an architecture critic can hope to find." And Nicolai Ouroussoff said that Libeskind's building had "succeeded spectacularly" and predicted that it would "endure as an important work of art."[76]

After the building opened to the public on September 11, 2001, however, more skeptical voices were heard. Certain critics argued that the installation of the exhibition in the previously empty building exposed its shortcomings as a museum, complaining that its awkwardly angled spaces were ill suited for display. Others griped about the exhibition's content, claiming that it provided German visitors with an all-too-easy opportunity to expose themselves to a "lite" version of the Jewish past and feel virtuous about helping to come to terms with the nation's Nazi legacy. Still others bristled at the inclusion of didactic texts bluntly telling visitors what reactions the architect expected them to have. Especially in the wake of Libeskind's 2003 victory in the competition for Ground Zero in Lower Manhattan, more than a few disenchanted critics began to refer to the Jewish Museum's symbolic features as "kitschy." Indeed, many wished that the building had been left empty as an abstract, de facto Holocaust memorial.[77]

This criticism notwithstanding, the Berlin Jewish Museum was crucial for establishing Libeskind's reputation as one of the world's most promising architects. The attention that he received paved the way for other commissions, many of which had a Jewish focus. Some were for museums and memorials related to the Holocaust. Others were for synagogues, Jewish schools, and community centers. In pursuing these projects, Libeskind confirmed his reputation as a Jewish architect who was committed to developing a new form of Jewish architectural expression.

Libeskind's next major project was the Felix Nussbaum museum in Osnabrück, Germany. Completed in 1998, the building had a clear Jewish focus, being devoted to chronicling the life and work of Nussbaum, a German Jewish painter and Holocaust victim.[78] As with his Jewish Museum, Libeskind aggressively placed the museum next to an existing edifice, Osnabrück's Museum of Cultural History (fig. 90), which served as a foil to his radical structure. The Felix Nussbaum-Haus, as it is formally called, is composed of three linear structures that intersect with one another at sharp angles: the first is a wood-clad structure called the Nussbaum House that displays Nussbaum's pre-1933 works

Figure 90. Daniel Libeskind, Felix Nussbaum Haus, 1998, aerial view. The museum is composed of three rectangular volumes: the Nussbaum House, center right; the shorter Nussbaum Bridge to its left; and the long, thin Nussbaum Passage. These volumes are aggressively situated next to Osnabrück's neoclassical Museum of Cultural History. The Nussbaum Passage points accusingly at the Villa Schlikker (top left), which was Nazi party headquarters during the Third Reich.

The Deconstructivists 191

and lies on an axis pointing admonishingly toward the site of Osnabrück's Rolandstrasse synagogue (destroyed on Kristallnacht). The second is a metal volume, called the Nussbaum Bridge, that is a suspended structure abutting the Museum of Cultural History and devoted to temporary exhibitions. The third structure, made of concrete and known as the Nussbaum Passage, is an extremely long and narrow space (a mere seven feet wide and over a hundred and fifty feet long) that displays Nussbaum's last paintings. Like the Berlin Museum's voids, this volume is the museum's defining symbolic space. Windowless and cramped, it gives visitors a sense of the claustrophobic circumstances under which Nussbaum painted while hiding from the Nazis. A range of other subtle design features — such as the Passage's spearlike thrust against another building on the site, the neoclassical Villa Schlikker, which once served as the city's Nazi party headquarters — further serve Libeskind's goal of fighting "against forgetting."[79]

Around the same time as he was working on the Osnabrück museum, Libeskind deepened his engagement with the Holocaust's legacy in two other unrealized projects in Germany. In 1993 he entered a competition to redesign the immense grounds of the Sachsenhausen concentration camp outside Berlin, submitting a proposal that opposed the plan to turn the site into a residential and commercial district. Arguing that the "former . . . death camp cannot be hidden or detached from . . . its historic context," he proposed tearing down the camp's crumbling Nazi buildings and flooding the site with water. He envisioned dikes upon which visitors could walk and gaze upon the camp's flooded ruins. And he proposed a long row of buildings housing various public services, whose placement at a sharp angle to the original site would disrupt its "monumental central axis" and undermine its authoritarian symmetry. Libeskind's plan drew considerable attention, but its radical thrust was opposed by historic preservationists and led to its defeat.[80] This was also true of Libeskind's entry in the 1998 competition for Germany's central Holocaust memorial in Berlin. Entitled "StoneBreath," his design featured six externalized voids — massive concrete monoliths perforated by gaping holes — that he described as the "precise solidification of the Void running through . . . the Jewish Museum." The forms were striking, yet Libeskind's convoluted explanation of their derivation and the fact that his Jewish Museum (then under construction) was already viewed as a Holocaust memorial in and of itself kept him from winning the competition. Still, these two projects helped Libeskind further refine his architectural strategy for confronting the Holocaust.[81]

Throughout these early Holocaust-related projects, Libeskind's architecture predictably tended toward the somber. His buildings' colliding volumes, slashed facades, and disorienting spaces — not to mention their elaborate historical and philosophical justifications — lent his work an overall feeling of rupture. His commitment to exploring such intangible concepts as absence, loss, and what he memorably described in the case of the Nussbaum museum as "the darkness, the inarticulateness, the opacity, and that which cannot become analysis," made his work intellectually challenging as well. For these reasons Libeskind's buildings pertaining to the Holocaust have been described as "antiredemptory" works of architecture that "never allow . . . memory . . . to congeal into singular, salvational meaning."[82]

Still, Libeskind's architecture resisted total despair and held out the possibility of hope. Beginning with the introductory text to his *Chamber Works* drawings of 1983, Libeskind injected expressions of optimism into all of his projects during the 1980s and 1990s. He described the flying beam of his

1987 Berlin City Edge submission, for example, as an "axis of Universal Hope." He described the projected "bar" of buildings in his Sachsenshausen memorial proposal as the "Hope Incision," while noting that the camp's flooded grounds would be the "site of a new baptism." He declared that his Felix Nussbaum museum testified to the "survival of the Jewish people and of European civilization." And his inclusion of soil from both Germany and Israel in his labyrinthine E. T. A. Hoffmann garden outside the Berlin Jewish Museum held out the possibility of reconciliation between Germans and Jews. The optimistic aspects of these Holocaust projects show that while Libeskind was committed to commemorating the past, he did not want it to block the way to the future.[83]

From Despair to Hope: Libeskind's Affirmative Jewish Architecture

After the mid-1990s, Libeskind's latent faith in hope found more explicit expression in new designs for synagogues and Jewish museums. In these projects Libeskind strove to develop a distinctly Jewish form of architectural expression. He did not pursue this goal naively, admitting that "there is no such thing as Jewish architecture." At the same time, he maintained that "there is an intuition about what makes spaces have a Jewish character. Usually it's something that is different [from the architecture of other religions]."[84] In these new projects, Libeskind tried to define that difference. His designs, whether completed or not, showed the possibility of creating Jewish architecture that moved beyond anonymous modernism and derivative postmodernism. They embraced a positive sense of Jewishness that acknowledged the Holocaust but were not brought down by its magnitude.

Libeskind articulated this agenda in two unrealized designs for synagogues in the German cities of Duisburg and Dresden. Both designs were assertively Jewish in their philosophical rationales and aesthetic form. Declaring that "new synagogue[s] today should reflect an optimism and independence of Jewish culture amid its neighbors," Libeskind planned his synagogues as physically prominent structures to show that they were now "part of the town and no longer [had to be] hidden behind other buildings." The Duisburg synagogue derived its form from the Hebrew letter Aleph, its three component parts—its head, body, and foot—housing the complex's foyer, sanctuary, and school (fig. 91). Connecting the latter two structures was a two-story library designed in the form

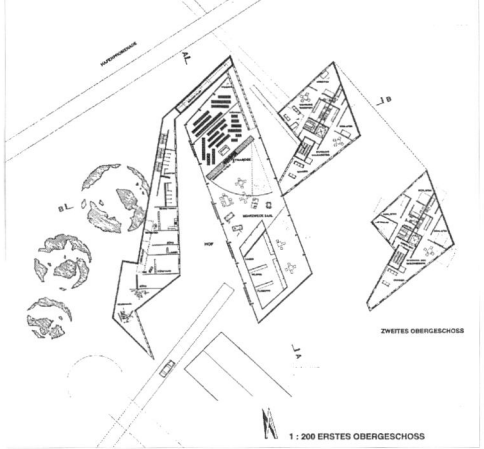

Figure 91. Daniel Libeskind, synagogue, Duisburg, Germany, 1996. The synagogue's spaces are formed by the separate parts of the Hebrew letter Aleph.

of an upright, open book, a form that affirmed the historic importance of education in supporting the "Jewish people's tradition across the desert of assimilation and annihilation." This gesture showed that the project was meant to be a hopeful marker of the "rebirth of the Jewish community" in Germany.[85] The Dresden design was equally hopeful, its ground plan being based on the Star of David in memory of the one artifact that was salvaged from the ruins of the city's famed Semper synagogue after its destruction on Kristallnacht. Libeskind did not get the commission for either of these projects, which were completed by other architectural firms (see Chapter 11). Still, his designs showed the evolution of his effort to develop an affirmative form of Jewish architecture that was conscious of but transcended the Holocaust.[86]

The most important milestone in Libeskind's evolution as a creator of Jewish architecture was his proposal for the Contemporary Jewish Museum of San Francisco (1998–2008). Following Eisenman's departure from the project in 1996, Libeskind was hired on the strength of a design entitled "L'Chai'm: To Life." Libeskind's design derived from his Duisburg proposal, as its ground plan was again based on Hebrew letters: this time, Chet and Yud, which spell chai, or life, in Hebrew. As he explained, "In the Jewish tradition, letters are not mere signs but are substantial participants in the story they create. Thus the spatiality of chai—a fundamental emblem of Jewish life—will be experienced as a full dynamic movement responding to the many levels of interpretation this word possesses." The two letters are difficult to discern in the museum's interior and are more visible in plan. They did, however, provide the structure with its major volumes: two long, horizontal wings (evoking the twin legs of the Chet) housed the core exhibition spaces, education center, and auditorium; a smaller vertical space, symbolizing the Yud, contained a special events gallery. According to the Jewish numerological tradition known as gematria, Chet and Yud make up the number eighteen, a lucky number in traditional Judaism. Libeskind's placement of thirty-six windows in the Yud volume thus represented "double-chai."[87]

Libeskind's design displayed additional Jewish meanings. One of the most interesting stemmed from his penchant for designing additions that were starkly juxtaposed to older buildings. As with his museum designs in Berlin and Osnabrück, Libeskind's San Francisco museum penetrated into, and appeared to be erupting out of, an existing structure: the neoclassical red-brick Jessie Street Pacific Gas and Electric Power substation (see fig. 72). Unlike his German museums, however, Libeskind's plan effectively transformed the existing building while adding on to it, thereby turning it into a parabuilding. Architecture critic Nicolai Ouroussoff proposed that Libeskind's adaptation and simultaneous transformation of the original building was an apt metaphor "for the Jewish struggle with issues of identity and assimilation." James Young added that the building's "self-effacing" character and respect for its neighbors made it a "model for Jewish integration." For his part, Libeskind said that the project "was about . . . the contribution Jews have made to society at large and to the world." He also described the building as radiating a sense of Jewish space, noting: "Even for those who know nothing about Hebrew or Jewish culture, they'll feel it. . . . The space will communicate . . . quintessential Jewish sensibilities. They will feel the relationship to the past, the optimism toward the future." Whether or not visitors to the museum have felt all this is unclear. Those who read Hebrew have undoubtedly recognized the four giant letters—Pey, Resh, Dalet, and Samech—spelling the word pardes (meaning orchard or paradise) slashed diagonally into the main wall of the entry lobby. Others have probably viewed the slashes as mere decoration. Libeskind's hermetic design, however, articulated his conviction that a "Jewish museum . . . should be Jewish."[88]

Another affirmative design was Libeskind's Danish Jewish Museum in Copenhagen. Completed in 2004, the museum represented an exception in Libeskind's work. It was ostensibly a Holocaust-related project in that it chronicled the experience of Danish Jews during the Second World War. Yet since their experience was fortunate (a majority of Denmark's Jews were ferried to safety in Sweden in the fall of 1943), Libeskind was less inclined to use the same brooding narrative style that he did in Germany. The Danish Jewish Museum was also exceptional architecturally in being an interior remodeling of two existing buildings: the seventeenth-century Royal Boat House and the nineteenth-century neo-Renaissance Royal Library, both of which were originally built for the Danish monarchy. Despite the project's lower profile, Libeskind approached it with his usual arsenal of symbolic references, rationales, and concepts. The theme was taken from the Hebrew word "mitzvah." Meaning both a commandment and a good deed, the term aptly described the actions of certain Danes on behalf of their Jewish fellow citizens during the Holocaust. As in his Duisburg and San Francisco projects, Libeskind took the four Hebrew letters that composed the word "mitzvah" — Mem, Zadi, Vav, and Hay — and used them to organize the interior corridor. Libeskind further provided a Jewish interpretation of the new interior, comparing its presence within the older building's vaulted space to a Talmudic "text within a text." Libeskind also clad his interior walls with wood to evoke the wooden boats that transported Danish Jews to safety. Sloping walls and the absence of right angles in the building produced a dizzying effect evoking choppy seas (fig. 92).[89]

Figure 92. Daniel Libeskind, Danish Jewish Museum, Copenhagen, 2004. The museum's wood-clad, angular interior evokes the boats that ferried Danish Jews over choppy seas to Sweden in 1943.

The predominantly Jewish focus of Libeskind's work in the 1990s led some architects to question whether he was someone who could "only design 'Jewish' spaces." Perhaps to preempt these suppositions, Libeskind pursued a variety of other commissions, mostly for cultural institutions. Yet even in these projects he revealed a clear Jewish sensibility and a creative debt to the Holocaust. In his proposal for the reconstruction of Berlin's Potsdamer Platz in 1991, for example, he cited the deportation of famous Jews, such as Paul Celan, and abstract concepts like "absolute absence," to justify his refusal to pursue the "illusory 'reconstruction' of [Berlin's] past" in favor of "laying new foundations" for a "heterogeneous, pluralistic reality." Jewish religious ideas, meanwhile, informed his Imperial War Museum of the North in Manchester, England (1997–2001). Designed in the shape of a shattered globe that had been reassembled in new, distorted form, the building's three colliding volumes—an Earth Shard, Air Shard, and Water Shard, each symbolizing theaters of war—suggested the Kabbalistic notion of *tikkun olam,* restoring the broken vessels from God's act of creation.[90]

The most vivid example of Libeskind utilizing his Jewish-inspired architectural vocabulary in a non-Jewish project, however, was his master plan for Ground Zero in lower Manhattan. Libeskind's professional experiences in Berlin a decade earlier enabled him to submit the most powerful design for the site's reconstruction. Just as many Berliners had hoped to suppress their own painful past by erasing its presence in the cityscape through a conservative program of architectural construction, some New Yorkers had hoped to evade the memory of the terrorist attacks by rebuilding the site as quickly as possible. In the initial architectural competitions for the site in July and December 2002, the designs of Norman Foster, THINK, United Architects, and the "dream team" of Richard Meier, Peter Eisenman, Charles Gwathmey, and Steven Holl, banished the past by envisioning gleaming new towers on a site that was essentially a graveyard. By contrast, Libeskind acknowledged the recent past in architectural form. As he wrote in his autobiographical *Breaking Ground,* "So little [of the destruction] was being conveyed by the architecture itself. Almost three thousand people had died, and we were treating the site of the tragedy as a tabula rasa, a clean slate to be filled with fashionable buildings." What was needed, he declared, "was a dramatic, unexpected, spiritual insight into vulnerability, tragedy, and our loss. And we need something that is hopeful."[91]

Libeskind's design, entitled "Memory Foundations," combined elements of his narrative architecture of commemoration with features of his increasingly ascendant architecture of hope. His master stroke was to preserve the World Trade Center's so-called slurry wall, an enormous concrete container that kept the Hudson River from flooding the site (fig. 93). For Libeskind, the slurry wall—which had been physically exposed by the twin towers' collapse—was not just an engineering barrier against nature but a symbolic barrier "against chaos and destruction" that simultaneously "seemed to attest . . . to the unshakable foundations of democracy." Having descended into Ground Zero's pit for commemoration, Libeskind's architectural vision ascended into the sky for inspiration. He envisioned five skyscrapers for the site, the tallest of which—known as the Freedom Tower—was invested with explicitly patriotic symbolism. At 1,776 feet high, in honor of the year of America's independence, the tower was an abstract Statue of Liberty, its off-center rooftop television antenna echoing Lady Liberty's upright arm and torch (see fig. 3). Libeskind's inclusion of gardens in the tower's upper portion "as a confirmation of life" underscored its affirmative message. Finally, his plan for Ground Zero envisioned a plaza called the "Wedge of Light," whose boundaries, he claimed, were formed by the position of the sun's rays at the precise times that the towers were respectively attacked and collapsed.⁹²

The story of how Libeskind's design won the competition for the World Trade Center site has been recounted elsewhere. His victory instantly made him a household name. Libeskind's design was popular among ordinary New Yorkers who wanted to see the destruction of 9/11 suitably commemorated. It also earned praise from architecture critics and gained him the fawning attention of the media, which raced to celebrate him—as *Time* magazine did in 2003—as "architecture's next star." Yet, as is so often true in American celebrity culture, Libeskind's placement atop an architectural pedestal inspired a backlash. Many critics who had praised his work in Berlin now stridently criticized his Ground Zero proposal. Muschamp decried it as a "demagogic" and "aggressive . . . war memorial" that bore an "Orwellian" similarity to the Bush administration's pursuit of peace through war. Filler suggested that Libeskind was beginning to act like an "entrepreneur of commemoration" and was in danger of becoming a "human Yahrzeit candle." Behind the scenes, Libeskind's stature was quietly being eroded. As a result of business decisions by the site's leaseholder and developer, Larry Silverstein, Libeskind was forced into an arranged marriage with Silverstein's preferred architect, David Childs of Skidmore Owings and Merrill, in 2003, and before long a new plan was adopted without much of Libeskind's original symbolism.

Figure 93. Daniel Libeskind, slurry wall, 2003. By exposing the World Trade Center's surviving slurry wall in his 2003 Memory Foundations proposal, Libeskind laid bare the 9/11 attacks' destructive legacy.

This setback notwithstanding, Libeskind's plan for Ground Zero was crucial for helping him refine his Jewish-inspired architectural philosophy. In *Breaking Ground,* he connected his philosophy to his personal story, writing:

> As someone who was born in the post-Holocaust world to parents who were both Holocaust survivors, I bring that history to bear on my work. Because of who I am, I have thought a lot about matters like trauma and memory. Not the trauma of a singular catastrophe that can be overcome and healed, but a trauma that involves the destruction of a community. . . . As an immigrant, whose youth often felt displaced, I've sought to create a different architecture, one that reflects an understanding of history after world catastrophes. I find myself drawn to explore what I call the void—the presence of an overwhelming emptiness created when . . . the continuity of life is so brutally disrupted that the structure of life is forever torqued and transformed.

Libeskind rejected modern architects' evasion of the Holocaust. As he put it, "Mies van der Rohe, Walter Gropius, and the other great modernist masters argued that buildings should present a neutral face to the world, but theirs is a philosophy that feels almost quaint now. Neutral? After the . . . devastations of the twentieth century, is it possible to embrace an antiseptic reality?" Libeskind's answer was to design buildings that helped "confront our histories, our complicated and messy realities, our unadulterated emotions." Doing so, he said, would help "create an architecture for the twenty-first century."[93]

Since his Ground Zero plan, Libeskind has embarked upon many new projects. Some are cultural institutions, such as his Denver Art Museum (2000–2006) and Royal Ontario Museum in Toronto (2002–7). Others, such as his Ascent at Roebling's Bridge in Covington, Kentucky (2004–8), are commercial residential commissions. Still others, such as his addition to the Dresden Military History Museum (2001–11), are more commemorative in character and display his brooding narrative style.[94] The reception of these works has been generally positive, but there is little doubt that since 2003, Libeskind's reputation has come back down to earth. Some critics have become bolder about highlighting what they call the kitschy aspects of his architectural philosophy.[95] Other commentators have questioned whether "[an architectural] language of loss . . . should be replicated from city to city" in mainstream structures.[96]

Still, to view the architect as "The Incredible Shrinking Daniel Libeskind," as a 2004 *New York Times* headline proclaimed, is to misread his stature.[97] Libeskind remains one of the world's most recognized architects, and his services continue to be in high demand. More importantly, thanks to his efforts to ground his design philosophy in Jewish ideas, he has played a singular role in enhancing the Jewishness of contemporary Jewish architecture.

Frank Gehry

If Peter Eisenman can be seen as the father of deconstructivism and Daniel Libeskind its most explicitly Jewish practitioner, Frank Gehry is arguably its most reluctant representative. Despite being included in the MoMA "Deconstructivist Architecture" exhibition of 1988, Gehry never wanted to belong to a larger movement. He has also been less interested than Eisenman and Libeskind in crafting theoretical or symbolic justifications for his work. Gehry has preferred to labor as an expressive artist, devising formally inventive designs for his projects, many of which — such as his Guggenheim Museum in Bilbao, Spain — have earned widespread acclaim. Thanks to such buildings, Gehry has become one of the most famous architects in the world today. He is, by extension, also the most accomplished Jewish architect. His buildings, however, are less obviously "Jewish" in orientation than those of Eisenman and Libeskind. Gehry has worked on fewer Jewish-related architectural projects, whether Holocaust museums, synagogues, or Jewish museums. His buildings have also been less defined by historical symbolism, narrativity, and memory. Still, Gehry's work shares similar origins to that of Eisenman and Libeskind. He has long been conscious of his Jewish identity because of youthful experiences with antisemitism. He has also perceived himself to be a Jewish outsider and has responded similarly to this condition, rebelling against the cultural norms of his environment by drawing on his Jewish identity to fashion structures that break radically with tradition. Unlike Libeskind and Eisenman, however, Gehry has shied away from emphasizing the Holocaust's legacy in his work, preferring a more ironic method of expressing his Jewishness with idiosyncratic symbolic forms. That said, Gehry has not avoided the Holocaust entirely; both in interviews and recent projects he has shown a growing readiness to wrestle with its legacy. Albeit in belated fashion, Gehry has come to display a profile similar to that of Eisenman and Libeskind.

Early Gehry

When Gehry first began to practice architecture, his work displayed few signs of a Jewish sensibility. After graduating from the University of Southern California School of Architecture in 1954, he studied for a time at Harvard and then worked at various firms before going into practice for himself in Santa Monica in 1962. In this period Gehry pursued a wide range of residential and commercial projects, few of which attracted attention. Among his more distinguished works were his starkly cubic Danziger Studio and Residence in Hollywood (1964 – 65), his O'Neill Hay Barn in San Juan Capistrano (1968), his studio in Malibu for the artist Ron Davis (1972), and his Santa Monica Place shopping mall (1973 – 80) (fig. 94). These were modernist, functional projects that used inexpensive materials, such as corrugated metal, plywood, and chain-link fencing. None

Figure 94. Frank Gehry, Danziger Studio and Residence, Los Angeles, 1964 – 65. This minimalistic design epitomized the modernist phase of Gehry's career.

helped Gehry break through to major prominence. Indeed, it took him more than twenty years to earn widespread attention. In this, he resembled Louis I. Kahn, who completed many works but achieved little distinction until he reached his fifties. Before long, however, Gehry would make bold moves that helped him inherit Kahn's mantle as the next great "creative genius" of the American architectural profession.[98]

The first project that got him noticed — the one that helped get him classified as a deconstructivist architect — was his own house in Santa Monica (1977–78). This was a renovation project in which Gehry took a modest 1920s Dutch colonial house and wrapped a new addition around it (fig. 95). His design differed dramatically from conventional additions, however, for instead of blending the new with the old, it sharply juxtaposed them. Gehry used many of the unconventional materials he had employed since the late 1960s to contrast the addition from the original house: corrugated metal for the addition's front and side facades, raw plywood for interior walls and ceilings, and chain-link fencing on the second story. He also crafted disjointed and sharply angled forms that seemed to be exploding out of (or crashing into) the house, especially a wood-framed glass cube that doubled as a kitchen window and skylight. The result was a novel structure of unprecedented hybridity.

Figure 95. Frank Gehry, Gehry House, Santa Monica, 1977–78. In this project, Gehry wrapped a metal-clad addition around an existing Dutch colonial house, punctuating his design with sharply angled forms such as the wood-framed glass cube (center).

At the time, few observers knew how to interpret the Gehry House. Although its new sections displayed a modernist love of formal invention, the preserved 1920s structure rejected a modernist tabula rasa mentality. Further confusing matters was the fact that the addition avoided any nostalgic postmodern revivalism yet was seen as "representing a *de-construction* kind of gesture" and, thus, a postmodern philosophical spirit. This assessment seemed particularly true in light of the similarities between Gehry's work and that of Peter Eisenman. In describing his Santa Monica house in the mid-1980s, Gehry seemed to agree with Eisenman's opposition to traditional architectural stability and enclosure; when he explained his refusal to give a finished look to his house, he noted: "The very finished building has security and it's predictable. I wanted to try something different. I like playing at the edge of disaster." While Gehry's approach did not stem from the same sources as Eisenman's, the impression left by his buildings was similar. Architecture critic Kenneth Frampton's claim that Gehry's house was "subversive" of existing architectural practice and an example "anti-architecture" summarized many views at the time.[99]

Gehry extended his assault against conventional architectural practice in the early 1980s by exploding the modernist "dumb box." In a series of attention-grabbing projects, he broke his designs into separate volumes, usually in the form of distorted Platonic shapes, which he juxtaposed to create highly sculptural architectural ensembles.[100] This new fragmentation strategy was visible in his private house designs, such as the Wosk residence in Beverly Hills (1982–84) and the Winton Guest House in Wayzata, Minnesota (1983–86). It also influenced the villagelike Loyola University Law School (1978), the staid Frances Howard Goldwyn Regional Branch Library in Hollywood (1983–86), and the quirky Edgemar Development complex in Santa Monica (1984–88) (fig. 96). Although stylistically diverse, these projects displayed sufficient conceptual unity to earn Gehry widespread attention in the American and international media and led to his inclusion in MoMA's "Deconstructivist Architecture" exhibition. His receipt of the coveted Pritzker Prize in 1989 confirmed his status as one of the world's most accomplished architects.

Figure 96. Frank Gehry, Edgemar Development complex, Santa Monica, 1984–88. This shopping complex was a highly sculptural architectural ensemble made up of discrete forms and represented Gehry's assault against the modernist "dumb box." Note the ghost cube at center.

The Birth of a Deconstructivist: Gehry's Jewish Identity

Explaining the deconstructivist turn in Gehry's career is challenging. Unlike many of his colleagues, the architect has written very little about his work and has not articulated any architectural philosophy in written form. As Witold Rybczynski has pointed out, even when the comprehensive retrospective of his work, *Frank Gehry: The Complete Works,* appeared in 1998, the architect did not even contribute an epigram.[101] One reason for Gehry's comparative silence is his nontheoretical bent. Compared to Eisenman and Libeskind, he spent far more time working on actual projects and devoted less time to teaching and writing. Gehry has given numerous interviews over the years, however, in which he has discussed key influences on his career. One of the most important was his willingness to make a sculpturally expressive turn in his work, a move that itself was predicated on his growing self-conception as a rebellious Jewish outsider.

The roots of Gehry's sculptural turn can be traced to the mid-1960s, when he began to develop friendships with artists and sculptors, such as Ron Davis, Robert Irwin, Ed Ruscha, Claes Oldenburg, and Richard Serra. Gehry has confirmed their influence on his creativity, declaring in 1986 that the reason his "approach to architecture is different" was that he sought "out the work of artists and use[d] art as a means of inspiration." Gehry's artist friends prompted him to trust his improvisational instincts, and his work consequently became more experimental. His decision to explode the traditional box into separate objects, for example, was influenced by the early twentieth-century still-lifes of the Italian painter Giorgio Morandi, whose arrangements of bottles, fruit, and other objects were echoed in Gehry's juxtaposed structures.[102]

In displaying an openness to the work of artists and sculptors, Gehry showed himself to be comfortable operating on the margins of the architectural profession. As he noted in 1999, "I think of myself as an outsider. I felt at home with the artists. . . . I was intellectually intrigued with their process, their language . . . , their ability to make things with their own hands. . . . I was hands-on and felt more comfortable. I became more and more detached from the architecture world. . . . [The] architects [in Los Angeles] were treating me like Joe Idiot anyway." Gehry was the antithesis of the commercially oriented businessman-architect epitomized by Morris Lapidus. Although he worked for the shopping mall pioneer, Victor Gruen, at the outset of his career, he eventually set out on a more individualistic path. This maverick streak helps explain why Gehry eagerly embraced unconventional materials like chain-link fencing in his buildings. It is telling that the exhibition catalogue for his 1986 retrospective exhibition opened with the boldly self-confident epigraph: "Being accepted isn't everything."[103]

More significantly, Gehry's inclination to see himself as an outsider can be traced back to his Jewish background. Architecture historians have long been aware of the Jewish aspects of Gehry's architectural work. Thomas S. Hines, Charles Jencks, and others have pointed out how the architect's conflicted sense of Jewishness and resulting self-conception as an outsider fueled his creative rebellion against his profession's norms.[104] What few scholars have highlighted, however, is how Gehry's identity crisis reflected broader trends in American Jewish society and culture in the twentieth century. Fewer still have systematically compared the substantial similarities between Gehry's career path and those of Eisenman and Libeskind. By examining these connections, the Jewish influences on Gehry's work can be better appreciated.

Gehry grew up with a strong sense of Jewish identity. He was born Frank Owen Goldberg in Toronto in 1929 to a Polish-born Jewish mother who emigrated to Canada as a child, and a Brooklyn-born son of immigrant Polish Jewish parents. Both sides of his family came from lower-middle and working-class origins and were politically left-leaning. This background notwithstanding, Gehry received a substantial Jewish education thanks to the influence of his maternal grandparents, who lived in one of Toronto's main Jewish neighborhoods and remained rooted in Orthodox tradition; his grandmother wore a wig, while his grandfather was president of the family's local synagogue. By contrast, his parents deliberately chose to live in a different neighborhood and thought "worldly" instead of "Jewish." Because Gehry spent much of his childhood in his grandparents' home, he had long conversations about Judaism with his grandfather, who had studied Talmud in Poland, and he later attended Hebrew school; he also celebrated his bar mitzvah at an Orthodox synagogue. At this age Gehry still felt positive about his Jewish identity. He recalls that as a thirteen-year-old he drew a portrait of Theodor Herzl in Hebrew school and proudly heard his Eastern European teacher tell his mother in Yiddish that he had "golden hands." He also liked to "study the Talmud," and he recalls being fascinated as a child with the "chanting of the Torah," especially "the ritual where the old men follow along the pages with a small silver pointer."[105]

Despite these positive elements in his Jewish upbringing, Gehry gradually became alienated from certain aspects of his background. One reason for this—and for his eventual development into a Jewish "outsider"—was his family's inability to relate to his artistic inclinations. Gehry received little support from his father, who was a businessman of modest achievement. Gehry recalls, "He didn't understand that I had any talent. He didn't get it. . . . I was never going to be any good at business. He wrote me off." Gehry's mother tried to nurture his artistic interests, taking him on visits to local art museums, but she could not overcome his father's lack of understanding. As Gehry put it, "I can relate to [the idea of being an outsider] because I was that in my own family. It was like maybe I was gay or something, maybe not quite as extreme as that, but I was close to that." These kinds of conflicts, of course, have always existed within families, regardless of religion. But in Gehry's case they reflected a familiar Jewish story: the gap in expectations between immigrant parents and native-born children. His parents' class standing was typical of new Jewish arrivals in North America, as was their social and cultural outlook. The fact that Gehry's father came from an impoverished background, had no formal education, and displayed working-class cultural traits (he had been an amateur boxer) meant that he was unlikely to understand what he took to be his son's less masculine inclinations. Gehry's description of himself during these years as "quiet" and a "sissy" reinforces this supposition. To be sure, his feelings of being an outsider were not brought about by any Jewish religious biases against artistic expression (as was true of the painter Chaim Soutine). But they did reflect the social and cultural expectations of many Jewish immigrant families at the time. The fact that other Jewish architects reported feeling misunderstood—Gordon Bunshaft, Morris Lapidus, and Stanley Tigerman were in the same situation—reveals that Gehry's experience was not uncommon. The tensions between his artistic inclinations and his Jewish familial and cultural background may well have led him to distance himself from the latter for the sake of pursuing the former.[106]

Gehry's distancing of himself was further encouraged by his weak commitment to traditional religious observance. Gehry says that his interest in religion faded after a demoralizing encounter with older congregants drinking schnapps after services at his Toronto synagogue. "I remember trying to talk to them about what the Torah meant, and what I'd read," he recalled. "I remember going home and saying to my father, 'You know, those guys didn't know anything about it. They were just there for the fucking drink.' And that's when I quit, right then. Never went back." After this point, Gehry embarked on a path of skepticism. When he and a friend read the Bible, he recalled, "We . . . found the contradictions and a whole bunch of stuff. And we would argue [with our teachers] . . . about atheism — that there was no God. And the word got out at school that we were atheists, and the girls wouldn't talk to us." Thereafter, Gehry refrained from formal affiliation with organized Judaism. Like Eisenman, Gehry today professes to being an atheist and is married to a Catholic woman. As he told the *New York Times* in 2003, "I don't believe in religion anymore. I go to a Catholic church with my wife." Indeed, Gehry's views of religion verge on outright hostility. As he told the German newspaper *Die Zeit,* "I would love it if religion were abolished worldwide, [as] all it does is cause misery and wars." Still, his attitudes toward religion are hardly doctrinaire. In 1995 he entered the competition for the Jubilee Church in Rome and has also expressed willingness to design a synagogue and a mosque.[107]

Despite being uninterested in Judaism as a religion, Gehry identifies with Jewishness in a sociopolitical sense. He has long expressed a commitment to social justice that is typical of the Jewish left-wing environment in which he was raised. Once he began his career, moreover, his left-wing idealism led him to embrace "values such as planning and saving the world" through architecture. Gehry pursued these goals at this early stage by designing social housing projects, and he has since reiterated "that we [architects] should all be trying to do that kind of housing." Most important, he sees his concern with social justice as Jewish in origin. In explaining his commitment to using architecture to solve social problems, Gehry has declared that "I'm a do-gooder Jewish liberal to the core." This political progressivism, combined with his distance from religion, allows Gehry to be viewed as a non-Jewish Jew, a man whose sense of self was molded by his ambivalent sense of Jewish identity.[108]

This ambivalence was further promoted by Gehry's boyhood experiences with antisemitism. The architect first became aware of anti-Jewish prejudice through his maternal grandfather, who frequently spoke of the antisemitic abuse he had suffered as a small businessman in Poland. Gehry personally confronted such prejudice himself while still a young boy. In 1938, when he was nine years old, Gehry moved with his family from Toronto to the small mining town of Timmins, Ontario, where he was the only Jewish child in his school. Before long, he was being regularly beaten up "for killing Christ." He also witnessed institutionalized antisemitism, in one case seeing "signs up in a lakeside community west of Toronto that no Jews were allowed in a restaurant." Finally, during the Second World War, many of Gehry's relatives who had stayed in Poland were killed by the Nazis, a fact that he later said scarred him profoundly. His awareness of his family's fate combined with his personal experiences of prejudice left him with the feeling that "you're the outsider."[109]

Gehry's encounters with antisemitism intensified his desire to assimilate further into the mainstream, an impulse hastened after his family left Canada for Los Angeles in 1947 because of his father's poor health and business prospects. During this period, Gehry was too poor to attend college and drove a delivery truck for a cousin's business. Fortunately, Gehry had relatives in Los Angeles who served as role models. His father's brother, Harry, was economically secure and had successfully assimilated. Like many other American Jews at the time, he had changed the family's surname from the Jewish-sounding Goldberg to the aristocratic-seeming Gaylord. Gehry's mother's family had earlier changed their surname from Caplanski to Caplan. These facts were no doubt in young Frank Goldberg's mind when he and his wife, Anita, decided to change their surname to Gehry—a name invented by his mother-in-law—in 1954.[110]

Gehry's decision to change his name was prompted by several factors. One was his growing desire to pursue a career in architecture. Gehry had gone to night school in the early 1950s and eventually found his way to the University of Southern California, where his cousin Hartley Gaylord was a student. He was admitted to the school of architecture, from which he graduated in 1954. His decision to change his name in that same year was partly driven by the dream of assimilation, as well as his enduring fears of antisemitism. He had experienced blunt anti-Jewish prejudice in the mid-1950s during a brief stint in the Air Force ROTC—where he was called "Kikey"—and continued to have encounters with it at USC. When a teacher called him over during his second year and said, "Frank, this isn't for you. You should get out of [architecture]," Gehry recalled, "It devastated me.... You could rationalize it as antisemitism." He was also told that he would not be able to gain admission to the university's architectural fraternity because of his Jewish background. Overall, he seems to have feared that he would have a more difficult time making a career in architecture with a Jewish-sounding surname. He also wanted to spare his future children the discrimination he experienced as a child. In a 2004 interview, Gehry acknowledged that antisemitism was "a factor in allowing myself to be convinced by my ex-wife that [changing my name] ... was the most important thing to do.... We were going to have our first child and there had been a lot of antisemitism [that] I experienced, [and that] she experienced, and she said she didn't want to bring a kid into the world to go through that." Gehry has also noted that his surname carried negative connotations, recalling, "The name at that time was a caricature. There was a radio program [at the time] called "The Goldbergs," ... and I took a lot of heat for it." In the end, Gehry was conflicted about his decision to change his name. He felt a good deal of guilt when his father resisted his plea to change their surnames for the sake of consistency. He recalls: "I didn't like the idea of changing [my name].... My father hated me for letting ... [my wife] do it.... After she did it I was so embarrassed." But he went ahead nonetheless.[111]

Gehry's attempt to escape from his Jewishness was further evident in his effort to craft a rough-and-tumble image for himself. To this day, Gehry's frequent description of himself as a "street fighter," his references to his time as a truck driver, his use of profanity in interviews, his studied avoidance of intellectualism, and his rumpled style of dress are integral components of this self-image. Some of these components reflect Gehry's upbringing in a milieu rife with physical aggression, one in which not just the children of Jews but of French Canadian Catholics were regularly beaten up. Significantly, Gehry did not shrink from this culture of physical violence but partook in it, recalling how, one day, after being attacked by an antisemitic Polish classmate, he "chased him [down] and beat him up." This pugilistic streak continued into adulthood, moreover, when Gehry took up boxing and full-contact ice hockey. The architect's embrace of toughness can be seen as part of a larger effort to distance himself from any traits—privilege, passivity, eggheadedness—that might be identified as Jewish. Having already felt misunderstood in his family because of his artistic inclinations,

The Deconstructivists 205

as well as having suffered the sting of antisemitism, Gehry was unwilling to be considered a "sissy" forever and moved decisively to create a new identity. Given this background, it is hardly surprising that his Jewishness played little role in his early architectural development.[112]

By the late 1970s and early 1980s, however, Gehry's repressed Jewish identity returned and drove him in a new direction. Like Peter Eisenman, Gehry returned to his Jewish background partly due to his decision to undergo psychotherapy. In the mid-1960s Gehry contacted the Los Angeles psychologist Milton Wexler to discuss a variety of marital, financial, and professional problems. Wexler recalls that when Gehry first came to see him, "he lacked a lot of confidence. He was talking often about being bankrupt and he meant more than just monetary bankruptcy. He meant bankrupt in his relationships, bankrupt in getting his clients to accept what he was doing." Gehry listened to Wexler's advice and ended his marriage to Anita in 1966. In the years that followed, therapy helped him mature, giving him the confidence to plunge into new relationships (he married his second wife, Berta, in 1975) and undertake a major shift in his professional life. Thanks to Wexler's and Berta's encouragement, Gehry decided in 1980 to abandon his commercial work for more creative projects. "It was like jumping off a cliff," he recalls. "[But] I was so happy from then on."[113]

Gehry's psychoanalysis helped him reconnect with his Jewish origins. As Michael Sorkin has noted, the architect's new experimental phase began at the same time that his personality assumed more explicitly Jewish features; it was at this moment "in which the Gehry persona, the bleeding-hearted Canadian nebbish . . . began to be thoroughly mythologized." Gehry's increasingly Jewish persona was alluded to in 1982 by the Canadian architecture critic Adele Freedman, who observed that the architect had begun to "disport . . . himself with the woebegone charisma of Woody Allen."[114] This was the period in which Gehry first began to discuss his Jewish background in explaining his work, crafting a coherent narrative that covered his family's immigrant origins, his experiences with antisemitism, and even his religious upbringing. Today, Gehry commonly refers to his Jewishness in discussing his career. In explaining why he decided to move beyond modernism, for example, Gehry noted in a 2002 interview: "I grew up in a Jewish family and I studied Talmud. And the Talmud starts with 'why?' And I guess I've got that kind of thing built into me. . . . I'm always questioning."[115] Such remarks may appear familiar today, but Gehry did not invoke his Jewishness until his work took a deconstructivist turn in the early 1980s.[116] The correlation between the course of his work and his manner of self-representation leaves little doubt: Gehry's architectural transition was partly inspired by the very Jewishness he had earlier rejected.

Gehry's Ichthy-tectural Turn

Gehry's return to his Jewish identity proceeded in unorthodox fashion. If Peter Eisenman acknowledged his Jewishness by embracing the role of the alienated Jewish outsider, and if Daniel Libeskind did so by becoming a custodian of Holocaust memory, Gehry expressed his Jewishness by making what might be called an ichthy-tectural turn in his work, seizing upon fish as a source of creative inspiration. However absurd the notion initially appears to be, fish forms have been a strikingly constant presence in Gehry's otherwise stylistically diverse work, appearing in his drawings, furniture designs, and many of his buildings. Architectural historians and journalists have frequently mentioned these forms' symbolic significance in passing, but few have explored their deeper meaning, sharing Charles Jencks's view that it is a "mistake to think that Gehry's fish means . . . anything profound."[117] Yet the fact that Gehry has frequently connected the fish to his Jewish background is revealing, for it reflects the growing sense of freedom felt by Jewish architects after the 1970s to inject Jewish symbolism into their work.

Gehry's fish fetish first surfaced in the early 1980s. At this time he began to seek inspiration in animal forms as alternatives to the historically derived ornamentation used by postmodern architects. In an unrealized proposal for the Smith house in Los Angeles (1981), Gehry drafted a colonnade made of animal forms: first eagles, and then fish. The fish motif surfaced again in 1981 in a jointly produced proposal with Richard Serra for a suspension bridge in New York City supported by a 150-story fish and in a tower for an unrealized revitalization plan for the central business district of Kalamazoo, Michigan (1981). Gehry soon incorporated fish forms in lamps, which he designed in the years 1983 – 86. One day, while experimenting with a plastic laminate called ColorCore, the architect threw a piece to the floor in frustration (an alternate version of the story has it "accidentally" falling) and watched it shatter into smaller fragments. Noticing that the fragments resembled scales, he and another artist decided to "make a fish" out of them, and the first fish lamp was hatched (fig. 97). Nearly thirty different designs followed, with some becoming permanent fixtures in Gehry's interior remodeling jobs, such as Rebecca's Restaurant in Venice, California (1982 – 85).[118]

This burst of productivity indicated that Gehry's fixation with fish had deeper psychological roots. Gehry has confirmed this connection, noting in many interviews that the fish has symbolized a variety of things for him during his career. At the artistic level, the fish symbolized his creative rebellion against postmodernism and classicism. In the early 1980s, Gehry — like Eisenman and Libeskind — was a fierce critic of postmodernism, believing that its nostalgic, historically evocative designs denied the reality of the contemporary world and represented a dead end for architecture. Yet rather than follow Eisenman's and Libeskind's post-structuralist strategy of subverting architec-

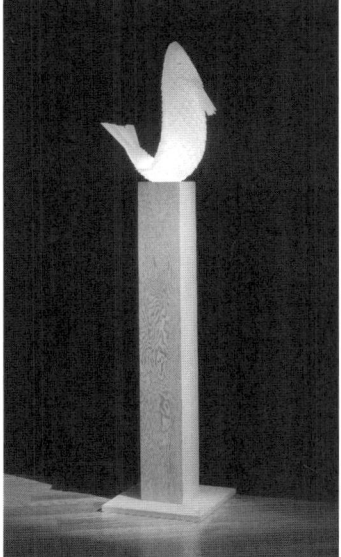

Figure 97. Frank Gehry, fish lamp, 1990. Gehry's fish fetish first found form in a series of lamps composed of ColorCore "scales."

tural "presence" with high theory, Gehry fought back with his fish. As he put it in an interview, "When my [architectural] brethren started to regurgitate the past in the postmodern movement . . . the past they were regurgitating was anthropomorphic. And I said: Well, if you're going to go back, you might as well go back three hundred million years before man to fish. . . . It was sort of a sarcastic remark. . . . I started drawing and . . . whenever I saw one of those postmodern buildings, I would angrily sketch in my book pictures of fish." The fish was Gehry's weapon against both postmodernism and classicism. In an interview with Charles Jencks he declared: "If everybody's going to say that Classicism is perfection . . . then I'm going to say fish is perfection, so why not copy fish? And then I'll be damned if I don't find reasons to reinforce why the fish is important and more interesting than Classicism." In seeking out his reasons, Gehry ended up claiming that the fish was a "critique on the anthropomorphism of classical architecture." By basing his architecture on animals he rejected the classical practice of basing architectural forms on the human body. In so doing, Gehry joined Eisenman in expressing the post-structuralist belief that mankind had been displaced from the center of the world and was no longer the basis of all measure. Finally, the fish did not just symbolize Gehry's artistic rebellion but his unrealized goal of artistic perfection. As he put it in a 1984 interview, "Whenever I'd draw something and I couldn't finish the design, I'd draw the fish as a notation . . . that I wanted [the design] to be better . . . [and] more beautiful."[119]

Significantly, the fish also symbolized Gehry's conflicted sense of Jewishness.[120] Gehry first highlighted the Jewish dimensions of the fish in 1984 when he declared: "When I was a kid I used to go to the market with my grandmother on Thursdays. We'd go to the Jewish market, we'd buy a live carp, we'd take it home to her house in Toronto, we'd put it in the bathtub and I would play with this goddamn fish for a day until the next day she'd kill it and make gefilte fish. I think maybe that has something to with [my interest in fish forms]." At one level, therefore, the fish was a symbol of familial togetherness. Gehry was extremely fond of his Orthodox grandmother and has attributed his interest in architecture to the many occasions when she would get down on the floor with him and play with scraps and blocks of wood from his grandfather's hardware store. Yet there was also a darker aspect to the fish's symbolism. The fact that the fish was trapped in a bathtub and destined to be turned into a meal meant that it symbolized imprisonment, helplessness, and unrealized potential. Gehry's later view of the fish as a symbol of unattainable artistic perfection may have been rooted in his awareness of the fish's fate.[121]

At a still deeper level, the fish was also a symbol of Jewish oppression and suffering. Beginning in the mid-1980s Gehry began to discuss his boyhood experiences with antisemitism. It was not just that neighborhood children had called him a Christ-killer. He also recalled how many of them, having gotten wind of his grandmother's peculiar culinary traditions, decided to call him such names as "Fish," "Fish Eater," and "Fish Head."[122] As a result of such painful tauntings, the fish assumed negative connotations for Gehry. Not only did it symbolize Christian hostility toward Jews but also Jewish powerlessness and shame.

That the fish possessed negative connotations for Gehry is further suggested by his habit in the 1980s of pairing fish forms with forms inspired by an even more threatening animal, the snake. Coiled snakes appeared alongside fish in several of Gehry's lamp designs (1983), in his unrealized architectural folly called "The Prison" (1983), and in his Fishdance Restaurant in Kobe, Japan (1986–87).

Scholars have paid little attention to the symbolism of Gehry's snakes, an oversight that reflects the fact that Gehry has not offered any comparable autobiographical tales to explain his interest in them. It is striking, however, that Gehry viewed snakes as psychologically powerful symbols. In the early 1980s he declared that "the snake . . . symbolizes hostility and invokes fear." Given the obvious links between hostility, fear, and the antisemitism that Gehry suffered in his youth, it is hard not to conclude that his fascination with both fish and snakes may have been rooted in boyhood traumas stemming from his vulnerability as a young Jew.[123]

That Jewish sources underpinned his views of both fish and snakes is further suggested by his description of "The Prison." In discussing this design — which envisioned a pair of snakelike and fishlike structures for transporting and confining prisoners — Gehry invoked the biblical story of "Jonah who lived inside the whale."[124] The snake's significance as a symbol of evil also had obvious biblical roots in the story of the Garden of Eden. Overall, it is not much of a stretch to conclude (even if it is impossible to prove) that the appearance of fish and snakes in Gehry's design for "The Prison" symbolized his feelings of being imprisoned within his Jewish identity. In the end, however, fish outnumbered snakes in Gehry's work and thus served as the primary symbol of his professional ambitions and personal travails. Not just a sign of unattainable artistic perfection, the fish stood for Gehry's indecision about whether to abandon or embrace his Jewish heritage.

To be sure, it is difficult to establish a direct causal relationship between Gehry's return to his Jewish identity and his artistic blossoming, and it would be an exaggeration to assert that Gehry's sense of Jewishness drove this rebellion. After all, he began his experimental phase with his own house in Santa Monica in 1977–78, before he began discussing his Jewish roots in public. Moreover, the absence of fish forms in this project highlights the irrelevance of Jewish considerations. Nevertheless, it is no coincidence that fish forms appeared in his work only after his watershed decision in 1980 to set aside his commercial work and embark on a new creative phase. It remains unclear whether the fish was truly a source of inspiration or merely a symbolic justification of his new path. Yet even if the fish primarily served as a retroactive method of rationalizing what he was already in the process of undertaking architecturally, Gehry's invocation of it was notable, for it links him to Eisenman and Libeskind, both of whom also cited their Jewish backgrounds in justifying the radical turns in their work.

Prior to the mid-1980s, Gehry used fish only for small projects — mostly lamps — and had emphasized fish scales as his major design element. A few years later, however, he began to enlarge the size of his fish and focus more on their broader anatomical features. In 1986, Gehry built an eight-foot-high, thirty-six-foot-long wooden fish sculpture for an exhibition at a fashion house in Florence, Italy. "It was [a] very kitsch . . . object," he recalls, but it "expressed movement," as did his seventy-foot-high fish sculpture at Fishdance Restaurant (fig. 98). Both of these fish were highly realistic, with scales, fins, eyes, and other features. Soon thereafter, Gehry produced more abstract fish by removing details and ending with mere torsos. First seen in the lead fish house that he designed for his Walker Art Center retrospective in Minneapolis (1986) and shortly thereafter in his fish torso conference room in Jay Chiat's temporary offices in Venice (1986–88), Gehry's abstracted fish culminated with his enormous copper fish sculpture at his Vila Olimpica in Barcelona (1989–92) (fig. 99). With this work, Gehry realized that he could strip the fish of its defining features and still retain the "sense of movement." The architect now recognized that he had made a breakthrough. "Quite accidentally, I found my [way] . . . into a language that I was really looking to find," he notes. "And I took that language into my buildings."[125]

Gehry's buildings in the 1990s reflected this new language in their dynamic, curvilinear forms and metallic, fishlike skins. Combined with his strategy of designing buildings as ensembles of separate forms, these new developments paved the way for new pathbreaking works. Fish forms, of course, were hardly the sole influence upon his architecture during this period. Without Gehry's embrace of CAD (computer-aided design) technology during this period, few of his ambitious designs could have been executed as planned. In particular, Gehry's use of the CATIA software program, which had been developed by the French aerospace industry, enabled him and his partners to map his designs in three dimensions and thereby bridge the traditional gap between the conception and execution of buildings.[126]

There is no shortage of stunning examples from this golden era of Gehry's career. It is notable that the first project in which he employed CAD technology was his Barcelona fish pavilion.[127] But a few years before, his buildings had begun to display dynamic curvilinear forms. The first work to exhibit a hint of the curves to come was his Vitra International Design Museum (especially its swooping exterior staircase) in Weil-am-Rhein in Germany (1987–89). The first designs to display metallic skins, which were applied in the form of individual rectangular sheets resembling scales, were the Frederick R. Weisman Art and Teaching Museum in Minneapolis (1990–93), the Center for the Visual Arts in Toledo (1989), and the Neue Zollhoff commercial development in Düsseldorf (1994–99). But the fish forms attained their apotheosis in his Guggenheim Museum in Bilbao (1991–

Figure 98. Frank Gehry, Fishdance Restaurant, Kobe, Japan, 1986–87. Gehry's fish forms assumed literal shape in this Japanese restaurant.

Figure 99. Frank Gehry, Fish Pavilion at Vila Olimpica, Barcelona, 1989–92. This enormous copper sculpture was a more abstract version of Gehry's earlier fish-inspired work.

Figure 100. Frank Gehry, Guggenheim Museum, Bilbao, Spain, 1991–97. In this project, Gehry reduced fish to dynamic curvilinear forms and metallic, scale-like skins. The largest gallery, left, was originally called the Fish Gallery.

97) (fig. 100), whose exterior cladding was made of thin, scale-like plates of titanium and whose interior featured a 450-foot-long and 50-foot-high space known as the Fish Gallery.[128] Subsequent buildings, such as the Walt Disney Concert Hall in downtown Los Angeles (1989–2003), had equally shimmering skins.

    The reaction to these works followed a familiar pattern. On the one hand, Gehry reaped worldwide attention for his eye-catching designs, earning numerous honors, accolades, and dozens of new commissions across the globe. On the other hand, like Eisenman and Libeskind, he has been criticized for having become too successful, too famous, too much of a "starchitect." While some critics have attacked Gehry's buildings as overpriced, unfunctional eye candy for the super-rich, others have decried his larger-than-life status—he once appeared as an animated version of himself on the hit television show *The Simpsons*—and have helped sustain the market for crudely hip "Fuck Frank Gehry" T-shirts. Still, despite this backlash, Gehry's professional reputation remains largely unsullied—a fact that was confirmed by *Time*'s inclusion of him on its 2004 list of the world's one hundred most influential people.[129]

Gehry and the Holocaust

Despite the immense attention that Gehry's work has received, however, one dimension has largely been ignored: its links to the Holocaust. Given the striking beauty of Gehry's buildings, such links initially seem preposterous. Certainly compared to the brooding architecture of Eisenman and Libeskind, Gehry's work seems unreservedly buoyant. As Ada Louise Huxtable put it in the late 1980s, "There are no gloomy buildings by Gehry; it is impossible to think of anything he has done without smiling."[130] Moreover, unlike Eisenman and Libeskind, Gehry has seldom mentioned the Holocaust in interviews and has generally refrained from designing Holocaust memorials or museums. While these differences suggest that the Holocaust has been relatively unimportant for his overall career, its presence has still been felt in subtle ways.

Despite their exuberance, Gehry's buildings have long exuded an aura of instability. His early works employed slanted wooden beams, metal struts, and other supporting elements that suggested imminent collapse. His Norton Simon Gallery and Guest House in Malibu (1974–76), for example, featured an exterior wooden trellis whose slats appear to be falling from the roof, while the angled struts supporting the canopies of his Chiat/Day Building in Venice, California (1985–91), and Schnabel Residence in Brentwood (1986–89) seemed poised to give way at any moment (fig. 101). Some of Gehry's other early buildings communicated insecurity more subtly, using ghost forms to convey a disquieting message of absence and loss. These included the fenestrated false facades of his World Savings and Loan Association in North Hollywood (1980) and the ghost cube of his Edgemar Development commercial complex in Santa Monica (1984–88) (see fig. 96). With Gehry's turn to computer-aided design in the early 1990s, the architect's buildings displayed instability more dramatically. His curvilinear, bright yellow Team Disneyland Administration Building in Anaheim (1987–95) appeared to be melting in the heat of an unseen explosion. The bulging forms of his brick-clad Vontz Center for Molecular Studies at the University of Cincinnati (1993–2000) seemed ready to burst from internal gaseous forces. And the dented, sharply sloping facade of his Ray and Maria Stata Center on the campus of MIT in Cambridge, Massachusetts (2004), appeared to have been hit by a hurricane (fig. 102). These buildings all communicated disturbing messages of past or future violence, although the originating events for their destabilized appearance were never defined.

Figure 101. Frank Gehry, Chiat/Day Building, Venice, California, 1985–91. The angled struts supporting the building's canopy on the right seem about to collapse. The oversized binoculars at left were designed by Claes Oldenburg.

Certain critics, however, have interpreted these buildings as influenced by the legacy of the Second World War. As early as 1980, one reviewer in *Progressive Architecture* likened Gehry's Santa Monica house to a war ruin, writing: "After gazing at the exterior, one is ready for the German wartorn apartments in Rainer Maria Fassbinder's film 'Marriage of Maria Braun': holes gouged out of peeling plaster walls, doors hanging by one hinge, [and] the roof caving [in]." Another commentator wrote that the crushed and disjointed forms of Gehry's Nationale-Nederlanden Office Building in Prague (1992–96) evoked the wartime bombing of its site and symbolized the "violence and destruction [that accompanied] . . . the extermination of Prague's Jewish culture by German occupying forces" (fig. 103).[131]

These comments have been exceptional among the many reactions to Gehry's buildings, but on rare occasions the architect himself has connected his work to the Holocaust. In an interview with the German newspaper *Die Zeit* in 2003, Gehry responded to interviewer Hanno Rauterberg's observation that his buildings seemed "fragile" and "provisional" by noting: "What you describe. . . . corresponds . . . [to the fact] that I have experienced much insecurity in my life and often had to begin over from scratch. I grew up as a Jew, after all." Although admitting that he was not religious, Gehry continued: "Despite all of my aversion, I will never separate myself from my Jewishness, I remain branded. For one's whole life, one belongs to it; for one's whole life, one has fear." The reason, Gehry went on to note, was the Holocaust. "Many of my relatives who hailed from Poland died in the Holocaust," he declared. "As a Jew, which I am, and yet am not, the thought haunts me that at any moment another Hitler can come along and stick you in the oven." "As you can see," he concluded, "I have been affected, and so presumably have my buildings." In response to a question about whether his architectural philosophy had anything in common with that of Eisenman and Libeskind, Gehry bluntly replied, "They have nothing to do with me." "I only know," he continued, "that I do not believe in an ideal or straight-lined world, nor can I build one. I have too much inner doubt to do so, doubt that surely is rooted in my own history."[132]

Figure 102. Frank Gehry, Ray and Maria Stata Center, Massachusetts Institute of Technology, Cambridge, 2004. The building's dented and slanted forms appear to have been hit by a hurricane.

Given Gehry's prior reluctance to discuss the Holocaust, these sudden references to it were significant. It is unknown what prompted him to make such personal disclosures about the German past, but they may have reflected unresolved feelings toward the land of the perpetrators. Although Gehry, like Eisenman and Libeskind, received numerous commissions from clients in Germany, he was much less comfortable working there. Like many American Jews of his generation, Gehry viewed Germany after 1945 with a mixture of suspicion and anxiety. When he first visited the country in 1960, he recalled: "I had trouble crossing the border—the border guys. I got this whole Nazi thing. It scared the shit out of me." He decided not to let his feelings get the best of him, however, noting that after he traveled there "a few times, . . . I sort of got over it [and] I became friends with a lot of German people." Today, he views Germany as "more liberal" in its political views "than most countries" and less antisemitic than France and Poland. Nevertheless, the fact that he has been so successful in Germany as a Jewish architect has left him with a sense of uncertainty. As he put it in a 1997 interview, "My first European buildings were in Germany. My best fans and clients are in Germany. It's funny, especially when you're a Jew, Germany doesn't have that cachet—you're kind of worried about it. Who are these guys that like me?" Gehry's suggestion that Germany lacked the same prestige as other countries reflected a commonly held view among postwar American Jews who disdained the country in various ways—refraining from visiting it or buying its products—because of its ugly past. His insecurity about being celebrated in Germany no doubt also reflected his uncertainty about how to respond to its postwar tradition of philosemitism.[133]

Perhaps for these reasons Gehry mostly refrained from thematizing the country's Nazi past in his designs. Most of his German projects, of course, were either for commercial buildings or social housing and were typically located in places (Weil am Rhein, Bad Oeynhausen, Düsseldorf, Hannover, Frankfurt) that were removed from major sites connected with the Third Reich. Yet Gehry did have two opportunities to build in Berlin, where he might have allowed himself—like Eisenman and Libeskind before him—to seek inspiration in the city's history. Yet, his unrealized design for the Berlin Museumsinsel (1991) ignored the fact that one of the site's major buildings, the Neues Museum, was still a ruin dating from the Second World War, while his DZ Bank headquarters on the Pariser Platz (1995–2000), adjacent to the Brandenburg Gate, was historically mute as well.[134]

Yet, even if Gehry did not overtly reference the Nazi past in his Berlin buildings, some of his public comments revealed that he supported the concept of using architecture to confront it. When German construction workers discovered the remnants of Albert Speer's bunker during excavation for the DZ Bank headquarters in 1995, for example, Gehry was shocked that no historic preservation efforts were undertaken at the site, declaring, "Everything that happened here I do not want to forget." To ensure that the guilty did not forget, he recommended in 1999 that the apartments in the rear of his DZ Bank Headquarters, which faced the future site of Eisenman's Holocaust Memorial, should be rented to ex-Nazis, who would thereby be forced to confront their deeds. More explicitly, Gehry revealed his views about architecture and the Holocaust in his praise for Libeskind's Jewish Museum. As he put it in 1997, "For me, architecture is about taking the emotions you have and getting through a process of building. . . . I've just been to Libeskind's Jewish Museum in Berlin. Now he comes from a Holocaust family, and he's very angry. I saw the building and I like it. . . . What's impressive to me is that it's the angriest building I've ever seen. . . . It's relentlessly anti-public-space. That anger comes through. And why not, in a building about the Holocaust. By the time I got through it, I was crying. I was very moved by it. And I was not expecting to feel anything." Gehry's comments were unusual for focusing on what he felt to be the expression of anger in the Jewish Museum. In contrast to Libeskind's own attitude toward the building, which combined a sense of sadness with hope, Gehry's response seemed charged with unmastered feelings about the past. Overall, the architect seems more comfortable avoiding direct confrontation with the Holocaust and leaving others to do the work of acknowledging it architecturally. This was suggested in a 2001 interview in Germany when he was asked about the dynamic rear facade of his comparatively staid DZ Bank headquarters. Gehry responded: "I was more interested in the front facade. On the rear facade, I thought: "Okay, there is this Holocaust thing [the Memorial to the Murdered Jews of Europe]. But that does not interest me." When asked by the interviewer "Why not?" Gehry responded, "Ask me something else." Gehry's abrupt cutting off of discussion on the Holocaust suggests, at the very least, that he is not entirely ready to address it in a German context.[135]

Figure 103. Frank Gehry, Nationale-Nederlanden Office Building, Prague, 1992–96. This warped building has been interpreted as displaying hints of wartime violence.

The Deconstructivists 215

Yet since the turn of the millennium, Gehry has come closer to the Holocaust in his work. This shift has taken place in the context of his newly awakened interest in pursuing Jewish commissions. In 2003 the architect was tapped to design the new Museum of the History of Polish Jews in Warsaw. Gehry expressed interest in this project partly because of his ancestral connection to Poland. He even agreed to waive his usual fee for the commission. Planned on the site of the former Warsaw Ghetto, next to Nathan Rapaport's 1948 memorial to the ghetto resistance fighters, the museum had as its main educational mission the narration of Polish Jewry's history from its early modern flourishing to its violent end, a mandate that required (as with Libeskind's Berlin museum) making sure that the devastation of the Holocaust did not overshadow the high points of Polish Jewish life. How Gehry would have tackled this challenge architecturally will never be known, however, as he quit the project after the Polish government could not secure the necessary funding. It is possible, though, that he would have used an exuberant approach for a place intended to foster Polish-Jewish reconciliation.[136]

This possibility seems likely given Gehry's design for another Jewish commission: the new Simon Wiesenthal Center for Human Dignity—Museum of Tolerance Jerusalem in Israel. When contacted in 2003 to work on the project, which is dedicated to "promoting unity and respect among Jews and people of all faiths," Gehry quickly accepted, observing that it held special importance for him as a Jew. Like Louis I. Kahn, Gehry noted the importance of working in Israel, remarking: "If you're raised a Jewish kid, Israel's the most important place in the world[,] where there's some sense of belonging when all else fails." He further demonstrated his personal connection to the project by reciting the first line of his bar mitzvah *haftarah* portion in one of his Jerusalem speeches.[137]

All the same, Gehry's views on Israel were complicated. In a 2007 interview he declared "I am not a Zionist" and stated "I could never live . . . [in Israel] myself right now" before adding: "I am pro-Israel." Like Eisenman, Gehry's strong Jewish identity did not necessitate a particular political stance on the Jewish state. Even so, the project in Jerusalem clearly motivated the architect. As one of his partners, Craig Webb, noted in 2001, "Frank is delving into his Jewish background in a way I don't think he's really done in the past," adding that the architect had developed designs revolving around the hexagonal Jewish star (as well as octagonal Islamic forms) in his effort to express the museum's mission of fostering tolerance, respect, and understanding. Gehry's remarks that the design aimed to foster "accessibility" more than anything else indicated that he agreed with the museum's goal of fostering the peace process in the region.[138]

In 2004, ground was broken for the building, which was to include a museum, a conference center, an educational wing, a library, and a theater. Not long afterward, however, the project ran into major problems. Widely criticized as conceptually flawed by skeptical Israeli, Palestinian, and American commentators, the project came to a halt in 2006 when a Muslim cemetery was discovered under the building site. In 2010, Gehry quit the project because of planning and financial disagreements. At the time of this writing, the museum's fate is uncertain.[139]

On balance, Gehry's buildings represent an affirmative version of deconstructivist architecture. Compared to the work of Eisenman and Libeskind, his buildings do not initially seem concerned with rethinking the discipline of architecture after Auschwitz. Indeed, Gehry might very well be seen as ignoring Adorno's injunctions against turning tragedy into art. Given Paul Goldberger's remark (made in reference to Gehry's Santa Monica house) that the architect proved that "it is possible to make . . . beauty out of ugliness," Gehry's architecture might be viewed as aestheticizing the very ideas of rupture, instability, and disorientation that Eisenman and Libeskind developed in less visually engaging form.[140] As with everything else in artistic expression, however, the truth lies in the eye of the beholder. While some regard Gehry's buildings as exuberantly cheerful, others, including the architect himself, have noted darker undercurrents. Gehry has remained largely tight-lipped about the historical sources of his architecture of instability. And perhaps because Eisenman and Libeskind have so demonstratively evoked the past in justifying their work, he prefers to remain relatively silent. For all of that, Gehry, too, has felt the Holocaust's legacy in his own way and incorporated aspects of it in his work.

Conclusion

Taken together, the deconstructivist work of Eisenman, Libeskind, and Gehry testifies to the unprecedented creativity and achievement of contemporary Jewish architects. All three rebelled against International Style modernism and revivalist postmodernism by seeking inspiration outside architecture, whether in scientific theories, philosophy, or sculpture. All their rebellions, moreover, were partly inspired by aspects of their Jewish backgrounds, most notably their experience of antisemitism, which made them feel like outsiders. To be sure, the three architects dealt with these feelings differently. While Libeskind remained proud of his Jewishness, Eisenman and Gehry tried to escape into self-denial, though neither maintained this evasive strategy permanently. At roughly the same time in their lives, both men became disaffected with their architectural careers and sought answers in psychoanalysis, thanks to which they reclaimed aspects of their Jewish identity and began to draw upon Jewish sources of inspiration in their work. Like Libeskind, Eisenman and Gehry repeatedly invoked their Jewish backgrounds to justify their radical architectural philosophies. Whether or not their Jewish backgrounds actually inspired their architectural transformations or were merely cited to justify them is less important than the fact that all three comfortably invoked their personal identities in discussing their work. This marked a novel development in the evolution of postwar Jewish architecture. While Jewish architects in the early years after 1945 were largely silent about being Jews, and while Louis I. Kahn only haltingly broke the silence, Eisenman, Libeskind, and Gehry successfully opened rich possibilities for the architectural exploration of Jewishness. Equally important, the Jewishness of their work has not stood in the way of their success. In striking contrast to the antisemitic responses to the architecture of Erich Mendelsohn or Marcel Breuer during the interwar period, the responses to Eisenman, Libeskind, and Gehry have been overwhelmingly favorable and shown no signs of bias. This fact, more than any other, reveals the paradoxical nature of Eisenman's, Libeskind's and Gehry's careers. While experiences of discrimination and feelings of outsiderness partly inspired their work, the waning of prejudice and the diminution of the fears once caused by it have enabled them to enjoy unmatched popularity and success. That said, the deconstructivist model is not the only one that explains Jewish architectural achievement in the postmodern era.

Chapter 9
Jewish Architects Between Alienation and Assimilation

In the Berlin suburb of Tegel, along the harbor area known as the Tegeler Hafen, stands a pair of adjoining apartment buildings that, at first glance, resemble each other closely. Both are clad in stucco, painted in yellowish hues, and display historicizing features, such as gambrel roofs, dormers, and mullioned windows. Both have occupied their sites since the late 1980s, when they were completed as part of the IBA exhibition's campaign to mend the torn urban fabric of postwar Berlin. Both, moreover, were designed by Jewish architects: the more flamboyant building by the Chicago-based Stanley Tigerman, the more refined structure by the New York–based Robert A. M. Stern. The buildings embody telltale features of postmodernism: historical reference, ornamentation, and attentiveness to urban context. In truth, though, they are based on completely different ideas. Aesthetically, Tigerman's design displays disruptive features—notably, a bright-red gridded glass foyer in the middle of the building's main facade—that sharply contrast with the architectural harmony exuded by Stern's more nostalgic design (figs. 104, 105). These aesthetic differences, in turn, reflect competing philosophical rationales. Tigerman's building embodies his conviction that architecture should express the traumas of the post-Holocaust world, while Stern's reflects the desire to provide refuge from them. Despite standing next to each other as ostensible good neighbors, the two Jewish-designed buildings represent contradictory world-views.

The two apartment houses point to a larger truth about the evolution of Jewish architecture in the wake of postmodernism: not all the important Jewish architects who became prominent during the period were interested in expressing Jewish concerns in their work. While some, such as Tigerman, displayed quasi-deconstructivist tendencies and reflected on issues of Jewish identity, others viewed such issues as irrelevant. The prominent Los Angeles–based architect Eric Owen Moss, for example, also designed buildings that exuded fragmentation, instability, and rupture, but he invoked no Jewish ideas to justify his approach. Equally uninterested in Jewish themes were architects who stood at the opposite end of the architectural spectrum. The New York–based Allan Greenberg, along with Stern, embraced postmodern classicism, designing revivalist buildings that were rooted in such venerable values as harmony, stability, and order. Predictably, these conservative works also exhibited few Jewish influences. The same can be said about major Jewish architects who remained loyal to

Figure 104. Stanley Tigerman, IBA Apartment House, Berlin, 1984–88. This ironic work of postmodernism features a disruptive glass and steel divider between the structure's two halves that illustrated Tigerman's fondness for "cleaving" buildings in two.

Figure 105. Robert A. M. Stern, IBA Apartment House, Berlin, 1984–88. Stern's nostalgic postmodern design harked back to the turn-of-the-century Jugendstil work of German architect and designer Bruno Paul.

mainstream modernism. One of the best known, Richard Meier, achieved prominence without drawing on his Jewish background or finding inspiration in Jewish ideas. In short, Jewish architects after the 1970s embodied postmodern pluralism in displaying diverse approaches to their work. Some continued to express a Jewish sense of alienation, while others displayed a penchant for assimilation.

Architects of Alienation: Tigerman and Moss

Two of the most prominent architects who expressed a sense of alienation in their work were Tigerman and Moss. Their buildings differed considerably in appearance. Tigerman's exhibited a lighthearted pop sensibility that borrowed from a wide range of historical sources, while Moss's were brooding and sculptural. Each, however, expressed a belief that the ruptured condition of the modern world required expression through an architecture of dislocation and fragmentation. That said, Tigerman and Moss disagreed about the rupture's origins, with the former pointing to specifically Jewish factors and the latter highlighting more abstract causes.

Stanley Tigerman

Few Jewish architects in the postmodern era displayed more signs of alienation than Stanley Tigerman. Tigerman's work resembled that of Eisenman, Libeskind, and Gehry in being partly influenced by reflections about Jewish identity in the post-Holocaust world. Yet, while he spoke frequently of exile, rupture, and loss, few of his buildings displayed the destabilized forms typical of deconstructivist architecture. Indeed, they were far less consistent in theoretical orientation and visual appearance. Tigerman turned this potential liability into a virtue, however, by claiming that his work's very eclecticism made it "Jewish." In the process, he emerged as one of the more openly self-professing Jewish architects of the postmodern period.

Born in 1930 in Chicago, Tigerman completed his architectural education at Yale in 1961 before joining the Chicago office of Skidmore, Owings, and Merrill. In 1964 he established his own practice as Tigerman and Associates (today Tigerman McCurry). During this initial phase of his career, Tigerman devoted his energies to designing office buildings and apartment complexes — at first in a Miesian idiom, later in a more brutalist vein — before turning his attention to more socially minded projects, such as his low-income Woodlawn Gardens Apartment Complex in Chicago (1963 – 69), his Five Polytechnic Institutes in Bangladesh (1966 – 75), and his Illinois Regional Library for the Blind and the Physically Handicapped (1975 – 78) (fig. 106). During these years Tigerman expressed some of the same left-wing political leanings as Frank Gehry. Indeed, in explaining his decision to "get involved" in social causes during the 1960s as the result of his "Marxist tendencies," Tigerman appeared even more radical in his political outlook.[1]

By the mid-1970s, however, the architect shifted to a more unconventional stance. This became clear in 1976, when he became the driving force behind the formation of the "Chicago Seven." Composed of Tigerman, James Ingo Freed, Stuart Cohen, Ben Weese, Laurence Booth, James Nagle, and Thomas Beeby, this group of architects sought to challenge the architectural traditions in the Windy City just as the New York Five had done in the Big Apple. In Chicago, that meant liberating architecture from the hegemony of Mies and his followers. As Tigerman put it in a 1998 interview, "I grew

Figure 106. Stanley Tigerman, Illinois Regional Library for the Blind and the Physically Handicapped, Chicago, 1975–78. This building represented Tigerman's commitment to socially minded architectural projects.

up in the city where the descendents of Mies . . . held sway like crazy for . . . the first thirty years of my life as an architect. . . . It was all Mies, one hundred percent." In 1978, Tigerman published a controversial, surrealist-inspired photomontage of Mies's famous Crown Hall building at IIT sinking into the ocean like the *Titanic* — a gesture that served as a shot across the bow of Mies's followers, whom Tigerman dismissed as epigones who had "contributed nothing" to the architect's formidable architectural legacy. Instead, Tigerman hoped, like the theoretically minded Eisenman, to reinvigorate the practice of architecture by convincing Mies's acolytes to abandon their master's antiintellectual dictum, "Build, don't talk," and open themselves to new ideas.[2]

In pursuing this goal, Tigerman set an example for others by abandoning his previous architectural philosophy and making a postmodern turn in his work. At this point, Tigerman had become disenchanted with Miesian formalism and increasingly interested in "cultural phenomena external to the discipline of architecture itself." He now believed that "one of the major functions of a building should be to communicate an idea, story, or fantasy." Many of Tigerman's projects from this period — primarily wood-clad residential commissions — began to embody this notion by displaying surrealistic, absurd, and even prurient traits. Projects like the Hot Dog House (1974–75), the Animal Crackers House (1976–78), and, above all, the Daisy House (1976–78) — whose plan evoked "an erect phallus, semen, and scrotum" — clearly expressed this lighthearted mindset and dovetailed with the playfully ironic ethos of the emerging postmodern movement (fig. 107).[3]

At the same time, Tigerman also began to display incipient deconstructivist impulses. In his designs of the late 1970s and early 1980s, he exhibited a tendency to "cleave" the plans of his buildings into "broken or ruptured parts." This tendency was visible in his unrealized designs for the D.O.M. Corporate Headquarters in Germany (1980) and Shaker Village Visitors Center in Pleasant Hill, Kentucky (1979), but it was epitomized by his unrealized plan for "A Symbolic Museum for a Painting That Will Never Go There," in Guernica, Spain (1981), which featured five Platonic solids — cone, pyramid, cylinder, cube, and sphere — that were sheared off "along the actual path the German bombers took" in their notorious aerial attack on the city in 1937. These disjointed designs contrasted sharply with Tigerman's earlier lighthearted work and signaled a new direction for him.[4]

Indeed, this phase was part of a larger Jewish turn in Tigerman's architectural career. Starting in the late 1970s and early 1980s, the architect began to refer to a variety of Jewish themes in his work. This trend was partly visible in the humorous names he gave to some of his projects, such as his Kosher Kitchen for a Jewish American Princess (an addition to a suburban Chicago home) in 1977–78.[5] At a deeper level, however, Tigerman's Jewish turn was expressed in his architectural writings, which contained extended reflections on the anti-Hellenic Jewish tradition of aniconism and the legacy of the Holocaust.

In making this turn, Tigerman was sorting through conflicted feelings about his identity. Tigerman's decision to seek inspiration in his Jewish background, like Eisenman's and Gehry's decisions, coincided with, and was partly influenced by, the onset of a midlife crisis. The late 1970s was a period that Tigerman describes as one when "[I began to] sense my own mortality.... [and] felt the need to reassess the way I wished to live the rest of my life."[6] In pursuing a path of introspection, however, Tigerman differed from Eisenman and Gehry in one important respect. While they had negative feelings about their Jewish heritage and reconnected to it only through psychoanalysis, Tigerman had a more affirmative attitude toward his background and returned to it without outside assistance. This was largely due to the fact that he had positive Jewish role models in his family. By far the most important was his paternal grandfather. During the Depression, financial difficulties in Tigerman's family forced him to move for an extended period of time into his grandparents' boarding house. While there, Tigerman spent countless hours with his grandfather, a deeply religious man who, after arriving in America in 1893 from his native Hungary, devoted himself exclusively

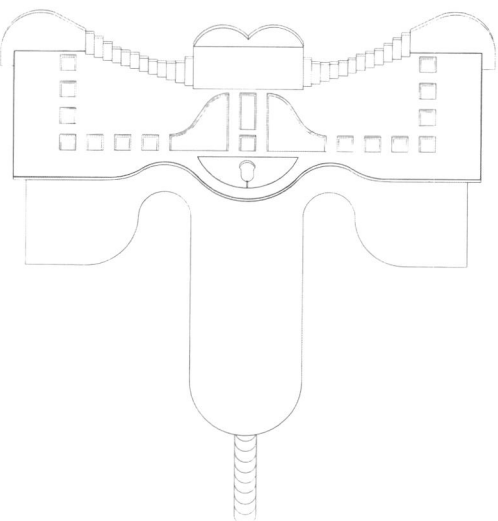

Figure 107. Stanley Tigerman, Daisy House plan, Porter, Indiana, 1976–78. The plan for this wood-clad residence possessed phallic imagery and expressed Tigerman's rebellion against Miesian modernism.

to the study of Talmud. The strength of character displayed by Tigerman's grandfather contrasted sharply with that of his father — a "sweet ... but ... weak man" who had "failed in his career as a chemist" — and profoundly shaped the architect's sense of Jewish identity. Thanks to his grandfather's influence, Tigerman was exposed to the Orthodox religious tradition and became fascinated with the Talmud — a fascination that would profoundly influence his later architectural writings. "My grandfather had a huge impact on my life," Tigerman noted in 2008. "He raised me, taught me how to walk, how to play pinochle, how to read English and Hebrew. We were incredibly close." Indeed, Tigerman has speculated that had he not gone into architecture, he might have followed in his grandfather's footsteps, asserting: "I should have been what my grandfather was. I should have been a rabbinic scholar."[7]

That said, not all of Tigerman's family members had a positive impact on him. Like Eisenman, Tigerman had a difficult relationship with his mother that left him conflicted about his Jewishness. He has described his mother as obsessed with money, though not due to privilege (as was true of Eisenman's mother) but to deprivation. Her obsession with money during the Depression made her unable to understand either her son's artistic inclinations or his later goal of becoming an architect. Speaking about his family in 1985, Tigerman recalled: "They understood neither what architecture was nor why I wished to become an architect. It was alien to my family." With his mother reinforcing negative stereotypes of Jewish acquisitiveness and his father being weak-willed, Tigerman gradually drifted from his early attachment to traditional Jewish practice. After his grandfather's death in 1938, Tigerman stopped going to the Orthodox synagogue and switched to a Reform congregation. Despite being bar mitzvahed, his religiosity effectively lapsed. Today Tigerman says, "I am not what I would call a practicing Jew."[8] In short, competing familial influences ultimately left Tigerman ambivalent about his Jewish identity.

This sense of ambivalence was further shaped by Tigerman's experiences with antisemitism. Tigerman first recognized the existence of anti-Jewish prejudice near the end of World War II when he learned about the Holocaust. His initial reaction as a young adolescent was to keep the genocide at arm's length; as he recently noted, "My own memory of the Holocaust is from a time when I was growing up in Chicago, having neither the capacity to process the information nor an identity sufficient to contend with the reality of what was happening in Europe. I was fourteen when the death camps were liberated, and yet all I did was to distance myself from what I saw in newsreels and read about in newspaper articles." After 1945, Tigerman's encounters with antisemitism became more direct, especially in high school and later in the U.S. Navy, where anti-Jewish prejudice was "rampant" among recruits from the American South. Tigerman also experienced antisemitism as an architect. He claims that he was "never considered for any number of architectural projects [because of antisemitism]," a fact he attributes to the long tradition of discrimination in the American architectural profession. He adds that he has amassed a large "hate mail file" expressing anti-Jewish sentiment.[9]

Taken together, these formative experiences understandably made Tigerman feel like an outsider. Like Eisenman and Gehry, however, he channeled his feelings of exclusion into creative rebellion. Having reached a crossroads in his career by the late 1970s, Tigerman decided to embrace the identity of a Jewish outsider as a way of giving new meaning to his architectural practice. Indeed, he now declared that his previous work's eclectic character was itself the embodiment of a Jewish sensibility.

Tigerman first advanced this claim in his 1982 book *Versus: An American Architect's Alternatives*. A highly philosophical study, *Versus* surveyed and tried to lend coherence to what Tigerman described as the nine phases of his career. The architect began the book by admitting that his work to date had been "uneven and faulty," confessing that it was defined by a "Svengali-like" meandering from one approach to another. Yet instead of bemoaning his work's "arbitrary" nature, Tigerman defiantly rejected the very notion of "finding a . . . right way of making . . . things" and instead endorsed the idea of "having more than one attitude in architecture." Instead of pursuing "perfection," Tigerman sought to live up to his book's oppositional title and emphasized his "perverse desire to confront" architectural tradition. Significantly, Tigerman stressed that this confrontational stance was innately Jewish. Throughout *Versus*, Tigerman cited Thorleif Boman and Bruno Zevi's theories about the historic rivalry between Hellenic and Hebraic thought in order to justify his new rebellious architectural philosophy. Tigerman asserted in the introduction, for example, that the antagonism between the two cultural traditions had long led him, as a Jew, to feel ill at ease within the architectural profession. Drawing on his own family experience, he declared: "For the past several years I have become increasingly aware . . . of the reason why no archetypal Jewish Mother ever boasts of 'my son, the architect' [as she would] 'my son, the doctor.' Just what is it about architecture that precludes it from inclusion in the cultural tradition of such a signal figure as the Jewish Mother?" The reason, he noted, was that the Hellenic values of "ideality and perpetuity — the bookends of architectural aspiration — have no place in the temporal thought contained within the tradition of Judaism." Tigerman expanded upon this idea in an interview the same year *Versus* was published, observing that "architecture is not a Jewish discipline, it's a Hellenic-Christian phenomenon. It deals with the making of icons. It deals with systems of life after death. To be a Jew deals with the sanctification of life alone. . . . Of course the Jews were always on the run . . . [and] weren't any place for two minutes, long enough to make anything worth a goddam, so they were never involved with beauty. Now to be an architect and to be a Jew is obviously to be schizophrenic." Rather than surrender to the contradiction between Jewish values and the principles of architecture, however, Tigerman embraced it, believing that the solution was "to confront these joint goals of ideality and perpetuity and to propose that architecture can hold a dialectical position within the dualistic tradition of simultaneity."[10]

Tigerman clarified his thinking in the last chapter of *Versus*, provocatively entitled "Post-Modernism Is a Jewish Movement." In it, he criticized modernist orthodoxy and postmodern historicism for being rooted in the perfectionist, Platonic tradition of idealism. According to Tigerman, modern architecture's embrace of "idealist objectivity" had deformed architecture by excluding any subjective "involvement . . . [with] the particular and idiosyncratic in life." Similarly, the Platonic embrace of "the perpetual and the ideal" underpinned the "historicism that became the crutch of Post-Modernism," which was also grounded in the same "values common to the Hellenic-Christian Tradition." Neither, he insisted, was appropriate for the current turbulent times. He was convinced that the "complexities of [a] . . . ruptured culture demanded a more comprehensive response than that provided by pure Platonic thought." In opposing Platonic tradition, Tigerman recommended what he called a more "dualistic," Aristotelian approach based on the willingness to embrace the "unsynthesized dialectic." Aristotle's guiding principle of the "mean between opposites" taught that it was preferable to hold "opposing values" in a state of unreconciled tension than to synthesize them into a harmonious whole.[11]

This Aristotelian idea particularly appealed to Tigerman because of its alleged Jewish features. Citing the Jewish philosopher Moses Maimonides's rediscovery of Aristotle's ideas in the Middle Ages, the architect claimed that the "unsynthesized dialectic" closely resembled Talmudic reasoning in rejecting "synthesis" and accepting "being torn" between opposing views. Rather than striving for the ideal, which was "used by mankind to express perpetuity," the Talmud recommended "search[ing] for the alternate dimension of things [and refusing] ... to remain content with simplistic solutions." Translated into architecture, this philosophical idea had important implications. As Tigerman put it, "It is possible in architecture to achieve an imperfect form of building representing the imperfect anthropomorphic condition of man.... In Judaism the basic question of morality is one of constant debate with oneself.... It is perfectly possible in one building to have a dialectic between a Platonic striving for perfection and the perverse desire to rupture that very perfection in order to represent the frailty of the human condition." Tigerman thus rejected an "architecture that is employed in the service of perpetual values" and instead demanded one that "interprets the dualistic tendencies expressed by contemporary civilization."[12] This kind of architecture would authentically express the ruptured nature of the postmodern world and avoid the pseudo-postmodern effort to evade it through a nostalgic neohistoricism. It would also be genuinely Jewish in embodying the Talmudic injunction for discursiveness and dualism instead of synthesis and idealism. In short, by philosophically reinterpreting his eclectic body of work as prototypically Jewish, Tigerman retroactively imposed a sense of coherence to his career and simultaneously appointed himself a spokesman for the eclectic postmodern movement then emerging.

In the years following the publication of Versus, Tigerman went on to cite other Jewish rationales for his new architectural philosophy. Among the more important was the tragic course of Jewish history, especially its culmination in the Holocaust. Although Tigerman mentioned the Nazi genocide in his writings as early as 1979, he began to do so more consistently a decade later following the publication of his book The Architecture of Exile (1988).[13] This deeply philosophical study sought to trace architecture's response to the modern world's ruptured condition by seeking its origins in antiquity. For Tigerman, the fact that the modern world was in a "state of exile, a state brought about by dislocation," could be traced all the way back to Adam and Eve's expulsion from the Garden of Eden. From that moment, human beings began to use architecture to try to return to Eden and recapture their lost innocence. Most of The Architecture of Exile surveyed the architectural results of this effort to overcome exile — examining the design of such edifices as Solomon's Temple in Jerusalem and analyzing its ensuing impact on western architectural history, especially since the Renaissance (the first epoch that willingly strove to "return to an earlier state"). But Tigerman also noted that the attempt to overcome exile had also found recent expression in "Postmodern America ... [which] also yearn[s] for another, simpler time."[14] Significantly, Tigerman partly attributed this impulse to the Holocaust's disastrous impact on modern history. It was the "aggregation of two world wars, a holocaust of unimaginable proportions, and the threat of nuclear destruction," he declared, which "create[d] a mood of hopelessness and despair." This remark suggests that Tigerman, like Eisenman, viewed the Holocaust less in particularistic terms, as a disaster that solely befell the

Jews, than in universalistic terms, as a paradigmatic catastrophe for humanity at large. He echoed this point in a 1989 essay entitled "Construction, (De)Construction, (Re)Construction," in which he wrote, in highly post-structuralist language, that "*members* of the human race are (dis)*membered* through their participation in, observation — or tacit acknowledgement of — a holocaust, which they all (sub)/(un)consciously (re)*member*."

The Holocaust, however, was not the only factor that explained the modern world's unsettled condition. Tigerman's reference in *Versus* to the "ruptured and agitated life of America in the 1960s and 1970s" — when the country "fell from grace" — suggests that the rupture partly stemmed from the social and political upheavals of those difficult years. Indeed, Tigerman singled out the U.S. defeat in the Vietnam War as an important reason why architecture "could no longer be construed as ideal . . . but . . . [now had to] speak to the imperfect in all of us." The Holocaust was thus not the sole trauma that influenced Tigerman's developing architectural philosophy. Nevertheless, it undeniably influenced his belief that architecture had to directly confront the realities of the post-Holocaust world. Its presence hovered over his declaration in 1989 that the "difficulties of any given era should be evident in architectural production; to do otherwise would be to abdicate moral responsibility. While architecture is essentially celebratory in nature, it is inconceivable to me that simply because many contemporary issues are repugnant they do not have expression in architectural form. . . . I am beginning to establish a body of work in which I attempt, through architecture, to express the ethical dilemma of our epoch, the salient feature of which is . . . disjunction."[15]

Fittingly, the Holocaust's legacy influenced some of Tigerman's designs for projects in Germany in the 1980s. Like Eisenman and Libeskind, he responded to the growing interest in Germany's Nazi past by thematizing elements of it in his work. In designing his apartment building at the Tegeler Hafen (1984–88), for example, Tigerman emphasized that the "site had been bombed" during the Second World War and had been scarred by the Nazi experience (see fig. 104). Thus, while he conceded that his design "drew upon the neoclassical language of Schinkel" and echoed the district's historicist architecture, he added that it "had to be ruptured, . . . [for] to use it unaltered would imply that nothing of significance had subsequently transpired." There was no mistaking Tigerman's building for a nineteenth-century one; its twin facades were painted neon yellow and "cleaved" by a red metal grid suggesting a "house under construction, or being torn down." Indeed, the exposed sides of the building's two halves, despite being painted in a black and white checkerboard pattern, resembled the scorched exterior walls of German buildings damaged during Allied bombing raids. They also symbolized the painful division of Germany into two parts, a legacy of the country's wartime defeat. The building was "my way of acting out against the Germans," Tigerman confessed in 2008, adding that, while in Berlin in the mid-1980s, he once "made a real pain in the ass of myself" at a party where he verbally "attacked . . . everybody my age or older asking where the fuck they were fifty years ago."[16]

A similar desire to remind the Germans of their recent past was evident in Tigerman's Berlin Wall Project of 1988. In this unrealized design, drafted for Berlin's 750th anniversary, the architect proposed planting four long rows of sycamore trees alongside the wall, thereby transforming the area around it into a linear park. Tigerman's aim was less recreational than commemorative, however, as was made clear by his desire for the park to preserve the "physical memory or scar of

[its] construction." For the middle of the park, Tigerman proposed placing two "freestanding columns of the Temple of Solomon," Jachin and Boaz, "on axis with the Brandenburg Gate" as symbols of "the two trees in the center of paradise," the Garden of Eden (fig. 108). Given that the twin pillars were iconic Jewish symbols of loss, destruction, and exile, their insertion into a German context drew attention to the ruptures of recent German history and served as beacons of remembrance. As he put it, "The wound that was inscribed in 1961 is as irreparable as the one that occurred in paradise. Neither memory can be erased; the palimpsest remains."[17] Although this remark focused strictly on Berlin's fate in the cold war, the fact that the city's division was itself a consequence of Germany's defeat in World War II suggests that Tigerman's park design, like his Tegel apartment building, was shaped by the desire to reflect on the legacy of the Nazi experience.

Tigerman's intermixing of Jewish and other themes in his writings during the 1980s raises the question about the causal role that Jewish concerns played in his work. Various observers have wondered whether Tigerman's theories inspired his designs or whether he merely chose to hide them, as the architecture critic Aaron Betsky surmised in 1983, "behind a smokescreen of authoritative academic words." In truth, both possibilities seem to have affected his professional development. On the one hand, Tigerman insisted in an interview with historian Betty Blum in 1998 that his tendency to "break . . . things apart" had defined his work "for almost a quarter century" and was consciously rooted in Jewish considerations. At the same time, he conceded that he may have supplied the Jewish sources of inspiration for his work after the fact. When Blum asked Tigerman,

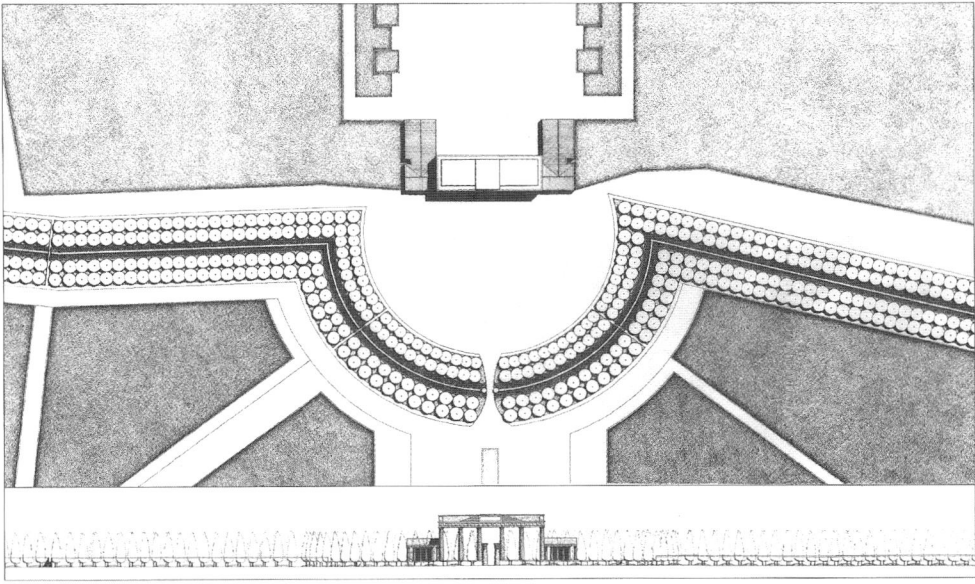

Figure 108. Stanley Tigerman, Berlin Wall Project, 1988. This project was for a linear park running along the Berlin Wall near the Brandenburg Gate. Tigerman lent Jewish symbolism to the project by placing two replicas of the columns that once fronted Solomon's Temple, Jachin and Boaz, directly opposite the gate. The columns are seen in the bottom image directly in front of the gate, while in the top image, they are the two tiny circles that nearly meet at the break in the curved section of the linear park.

"When patterns emerge [in your work], do you ten or fifteen years later sort of categorize these things and find reasons for them?" He replied, "You're really cynical!" but then noted, "Yeah. Well, I find reasons for them. Maybe these were reasons that finally came out." Certain skeptics might interpret these remarks as proof that Tigerman's talk about Jewishness in architecture is mere rhetoric disconnected from his actual work. Others could point to Tigerman's classically inspired buildings from the late 1980s as proof that he has never fully lived up to his allegedly principled opposition to classicism.[18] Yet the fact that Tigerman would later draw on many Jewish ideas in designing his Illinois Holocaust Museum and Education Center in Skokie (discussed in Chapter 10) shows the sincerity of his Jewish architectural turn.

In the end, the diversity of Tigerman's output shows that Jewishness in architecture is more about pluralism than purity. It also reveals that architectural Jewishness is less about aesthetics than ideas. The fact that Tigerman followed Eisenman, Libeskind, and Gehry in framing his architectural rebellion in Jewish terms confirms how certain Jewish architects were willing to seek creative inspiration in their heritage in the postmodern era.

Eric Owen Moss

The opposite is true of the work of Eric Owen Moss, whose career casts a different light on the Jewish dimensions of deconstructivism. Moss has frequently been called a deconstructivist, although, like most architects, he dislikes labels.[19] His buildings have nevertheless displayed a deconstructivist bent in rejecting both postmodern historical reference and modernist abstraction in favor of a sculptural aesthetic of instability. Moss has also exhibited deconstructivist tendencies by citing factors outside of architecture to explain his works' sources of inspiration. Yet, in sharp contrast to Eisenman, Libeskind, Gehry, and Tigerman, he has refrained from justifying his work with references to Jewish history, culture, or identity. The absence of Jewish themes in Moss's writings and buildings confirms a point that bears repeating: deconstructivism has no *inherent* connection to sources of Jewish inspiration. Indeed, the fact that a Jewish architect like Moss could embrace a deconstructivist approach without linking it to his Jewish identity shows that an architecture of alienation could easily be rooted in a mindset of assimilation.

Moss enjoys an international reputation, but most of his realized work has been centered in his home city of Los Angeles.[20] After receiving his master's degree in architecture at the University of California at Berkeley in 1968 and a second master's at Harvard University in 1972, Moss opened his own firm in Los Angeles in 1976 and quickly gained attention for housing designs that exhibited quirky traits, like those of Frank Gehry. His 708 House (which he built for himself in 1979 – 82) displayed incongruous features, such as a false gable and a protruding glass-paneled "flying door" supported by a sharply angled "flying buttress" made of steel, while his Petal House (1982 – 84) featured an anti-roof that, like a flower, seemed to be unfolding and opening to the sky (fig. 109). Moss's best-known buildings have appeared since the late 1980s in a formerly derelict industrial warehouse district in the Los Angeles neighborhood of Culver City, where he has built and renovated numerous buildings for the developers Frederick and Laurie Samitaur Smith.[21] These buildings display many deconstructivist features: colliding volumes, disjointed forms, and the juxtaposition of diverse materials, such as wood, steel, stucco, and acrylic. Many of his designs also qualify as parabuildings, in that they were renovations of existing buildings, the original structural elements of which (wooden bowstring trusses, sawtooth roofs, and so forth) were gutted and exposed in a kind of architectural autopsy.

Moss's Culver City buildings all exuded instability. His early works, like Gehry's, employed angled beams, struts, and columns to suggest the possibility of structural collapse. His Paramount Laundry building (1987–89), for example, featured a portico supported by columns made of vitrified clay pipe, one of which was bent at a sharp angle and appeared ready to fall. A similar mood of unease was communicated in the street facade of the Gary Group office building (1988–90), which displayed faux boarded-up windows and a voided wall segment tilted backward, as if poised to topple into the parking lot behind it (fig. 110). Later works radiated a more enigmatic aura of uncertainty. His Samitaur office building (1989–95) was a three-hundred-foot-long structure, elevated fourteen feet above the ground on steel girders, whose facade bore jagged, protruding, and slashed features, including the uncanny visage of a smiling jack-o-lantern (fig. 111). Not far away, a warehouse renovation known as the Beehive (1996–2001) was a cylindrical, steel-clad structure featuring a surrealistic roof composed of three ascending and descending staircases reminiscent of M. C. Escher. Finally, other buildings displayed hints of trauma, such as his bruised and bulging "What Wall?" warehouse renovation (1996–99), and his Umbrella Building (1996–99), which looked disemboweled (fig. 112).

At first glance, the similarity of Moss's destabilized designs to those of other deconstructivists strongly suggests that he was committed to an architecture of alienation. Many critics interpreted Moss's work in this way, asserting—as Anthony Vidler did in 1996—that his buildings' evocative "half-ruins and fragments," their "shattered wholes," and their "violence . . . against geometry" were linked to the "present fin-de-siècle and its formal and social disruptions." Moss himself seemed to support these interpretations in his writings and interviews, as in 1991, when he affirmed that his buildings were part of a "social and political commentary on the world and the way it works." To be sure, the specific nature of Moss's commentary remained abstract. In declaring his desire in 1996 to "build instability . . . [and] then obviate it," he opaquely explained that "instability is related to an unsteady psychological state in . . . the culture. Architecture should look at that condition and say something about it." He added in a 2002 interview that he was "interested in communicating some-

Figure 109. Eric Owen Moss, 708 House, Los Angeles, 1979–82. This house features supergraphics on its facade (now faded), a false gable (top right), and a protruding glass-paneled "flying door" supported by a steel "flying buttress" (lower right).

Figure 110. Eric Owen Moss, Gary Group office building, Culver City, California, 1988–90. This building in an industrial part of Los Angeles displays faux boarded-up windows (left) and a voided wall segment (top) that, when viewed from the side, appears tilted and ready to fall backwards into the parking lot behind it.

thing of [the] intrinsic uncertainty and unknowing [of life]" and concluded that the "power of . . . not knowing can be communicated in architecture."[22]

In advancing these ideas, Moss revealed the influence of post-structuralist thought. His declaration that "there's a perpetual fight between trying to know and understanding that you can't know" expressed his resistance to the idea of singular truth. And his remark that "the ideology ought to be that there's no ideology" reflected his rejection of all-encompassing metanarratives. The architectural implications of this outlook were clear. In contrast to the modernist goal of creating a style of universal validity, Moss spoke of "making something and then contesting its validity." Rather than pursuing the goal of architectural "resolution," he preferred to pursue "articulate irresolution." In his embrace of indeterminacy, in short, Moss exhibited deconstructivist tendencies.[23]

These tendencies found their most systematic expression in Moss's highly personal book *Gnostic Architecture* (1999). Touted as the "definitive statement" of his "design theory," the book provided a new package for Moss's embrace of architectural indeterminacy. For Moss, gnostic architecture was defined by the recognition "that there are always useful contradictory points" within any worldview and by the notion that "[any] paradigm has to include suspicion of itself." For this reason, Moss further wrote that "gnostic architecture is not about faith in a movement, a methodology, a process, a technique, or a technology. It is a strategy for keeping architecture in a perpetual state of motion." Yet gnostic architecture was not solely about skepticism. It was also informed by the individualistic

Figure Figure 111. Eric Owen Moss, Samitaur office building, Culver City, California, 1989–95. This elevated 300-foot-long structure displays jagged, protruding, and slashed features, one of which resembles a grinning jack-o-lantern (left).

Figure 112. Eric Owen Moss, Umbrella Building, Culver City, California, 1996–99. The building, which was originally designed as an outdoor performance space for the Los Angeles Philharmonic, appears to have been disemboweled.

quest for the elusive idea of gnosis, or transcendent knowing. Crucial to this goal was Moss's idea of the "dialectical lyric." This hazy idea referred to what Moss termed the "lyrical resolution" of the "intellectual dialectic" in built form. As he wrote: "The dialectic locates the tension. The lyric subsumes it. The process of making a building is the process of making that cerebral subject matter tangible as the experience of the building. If you can sense that contradictory quality instinctively without . . . dealing with it in an intellectual way, then it's there." While it is difficult to attain, he continued, the possibility of "rendering the dialectic so sharply . . . that a transcendent lyrical experience becomes available in . . . architecture" was a worthy ideal to pursue. The resulting poetic experience would lead to the essence of gnosis: a kind of "tentative understanding that would be forever tenuous and . . . arrived at personally." For Moss, the poetry of architectural form could somehow resolve the dialectical tensions that he hoped to preserve in all of his buildings.[24]

In pursuing the idea of dialectical tension in architecture, Moss seemed to follow Tigerman, whose idea of the unsynthesized dialectic was central to his work in the early 1980s.[25] Yet unlike Tigerman, Moss refrained from invoking Jewish sources of inspiration to explain his version of the idea. Moss was not reluctant to cite factors outside architecture to explain his architectural philosophy, as was shown by his reference in *Gnostic Architecture* to the novels of James Joyce, the sculptures of Henry Moore, the music of John Cage, the Heisenberg principle, the Mayan temple of Chichén Itzá, Mars's moon of Phobos, Kyoto's Ise Shrine, the *Epic of Gilgamesh,* the military thinking of Carl von Clausewitz, Greek mythology, Edgar Degas's paintings of ballerinas, and many others. Given the range of Moss's sources of inspiration, it is notable that none of the factors invoked by other Jewish deconstructivists — the role of antisemitism, the idea of Hebraism in architecture, or Jewish outsiderness — appeared at all. Most significant was the absence of references to the Holocaust. Especially because Moss's affirmation of indeterminacy owed its existence to post-structuralist ideas that themselves were partly related to the Holocaust's legacy, his failure to invoke its significance is surprising.

Moss's silence on Jewish themes was largely due to his assimilated background. Born in 1943 in Los Angeles, Moss was the son of educated, left-leaning parents. His mother was a long-time representative of the Amalgamated Clothing Workers of America, and his father was a writer for the *Los Angeles Herald-Examiner*. Moss describes them as having rejected "sectarian allegiances" and recalls that they did not keep him out of school for Jewish holidays. They were not entirely secular, however. Because his parents "thought it was important to acknowledge [Jewish tradition] in a cultural and historical way," they hired a Hebrew teacher to come to the house. By all indications, however, this experience left little impression. "I remember it being a pain in the neck," Moss says. Another factor that contributed to his ambivalent stance on Judaism was his father's philosophical orientation. Moss had a very close relationship with his father, Morton Moss, a man whom he describes as having embraced a radical skepticism and a kind of "existential hopelessness" in his general outlook. A voracious reader who maintained an "astonishingly huge library," the elder Moss was deeply committed to studying "profound philosophical questions" throughout his life, mostly through poetry, which he wrote on the side under his nom de plume, Moss Herbert. His resulting universalistic orientation precluded a particularistic commitment to Judaism. While Moss describes his father as the "most religious man I ever met," he adds that "he didn't sign up with anybody" in the sense of giving his allegiance to a particular faith. It was small wonder that the younger Moss became a religious skeptic. This mindset was reflected in his Petal House of 1982, which included a garage/guest house with a "sort of rose window" that Moss called the House of the Holy Mercedes, adding that it was sacrilegiously meant to "[abuse] religious symbolism." Moss's observation that "sometimes it's hard to believe in the idea of believing" further shows that his world-view was unlikely to welcome traditional Jewish religiosity.[26]

Yet Moss has not completely disavowed his Jewish background. In a 2008 interview, he admiringly observed that "Jews [have been] . . . a tough, fascinating, resilient, and extraordinary group of people over time. . . . I don't think there's anything comparable." He further noted that his friend, the Austrian architect Wolf Prix, of the firm Coop Himmelb(l)au, has frequently referred to him as a rabbi "in terms of [my] talking." He added that he was "disappointed" that his father (or grandfather, he does not know who) shortened the family name to Moss after arriving in America several generations ago. "I was hurt that [my father] didn't tell me about it," he declared. "It was never discussed with me." If presented with a similar choice today, Moss affirms, "I wouldn't change my name, [even] if it was Gazakowatsky"—a claim that reflects a willingness to embrace his ethnic identity (and that contrasts with the actions of the young Frank Goldberg/Gehry). In the end, however, Moss has resisted most conventional forms of Jewish identity. Believing that "Jewishness is . . . bigger and deeper than any ability to describe it," he has avoided any direct connection to it. As he concluded in 2008, "I've always been reluctant to assign any of the things I've done [in my career] to a particular allegiance, either a religious allegiance or a political allegiance. . . . It's not so much that I'd have to convince you about it, I haven't convinced myself about it."[27]

Beyond his secular upbringing, Moss's assimilated identity is also explained by his lack of exposure to antisemitism. Although he recalls an episode in the early 1960s when his then-girlfriend's parents lamented the possibility of having Jewish grandchildren, anti-Jewish prejudice played little role in his life. Moss thus differed substantially from Eisenman, Libeskind, Gehry, and Tigerman, all of whom directly experienced anti-Jewish prejudice and came to view themselves as outsiders. It is true that Moss has long viewed himself as an outsider, saying, "In a psycho-therapeutic sense . . . I've never felt quite like I fit [in]." Yet, he hastens to add, "I don't know that it has anything at all to do—even in retrospect—with being Jewish."[28]

Moss's assimilated identity may explain why he was disinclined to reflect deeply on the Holocaust in his work. Without feeling a specifically Jewish sense of outsiderness, he did not feel drawn to the subject like his deconstructivist colleagues. That said, Moss's stance remains puzzling. Not only was Holocaust consciousness spreading throughout America at the same time he was developing his signature style, it had become increasingly important within his own family. In the early 1980s, Moss's father wrote an epic poem entitled *Holy Holocaust*, a passionate indictment of Christian antisemitism. This fact alone suggests that the architect was likely aware of the Nazi genocide's increasingly prominent legacy. Moss's active role in getting the poem published after his father's death in 1991—and the fact that he took the book's cover photograph of the Mauthausen concentration camp's infamous "stairway of death"—provides further evidence of Moss's awareness of the Holocaust. Finally, the father's dedication of the book to his son suggests the importance of the Nazi genocide to both. Nevertheless, that importance remained limited for the younger Moss. In 2008 he acknowledged that the Holocaust was "horrendous," but quickly added that he was also horrified by the Soviet Gulags. Moreover, although he asserted that he relates to the Holocaust "as a Jew," he hinted that he is unwilling to exploit it for particularistic purposes, saying he is "not interested in my side against your side in terms of . . . religious insight." Perhaps most revealing is Moss's blunt explanation of why he visited the Mauthausen concentration camp in the mid-1990s: "I needed to go to a concentration camp. I probably needed to go forever." These pregnant remarks suggest that Moss, like Gehry, may possess unresolved feelings toward the Holocaust and simply prefers for them not to affect his work.[29]

That these feelings could not be kept entirely silent, however, was revealed in 1996, when Moss submitted a design for the Jewish Museum of San Francisco. By this time, museum officials had abandoned Peter Eisenman's proposal for the adaptive reuse of the Jenny Street substation and were searching for new options. Moss responded by drafting a plan, entitled "Recollecting Forward," which was notable for being the first in his career to be influenced by Jewish considerations. The project's title referred to Moss's longstanding practice of producing new spaces through the incorporation of older ones, but this time the architect gave it a Jewish spin, noting that his combination of the old and new echoed the idea of "Judaism as . . . dialectical/a dialogue." In practice, Moss's concept of the museum's spaces "as dialogues between spatial alternatives" revealed few clear Jewish influences. Although he proposed transforming the plaza in front of the museum into a "plaza of Abrahamic ecumenicism," its architectural expression remained unclear. The same was true of Moss's brief invocation of the Holocaust, which he alluded to by mentioning his 1996 visit to Mauthausen's rock quarry stairway and asking how it might be possible "to incorporate that experience . . . in the conception of a building that says life goes forward." Moss may have elliptically tried to answer his own question by quoting a line from Franz Kafka's novel *The Trial,* about the "inextinguishable radiance of light," and noting that he planned to use the museum's existing skylights to symbolize "optimism, but not a naive optimism." If so, then Moss may be seen as borrowing Louis I. Kahn's strategy of using light as a response to the Holocaust. In the end, however, Moss's efforts came to naught, as disagreements with museum officials prevented the design's approval.[30]

On balance, Moss remains a brilliantly inventive but enigmatic architect. Because his sources of inspiration are so broad, it is impossible to identify clear lines of influence in his work. No doubt Moss prefers it this way, even if critics occasionally have faulted him on his laundry list approach to explaining his designs.[31] What is apparent, however, is that Jewish sources of inspiration have played little overt role in his career. While his architecture suggests a mentality of alienation, the roots of this sentiment have little to do with his Jewishness. Moss's professional ascent testifies to the possibility of combining a radically unconventional architectural practice with a conventional personal stance of assimilating into mainstream American society. In the final analysis, he represents a postmodern version of the early postwar era's many non-Jewish Jewish modernists.

Architects of Assimilation: Greenberg, Stern, and the Classical Tradition

By contrast, a more consistent model of assimilation, merging the personal with the architectural, is offered by the careers of Allan Greenberg and Robert A. M. Stern. While Tigerman and Moss explicitly rebelled against architectural tradition, Greenberg and Stern worked to uphold it, laboring to promote the venerable movement of neoclassicism. It may seem odd, at first glance, for any Jewish architect to embrace the classical tradition, given the insistence of Boman, Zevi, and others that classicism embodies values that are antithetical to a "Hebraic" (and, by extension, Jewish) mindset. Yet, no matter how famous this argument may be, its basic essentialism impedes rather than contributes to genuine historical understanding. In reality, there is no reason why Jewish architects cannot work in a classical vein, a fact shown not only by the careers of Greenberg and Stern, but countless earlier Jewish classicists as well. That said, the two architects' embrace of classicism does, in fact, reflect the relative unimportance of Jewish concerns for their work. Unlike their deconstructivist colleagues, Greenberg and Stern were largely uninterested in confronting the Holocaust's legacy for western architecture. In embracing classicism, both rejected the idea that Auschwitz exposed the bankruptcy of western architectural traditions and created a rupture that needed to find distinct architectural expression. Greenberg and Stern furthermore displayed little interest in drawing on their Jewish backgrounds in their work. Rather than producing individualistically expressionistic designs and justifying them with rationales drawn from Jewish sources, they produced conservative designs that they justified with references to tradition. In doing so, they showed that they did not see themselves as outsiders within their discipline. Instead of exhibiting a sense of alienation, their buildings reflected a commitment to assimilation.

Allan Greenberg

Of the two architects, Greenberg is the more rigorous in his embrace of classicism. His buildings' careful adherence to classical principles of composition and ornamentation confirms that he belongs to the nostalgic rather than the ironic wing of the postmodern movement. The overall seriousness, stateliness, and sobriety of Greenberg's designs have made him a leader of a group that the *New York Times* in 1995 glibly called "architecture's young old fogies." By virtue of his many classical designs for governmental and educational institutions, as well as private homes, Greenberg has become known as the most accomplished classical architect in the United States. As Paul Goldberger wrote in 1995, Greenberg was "the most skillful, and surely the most thoughtful classical architect practicing in the world today." No wonder that in 2006 he was awarded the Richard H. Driehaus Prize, classical architecture's version of the Pritzker.[32]

Paradoxically, Greenberg's embrace of classicism arose from a spirit of rebellion. Like many other architects of his generation, Greenberg was trained as a modernist. He began his study of architecture at the University of Witwatersrand in Johannesburg, South Africa, where he obtained his B.A. in architecture in 1961 before moving on to pursue a master's degree at Yale, which he completed in 1965. At both institutions Greenberg received a modernist education and came to admire the work of Le Corbusier and Paul Rudolph. After he began practicing on his own in the late 1960s, however, the crisis of modernism prompted him to reconsider his principles. In doing so, Greenberg was hardly alone. Yet while many of his peers, such as Libeskind, Eisenman, Tigerman, and Moss, responded by embracing an experimental architecture oriented toward the future, Greenberg found himself returning to the past.

Indeed, his turn to classicism was rooted in his critique of modern architecture. In the late 1960s and early 1970s, while he was teaching at the Yale School of Architecture, Greenberg also worked for the New Haven Redevelopment Agency and witnessed the social upheaval and architectural destruction caused by the city's modernist-inspired urban renewal projects. Although he initially "could not understand why beautiful and urbane older buildings were being demolished to subsidize mediocre speculative development," he quickly realized that "it was a tawdry reflection of Le Corbusier's ideal city: the Ville Radieuse," a utopian city planning concept that was hostile to the historic urban fabric. Greenberg was also put off by the inability of modern buildings to communicate with ordinary human beings. As modern architects rejected the inherited truths of architectural tradition, Greenberg argued, they increasingly looked "to disciplines that have little to do with architecture for sources of inspiration" and ended up reducing "architectural design . . . [to a] medium for architects to express a personal style." The individualistic character of modernist designs, however, made them bad neighbors to existing buildings and eroded the historically evolved urban environment.[33]

As a result of these insights, Greenberg increasingly embraced classicism in his work. In designing his first major building, the West Wing Addition to the Connecticut State Library and Supreme Court in Hartford (1968–77), he quoted elements of the existing neoclassical structure (built in 1901) in his otherwise modern building (fig. 113). He soon concluded, however, that the relationship between the new and old structures was not as harmonious as it could be. When asked to design an addition to a seventeenth-century farmhouse in Guilford, Connecticut, in 1978, therefore, he provided it with historicist detailing that blended with the original structure. So pleased was Greenberg with the results that by the end of the decade, he later recalled, "I decided to pursue a career as a classical architect."[34]

With this decision Greenberg partly returned to his roots. Even though he was trained as a modernist, his architectural education in South Africa began with a two-year course of study in classical architecture, which gave him a deep respect for the British neoclassicist Sir Edwin Lutyens. In returning to his classical roots Greenberg followed Louis I. Kahn, whose own classical turn in the mid-1950s was partly inspired by his earlier Beaux-Arts training; unlike Kahn, however, Greenberg refused to synthesize classicism with modernism. He also rejected the irony of postmodern classicism, believing it to be a "parody of traditional forms."[35] Instead, he aimed to revitalize a purer classical tradition.

Figure 113. Allan Greenberg, Connecticut State Library and Supreme Court, Hartford, 1968–77. Despite being modernist in form, Greenberg's addition at right echoes the proportions and materials of the older neoclassical structure.

Figure 114. Allan Greenberg, courthouse, Manchester, Connecticut, 1981. This building displayed signs of ironic postmodernism, for example, in the exaggerated banding surrounding the entrance.

Figure 115. Allan Greenberg, Gore Hall, University of Delaware, Newark, Delaware, 1995–98. This academic building represents a purer form of Greenberg's classicism.

In the years that followed, Greenberg's work evolved in an increasingly purist direction. Some of his institutional commissions, such as his neoclassical courthouse in Manchester, Connecticut — a creative renovation of a defunct supermarket — displayed a somewhat mannered classical syntax and betrayed signs of ironic postmodernism (fig. 114). But his domestic work of the period was more historicist, as was shown by his Farm House in Greenwich, Connecticut (1979–83), which was a small-scale version of George Washington's Mount Vernon, and his Italianate Huckleberry House in nearby New Canaan (1983–85). This trend continued with his prestigious interior remodeling of the Offices of the Secretary and Deputy Secretary of State and the Treaty Room Suite at the U.S. Department of State in Washington, D.C., which he completed for Secretary of State George Schulz in 1987–92. In the years that followed he designed a variety of classically inspired university buildings, such as Gore Hall at the University of Delaware (1995–98), and private homes for wealthy clients, such as Martha Stewart (fig. 115).[36]

Around this same time, Greenberg was striving to legitimize classicism in various publications, promoting it as a humanistic form of architecture. As he put it in 1994, "Classical architecture is . . . rooted in the physiology and psychology of the individual human being." "The classical column," he declared, "has both gender and character. The doric column is male, strong, and heavy; the ionic is matronly, thinner and more elegant; and the corinthian is maidenly, even more slender and the most . . . ornate. Thus the rows of columns supporting the roof of . . . any truly classical building . . . are also people." Greenberg added that classical buildings were easily comprehensible to ordinary human beings and provided them with "psychological comfort." In contrast to modernist buildings, which were excessively individualistic, classical buildings were communally oriented and more likely to meet with mass approval, especially given the classical layout of many American cities.[37]

Greenberg also insisted that classicism was essentially democratic. "A Classical approach to design," he noted, "fulfills architecture's most basic responsibility: to communicate to citizens the mission of our civic, religious, and educational institutions. . . . This is particularly important in the United States, where our system of government is based not on ideals of blood, tribe, or land, but on the natural rights that the Declaration of Independence tells us belong to all human beings." Throughout their history, Greenberg argued, Americans had taken classical forms and adapted them to express their democratic ideals. In the process, "forms once used to designate royal authority and religious privilege became symbols of democracy." Greenberg stressed that George Washington and Thomas Jefferson had been inspired by the political and architectural traditions of the Roman Republic and believed they could express the "majesty of the people." This belief was best expressed in the U.S. Capitol building, whose dome crowned a space that Jefferson originally designed as the "Hall of the People" (today's Capitol Rotunda). In short, Greenberg believed that classicism's humanistic and democratic credentials made it the "appropriate language of architecture in the United States for the twentieth as well as the twenty-first centuries."[38]

In embracing this patriotic architectural philosophy, Greenberg did not seem motivated by considerations related to his Jewish background. If anything, his view of classicism as the architecture of democracy was influenced by his identity as an immigrant who came to America from strife-ridden South Africa. Greenberg was born in the troubled nation in 1938 and lived there until the early 1960s. As he wrote in the autobiographical introduction to his book *The Architecture of Democracy*: "I fled from South Africa because of its Apartheid system. Like so many who came here from lands beset by oppression, I remain awed by the American political system. . . . I have long regarded the nation's founding documents — the Declaration of Independence, the Constitution, and the Bill of Rights — as miraculous creations, on the order of the tablets of the law God handed Moses." Greenberg did not embrace merely the political ideals of his adoptive home, however, but also what he saw as its dominant architectural traditions. For him, classicism embodied timeless ideals that offered an escape from injustice. Significantly, this was true of both his former home, South Africa, and his new home, America. Reflecting back on the turbulent 1960s, Greenberg asserted that the "protests against the war in Vietnam, racism, imperialism, military recruitment on campus, poverty, [and] urban renewal" unsettled him profoundly at the very moment that he was reassessing his views toward modernism. In this climate of unrest, Greenberg recalled that he "craved something solid and coherent," and he eventually reaffirmed his commitment to classicism. In a sense, Greenberg's desire for a sense of rootedness led him to suppress his origins as an outsider in favor of becoming an insider.[39]

That said, Jewish concerns were not irrelevant to his views of the era's crises. His disgust with the Apartheid regime in South Africa was partly rooted in a Jewish commitment to social justice. Greenberg grew up with a keen ethical sense due to his family's roots. His grandparents had fled to South Africa in the early 1900s from the Russian empire, where they had experienced acute antisemitism. For this reason, they originally viewed their adopted country as a refuge. With South Africa's formalization of Apartheid in 1948, however, Greenberg's family became increasingly uncomfortable living there as Jews, a feeling sharpened by the fact that the country was "very antisemitic." The result was that Greenberg "felt very much like an outsider" and developed a "tremendous identification with blacks," a stance he says was reinforced by constantly being in the company of black child-care providers as a young boy. The fact that Jews were overrepresented among the white opponents of Apartheid rule during the postwar period, and the fact that tens of thousands left the country after the early 1970s, further supports the idea that Jewish considerations subtly influenced Greenberg's decision to emigrate in 1961.[40]

Once in America, however, Greenberg strove to leave his foreign origins behind him. The significance of Greenberg's immigrant roots should not be exaggerated. His career path, after all, differed considerably from that of another Jewish immigrant, Daniel Libeskind, who was equally fond of America's political values but rejected its architectural traditions. Yet, Greenberg's Jewishness was not irrelevant. To the extent that the particularistic features of his identity fostered his embrace of the universal style of classicism, he resembled earlier non-Jewish Jewish architects.

And yet, while Greenberg's classical orientation may have indirectly originated in his Jewish identity, he refrained from consciously drawing upon it in his work, preferring a more assimilationist path. That he did so is partly explained by the fact that he encountered few barriers in his quest to integrate into American society. Unlike Eisenman, Gehry, and Tigerman, Greenberg never experienced antisemitism in the United States and never developed the outsider persona that led others to thematize their Jewishness in their work. His autobiographical first chapter of *The Architecture of Democracy* notably makes no mention of his Jewish background. Instead, it minimizes the particularities of self in favor of celebrating the universal truths of the classical tradition. This emphasis may partly explain why Greenberg has done little work for Jewish institutional clients.[41]

This is not to say that Greenberg is ambivalent about his Jewishness. Like Eisenman, Tigerman, and Moss, he says he is not a "religious person," but in conversation he shows knowledge of Jewish history, religion, and philosophy, quoting biblical passages, Talmudic tractates, and peppering his observations with references to Philo, Rashi, and Samson Raphael Hirsch. He has also shown interest in the influence of Jewish traditions on architecture. In *The Architecture of Democracy,* for example, he noted that "the Puritans thought of themselves as the new children of Israel, building the new promised land.... They read Hebrew and knew that in Hebrew, buildings are named as houses. You say, *beit hamidrash,* study house, and *beit din,* judgment house. And that's where I believe the Puritans got their meetinghouse." He later added that this Jewish connection "means a lot" to him personally. Nevertheless, Greenberg has never linked his own work to Jewish sources of inspiration. He does not believe that the postwar success of American Jewish architects has much to do with their Jewish backgrounds, saying, "I don't think the fact of being Jewish has any architectural implications at all." As for the idea of Jewish architecture, he observed: "Jews . . . have [an] . . . eclectic tradition of building. . . . I think there is some deep element of skepticism in the Jewish people about the notion of beauty in buildings, beautiful things, admiring artifacts, as worshipping a false God. I think there's a kind of deep ambivalence." When asked if he felt that ambivalence, Greenberg replied: "I don't. But I'm not sure I'm a very good Jew. The older I get, the more complicated everything seems to become. . . . But there is no doubt that the pursuit of beauty . . . for its own sake may compromise the pursuit of religion." Given the course of his career, Greenberg seems to have sided with the former over the latter.[42]

Greenberg has also refrained from confronting the legacy of the Holocaust in most of his work. Unlike Eisenman, Libeskind, Gehry, and Tigerman, Greenberg did not view the Holocaust as a historical rupture that necessitated the creation of a new architecture. "I don't know that the Holocaust . . . suggests any architectural implications," he noted in 2008. This view was symbolically expressed in his buildings, which affirmed the unbroken continuity of the classical tradition. But it was also visible in his reading of twentieth-century architectural history. In *The Architecture of Democracy*, Greenberg followed Leon Krier in rehabilitating neoclassicism by reassessing its relationship to the Nazi architecture of Albert Speer. Unlike Krier, however, Greenberg did so by denying that Speer's work was classical to begin with. For Greenberg, the colossal size of Speer's buildings, such as the (unrealized) Grosse Halle in Berlin, violated traditional classical anthropomorphism, which disqualified them as true works of classicism. Reflecting the fact that "in the Nazi cosmos, human beings . . . merely [existed] to serve the Führer," the Grosse Halle embodied a "cosmos with Hitler at its center" and abandoned "any connection to anthropomorphism." For Greenberg, this grandiosity was the antithesis of the classical spirit. Echoing Krier's arguments, Greenberg insisted that the Nazis' architectural philosophy was distinctly *modern* in its disregard of architectural tradition. It was thus irrelevant that Speer used neoclassical forms; they were "so much larger" that they were "anti-anthropomorphic and antihuman." More significant for Greenberg was Hitler's goal of "obliterating the past . . . to build new cities and towns that would. . . . celebrate the triumph of National Socialism." In pursuing this goal, Hitler "actually followed in the footsteps of early modernist architects of the 1920s," such as Le Corbusier, whose Plan Voisin proposed demolishing as much of Paris as Hitler planned to demolish of Berlin. As Greenberg asserted, "Le Corbusier and Hitler designed their versions of Paris and Berlin to celebrate the application of industrial technology and the new social and economic organization of their different forms of socialist utopia." In the end, he believed, the Nazi experience taught that it was modernism rather than classicism that was politically suspect, for modernism had "espoused authoritarian political principles that were antithetical to individual freedom and the democratic process." By rebranding Hitler and Speer as modernists, Greenberg hoped to rehabilitate neoclassicism by freeing it of its associations with political extremism.[43]

To do this, however, Greenberg had to overlook Hitler's and Speer's deep interests in classicism and their use of Greek and Roman traditions to justify the Nazis' mission of safeguarding the future of the Aryan race.[44] Greenberg's elision of these links was not unique among traditional architects and echoed the same apologetic strategies utilized by postmodernists during the Architects' Debate. It was unusual, however, for a Jewish architect to embrace such relativistic views of the Nazi period, given their popularity on the German political right. To be sure, Greenberg shared no political affinities with this camp. But by reinterpreting Nazi architecture in such a way as to bolster his classicist agenda, he showed how, at least in this instance, a commitment to beauty prevailed over a commitment to memory.

That said, Greenberg was hardly indifferent to remembrance. In the early 1980s he proposed an unrealized design for a Holocaust memorial in New York's Battery Park. Greenberg worked independently of survivor organizations and city leaders in producing his unsolicited design. His primary motivations were personal, as his family lost many relatives in the Nazi genocide. As a boy in South Africa in 1943, Greenberg witnessed his distraught parents react to the news of their relatives' murder in Eastern Europe — he recalls hearing that they had "been turned into soap and . . . lampshades." Ever since, he notes, "I've spent all of my life trying to deal with that knowledge." Greenberg says that he has read "hundreds of histories of Germany, of World War II, of the Jews" and has thought about "all of the difficult questions that all Jews raise." His specific decision to commemorate the Holocaust with a memorial, however, dates back to the late 1970s when he was on a trip to northern France to see World War I memorials and cemeteries. While there, he found himself wondering "why Jews did not recognize the Holocaust" in the United States in a similar way. His reading of André Schwarz-Bart's "extraordinary" Holocaust novel, *The Last of the Just,* on the same trip intensified his commitment to commemorating the genocide.[45] And so once he returned home, he drafted a design in the hope of succeeding where Eric Mendelsohn, Percival Goodman, and Louis I. Kahn had failed.

Greenberg's design differed dramatically from theirs, however, by virtue of its neoclassical character. His memorial assumed the form of a massive quadrifrons stone arch topped by a monumental conical shape containing an interior oculus (fig. 116). Greenberg's elaborate description of the memo-

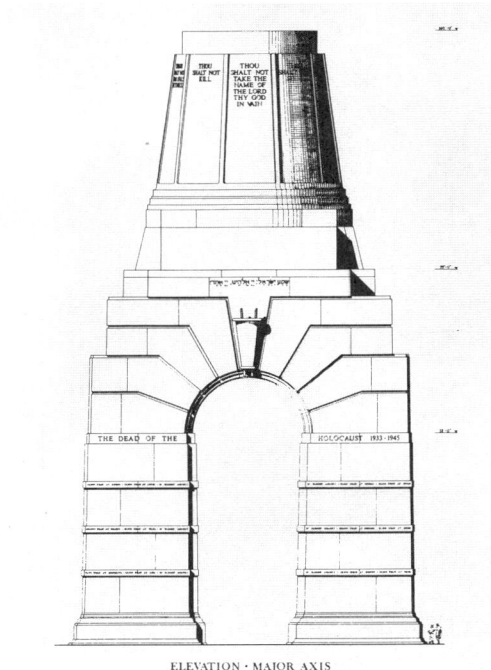

Figure 116. Allan Greenberg, Holocaust Memorial proposal, New York, 1984. The design featured a mix of religious imagery and Holocaust references. Note the inclusion of a Torah scroll above the arch where the keystone would normally be, along with the engraved text of a Jewish prayer, the "Shema."

rial's symbolic content mixed religious imagery with Holocaust iconography. The conical shape was engraved with the Ten Commandments, while a Torah scroll was located in the spot typically reserved for the keystone above the arch. Above the scroll was the engraved text of the Jewish prayer, the "Shema," while below was engraved the death toll of Jews at specific ghettos and camps followed by the words "in blessed memory." On the interior, Greenberg planned four pilasters, topped with stone menorahs and commemorative books "containing the names of the dead."[46]

Greenberg's design was not widely publicized, but the responses that did appear were generally negative. One of his friends, the sociologist Philip Rieff, found his inclusion of concentration camp names in the arch misguided. Critic Michael Sorkin admired Greenberg's initiative, but found his architectural language to be "tendentious" and of questionable appropriateness. Greenberg's design also suffered from symbolic confusion that revealed the difficulty of commemorating the Holocaust with classical forms. Greenberg explained that the conical form atop the arch corresponded to the biblical site of Mount Ebal (from which Moses gazed upon the Promised Land) and to the altar that God commanded Moses to build on top of it (where Joshua wrote down the divinely bestowed Law of Moses). Greenberg's decision to engrave the Ten Commandments onto the cone lent the shape a quasi-sacred meaning, implying that six million Jews had been unable to reach the Promised Land of America and had been left stranded in Europe, their burial site. This was an eloquent message, but Greenberg confused matters by noting that the conical form was also meant "to recall . . . the chimneys of the death camps" — a message that became doubly confusing when he added that the chimney was "also a symbol of hope because it is open to the sky." Adding to the symbolic cacophony was the memorial's striking resemblance to Nazi architect Wilhelm Kreis's classically inspired memorials for German war dead. In using such classical forms, Greenberg signaled his refusal to accept the idea, associated with deconstructivists such as Eisenman, Libeskind, and even Gehry, that the Holocaust proved the bankruptcy of classicism and necessitated an architecture of rupture, displacement, and loss. Instead, he expressed a message of hope. His message ultimately did not resonate with local Jewish officials, however, and the project was abandoned.[47]

On balance, the absence of Jewish traits in Greenberg's work is not due to any inherent incompatibility between classicism and "Hebraic" or Jewish values. Rather, it reflects the need of classical architects to adhere to their venerable tradition's universal principles and forswear particularistic allegiances that might undermine them. This obligation, in addition to Greenberg's endorsement of classicism's timelessness, explains why the architect has largely avoided the Holocaust in his work.

Robert A. M. Stern

Although not a purist like Greenberg, Robert A. M. Stern has been an equally ardent supporter of the classical architectural tradition. In the 1970s, his postmodern buildings were more lighthearted and displayed a greater sense of irony than Greenberg's. Yet, over time, his designs have become more conservative and wedded to a strict revivalist mentality. Stern is distinguished by the sheer volume of his work. The output of his enormous firm, which employs more than three hundred people, spans everything from commercial and cultural buildings to private residences. Yet Stern is an intellectually minded academic and not just a profit-oriented commercial architect. He taught at Columbia University's School of Architecture, Planning, and Preservation before becoming dean of the Yale

School of Architecture in 1998. He has written on many topics pertaining to architecture and has been central to major debates within the profession. As a result, Stern is one of the profession's most public faces and the heir to Philip Johnson as the gray eminence of the New York architectural scene.[48] He is also a national leader in the world of classical architecture, a fact recently confirmed by his receipt of the Richard H. Driehaus Prize in December 2010.

Like Greenberg, Stern turned to architectural tradition in a spirit of rebellion. Although he studied architecture at Yale in the early 1960s during modernism's postwar heyday, he distanced himself from the modern movement after establishing his own practice in 1969 (which has been known as Robert A. M. Stern Architects since 1977). This shift was partly rooted in a lifelong love of historicist architecture. As he recalled in 1986, "I always wanted to be an architect . . . [and] make buildings like those I saw in the Manhattan skyline of the twenties and thirties, soaring towers filled with dreams of modern power married to ancient form." Stern predictably disapproved of the modernist buildings that were erected in New York after 1945, calling them "insensitive, uniform boxes" that were "so bland, so inarticulate, so boring." He thus welcomed the first signs of the postmodern movement in the work of Robert Venturi in the 1960s. Venturi's influence was visible in Stern's early housing designs, which combined modernist plans with hesitant nods to tradition. His Wiseman Residence (1965–67) and Beebe Residence (1971–72)—both in Montauk, Long Island—featured abstracted historical forms and were clad in traditional wooden shingles, while his Lang House in Washington, Connecticut (1973–74), was a starkly rectilinear design enlivened by a decorative arched molding over its front door (fig. 117). Other examples of Stern's ironic embrace of tradition appeared later in the decade in houses and commercial buildings that featured classical columns rendered as negative silhouettes. Stern earned attention for these designs but later regarded them as "schizophrenic." Like Greenberg, he was more comfortable working in an entirely traditional vein, as he did when renovating Shingle-Style summer homes in the mid-1970s. Thanks to this experience, Stern realized that he had suppressed his "natural instincts to see architecture in traditional terms" and by the late 1970s decided to abandon modernism in favor of "forms rooted in tradition."[49]

Figure 117. Robert A. M. Stern, Lang House, Washington, Connecticut, 1973–74. With its decorative arched molding over the front door, this residence displayed early signs of Stern's turn to classicism.

Figure 118. Robert A. M. Stern, Point West Place, Framingham, Massachusetts, 1983–84. This office building embodied postmodern hybridity in combining a conventional glass and steel modernist box with a stylized but monumental stone-faced classical portico.

Like a convert to a new faith, Stern took his message public in numerous publications of the 1970s and 1980s, speaking out about modernism's flaws and classicism's merits. In 1972 he enlisted Allan Greenberg and three other architects to attack the modernist position of the New York Five in essays grouped under the title "Five on Five." In his essay, Stern found fault with a "conception of architecture [that is] insistently new, abstract and divorced from . . . its landscape and . . . its architectural traditions" and instead advocated Venturi's idea of architectural inclusivity. As he later put it, "Modernism emphasized innovation over invention, disruption over continuity, interior monologue over public discourse. In arbitrarily rejecting the time-honored forms that resonate with a culture . . . it introduced a kind of tyranny of the present . . . that stripped away the rich historic complexities of street ensembles, neighborhoods, and sometimes entire cities, as it reveled in the very personal and self-important thrill of isolated invention." By the end of the 1970s, Stern embraced the emerging postmodern movement's principles of "contextualism," historical "allusionism," and "ornamentalism." He later distanced himself from the label "postmodern" in favor of a "new-old approach" that he termed Modern Traditionalism. But he remained true to his belief that "architecture must . . . go backward in order to go forward."[50]

At the core of this mission lay Stern's conviction that architecture's future lay in a return to classicism, which was the "only codified, amplified, and perennially vital language of architectural form." Unlike Greenberg, Stern was not advocating a revival of classicism but a "process of hybridization" that embodied the "interaction of the classical, the vernacular, and the mechanical components of modernism." That synthesis, he believed, could form the basis of a postmodern architecture that could restore representation and narrativity. Architecture, he declared in 1981, had a "story-telling role" and an "obligation to . . . convey meanings besides its own inherent qualities." In arguing for an "architectural culture in which buildings can be 'read,'" Stern joined Venturi, Charles Moore, and Michael Graves as one of postmodernism's most important American representatives.[51]

Stern also practiced what he preached. His designs of the 1970s and 1980s drew on historicist forms, yet their continued reliance on modernist principles ensured hybridity. His Point West Place office building in Framingham, Massachusetts (1983–84), for example, combined a conventional glass and steel modernist box with a stylized but monumental stone-faced classical portico (fig. 118). His buildings for the Walt Disney Corporation, especially his Casting Center Walt Disney World in Lake Buena Vista, Florida (1987–89), and his Animation Studios in Burbank, California (1994), displayed more whimsical hybridity by integrating enlarged wizards' hats, Mickey Mouse silhouettes, and the like into the facades. In the 1990s, by contrast, Stern's buildings became more literally classical. Stern designed an enormous number of buildings during this period, among them his neo-Georgian office building on Berkeley Street in Boston's Back Bay (1986–91), his neoclassical Norman Rockwell Museum at Stockbridge, Massachusetts (1987–92), and stately public libraries and university buildings across the country (fig. 119). He also became known for his New Urbanist planning work and his master plan for the Disney-created town of Celebration, Florida (1997). He continued to design opulent neo-Shingle-Style and Mediterranean style suburban mansions and luxurious apartments in Manhattan, such as 15 Central Park West (2007). But he also produced a high-tech design for the Comcast Center skyscraper in Philadelphia (2008). For his most high-profile commission, however, he returned to his conservative roots, producing a classically inspired design for the George W. Bush Presidential Library in Dallas (2007–).[52]

Stern, in short, is one of the most prolific Jewish architects practicing in America, yet little of his work has displayed Jewish influences. Although he emulated Eisenman, Libeskind, Gehry, and Tigerman in using rebellion as a tool of creativity, he differed by refraining from drawing on his experiences as a Jew. Unlike Eisenman and Libeskind, Stern never took note of the Holocaust in his

Figure 119. Robert A. M. Stern, Norman Rockwell Museum, Stockbridge, Massachussetts, 1987–92. This building exhibited a more traditional, albeit mannered, classical form.

architectural philosophy. Unlike Gehry and Tigerman, he was uninterested in the complexities of being a Jewish outsider. In a sense, of course, Stern embraced an outsider identity by accepting classicism at a time in which modernism's dominance made it marginal. But this radical step was unrelated to his Jewishness. In fact, in rebelling against modernism by returning to the architectural past, Stern deemphasized his Jewishness for the sake of fitting in to a larger and venerable tradition. His rebellion was thus predicated on a stance of assimilation.

Born in 1939 in Brooklyn, Stern grew up in an assimilated family. His grandfather became a Christian Scientist shortly after coming to America in 1880 and passed little Jewish identity to Stern's father. His Russian-born mother was reared in a more traditional Jewish household. "But by the time I was growing up," Stern recalls, "[she had] given up many of the traditional aspects of [Judaism]." Although he celebrated his bar mitzvah at a Conservative synagogue, he says it was "against [my] ... wishes. ... I vowed ... that I would never go there again." Ever since, Stern has not been "religious or practicing." Beyond his distance from traditional Jewish life, Stern displayed few signs of being a Jewish outsider. Unlike Eisenman, Libeskind, Gehry, or Tigerman, he did not experience any significant antisemitism. He met with no family resistance, moreover, when he announced his plan to become an architect—in fact, he recalled, "they supported me." Stern thus found it easy to assume an assimilated stance in his life and work.[53]

This stance was best expressed by his embrace of American architectural tradition. Describing his work in the early 1990s, Stern declared: "The story I seek to tell is that of America, or more precisely what it means to be an American." There is little reason to doubt the sincerity of Stern's words. But it is notable that various observers, both supporters and critics, have interpreted his stance as a denial of his Jewishness. Tigerman, a longtime friend, noted in 1998 that "Bob Stern ... basically is not Jewish as an architect, ... [as his] pretensions have always moved him towards Christian beliefs." A more skeptical position was advanced by Michael Sorkin, who, in his review of Stern's 1986 PBS television series *Pride of Place,* wrote, "This is ... a memoir of attempted assimilation. Whatever its nominal subject matter, it's actually about how a Jewish boy from the Bronx [sic] can make it among the goyim, conquer Plymouth Rock, design ersatz classical architecture as if to the mannerism born. ... Our pilgrim's progress begins at Yale ... and never strays too far from the bowers of power. Down to the University of Virginia to chat about Mister Jefferson, a stroll in New Canaan with Philip Johnson ...a visit to Princeton, a virtual compendium of formerly restricted environments, a Cook's tour of Episcopal nirvana." Sorkin went so far as to claim that Stern's emphasis of his initials "A. M." in his firm's name was meant as an assimilationist gesture as well. In commenting on a 1986 real estate advertisement promoting a Stern-designed housing development, he noted, "To compensate for the troubling Our Crowd character of the 'Stern,' there's the impressive inscription of the 'A. M.' ... [It] adds an implicitly Latinate, classicizing tone ('ante meridiem') ... [and] invokes the morning and the man ready to confront it—the Protestant work ethic spelled out." Given that Frank Gehry had changed his name from Goldberg, the idea that Jewish architects might fashion their names to fit into a conservative profession was plausible. Unlike Gehry, who later reembraced his Jewish identity, however, Stern never wavered from assimilation.[54]

This is not to say that Stern tried to suppress his Jewish heritage in his work. He displayed a greater readiness than did Allan Greenberg to take on Jewish commissions. The most important of these was his design for the Kol Israel Synagogue in Brooklyn, completed in 1989 (fig. 120). He also produced an unrealized design for Sephardic Study Center, Brooklyn (1984), and for a social hall at the Congregation Shaare Zion synagogue in Brooklyn (1984). For secular Jewish purposes, meanwhile, Stern designed the Center for Jewish Life at Princeton University (1986–93). In none of these projects, however, did he strive to articulate a Jewish style of architecture. His design for the Kol Israel Synagogue was faintly Romanesque, its mixture of brick, stone, and red tile roof being intended to "complement the watery Mediterranean quality of the surrounding houses." The Center for Jewish Life was built in a classical style in keeping with its surroundings.[55]

The minimal importance of Jewish themes in Stern's work was most visible in his reluctance to reflect on the Holocaust's implications for his broader architectural philosophy. Having never experienced much antisemitism and having never developed an outsider identity, Stern was less drawn to the Holocaust than were the deconstructivists. In theory, of course, the architect's belief in the "power of memory . . . to infuse design with . . . meaning," like his conviction that it was the architect's job to "interpret the past in its fullest complexity," should have left Stern open to taking seriously the Holocaust's legacy. In practice, however, he opposed exposing architecture to the influence of trauma.[56]

For Stern, the danger of allowing traumatic events to shape architecture was obvious from the history of modernism. Modern architecture's initial emergence, he claimed in 1986, had largely been a response to the "havoc, destruction, and disillusionment" of World War I. Mies and Gropius believed that the "modern world would benefit from its liberation from the historical tyranny of the establishment that had conspired behind the stone walls of palaces." Later, when Americans experienced a crisis of confidence during the Great Depression, "bare-boned" modernism was widely embraced as a "tonic to the luxurious architectural expression of a consumer society that seemed . . . to have failed." After 1945, Stern continued, Gropius's and Mies's identities as "refugees from . . . Nazism" made them appear as "cultural ambassadors" to Americans and gave their work added moral credibility. The result, he implied, was that modernism's ensuing association with democratic values eased its postwar acceptance — to the detriment of all.[57]

Stern therefore opposed using the Nazi experience to support modernism's claims to moral and political superiority. Like Greenberg, he rejected the claim that modern architecture represented a

Figure 120. Robert A. M. Stern, Kol Israel Synagogue, Brooklyn, 1989. The revivalist design incorporated Romanesque and Mediterranean elements.

democratic alternative to authoritarian classicism. Instead, he defended classicism, noting that it "was as popular among democrats as fascists" during the interwar era. "Classicism embodies no specific political . . . agenda," he insisted. Yet, like Greenberg, Stern went further and accused modernism of authoritarian tendencies, noting that "an innovation that is based . . . on a radical imposition of something new for its own sake is a form of totalitarianism." Stern even implied the existence of affinities between the "International Style in architecture . . . [and] National Socialism in the politics of the 1920s and 30s" by pointing to their mutual pursuit of a "falsely monolithic" form of "cultural coherence."[58]

Stern also criticized how the Nazi past was used to legitimize deconstructivism. He opposed Eisenman's and Libeskind's efforts to make architecture reflect the bleakness of the postmodern, post-Holocaust world. As early as 1980 he dismissed what he called Eisenman's "schismatic postmodernism" by noting that efforts to do justice to the "crises of mid-century life" had resulted in an architecture of "unparalleled abstraction and hermeticism" that left human beings "alone, naked." For Stern, Eisenman's nihilistic strategy represented little more than a fashionable pose. It was easier, he observed, for architects "to hide behind the headlines and profess the hopelessness of a world in holocaust" than to wrestle with their ungrounded biases against classicism. As he put it, "Enduring art cannot be founded on a negative statement."[59]

Instead, Stern declared that architecture should provide refuge from contemporary problems. "Believing as I do in the continuity of tradition," he wrote in 1986, "I try to create order out of the chaotic present by entering into a dialogue with the past . . . because a knowledge of the past can nourish us . . . and reestablish a sense of decorum to our stridently individualistic present." To be sure, the past in question had to be positive in nature. "Architecture is . . . an art of affirmation," Stern declared. It was a discipline that should help "formulate and sustain a usable past." Asserting that "architecture . . . reaches lyrical heights when it . . . builds a dream [rooted in] . . . new hope for the future," Stern suggested that a forward orientation was the best way for architecture to fulfill its primary mission of shoring up humanistic values. As he noted, "Architecture is perhaps the last stronghold for humanism, the last discipline dedicated to the celebration of the intellectual and cultural traits that permit men and women to coexist, to communicate, to share." This communal vision left little room, of course, for the post-humanist ideas and jarringly individualistic designs of Eisenman and Libeskind. Declaring that architecture is the "least personal" of the arts, Stern asserted that its task was neither to express the "architect's tortured soul" nor the "crisis of our times" but to affirm "public values."[60]

As a result, Stern's built work has largely avoided confronting the Holocaust's legacy. This is true even of his designs in Germany. Unlike Eisenman, Libeskind, and Tigerman, Stern chose not to thematize Germany's Nazi past in his buildings, observing in 2008 that "none of my work in Germany has been predicated on some sort of punishment . . . for German misdeeds." Unlike Gehry and Tigerman, he felt no ambivalence about working in the Federal Republic, a country for which he feels a "special fondness." These feelings were visible in Stern's apartment house at the Tegeler Hafen in Berlin (1985 – 89), which, in the effort to heed the IBA mandate to mend the city's torn urban fabric, drew inspiration from Germany's architectural heritage, specifically the "multifamily housing of the fin de siècle, the so-called 'urban villas' of Dahlem . . . as well as the cool classicism of Bruno Paul." In pursuing this nostalgic approach, Stern differed dramatically from Tigerman, whose adjoining building at the site called attention to its violent past. More recently, in his design for a Residence and Office Building at the Quartier am Tacheles in central Berlin, Stern ignored the site's best-known building — the hulking ruin of a prewar Jewish-owned department store that was later used by the Nazis — in producing an ensemble of commercial historicizing New Urbanist buildings that German critics have likened to a theme park. These examples — like Stern's support in 2001 for reconstructing Berlin's vanished Hohenzollern Palace — showed the architect to be less interested in preserving the scars of history than in manufacturing feel-good simulations of it.[61]

Stern did not completely ignore Germany's Nazi past, however. In 1987 he submitted a design for a Holocaust memorial in Frankfurt as part of the city's plan to commemorate the Nazis' destruction of the Jewish community's main synagogue on the Börneplatz in 1938. Stern proposed a full-scale abstract replica of a half-timbered house, the kind that, for centuries, had lined the Frankfurt ghetto's main street, the Judengasse (fig. 121). His interesting twist was to build it entirely of glass and to place a brazier and eternal flame inside it. Aesthetically, the proposal was ambitious. Influenced most

Figure 121. Robert A. M. Stern, Holocaust memorial proposal, Frankfurt, 1987. The design featured a full-scale, abstract replica of a half-timbered house made of glass containing an eternal flame.

likely by O. M. Ungers's German Architecture Museum in Frankfurt (1979–84), it convincingly applied the methods of postmodern neohistoricism to the task of commemoration. Like Greenberg's neoclassical Holocaust memorial design for lower Manhattan, however, its symbolism was somewhat confused. In his proposal, Stern declared that the eternal flame was meant to "recall . . . Kristallnacht" and asserted that the overall design was meant to be an "optimistic monument to that most enduring yet fragile of human emotions, hope." Why the flame, as opposed to the memorial's glass form, was meant to evoke Kristallnacht was left unexplained, as was the reason the monument should be hopeful. Perhaps because of its conceptual muddiness the memorial remained unrealized, but it highlighted the difficulty of applying Stern's optimistic architectural philosophy to a project commemorating tragedy.[62]

The same can be said about another unrealized German project that Stern worked on at the same time: the new headquarters of the Academy of Sciences in Berlin. The site of the project was the war-damaged Italian Embassy, a monumental neoclassical building built in 1939–42 by the German architect and colleague of Albert Speer, Friedrich Hetzelt. The site's history shaped the competition guidelines, which specified that all architects should pursue a modern solution that would explicitly contrast with the building's neoclassical heritage. Stern adhered to this stipulation, embracing the same politically charged modernist view of neoclassicism that he had earlier rejected. In his project proposal, Stern described the classical building as "dehumanizing in its architectural expression" and vowed to "humanize" it by utilizing materials and forms that "challenge . . . the monumentality of . . . Hetzelt's design . . . [and symbolize] . . . the democratic order." Stern even preserved a war-damaged classical pergola by incorporating it into a "kinetic" outdoor room free of any "static, axial" character. These design decisions were out of character for Stern, but elsewhere in his proposal he reverted to type. He called for restoring the building's classical rooms to their original form, arguing that the "classical tradition" in which the building had been designed retained its "architectural validity" despite its fascist origins. As with his Frankfurt memorial proposal, the symbolism of Stern's design displayed internal contradictions.[63]

The mixed character of Stern's projects in Germany is instructive for understanding his view of the Holocaust's architectural implications. If his Tegel apartment building and Tacheles project reflected a desire to ignore the Second World War's legacy, his Holocaust memorial and Academy of Sciences proposals seemed to acknowledge it. These proposals' lack of symbolic clarity, however, suggests that Stern was mostly uninterested in reflecting deeply on the Nazi era's significance for his architectural practice. Committed to defending principles of classicism, he never seriously contemplated breaking with tradition and fashioning an architecture of commemoration comparable to that of the deconstructivists.

The Eternal Modernist: Richard Meier

If Greenberg and Stern represented an assimilationist mentality as postmodernists, Richard Meier did the same as a modernist. Meier is one of the best-known modern architects in the United States today. For decades he has pursued a strict version of modernism devoted to formalism and abstraction. His buildings are instantly recognizable by virtue of their brilliant white exteriors (usually in the form of square, porcelain-finished steel panels laid out in gridlike patterns), unfinished geometric shapes, multistory interior spaces, wide expanses of glass, metal pipe railing, voided wall slabs, and ramps. Perhaps the most defining trait of Meier's career has been consistency. He became the youngest winner of the Pritzker Prize at the age of forty-nine in 1984. His reputation was solidified with his celebrated design for the Getty Center in Los Angeles (1984–97).[64]

After earning his degree in architecture at Cornell in 1957, Meier worked for SOM and Marcel Breuer before establishing his own practice in 1963. From the start, his work displayed the influence of Le Corbusier, which was visible in a series of widely acclaimed private houses in the late 1960s and early 1970s. His Smith House in Darien, Connecticut (1965–67), Saltzman House in East Hampton, New York (1967–69), and Douglas House in Harbor Springs, Michigan (1971–73), all displayed pristine white facades, open plans, overscaled windows, and intricately interpenetrating volumes that took full advantage of their dramatic natural settings (fig. 122). These designs revealed that Meier never wavered in his allegiances. In contrast to other Jewish architects whose buildings

Figure 122. Richard Meier, Smith House, Darien, Connecticut, 1965–67. This early residence perfectly embodied Meier's purist modernist aesthetic.

began to show major shifts at the same time, Meier, in the words of Joseph Rykwert, seemed to work "as if no possible alternative [to early twentieth-century modernism] existed."[65]

Meier was fully aware of the postmodern critique of modernism, but he was never tempted to return to the past, noting in 1981, "I find postmodernism literal, uninspired and lacking in spatial richness. To quote verbatim from the past doesn't interest me. And the fascination with ornament wears off very quickly." Meier admitted that "we cannot help learning from history," but he refused to regard history merely as "a copy book from which to re-create the past." For him, history was a source of "timeless ideas, which, reinterpreted, can be meaningful for our time, and perhaps, for all time." His goal was to use the past "to say something new." In practice, therefore, Meier's modernism was subtly influenced by a postmodern sensibility. His desire to embrace yet move beyond the early twentieth-century buildings of Le Corbusier precisely embodied the tension between past and present. Meier's work has thus been seen as representing a "neo-Modernist" form of architectural revivalism.[66]

Yet Meier's designs moved beyond a Corbusian revival, as was shown by larger commissions that came his way after the late 1970s. In the Atheneum in New Harmony, Indiana (1975–79), the Museum of Decorative Arts in Frankfurt, Germany (1979–85), and the High Museum of Art in Atlanta (1980–83) Meier produced ambitious buildings on a scale that exceeded the iconic modernist works of the 1920s and 1930s (fig. 123). In subsequent public commissions, such as his Exhibition and Assembly Building, or Stadthaus, in Ulm, Germany (1986–93), his Museum of Contemporary Art in Barcelona (1987–95), and his City Hall in San Jose, California (2004–7), Meier broke up the modernist box and designed elaborate groupings of geometric forms clad in his trademark white. His grandest achievement, however, was the much-publicized Getty Center in Los Angeles (1984–97), where he moved beyond his white panels and embraced new materials, such as travertine cladding, to ground his design more deeply in the rugged landscape of the Santa Monica mountains (fig. 124). More recently, his upmarket apartment and condominium towers on the west side of Manhattan and Miami Beach have featured a more expansive use of glass, while his Jubilee Church in Rome displayed a turn toward sculptural expressiveness.

None of these buildings, however, displayed any signs of Jewish influence. Unlike the deconstructivists, Meier did not wrestle with the Holocaust's legacy in his work, refraining from participating in many of the historically freighted architectural competitions in Germany in the 1990s. He also did

Figure 123. Richard Meier, Atheneum, New Harmony, Indiana, 1975–79. This building displays many of Meier's trademark forms, including intersecting volumes, white square porcelain panels, metal railings, and ramps.

Figure 124. Richard Meier, Getty Center, Los Angeles, 1984–97. In this celebrated project, Meier introduced new materials, such as travertine, to go along with his traditional white forms.

not take any significant inspiration from his family's Jewish background, rarely invoking this side of his identity in his writings or interviews. He likewise remained distant from Jewish-related projects, although he says that he would be "delighted" to design a synagogue.[67] Meier has thus registered his notable achievements in spite of his Jewishness rather than because of it.

The absence of any Jewish dimension to Meier's work reflects his assimilated Jewish identity. Born in 1934 in Newark, New Jersey, Meier hailed from a middle-class German Jewish background that was relatively unobservant. Like his fellow New Jerseyan and cousin Peter Eisenman, Meier had a secular upbringing. Although he occasionally attended Friday night services as a child, Meier today is unaffiliated, declaring, "I don't feel part of a . . . 'Jewish community.'" He is married to a Catholic woman and celebrates both Jewish and Christian holidays with his two children. Overall, Meier has a privatized sense of Jewish identity. "If I observe the holidays now," he recently declared, "I observe them at home. It's something which I think is for me and my immediate family."[68]

Meier nevertheless has positive feelings toward his Jewish heritage. He displayed a keen interest in synagogue architecture at the beginning of his career, organizing the 1963 exhibition "Recent American Synagogue Architecture" for the Jewish Museum in Manhattan. And, like Louis I. Kahn, he displayed strong Zionist inclinations, visiting Israel on numerous occasions and accepting Jerusalem mayor Teddy Kollek's request to develop ideas for the city's urban development in the early 1970s. Meier has not displayed much interest in the Holocaust, however. Although, like Eisenman, he has childhood memories of listening to radio broadcasts and being "concerned" about events going on in

Nazi Germany, the war years did not haunt him. This may have been due to the fact that, unlike Gehry and Libeskind, he did not lose any relatives in the Holocaust. It also may reflect the fact that he never had any significant personal experiences with antisemitism. Although he recalls that, as a teenager, he was once rejected by a girl because he was Jewish, his reaction was one of surprise rather than anguish. He adds that anti-Jewish prejudice never impeded his career. Meier's experiences thus resembled those of Stern and Greenberg rather than Eisenman, Libeskind, Gehry, and Tigerman. Unlike the latter group, he never developed an outsider's identity. Instead, assimilation has afforded him the luxury of considering himself an insider.[69]

Meier's disinterest in drawing on his Jewish identity in his work also reflected his modernist architectural principles. Like earlier Jewish modernists, such as Neutra, Bunshaft, and Breuer, Meier has embraced the universal and avoided particularism in most of his work. He has noted that his "fundamental concerns" have always been "space, form, light, and how to make them." Abstraction, he says, "allows architecture to express its own organizational and spatial consequences . . . . [It] permits the creation of space without confusing its volume with any superimposed system of meaning." For this reason, Meier logically declared that his interest in architecture "is not representational." As he later put it: "The theme of my architecture is architecture." Unlike postmodernists and deconstructivists, Meier has refrained from connecting his buildings to larger cultural trends, historical events, or phenomena of symbolic significance. In refusing "to rely on symbols to impart meaning," Meier affirmed that his architecture is internally rather than externally focused.[70]

The optimism of Meier's architectural philosophy is a further reason why he has shown little interest in exploring the Jewish historical experience, especially its tragic dimensions. Nothing better symbolizes Meier's commitment to an affirmative view of human existence than his adherence to the color white. Declaring that white had traditionally been associated with "purity," "clarity," and "perfection," Meier noted in 1984 that it served his "primary preoccupation, which is the molding of space and light." Meier has also suggested that whiteness was well suited to counter the darkness that, according to deconstructivists, architecture needed to confront. While Eisenman demanded that architecture take account of the crises of the postmodern world, Meier reaffirmed the project of modernity. As he wrote in 1990, "Much has been made of . . . the fact that we live in a disordered, chaotic society. . . . However, rather than reflect that chaos, I try to make order out of it." Meier rejected Eisenman's attempt to create a decentered architecture, saying: "I don't see why I should become involved with his particular obsessions." Instead, he proclaimed: "Architecture at its best is joyful [and] exhilarating." In this sense, Meier embraced a modernist version of Greenberg's and Stern's classicism. Like their architecture, Meier's modernism aimed to be uplifting. As he put it in a 2010 interview, if his architecture had any relationship to the Holocaust's legacy it was to promote "healing." "Modernism," he noted, expresses "a recognition [that] allows us to move on" in the sense that it acknowledges that the Holocaust existed. "We can't deny it, but that doesn't mean that what we do is hemmed in because of it."[71]

This approach was particularly visible in several projects that Meier completed in Germany in the 1980s and 1990s. Like Eisenman, Libeskind, Gehry, and Tigerman, Meier received numerous commissions from German clients, but his designs did not dwell on Germany's dark past. More than a few of his projects were located at or near historically burdened sites. His Stadthaus in Ulm

(1986–93), for example, was situated on the city's central Münsterplatz, which lost nearly all of its historic architecture, except its gothic cathedral (the tallest in Europe), in wartime bombings. Yet instead of thematizing the wartime damage as Eisenman and Tigerman had done in Berlin, Meier aimed to mend its effects by nostalgically quoting the gabled roofs of the adjacent neohistoricist postwar buildings in his Stadthaus's pitched roof glass skylights (fig. 125). Similarly, his Siemens Headquarters building in Munich (1983–99) ignored the nearby presence of the former site of the Gestapo headquarters on the Briennerstrasse. And his Potsdamer Platz Master Plan proposal (1992) refrained from wrestling with Berlin's Nazi past as Libeskind's proposal did. These omissions were hardly surprising given Meier's architectural philosophy, but they underscored his avoidance of Germany's dark history as a source of creative inspiration.

That said, Meier's modernist designs did possess a special historical resonance in Germany, for they represented the return of an architectural style to a country that had largely expelled it with the rise of the Nazis in 1933. When the Museum for Decorative Art opened in Frankfurt in 1985, Meier recalled, "I saw how important it was for me to do the building as an American, an architect and Jew because I had helped to build a link between what was destroyed in World War II and the present." Similarly, Meier knew that the city of Ulm's mayor regarded his Stadthaus design "as being politically important as a statement of the best . . . new building, the best personification of a moment in time in which Germany . . . wiped out an important intellectual part of its population." Indeed,

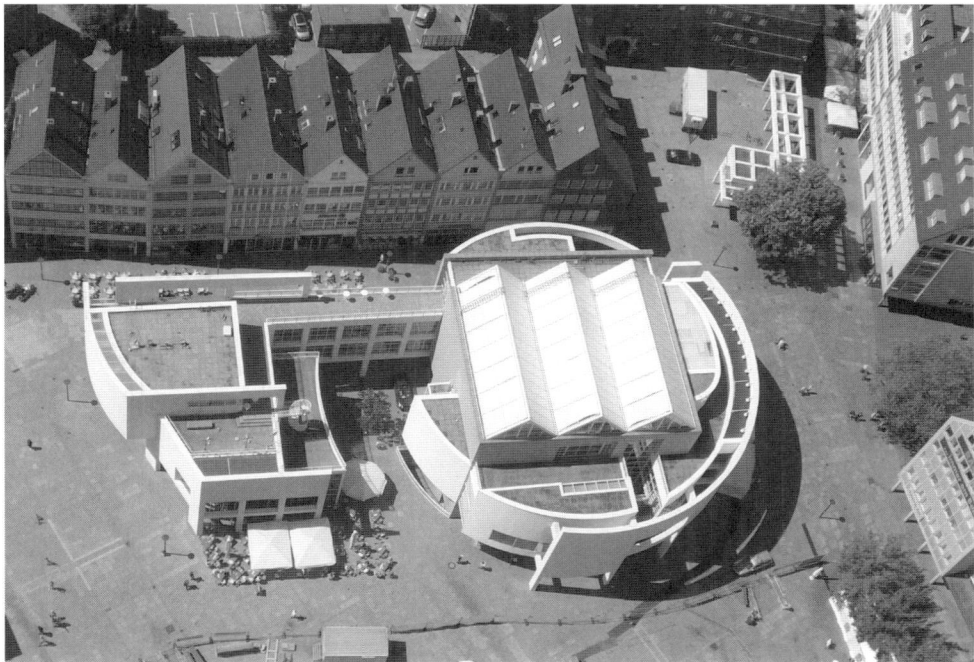

Figure 125. Richard Meier, Stadthaus, Ulm, Germany, 1986–93. Meier's otherwise modernist building (at bottom) exhibited a dash of postmodern contextualism with its pitched skylights echoing the gabled roofs of the adjacent neohistoricist postwar buildings (at top). This touch reflected the architect's effort to help heal the damage suffered by Ulm's central Münsterplatz in World War II.

Meier recognized that there was a desire in the city to "bridge a gap that was artificially [ruptured]" and acknowledged that the commission represented an effort to "heal wounds" left by the Nazi era. Meier viewed these designs as particularly significant, moreover, because of his German Jewish origins. In short, he viewed his work in Germany, at least in part, as promoting "reconciliation" between Germans and Jews.[72]

A related goal, that of Catholic-Jewish reconciliation, was visible in one his most symbolically resonant buildings, the Jubilee Church (La Chiesa di Dio Padre Misericordioso) in Rome (1996–2003). Like the Getty Center, this building represented a departure for Meier in being more sculpturally expressive, its three concentric shells dramatically connected by gridded glass walls to geometric forms including a bell tower (fig. 126). Meier did not intend the building's forms to have any specific symbolic resonance related to Jewish-Christian relations. Indeed, he initially saw little symbolic significance in the fact that he was a Jewish architect designing a Catholic church, explaining that he simply "thought about what it is to make a religious space; whether Catholic or Jewish, it didn't matter: it's religious space." Yet, while Meier downplayed the importance of his Jewish identity, others saw it as significant. In 1996, Bruno Zevi declared, "I do not think that anyone realizes the novelty of this. You must remember that for centuries . . . the Jews were . . . accused of murder, of procuring the death of the symbol of humanity, of the Son of the Father, of the Son of God." But in commissioning a Jew to build a new church, the Vatican ushered in the dawning of a "new Christianity, . . . a fabulous age in which a pope, John Paul II, after two thousand years of anti-Jewry, came to the synagogue to re-embrace his 'major brothers.'" At a time when the Catholic Church was seeking to atone for its historic sins at the millennium, its decision to commission a Jewish architect to build a church—probably the first in its entire history—was important. Tellingly, this reaction surprised Meier, who confessed that he "never thought [his Jewish identity] was particularly significant" for the project. In the wake of all the attention, however, the architect eventually changed his tune and has recently declared that he feels "extremely proud" to be the first Jew to design a church for the Vatican. He has further expressed his hope that his achievement "breaks down barriers. . . . and promotes understanding."[73]

Given the historically inflected reactions to Meier's buildings in Germany and Italy, it is tempting to view his architecture as a unique form of post-Holocaust modernism devoted to the cause of

Figure 126. Richard Meier, Jubilee Church (La Chiesa di Dio Padre Misericordioso), Rome, 1996–2003. Defined by its striking concentric shells, this building marked a sculptural turn in Meier's work. Some observers claimed that the building possessed deep symbolic significance for Catholic-Jewish relations.

healing. In truth, however, such a reading overstates the extent to which Meier's work has been influenced by Jewish sources of inspiration. While his purist modern designs promise the vision of a restored and reconciled world after Auschwitz, they were conceived less through a direct confrontation with, than an avoidance of, the Holocaust's legacy.

Conclusion

As is shown by the buildings of Tigerman, Moss, Greenberg, Stern, and Meier, Jewish architects ranged between alienation and assimilation after the 1970s. While some reflected on the complexities of post-Holocaust Jewish identity in their creative work, others did not. Underpinning these architects' diverging responses were their differing views of the Holocaust's relevance. Among the more important reasons for this divergence were their personal upbringing and ability to accommodate the historical weight of the Nazi genocide to their architectural philosophies. Those who came from relatively strong Jewish backgrounds or embraced untraditional architectural philosophies could most easily forge a compatible relationship between the two. This was especially true of Tigerman, who perceived his semi-deconstructivist idea of architectural dualism as an appropriate and specifically Jewish response to the post-Holocaust world. Deconstructivists who were more assimilated, however, such as Moss, had little incentive to add a Jewish gloss to their architecture. Those architects who adhered to tradition, meanwhile, such as Greenberg and Stern, found it difficult to embrace the Holocaust's legacy. Given the stigmas surrounding neoclassicism, any architect who wanted to utilize the style had to rehabilitate it by relativizing the significance of the Nazi experience and keeping the Holocaust at arm's length. Of course, Stern's and Greenberg's relatively assimilated identities may have made them disinclined to consider the Holocaust's relevance to begin with, a possibility that raises a question of causality: Did the minimal significance of these architects' Jewishness (and by extension their minimal interest in the Holocaust) facilitate their acceptance of classicism; or did their preexisting commitment to classicism lead them to deemphasize their Jewishness? Both factors probably contributed to the largely non-Jewish character of their work. The same can be said about Richard Meier, who also had to minimize the Holocaust's significance in order to defend his modernist principles.

The successful careers of all these men demonstrate that Jewish architects were able to rise to prominence without having to draw on their Jewish identities. Their success can be attributed to their innate talents, their ability to gauge the mood of the times, and their skill in tailoring their work to different clients. Moss's adventurous clients were entirely different from those who commissioned the classical buildings of Stern and Greenberg. Likewise, Tigerman's early pop designs and socially conscious commissions were far removed from the grand civic and cultural buildings produced by Meier. Thanks to the emergence of an increasingly pluralistic architectural culture after the 1960s, all of these architects were able to thrive. Whether their achievements will be as enduring as those of the deconstructivists remains an open question, but their example shows that the postwar achievements of Jewish architects were not predicated on their architecture becoming more Jewish. Significantly, the opposite is true of another branch of Jewish architecture in the pluralistic postmodern era — Holocaust museums.

Chapter 10
Holocaust Museums
A New Form of Jewish Architecture?

Most motorists driving on Orchard Lake Road in the Detroit suburb of Farmington Hills are probably too focused on the stresses of their daily commute to pay attention to their surroundings. Little of architectural interest graces the tree-lined road, which is defined by low-slung office complexes and parking lots. Drivers must be surprised, therefore, to encounter an unusual structure that abuts the street's edge. If traffic is moving slowly, they will easily spot a large brick wall fronted by vertical steel pillars and horizontal strands of wire resembling a prison camp's electrified fence. They will also note a massive, metal-clad volume displaying blue and gray stripes evoking a prisoner's uniform. Perhaps they will glimpse an ominous chimney near the building's entrance. First-time drivers on Orchard Lake Road may wonder about the building's identity, but veteran commuters know that it is the Holocaust Memorial Center of Michigan (1999 – 2004) (fig. 127).[1]

The Holocaust Memorial Center's liberal use of concentration camp iconography reveals an important fact about the Holocaust's impact on western architecture in recent years. While the legacy of the Nazi genocide indirectly influenced deconstructivism, it played a major role in the rise of an entirely new genre of architecture, Holocaust museums. Beginning in the late 1970s and early 1980s, the establishment of museums dedicated to documenting the Nazi genocide became a conspicuous trend in the United States and elsewhere. The chartering and eventual construction of the United States Holocaust Memorial Museum in Washington, D.C., between 1980 and 1993 represented the first and most prominent example. Other major museums soon followed in New York, Los Angeles, Houston, Detroit, and Chicago, while more modest research and education centers were established in other cities. Today, there are around two dozen Holocaust museums in the United States, while a comparable number exist in Europe, Israel, Africa, and Australia.[2]

The architecture of these museums has varied widely, largely owing to the different contexts in which they were built. European and American Holocaust museums have generally diverged in their degree of architectural innovation, with the former being less ambitious than the latter. Due to Europe's abundance of significant historical sites related to the Holocaust, exhibitions devoted to documenting it have mostly been established in preexisting architectural settings and have thus tended to entail historic preservation work rather than new construction. This has been especially true in Germany, which, beginning in the 1960s and continuing through the 1970s, saw the creation of Holocaust exhibitions at many of the country's major concentration camps.[3] Historic preservation continued to trump new construction in the decades that followed, when a number of "documentation centers" devoted to the study of National Socialism arose at other existing Nazi perpetrator sites, such as the Gestapo Headquarters of Cologne (1981), the ruins of Heinrich Himmler's Reich

Figure 127. Neumann/Smith and Associates, Holocaust Memorial Center of Michigan, 1999–2004, detail. The building's facade evokes a concentration camp with its allusions to brick walls, barbed-wire fencing, and striped prisoner uniforms. The six pyramidal shapes refer to the murdered six million Jews. The small striped volume protruding out of the brick wall near the street symbolizes a concentration camp inmate escaping. The white elliptical volume at left houses the International Institute of the Righteous.

Main Security Office in Berlin (1987), and Hitler's Obersalzberg mountain retreat at Berchtesgaden (1999). To be sure, there have been exceptions, as is shown by the construction of recent documentation centers in Nuremberg (2001), Bergen-Belsen (2007), Dachau (2009), and Berlin (2010), which are all new works of architecture.[4] But apart from these very recent examples, most European museums dealing with the Holocaust have been established in preexisting architectural spaces and do not constitute a larger architectural phenomenon.[5]

In the United States, by contrast, Holocaust museums have been defined by a higher degree of architectural innovation and thus deserve closer examination as a coherent architectural genre. For obvious reasons, historically resonant sites of the kind that exist in Europe are absent in the U.S., and so when Holocaust museums started to be established there, they were typically housed in new buildings. This reality, in turn, forced architects to consider what kinds of structures were best suited for representing the Nazi genocide. Most architects were initially unprepared to respond to the Holocaust's representational challenges. During the early postwar decades when modernism held sway, most architects never bothered to consider the possibility that the Holocaust might have any architectural implications at all. With the rise of postmodernism and the rehabilitation of architectural representation, however, architects acquired the tools to grapple with Auschwitz's architectural legacy. Especially as commissions for Holocaust museums began to proliferate, architects began to reflect on what kind of buildings would do the subject justice. In the process, they belatedly confronted the cultural and philosophical questions implicitly raised by Theodor Adorno decades earlier about the proper response of architecture to atrocity.

In the United States, architects pursued different strategies in wrestling with the challenges posed by the Holocaust. Some chose to design museums according to modernist principles and abstained from historical reference. Most, however, displayed a postmodern sensibility and produced historically informed designs defined by narrativity and didacticism; indeed, most embraced the idea of *"architecture parlante"* ("speaking architecture") by making their buildings visually disclose their underlying function and identity. These buildings alluded to the Holocaust in different ways. Some displayed concentration camp iconography in their exterior form, whether guard towers, crematoria, chimneys, barbed wire, or striped prisoner uniforms. Others employed design strategies related to the number six — for example, hexagonal floor plans — to recall the six million Jews killed by the Nazis. Still other museums used interior spatial effects to heighten their exhibits' narrative power — for example, by having visitors begin their tours in cramped, dark spaces and allowing them to emerge into light-filled spaces fit for contemplation. In all of these ways, architects demonstrated a new willingness to reflect on the Holocaust in their work. Significantly, they were not alone, for the enthusiastic popular response to their designs confirmed that the general public also believed the Holocaust had architectural implications worth expressing.

The Emergence of Holocaust Museums

Most scholarly studies of Holocaust museums have focused on how their permanent exhibitions represent the Nazi genocide.[6] These analyses have mostly addressed curatorial issues, such as how artifacts, survivor testimonies, and new media are incorporated into exhibitions, as well as the manner in which they reflect diverging models of national, ethnic, and religious identity. By contrast, few scholars have systematically examined Holocaust museum architecture. Many questions thus remain unanswered. Do Holocaust museums exhibit a sufficient degree of stylistic or functional unity to qualify as a distinct architectural genre? If so, why did they appear when they did? What considerations have influenced the architects of Holocaust museums? How have their designs been viewed by architecture critics and the general public? Finally, to what extent can Holocaust museums be regarded as a branch of Jewish architecture?

To answer these questions, it helps to survey the evolution of Holocaust museum architecture, beginning with that of the world's first Holocaust museum, the Yad Vashem Holocaust Martyrs' and Heroes' Remembrance Authority in Jerusalem. When the original complex was built in the late 1950s and early 1960s, the library, archive, and administrative building (1957), the Hall of Names and Synagogue building (1965), and the history museum (1973) were modern, functionalist structures clad in Jerusalem stone. Their sober design was in keeping with the era's modernist architectural principles. But their restraint also reflected the Holocaust's marginalized place in public discourse in Israel, Europe, and the United States. The architects of the Yad Vashem complex, according to Yosef Lishinsky, were guided by a "rigorously minimalist and bare aesthetic [mindset] . . . , which would not impose itself on the visitor but rather would arouse the rational and the sensitive in him while leaving him free to concentrate on the essence." Given that many visitors were survivors who were familiar with the past's horrors, subtlety and restraint rather than exaggerated literalism and "spectacular effects" in the complex's architecture were in order.[7]

The one partial exception was the most symbolic building of the museum complex, the Ohel Yizkor, or Hall of Remembrance (1961). Designed by the Israeli architect Arieh Elhanani, it combined modern and ancient forms to create a powerful, albeit abstract, memorial edifice. The building's square cement base and rough-hewn concrete roof reflected the tectonic orientation of the New Brutalist movement, while the inclusion of hundreds of small basalt boulders in the base's facade evoked the first crude monument mentioned in Genesis: the so-called *gal-ed* (fig. 128). Set against the rugged Judaean hills, the building's rocky form lent it a timeless, sacred feel. In effect, the hall resembled a large tomb, a reading reinforced by its allusion to the Jewish practice of leaving small pebbles on gravestones in memory of the departed. Yet while the visceral power of the building's primal forms has earned it praise as Yad Vashem's "architectural and emotional centre of gravity," its aura of "unchanging eternity" contributed to its historically unspecific character. While it was clearly devoted to honoring the dead, there were no exterior references to the cause of their demise. As a result, the Holocaust was not overtly referenced in the building's outward form.[8]

Figure 128. Arieh Elhanani, Ohel Yizkor, or Hall of Remembrance, Yad Vashem, Jerusalem, 1961. The building combines ancient and modern materials—basalt boulders in its base with a New Brutalist concrete roof—to create an evocative memorial to the victims of the Holocaust.

Until the early 1980s, Yad Vashem was the world's only autonomous Holocaust museum. Although Jews established scattered commemorative exhibitions in the United States and Europe, they were commonly housed in synagogues and other community buildings. It was not until the early 1980s that freestanding Holocaust museums began to appear, mostly in American cities. These buildings were largely nondescript, functional structures with few narrative pretensions. Nevertheless, they attracted a respectable number of visitors, ranging from community members to local schoolchildren. By the 1990s, however, as Holocaust consciousness began to swell, the popularity of these early museums increased so much that they paradoxically became a victim of their own success. As museum officials in many cities recognized that their existing buildings could no longer accommodate the growing crowds, they decided to move their institutions to new locations and prepared ambitious plans for expansion.

The debates that accompanied this planning, however, revealed the absence of a consensus about the kind of architecture that was best suited for Holocaust museums. Thanks to the growing split within the architectural profession between modernists and postmodernists, multiple design options existed, yet they all presented dilemmas. Selecting a sober and rational modern building for a Holocaust museum, for example, possessed the advantage of allowing its exhibits to remain the focus of attention; yet the ahistorical silence of such a building could easily be seen as evading the Holocaust's architectural implications. The alternative was for Holocaust museums to represent the event more explicitly, in postmodern fashion. But this option risked making the museum's architecture the main focus, thereby distracting attention from its exhibits and trivializing the genocide. Finally, there was the problem of architectural beauty. Because architecture as a discipline had long been associated with the Vitruvian notion of aesthetic delight, the idea that a Holocaust museum could be beautiful seemed to ignore Adorno's warning against deriving aesthetic pleasure from atrocity. On the other hand, if a Holocaust museum's architecture was ugly or repellent, it risked sabotaging its mission of drawing in and educating visitors.[9]

The United States Holocaust Memorial Museum

Many of these questions were first raised in the discussions that accompanied the planning and construction of the United States Holocaust Memorial Museum (USHMM) in Washington, D.C. The long story of the USHMM's founding has been expertly told elsewhere. What is worth emphasizing is how the museum's backers wrestled with architectural questions in pursuing their mission. As in most other American cities, the impetus to establish the USHMM came from Holocaust survivors who, beginning in the 1970s, became strongly committed to preserving the memory of their experiences in a permanent institution. Once a number of these figures received recognition by President Jimmy Carter and were formally appointed to the President's Commission on the Holocaust, they began discussing their goals for a museum. Questions of architecture did not figure prominently at first. In the group's 1979 *Report to the President,* for example, the commission laconically recommended that a "National Holocaust Memorial/Museum . . . must be of symbolic and artistic beauty, visually and emotionally moving in accordance with the solemn nature of the Holocaust." The commission's desire for the building to be emotionally moving was predictable. But the desire for it to be "beautiful" reflected a lack of awareness about the deeper question of whether a building commemorating the Holocaust should be informed by a seemingly contradictory aesthetic principle.[10]

This lack of awareness was also visible in the ensuing discussion about whether the museum even needed to be housed in a new building. Many members of the Holocaust memorial commission did not believe that a new structure was needed. In 1981, the federal government turned over to the commission's successor body, the Holocaust Memorial Council, a prime piece of land just off the National Mall between 14th and 15th Streets, then occupied by a dilapidated set of turn-of-the-century annex buildings associated with the late nineteenth century neoromanesque Auditors Main Building. Some commission members, such as Elie Wiesel, thought that the annexes' crumbling brick facades evoked concentration camp structures and believed that they might serve well as the museum's future home. Wiesel had difficulty imagining how any new building could convey the reality of the Holocaust, a position consistent with his belief that only survivors had access to its horrific truth. Other commission members preferred a new building whose design could somehow evoke the Holocaust's bleak reality. In 1981, the eminent Holocaust historian Raul Hilberg insisted that the building "should be a contemporary statement about the Holocaust. It should . . . not be erected with smooth lines. Its atmosphere should not be 'serene.' In no conventional sense should it be 'beautiful.' The materials must be rough and they should evoke the primitive, elemental forces that generated the Holocaust." Once it became clear that the annexes of the Auditors Main Building would be too small to accommodate the museum's ambitious exhibition and educational objectives, council members agreed to consider a new structure.[11]

Despite having the enviable opportunity to make what one council member described as an "architectural statement about the Holocaust," however, there was initially little inclination to pursue an ambitious building. The council did not bother to organize an international architectural competition and instead solicited designs from architectural firms known to council members through business and personal connections. In 1985, the council favored a design by a local architect, Karl Kaufman, that proposed a stone-clad, neoclassical structure featuring a hall of remembrance suspended over a central plaza. Later that year, however, the Washington, D.C., Commission of Fine Arts rejected the design as overly massive and unsuited for commemorating the Holocaust's human dimensions. Indeed, the claim by more than a few observers that the monumental design resembled fascist architecture helped seal its fate. The comments made clear that any Holocaust museum should not mimic the architectural styles of the perpetrators and should instead honor the victims. At this point the council members regrouped and accepted the advice of a newly hired consultant, MoMA curator Arthur Rosenblatt, to seek a more prominent and experienced architect. The first architect they consulted, I. M. Pei, was unavailable, but Pei informed the commission that his partner, James Ingo Freed (1930–2005), might be interested.[12]

In Freed, the USHMM found an architect who was uniquely qualified to design the nation's first major Holocaust museum. Born in the German city of Essen in 1930, Freed had witnessed the rise of the Nazis as a child and had remained deeply affected by what he saw. The sight of Essen's main synagogue burning on Kristallnacht, in particular, remained with him as an indelible reminder of a traumatic childhood. Freed was lucky, however. Thanks to the fact that his father had relatives living in America, Freed was able to leave Germany in 1939 and eventually settle in Chicago. By contrast, much of his mother's side of the family perished in the Holocaust.[13]

After becoming an architect, Freed displayed little interest in drawing on the Holocaust in his work. Like fellow German Jewish refugees Eric Mendelsohn and Marcel Breuer, Freed channeled his creative energies into ahistorical modernism. He was much younger than Mendelsohn and Breuer, of course, and received his education in the 1950s at IIT, where he studied with Mies. After graduating, he joined the firm of I. M. Pei and Henry Cobb and designed such modernist structures as the Jacob Javits Convention Center in Manhattan (1979–86). Until he was contacted to consider the USHMM project he had ignored his Jewish heritage. "There was a conspiracy of silence about the Holocaust and about our being Jewish," Freed remarked about his family. "I did what a lot of people . . . did—we just forgot about it, took it out of our minds." As he put it in 1997, "My parents disconnected after World War II. . . . They did not want to speak German, so we never spoke the language after 1945. My mother said her parents were burned in the ovens. We got a letter informing us, it was really horrible. She couldn't talk about it. She collapsed. . . . Somehow we disconnected and that was that." After agreeing to draft a design for the museum, however, Freed decided to reclaim his past, reconnecting with his Jewish origins and his painful childhood experiences. A pivotal experience was his visit to Auschwitz in October 1986, an event that he said stirred up "archaic memories" and served as a emotional "turning point" for him. Standing in the crematorium, he recalled, "I stood in a time warp, realizing that, except for good fortune, I would have been brought to such a place to die."[14]

As a consequence of this experience, Freed realized that the Holocaust museum's architecture had to be appropriate for its weighty subject matter. It could neither be a neutral modernist box nor an exhibitionistic high tech design, but rather "a disruptive building" that was "expressive of the event." It had to be "a building where the container has to join with the contained," where the interior exhibit influenced the exterior form. Freed had arrived at his Adornian moment. Recognizing that the emotional experience of confronting the Holocaust's legacy had "exhausted my store of known architectural strategies" and "caused an internal reconstructing . . . of my work in architecture," Freed realized that to design the building he had to abandon his existing modernist principles and start afresh. In coming to this awareness, Freed followed in the path of Eisenman, Gehry, and Tigerman by allowing his Jewish identity—particularly his memories of childhood persecution—to influence his design.[15]

In planning the museum, Freed turned toward postmodernism, but with a twist. His design was committed both to historical reference and representation, but not in a nostalgic or ironic vein. Freed made clear that he was uninterested in explicitly "resuscitating the forms of the Holocaust" and preferred to allude to the event metaphorically with "symbolic forms that . . . are [both] banal, abstract and open-ended." In so doing, he hoped to create an emotionally affecting building. "I don't believe that you could ever understand the Holocaust with the mind," Freed wrote. "Feeling may be a better way of getting at it because horror is not an intellectual category." While avoiding literalism, therefore, the museum's forms and materials were meant "to stir the emotions, allow for horror and sadness, [and] ultimately to disturb." In short, while Freed wanted the museum to be a "resonator of memory," he displayed a postmodern suspicion of metanarratives by resisting the imposition of a singular totalizing message.[16]

Allusions to the Holocaust are everywhere in Freed's museum. Its brick and limestone exterior was partly determined by the architect's postmodern desire to relate the building to its immediate neighbors (the nineteenth-century brick Auditor's Main Building to the north and the limestone-clad, neoclassical Bureau of Printing and Engraving to the south), but it also had historical significance. The museum's main brick-clad volume was intended to evoke concentration camp guard towers (fig. 129). Meanwhile, the museum's two limestone-clad, neoclassical wings — the curved entrance on 14th Street and the hexagonal Hall of Remembrance on Raoul Wallenberg Place — were meant to critique what Freed called the "Nazi appropriation of monumental classicism" (fig. 130). The fact

Figure 129. James Freed United States Holocaust Memorial Museum, Washington, D.C., 1988–93. View from Raoul Wallenberg Place. The museum's brick-clad volume (left) evoked concentration camp guard towers, while the hexagonal Hall of Remembrance (right) features blocked-out windows suggesting entrapment.

Figure 130. United States Holocaust Memorial Museum. The building's curved entrance on 14th Street is a false facade that seeks to undermine Nazi strategies of architectural subterfuge.

that the curved limestone entryway on 14th Street is a false facade (a "lie," in Freed's words) alludes critically to Nazi strategies of architectural subterfuge. Similarly, the Hall of Remembrance's limestone-sealed false windows, by suggesting entrapment, subverts neoclassicism's claims to grandeur.[17]

The museum's interior is also laden with considerable symbolic meaning related to the Holocaust. An interior focal point is the soaring Hall of Witness, designed with rough industrial materials — especially brick and steel — that evoke both the train stations from which many Jews were deported and the extermination camps (fig. 131). Diagonal steel cross-bracing in the brick walls above the semicircular arched doorways was inspired by the steel banding used to keep Auschwitz's brick crematoria from exploding due to extreme heat.[18] Suspended steel bridges between the guard towers evoke the elevated wooden walkways built to carry Jewish pedestrians over inaccessible streets in the Warsaw Ghetto. The staircase on the west wall was designed to look like a railroad track, while the steel-gated entrance at its end resembles a concentration camp gate. The eccentrically pitched steel beams of the ceiling skylight and the tilt of the monumental staircases contribute to a feeling of disorientation. And the sight of pedestrian bridges overhead with blurred figures walking by create a sense of being under surveillance.

The unease inspired by these forms is alleviated in the Hall of Remembrance (fig. 132). Clad in cool limestone, it is a contemplative, minimalist, and quasi-religious space illuminated by a domed skylight. The space's center is empty, symbolizing missing Jews.[19] An eternal flame at the side commemorates more traditionally. The hall's hexagonal shape alludes both to the six-pointed Star of David and the six million Jews killed by the Nazis. Triangular openings in its walls evoke the triangular patches on concentration camp uniforms. Finally, engraved quotations on the walls — such as, "For the Dead and the Living We Must Bear Witness" — signify the space's function as one of remembrance.

Today, the USHMM's evocative architecture is considered one of its most notable features, but while the museum was still in the planning stages, it was unclear whether Freed's design would be built as planned. Council members and outside critics questioned whether the design should accentuate the Holocaust's horror or mitigate it with a more hopeful message. Certain council members found elements of Freed's original design hard to bear and asked that they be softened. For example, the architect originally planned to include a "large steel plate projecting above [the 15th Street entrance,] creating a real sense of discomfort," but he had to withdraw the idea. He also originally proposed sealing the false recessed windows in the facade of the Hall of Remembrance with brick to evoke the sealed buildings of Polish ghettos. Yet after council members urged him to open the windows to admit more light (and, symbolically, hope) he compromised by using limestone to block the windows, producing a less jarring effect. He rejected requests for more windows in the Hall of Remembrance, however, through which museum visitors would be able to see the Mall's reassuring landmarks. Rejecting the claim that he was deliberately "blocking . . . symbols of America," Freed wanted visitors to concentrate on the museum's overriding theme and not be distracted by the outside world. He added that the narrow slits between the walls of his hexagonal Hall of Remembrance would provide visitors "just barely [a] glimpse" of the Mall's sights and inspire hope. In the end, Freed convinced officials "that this is not a typical 'good times' building." Reflecting back on the constant efforts of both city officials and council members to mute his design, Freed remarked: "There

Figure 131. United States Holocaust Memorial Museum. Inside the museum's soaring Hall of Witness, the use of brick and steel evokes the train stations from which Jews were deported to extermination camps. The staircase is designed to look like a railroad track, while the steel-gated entrance at its end resembles a concentration camp gate.

Figure 132. United States Holocaust Memorial Museum. The Hall of Remembrance's hexagonal shape symbolizes the six million Jews killed by the Nazis. The triangular openings refer to the patches worn by concentration camp prisoners. Glimpses of the National Mall can be seen through the vertical slits in the wall (left).

Holocaust Museums 267

was always the unadmitted drive to neutralize [it], to make it less potent. They would like things to be more heroic, with more marble, more central spaces. . . . I have to make a building that allows for horror, sadness. I don't know if you can make a building that does this, if you can make an architecture of sensibility. Because that is really what it is."[20]

When the building was dedicated in 1993, architecture critics praised it for evoking horror without descending into false pathos and kitsch. While initially fearful that the architect's embrace of postmodern representation might lead him to "produce a Holocaust theme park," Herbert Muschamp concluded that Freed had "designed a work of such enormous power that it . . . defie[d] language." Other critics praised Freed for designing an impassioned rather than coolly objective building. As Mildred Schmertz wrote, "Freed appears to have been right to put his feelings at the center of the design process." The resulting museum was widely seen as a masterpiece. Architecture historian Joan Branham called it "one of the 20th century's most successful examples of architectural form in dialogue with its very contents, an external shell intimately . . . dictated by internal matter." In effect, Freed had succeeded in producing a dark *architecture parlante* by placing the museum's formal dimensions in the service of larger symbolic purposes. Indeed, Raul Hilberg went so far as to say that Freed had successfully "built a concentration camp on the mall."[21]

That the few negative reviews faulted Freed's design for being too "restrained" in evoking the Holocaust's horror further vindicated his bold architectural leap. Responses to the USHMM revealed that Americans were willing to accept an architecture that alluded to atrocity without being unduly alienating. To have confounded "normal expectations" of what architecture was supposed to embody, to have turned "certainties . . . [into] doubts" without eliciting a backlash meant that Freed's "significant, singular, [and] intentionally troubling [building]" had been accepted.[22]

The museum was a turning point in Freed's career. When asked in a 1998 interview about his greatest accomplishments, he admitted that he had reservations about being "known as the Holocaust Memorial architect only" but concluded: "I guess it really has to be the Holocaust Museum. It's the only really coherent building I have ever done."[23] In making this admission, Freed acknowledged that he had something in common with his deconstructivist contemporaries. Although his work was stylistically far removed from that of Eisenman, Libeskind, and Gehry, his willingness to draw on his Jewish background and reflect deeply on the Holocaust's architectural implications enabled him to produce a building of profound originality.

The Museum of Jewish Heritage — A Living Memorial to the Holocaust

The creation of New York City's Museum of Jewish Heritage — A Living Memorial to the Holocaust (MJH) was, like its name, a more convoluted affair. Ever since 1947, the effort to build a Holocaust memorial in New York had been unsuccessful. Following the failure to realize Louis I. Kahn's glass cube memorial in Battery Park in the late 1960s, survivors continued to search for a place to build a suitable memorial or other commemorative institution.[24] They finally achieved success in 1984 when a Holocaust memorial commission established by Mayor Ed Koch three years earlier announced its decision to establish a permanent museum commemorating Holocaust victims and documenting Jewish life in Europe and the United States. The success proved short-lived, however, as the announcement sparked a debate that delayed the museum's construction for more than a decade.

The New York debate was over the same question that initially confronted Holocaust commission members in Washington, D.C.: whether the museum should be housed in an existing building or a new one. Koch's commission initially proposed creating a museum inside a historic edifice, the Beaux-Arts United States Custom House, built in 1902–7 according to the design of Cass Gilbert (fig. 133). The once-opulent Custom House, located at Bowling Green, had stood empty for more than a decade following the relocation of its offices to the World Trade Center in the early 1970s. Its status as a historically significant landmark, however, attracted the attention of several real estate developers on the commission, who believed it could be inexpensively renovated.[25]

For many observers, however, the building's grandeur was incompatible with its intended function as a Holocaust museum. In 1984, the chairman of the New York Landmarks Conservancy, Brendan Gill, declared in the *New York Times* that the idea of transforming an "enormous neo-Renaissance palazzo—dedicated to a manifestation of power, money, and nothing but money—into a museum of the Holocaust is . . . offensively ironic." Equally offensive, for the *Wall Street Journal,* was the fact that the building displayed statues of historic figures, such as King Ferdinand and Queen Isabella of Spain, who had persecuted Jews. Supporting this sentiment, the *Times* opined that the Holocaust would be "trivialized" in such an "extravagantly decorated" building and concluded that the event "requires a building expressing its tragic significance." In the end, the fact that powerful interests were opposed to locating the museum in the Custom House (Governor Mario Cuomo wanted to move state offices there) ended up defeating the idea. But the building's perceived unsuitability as a Holocaust museum was also crucial. Indeed, it pointed to the growing belief that a Holocaust museum required a form of architecture commensurate with the seriousness of its commemorative mission.[26]

In 1985, therefore, sentiment shifted in favor of housing the Holocaust museum in a new building. After Governor Cuomo offered the museum a prime site in Battery Park at no charge, commission members—many of whom were real estate developers—conceived of a plan to finance the museum by building it in conjunction with a thirty-two-story condominium tower. This mixed-use project (which followed the model used in the Museum of Modern Art's expansion in 1985), was intended to

Figure 133. Cass Gilbert, United States Custom House, New York City, 1902–7. This building was selected in 1984 as a possible site of New York City's Holocaust Museum, but widespread criticism of the idea quickly led to its cancellation.

provide rental revenue to the museum, and it appealed to many commission members' business sense.[27] Having seemingly secured the museum's financing, the commission in 1985 contacted architect James Stewart Polshek to plan its design.

With Polshek, the commission engaged a major figure who in some ways resembled Freed. Born in the same year, 1930, Polshek was also a modernist, having studied at Yale in the 1950s with Louis I. Kahn. For a time, he even worked with Freed in the office of I. M. Pei until he established his own practice in 1963. Before being asked to design the New York City Holocaust museum, Polshek had never worked on any major Jewish projects. Like Freed, he hailed from an assimilated, non-observant background. His Hungarian-born father was a militant secularist who gravitated to left-wing politics, while his mother was devoted to high culture and uninterested in religion. Prior to the mid-1980s he was best known for working on mass housing projects and for his respected tenure as the dean of Columbia University's School of Architecture. He later designed such major works as the Rose Center for Earth and Space at New York's Museum of Natural History (2000), the William J. Clinton Presidential Center in Little Rock (2004), and the Newseum in Washington, D.C. (2008). Neither these nor his earlier works, however, indicated that he was prepared to work on a Holocaust museum. As he put it, "The Holocaust had always been an abstraction to me — grotesque, unspeakable, but remote." Nevertheless, he resolved, like Freed, to seek ideas by traveling to concentration camps, such as Dachau and Auschwitz, as well as Yad Vashem.[28]

Polshek approached his design task quite differently from Freed, however, by rejecting a postmodern solution. His design, which was unveiled in 1986, may have been inspired by Kahn's Holocaust memorial proposal from two decades earlier. Its primary feature was a sixty-foot-high memorial cube that the architect described as "made of cast glass and stone panels. . . . [The memorial cube] will be illuminated twenty-four hours a day to symbolize the Eternal Light. A portion of the Memorial's cladding will appear to be partially incomplete. . . . It is an accepted practice [in Jewish tradition] to leave a portion of a new dwelling unfinished as a reminder of the destruction of the Second Temple in Jerusalem. The Hebrew word for destruction is *churban*. The same word was an early term for the Holocaust used by survivors. The choice of a monolithic, Platonic six-sided geometric figure is also meant to convey the indivisibility and survivability of the Jews." In function, the cube represented Polshek's version of Freed's Hall of Remembrance at the USHMM and was intended to mark the culmination of the museum visit. The museum itself was an independent structure, separated from the memorial by a massive stone wall (intended to recall the "walls of the Second Temple") that led through a portal down a flight of stairs to a soaring entry chamber (called the Prologue) and an exhibit space laid out along a wide arc describing the course of Jewish history.[29]

These features lent the museum its share of symbolic content, but the design alluded to the Nazi genocide less explicitly than Freed's USHMM. While Polshek's memorial cube, like Freed's Hall of Remembrance, strove for a "mood of profound solemnity . . . [and] silence," his museum wing did not attempt to jar visitors with disturbing iconography related to the Jews' actual deaths. One reason for this comparative restraint may have been that Polshek lacked a personal connection to the Nazi genocide. But commercial considerations were probably also involved. In light of the commission's desire to sell apartments in the adjacent condominium tower, Polshek's museum design had to be comparatively muted lest it scare off prospective buyers. These considerations also explain the commission's decision in 1986 to call the museum the Museum of Jewish Heritage — A Living Memorial to the Holocaust (a name that placed the Holocaust in a subordinate and less threatening position).[30]

In the end, Polshek's design remained unrealized. The most immediate reason was the stock market crash of October 1987 and the ensuing collapse of the New York real estate market, which hurt the commission's ability to raise money for the museum through the sale of apartments. Also playing a role, however, was the growing discomfort of certain commission members with the idea of combining a Holocaust museum with a commercial real estate venture. When Polshek's plans for a condominium tower attached to the museum were publicized, commission members reacted with "sarcastic comments about naming the residential complex 'Treblinka Tower' and the surrounding streets 'Auschwitz Avenue' and 'Birkenau Boulevard.'" Journalists also reacted negatively, with Michael Sorkin writing: "I find something profoundly disquieting about this arrangement.... One wouldn't add a condo at a cemetery, at the Lincoln Memorial, [or] at Treblinka itself." Critical comments persisted through the early 1990s, most strongly in a 1993 *Forward* article entitled the "Harrowing Tale of 'Holocaust Heights'" that attacked the mismanagement of the delay-plagued project. These attacks revealed that there was a basic problem with the commission's desire to build the "best possible museum at the least cost." By necessitating the construction of a profitable residential tower to finance the museum, the commission's business plan undermined any enthusiasm that the project might have generated. Like its earlier failed effort to establish the museum in the Custom House, the commission's failure to realize Polshek's design stemmed from the growing conviction that Holocaust museums required a unique form of architecture.[31]

Plans began to move forward again only in 1993 when the commission put its finances in order and hired the firm of Kevin Roche John Dinkeloo and Associates to design the museum. The reasons for the shift remain unclear, but by the time planning resumed, the opening of the evocative USHMM had raised the bar for Holocaust museum design and may have made Polshek's modernist proposal seem bland. The commission's decision to hire Roche's firm was tinged with irony. Although the New York museum was more "Jewish" in its mission (being devoted to chronicling not merely the Holocaust but the American Jewish experience more broadly), its leaders decided to hire a Christian architect to design it. An Irish-American born in 1922, Roche, together with John Dinkeloo (1918–81), took over Eero Saarinen's firm after the architect's death in 1961 and proceeded to build many modernist structures, such as the Ford Foundation Building in Manhattan (1963–68), the muscular Knights of Columbus Tower in New Haven (1965–69), and several additions to New York's Metropolitan Museum of Art (1967–85). Roche came to the attention of the commission thanks to his renovation of Manhattan's Jewish Museum (1988–93), for which he uncharacteristically designed a historicist addition to match the original neogothic mansion designed by C. P. H. Gilbert in 1908. Neither this commission nor any previous work had prepared him to design a Holocaust museum. Like Freed and Polshek, Roche recognized that the MJH "carrie[d] . . . an enormous emotional burden." Yet, unlike them, he did not travel to Europe to seek inspiration from sites related to the Holocaust. Instead, he produced a design that was more abstract in its symbolism.[32]

Roche's plan for the museum echoed some of the elements of Freed's USHMM while avoiding its more explicit features. Pyramidal in form, Roche's design confronted the Holocaust by its many

Figure 134. Kevin Roche John Dinkeloo and Associates, Museum of Jewish Heritage—A Living Memorial to the Holocaust, New York City, 1993–97. The original museum, left, displayed many allusions to the number six. It was hexagonal in shape, had six windows on each of its sides, and six tiers or "louvers" atop its base. In 2003, the museum was separated from the skyscrapers at the right by the construction of the new Morgenthau wing.

allusions to the number six (fig. 134). Its plan was based on the same hexagonal form used by Freed in his Hall of Remembrance. Each side of its granite-faced base also displayed a horizontal row of six windows. Atop the base, six tiers or "louvers" narrowed as they ascended. Roche noted that because the building's roof would be illuminated by the sun, it would "act like a beacon, sending a subtle message that we must never forget the Holocaust." He also emphasized the museum's modernist pedigree. In a subtle dig at Freed's USHMM, Roche described how he "didn't want to be specific" in designing the MJH and refused to "borrow from classical architecture" in the hope that the museum would "have meaning for different people at different times."[33] Unlike Freed's design, Roche's included no overt references to concentration camp iconography, and the interior's conventional exhibition spaces lacked the USHMM's emotional force. Like Freed's museum, however, this one also had a redemptive conclusion. Just as visitors to the USHMM could glimpse the Mall and its monuments of democracy in the Hall of Remembrance, visitors to the MJH were rewarded at the building's summit with inspiring views of the Statue of Liberty and Ellis Island.

Compared to the effusive response to the USHMM, the reaction to the Museum of Jewish Heritage after its dedication in 1997 was mixed. Although some observers wondered whether another

Holocaust museum was needed, most concluded that the New York museum's powerful exhibits, especially the video testimonies of survivors, confirmed the merits of commemoration. Critical voices were also heard, however. Herbert Muschamp compared the MJH unfavorably with Freed's building, noting that Roche's design had recycled the pyramidal forms of his Lehman Wing at the Metropolitan Museum of Art (1975) and had not been inspired by any consideration of the Holocaust. Indeed, although Roche claimed that the number six guided his design decisions, a model of the building from 1994 revealed five (not six) windows on each side of is hexagonal base and eight (instead of six) pyramidal louvers above it. Muschamp also chided Roche for failing to follow Freed's example and "challenge . . . himself to reckon with ideas outside his usual frame of reference." In the absence of any such reflection, Muschamp noted, the museum was unable "to arouse empathy or express ideas" and fell short of becoming a "work of art." He concluded, "Regrettably the building that houses the museum fails to wrap itself around the intelligence displayed inside."[34]

The completion of the Museum of Jewish Heritage represented an anticlimactic end to the fifty-year effort to create a Holocaust memorial in New York, but the fact that the museum was completed at all was an undeniable achievement. In 2003, the museum dedicated its new 80,000-square-foot Morgenthau Wing, housing a theater, exhibition galleries, an educational center, cafe, and memorial garden. The fact that the four-story building, also designed by Roche, refrains from any sort of Holocaust-related symbolism suggests that the museum had no interest in competing with the USHMM architecturally. It has proved to be a vibrant institution, but the Museum of Jewish Heritage — true to its name — chose, at least architecturally, to deemphasize its status as a Living Memorial to the Holocaust.

The Holocaust in the Heartland: The Museums of Houston, Detroit, and Chicago

In Houston, Detroit, and Chicago, Holocaust museums were established that went far beyond the USHMM and MJH in incorporating explicit Holocaust iconography into their designs. These museums sparked occasional criticism, but their favorable critical and popular reception revealed that their underlying narrative strategies were widely accepted.

The origins of the Holocaust Museum Houston (HMH) resembled those of the museums in Washington and New York. In the early 1980s, Holocaust survivors in the Texas metropolis also concluded that aging survivors' memories of the past could be preserved only in a permanent institution. Initially, the Holocaust Education Center (HEC), as it was called when it was established in 1990, was housed in the offices of the Houston Jewish Federation. Yet, as was true in other cities, its founders quickly realized that it needed a larger space. In developing their plans, the museum's founders sought a location in the city center that would be "accessible to large multicultural audiences," eventually settling on a low-slung medical office building in Houston's museum district. HEC officials next hired a local architect, Mark Mucasey, to draft plans for what would have been a functional but nondescript home for the museum. After consulting Ralph Appelbaum, the respected designer of the USHMM's permanent exhibition, about his willingness to produce their own museum's exhibition, however, museum officials followed his suggestions to broaden their vision, double the project's size, and build a new, more representational wing adjacent to the existing building.[35]

Following additional fundraising for the $7 million project and several years of construction, the 18,000-square-foot Holocaust Museum Houston was finished in 1996. Touted as the "second museum in the nation totally dedicated to telling the story of Nazi Germany's campaign to eradicate Jews," the HMH displays exterior features that vividly evoke the Holocaust's legacy.[36] As is visible in the plan of the two adjacent structures, Appelbaum embraced a deconstructivist technique in violently thrusting the permanent exhibition addition into the existing classroom and temporary exhibition building. The new wing is a reinforced concrete wedge that begins at ground level near the museum's entrance and rises precipitously to a height of forty feet (fig. 135). Stone plates bearing the names of lost Jewish communities are embedded in the wedge, making it resemble a massive gravestone. The wing's most visually arresting feature is an enormous dark brick cylinder that bisects the wedge and appears to be perched on top of it. This structure, which houses a theater, bears an obvious resemblance to a crematorium smokestack and is the museum's most historically resonant element. It was not the only one, however, for in front of the building, six upright steel girders connected by strands of wire symbolize the Holocaust's six million victims and evoke the electrified concentration camp fencing.

Holocaust symbolism also pervades the building's interior. Like the USHMM, the museum's liberal use of brick and steel evokes the Nazis industrialized system of killing. The exhibit's circulation pattern powerfully communicates the progressive suffering of the Jews in Nazi Germany by

Figure 135. Ralph Appelbaum Associates with Mark Mucasey, Holocaust Museum Houston, 1996. The museum's main feature is an enormous tilted concrete wedge topped with an oversized cylindrical form evoking a smokestack. It is fronted by six steel girders connected by strands of wire.

starting in the most spacious section of the inclined wedge (where its ceiling height is generous) and gradually leading into its more cramped spaces, concluding inside the cylindrical smokestack space, where survivors' testimonies play on video screens. The museum concludes in a light-filled memorial hall featuring an abstract sculpture of colored glass tiles known as the Wall of Tears, where visitors can reflect on their experience.[37]

In designing the HMH, Appelbaum hoped to duplicate the success of Freed's USHMM and produce a building that would affect visitors emotionally. Deciding that simply renovating the original structure "would not do the exhibit justice," Appelbaum and his design team believed that the HMH's architecture should be "deliberately assertive." As Appelbaum put it, "We wanted to trigger moral and ethical discussions in the community to alert people to what hate and racism can do." Or, as museum officials declared: "The building's stark forms and materials place the Museum in opposition to adjacent buildings and emphasize its distinctive theme: cruelty and carnage are close by, and we must continually stand against them. Even before they enter, visitors arriving at Holocaust Museum Houston become aware that it has staked out a claim to attention, a claim embodied in its physical presence and . . . primary spaces." Judging by the fact that the museum has drawn some 70,000 annual visitors and recently registered its one millionth, its architecture can be viewed as having successfully drawn the public's attention to the Holocaust.[38]

By contrast, the case of the Holocaust Memorial Center of Michigan (HMC) showed how historically evocative buildings could cause controversy. As in Houston, plans for the museum originated with local survivors in the early 1960s. They finally realized their goal in 1984 with the completion of the nation's first freestanding Holocaust memorial center on the grounds of the Jewish Community Campus (JCC) in suburban West Bloomfield. The museum was a success, drawing 2.5 million visitors from the date of its founding to the end of the 1990s. Yet the museum's directors, like their colleagues in Houston, came to believe that the existing space was insufficient for its future needs. In 1999, therefore, they announced plans to expand the museum on its existing site. This process took several years to unfold, and as the planning progressed, Holocaust imagery became more rather than less explicit in the museum's design, reversing the situation in New York.[39]

In the first stage, the proposed 41,000-square-foot addition to the HMC displayed few symbolic references to the Holocaust. This was partly due to the new complex's broad mission, which included a Museum of European Jewish Heritage and an International Institute of the Righteous. These institutions were intended to counter the Holocaust museum's somber narrative by providing visitors with a "comprehensive view of Jewish life in Europe before the Holocaust and an inspirational look at the people and institutions who performed brave acts of altruism throughout history in the face of evil or great danger." As a result, the initial plans by the Detroit-based architecture firm Neumann/Smith and Associates paid greater attention to the positive features of Jewish history and made special efforts to lend its design a clearly "Jewish" character by having it "be reminiscent of [a] shtetl." Because the HMC's founder, Rabbi Charles Rosenzveig, believed that the initial draft was "too beautiful," however, the architects shifted gears and proposed renovating the existing Holocaust museum with a design incorporating "forms commonly associated with the Holocaust experience," such as an "entry gate, observation towers, fences of barbed wire, gallows and naked red brick." This change reflected the architects' growing desire to "make the architecture [of the complex] express ideas" and evoke the Nazi genocide's "hideousness." The new imagery was also meant to "assist the Center's mission [of] . . . keep[ing] alive the idea of remembrance." As Kenneth Neumann put it, "I think you need a building that, when those who survived are gone, is strong enough to . . . make people . . . come inside." "Visitors," he declared, "[will] leave with a stronger impression if the architecture reinforces the exhibits within."[40]

Despite the architects' commitment, plans for the museum changed for a third and final time in 2001, when the museum's directors decided not to renovate the existing HMC but to relocate to Farmington Hills, five miles away. This shift reflected the directors' desire to double the exhibition's size and provide room for a large auditorium and library. Strictly speaking, the building was not an entirely new structure, as it incorporated the steel frame of an old movie theater on the site. When the museum was completed in June 2004, however, it gave the impression of being an entirely new edifice. The HMC's description of the new building as the "nation's first freestanding museum dedicated to the memory of the Holocaust" was misleading, but it was a striking structure nonetheless.[41]

The HMC displays multiple references to the Holocaust. Its two-story-high brick entrance evokes a concentration camp gate (fig. 136). Behind it stands an equally high red brick wall, in front of which rise vertical steel beams crisscrossed with metal wire, suggesting an electrified concentration camp fence. To the right of the entrance, a glass enclosure encased in red brick is supported by inverted L-shaped beams; their horizontally protruding ends resemble camp gallows. The enclosure is also pierced by a soaring red brick elevator shaft evoking a crematorium smokestack. To the left of the entrance, the sight of red brick gives way to a long, rectangular, metal-clad volume painted in blue and gray vertical stripes to refer to concentration camp uniforms. In front of this volume, which houses the exhibition, a long red brick wall also features vertical steel beams and horizontal bands of wire, suggesting incarceration. (In a clever gesture, a small section clad in striped metal protrudes from part of the wall, symbolizing a prisoner trying to escape.) Between the striped volume and the

Figure 136. Neumann/Smith and Associates, Holocaust Memorial Center of Michigan, Farmington Hills, Michigan, 1999–2004. The entrance of the museum (left) is meant to evoke a concentration camp gate (note the Star of David in the skylight). To the right is a glass enclosure pierced by a tall brick elevator shaft resembling a crematorium smokestack. The enclosure's roof is supported by horizontally protruding beams resembling camp gallows. Compare with fig. 127.

wall stand six, fifteen-foot-high glass pyramids that, at night, glow like memorial flames for the six million murdered Jews. Even the redwood trees planted around the building were selected to look "gnarly" in winter and "be expressive of the time." The sole structure that lightens the oppressive atmosphere is a white elliptical volume at the museum's south end that houses the International Institute of the Righteous. Like Freed's Hall of Remembrance, it is a more hopeful space where visitors end their museum tour.[42]

In contrast to the museums in Washington and Houston, the HMC aroused considerable criticism. Many observers found the building's resemblance to a concentration camp disturbingly literal. Holocaust survivors reported that the building's vivid imagery brought back painful memories. Calling it "grotesque," one survivor observed, "I have enough nightmares as it is. I don't need to be reminded when I drive by that building. I don't want to see chimneys and stripes." Another called the museum "frightening" and compared driving past it to "being punched in the face." One reason for these reactions was the building's public presence along Orchard Lake Road, a busy thoroughfare. Unlike museums and memorials that are visible only to those who seek them out, the HMC's public presence may have represented an unwanted intrusion into the daily routine of more than a few local residents. (That the Michigan state legislature decided in 2006 to rename a nearby stretch of the nearby Northwestern Highway the Holocaust Memorial Highway did little to lessen this feeling.) With the Holocaust penetrating everyday life in suburban Detroit, some observers feared a surfeit of memory. As one survivor warned: "There is going to be a backlash.... People are going to be desensitized."[43]

Despite these comments, the building had plenty of defenders. Rabbi Rosenzveig conceded that the building was "intended to be in your face" but noted that it "was meant to represent a horrible period in history" and was not an "entertainment building." One survivor added that while the museum was painful, imprisonment itself was "not a pretty experience. I don't think the building should be pretty." Neumann regretted upsetting people with his design but declared, "It's violent as that time was violent. Most have felt this is a positive thing. It tells their history. Many want the story to be retold. You want to show young people the result of not caring about their fellow man." That this sentiment was widely shared was shown by the architects' receipt of an award for the building from the Michigan chapter of the AIA. Recently announced plans for an expansion to make room for a larger library and children's wing—the design of which also employs brick and striped metal cladding—further testify to the museum's success.[44]

Perhaps the final vindication of the HMC's architectural strategy can be found in the fact that one of the most recent Holocaust museums to open in the United States has followed its lead in employing highly symbolic forms. In April 2009, the Illinois Holocaust Museum and Education Center (IHMEC) was dedicated in the Chicago suburb of Skokie. The building traces its origins to the late 1970s, when the threat of neo-Nazi marches in the city galvanized survivors to band together behind the cause of Holocaust education. In the early 1980s they formed the Holocaust Memorial Foundation of Illinois and, in 1985, established a headquarters and small museum in a storefront in Skokie. The 6,000-square-foot exhibit was viewed by some 30,000 annual visitors. But by the millennium it had outgrown the space. In 1999, museum officials set out to build a new facility intended to serve an expected 250,000 annual visitors, many of them Chicago-area schoolchildren. They hired Stanley Tigerman to design the structure, and he quickly developed plans for the 65,000-square-foot, $35 million building. Before any work could proceed, however, problems erupted over its intended site. Museum officials originally hoped to build the museum in a residential neighborhood on land purchased from a Hebrew day school. But local residents objected that the museum would bring too much traffic to the neighborhood, and in 2002 the Skokie village board rejected the plan. Whether or not the opposition was partly due to antisemitism (local Jews speculated that some residents were sick of being "reminded of the Holocaust"), the decision forced museum officials to seek a new location. After threatening to take the museum out of Skokie altogether, officials and village leaders agreed a year later on a new site two miles from the original museum, and in 2006 ground was finally broken.[45]

The IHMEC was unique in having been designed by an architect who had spent many years thinking about the Holocaust's architectural implications. Even though he had never before designed a Holocaust museum, Tigerman was better prepared than architects who were confronting the subject for the first time. In keeping with his intellectually ambitious design philosophy, Tigerman conceived a symbolically elaborate plan that sought to integrate aspects of the Nazi genocide into the building's architectural form. The design for the IHMEC features two major structures and a smaller third wing connecting them. All relate to one another as integral parts of what Tigerman envisioned as a tightly controlled, highly didactic, and transformative museum experience. The Holocaust museums of Washington, Houston, and Detroit adhered to this idea as well, but Tigerman took it to a new level in Skokie. For one thing, his was the only museum that visitors could not enter and leave from the same location. Tigerman intended this controlled path to evoke the fact that, in the Holocaust, "there were no options . . . there was only one way . . . [and it was to] the furnace." He further declared that it would symbolize his hope that visitors who experienced the building would have an "epiphany" and not leave it as the same people who entered.[46]

Visitors enter the IHMEC through an ominous-looking structure clad entirely in gray anodized metal (fig. 137). The building exhibits various neoclassical features, most notably two gabled volumes fronted by an entry portico topped with a pediment. Tigerman wanted the forms to recall that "Jews in concentration camps were kept in horse barns that had gabled roofs." This wing contains the museum's permanent exhibition, which is devoted to prewar Jewish life and the path to extermination. After making their way through this part of the museum, visitors proceed to the linking structure — which Tigerman called the "cleave" — that serves as the museum's memorial space. Its fan shape is meant to evoke a "book of remembrance," and its main feature, a cylindrical form at the western end, is engraved with the names of Jewish victims — just "as Jews had their numbers burned into their arms." In the cleave, visitors encounter one of the museum's main artifacts, an early twentieth-century railway boxcar of the kind used to transport Jews to the death camps. From here, visitors proceed to the second major structure, the education center, which is clad in pure white anodized metal. It chronicles the liberation of the camps and the struggle of survivors to make new lives in North America, Israel, and beyond. Finally, visitors proceed to the Hall of Reflection, designed for contemplation, and only then go to the building's exit.[47]

Some of these design elements are found in other American Holocaust museums, but Tigerman's building is distinguished by its deeply encoded "Jewish" features. First of all, the facades of the

Figure 137. Stanley Tigerman, Illinois Holocaust Museum and Education Center, Skokie, 2006–9. The museum is composed of two primary structures: the gray building houses the main exhibition (left), and the white building contains the education center (right). They are linked by the museum's main memorial space (center), known as the "cleave." In front of the museum are two metal ghost versions of the pillars Jachin and Boaz.

museum's gray and white wings face east for religious reasons. The gray structure, Tigerman noted, is "orientated toward the Western Wall of Jerusalem's Temple Mount," presumably to hold its destruction in memory. The white structure is "oriented due east in anticipation of a Messianic Age." Secondly, Tigerman notes that the "three parts of the complex can also be interpreted as the three parts of Lurianic Kabbalah." The cleave — what he also called the "wound" — symbolizes the act of *zimzum,* God's original contraction into himself to create the universe. The dark building represents the moment of *shevirat ha-kelim,* when the divine light produced by the act of zimzum shattered the vessels containing it and gave rise to evil in the world. The white building, finally, represents the task of *tikkun olam,* repairing the damage — in this case, through the process of education and remembrance.[48] This subtle symbolism is notable. Although earlier works of Jewish architecture, such as Barnett Newman's synagogue design from 1951 and Louis I. Kahn's Mikveh Israel plans from 1962, explicitly or implicitly drew on Kabbalistic thought, neither directly linked it to the Holocaust. Tigerman not only connected the two, he was the first Jewish architect to complete a building informed by the pairing.

In adding this religious symbolism to the building, Tigerman courted controversy, for his design might be seen as suggesting that the Holocaust had divine origins. To be sure, Tigerman is a secular Jew who rejects the idea, common among certain ultra-Orthodox sects, that the Holocaust was divine punishment for the Jewish people's modern waywardness. And yet he hinted that European Jews prior to the Holocaust were unable to sense the direness of their situation. In a 2007 lecture at Yale he bluntly noted that the "tribal nomad, the wandering Jew, who in the twentieth century wandered into a Holocaust of unimaginable proportions by denying the realities of one increasingly unsympathetic state, would have been better off remaining an outsider."[49]

This comment focuses attention on what is probably the most iconic Jewish element of Tigerman's design: two thirty-five-foot-high "evacuated columns" flanking its front entrance. Made of metal lattice, the see-through columns are ghost versions of Jachin and Boaz, the legendary pillars that stood in front of Solomon's Temple in Jerusalem until destroyed by the Babylonians in 586 BCE. Symbols of absence, they evoke Jewish loss, exile, and suffering. They also stand as implicit warnings against assimilation. Provocatively placed in front of a Holocaust museum, these symbols of Jewish exile pessimistically suggest that Diaspora Jews' method of coping with their outsider status — trying to become insiders — is doomed to failure. In 2008, Tigerman suggested as much, pointing to the recent worldwide surge in antisemitism and declaring: "If Jews think that they will [be able] through assimilation [to] get rid of the antagonism that is so innate and so deep and so old, they're smoking something and I don't know what it is. You'll never get rid of it. . . . One needs to remain vigilant." These comments point to the final aspect of the IHMEC's Jewishness. Whereas most American Holocaust museums have embraced the universalistic lesson that intolerance poses dangers to all people, the IHMEC offers a more particularistic message aimed specifically at Jews: remember the Holocaust, and assimilate at your own risk. It is too early to know whether the museum's architecture has successfully communicated this sober message to ordinary visitors. Architecture critics have disagreed in their assessments of the building's symbolism, with some calling it "esoteric" and others describing it as "visually arresting . . . and intellectually satisfying."[50] For now, what is undeniable is that by injecting deeply personal ideas about the modern Jewish condition into the design of the IHMEC, Tigerman has produced the most self-consciously Jewish Holocaust museum of the past generation.

Shadows in Sunshine: Holocaust Museums in Southern California and Florida

If the Holocaust museums built on the East Coast and in middle America explicitly evoked the Nazi genocide in their physical form, those established in the sunbelt states of California and Florida shied away from doing so almost entirely. Four museums were established between the early 1990s and the end of the first decade of the new millennium: the Simon Wiesenthal Center's Beit Hashoah — Museum of Tolerance in Los Angeles (1988–93), the Los Angeles Museum of the Holocaust (2007–10), the Florida Holocaust Museum in St. Petersburg (1998), and the Holocaust Documentation and Education Center in Hollywood, Florida (2007). While the buildings differed in their architecture, their designers' aversion to visually representing the Nazi genocide contrasts sharply with the more explicitly Holocaust-influenced architecture elsewhere.

The most prominent of the four museums is the Simon Wiesenthal Center's Beit Hashoah — Museum of Tolerance. The origins of what today is simply called the Museum of Tolerance (MOT) diverge from those of other museums in that the project did not originate with local survivors. Plans for the museum date back to 1977, when the Orthodox rabbi Marvin Hier settled in Los Angeles and established the Simon Wiesenthal Center, an institution that describes itself as a "Jewish human rights organization" devoted to combating "antisemitism, hatred, and terrorism." The fledgling institute was housed, along with a small yeshiva (also founded by Hier), in a small building on Pico Boulevard in the heavily Jewish Pico-Robertson neighborhood of West Los Angeles. In the Wiesenthal Center's original headquarters, Hier set up a small exhibit devoted to the Holocaust. His motives in doing so are unclear, but he seems to have been eager to reproduce a version of Yad Vashem on American soil. The museum opened to the public in that year and attracted a respectable number of visitors to its traditional, artifact-based exhibit. The museum's success soon raised expectations, and in 1987, Hier announced grand plans for a stand-alone institution.[51]

Six years later, in the spring of 1993, the $50 million, 165,000-square-foot headquarters opened and immediately attracted attention. Nearly all of it centered on the museum's high-tech, multimedia approach to representing the Holocaust. Few observers bothered to discuss the building's architecture, which was described as "nothing special."[52] This absence of attention was fully understandable, given the MOT's lack of symbolism. The granite-faced building featured stacked cubic masses on its main north facade that rose in height as they retreated from the street (fig. 138). The building's south facade revealed a wide expanse of glass (fig. 139). The only defining element was a squat dome on the roof.

The museum's uncommunicative appearance partly reflected the architectural principles of its designer, the Los Angeles–based architect Maxwell Starkman (1921–2004). Like Frank Gehry, Starkman came to Los Angeles from Toronto after World War II and worked briefly for Richard Neutra before establishing his own practice in 1953. Working primarily with major commercial real estate developers, his busy firm, Starkman and Associates, produced an estimated twenty thousand

Figures 138 and 139. Starkman and Associates, Museum of Tolerance, Los Angeles, 1987–93. The north facade of the building is dominated by stone-clad, cubic forms and a narrow vertical slit of glass. The museum's south facade is defined by an open expanse of glass. Both facades display hints of religious symbolism in respectively evoking closed and open Torah scrolls.

single-family homes during its thirty-year existence. In the 1980s it was ranked as the fourth-largest architecture firm in the United States. Starkman also designed major commercial buildings in Los Angeles, such as the glass and steel Sunset Media Tower in Hollywood (1971) and the Sony Pictures Plaza in Culver City (1988). Since all of Starkman's work was squarely within the modernist tradition, it was unlikely that he would change his methods for the last project of his career, the Museum of Tolerance. It is unknown whether Starkman, who was born of Polish Jewish immigrant parents, lost family members in the Holocaust. But he fought in the U.S. Army, participated in the D-Day landing of 1944, and was later described by his brother as having "read every book on the Second World War." Like other Jewish architects who served in the war, such as Gordon Bunshaft, Max Abramovitz, and Bertrand Goldberg, however, Starkman did not permit his feelings about the Nazi era to challenge his architectural principles. Even though the Holocaust had become a topic of great interest for American Jews and had led some, such as Freed, to reconsider their previous approaches to their craft—and even though Starkman apparently "poured his heart and soul into the project," as his brother recalled—the architect did not allow emotion to influence his design for the MOT.[53]

The museum's historical muteness also reflected the priorities of Starkman's client. By all indications, the MOT's founders were uninterested in having the building's architecture allude to the Holocaust. At the time that Starkman was working on his design, Hier and other museum officials would have been aware of Freed's symbolically evocative plans for the USHMM, which were finalized by the spring of 1987. Yet while the MOT was in implicit competition with the Washington museum, and despite Hier's aggressive efforts to raise the museum's national profile, he refrained from going in the same design direction. One reason may have involved his Jewish religious beliefs. Not long after the museum's opening, journalist Edward Norden wrote in *Commentary* that the building's nonnarrative architecture reflected the fact that "orthodox Jews do not especially go in for appearances."[54]

While suggestive, Norden's observation was off the mark, for the MOT did, in fact, exhibit an abstract kind of Jewish symbolism. Architecture critics who saw the building's plans when they were first publicized in the late 1980s remarked that its squat dome "alludes to Middle Eastern architecture," thus implying a degree of Jewishness. The dome's resemblance to a yarmulke, indeed, was in keeping with the client's modern Orthodox brand of Judaism. The split running down the museum's front facade, moreover, could be interpreted as an allusion to the twin tablets of the Ten Commandments. The divided facade can also be seen as a closed Torah scroll—a reading supported by the MOT's rear facade, whose convex glass curtain wall flanked by twin stone-faced piers resembles an unrolled scroll displaying its sacred parchment. Whether Starkman intended these readings is unknown. But given Hier's religious priorities and the fact that the MOT was originally connected to a yeshiva, such symbolism is not inconceivable.[55]

The museum's lack of architectural legibility may have also reflected tensions surrounding its overall mission. Not only did the MOT have to reconcile its religious past with its secular present; it also had to balance the particularistic fight against antisemitism with the universalized campaign against intolerance more broadly. Of all the museums built in the United States at the time, the Museum of Tolerance embraced the most universal vision of the Holocaust, as illustrated by the institution's very name. It was conceived as the Beit Hashoah, which translates to House of the

Holocaust. But as Hier went about soliciting financial and political support for his project, he found himself broadening (and Americanizing) its mandate. Soon, museum officials hyphenated its name to read "Beit Hashoah — Museum of Tolerance." Before long, the subtitle took over entirely, hence its present official name. The museum's exhibit also echoed this universalizing impulse by linking the Holocaust to countless past and contemporary acts of injustice, prejudice, and bigotry. Against this background, the building's architecture may have deemphasized the Holocaust's historical specificity for the sake of emphasizing its universal mission.[56]

Whatever the case may be, the inconspicuous architecture of the Museum of Tolerance was echoed in a second Holocaust museum built several miles to the east, the new Los Angeles Museum of the Holocaust (LAMH). Ever since plans for the new museum were announced in 2007, many observers have wondered whether any city needs two Holocaust museums. In reality, the Museum of Tolerance was the second Holocaust museum in Los Angeles. Survivors had already come together in the early 1960s to found a one-room exhibition that opened to the public in 1978 as the Los Angeles Martyrs Museum in the Jewish Federation building on Wilshire Boulevard. One year earlier, in 1977, they had commissioned a Holocaust memorial, which was ultimately erected in nearby Pan Pacific Park in the heavily Jewish neighborhood of Beverly-Fairfax in 1991. This activity notwithstanding, local survivors were upstaged by the opening of Hier's MOT, and during the 1990s, the Martyrs Museum remained a modest operation, drawing on average only twelve thousand visitors a year. Museum officials remained convinced, however, that their institution offered a more Jewish-focused portrayal of the Holocaust than the universalistic one at the MOT, and so they decided in 1991 to upgrade the museum, moving it to a larger exhibition space next door.[57] Unfortunately, multiple setbacks ensued in the years that followed. Due to earthquake retrofitting work, the museum had to move its location several times, and in 2004 it had to close altogether when the building in which it was housed was sold to a developer. Nevertheless, museum officials remained persistent and redoubled their efforts to find a permanent home for their institution. These efforts finally paid off in 2007 when, after a successful fundraising campaign, officials announced their plans to establish the Los Angeles Museum of the Holocaust in Pan Pacific Park next to the existing Holocaust Martyrs' Memorial.[58]

Designed by the Los Angeles firm of Belzberg Architects and dedicated in the fall of 2010, the new edifice represents a notable departure from previous Holocaust museums. The 32,000-square-foot building is similar in size to others, but it is unique in being located largely underground. Built directly into a hillside in Pan Pacific Park, the LAMH merges gracefully with its natural surroundings (fig. 140). Its roof is covered with triangular sections of grass that spread into the park's adjoining green fields. The museum's organic feel is emphasized further by its streamlined curves, which — visible both inside and out — echo the park's rolling hills. In a sense, the museum can be seen as a work of environmental sculpture or landform architecture that blurs the line between building and setting. In adopting this form, Belzberg Architects followed the example of other contemporary builders who have produced similar designs, such as Peter Eisenman's City of Culture of Galicia, in Santiago de Compostela, Spain (under construction since 1999), and Enric Miralles's Scottish Parliament complex, in Edinburgh (1998–2004), both of which partly merge with the contours of their surrounding landscapes. What is most notable about the museum's landform design, how-

Figure 140. Belzberg Architects, Los Angeles Museum of the Holocaust, 2004–10. The museum is located largely underground and merges with the grassy environment of Pan Pacific Park. The Holocaust memorial is the black object at top center.

ever, is its relative inconspicuousness. Unlike the explicit architecture of the museums in Houston, Detroit, Chicago, and Washington, D.C., the LAMH resembles a stealth museum that nearly disappears into its natural surroundings.

The building's subterranean setting is significant for several reasons. At the most prosaic level, the LAMH's location reflected practical considerations on the part of the architect. Aware that the Los Angeles parks and recreation department feared the museum might adversely affect the park's atmosphere, the firm's founder, Hagy Belzberg, reassured skeptics that his intent was "to integrate the building into the park and minimize [its] visual impact." Yet there were deeper reasons for the building's underground location. In one sense, the building's self-effacing character might be seen as reflecting an assimilationist reflex on the part of the Los Angeles Jewish community. After all, some of the city's most important Jewish institutions, such as the Museum of Tolerance and the Skirball Cultural Center (designed by Moshe Safdie in the years 1986 to 1995 and discussed in Chapter 11), have strived not to appear architecturally Jewish in any way, a strategy that echoes their universalistic mission of reaching out to non-Jewish audiences. Belzberg's recent remark that the LAMH deliberately has "no Jewish identification" and that it aims to "attract people already in the park who might not have come there intending to step foot in a Holocaust museum," suggests that the building indeed may be following in a longer local tradition.[59]

Yet the LAMH's underground location actually has more to do with the meaning of the Holocaust or, more precisely, with the question of how architecture should properly address its legacy. Like other Jewish architects, Belzberg came to reflect on this question partly for personal reasons. Born in 1964, he was too young to have been directly affected by the genocide, but his Polish-born father had lost most of his relatives during the war (his Israeli-born mother's family was spared). Having been "brought up in a household of remembrance," as he puts it, Belzberg was naturally inclined to pursue the museum commission. Yet, prior to doing so, he had not reflected much on the Holocaust's architectural implications. Indeed, since opening his own practice in 1997, his mostly residential and commercial work was exuberantly sculptural, marked by sinuously swerving forms that exuded a vital optimism. In approaching the LAMH commission, he utilized many of the same forms, but he now invested them with new significance. Belzberg partly adopted this approach because of his opposition to postmodern literalism. As he put it in 2008, the tendency of postmodern architects to utilize such historically symbolic forms as "barbed wire and bricks" in the design of Holocaust museums was improper because "architecture has nothing to do with the Holocaust. It was the people that had to do with [it]." Instead, Belzberg embraced a more deconstructivist strategy of dramatic allusion. In 2008, he noted that embedding the LAMH into the natural environment of a public park represented a commentary on how the Holocaust transpired in the midst of ordinary German life. Citing Peter Eisenman's Memorial to the Murdered Jews of Europe, in Berlin, whose location in the heart of the busy metropolis lends itself to such prosaic activities "as picnicking and playing Frisbee," Belzberg observed that the daily occurrence of these same activities near the LAMH would symbolically underscore the chilling fact that during the Holocaust, "people knowingly or unknowingly went on with their lives while extraordinary events were taking place." Given this claim, the museum's relative inconspicuousness as architecture does not so much hide as illuminate one of the more disturbing facts of the Holocaust: the coexistence of atrocity and normalcy.[60]

Whether this subtle message will be grasped by parkgoers is unclear. It may not register with casual passersby, but visitors who enter the museum and see its exhibit will probably understand it. In a symbolically powerful move, Belzberg guides visitors into the museum by directing them, from their aboveground arrival point, down a long ramp to the museum's entrance, thirteen feet below grade. As they leave the sunlight above, they enter progressively smaller and darker spaces that echo the exhibit's powerful narrative of worsening anti-Jewish persecution. By the time the exhibit arrives at the war's end and liberation, the spaces open up again and become lighter. To be sure, these effects were also utilized in Houston and Skokie, but in Belzberg's comparatively compact and inconspicuous design, they assume greater significance. Indeed, Belzberg's juxtaposition of light and darkness effectively drives home his claim that the distance between normalcy and atrocity is small. It is too early to know how the LAMH will fare given the existence of its competitor, the MOT, several miles to the west. The initial reactions to the museum have been mixed, with reviewers disagreeing in their assessment of its self-effacing character. While some have questioned the museum's "oddly deferential" relationship to its setting, others have praised it for "step[ping] . . . aside to make room for the forces of history" so powerfully portrayed in its exhibit.⁶¹ Whether or not this disagreement will persist and how it will affect the LAMH's relationship with the MOT is unclear. In the meantime, Los Angeles's two museums will remain intriguingly linked by their shared reluctance to refer directly to the Holocaust in their physical form.

Across the country in Florida, two other Holocaust museums revealed a similar trend. One was the Florida Holocaust Museum (FHM), which opened in St. Petersburg in 1998. In the late 1980s, local Jewish leaders, headed by a German Jewish refugee, Walter Loebenberg, hoped to preserve the Holocaust's lessons in memory. They first established a small exhibition in the Jewish Community Center of Pinellas County in 1992. Known as the Tampa Bay Holocaust Memorial Museum and Educational Center, the exhibition became surprisingly popular, and museum officials soon decided to move to a larger site in downtown St. Petersburg. In the mid-1990s they bought a nearly 27,000-square-foot structure, the former First Florida Bank, and hired an area architecture firm, Nick Benjacob and Associates, to renovate it. The building's location on a restricted lot limited its ability to be architecturally adventurous, but the architects attempted to convey something of the Holocaust's magnitude in their design.⁶²

The FHM betrays its mundane origins in its rigid rectilinear form and heavy black cornice, but the architects enlivened its facade by symbolically using triangular shapes. Evocative of concentration camp uniform patches and incomplete Stars of David, triangles had appeared in James Freed's Hall of Remembrance at the USHMM but they had never been used as central design elements elsewhere. Benjacob, the Israeli-born founder of the firm, said that he used triangular forms for a precise reason: "The era of World War II is so depressing that I did not want to do anything with either circles or squares because they are whole shapes." Instead, he affirmed, "I wanted a broken shape. A triangle is a . . . hard shape and I wanted to design a feeling for . . . visitors before they even entered the museum."⁶³ The museum's main entrance is a large triangle (as is its parking lot entrance), while outside there are six metal triangular gas lamps on one wall and five on another (symbolizing eleven million Holocaust victims, a total revealing the museum's expansive conception of the genocide) (fig. 141). The triangles' symbolism notwithstanding, the FHM was more visually subtle than the museums of Washington, Houston, and Detroit.

Figure 141. Nick Benjacob and Associates, Florida Holocaust Museum, St. Petersburg, 1996–98. The museum features multiple triangles, seen in the front and side entrances, as well as in the eleven commemorative lamps on the front and side facades.

The state's other major Holocaust museum is the Holocaust Documentation and Education Center in the Miami suburb of Hollywood. Founded in 1979 by members of the country's second-largest survivor community, the institution was located for years in a one-room trailer on the north campus of Florida International University until it found a permanent home in the fall of 2007. Like the FHM, the HDEC was established in an older structure. The major difference — a jarring one — was that it was a cheerful, pastel-colored Art Deco building from 1930. It may seem incongruous for a Holocaust museum to be housed in such a structure, yet the decision to do so did not reflect any conscious design strategy; the site was chosen for practical reasons, having been generously donated to the HDEC by the city of Hollywood. Moreover, it proved temporary. In 2008, the HDEC's board undertook renovation work that muted the building's deco appearance, and it has since commissioned the firm of Gallagher and Associates to design a $20 million, 30,000-square-foot addition next door. The future building, to be known as the South Florida Holocaust Museum, promises to be a major institution. But its design remains unclear and will ultimately be determined by the success of fundraising efforts.[64] For the time being, therefore, Florida's other Holocaust museum continues to conform to a sunshine state penchant for self-effacement.

In light of the California and Florida museums' relative inconspicuousness, it is tempting to engage in geographical determinism and hypothesize that sunny, warm climates may somehow impede the architectural representation of the Holocaust's horrors. It is especially tempting given the fact that most of the symbolically resonant museums — those in Detroit, Chicago, Washington, D.C., and New York — are in colder and comparatively gloomier climates. This trend is somewhat counterintuitive, for one would think that in sunny regions, where outdoor leisure culture is pronounced, museums would have to be even more architecturally striking to draw people inside. Does the self-effacing character of these museums perhaps reflect the desire not to spoil the illusion of being in a garden paradise? It is impossible to answer this or related questions with any certainty. What is clear, however, is that the sunbelt Holocaust museums show that an architectural confrontation with the genocide's legacy does not have to be explicit.

The New Holocaust Museum at Yad Vashem

Holocaust museum architecture is not only about buildings in the United States, as is shown by a major new complex dedicated in 2005 at Yad Vashem in Jerusalem. The origins of the new complex date to the early 1990s, when the completion of the American Holocaust museums in Washington, Los Angeles, and New York made Israeli officials fear that they were becoming marginalized in the international Holocaust museum landscape.[65] Beginning in 1993, they contemplated expansion, and in 1997 they commissioned the renowned Israeli-Canadian architect Moshe Safdie to design a new $56 million, 40,000-square-foot historical museum as part of a $100 million redesign of the Yad Vashem complex.

In selecting Safdie, Israeli officials were choosing an architect of international stature, albeit one difficult to categorize. Born in Israel in 1938, Safdie moved to Canada at the age of sixteen and later studied architecture at McGill University. After graduating in 1961, he worked briefly with Louis I. Kahn before setting up his own practice. Safdie gained recognition at the age of twenty-nine with his famous Habitat mass housing scheme at the Montreal World Exposition of 1967. His prefabricated interlocking cubic apartments seemed to promise a humane alternative to the dull high-rises of the early postwar period and established him as a visionary representative of the modern movement's younger generation. Safdie had difficulty living up to this breathtaking debut in his subsequent work, but he remained active, designing an array of projects all over the world.

His architectural philosophy evolved considerably during his career. In the late 1960s and early 1970s, Safdie continued to design modernist mass housing schemes featuring modular, polyhedric forms. Yet over time, his designs began to exhibit a Kahnian sensitivity to monumentality and subtle historical reference. Like Kahn, Safdie had been exposed to the rich historical urban environment of Jerusalem (where he produced most of his work in the 1970s) and was thus attentive to site and context: his Yeshivat Porat Yosef (1971–77) and Mamilla residential development (1972–99), for example, both displayed arches and domes that deferred to the forms of the Old City while still asserting their modern character. Despite this historicist turn in his work, Safdie was a fierce critic of postmodern revivalism, condemning its supporters in a famous 1981 essay for incorporating obscure architectural details in new buildings — a practice that he compared to telling "private jokes in public places." By the 1990s, however, further historicist elements were creeping into his work. His Public Library and Federal Government Headquarters (1992–95) in Vancouver displayed classical forms that prompted comparisons to the Roman Colosseum, while his Skirball Cultural Center in Los Angeles (1986–95) exhibited signs of Spanish colonial influence. As a result of these switches — and in the absence of a consistent style — critics have found Safdie difficult to classify. Although his attentiveness to context distances him from the extreme modernist camp, his aversion to representation prevents him from being called a postmodernist.[66]

Safdie's strategy for designing the new Yad Vashem complex was thus difficult to predict. One thing that seemed clear, though, was his opposition to any deconstructivist approach. In various interviews in the 1990s, Safdie rejected the "preoccupation with imbalance" and the emphasis on "destruction . . . [and] pessimism" that defined the work of Eisenman and Libeskind. He believed it was misguided for architects to emphasize "chaos" and produce "buildings . . . that look like an earthquake shook them." Without saying so explicitly, Safdie appeared to deny the Holocaust any role in shaping present-day architecture. While conceding that "our century has been marked by greater destruction of human life than any preceding century," he declared that it amounted to "supreme arrogance" to react to the world's conditions of "violence . . . [and] disjuncture" by attempting "to glorify them" architecturally. Instead, he noted, "I feel increasingly committed to a search for calmness and serenity in my own work."[67]

Yet Safdie was not entirely averse to recognizing the Holocaust's architectural relevance. He had already commemorated the Nazi genocide several years earlier at Yad Vashem in two memorials: the poignant Children's Memorial (1976–87), which was a darkened, mirrored room featuring the infinitely reflected light of a single candle; and the dramatic Memorial to the Deportees (1991–94), which featured a historic railway boxcar poised to topple off of a fragmented wooden bridge into an abyss. Safdie's involvement in these projects reflected a personal commitment to preserving the memory of the Holocaust. As a Jew of Sephardic background (his father's family hails from Aleppo, Syria), Safdie did not lose any relatives to the Holocaust, but his first wife experienced the war's horrors as a child hidden in Poland, while his second wife is the daughter of Hungarian survivors. His Israeli upbringing also sensitized him to the event's magnitude. Given this background, Safdie's earlier opposition to deconstructivism may have reflected his belief that the Holocaust's influence should not intrude into the ordinary built environment but be limited to buildings specifically intended to commemorate it. He readily admitted the Holocaust's significance for his Yad Vashem design, explaining that in preparing it, he had rejected a "business as usual" approach, being convinced that the new museum could not "be accommodated in a conventional building." The story of the Holocaust, he declared, was "too terrible . . . in the annals of civilization . . . to be told in normal 'galleries.'"[68]

In his ensuing design, Safdie rejected both the neutral modernism of the Museum of Tolerance and the symbolic postmodernism of the USHMM in favor of a plan that, ironically enough, displayed the influence of deconstructivism. As with many of Eisenman's and Libeskind's designs from the

Figure 142. Moshe Safdie, Yad Vashem, Jerusalem, 1997–2005. The museum is housed in a 600-foot-long triangular shaft (center) that penetrates the western slope of Mount Herzl and emerges at the other end, its sides flying apart in an explosive gesture of final release. The square building to the shaft's center left is the Hall of Remembrance.

Holocaust Museums 289

1990s, Safdie's proposal for Yad Vashem attacked the existing site by thrusting radically new forms into it. The architect preserved the existing administration building, the Hall of Remembrance, and the original Hall of Names building but replaced the other structures with a new historical museum, visitors center, synagogue, sunken courtyard, and cafe. The most dramatic feature of Safdie's ground plan was a 600-foot-long triangular shaft housing the museum that violently penetrated the western slope of Mount Herzl and burrowed deep into the ground only to emerge at the other end, its sides flying apart in an explosive gesture of final release (fig. 142).[69] Anticipating Belzberg's underground design in Los Angeles, Safdie's plan called to mind Libeskind's designs in Osnabrück and Berlin, both of which also featured long, barlike shapes slamming into existing sites.

Safdie's design contended with the Holocaust's legacy in metaphorical rather than literal terms. The thrust of the spearlike shaft created a wound that evoked the Holocaust's violence. As Yad Vashem director Avner Shalev put it, "The rupture in the continuity of the mountain represents the rupture [that took place] in the European Jewish world." Safdie's use of triangular forms was another example of his symbolic approach. As with Freed's museum in Washington and Benjacob's museum in St. Petersburg, the presence of triangles in the shape of the shaft and its overhanging skylights evoked both the triangular patches of concentration camp uniforms and fractured Stars of David. Safdie's use of materials was significant as well. Refusing to abide by the city of Jerusalem's mandate that all buildings be clad in local limestone (which he thought would be "too beautiful"), Safdie won permission to craft the entire building out of concrete in order to evoke the Holocaust's industrial character.[70]

The museum's interior spaces are similarly metaphorical. Safdie avoided the programmatic use of darkness and light in his skylit galleries, but, like Tigerman, he controlled visitors' movements through them. Once inside the triangular prism, visitors can see to its far end, but they cannot walk in a direct line toward it (fig. 143). Instead, their path is blocked by inaccessible cuts in the floor—"as if an earthquake ripped it apart"—fronted by fencelike strands of metal wire. These blockages force visitors to zigzag through adjacent exhibition galleries that guide them back to the central shaft. This directional flow echoes the twists and turns that defined the Jewish experience of the Holocaust and recalls the zigzag form of Libeskind's Jewish Museum in Berlin. Safdie also intensified the psychological dimension of his museum's interior. As in the Holocaust Museum in Houston, Yad Vashem's triangular space becomes more cramped as its exhibit continues, assuming the form of a narrow isosceles triangle at the exhibit's narrative nadir—Auschwitz—only to widen into an equilateral triangle at its redemptive conclusion. Here one sees the museum's most expressionistic feature. As the prismatic shaft explodes out of the hillside, it separates into a pair of curvilinear bands of concrete cantilevered over its edge. This dramatic feature has been interpreted as a pair of wings or the triumphant blast of a horn. Experienced from the inside, the space provides visitors with a sweeping vista of the Jerusalem hills, dotted with settlements. This view confirmed the continuation of life after the Holocaust and validated Israel's identity as a place of Jewish refuge. It confirmed Safdie's belief that "life prevailed. We prevailed." Like so many architects, ranging from Louis I. Kahn to James Freed, Safdie ended his architectural journey by reemerging into light.[71]

The reaction to Safdie's building confirmed it as a major achievement. Israeli government officials organized a dedication ceremony that was attended by representatives of more than thirty coun-

Figure 143. Yad Vashem. Inside the museum, visitors cannot walk in a direct line but are guided along a serpentine path into the galleries through the side entrances. The triangular interior space contracts from that of an equilateral triangle at the beginning to a narrower isosceles triangle in the middle.

tries. Journalists and architecture critics called the building "breathtaking." To be sure, given the polarized politics of present-day Israel, critical remarks were predictably voiced as well. Observers accused Safdie's design of, among other things, putting architecture ahead of the museum's exhibition, Disney-fying the Holocaust, and emulating the separation wall running through Palestinian lands. Most people, however, hailed the design as a resounding success. In the end, Safdie's design proved that Holocaust museum architecture could be evocative without being overly literal.[72]

Conclusion

The emergence of Holocaust museums constitutes a coherent and important architectural phenomenon. No single architectural strategy has emerged as the preferred method for representing the Holocaust, as modernist, postmodern, and deconstructivist approaches have all found expression. Holocaust museum designs, however, have become increasingly explicit in representing the Nazi genocide. This development reveals that architects have finally begun to confront the Holocaust's implications for their discipline. However belated it may be compared to other fields of cultural expression, architecture's increasing confrontation with the Nazi genocide has been serious. The growing willingness of architects to incorporate iconography and spatial effects drawn from the Jews' experience in the Nazi era testifies to a deepening recognition of the Holocaust's architectural legacy.

The proliferation of Holocaust museums raises the question whether they should be classified as a branch of Jewish architecture. For some observers, the answer is clearly no. Allan Greenberg, for one, has declared that since "concentration camps are not Jewish," modeling buildings after them represents "twisted thinking."[73] Those accustomed to thinking of Jewish architecture strictly in terms of synagogues, moreover, would also likely balk at including Holocaust museums. And yet, if Jewish architecture is defined as those buildings that reflect the Jewish historical experience, Holocaust museums should be considered as well.

This claim will probably not persuade those who believe Jewish architecture is best defined in a religious sense and restricted to synagogues. Yet even if we adhere to a religiously based definition, Holocaust museums may still deserve inclusion, for in their own way they have displayed quasi-religious features. In recent years, scholars have pointed out that the Holocaust has acquired a semi-sacralized status in modern Jewish life — a fact illustrated by Elie Wiesel's frequent comments about the Holocaust's ineffability, the treatment of its artifacts as holy relics, and — most significantly — Arthur Hertzberg's description of the USHMM as a "Jewish national cathedral." Of course, holiness in Judaism does not inhere in the architecture of its religious edifices but in the prayers that are recited inside them. Still, like churches and synagogues, Holocaust museums have begun to develop their own ritualized iconography and symbolism. The exterior allusions to concentration camps and the interior manipulation of dark and light have become common to nearly all Holocaust museums. They have also become pilgrimage sites where people may pay respects to the dead, educate themselves, or simply remember. All Jews may not agree about this sacralized view of Holocaust museums, but enough probably do to describe the museums as a Jewish architectural phenomenon.[74]

A second question involves the future evolution of Holocaust museum architecture. Until now, the public has accepted the visually explicit character of Holocaust museums, yet occasional complaints raise the question of whether there are limits to the architectural representation of the Holocaust. Holocaust museums currently include allusions to barbed wire, guard towers, and crematoria chimneys; is it merely a matter of time before more graphic images — ovens, gas chambers, human remains — find their way into designs? Standards of taste should prevent the incorporation of extreme elements in museum architecture, but the vivid symbols seen in suburban Detroit, Houston, and Washington were also probably unimaginable at one time. For this reason, it is conceivable that future museum architecture may become increasingly explicit. As architecture critic Ziva Freiman wrote after visiting the USHMM a decade ago, "I still maintain that architecture has a deeper potential [to represent the Holocaust] than we have yet plumbed. . . . [The] most potent [architecture] may arise from a capacity to deliver an inkling of the victims' torment by approximating physical aspects of their experience — becoming an architecture of empathy, rather than spectacle. If we have the stomach for it, we may go even further to imagine a shocking, manipulative architecture that confronts us with what is most base in our humanity."[75]

If Holocaust museum architecture continues to develop in this way, there is a risk that it may incite a backlash. Some signs of this have already appeared. During the early 1990s, the heated debates about the wisdom of building Holocaust museums included implicit indictments of their architecture. This was most visible in certain critics' observations that Holocaust museums reduced the Nazi genocide to the status of theme parks.[76] For these critics, the discipline of architecture was complicit in a worrisome trend. Yet while Holocaust museums and buildings designed for the Walt Disney Corporation in the 1990s were both influenced by postmodernism — and while the Holocaust Memorial Center near Detroit looks strangely similar to Robert A. M. Stern's Disney Animation Studios in Burbank (figs. 144, 145) — the buildings' vastly different aims (education versus entertainment; piety versus profit) show that the museums' architecture aspires to nobler ends.

For all that, Holocaust museums continue to be criticized. Tova Reich lampooned them in her 2007 novel *My Holocaust* (albeit without devoting much attention to architecture). But the most direct swipe at Holocaust museum architecture in the last several years may be the most representative. In his farcical 2006 novel *Absurdistan*, Gary Shteyngart spoofed the wave of symbolically resonant Holocaust museums by portraying his protagonist, Misha Vainberg, proposing the creation of a Holocaust museum in a fictional Central Asian country. Vainberg's "modest proposal" pays particular attention to the museum's symbolic architecture:

> Some of the world's most remarkable recent architecture has been built in commemoration of the Holocaust, but much of it is too abstract and cerebral. . . . The Institute for Caspian Holocaust Studies [by contrast] will take the shape of a giant broken matzoh, in reference to the tragedy that befell our people and as a reminder of the Passover meal, which, among all the traumas of a Jewish upbringing, consistently rates as the "least scarring." . . . The main exhibition space of the broken matzoh will lead to a titanium-clad lamb shank (hint: Frank Gehry) symbolizing both the forearm of the Almighty and our own newly found brute strength.

The tone of this passage is mocking, but it is ultimately a gentle form of criticism.[77]

Future criticism of Holocaust museums will likely be equally mild, largely because the great wave of Holocaust museum construction in the United States is probably behind us. By now, most

Figures 144 and 145. Neumann/Smith and Associates, Holocaust Memorial Center of Michigan, and Robert A. M. Stern, Disney Animation Studios, Burbank, California, 1994. The Holocaust Memorial Center of Michigan and the Disney Animation Studios exhibit striking similarities in their use of conical shapes and striped facades.

major American cities with sizable Jewish populations have constructed their own museums. And those that are still establishing them, such as Miami and Dallas, are few in number.[78] For this reason, while the designs of future museums will surely serve as bellwethers of the Holocaust's evolving architectural legacy, that legacy may in fact be more apparent in other structures. Nowhere is this clearer than in many of the Jewish synagogues, community centers, and museums that have recently been constructed in Germany and the United States.

Chapter 11
Jewish Architecture Between Nightmare, Nostalgia, and Normalcy

Anyone who strolls through the historic old town of Dresden, as I did in the summer of 2008, sees a city rushing to recover its past. Many of the city's war-damaged buildings, such as the sprawling royal palace, are being restored, and some that were once mounds of rubble, such as the domed Frauenkirche, have been entirely reconstructed. From certain vantage points near the Elbe River, Dresden's dark sandstone buildings almost give the impression of a city untouched by the destructive course of recent history. Yet a mere several blocks from one of Dresden's most famous overlooks stands a building that counters the city's backward-looking tendencies. Anchored firmly to the ground, the stone-clad cubic building looks as if it is being twisted several degrees counterclockwise (fig. 146). It is probable that few pedestrians who walk by the new synagogue of Dresden (1998 – 2001) know the reason for the twist. But the architecture firm that designed the building, Wandel Hoefer Lorch and Hirsch (WHLH), rotated it to duplicate the ground plan of the mid-nineteenth-century synagogue by Gottfried Semper that originally stood on the site. In referring to the former synagogue, the architects had clear commemorative motives in mind. For, like so many other synagogues in Germany, Semper's building was destroyed on Kristallnacht. The twist in Dresden's new synagogue is thus an architectural gesture of remembrance that alters one's understanding of the building. Instead of appearing as a playful gesture, the twist can be interpreted as the start of a violent tornado destined to culminate in unprecedented destruction.

The new synagogue of Dresden reveals that Jewish architecture during the postmodern era has not been limited to pathbreaking works of deconstructivism and pathos-laden Holocaust museums. Traditional types of Jewish buildings, such as synagogues, community centers, schools, and museums, have been erected as well. Unlike the situation in the early postwar years, however, their forms have displayed a greater sense of Jewishness. Influenced by the era's postmodern spirit, they have looked to the past and taken their impetus from different aspects of Jewish history. The nightmare of the Holocaust has continued to influence the design of Jewish buildings, finding echo for the first time in synagogue architecture. But nostalgic visions of the Jewish historical experience have found expression as well. Bygone historical styles of synagogue architecture, especially that of Polish wooden synagogues, were revived during this period as part of the postmodern return to history. Still other buildings reflected the influence of Jewish religious and intellectual traditions, such as the Talmud, the Kabbalah, and even the Hebrew alphabet. Significantly, some important works of Jewish architecture refrained from expressing a sense of Jewishness entirely and instead aimed for a condition of normalcy. Yet even these buildings betrayed signs of the era's increased expectation that Jewish buildings should exude a sense of Jewish identity. In all these ways, the diverse forms of Jewish architecture perfectly fit the period's pluralistic postmodern mood.

Figure 146. Wandel, Hoefer, Lorch and Hirsch, New Synagogue, Dresden, 1998–2001. The stone-clad building is distinguished by its distinct twist, which exudes a sense of instability.

Lingering Nightmares: Jewish Architecture in Germany

During the postmodern era, the Holocaust gradually made its presence felt in German synagogue architecture. In the 1970s and 1980s, the Jewish community's lack of growth meant that relatively few synagogues were built. Those that were, however, displayed the new representational possibilities afforded by postmodernism. This potential was fully unleashed following the epochal events of 1989–90, when German reunification and the rapid expansion of the Jewish population sparked a new wave of synagogue construction. Significantly, while these new buildings were diverse in appearance, they were linked by their commitment to remembrance.

The turn to memory in German Jewish synagogue architecture reflected the surging attention to Germany's Nazi past in the 1980s. Following the broadcast of the NBC docudrama *Holocaust* on German public television in 1979, the Nazi genocide became a subject of intense public fascination, as was shown by the Bitburg Affair of 1985, the Historians' Debate of 1986–87, and the marking of the fiftieth anniversary of Kristallnacht in 1988. That last event was significant for the evolution of

Jewish architecture in Germany, as it redirected attention to one of the Third Reich's main architectural legacies, the mass destruction of Jewish synagogues. In towns, cities, and villages throughout the Federal Republic, books were published on the history of local synagogues; historic preservation efforts were launched; and, in a few cases, efforts to build new synagogues were accelerated to coincide with the anniversary as symbolic gestures of atonement.[1] All these examples revealed a growing tendency to view Jewish architecture from a perspective colored by an awareness of Germany's Nazi past.

A clear sign of this trend was the opening of a major exhibition on synagogue architecture, "The Architecture of the Synagogue," at the German Architecture Museum in Frankfurt in 1988. In the exhibition catalogue several contributors pointed out the links between Jewish architecture and the memory of the Nazi period. None did so as perceptively, however, as the German Jewish architect Salomon Korn. In his essay "Synagogue Architecture in Germany After 1945," Korn surveyed the shifting relationship of German synagogues to the legacy of the Holocaust, arguing that while the reluctance of Jews to pursue an architecture of admonition in the early postwar period made sense in light of their fragile psychological state, the growing attention to the Nazi past in the 1980s rendered this hesitant stance obsolete. In what amounted to a manifesto, he called for a historically informed synagogue architecture that called attention to the Holocaust's legacy, writing: "Perhaps a generation needed to pass ... before the victims' descendants ... could speak with fewer inhibitions. It is high time for this [to happen], for only the honest baring of the still painful historical wounds can lead to their healing.... There now appears to be [a] possibility of bringing into the open that which has long been repressed.... The time has come for synagogue architecture to shift from a ... stance of reticence towards a painful, but necessary, one of remembrance."[2]

Korn's commitment to confronting the Holocaust in architectural terms was rooted in his own experiences. Born in 1943 in Nazi-occupied Lublin, he and his parents lived in a DP camp outside Frankfurt after the war. Like many other refugees, they had not planned on staying in Germany but did so nonetheless. After studying architecture and sociology in the 1960s, Korn became interested in the history of synagogue architecture in the early 1970s, the same time that he began to study the history of the Third Reich. By the 1980s he had become active in German Jewish affairs as head of the Frankfurt community. Since 2003 he has been vice president of the Central Council of Jews in Germany. Korn thus came to be involved in many postreunification debates about Germany's Nazi past, including the planning for Peter Eisenman's Berlin Holocaust memorial. It is no surprise, therefore, that Korn was in advance of his coreligionists in striving to thematize the Holocaust in architecture.[3]

Korn strove to implement his recommendations in his own architectural work, most notably in his Jewish Community Center of Frankfurt (1980–86). In designing this building, Korn made the "historical cracks ... and fractures of German-Jewish history the point of departure." "Architectural metaphors," he believed, could help "thematize the ambivalent situation of the Jews in Germany" and "symbolize the past's effect on [their] ... present." In embracing this perspective, Korn was influenced by the precedent set by the Berlin Jewish Community Center building of 1959. He was able to follow it only to a limited degree in Frankfurt, however. Since there were no architectural remnants of the prewar synagogue that could be incorporated into the new building, Korn instead selected Jewish symbols to "transform admonition and memory into architecture." His chief symbol was the Ten Commandments, which he alluded to by placing a single giant tablet at the building's entrance (fig. 147). More significant was the presence of several cracks on the tablet's surface and the absence of Hebrew letters, both of which served as a "warning of the fragility of German Jewish relations over the course of... history." Korn stressed this point by placing beneath the tablet a cornerstone listing the ten thousand Frankfurt Jews deported by the Nazis. At a time when many local Jews were incensed by the Frankfurt city council's decision in 1984 to build a new administrative building on the former Börneplatz in the old Jewish ghetto, a reminder of Jewish victimization sent a powerful message.[4]

Yet Korn did not want his building to be merely an architectural admonition. He also lent the building a more optimistic dimension by including three stylized menorahs in its facade as a "symbol of hope." "It is between the enduring memories of destruction and the... uncertain hope for the future," Korn asserted, "that Jewish life in Germany continues to oscillate." This tension between hope and uncertainty also influenced the building's floor plan. To illustrate the theme of rupture, Korn separated the complex into two parts bridged with a peaked glass skylight over the building's foyer at a juncture he called the bend. This space was open and filled with light. But it was fully exposed to, and partly merged with, the outside world, thereby symbolizing the reality of life in the Diaspora—a place where Jews "never knew if [they were]... secure." At the same time, the interior's openness was meant to counter the Jewish community's early postwar "spiritual provincialism" and encourage an "openness to the world" that could guarantee its future creativity. This optimistic vision was epitomized by Korn's much-quoted observation about his project's significance: "Whoever builds a house wants to stay."[5]

Figure 147. Salomon Korn, Jewish Community Center of Frankfurt, 1980–86. A single tablet of the Ten Commandments, marked by cracks, stands at the building's entrance as a symbol of the ruptures of German Jewish history. A stylized menorah is visible at center right.

Korn's architectural philosophy remained tinged with pessimism, however. Although he wanted German Jewish synagogues to be more open in representing the Holocaust's rupture, he lamented in 1988 that "it appears as though [the impulse to acknowledge the Holocaust] . . . has come too late! Most Jewish communities in the Federal Republic are too small and old to survive into the next several decades. In the near future there will only be around two dozen Jewish communities and there is already no shortage of synagogue space in them. . . . Today with the gradual end of the postwar era, . . . the construction of synagogues and community centers is largely complete. . . . While [some] . . . will certainly be built here and there, synagogues as a category of architecture have no meaningful future . . . in Germany."[6]

The irony of Korn's observation is that Jewish life was about to be radically transformed. The end of the cold war and the ensuing reunification of Germany infused the German Jewish community with thousands of Jewish immigrants from the former Soviet Union.[7] From a Jewish population in 1989 of about 25,000 members, the number in the Federal Republic of Germany quadrupled to over 100,000 who were affiliated with the official community and another 100,000 unaffiliated. Individual cities reveal the extent of the influx. Munich had around 2,200 Jews before 1989 but today has around 9,000. More dramatically, Wuppertal's Jewish population grew from 65 to 2,000, Duisburg's from 50 to 1,200, and Dresden's from 60 to 350. Depending on how one measures it, the Jewish population of Germany has risen to between 20 and 40 percent of its size before 1933.[8]

The New Conspicuousness: German Synagogues Since Reunification

The growth of the German Jewish community had immediate architectural consequences as it forced congregations to expand their buildings or construct new ones. Between 1989 and 2010, plans for about thirty synagogues were considered, and over twenty were constructed.[9] Their architecture was of a noticeably higher standard than that of the early postwar period. Government subsidies were more generous than in the comparatively poor 1950s, with a combination of state and city funds, private donations, and Jewish community resources covering the substantial building costs. To be sure, the new synagogues faced challenges. Jews of differing religious leanings (both Orthodox and Reform) often had to be accommodated within a single sanctuary. Sufficient social and educational space was needed to help Eastern European Jews integrate into their new surroundings. Security needed to be considered, especially following the March 1994 bomb attack against the synagogue in Lübeck, the foiled 2002 attack against the synagogue then under construction in Munich, and ongoing threats from Muslim terrorists. Despite these challenges, palpable optimism surrounded Germany's new synagogues. Unlike the early postwar era, when Jewish houses of worship were defined by privacy, insularity, and anonymity, those built since 1990 have been far more conspicuous.

They have also dealt more directly with the legacy of the Holocaust. Thanks to the rise of postmodernism and the intensifying German debate about the Nazi past, architects in Germany — Jewish as well as Christian — have become more committed to reflecting on the Nazi genocide's implications for synagogue design. In doing so, they have pursued different architectural strategies. The major Jewish architect responsible for designing many recent synagogues, Alfred Jacoby, has produced mostly abstract, nonrepresentational buildings that have attempted to provide Jews with a sense of normalcy by symbolically healing the scars of the Holocaust. By contrast, Christian German architects, such as the firm of WHLH, have drawn more overtly on the Holocaust's legacy, as well as Jewish religious traditions, in their allusive modernist work as part of a conscious effort to prevent German society from forgetting the crimes of the Nazi era. Finally, certain Jewish architects working in Germany, such as Zvi Hecker and Manuel Herz, have created a dramatically expressive form of synagogue architecture, rooted in Jewish textual traditions, that confidently signals the Jewish community's readiness to reestablish its physical presence in the German built environment and transcend its early postwar inhibitions rooted in the traumas of the Holocaust. In short, although diverse in form, recent synagogues in Germany have been defined by an unprecedented degree of assertiveness.

The Synagogues of Alfred Jacoby

Alfred Jacoby has been the most prolific synagogue designer in Germany since reunification. A professor at the Dessau Institute of Architecture who also maintains an office in Frankfurt, Jacoby has designed nearly a dozen synagogues since 1988, completing seven. Compared to the early postwar synagogues of Hermann Zvi Guttmann and Helmut Goldschmidt, Jacoby's buildings have displayed much more formal experimentation and refinement, but, like theirs, they have generally shied away from directly confronting the legacy of the Holocaust. In sharp contrast to Salomon Korn, who called for a symbolically allusive form of German synagogue architecture that could lay bare the scars of the recent past, Jacoby has employed a more restrained modernism in the effort to heal them.

Jacoby's strategy reflected his background. Born in Offenbach in 1950, he was the son of Holocaust survivors from Poland and was well aware of the genocide's impact on his family. Given that his parents had suffered in forced labor camps (and had lost their own parents in the gas chambers), it is understandable to hear him describe his parents as "sad people." "They have nightmares," he noted in 2000. "It haunts them."[10] Jacoby's traumatic family history made him ambivalent about living in Germany, and he spent a good deal of time abroad. At age fifteen he left for Great Britain, and he received his B.A. in architecture from Cambridge University in 1973. He continued his study of architecture at the Eidgenössische Technische Hochschule (ETH) in Zurich from 1973 to 1977, where he worked with Aldo Rossi. He returned to Germany only in 1980, moving to Frankfurt, where he set up his architectural practice. At this time, Jacoby, unlike Korn, had neither much inclination to dwell on the Holocaust nor much interest in synagogue architecture.

Jacoby's feelings changed dramatically in 1986, however, when he was invited to enter the competition for the new synagogue of Darmstadt. Even though he had no experience designing synagogues, his identity as one of Germany's only Jewish architects earned him a chance to secure the commission. The Darmstadt synagogue was one of the very few planned in the Federal Republic during the 1980s. It possessed special symbolic resonance because its construction and dedication coincided with the fiftieth anniversary of Kristallnacht. Indeed, local political officials viewed the project as a form of reparations — a fact that explains the outlay of substantial government funds on a building for a community that numbered only one hundred members.[11]

Jacoby's ensuing plan for the Darmstadt synagogue was somewhat anomalous in being his only design that displayed postmodern influences. Its defining feature, a large central dome flanked by two smaller domes, displayed echoes of the Moorish revival style that had been pioneered in the mid-nineteenth century by Gottfried Semper in his Dresden synagogue (fig. 148). This historic evocation carried over into the synagogue's interior, which featured an ornate domed ark. To be sure, this was no pure revival; the synagogue's yellow sandstone facade was spare, without ornamental flourishes (even if it tried to evoke Jerusalem stone), while its glass and steel domes looked high tech. Still, the overall impression was of nostalgia for the golden era of German Jewish synagogue design. The synagogue aimed to satisfy the hopes of both local Jewish community and city officials that the building could help reestablish a "continuum" with the pre-Nazi period and stand in the "best tradition of Jewish-Christian interaction."[12]

Jacoby's design reflected his views of the recent past. At the 1988 dedication of the synagogue, he explained that its architecture expressed a new sense of German Jewish confidence. In contrast to early postwar synagogues, which he said were symbols of "insecurity" that failed to engage with their surroundings, his Darmstadt design "self-confidently [aimed to] make itself recognizable" as a Jewish house of worship. This was the reason, he explained, that he positioned it "directly on the street." It was also the reason he drew on historicist traditions: because only an "old typology

Figure 148. Alfred Jacoby, Synagogue, Darmstadt, 1986–88. Displaying prominent domes and interior ornamental flourishes, this postmodern building represented a partial revival of nineteenth-century historicist synagogue architecture.

in a modern form would make the building legible as a synagogue." This desire to be noticed represented a new approach in postwar German Jewish architecture. In declaring "we must confidently display our Jewish identity," Jacoby, unlike Korn, wanted to break free of the inhibitions rooted in the Nazi experience. "A synagogue should not be an architectural memorial to the Holocaust," he flatly asserted. Rather, it should be a "place of prayer . . . and meditation . . . in which the belief in humanity can be realized." This, he concluded, represented the best hope of "combating the evil that people perpetrate."[13]

Local officials and Jewish community representatives hailed the synagogue as an important step toward German-Jewish reconciliation. Echoing Darmstadt mayor Günther Metzger's description of the building as a symbol of "hope," Josef Fränkel, the head of the Jewish community, declared that the synagogue constituted a sign of progress in the Germans' long-delayed task of "confronting the past." Yet, dissenting voices were heard among Jewish critics. One of the most outspoken was Korn himself, who argued that the building's neohistoricist design "glossed over [the] . . . scars left . . . by the destruction of Jewish architectural culture in Germany." Korn, however, overlooked the stained-glass windows, designed by the British artist Brian Clarke, which abstractly alluded to the Nazi years. A set of red windows, called the "Wall of Suffering," was meant to suggest the destruction wrought on Kristallnacht, while a set of blue windows flanking the ark, entitled the "Wall of the Future," symbolized hope. The windows showed that while Jacoby was reluctant to have the building itself allude to the Holocaust, he was willing to include art that did.[14]

During the 1990s, Jacoby's architecture shifted in style. By the time he received his next commissions, postmodernism had lost its appeal, and his later synagogues instead displayed the neo-Rationalist influence of Aldo Rossi. Like Rossi, Jacoby employed a hybrid approach, combining unadorned modernist spheres, ellipses, and cylinders with classical symmetrical plans. Jacoby's version of modernism was, like Rossi's, opposed to the functionalist ethos that underlay many early postwar modern synagogues. Instead, he strove to produce identifiably sacred Jewish spaces.

This assertive approach reflected the effort of Jews in post-reunification Germany to move confidently into the future without neglecting the past. In writings, speeches, and interviews, Jacoby struggled to balance the imperatives of remembrance and the desire for normalcy. On the one hand, he repudiated the nostalgic principles that informed his postmodern Darmstadt design. "You can't go back to early synagogue tradition," he declared in 2001, "because it would ignore the terrible historical event called the Holocaust" and produce buildings that were little more than "kitschy . . . recollection[s]." Yet while Jacoby seemed to adopt Korn's view that the Holocaust needed architectural acknowledgment, he did not pursue an architecture of dislocation. Unlike the deconstructivists, he rejected the idea that the Holocaust was a byproduct of Enlightenment rationality, declaring in 2002: "I still believe in the forces of Enlightenment." He also declared that he did not "want to make . . . Holocaust memorial[s]" out of his synagogues. Jacoby rejected this commemorative approach, believing that the Holocaust was beyond conventional representation. He further justified his abstract philosophy by citing Ludwig Wittgenstein's credo: "Whereof one cannot speak, thereof one must be silent." Finally, his architectural reticence respected the wishes of elderly congregants not to be reminded of the past. "The people going into the synagogue remember [the past]," he noted in 1997. "Why make them relive it?"[15]

Declaring that it is "important to have a vision of the future," Jacoby decided to design his synagogues "In a New Spirit," as the title of an exhibition of his work proclaimed in the late 1990s. He rejected admonitory architecture in favor of buildings informed by the "perspective of healing." Jacoby conceded that the "material and spiritual destruction . . . imposed on the Jews . . . during the Nazi period" was "irreversible" and could not be "undone through any healing process." So he designed for the "survivors and those born after the war who needed a beneficial future orientation." Quoting historian Fritz Stern's assertion that reunification in 1990 gave Germany a "second chance" to do right by history, Jacoby declared: "The new synagogues are stone vessels, within which a second chance for Jews and non-Jews to coexist in this country might be able to germinate."[16]

This agenda was expressed in the synagogues that Jacoby designed from 1994 to 2008 in Heidelberg, Aachen, Kassel, Offenbach, Chemnitz, and Speyer. Unlike early postwar synagogues, which he said "did not seek any relationship to their surroundings," his designs strove "to become part of the city's fabric." They avoided anxious anonymity in favor of self-confident normalcy. Many of these traits were visible in his Aachen synagogue (1991–95). Built on the Synagogen Platz, empty since the destruction of the prewar synagogue, Jacoby's building fulfilled a long-deferred goal of mending the city's ruptured urban fabric (fig. 149). Yellow local brick in its facade adhered to regional building traditions while resembling Jerusalem stone. The synagogue's flat dome evoked prewar houses of worship, and the presence of a Hebrew text on the front facade made the building's identity clear. The synagogue strove to communicate a sense of openness. The wide expanse of glass in its facade allows views of the activities inside the building, while the Hebrew text, "For my house shall be called a house of prayer for all peoples" (Isaiah 56/7), broadcasts an ecumenical message.[17]

Jacoby's other synagogues echoed this self-confident neighborliness. They generally displayed sober circular and elliptical plans for their sanctuaries (as in Heidelberg, Chemnitz, and Aachen) and simple rectilinear plans for the community spaces. The curvilinear forms have no esoteric historical significance (unlike Hermann Zvi Guttmann's parabolas from the 1960s); instead, Jacoby chose them to highlight the central location of the bima and to symbolize the idea of a single God.[18] He often included explicit Jewish symbols in his facades — the most overt being oversized Ten Commandments in the circular facade at Heidelberg.

Explicit signs of the Holocaust's legacy were played down, but they were not entirely absent. In Offenbach, Jacoby encased Guttmann's original synagogue in a lens-shaped structure composed of multiple panes of glass. The panes were colored deep blue except at their end point, where they were left clear to provide a direct view of the monumental, domed Goethestrasse Synagogue, built in 1916, across the street. In deliberately placing the outermost point of the lens on a direct axis to the old synagogue — which was damaged on Kristallnacht and transformed into a theater after 1945 — Jacoby directed congregants' attention toward the remnants of prewar Jewish life in Germany. An equally subtle gesture appeared in his synagogue in Kassel. Probably his most restrained design, the building was a spare white edifice in the unadorned style of the Bauhaus, except for its sanctuary, whose exterior was clad in dark cedar wood. The synagogue's most distinctive feature was its ark, which displayed a long crack down its two twenty-one-foot-high glass doors, reminiscent of the cracked Mosaic tablets of Korn's Frankfurt JCC. The ark's designer, Johannes Schreiter, referred to

Figure 149. Alfred Jacoby, Synagogue, Aachen, 1991–95. The synagogue strives to establish a sense of normalcy for the Jewish community by blending into its site, using local materials, and communicating a sense of openness with its glass facade.

the cracks in universalistic terms as "ciphers for the unpredictable, for forces that man is constantly exposed to." But other observers saw them as references to the Kristallnacht pogrom. These symbolic gestures — like the Darmstadt synagogue's stained-glass windows — showed that Jacoby was open to acknowledging the Holocaust's legacy. But their subtlety within the otherwise normalized Jewish spaces highlighted the architect's desire to deemphasize the past in favor of the future. As he concluded, "I want to build in a way that those who wish to be reminded will see . . . and those who want to have a moment to forget can find comfort."[19]

Other Synagogues: German Architects Confront the Holocaust

If Alfred Jacoby's work represented the effort of a German Jewish architect to strive for normalcy by moving beyond the past, other synagogues, designed by non-Jewish German architects, reflected the desire to hold its lessons in memory.[20] This situation ironically represented something of an inversion of the early postwar pattern, in which Jews admonished Germans not to forget the Nazi era. As part of Germany's larger effort in the 1990s to come to terms with the Nazi legacy, the synagogues designed by German architects were defined by the well-intentioned effort to make up for earlier shortcomings. These synagogues did two things: they attempted to atone for the Holocaust by allowing its legacy to influence their designs; and they strove to express respect for Jewish religious and architectural traditions by articulating a sense of Jewishness in built form. In so doing, however, they worked at cross-purposes to Jacoby's synagogues, for instead of promoting the normalcy of Jewish life, they underscored its enduring exceptionality.

One of the most significant buildings was the new synagogue and community center complex of Dresden (1997–2001). Designed by the Saarbrücken firm of Wandel Hoefer Lorch + Hirsch (WHLH), the building was influenced by the Holocaust's legacy in several ways. As was true of new synagogues in other German cities, Dresden's was built on the site of its predecessor, Gottfried Semper's famous synagogue, destroyed on Kristallnacht. The firm's design was modern, in keeping with the Jewish community's preference for a new building instead of a reconstruction of the Semper building, which some locals had proposed. In submitting their design, the architects sided with the Jewish community's decision, saying that it symbolically acknowledged that the "Jewish history of Dresden [was one] . . . of destruction, not continuity."[21]

Committed to illustrating the reality of "historical rupture," the architects adopted a version of Eisenman's deconstructivist idea of "artificial excavation" and oriented their plan to that of the vanished synagogue. The architects' design comprised two structures: a synagogue and a separate community center separated by a small empty plaza where the original synagogue once stood. The new synagogue was a minimalist cube made of concrete blocks that twisted noticeably, so that it appeared unbalanced. This feature resulted from the architects' decision to situate the synagogue's plan perpendicular to the street but then to torque it from above by some fifteen degrees to make it parallel with the floor plan of the vanished Semper synagogue (figs. 150, 151). Between the synagogue and the community center across the plaza, the architects traced the outlines of Semper's building in glass shards, evoking the destruction of Kristallnacht. They also included fragments of the original synagogue, inserting stones salvaged from its excavated foundation into the retaining wall around the complex and reusing the original Star of David from the synagogue's roof over the entrance to the new sanctuary.[22]

The synagogue did not just meditate on the Holocaust, however, but on broader aspects of Jewish history and identity. In reflecting on the idea of "what a synagogue actually is today," the architects rejected the nineteenth-century reliance upon "Christian precedents" and instead embraced the "primeval architectural experiences of the Jewish people." Their design related the permanent to the temporary, as exemplified by the contrast between two paradigmatic structures, the Temple and the Tabernacle. The synagogue's exterior paid homage to the Temple by its use of precast concrete blocks resembling Jerusalem stone. The interior, by contrast, evoked the biblical Tabernacle. In a bold move, the architects enveloped the sanctuary's simple wooden seating area in a shimmering, tentlike net suspended from the ceiling and woven of thousands of tiny metallic Stars of David. By situating the tentlike interior inside the fortress-like exterior, the architects hoped to visually articulate the "historic conditions of Judaism in an architectural context." Whereas the temple interior symbolized the "flexible and dynamic (*aufbrechend*) quality of Judaism," the temple-like exterior symbolized the "inextinguishability of Jewish belief."[23]

After it was dedicated in 2001, the building earned widespread praise and won several prizes, including the 2002 World Architecture Award. Many observers hailed the synagogue for communicating a sense of historical awareness without resorting to deconstructivist pyrotechnics. One critic wrote that the "synagogue beats any number of Jewish museums and memorials, particularly those in the Daniel Libeskind mode, that try to express the crisis of description that has struck so many artists and theorists of the holocaust." Summing up the consensus, another commentator praised the architects' refusal to mimic Libeskind's "aesthetic of rupture" and argued that the synagogue's self-confident assertion of the "right to difference expressed in space" meant that the Holocaust "no longer stands in the foreground."[24]

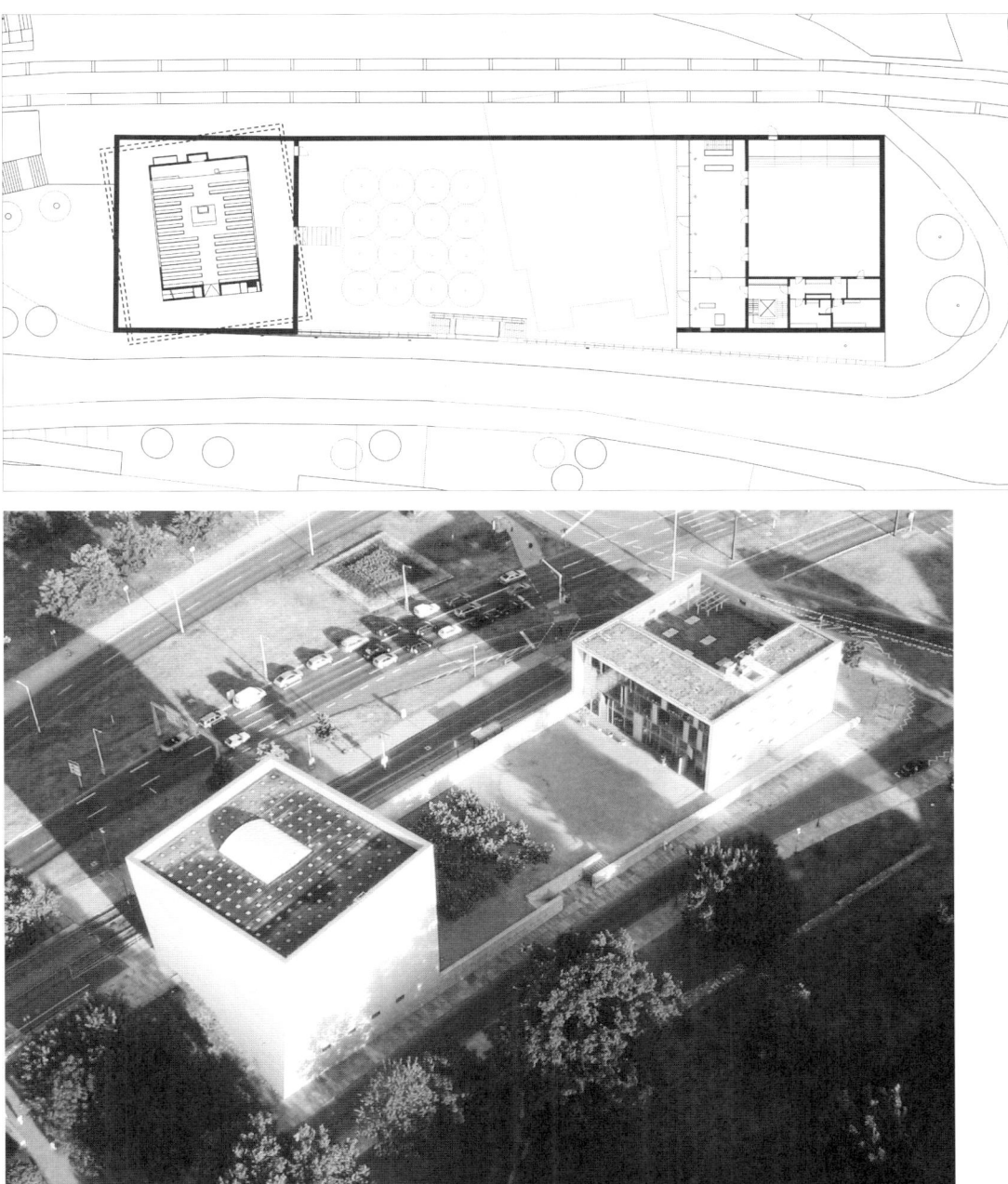

Figure 150. Wandel, Hoefer, Lorch, and Hirsch, Synagogue, Dresden, 1998–2001. The new synagogue (left) is situated perpendicular to the street but is torqued from above to make it parallel with the plan of the original synagogue on the site (center), which was designed by Gottfried Semper in the mid-nineteenth century and destroyed on Kristallnacht.

Figure 151. Synagogue, Dresden. This aerial view shows the synagogue at left and the community center at right. Between is the empty plaza where the Semper synagogue once stood.

Yet if the synagogue was an expression of self-confidence, it was very different from that articulated by the synagogues of Alfred Jacoby. In their openness, attention to context, and downplaying of the Holocaust, Jacoby's synagogues expressed the hope of a Jewish architect that Jewish and Christian Germans were finally ready to pursue reconciliation. By contrast, the Dresden synagogue was more strident. Its modern form refused to adapt to the city's baroque skyline, its location atop a walled-off enclosure removed it from the street, and its windowless facade lent it the appearance of a fortress. On its perimeter, the synagogue was the antithesis of openness, a fact that was reflected in local complaints that the building resembled a "concrete bunker."[25]

This assertiveness reflected the ambitions of its Christian German designers to admonish German society not to forget the lessons of the past. The founding members of WHLH (Andrea Wandel, Rena Wandel Hoefer, Andreas Hoefer, Wolfgang Lorch, and Nikolaus Hirsch) were committed to confronting Germany's Nazi legacy. Born between 1955 and 1964, they came of age in the 1970s and 1980s at precisely the time that debates about the Third Reich were taking center stage in the nation's cultural life. They supported an honest reckoning with the Nazi legacy, as was suggested by their work on a range of Holocaust memorials, such as their cubic Börneplatz memorial in Frankfurt (1992–96), their Track 17 memorial marking the deportation of Jews from the Grunewald train station in Berlin (1998), and the memorial site at the Hinzert concentration and forced labor camp near Trier in 2005. It was no surprise that the firm's synagogue in Dresden demanded to be noticed. As German critic Hanno Rauterberg observed, the building "inserted itself self-confidently" into the city "as if nobody should be able to overlook the return of the Jewish community." Unlike Jacoby's synagogue, it displayed "no hope in reconciliation" but simply sat there "stoically" and a bit secretively. The irony, of course, is that however well-intentioned the architects' goals may have been, their depiction of the Jewish community reproduced the nineteenth-century tendency of German architects to portray the Jews as different, just as Semper himself had done with his synagogue. In striving to preserve memory, they undercut Jacoby's goal of normalcy.[26]

Similar conclusions can be drawn about WHLH's new Ohel Jakob synagogue in Munich (1999–2006). For years city officials had mulled over building a replacement for the main synagogue on the Herzog-Max-Strasse, which was demolished on Hitler's orders in June 1938, five months before Kristallnacht. But it was only with the growth of the Jewish community in the 1990s that plans moved forward. In 1999, partly on the basis of its success in Dresden, WHLH won the commission to design the new synagogue. There were major differences from, as well as similarities to, their Dresden design. The Munich building was not built on the site of the original synagogue, which had been sold to a department store in the 1950s, but it was nonetheless erected at a prominent location within the historic Altstadt, on the Jakobsplatz. As was true of the site of Jacoby's synagogue in Aachen, the site had never recovered from wartime bombings and was undistinguished, apart from the presence of the late medieval city museum.

The architects planned the synagogue, a community center, and a Jewish museum as simple cubic modernist forms. Yet, as in Dresden, the architects invested the synagogue with clear Jewish architectural symbolism, again based on the Temple and Tabernacle. The Temple's influence was visible in the synagogue's hefty twenty-six-foot-high base, which was clad in rough travertine evoking the Western Wall in Jerusalem (fig. 152). Above the base was a smaller cube, made of glass and steel, whose diaphanous quality was meant to evoke the transitory qualities of the biblical Tabernacle. This symbolism may have escaped local community members, who have variously likened the building to a tefillin box and, more irreverently, to the Kaaba in Mecca. Still, the overall effect was of an assertive building that did not try to blend in with the Jakobsplatz's medieval gables and turrets.[27]

In contrast to the Dresden synagogue, however, the Holocaust had a less prominent influence on the Munich synagogue. Since the building was not erected on its original site, no archaeological references could be made in the building's plan. Munich's synagogue thus lacked Dresden's twist. Yet, in a subterranean passageway between the synagogue and the community center, the architects created a memorial documenting the names of the forty-five hundred local Jews killed in the Holocaust. The building itself, however, was little influenced by the German past and thus stands as a more hopeful building than its admonitory Dresden counterpart. Thanks to its connection to the adjoining Jewish Museum, whose wide expanse of glass opens up invitingly to the Jakobsplatz, it has a more welcoming presence. Compared to the community's previous main synagogue on the Reichenbachstrasse, which is a more anonymous structure, it reached out to the local community as a place of cultural interchange. It was to be expected, then, that architecture critics echoed Zentralrat president and former Munich community chief Charlotte Knoblauch, who in 2006 said the synagogue signaled that Munich's Jews were abandoning their insular, "rear courtyard existence" for a more public presence.[28]

The notion that new synagogues could foster improved relations between Jews and Christians in Germany found further confirmation in the new Bergische Synagoge in Wuppertal-Barmen (2002). Designed by the firm Goedeking and Schmidt, the synagogue was unique for being built directly next to a church, the Gemarker Kirche, on land that the church had donated as a gesture of reconciliation. The Gemarker Kirche had a history of opposition to Nazism, having served in 1934 as the place where the Protestant "Confessing Church" issued its famous Barmen Declaration resisting the Nazis' attempts to subsume the church within the German Christian movement. This declaration was courageous, but since it did not mention the plight of the Jews, church members later saw it as deficient. As Pastor Werner Jacken put it in 2002, of the declaration's six theses against Nazism, a "seventh thesis was lacking, a declaration of solidarity with the Jews. This thesis now stands hewn in stone: a

Figure 152. Wandel, Hoefer, Lorch and Hirsch, Synagogue, Munich, 1999–2006. The building's rough travertine base alludes to the Temple in Jerusalem, while the glass and steel structure atop it evokes the transitory qualities of the biblical Tabernacle.

synagogue on former church land."²⁹ The synagogue was thus a belated attempt to atone for the church's failure to act.

The architects, in turn, tried to communicate this sentiment by respectfully incorporating Jewish motifs in the synagogue's design. As with the synagogues of Alfred Jacoby and WHLH, the symbols were subtle and embedded in an otherwise nonrepresentational modernist aesthetic. Natural stone cladding on the synagogue's exterior evoked Jerusalem stone. On the western facade, nine narrow vertical windows (eight of which were grouped together and a ninth set apart) symbolized the candles of a Hanukkah menorah (fig. 153). A tall thin pyramid on the roof evoked the biblical Tabernacle. Two freestanding cylindrical columns at the synagogue's entrance represented Jachin and Boaz.³⁰ In all of these ways, the synagogue showed respect for Jewish religious and architectural tradition.

On balance, the synagogues of Dresden, Munich, and Wuppertal-Barmen embraced a design strategy that can be called allusive modernism. They abstained from overt historical references to nineteenth-century synagogues in favor of a nonrepresentational approach featuring abstract, geometrical shapes. Yet they were able to infuse them with symbolic weight through their attention to site, their use of materials, and their incorporation of forms rooted in Jewish architectural tradition. While the Holocaust never found overt expression—as, for example, in American Holocaust museums—its legacy explains why German architects attempted to lend their designs a Jewish image. These didactic buildings were meant to symbolize a commitment to remembering the past as a way to a better future. The fact, finally, that each of the synagogues was dedicated with the highest level of pomp—German president Johannes Rau and Israeli president Moshe Katsav were on hand at Wuppertal—underscored the belief that the buildings were intended to promote the laudable goal of German-Jewish reconciliation.³¹

Jewish Architects and the Turn to Expressionism

The allusive modernist synagogue designs of Christian German architects may have surpassed the synagogues of Alfred Jacoby in articulating a sense of Jewishness, but they were themselves exceeded by several radical works designed by two other Jewish architects. The designs of the Berlin-based Israeli architect Zvi Hecker and the Basel-based architect Manuel Herz represented the most dramatic attempts to forge an explicit form of Jewish architecture by seeking inspiration both in religious tradition and historical memory.

The first realized design was Hecker's Jewish community center and synagogue complex in Duisburg (1996–99). As in other German cities, the complex replaced the city's prewar synagogue, destroyed on Kristallnacht, and accommodated its growing Jewish population (fig. 154). Hecker's plan featured five narrow concrete fins that connected the complex's religious, social, and educational spaces. The fins served no obvious function and could be viewed as extraneous sculptural flourishes. Yet they had symbolic meaning. Hecker intended the fins to resemble the pages of an open book, specifically the five books of the Torah (fig. 155). In its consonance of forms and symbolism, the building was an obvious example of *architecture parlante*. Hecker sought additional Jewish meanings in his design as well. The end points of the fins were meant to correspond to abstracted versions of the first five letters of the Hebrew alphabet. These gestures reflected Hecker's desire for the building to exude a positive sense of Jewish identity, especially the Jewish people's intellectual and religious history as the "people of the book." In his own formulation: "Jewish culture and Jewish identity thrived mainly through writing. It was the Book that bound together . . . the scattered communities in [the] Diaspora. In Jewish history, text replaced territory, the Book a kingdom."[32]

Hecker further intended his JCC to be a memorial to the Holocaust. The building's fins, while symbolizing a book's pages, also resembled the five fingers of a hand — the Hebrew word for which, *yad,* also means memorial (as in Yad Vashem). Hecker further made his commemorative purpose clear in declaring that "any new building for the Jewish community . . . in Europe . . . is also for those who didn't survive." He added that each fin referred to a significant event in the Duisburg Jewish community's history. One in particular was aligned on an axis that pointed to the destroyed synagogue of 1938 — a design idea previously used by Daniel Libeskind and Alfred Jacoby. The building was not meant to be merely admonitory, moreover, but also inspirational. Hecker claimed that the Jewish tradition of writing could be viewed as redemptive in the sense that it expressed the Jews' response to catastrophe. As he put it: "Writing was also the testimony of the survival of the Jewish people in violent times."[33]

Figure 153. Goedeking and Schmidt, Synagogue, Wuppertal-Barmen, 2002. The building's Jewish features are visible in its stone cladding, reminiscent of Jerusalem stone, the conical shape on the roof, suggesting the biblical Tabernacle, the presence of two columns in front of the entrance, evoking Jachin and Boaz, and the grouping of nine windows on the facade (at right) symbolizing the candles on a menorah. At the rear left is the Gemarker Kirche.

Figures 154 and 155. Zvi Hecker, Synagogue and Jewish Community Center and plan, Duisburg, 1996–99. The building's plan features five narrow concrete fins connecting the complex's religious, social, and educational spaces. The fins symbolize the pages of an open book or the fingers of a human hand. The synagogue is located in the triangular structure at top right.

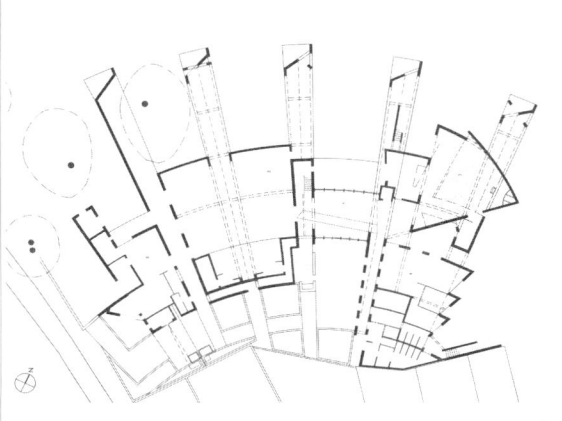

In developing the symbolism of his Duisburg project, Hecker revealed something about his own background. Born in 1931 in Krakow, Poland, he escaped the ravages of the Holocaust when his parents moved the family to Samarkand in Uzbekistan, where he spent the war years. Like Libeskind's parents (who had also spent the war in Soviet Central Asia), Hecker returned to Poland after 1945, where he studied architecture, and then moved to Israel in 1950. After receiving his degree in architecture from the Technion in 1955 and opening his own practice in 1959, Hecker built institutional and residential structures in Israel. His early designs from the 1960s, such as his city hall in Bat Yam (1960–63), displayed a fondness for the era's polyhedric, cellular plans, but after the 1970s he settled into a more expressionistic mode. In such buildings as the Spiral Apartment House in Ramat Gan (1981–86), Hecker mixed complex geometric plans and eclectic materials, just as Bruce Goff, Ralph Erskine, and Lucien Kroll were doing at the time.[34] Until this point, Hecker had not addressed the Holocaust in his work. But this changed after he moved his office to Germany in the early 1990s.

In 1991, Hecker settled in Berlin to oversee the completion of his first major German commission, the Heinz-Galinksi School (1990–95). The first Jewish school to open in Germany since the end of the Nazi era, the building was designed in the shape of a spiraling sunflower and displayed few signs of a specifically Jewish mindset, let alone of the Holocaust. But Hecker's years in Germany eventually led him to confront the legacy of the Nazi genocide. By the mid-1990s he had become increasingly involved in designing Holocaust memorials. In 1996 he collaborated with two fellow Israelis, artist Micha Ullman and architect Eyal Weizman, on the memorial for the Lindenstrasse synagogue in Berlin Kreuzberg. And in 1998 he submitted an unrealized design for the central Memorial to the Murdered Jews of Europe. Both projects dealt with writing. For the Lindenstrasse synagogue project, entitled "Page," Hecker reproduced concrete versions of the synagogue's original wooden benches and placed them between the many trees that had since grown at the historic site. Seen from above, the benches resemble abstract lines of text on a single page of the Talmud. Hecker's unrealized entry for the Berlin Holocaust memorial was entitled "Torn Pages" and exhibited the finlike design of the Duisburg complex. Taken together with his Heinz Galinski School, which was also functionally related to the theme of Jewish learning (a school in Hebrew is known as a House of the Book, or *Bet Sefer*), these projects make clear that Hecker's Duisburg synagogue and community center complex fit into a larger pattern of conceiving of Jewish space in terms of the Jewish intellectual tradition.[35]

Hecker's Duisburg synagogue and community center provided yet another example of how the experience of working in Germany on Jewish-related projects led certain Jewish architects to reflect on the relevance of the nation's history for their own architectural work. The result was an innovative design of unusual complexity whose significance was tied to the experience of the Holocaust. No doubt, for many visitors, the sources of inspiration for the Duisburg JCC may not be apparent in its building's exterior. But the design's symbolic rationale impressed architecture critics and earned the building considerable praise. Taking note of the synagogue complex's "neighborly" relationship to nearby buildings, one German critic keenly observed that its "five fingers [were] . . . not a fist" (and thus a symbol of Jewish historical resentment) but rather "expressed the hope for Jewish and Christian coexistence." Other observers echoed this redemptive assessment by praising the building for creating a "triumph out of destruction." These remarks reveal that the building owed not merely some of its origins, but also some of its critical success, to its strategy of dealing with the Holocaust's legacy.³⁶

The same year that the Duisburg synagogue was dedicated, an even more expressionistic design appeared with Manuel Herz's 1999 proposal for a new synagogue in Mainz. This project resembled Hecker's in being inspired by Jewish textual sources. But while Hecker found inspiration in the visual image of a book, Herz based his design on a sacred Hebrew word—*kedusha*. Denoting the idea of "holiness," the word strongly influenced the synagogue's irregular sawtooth form. Herz took the word as it appeared on the written page and traced an irregular line above its five individual letters—Kuf, Daled, Vav, Shin, and Hay—arriving at a jagged segment that formed the contours of the building's exterior (fig. 156). In explaining his design, Herz cited the traditional Jewish idea that the letters of the Hebrew alphabet were divinely given and possessed "architectural qualities." He further pointed out that each of the five letters corresponded to different spaces in the complex. The tallest and most visually striking one was formed by the letter Kuf, which corresponded to the synagogue sanctuary and which Herz likened to an upright shofar, a form that he explained had multiple meanings (fig. 157). Herz first pointed to its theological significance, noting that the "hornlike" shape's eastern orientation toward the sky expressed a "listening to God." He added that it also had a social function in that it helped to "call together the Jewish community" and "represented a belief in the future." Shifting from an auditory to an optical metaphor, Herz observed that the sanctuary's shofar-like form, which was capped by a large skylight with mullions shaped like a page of the Talmud, "allowed a light to shine in the diaspora." This observation echoed the design's title, "Light of the Diaspora," which honored Mainz's famous medieval rabbi, Gershom ben Judah, whose immense Talmudic learning earned him his legendary reputation. In all these ways, Herz hoped to "take up the centuries old Jewish teaching [and reenvision it] in modern form."³⁷

Like Hecker's Duisburg complex, Herz's design for Mainz was also partly influenced by the legacy of the Holocaust. In his project description he alluded to the past persecutions of Mainz's Jews, noting that the millennium of Jewish life in the city was just as defined by "suffering" as "learning." To mark this reality, Herz preserved the architectural remnants—four fluted columns from the entry portico—of the original neobaroque synagogue (1912) that remained at the site, a decision that echoed the effort to preserve the signs of the past at the Jewish community center on the Fasanenstrasse in Berlin. Still, Herz ultimately chose to transcend, rather than dwell on, the

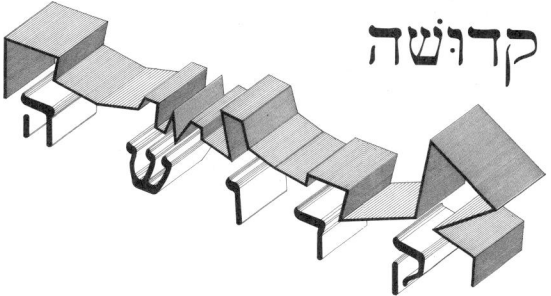

Figure 156. Manuel Herz, Synagogue and Jewish Community Center, Mainz, 1999–2010. The Hebrew word *kedusha* (holiness) provided part of the inspiration for the building's form.

Figure 157. Synagogue and Jewish Community Center, Mainz. The tall angular structure at right is the synagogue sanctuary. Its form derives from the letter Kuf in "kedusha" and alludes to a shofar. The stone columns at left are remnants of the prewar synagogue.

Holocaust's legacy. Pointing out that, even after the Holocaust, a "small number of Jews returned to . . . [Mainz] to rebuild their community anew," Herz argued that the synagogue project, with its guiding idea of kedusha, or holiness, demonstrated the community's capacity for renewal. Just as the idea of holiness "takes something out of the realm of the ordinary into the realm of the special," he noted, it was "precisely . . . [an act of uplift] that the Jewish community of Mainz deserves to experience." For this reason, Herz rejected suggestions that his building refer to the previous Mainz synagogue that had been destroyed on Kristallnacht. Insisting that alluding to the "Nazis' act of destruction" in the synagogue would amount to a form of self-imprisonment, Herz concluded, "It is impermissible for the Holocaust . . . to become the foundation of the new. The Nazis would thereby become the co-authors of the new synagogue, and I do not want that." Instead, emphasizing the continuity of Jewish religious traditions provided the best way of pointing the community forward.[38]

With its emphasis on hope, Herz's assertive brand of Jewish architecture partly reflected the influence of Libeskind. Like him, Herz embraced a deconstructivist form of architectural expression, the zigzagging elements of his Mainz synagogue echoing the forms of Libeskind's Berlin Jewish Museum. Herz also shared Libeskind's readiness to draw on Jewish sources of inspiration. These similarities were not coincidental. Herz worked in Libeskind's office in Berlin from 1995 to 1997, at the precise time that Libeskind was producing his unrealized 1996 design for the Duisburg synagogue and community center, whose plan was based upon the Hebrew letter Aleph. Herz's idea of basing the Mainz synagogue on an entire Hebrew word can be seen as an extension of Libeskind's idea for Duisburg, and also of his later plan for the Jewish Museum of San Francisco, which was based upon the word *chai*.

Herz was no carbon copy of Libeskind, however, as is revealed by his biography. Born in 1969 in Düsseldorf, he was a full generation younger than Libeskind and two generations younger than Hecker. As a result, he had a less personal relationship to the events of the Holocaust. His parents were not Holocaust survivors, and they had not lost any family members in the Nazi genocide. This is not to say that Herz felt completely at home in Germany. Like Jacoby, he was ambivalent about living in the land of the perpetrators and responded by following something of an international existence; he pursued his architectural studies at the AA in London and has since held teaching positions in Switzerland, Sweden, and the Netherlands. Still, Herz's generational identity liberated him to express his Jewishness. Herz implied as much in a 2001 interview when he noted that the "generation that is influencing contemporary Jewish life in Germany . . . no longer sees the Holocaust as the single defining moment in the Jewish community."[39]

Herz drew the logical architectural consequences of this belief by calling on German Jews to represent themselves more overtly in German public space. Declaring that it was no longer possible for them to "integrate by being inconspicuous," Herz challenged German Jews to display a new kind of "visibility" in the built environment by embracing an extroverted variety of synagogue architecture rooted in distinctively Jewish forms. Herz claimed that his design for Mainz followed in the tradition of recent synagogues "that did not find inspiration in the structure of churches but attempted to realize a Jewish conception of space." Rather than embracing a sense of "modesty," which he defined as a "Christian . . . concept," Herz proclaimed an affinity for the "absurd" and the "contradictory" in his architecture. In seeking a more identifiably Jewish form of architectural expression, Herz differed from Jacoby, whose designs made Jews more conspicuous but with an eye toward having them fit in rather than stand out. By contrast, Herz wanted his assertive architectural philosophy to shake up German culture. His hope that the synagogue would "elicit attention, raise questions, . . . and awaken doubt" suggests that he may have been working through his own ambivalence about his identity while producing his design.[40]

As events played out, Herz had to wait years before his vision was realized. While his proposal immediately earned positive reactions — one critic hailed it as a "sign, after decades of abstinence, of the emergence of a new . . . tradition of Jewish architecture in Germany" — financial disagreements between city and federal authorities made it uncertain that it would ever be finished. As the design hung in limbo, Herz considered realizing a slightly altered version of it in Smolensk, Russia. But in 2008, local Mainz officials and federal government agencies finally agreed to share the cost of the 10 million euro synagogue project, and the cornerstone was laid in November of that year. The building finally opened in September 2010. In its completed form, the synagogue fulfills Herz's goal of creating an attention-grabbing edifice, not only by virtue of its unusual angled shape but also by its unusual cladding in a gray grooved ceramic material meant to evoke the natural striations of a shofar. Thanks to these features, the building has received considerable attention, all of it positive.

The dedication ceremonies were notable for attracting, beyond the customary array of local politicians, the German federal president, Christian Wulff. Some ten thousand local citizens stood in line for hours to tour the building as part of an open house day of festivities. Architecture critics, meanwhile, have hailed the synagogue, calling it "bold like few other new buildings" and predicting that it would be seen as "the most important Jewish center in over seventy years in Germany." Predictably, other observers saw the synagogue as a sign of German-Jewish reconciliation, with President Wulff describing it as a "symbol of trust in our country."[41] Whatever the precise views, the consensus was that the building was a remarkable success.

By any standard of measure, the Jewish houses of worship built in Germany over the past two decades have displayed unprecedented inventiveness and redefined the genre of synagogue architecture. That they have done so is largely due to their architects' refusal to ignore Germany's dark past, in which they have frequently found creative inspiration. While some, such as Alfred Jacoby, have tried to heal the wounds of the Holocaust by designing affirmatively Jewish buildings that blend into the German built environment, others, such as Zvi Hecker and WHLH, have tried to highlight the Holocaust's legacy by producing eye-catching edifices that draw attention to themselves. All of these innovative structures attest to the vibrancy of contemporary German and German Jewish culture, a trend that will be further confirmed if Libeskind succeeds in realizing his newest commission, a synagogue for the liberal congregation Beth Shalom, in Munich.[42]

That said, there has been more than a little skepticism toward the idea that recent synagogue architecture testifies to German Jewish cultural vibrancy. In 2001, the German Jewish writer Richard Chaim Schneider voiced the suspicion that the construction of the new Ohel Jakob synagogue in Munich was less about genuine German-Jewish understanding than the desire of local politicians to bury memories of the Nazi past and prove that Munich had finally become an "open and liberal city." A similar suspicion was expressed in 2005 by Manuel Herz, whose essay "Institutionalized Experiment: The Politics of 'Jewish Architecture' in Germany" offered a pessimistic assessment of the country's wave of synagogue construction. While he praised the unconventional quality of the new synagogues and argued that their "anarchic" penchant for "breaking the rules" served to "critique . . . [the] established values of German society," he claimed that their radicalism served the aims of the German state. The only reason why German political authorities devoted so many economic resources to constructing synagogues, he insisted, was that they provided the means of pointing to the Jewish community's "secured . . . presence in Germany," thereby "closing . . . [a] shameful chapter [of] history."[43]

It is true that German authorities were eager to show themselves and their nation in a positive light by promoting the construction of new synagogues. Yet they did not do so merely for public relations, but to confront the real political threat of right-wing extremism. Political authorities in Dresden, for example, advanced the synagogue project there only following the intensification of neo-Nazi activity in the city and in Saxony at large. Authorities in Munich had to contend with similar extremist elements, some of whom tried to blow up the Ohel Jakob synagogue while it was under construction in 2003. Some German politicians may have viewed new synagogues as architectural fig leaves that could distract attention from homegrown political extremism and reassure outsiders about the country's enduring commitment to democratic values. Yet, precisely because of

Germany's ugly history, the existence of state support for Jewish institutions is significant and should not be taken for granted. Herz's concluding observation that Jewish architects in Germany were serving as the "court's fool[s]" by helping to "reinforce . . . the established and conservative society" can thus be seen as overly pessimistic. The new Jewish synagogues of the Federal Republic of Germany testify to the realization of the German government—and, it is to be hoped, the German people—that facing the nightmares of the past is a precondition for a normalized present.[44]

From Nostalgia to Normalcy: Recent Jewish Architecture in the United States

In the United States, by contrast, Jewish architecture during the same period developed differently. A broader range of Jewish-related buildings emerged in the years after the 1970s—synagogues, schools, community centers, museums, and university student centers. These buildings followed the same postmodern pattern visible in Germany by seeking inspiration in the past. Yet they expressed a wider array of influences. Some expressed lingering nightmares from the Holocaust by evoking Polish wooden synagogue architecture. Others alluded to Jewish religious iconography, ritual objects, and mystical thought. All of these buildings displayed an eagerness to articulate Jewishness in physical form. Yet not all works of Jewish architecture did so, as a third category of buildings, museums, strove for an architecture of normalcy.

Neo-Shtetlism: The Impact of Polish Wooden Synagogue Architecture

The rediscovery of Polish wooden synagogue architecture was the first indication of the postmodern turn in Jewish architecture. Strictly speaking, the renewed interest in the style was a proto-postmodern phenomenon, as its first signs appeared as early as the 1960s. Prior to that point, there had been little knowledge of or interest in this unique Jewish architectural legacy. During the 1920s and 1930s, isolated scholars and artists in Eastern Europe became aware that many wooden synagogues had been damaged during World War I and made efforts to catalogue them. They were disillusioned, however, that the "Jewish population as a whole has been indifferent to their fate."[45] This indifference continued after 1945 as the mammoth challenges of postwar reconstruction in Eastern Europe overshadowed the fact that wooden synagogues had almost disappeared. It was a decade and a half after the war's end before these buildings began to inspire architects in their work. The renewed interest in Polish wooden synagogues represented a specifically Jewish version of postmodern revivalism. Yet it also represented a growing willingness to acknowledge the Holocaust's legacy. Given the fact that Polish wooden synagogues were deliberately targeted for destruction by the Nazis, the revived interest in them reflected a commitment to rescue a rich cultural legacy from oblivion.

This new attitude was largely due to the publication of Maria and Kazimierz Piechotka's *Wooden Synagogues* in 1959. The book was a richly illustrated compendium of photographs, plans, and descriptions of nearly seventy synagogues from prewar Poland. Its analysis focused on the Jewish architectural style's origins and relationship to Polish architecture. The book's power, however, resided in its illustrations. Exterior shots of the synagogue's slanted roofs and interior pictures of their richly decorated sanctuaries provided a detailed portrait of a "world irrevocably lost to us," as Alfred

Werner put it in a 1960 *Commentary* review, and vividly underscored the magnitude of Jewish loss. Published at a time of increasing western awareness of the Nazis' crimes, the book could not help but be viewed from an emotional perspective shaped by the Holocaust's legacy.[46]

The book's influence was visible in the synagogue designs of Jewish architects in the 1960s. In his introduction to the catalogue of the Jewish Museum of New York's exhibition, *Recent American Synagogue Architecture,* in 1963, Richard Meier highlighted the significance of the "marvelous Polish buildings of the seventeenth and early eighteenth centuries, like those at Wolpa, Grodno, and Zabludow." These synagogues clearly influenced two synagogues profiled in the exhibition: Davis, Brody, and Wisniewski's design for the Orthodox Congregation Sons of Israel in Lakewood, New Jersey (1963), and Oppenheimer, Brady, and Lehrecke's Temple Shalom in Norwalk, Connecticut (1966) (fig. 158). A third architect, Louis I. Kahn, was only several years away from completing his design for Temple Beth-El in Chappaqua, New York. All these synagogues had hexagonal or octagonal plans, were clad in wood, and displayed roofs marked by multiple gables and peaks. Their architects (and the rabbis for whom they worked) openly acknowledged the influence of Polish synagogue architecture.[47]

It is unclear whether these synagogues' architects saw their designs as memorials to the Holocaust. Yet it is worth noting that in the introduction to *Wooden Synagogues,* Stephen Kayser pointed to such a connection, writing, "Two decades have passed since [the] . . . wanton destruction [of Polish wooden synagogues] began. . . . Now that practically all of them have fallen to the destructive madness of the Nazi horde, they deserve to be remembered like the six million human beings who perished with them in unspeakable agony." Few architects in the 1960s explicitly connected their work to the Nazi genocide. But Herbert Oppenheimer, describing his design for Temple Shalom in Norwalk in 1966, commented: "I wish to make this building tangible proof that Polish synagogues have not been completely destroyed, but that their spirit in some way continues." Given this remark, it is possible that the desire to acknowledge the Holocaust's legacy may have influenced at least some of the architects who found creative inspiration in wooden synagogues. If so, it is likely that this desire was rooted in a redemptive view of the past — one that, like Louis I. Kahn's unrealized Holocaust memorial proposal, asserted Jewish survival in the wake of catastrophe.[48]

Figure 158. Oppenheimer, Brady, and Lehrecke, Temple Shalom, Norwalk, Connecticut, 1966. This building was one of the first postwar synagogues influenced by Polish wooden synagogue architecture.

After the mid-1960s, interest in Polish wooden synagogue architecture lapsed for several decades, but it returned in the 1980s. The rise of postmodernism played an important role, as did the growth of Holocaust consciousness in the United States. In 1985, the *Wall Street Journal* referred to Polish wooden synagogues during the larger debate over the location for the New York City Holocaust museum. In opposing the plan to locate the museum in the U.S. Custom House, the newspaper instead recommended that the "commission should consider building a replica of one of the Polish wooden synagogues razed by the Nazis and their collaborators. Like their congregants, virtually all of the Polish wooden synagogues are gone. But . . . photographs . . . of these martyred buildings were miraculously preserved [in] . . . Maria and Kazimierz Piechotka['s] . . . book . . . [which] is a Holocaust memorial all by itself. . . . [Any] architect today, working from its pictures and other archival material, could draw up practical plans." This proposal went nowhere, but it was not the last time that this style of architecture was linked to the Holocaust. One year later, in 1986, Percival Goodman reviewed Carol Krinsky's book on European synagogue architecture by highlighting the legacy of Polish wooden synagogues, which he described as having suffered "depraved attacks" by the Nazis and which he said were inseparable from the "ghosts of 6 million people murdered in our time because they worshipped their God in the buildings . . . examined in this book."[49]

By the late 1980s, the style began to find its way once more into synagogue architecture. One of the best-known buildings to display its influence was Norman Jaffe's Gates of the Grove synagogue in East Hampton, New York (1985–89). This synagogue's plan and richly symbolic interior is discussed in greater detail below, in the context of Kabbalah, which was its primary source of inspiration. But its exterior was explicitly influenced by Polish wooden synagogue architecture. Jaffe had been given a copy of the Piechotkas' book by the synagogue's rabbi early in the design process, and he used the famous Volpa synagogue in Belarus as inspiration for his synagogue's street facade.[50] The shingled facade featured several gabled roofs cascading downward in the fashion of many Polish synagogues (fig. 159). Jaffe himself acknowledged this influence, writing that the Polish Jewish tradition of "[piling] roof upon roof" was echoed in his synagogue's own "stepping [of] shingled roofs ascending like a woven wood stair to the sky." Meanwhile, architecture critics, such as Paul Goldberger, described the building as reflecting Jaffe's desire to "merge the deep beauty . . . [of] the

Figure 159. Norman Jaffe, Gates of the Grove, East Hampton, New York, 1985–89. Beyond being influenced by the architecture of Polish wooden synagogues, the building featured rows of shingles shaped like Stars of David (visible to the left of the horizontal wooden beam at right).

wooden synagogues of Poland with his love of modernist form." Unlike Herbert Oppenheimer, however, Jaffe did not allude to the Holocaust as a reason for his embrace of the style.[51]

The same is true of M. Louis Goodman's Temple Israel in Greenfield, Massachusetts (1991). Temple Israel combined the influence of Polish wooden synagogues with the austerity of rural New England colonial architecture. Two white columns flank the entryway (a reference to Jachin and Boaz), but otherwise, Platonic shapes prevailed: squares and circles for windows and triangles in the roof's gables. The design was not literal, as was shown by its metal roof. Goodman affirmed its contemporary identity, saying, "Every building has a story, and I'm trying to put the story on the bones of modernism." Goodman also confirmed that the building was meant to evoke Polish wooden synagogues, disclosing that he became interested in them while working for Louis I. Kahn in the 1960s. Like Kahn, he had read the Piechotkas' book and had come to realize that "they were . . . beautifully proportioned . . . [and] intelligently made." Like Jaffe, however, Goodman did not embrace the style in order to commemorate the Holocaust.[52]

By contrast, a sense of historical responsibility informed another synagogue that merged Polish wooden synagogue architecture with vernacular New England building traditions: Beth Sholom Rodfe Zedek in Chester, Connecticut (1998–2001). Executed by the Connecticut architect Steven L. Lloyd, the synagogue was based on the design of the minimalist artist Sol LeWitt, who was a congregant and major donor to the synagogue. LeWitt said that in conceiving the design, he was "inspired by the old wooden synagogues [that were found in] the shtetls in Eastern Europe," calling his style "neo-shtetl." The synagogue is an octagonal building with an exterior displaying a series of sloping roofs. Its lofty interior is dominated by interlacing wooden beams that come together at the ceiling in the form of a Star of David. An ark by LeWitt featuring a multicolored Star of David set inside of a circle adds color to the interior's otherwise minimalistic arrangement of white walls and wood. It is unclear whether LeWitt specifically intended to commemorate the Holocaust, but he had displayed a keen interest in doing so in his own artistic work. In 1989, his minimalist sculpture, *Black Form: Dedicated to the Missing Jews,* was installed in front of the Town Hall in the German city of Altona outside Hamburg. And his set of five paintings, "Consequence," was installed at the United States Holocaust Memorial Museum in 1993. Given LeWitt's interest in the Nazi past, it is highly likely that his design for the Chester synagogue was meant partly as an act of commemoration.[53]

In the 1990s, Polish wooden synagogue architecture also began to influence secular structures, most notably the National Yiddish Book Center in Amherst, Massachusetts (fig. 160). In the early 1980s, its founder, Aaron Lansky, conceived the idea of rescuing unwanted Yiddish books and, after collecting over a million volumes, decided to establish an institutional home for them. In thinking about the design for what was to become the National Yiddish Book Center in the early 1990s, Lansky wanted a building "with a sense of historical memory." He rejected more than twenty architects until he settled on the Boston-based Allen Moore. A Christian "old-line Yankee architect" who employed New England building traditions in his work, Moore, like Jaffe, Goodman, and Lloyd, nevertheless also sought inspiration in Polish wooden synagogue architecture. A photograph of the Volpa synagogue made a particularly strong impression on him, and the similarities he perceived between the Polish and New England countryside convinced him that a design inspired by Polish wooden synagogue architecture would fit well into the Center's site on the campus of Hampshire

College. The resulting building, which was dedicated in 1997, features pitched roofs and gables of varying staggered heights that evoke organically evolved structures. Lansky referred to the design as "heimish modern," a blending of historical motifs and modern conveniences, while other journalists described it as a "postmodern shtetl."[54]

It is hard to say how much the Holocaust's legacy influenced the building's design. Lansky wanted to view the institution as a "place where young people can learn about Jewish culture in a context that is not just about victimization." Indeed, he viewed the center "as a counterweight to the [United States] Holocaust Memorial Museum," in the sense that it provided a "glimpse not of how Europe's Jews died but of how they lived." Unlike James Freed's museum, Moore's design did not allude to the Holocaust. After one of Moore's Jewish friends complimented his early sketches for the building by saying, "This will be the first Jewish building in America that nobody's going to feel guilty in," the architect cited the task of avoiding a "guilty building" as a guiding principle of the project. At the same time, though, Lansky invoked the Nazi past to lend urgency to the institution's book-rescuing mission. A fundraising letter from the 1990s highlighted the "alarming fact" that "throughout North America, . . . thousands of priceless Yiddish books . . . that had survived the ravages of Hitler and Stalin . . . were being discarded and destroyed: not by anti-Semites, but by Jews!"[55]

On balance, Lansky invoked the Holocaust to emphasize Jewish survival and renewal. In a speech at the center's dedication in June 1997, he remarked: "I think this building proves that . . . Yiddish as a language, as a culture, as a sensibility, is not dead," adding that its creation was motivated "not by nostalgia . . . or a sense of . . . bemoaning the depredations . . . of the past . . . [but by] faith in the future." Lansky saw the institution as heralding a "Jewish revival," for it symbolized the courage "to reclaim our own culture without embarrassment" and give up the notion that "cultural abandonment" was still the "price of admission to America." These remarks — like Lansky's claim that the center was "surely . . . the most beautiful Jewish building in America" — suggested that the National Yiddish Book Center was an architectural rejection of assimilation and an assertion of

Figure 160. Allen Moore, National Yiddish Book Center, Amherst, Massachusetts, 1997. The wooden building's sloping roofs evoked the vanished wooden synagogues of Poland.

Jewish ethnic pride.[56] Not only in its mission but in its particularistic architectural form, the building symbolized another way in which Jews during the postmodern period affirmed their identities.

The interest in Polish wooden synagogues, finally, found expression in efforts to replicate them. In Berkeley, California, in 1999, the Orthodox Congregation Beth Israel announced plans to re-create a version of the eighteenth-century synagogue of Przedborz to replace its own structure from the 1920s. In explaining their plan, congregants denied that the Holocaust had anything to do with it. "We want this to be a living, breathing building, not a Holocaust memorial or a mausoleum," one congregant affirmed. Yet synagogue leaders had trouble articulating what the restoration plan was meant to achieve beyond creating a "symbol of something old and enduring." Critics of the plan attributed it to simple nostalgia, while one went so far as to see it as a sign of "Jewish neurosis." The reconstruction plan attracted support from major Jewish figures, such as Elie Wiesel and Tony Kushner, but a lack of funds led to its abandonment in 2003. The impulse behind it, however, lives on. A plan announced in 2003 to build a full-scale replica of the Zabludow synagogue as part of a larger folk architecture museum in Bialystok, Poland, shows that the fascination with wooden synagogue architecture continues.[57]

The implications of this trend for Jewish memory are unclear. The interest of Jews in wooden synagogue architecture can mostly be attributed to the nostalgic mindset and renewed sense of ethnic pride that defined American Jewish life in the postmodern era. The support for these synagogues also reflected the growing Jewish interest in Diaspora culture during the 1990s.[58] In the end, though, the memory of the Holocaust probably lies behind the phenomenon as well. To be sure, it was a different form of remembrance from that which fostered the rise of deconstructivism, as it focused on renewing Jewish life after the Holocaust instead of dwelling on its ruptures. Still, in seeking inspiration in a vanished Jewish architectural tradition, American Jews indirectly testified to the Nazi genocide's enduring impact.

Jewish Architecture and the Revival of Religious Symbolism

The postmodern turn in Jewish architecture was also reflected in the tendency of synagogues and secular Jewish buildings to allude to Jewish religious traditions. This development contrasted sharply with the early postwar era, when Jewish buildings strove for a universal, modern appearance and distinguished themselves as Jewish only through applied ornament. Now architects imported Jewish themes into their designs' overall conception and appearance. Given the pluralism that has long defined Diaspora Jewish life, no single style emerged in this period; rather, a multiplicity of methods communicated Jewish identity in architectural fashion by seeking inspiration in the Jewish religious past. There was no idealistic expectation that returning to history could produce an authentic form of Jewish architecture. The skeptical postmodern belief that everything original had already been tried and that the past's remains could only be recycled shaped the designs of this period. Still, the desire to inject a sense of Jewishness into Jewish architecture was no less heartfelt.

Beginning in the late 1970s and early 1980s, American synagogues displayed postmodern influences by embracing stylistic revivalism, ornamentation, and narrative. The Chicago architecture firm of Hammond, Beeby, and Babka's award-winning sanctuary and social hall for the North Shore Synagogue in the Chicago suburb of Glencoe, Illinois (1979–83) combined a neoclassical brick-clad exterior with interior arches reminiscent of John Soane's Bank of England (1788–1830). Pietro Belluschi's domed design for United Hebrew Congregation outside of St. Louis (1986–89) was inspired by Brookman Whitehouse's neo-Byzantine Temple Beth-Israel in Portland, Oregon (1927). Other synagogues, such as Travis Price's domed Oseh Shalom in Laurel, Maryland (1992), and Judith Capen and Robert Weinstein's gabled design for Temple Micah in Washington, D.C. (1995), were more eclectic, evoking such varied Jewish symbols as tallis fringes and tefillin straps (fig. 161). Finally, Stanley Tigerman's unrealized proposal for the Reform Or Shalom congregation in suburban Chicago envisioned an entryway flanked by unfinished versions of the columns Jachin and Boaz in order to symbolize the "anxiety of an exilic people."[59]

Secular Jewish buildings also drew on religious traditions. Rothschild Doyno Architects took up the motif of the biblical "pillar of fire" in designing the Hillel Jewish University Center near the University of Pittsburgh (2001). Herbert S. Newman and Partners' pyramidal Jewish Center at Williams College (1991) was inspired by Mount Sinai. James Rossant's Ramaz School in Manhattan (1981) alluded to Hebrew letters in the staggered windows of its aluminum-clad facade (fig. 162). And the important Jewish structure known as a sukkah—a temporary hut erected for the harvest holiday of Sukkot—inspired such buildings as Moshe Safdie's Harvard-Radcliffe Hillel building (1995), Roth and Moore's Slifka Student Center at Yale (1995), and Daniel Libeskind's glass courtyard addition to

Figure 161. Judith Capen and Robert Weinstein, Temple Micah, Washington, D.C., 1995. The postmodern structure's facade displayed such Jewish symbols as the Ten Commandments, the columns Jachin and Boaz, a diagonal Star of David pattern, and a blue cornice evoking a tallis stripe.

Figure 162. Herbert S. Newman and Partners, Jewish Center, Williams College, Williamstown, Massachusetts, 1991. The building's ziggurat-like dome was inspired by Mount Sinai, while the corner chimneys allude to concentration camps.

the Jewish Museum of Berlin (2004–7). None of these architects claimed to have created a unique form of "Jewish architecture." But by drawing so explicitly on Jewish sources of inspiration, they transcended mere functional ambitions and lent their work a more particularistic character.[60]

Synagogue Architecture and the Kabbalah

Perhaps the most notable way in which religious symbolism influenced Jewish architecture was in buildings inspired by the Kabbalah. Given its emergence as a major cultural phenomenon in the United States in recent years, it was probably only a matter of time before Kabbalah influenced synagogue design.[61] There were precedents in Louis I. Kahn's synagogues from the 1960s, but his interest in Kabbalistic ideas has never been determined with certainty. By contrast, beginning in the 1980s, Jewish architects openly sought inspiration in Kabbalistic themes and imagery. Two of the most important were Norman Jaffe and Alexander Gorlin, both of whom designed synagogues that rank among the more innovative of recent years.

The case of Norman Jaffe's Gates of the Grove synagogue in East Hampton, Long Island (1985–89), highlights the forces that made Kabbalah a cultural phenomenon in the United States. Like other American Jews, Jaffe was attracted to Jewish mysticism as part of a larger New Age quest for spiritual sustenance. Like Eisenman, Gehry, and Tigerman, Jaffe reembraced his Jewish background because of a midlife crisis. Born in 1932 in Chicago, he belonged to the same generation as his deconstructivist peers and shared their experience (Eisenman excepted) of having been raised by immigrant parents who exposed him to an Orthodox tradition from which he quickly strayed. Until the mid-1980s, little in Jaffe's life or work displayed Jewish influence. After establishing his own firm in the 1960s, he was best known for a series of modernist vacation and beach homes for wealthy clients on Long Island. As he was nearing the age of fifty in the early 1980s, however, the pressures of success and the lack of a stable personal life (he remained single after his estranged first wife died in a car accident) left him feeling spiritually empty. For a time he experimented with Eastern religions, traveling to meet with a swami in India, becoming a vegetarian, and taking up yoga. Finally, a new opportunity for religious identification appeared in 1985 when he learned that the Jewish Center of East Hampton was planning to build a new sanctuary. Even though he had never designed a synagogue, Jaffe eagerly sought the commission, and, after producing his plan (and waiving his fee), he persuaded the congregation to let him go ahead with it.[62]

Jaffe's proposal displayed a wide range of Jewish influences, but the most novel were Kabbalistic in inspiration. The architect based his design on the number ten, symbolizing the ten holy attributes of God contained in the mystical sefirot. Jaffe created ten prayer alcoves in the synagogue's interior, each of which was located at the end of five rows of bent cedar columns that became taller in height (and longer in plan) the farther they were from the bimah. At each end of the five rows was a separate alcove, the wooden wall of which was carved with the Hebrew words for the divine attributes: *malkhut, din, rakhamim,* and so forth (fig. 163). Jaffe also claimed that the bent columns were inspired by the Hebrew letter Yud, the tenth letter of the alphabet. Ten windows on the building's north and south facades further played on the number ten's significance. Skylights had additional Kabbalistic meaning by allowing natural light to enter the sanctuary's interior. As Jaffe explained, "Light is used in cabalistic literature as a metaphor to represent . . . the various . . . emanations . . .

Figure 163. Norman Jaffe, Gates of the Grove Synagogue, East Hampton, New York, 1985–89. The synagogue's interior is deeply influenced by Kabbalistic ideas, most notably the symbolically significant number ten.

of Divinity." Yellow cedar wood throughout the building's interior expressed Jaffe's belief that the synagogue was "the tree of the Kabala, whose roots are in heaven, whose meaning is incomprehensible." Finally, the synagogue's location in a grove of old trees (which provided the building with its name) and Jaffe's description of his structural porticos as treelike forms that "ask to echo the forest" underscored his design's origins in the Kabbalistic idea of the (sephircthic) tree.[63]

What led Jaffe to the Kabbalah is unknown. Some of his pronouncements about light — "the light meets the wall . . . the wall delights in the light" — suggest the influence of Louis I. Kahn. But there is little doubt that his Kabbalistic interests reflected his personal circumstances. Notes that Jaffe drafted during the design process suggest that he may have seen the Kabbalah as a means of crafting a spiritually genuine form of Jewish architecture that could counteract the materialistic nature of his previous architectural practice. In one instance, Jaffe cited the Second Commandment against making graven images, observing that its historic purpose may have been "to release the mind from the familiar material aspects of existence. If the mind is occupied with making . . . [a] picture, there is less space for worship." Given his disenchantment with designing for wealthy clients, planning a synagogue according to Kabbalistic principles made perfect sense. Whatever Jaffe's motives, his design was praised by architecture critics as "spiritual and inspired," and he went on to pursue further synagogue commissions. Tragically, Jaffe's death in a drowning accident in 1993 prevented him from fully tapping his potential as a synagogue architect.[64]

By contrast, the synagogues of Alexander Gorlin reveal how Kabbalistic motifs continue to influence contemporary Jewish houses of worship. Gorlin is best known for his residential work, especially his much-publicized apartment for Daniel Libeskind in 2004, but as early as the late 1990s he was branching out into religious architecture, producing designs for seven synagogues and synagogue additions in the New York metropolitan area. His best known, the North Shore Congregation in Kings Point, Long Island (1998–2001), eloquently expressed the architect's interest in the Kabbalah. Unlike Jaffe, who gravitated to the mystical tradition out of a sense of spiritual emptiness, Gorlin embraced it from an intellectual perspective that reflected his Jewish background. Born in Brooklyn in 1955, Gorlin grew up in a household that was committed to Conservative Judaism and

Figure 164. Alexander Gorlin, North Shore Congregation, Kings Point, Long Island, 1998–2001. The skylight above the ark is explicitly influenced by the Kabbalistic idea of zimzum.

counted several Orthodox rabbis in the family tree. During his childhood, his mother took him and his sister to a "Kabbalistic astrologer" who had long advised his parents about careers, personal relationships, and the like. These experiences gave him a passing familiarity with the subject, but it did not inform any of his early architectural work. This is not to say that Gorlin was uninterested in the Jewish dimensions of architecture; while a student at Cooper Union in the late 1970s he reconstructed Ezekiel's vision of the Temple for his thesis project. Yet after earning his master's degree from Yale in 1980 and opening his own practice in 1986, he found little opportunity to explore Jewish themes in his mostly residential work.[65]

Gorlin's avoidance of Jewish subjects changed in 1998, however, when he received the commission for the North Shore synagogue. "I was looking for some inspiration," he recalls, "and was surprised that the Rabbi didn't provide any direction." He knew that he did not want to do a "19th century pastiche" for the project, but could not determine how to express a sense of Jewishness in modernist fashion. Inspiration came from the work of Kahn. As Gorlin recalled in 2008, "My interest in [Kabbalah] came from my realization that Kahn—whether or not it was true—may have referenced [it in his synagogues of the 1960s]." Gorlin's interest in the Jewish dimensions of Kahn's work dated back to 1985, when he published an essay, entitled "Biblical Imagery in the Work of Louis I. Kahn," that was influenced by and helped perpetuate Jeffry Kieffer's theory about Kahn's interest in Kabbalistic imagery. Gorlin later plunged into the academic literature on Jewish mysticism, reading the works of Gershom Scholem in planning the North Shore synagogue. So interested did he become in the subject that he has begun work on a new book, *The Architecture of Kabbalah*.[66]

Gorlin's North Shore synagogue was directly informed by the Kabbalistic idea of zimzum (the withdrawal of God into himself at the moment of creation) and the resulting *shevirat ha-kelim* ("breaking of the vessels"). The architect explored these ideas in the area above the ark (fig. 164). There Gorlin placed a skylight in the form of a steel-framed cube containing two inverted triangles of clear glass. Depending upon the angle from which one views the cube, the otherwise skewed-looking interior triangles merge to form a Star of David. But the cube's main significance is to signify the "Holy of Holies [in Solomon's Temple], which is described exactly as a cube." Functionally, the cube serves as a skylight to the outside. But symbolically, the light shining through its fractured form signifies the moment when the "vessel of the synagogue has broken . . . and the light pours in." Kabbalistic ideas of light further influenced Gorlin's eternal light, which echoes the inverted triangles of the cube to evoke the highest of the sephirot, God's crown (*Keter*). He also designed the brightly colored curtain (*parokhet*) for the ark with a diagram of the sephirot. The synagogue's design thereby physically embodied the Kabbalistic epic of divine creation.[67]

Gorlin continued his interest in the Kabbalah in his subsequent work. His unrealized proposal for an addition to Temple Sinai in Roslyn, New York (2006), took the cube from the North Shore Synagogue and made it the basis of his entire synagogue plan. His design for the Summit Jewish Center in New Jersey (in progress) assumed the form of an unfolded Star of David. More recently, Gorlin has been commissioned to design an addition to Louis I. Kahn's Temple Beth-El in Chappaqua, a proposal that its current rabbi has likened to a "shtetl."[68] While the design has yet to be finalized, it is fitting that an architect whose devotion to Kahn helped inspire his first successful Jewish commission has been granted the honor of adding to the master's work.

Kahn's influence raises the question of whether Gorlin's interest in the Kabbalah can be connected to the legacy of the Holocaust. While Kahn's use of Kabbalistic imagery may have reflected his desire to "repair the world" during a period of growing Holocaust awareness, Jaffe's interest in Jewish mysticism was largely motivated by personal spiritual considerations. Gorlin, by contrast, has openly pointed to the Nazi genocide's influence on his work. As someone who grew up in a multifamily building with several Holocaust survivors, he has noted that "Holocaust awareness was an integral part of my early Jewish identity." More important, it shaped his interest in Kabbalah—at least insofar as he says he "understand[s] the Holocaust in a... simplistic Kabbalistic way," one related to the idea of the "withdrawal of God." The Holocaust may not yet have found overt expression in Gorlin's synagogue designs. But he holds open the idea that it could find expression in his future work, noting: "I could see the Holocaust as a starting point for the design of a synagogue as part of the yin-yang of the dialectic of the broken vessels and *tikkun olam*."[69] For this reason, the recent turn to the Kabbalah in synagogue design can be seen as another sign of the Holocaust's legacy.

Toward Normalcy: Non-Jewish Jewish Architecture

Jewish-related buildings did not always express Jewishness in their architectural form, however, as was shown by three prominent Jewish museums in Los Angeles, Chicago, and Philadelphia.[70]

Figure 165. Moshe Safdie, Skirball Cultural Center, Los Angeles, 1985–96. The museum displays no visible Jewish features, although its bell tower (far left) and abstract rounded gables suggest the influence of Spanish colonial architecture.

These buildings were designed either according to local vernacular traditions or the universal style of modernism and can thus be described as examples of architectural assimilation. Indeed, they can arguably be viewed as "non-Jewish" works of Jewish architecture. Despite being conceived as specifically Jewish institutions, they were marketed in universalistic terms by their founders, who hailed them for their openness and accessibility to the general public. This marketing strategy, however, ran up against a certain amount of resistance. In an era in which postmodernism valorized expressions of ethnic particularism, architects as well as critics projected Jewish meanings onto buildings whose true inspirations lay elsewhere.

One example of this pattern is Moshe Safdie's Skirball Cultural Center in Los Angeles (1985–96). Built to house the Los Angeles branch of Hebrew Union College's vast collection of Judaica, the 125,000-square-foot, $65 million museum complex is located in the Santa Monica Mountains, a mile north of Richard Meier's Getty Center. The Skirball Center is typical of Safdie's buildings in that its combination of modern and traditional elements makes it difficult to categorize stylistically. His building displays few Jewish markers, however. In plan, the complex comprises a sprawling set of primary and secondary structures, geometric in shape, connected by trellised courtyards and surrounded by lush greenery. The forms are unadorned and mostly modern in appearance, yet their materials betray signs of a postmodern sensibility. The most obvious example is the museum's distinctive roofline, which is made up of seven stainless steel roofs featuring rounded gables (fig. 165). The gables strongly resemble those of Spanish missions, an impression reinforced by an abstracted Spanish colonial bell tower at the complex's southern edge. These features suggest that, in designing the complex, Safdie adhered to one of California's original vernacular traditions and pursued a path of architectural assimilation.

This supposition was strongly supported by the Skirball's overall mission. Ever since it was conceived, the museum embraced an integrationist vision of the American Jewish experience. The museum's very name does not even include the adjective "Jewish." Moreover, museum officials stressed that the institution was "not an exercise in ethnic vanity" but an "attraction for a larger public" that would "strengthen understanding" among all people in Los Angeles. For this reason the institution portrayed Jewishness universalistically, stressing the "parallels between Jewish values and American democratic principles," Judaism's respect for the "sanctity of life," and its desire to make the world "more just and ... compassionate." The lack of particularistic emphasis was epitomized by the declaration: "We [Jews] have thrived as a distinctive thread in the multicolored fabric of the human family. The Jewish thread is no more precious — and no less — than any other."[71]

This avoidance of ethnic particularism explains why museum officials steered Safdie away from overt expressions of Jewishness in the building. Early on they rejected the idea of using Jerusalem stone as an homage to Israel. They also rejected including allusions to the Holocaust. The refusal to evoke either of these themes reflected the desire of the Skirball's founder, Rabbi Uri Herscher, to make the museum unique among Jewish institutions. "We have Holocaust centers, we have Israel-oriented centers," he noted in 1996. "The Skirball Cultural Center is designed to tell the story of how Jewish tradition, Jewish values, and Jewish vision intersect with the fabric of American life." Herscher's desire to keep the Holocaust's influence at arm's length was notable in light of his personal background: he is the son of German Jewish refugees who fled to Palestine in the 1930s, and he later lost numerous relatives in the Nazi genocide. In explaining the Skirball's aversion to "emphasizing the last 50 years of history," he noted, "I really wanted to tell a story that was not mournful. . . . There were 18 Herschers, at least, who perished in the Holocaust, and I think . . . the best memorial to them is to repair a little corner of the world." Since overt expressions of Jewishness would have cast doubt on the museum's mission of celebrating Jewish integration into American life, its architecture had to be assimilationist.[72]

Safdie was himself sympathetic toward this assimilationist mission. When asked by journalists whether the building had any Jewish sources of inspiration, he noted that over the course of history, "Jews built in the architecture [style] of the place [where they lived]." This comment might have led Safdie to admit the influence of Spanish colonial architecture on his design, which was perceived by certain commentators. Instead, he explained the Skirball Center's origins as outside the realm of architecture. When pressed about the building's Jewish dimensions, Safdie replied that if any such thing as Jewish architecture existed, it would "come out of a respect for nature." This remark was admittedly opaque, but it reflected the fact that the Skirball Center's core idea was less architectural than horticultural. In developing his design, Safdie declared, "Los Angeles is a city of oases in the wilderness . . . I've tried to make the Skirball an oasis." His 1991 comment that "I have tried to design a place that . . . responds to its natural setting" begged the question of how his architecture was actually influenced by it. But his description of the complex as an "essay in calmness . . . and harmony with nature" revealed that he was mostly inspired by the site. The frequent questions about his sources of inspiration for the center eventually led Safdie to locate Jewish significance where none originally existed. By 1996 he was claiming that the complex was inspired by the idea of a garden, saying that "the Jews . . . were the first people to imagine a paradise on earth." This description sidestepped the Skirball's actual architecture, but it was notable for conceding, at least rhetorically, the presence of Jewish inspiration.[73]

The fact that other observers assigned Jewish significance to the Skirball highlighted the paradoxical nature of "non-Jewish" Jewish architecture in the postmodern era. After the museum was dedicated in 1996, Karen Stein, writing in *Architectural Record,* identified the building's Jewish character in Safdie's combination of traditional and modern materials, which succeeded in creating a "hybrid of foreign culture and new place—the architectural equivalent of an immigrant." Similarly, Herbert Muschamp in a major *New York Times* piece highlighted the Skirball's desire to "be a good neighbor" by "blend[ing] into its rugged desert terrain" while simultaneously trying to attract attention with its modern forms. The fact that Muschamp used the Skirball as a jumping-off point for meditating on the contemporary achievements of Jewish architects reflected the increasing inclination to assign Jewish significance to buildings unrelated to Jewish sources of inspiration. By the mid-1990s, the expectations that people brought to works of Jewish architecture had changed. In an era when postmodernism made architectural expressions of ethnicity acceptable, Jewish buildings were expected to communicate a sense of Jewish identity. This expectation ironically led both architects and critics to read Jewish exceptionality into buildings whose primary goal was normalcy.[74]

A similar pattern was visible in another major Jewish cultural complex, the Spertus Institute of Jewish Studies in Chicago (2008). Built to house Spertus College, the Spertus Museum, and Asher Library, the building was designed by the Chicago firm Krueck and Sexton on a prime site on

Michigan Avenue overlooking Grant Park. The building is a ten-story glass and steel tower that contrasts sharply with the nineteenth-century masonry buildings nearby. Unlike Chicago's many glass and steel modernist towers from the early postwar period, the Spertus Institute's facade was intricately designed to look like a faceted diamond, its crystalline form composed of 726 separate panes of glass in more than 556 shapes (fig. 166). The facade possesses great aesthetic appeal, but, like Safdie's Skirball Center, the Spertus Institute does not exhibit any overtly Jewish features. Its resemblance to Christian de Portzamparc's prismatic LVMH Tower in New York (1995–2000) and Jean Nouvel's proposed design for a faceted skyscraper next to the Museum of Modern Art (2007–) suggests that it was beholden mostly to new structural and formal trends within the architectural profession.

The building's appearance reflected the institute's effort to couch its mission in universalistic terms. Although founded as an educational institution for the promotion of Jewish learning, the Spertus Institute stressed that the new building "welcomes all who are eager to learn, whatever their background." As the institute's president, Dr. Howard A. Sulkin, put it, the openness of the building's glass facade "communicates this [message] by providing a physical invitation to come inside

Figure 166. Krueck and Sexton, Spertus Institute of Jewish Studies, Chicago, 2008. The building's glass facade was seen by some as symbolizing the Spertus Institute's Hebrew motto "yehi or" (Let there be light).

and engage in the educational and cultural programming that Spertus offers." Sulkin stressed how this openness differed from the "typical Jewish approach of building . . . barriers" in front of their institutional buildings in the wake of 9/11. The Spertus Institute, he insisted, was a "totally optimistic building" that welcomed all with an "inviting . . . atmosphere."[75]

Sulkin also invested the building with Jewish significance. When asked in 2008 about the lack of identifiable Jewish symbols in the museum's glass facade, he replied: "We wanted this to be a Jewish building . . . of the 21st century . . . and you can't have a 21st century building without lots of glass and abstraction." He asserted that glass symbolized the institute's educational mission, pointing out that, by allowing the influx of light, it symbolized the institute's Hebrew motto "yehi or" (Let there be light). Sulkin also emphasized how the skyward thrust of the building's jagged crown expressed the limitless striving of the Jewish educational tradition. Others notably followed Sulkin's interpretive lead. The firm of Krueck and Sexton declared that the role of light was "fundamental to Jewish religious and intellectual traditions." Similarly, *Chicago Tribune* architecture critic Blair Kamin praised the Spertus as a "creative essay in Jewish architecture, eschewing facile iconography or familiar historicism for its beguiling study in light." He also praised the building for avoiding "overt religious symbolism" and the "jagged and aggressive . . . [forms] of Daniel Libeskind." In so doing, Kamin elevated the Spertus's abstract, universalistic form of Jewishness above the historically influenced, particularistic forms associated with postmodernism and deconstructivism. As he concluded, "The new Spertus can be understood as an expression of the cultural confidence now felt by once-marginalized American Jews. . . . [Indeed,] coming from a people who have borne witness to so much darkness . . . [it is] a gift of light."[76]

This optimistic desire to root Jewish architecture in the future instead of the past also informed a third Jewish museum, the National Museum for American Jewish History (NMAJH) in Philadelphia (2007–2010). Designed by James Stewart Polshek's newly renamed firm, Ennead Architects, on a prime corner spot directly on Independence Mall across from the Liberty Bell, the $150 million, 100,000-square-foot museum resembles its counterparts in Los Angeles and Chicago in lacking overt Jewish symbolism. Polshek's design features two four-story boxlike volumes: one, facing the Mall on Market Street, is clad in glass; a second, along Fifth Street, is clad in terra-cotta (fig. 167). The latter building, which contains most of the museum's exhibits, is set somewhat back from the Mall, while the glass structure directly fronts it. The glass facade is largely unadorned, although it features a large horizontal cut on one of its upper stories that serves as a balcony. It also features an eight-foot-high "eternal light" at the top of its hundred-foot atrium in the form of an LED light sculpture (which was originally conceived as an actual flame). In short, the modernist edifice displayed little that could be identified as specifically Jewish iconography.

As was true of the Skirball Center and Spertus Institute, this fact reflected the NMAJH's universalistic mission. The museum's function, according to museum officials, was to educate "Jews and non-Jews alike about how Jews used the opportunities of freedom to make diverse contributions to American life, while also recording the experiences of other ethnic groups." This being the case, James Polshek predictably interpreted the building's ample use of glass as a sign of openness and universalism. As he put it, the museum's facade remained unadorned so as to "attract visitors who are interested in experiencing how America's promise of freedom shaped the evolution of one cultural group, rather than a specifically Jewish audience." The museum's universalistic modernist form thus symbolically reflected the important role of assimilation and integration in the success of American Jews.⁷⁷

At the same time, however, the NMAJH's abstract form was seen as possessing more explicit Jewish symbolism. None other than Polshek himself confirmed this, noting in 2002 that the building's "transparent exterior . . . embodies the idea that today, in America, Jews do not have to hide and that America is inseparable from Jewish life." The architect reinforced this point by proposing the inclusion of a quotation by Louis Brandeis in the museum's glass facade that read, "The highest Jewish ideals are essentially American." Just as this quotation (which was not in the final design) underscored the two cultures' common values, so, too, did the museum's most ostensibly Jewish feature, its eternal light. This beacon, Polshek asserted, "represented both American freedom—a reference to our beloved Statue of Liberty—and the permanence of the Jewish people, as represented by the Eternal Light. This light will shine as long as Americans embrace and defend freedom of religion and cultural expression."⁷⁸

Yet no matter how positively the NMAJH's Jewish symbolism was portrayed, other associations surrounding the museum were more ambiguous. More than a few questions were prompted by the meaning of the building's glass façade. For one thing, if the museum's creation confirmed that American Jews no longer needed to hide, why was the building's terra-cotta volume hidden behind

Figure 167. Polshek Partnership, National Museum for American Jewish History, Philadelphia, 2010. The museum's glass facade displays no Jewish traits apart from an eternal light at top. However, the facade's resemblance to Polshek's 1986 design for New York's Museum of Jewish Heritage—A Living Memorial to the Holocaust (which also featured a glass cube containing an eternal light), suggests the subtle influence of the Holocaust's legacy.

what Ennead partner Joseph Fleischer called a glass "veil?" In 2008, Polshek ventured something of an answer in declaring that the former structure symbolized "permanence and protection" while the latter symbolized "impermanence and fragility." In making this connection, however, Polshek raised still further questions, for his comment profoundly altered the traditional metaphorical meaning of glass. For much of the twentieth century, glass in modernist practice was typically seen as a confident symbol of democratic openness. Polshek, however, offered a new political interpretation in declaring that the "amount of glass [used in the museum] implies that one should not take for granted the freedoms supplied by a democracy."[79]

Polshek did not offer any reasons for this sobering admonition, but since it undercut the museum's otherwise buoyant message, its provenance is worth exploring. It is possible, first of all, that the admonition partly reflected the impact of the 9/11 attacks, which clearly underscored the threat of Islamist terrorism to Western democracy — just as the World Trade Center's destruction highlighted the fragility of modern glass and steel architecture. A second and possibly more significant source of the building's ambivalent symbolism, however, may be the legacy of the Holocaust. Why else, but for the Jewish experience in the Third Reich, would one stress that glass symbolizes the "fragility of democracy?" Democracy, after all, has never been seriously threatened in more than two centuries of American history, yet it was destroyed in Germany. This being the case, it is hard not to interpret Polshek's comment about the fragility of glass as anything but an allusion to Kristallnacht, the Night of Broken Glass. For it was then that German Jews realized both the fragility of their shop windows and of German democracy. The fact that Polshek had proposed a glass cube for the memorial wing of his New York Holocaust museum two decades earlier — and the fact that this design may itself have been influenced by his teacher Louis I. Kahn's glass Holocaust memorial proposal from the late 1960s — further reinforces the connection between glass and fragility (especially given the presence of eternal flames in both of Polshek's designs). Finally, glass may have been connected to the Holocaust in the way it helped to emphasize the event's status as a foil to the American Jewish experience. As discussed in Chapter 10, the Holocaust museums of Washington, D.C., and New York each provide visitors with redemptive views of the present-day democratic world, embodied respectively in the National Mall and the Statue of Liberty. The NMAJH employs this strategy as well, but with a twist. Instead of waiting until the exhibition's conclusion, the museum's glass facade provides visitors on all floors with a direct view of Independence Hall and the Liberty Bell throughout their visit. This proximity to the comforting icons of American democracy provides the reassuring message that America is not Europe. Indeed, it helps explain Polshek's comment about why American Jews — unlike their European brethren once upon a time — do not have to "hide."

Despite this upbeat message, however, signs of ambivalence remain. One involves the decision to switch the form of the building's eternal light, originally planned as a large flame, to an LED-powered light sculpture. The reason for this change is unclear, but the fact that the light is not visible in the daytime weakens its symbolic affirmation of Jewish "continuity." Moreover, the building's symbolic faith in liberty may be seen as somewhat qualified by the relocation of a historic monument — Sir Moses Jacob Ezekiel's 1876 marble sculpture *Religious Liberty* — in front of the building. While this allegorical celebration of the separation between church and state clearly endorses of one of

America's founding ideals, its upright arm can be interpreted as attempting to ward off potential threats, a gesture that gives the monument the impression of serving as an insurance policy. In short, even if the NMAJH celebrates the successes of American Jewish history, its architecture shows lingering signs of insecurity rooted in the realities of the modern European Jewish experience.

That said, few observers have taken note of these ambiguities since the building's opening in November 2010. Following festive dedication ceremonies presided over by Vice President Joseph Biden and a host of major celebrities, architecture critics weighed in with their assessments. While some pointed out certain functional shortcomings in the building, most hailed it as a success. Few, however, tried to read any signs of Jewishness into the museum's design beyond the familiar talking points offered by Polshek himself. The absence of the same kind of subjective interpretations seen with the Skirball and Spertus museums probably reflects Polshek's success in controlling the museum's symbolism. The result, however, was that the NMAJH's symbolic ambiguities were overlooked. Indeed, Paul Goldberger's remark at an architectural symposium that "any notions of a Jewish approach to architecture [were] wisely abandoned" in the museum's design suggested that critics were content to take the architect at his word about the building's meaning and preferred not to delve deeper into its more complex sources of inspiration.[80]

Taken together, the Jewish museums of Los Angeles, Chicago, and Philadelphia reveal an important irony about Jewish architecture in the postmodern era. Although there was little that was architecturally Jewish about these otherwise modern buildings, the desire of critics, the general public, and, at times, even the architects themselves to locate Jewish significance in them ended up investing the buildings with a greater sense of Jewish meaning than they objectively had when they were designed. It is difficult to know how representative these three cases are, but Jewish museums in America may be particularly prone to displaying the conflicting desires of Jews to both fit in and stand out. No wonder, then, that Daniel Libeskind's proposed design for Boston's new Jewish museum — the neutrally named New Center for Arts and Culture (a project currently in limbo) — entirely lacks the overt Jewish symbolism visible in his other projects.[81] Still, no matter how conflicted they may be about exuding a sense of Jewish identity, Jewish museums further attest to the vibrancy of contemporary Jewish architecture.

Conclusion

As is shown by the diverse buildings erected in Germany and the United States in recent years, Jewish institutions, both religious and secular, have displayed a keen interest in having Jewish buildings communicate a sense of Jewishness. The meaning of Jewishness has spanned everything from the tragedies of Jewish history to the spiritual elements of the religion. But whatever the source of inspiration, the desire for Jewish architecture to somehow appear "Jewish" is an undeniable trend of recent years. So powerful has it become that buildings unrelated to Jewish influences have been described by their architects and critics as Jewish in various ways. Whether or not this trend will last, whether it has produced good architecture, whether it should be welcomed or bemoaned — all of this remains unclear. What is now fully evident, however, is that Jews have come to expect that their community's buildings will stand as reflections of Jewish identity.

Conclusion

Figure 168. Daniel Libeskind, Berlin Jewish Museum. The iconic building, seen here from the Lindenstrasse, is probably the world's best-known example of contemporary Jewish architecture.

When I first saw Daniel Libeskind's Jewish Museum in Berlin in the summer of 1998, it was still under construction. Its slashed, zinc-clad facade was more or less complete, but it remained partly hidden behind billboard-clad fencing. I was unable, therefore, to draw any of my own conclusions about the building's evocative interior spaces. Press reports in the years that followed, however, identified those spaces as representing the building's soul. When I read that several hundred thousand visitors had taken the time to tour the museum even before its permanent exhibit had been set up, it became clear that Libeskind had accomplished something special. It was thus with great anticipation that I visited the museum in 2008 (fig. 168). I expected an emotional experience but instead found the building's power muted by its success. Throngs of tourists made it difficult to sense the bleakness described by early writers. It did not help that one of the museum's most powerful interior spaces — the multistory memory void — was closed "until further notice." And my impression of the evocative Holocaust tower was lessened by the presence of a smiling, helpful museum employee who, by courteously opening its door for me, mediated what I had hoped would be a more personal experience. Still, as I looked at all the tourists snapping photos of the museum, I recognized that Libeskind had registered a major achievement. If his victory in the Ground Zero competition had made him one of the world's most prominent Jewish architects, the success of his Berlin Jewish Museum made it one of the world's best known examples of Jewish architecture.

Jewish Architectural Achievement

As is shown by Libeskind's Jewish museum in Berlin, Jewish architects and Jewish architecture have gained tremendously in prominence since the end of the Second World War. No distinctly Jewish style of architecture has emerged, but the accomplishments of Jewish architects and their impact on the western architectural profession prove that the stubborn notion of Jewish architectural underachievement should be consigned to the past.

Jewish architects since 1945 have not simply entered the ranks of what was previously an exclusive "gentleman's profession," but they have become some of its most influential leaders. In the early years after World War II, Jewish architects, such as Gordon Bunshaft, Richard Neutra, Marcel Breuer, and Max Abramovitz, helped refine modernism's architectural language and constructed some of its most recognizable icons: the Lever House, the Kaufmann residence, the Whitney Museum, and the United Nations headquarters. Jewish architects also pointed the way beyond modernism, none more influentially than Louis I. Kahn. By seeking inspiration in the past he helped to break the International Style's dominance of western architecture in the 1960s and paved the way for the architectural movements of the postmodern era. When these movements emerged, they, too, boasted Jewish architects among their leaders. Robert A. M. Stern and Allan Greenberg helped usher in the neohistoricist variant of postmodernism, while the deconstructivist rebellion against postmodernism is unthinkable without the efforts of Peter Eisenman, Daniel Libeskind, Frank Gehry, and Eric Owen Moss. Finally, the modernist movement itself has continued to thrive thanks to the creative work of Richard Meier, Moshe Safdie, and James Stewart Polshek, all of whom have helped expand its formal vocabulary and preserve its vitality. Based on the accomplishments of these and other architects, the Jewish contribution to western architecture during the postwar period has been substantial.

Numerous factors account for the unprecedented success of Jewish architects in recent decades. One of the most important was the removal of the barriers that had long prevented Jewish advancement in the profession. If the chronic insecurity of Diaspora Jewry had traditionally inhibited Jewish architectural achievement, the security that Jews enjoyed after 1945 helped them accomplish more than ever before. Not surprisingly, the accomplishments of Jewish architects have largely taken place in the United States, the country where Jews have enjoyed the greatest freedom in the modern era. The postwar openness of the American architectural profession — like American society in general — also enabled Jewish architects to reach their full potential. These sociological and institutional factors have been rightly cited by Jewish architects themselves as crucial preconditions for contemporary Jewish architectural achievement.

Another possible factor is Jewish group solidarity. Scholars have noted how Jews in diverse commercial and cultural fields, such as banking, the garment industry, film, and theater, have historically thrived by supporting each other through "corporate kinship."[1] The possibility that a similar dynamic may have helped Jews in the architectural profession was recently proposed by the African-American architect Melvin Mitchell in his book *The Crisis of the African-American Architect*. In this study, Mitchell bemoaned the small number of African-Americans in the field of architecture and enviously contrasted their situation to that of American Jews, noting that the combination of an "informal mentoring system," a major Jewish "patron base," and the presence of Jews in the "mainstream architectural press" were all responsible for postwar Jewish architectural achievement.[2] Mitchell's analysis is overly simplistic, but it bears considering. Jewish architects in Europe long benefited from the patronage of Jewish clients. Moreover, Jewish architects both in Europe and the United States have frequently worked closely with, and sometimes mentored, one another. Richard Neutra worked for Erich Mendelsohn and collaborated on several projects with Rudolf Schindler. Louis I. Kahn taught James Stewart Polshek and employed Moshe Safdie. Richard Meier worked for both Marcel Breuer and Gordon Bunshaft; he employed Robert A. M. Stern; and he went to school with (and is related to) Peter Eisenman. Both Meier and Eisenman briefly employed Daniel Libeskind. And Libeskind, in turn, employed Manuel Herz and was a client of Alexander Gorlin's.

These connections alone, however, do not explain Jewish architectural success. The important role of Christians in mentoring Jewish architects (for example, Philip Johnson's support for Eisenman and Stern); the existence of Jewish-Gentile partnerships (Harrison and Abramovitz); the rivalries between Jewish architects (Eisenman versus Libeskind; Eisenman versus Stern); and the success of maverick architects outside the East Coast establishment (Frank Gehry and Eric Owen Moss in Los Angeles, and Stanley Tigerman in Chicago) demonstrate that there is no such thing as a monolithic Jewish architectural "club." The same can be said about Jewish patronage. While Jewish patrons have frequently hired Jewish architects (for example, Edgar Kaufmann's commissioning of Richard Neutra) they have just as often hired Christians (for instance, Samuel Bronfman's selection of Mies to design the Seagram Building). Moreover, the role of Jewish architecture critics has hardly been decisive in establishing the success of Jewish architects. Herbert Muschamp and Paul Goldberger may have played a role in making stars of a few postwar Jewish architects, yet they have done the same for Christian architects (as have Christian architecture critics).[3]

Perhaps the most intriguing possible reason for postwar Jewish architectural success is the growing willingness of Jewish architects to make their work more Jewish. Beginning with Louis I. Kahn and continuing with such figures as Eisenman, Libeskind, Gehry, and Tigerman, Jewish architects in the years since 1945 have strived as never before to seek inspiration in Jewish ideas, themes, and experiences. Indeed, it is arguably the case that the most famous Jewish architects of the postwar period have been the ones whose buildings have exhibited the most Jewish traits. This claim is debatable, but the success of these architects cannot be appreciated fully without considering their work's Jewish dimensions. Of course, the achievements of Kahn and the deconstructivists were enabled by numerous factors. The weakening of the modernist movement and the rise of postmodernism helped clear a path for architectural innovation; the rise of multiculturalism liberated architects to express a sense of ethnic identity; and new technologies, such as CAD, enabled them to pursue formal innovations that were unimaginable earlier.

Although these developments were crucial for the success of Jewish architects, so was their willingness to break with architectural convention and embrace innovation. It is impossible to trace the origins of any artist's creativity to a single source. Yet, to an important degree, the creative rebellion of many postwar Jewish architects was sparked by their sense of themselves as outsiders. That sense, in turn, was related to their sense of themselves as Jews. Owing in part to their encounters with antisemitism, they brought a sensibility to their work that directly shaped their creativity. It is striking that Kahn, Eisenman, Libeskind, Gehry, and Tigerman all reached high points in their careers only once they began to seek creative inspiration in their Jewish identities. The more they took on Jewish commissions and conceived of their design philosophies in Jewish terms, the more their work and reputations benefited. It is possible, of course, that these architects might have been inclined to rebel against architectural convention even if they had not been Jewish. Robert Venturi and Zaha Hadid, among many others, rebelled in similar ways around the same time. But Jewish architects often went out of their way to validate their philosophies in Jewish terms, which suggests that their tendency to rebel was partly an outgrowth of their heritage.

To be sure, other Jewish architects achieved notable success without assigning Jewish meaning to their work. This was true of early postwar modernists, such as Neutra, Bunshaft, Breuer, and Abramovitz, as well as their younger colleagues, Meier, Polshek, and Safdie. They all established world-class reputations by designing rational, ahistorical buildings without trying to infuse them with Jewish traits. The same can be said for postmodernists, such as Robert A. M. Stern and Allan Greenberg, whose classically inspired buildings also lacked discernible Jewish features. In varying degrees, these accomplished figures, whether modernists or postmodernists, can be considered "non-Jewish" Jewish architects in the sense that they refrained from drawing on their religious and ethnic heritage for the sake of embracing broader universal ideals. It is true that many of these architects have occasionally worked on Jewish commissions, whether synagogues, schools, or museums, yet they rarely incorporated elements of Jewishness into them. Moreover, the bulk of their work remained unaffected by Jewish ideas. Whatever their other interests, their buildings can partly be seen as expressions of a larger assimilationist impulse.

Which variety of Jewish architecture — the alienated or the assimilated — will posterity find more significant? Standards of evaluation are subjective and change over time. Should one prioritize innovation or continuity in architecture? Individualistic expressiveness or rational restraint? Aesthetic dissonance or harmony? The creation of eye-catching monoliths or the preservation of the urban fabric? All of these questions boil down to a deeper one: Which is more important, change or tradition? Where one stands on these issues invariably determines how one evaluates the major architectural movements of the postwar period—whether modernism, postmodernism, or deconstructivism. Those critics who favor innovation will probably reserve their greatest praise for the pathbreaking work of Jewish deconstructivists; critics would rank the achievements of Jewish modernists as less notable; and they would place the derivative designs of postmodernists last. More conservative critics, by contrast, will view deconstructivism as a transient phenomenon and grant greater respect to the evolving modernist and postmodern traditions. At present, the prevailing tendency of architectural historians and critics to reward innovation may mean that the deconstructivists remain admired, while the modernist and postmodern buildings of other Jewish architects fare less well. And yet, since no reputations are permanent, the achievements of Jewish architects will be debated well into the future.

One thing is clear, however: the very diversity of the buildings designed by Jewish architects since 1945 makes it impossible to speak of Jewish architecture in any monolithic sense. Not only have their buildings differed dramatically in appearance, but they also have been informed by varied purposes and philosophies. The most basic difference is between those architects who have assigned their work Jewish significance and those who have not. But even those who have done so have differed in the ways in which they have lent their architecture Jewish meaning. They have claimed that their work expresses the reaction of alienated Jewish outsiders against architectural tradition; they have invoked ideas of "Hebraic" values in opposition to classical Hellenic values; they have pointed to the legacy of the Holocaust as justifying an architecture of rupture and fragmentation; they have been inspired by the Jewish religious tradition, drawing on the Talmud, the Kabbalah, and even the Hebrew alphabet in their designs; they have drawn on the Jewish architectural past, evoking the legacy of Polish wooden synagogue architecture; and they have incorporated Jewish iconography into the plans and structures of their buildings. Even those Jewish architects who did not deliberately strive to invest their work with Jewish meaning can be seen as having done so unintentionally, for those who have embraced modernism or classicism have paradoxically exhibited one of the more identifiably "Jewish" behavior patterns in the modern era—the attempt to transcend their Jewishness by embracing universal principles. Given such a wide range of intentions, it is no surprise that the forms of Jewish architecture have been equally diverse. They have been individualistically expressive and coolly rational. They have stood out in their environments and blended into them. They have been whimsical and serious. They have been religious and secular. They have even been Jewish and non-Jewish. As a result of this diversity, it is impossible to identify the emergence of a distinctly Jewish architectural style.

Nevertheless, the fact that Jewish architects have increasingly drawn on Jewish sources as inspiration for their work makes it arguably more Jewish than the work of previous Jewish architects. In earlier eras, Jewish architects were occasionally prompted to explore Jewish themes in their designs for synagogues, but they did not do so in their secular work. That has now changed. Today, Jewish architects also reflect on Jewish concerns in devising their broader architectural philosophies and their designs for ordinary buildings. This development reflects the fact that in today's multicultural world, Jewish architects no longer have to stifle their identities as their predecessors did in more assimilationist eras. Had architects such as Gehry and Eisenman lived a generation or two earlier, they probably would have followed in the path of such "non-Jewish" Jewish architects as Neutra and Bunshaft, neither of whom sought inspiration in their heritage. Now that ethnic difference is accepted, however, Gehry regrets having changed his name from Goldberg, while Eisenman proudly asserts his identity as a Jewish outsider. Indeed, Jewishness has become so accepted in today's society that even Christian architects have tried to lay claim to Jewish identities. The fact that the acclaimed Catalonian architect Santiago Calatrava has proudly spoken of his heritage as the descendant of Spanish crypto-Jews (conversos who "never really converted") strikingly illustrates this shift.[4] This open declaration of solidarity with the Jewish people would have been unthinkable in earlier eras, when Jewish architects faced greater hostility and tried to evade detection. The fact that it can occur in today's world is a sign of just how far Jewish architects have come in being able to freely express themselves in their professional work.

Jewish Architecture and the Memory of the Holocaust

That they have been able to do so in the years since 1945 is also a reflection of the Holocaust's legacy, which is yet another important cause of postwar Jewish architectural achievement. The Nazi genocide has reinforced the ethnic identity of certain Jewish architects and provided them with a new and powerful source of architectural inspiration. It took some time, of course, before Jewish architects were prepared to confront the Holocaust's ramifications in their work. The first to do so was Louis I. Kahn. His approach in the 1960s was tentative, however, and his attempt to provide a sense of solace through an architecture of light and healing reflected a largely redemptive view of Jewish history in the wake of catastrophe. By contrast, Jewish architects a decade later began to confront the genocide's bleaker dimensions more directly. Beginning in the late 1970s and early 1980s, the deconstructivists Eisenman and Libeskind, as well as Tigerman, began to cite the Holocaust as necessitating a break with architectural tradition and the embrace of architectural rebellion. Their reasons for doing so varied, but the fact that they had all experienced wartime or early postwar antisemitism — and were willing to wrestle with their feelings about it — explains why they were the first within their profession to display signs of the new Holocaust consciousness that was beginning to emerge within western cultural and intellectual life. It is difficult to determine whether these architects' reflections on the Nazi genocide inspired their radical architecture or whether it merely provided a convenient rationale for it. The likelihood is that the latter was more the case than the former. But the fact that they chose to link their architecture to the Holocaust's legacy in any way whatsoever reflected the event's increasing influence.

The Holocaust's legacy went beyond influencing the movement of deconstructivism. It also gave rise to a new genre of architecture, Holocaust museums. The architects who were responsible for designing these institutions believed that ordinary architectural strategies were inappropriate and strove to develop a kind of architecture suitable for their mission. The buildings that resulted, such as Freed's USHMM, Safdie's new complex at Yad Vashem, and Tigerman's Illinois Holocaust Museum and Education Center, all tried to acknowledge the Holocaust's impact, whether by utilizing Holocaust-related iconography or embracing disruptive deconstructivist design principles. The Holocaust also influenced synagogue architecture. In Germany, it found both explicit and implicit expression in the designs of Salomon Korn, Zvi Hecker, and the firm of WHLH. In the United States, meanwhile, the Holocaust's echoes were felt in synagogue designs inspired by the wooden synagogues of prewar Poland.

All these buildings confirm Aaron Betsky's hypothesis that "it took the Holocaust to create a Jewish architecture."[5] Betsky's remark was made in passing over a decade ago, but he correctly implied that the Nazi genocide contributed something that Jewish architecture had long lacked. If architectural historians are right that a major impediment to the emergence of a Jewish style of architecture has been the diversity of the Jewish historical experience, the Holocaust's status as a unifying event for Jews the world over has provided a basis for a new form of Jewish architectural expression. In reality, of course, the Holocaust has not given rise to a monolithic style of Jewish architecture, but without the genocide's prod to conscience and creativity, many of the most important works of postwar Jewish architecture would not have come into being.

Just as the Holocaust's legacy helps explain the evolution of postwar Jewish architecture, that history sheds light on lingering questions about the Holocaust's legacy. One is how the Nazi genocide has shaped western culture since 1945. For years, scholars have traced the responses to Adorno's demand that western culture somehow acknowledge the Holocaust's magnitude. The postwar history of Jewish architecture reveals that, while Adorno's plea was initially ignored, it was eventually heeded. The Nazi genocide's role in giving rise to the deconstructivist movement, in determining the design of Holocaust museums, and in influencing synagogue architecture reveals that its legacy has helped to shape our physical world. Just as the Holocaust has influenced the books we read, the films we watch, and the ideas that guide our thinking, it has also shaped some of the buildings that compose our urban environment. Most people are probably unaware of this reality. But to gaze on the oddly contorted forms of a deconstructivist building is, at least in part, to see a physical embodiment of the Holocaust's legacy of disruption, fragmentation, and disorientation. This connection is most readily apparent in major public buildings related to German Jewish history, such as Libeskind's Berlin Jewish Museum. But deconstructivism's historical associations can be seen as extending to all kinds of public buildings, and not only those designed by Libeskind, Gehry, and Eisenman. Indeed, the deconstructivist aesthetic — and by extension, the Holocaust's legacy — has even spread to ordinary commercial architecture, as is shown by the similarity between a Best Buy store in Bloomington, Indiana, and Libeskind's Contemporary Jewish Museum in San Francisco (figs. 169, 170). It is unclear what Adorno would say about this development, but it is evident that architects have finally begun to take note of the Holocaust's significance for their discipline.

Admittedly, it took them a long time to do so. Yet this fact itself helps address another question that has long interested historians: namely, how to periodize the evolution of Holocaust memory. In trying to determine *when* the Holocaust assumed a central place in western consciousness, historians have argued over whether attention toward the event emerged only after the late 1960s and early 1970s or whether it had emerged earlier. The case of architecture reveals a different picture. Of all the major fields of cultural endeavor — film, literature, art, theater, music — architecture has

Figures 169 and 170. Best Buy Store, Bloomington, Indiana, date unknown, and Daniel Libeskind, Contemporary Jewish Museum of San Francisco, 1996–2008. Both buildings display blue wedges piercing red brick classical facades.

arguably been the last to take note of the Holocaust, doing so only in the 1980s and 1990s. The belated nature of architecture's confrontation with the Holocaust suggests that it is difficult to draw generalizations about the rise of Holocaust consciousness in western culture. What may have been true for certain branches of cultural expression may not have been true for others; what poets and painters were able to do soon after the war architects took decades to accomplish. Architecture, as a result, should be seen as occupying the outer margin of the cultural confrontation with the Nazi genocide. Does this mean that architecture is nonrepresentative of western society's awakening to the Holocaust's legacy? No, for there is something profoundly revealing about architecture being last in line. Architecture is arguably the most conservative and public of the arts, which may explain why it has been the last to register the Holocaust's impact. Time had to pass before western society was emotionally ready to institutionalize memory in built form. Only after the ground had been prepared by the recollections of memoirists, the verses of poets, the canvases of painters, the stories of novelists, the speeches of politicians, the analytical accounts of historians, and the commemorative monuments erected by towns and cities throughout the west could clients commission, and architects design, buildings—the most prominent and least avoidable testaments of all—that grappled with the meaning of the Holocaust. Only by being aware of this reality can we grasp the full extent of the cultural confrontation with the Nazi genocide's legacy.

The Elephant in the Building: The Case of Israel

The story of postwar Jewish architecture, however, is not only about the Holocaust. By now, more than a few readers may have wondered how it is possible to write an entire book about Jewish architecture without considering the architecture of Israel. The subject deserves a book-length study of its own, especially as there are few comprehensive surveys of it in English.[6] The following reflections cannot do justice to the topic's complexity, but a few observations are in order.

I begin with a riddle: When is Jewish architecture not Jewish architecture? The answer: When it is Israeli architecture. The question of the relationship between Israeli and Jewish architecture was implicit in a remark that Peter Eisenman made in the winter of 2006: "People in Israel," he said, "are not Jews; they are Israelis. For me, a Jew lives in the Diaspora."[7] Eisenman's words were too categorical, of course. Most Israelis are Jews; not all Jews live in the Diaspora. Yet Eisenman was correct to call attention to the differences between Diaspora Jewish identity and the identity of Jewish Israelis. Scholars have shown the many ways in which Israeli culture and Diaspora Jewish culture have diverged.[8] It is well known, for example, that the Zionist mission was based on the paradoxical notion that, in order to renew Jewish life for the future, it was necessary to turn away from the Jewish past. This belief was summed up by the idea of "negating the Diaspora," an idea that, in cultural practice, meant that Jews in the early Yishuv (the pre-state Jewish settlement in Ottoman/British Palestine) and the later state of Israel were less interested in asserting traditional Jewish forms of identity than in inventing a new and reinvigorated form of Hebrew (and eventually Israeli) identity. Admittedly, this new form of identity was also understood to be Jewish, but it was envisioned as transcending undesirable forms of Diaspora Jewishness. Translated to the realm of architecture, this view meant that Jewish architects in Palestine (and later Israel) operated with different priorities from those in the Diaspora. Rather than exploring aspects of Jewishness in their work or trying to create a distinctly Jewish form of architecture, architects in Palestine and Israel focused on fashioning a "Hebrew," "Zionist," and, eventually, an "Israeli" national style of building.

This quest was partly a response to the perception that the existing built environment of the fledgling Jewish state was deficient. Early Jewish visitors to Palestine complained that the "flimsy homes" and "narrow streets" of Jewish villages displayed lingering signs of a Jewish "ghetto" mentality. They especially found fault in the early architecture of Tel Aviv, whose alleged ugliness they saw as proof of "Jewish inexperience in building" and typical of a "people given to the arts of time rather than . . . space." Given the fact that Jewish settlements compared especially poorly with the indigenous architecture of Arab villages, early Jewish architects in Palestine drew on "oriental" building traditions in formulating a style of architecture appropriate to the new Jewish homeland. This preference was visible in Joseph Barsky's design for the Herzliyah Gymnasium in Tel Aviv (1909) and Alex Baerwald's design for the Technion in Haifa (1912–24), both of which employed an eclectic mix of Islamic, Assyrian, and other motifs, such as domes, pointed arches, and crenellated cornices (fig. 171). An equally historicist, if somewhat more intentionally Jewish, approach was visible in Y. C. Tabatchnik's Palm House in Tel Aviv (1922), which incorporated Jewish symbols, such as menorahs, into its iron balconies and attempted to devise a Jewish order of columns. Most Jewish architects eventually realized, however, that such backward-looking approaches could not succeed in creating a truly Jewish form of architecture. The fundamental problem, as the architect Yohanan Ratner saw it in 1933, was not merely the absurdity of copying Arab traditions of building; it was the near total absence of "original Hebrew buildings" in the country that might be able to point the way to a true "Hebrew style." Without their own real historical legacy to fall back on, most Jewish architects in the Yishuv believed it was futile to look to the past for inspiration.[9]

Instead, Jewish architects looked to the future and embraced the modern movement. Especially once Bauhaus-trained, German Jewish architects began to arrive in Palestine after the Nazi seizure of power in 1933, the International Style became the style of choice. It was most visible in Tel Aviv, whose many modernist buildings, such as Zeev Rechter's Engel House apartment complex (1933), made it known as the "White City" (and earned it UNESCO status as a World Cultural Heritage

Figure 171. Alex Baerwald, Technion, Haifa, 1912–24. Home to the Israel Institute of Technology, the Technion embraced an eclectic mix of Islamic, Assyrian, and other "Oriental" motifs in the effort to create a Hebrew style of architecture.

Site in 2003) (fig. 172). An important reason for modernism's success was the fact that its utopian character dovetailed with the Zionist goal of negating the Disapora and creating a new Jewish urban reality. Some architects tried to invest modernism with Jewish significance. Commenting on the buildings at the 1934 Levant Fair in Tel Aviv, the Jewish engineer Willie Weltsch described the International Style as a form of "modern Jewish architecture" whose dynamism expressed the "unprecedented revival" of a people that had long been "subjected to the deepest degradation." Most Jewish architects, however, avoided defining modernism in Jewish terms. Ratner, for example, was convinced by the early 1930s that "conscious efforts" to create national styles of architecture were destined to fail; they could develop only over time. For this reason, he counseled patience and suggested that the "new style" in Palestine might eventually "gain . . . certain national characteristics." By the early 1940s, most architects in Israel had come to support this position. While there were fleeting attempts by architects such as Erich Mendelsohn to synthesize modern trends with Arab vernacular building traditions (he idealistically aimed to create a "semitic" brand of architecture appropriate for a binational state), they found little resonance. Especially as tensions between Jews and Arabs increased in the 1930s, most Israeli architects abandoned vernacular visions and hoped that a national style might arise through the modern movement.[10]

This hope persisted, albeit with diminished urgency, after the creation of Israel in 1948. While certain Israelis expressed frustration that a national style had not been established, the many challenges facing the young country made the intense pursuit of style an unaffordable luxury. After fending off Arab military attacks in 1947–48, the state of Israel had to integrate hundreds of thousands of refugees arriving from war-torn Europe. Functionalist solutions to pressing problems were in high demand, and priority was given to issues of city planning, refugee housing, and infrastructure. Little attention was given to issues of architectural representation. This understandable neglect contributed to the mediocre quality of the nation's architecture. Observers at the time said as much, declaring, as the journal *Architectural Record* did in 1952, that the monotony of the country's architecture reflected the "lack of resolution . . . of what constitutes a Jewish, or an Israeli expression . . . in the art of building." This question found no resolution even after stability was restored by the late 1950s and early 1960s. The major structures built in this period exhibited little Jewish

Figure 172. Zeev Rechter, Engel House, Tel Aviv, 1933. This apartment building was an important early example of International Style modernism that helped earn Tel Aviv the nickname White City.

character. This was equally true of Joseph Klarwein's classically inspired design for the Knesset (1958–66) and Alfred Mansfeld and Dora Gad's Miesian Israel Museum (1965) (fig. 173). On balance, this period, which was dominated by the "second generation of Israeli architects," such as Ram Karmi, Yacov Rechter, and Eldar Sharon, focused on function instead of representation.[11]

After the 1967 war, however, Israeli architecture headed in a new direction. With the reconquest of Jerusalem and the occupation of the West Bank, Israelis began once more to find inspiration in their country's architectural past. The rise of postmodernism, with its valorization of history, memory, and identity, sustained this trend as well. Many major projects pursued in this period drew on regional building traditions. Moshe Safdie's Mamilla residential development (1972–93) used stone facing, arches, and domes, while his new campus for Hebrew Union College (1976–89) featured stone-clad buildings that surrounded interior courtyards graced with trellised arcades (fig. 174). These trends continued into the 1990s, if in less revivalist fashion, as were shown by Ram Karmi and Ada Karmi-Melamede's Israel Supreme Court building (1986–92), which drew upon Roman, Hellenistic, and modernist forms, and the Canadian Jewish architect Jack Diamond's design for the Jerusalem City Hall (1997), which used Mamluk stonework and other Arab design elements. Throughout this phase, various architecture critics remained watchful for signs that an "Israeli architectural identity" or an "Israeli style" might be emerging.[12]

Figure 173. Joseph Klarwein, Knesset, 1958–66. Israel's national parliament shows the influence of classical principles. There is no evidence of a national Israeli style.

Figure 174. Moshe Safdie, Mamilla development, Jerusalem, 1972–93. The apartments, seen in the foreground, employ building materials, such as limestone, and design elements, such as arched windows and domes, that have regional roots and blend into their historic environment. The walls of Jerusalem's Old City are in the background.

Conclusion **347**

The irony, of course, was that this historically minded turn in Israeli architecture once more brought it closer to the region's non-Jewish (and frequently Arab) vernacular architectural traditions. To be sure, there were efforts to read Jewish qualities into Arab architecture by those who saw it embodying ancient biblical traditions. But as Israeli architects increasingly emphasized relating to the land, they tended to deemphasize Jewish qualities in favor of connecting to larger regional, especially Mediterranean, traditions. By doing so they questioned the degree to which Jewish elements were necessary to Israeli architecture. This conceptual problem reflected larger problems of Israeli identity. The fact that Israel counts among its citizens a large non-Jewish Arab minority (as well as Druze and others) makes it difficult to restrict the idea of "Israeli architecture" only to buildings built by and for its Jewish citizens. This point was driven home in 2004 when Zaha Hadid was chosen to design a major new museum of Palestinian Art and Culture in the Israeli Arab town of Umm al-Fahm. While Hadid has since bowed out of the project, the question remains: Once the museum is completed, will it qualify as Israeli architecture despite having no Jewish features? At one time, the answer would have been no, but as Israeli architects draw upon their country's diverse architectural traditions, issues of architectural Jewishness may become less significant.[13]

To be sure, there has been interest in Jewish architecture in Israel. Especially since the rise of postmodernism, the desire to invoke Jewish architectural precedents has been visible in synagogue architecture. The Great Synagogue of Jerusalem (completed in 1982 next to the Chief Rabbinate), for example, was modeled by architect Alexander Friedman after Solomon's Temple. Other synagogues have been more nostalgic and closely imitated historic buildings. In 2000, the Belzer Hasidim completed construction on their new Great Synagogue in Jerusalem, which is an enlarged replica of their nineteenth-century headquarters in Poland and reputed to be the largest synagogue in the world (fig. 175). Other examples of this nostalgic mentality include the reconstruction of the ruined Hurva synagogue in 2010 and the current planning for Israel's first shtetl theme park (known as The

Figure 175. Yitzhak Blatt, Belz World Center, Jerusalem, 1985–2000. This synagogue, reputed to be the largest in the world, is a replica of the original nineteenth-century synagogue used by the Belzer Hasidim in Poland.

Shtetl—The Living History Museum of the Jewish World) in Rishon LeZion, complete with reproductions of Eastern European "Jewish architecture." These projects reveal that interest in Jewish architecture continues in Israel. And yet its derivate character prevents it from being at the forefront of Israeli architectural creativity.[14]

As is shown by this brief survey, Israeli architecture has diverged in key ways from Jewish architecture in the Diaspora. Israeli and Diaspora Jewish architects have embraced many of the same movements during the postwar era, such as modernism and postmodernism, but have employed them to different ends. While Jewish architects in the Diaspora have been interested in exploring aspects of Jewish identity in their work, Israeli architects have been more interested in creating an Israeli national style of building. Perhaps the most telling difference is the two groups' differing responses to deconstructivism. While certain buildings in Israel exhibit deconstructivist influences, such as Yacov and Amnon Rechter's Law Faculty Building at the College of Administration in Rishon LeZion (1995) and Bracha and Michael Chyutin's Theater in Givatayim (1996), the movement does not seem to have taken off in Israel as it has in the United States.[15] For obvious reasons, the anxious feelings of rootlessness and outsiderness that underpin the work of American Jewish deconstructivists have found little resonance in Israel. In the Jewish state, Israeli architects have expressed rootedness by taking inspiration from the landscape and surrounding physical environment. Being a majority in their own state, moreover, Israeli architects have not felt like outsiders as have certain American Jewish architects. They also seem less inclined to cite the Holocaust as grounds for embracing an architecture of instability. Perhaps because the country faces many present-day threats and has many Holocaust survivors (in addition to the central memorial site, Yad Vashem), the cultural climate has been less hospitable to deconstructivist architecture.[16] This suggests that the oppositional impulses that have animated much of the creative vitality of Diaspora Jewish architecture have been lacking in Israel. Instead of feeling the need to fight against and overturn traditions, Israeli architecture has been defined by more affirmative impulses. Living in the Jewish state and being able to relate their work to a Jewish spatial context, Israeli architects have felt little need to invest their architecture with explicit Jewish significance. Like much of life in Israel overall, Jewishness is widely seen to exist naturally and does not have to be fashioned.

That said, Israeli architecture has hardly lacked for oppositional impulses. In recent years, some Israeli architects and historians have examined the role of architecture in the occupation of Palestinian lands, accusing the Israeli architectural and political establishments of colluding in policies seen as detrimental to the country's interests. Other scholars have invoked the Arab-Israeli conflict to cast a negative light on Tel Aviv's Bauhaus architectural legacy, charging that those who celebrate it are attempting to distract attention from the departure and/or expulsion of Arabs from the neighboring city of Jaffa in 1948. These critical stances stand in contrast to more affirmative evocations of the Israeli military tradition. Zvi Hecker's evocative Palmach History Museum in Tel Aviv (1999) commemorates the Yishuv's elite commando unit with a design whose coarse stone facade, seemingly just quarried, symbolizes the toughness of the soldiers who defended the fledgling state. Given the political polarization in contemporary Israeli life, it is no surprise that political tensions have found their way into Israeli architecture. But their increasing presence (combined with their absence from Diaspora Jewish architecture) constitutes yet another example of divergent paths.[17]

For many reasons, then, Israeli architecture does not fit neatly into a discussion of postwar Jewish architecture in the Diaspora. The forces that have shaped the achievements of Jewish architects in the United States and other western countries have differed from those that have shaped developments in Israel. Deconstructivism and the Israeli-Palestinian conflict are merely two examples. Others would include the utopian streak within Israeli architecture (seen in such agricultural settlements as kibbutzim and moshavim), the architectural implications of the country's military culture, and the impact of its secular/religious divide upon the built environment.[18] As scholars investigate these and other ways in which Israeli and Diaspora Jewry have diverged from one another, we will be better able to answer what is perhaps the most interesting question of all: namely, why Israel, despite having the same-sized Jewish population as the United States, has produced fewer distinguished architects. The most famous figures of the early postwar generation, Ze'ev Rechter, Arieh Sharon, and Dov Karmi, are largely unknown outside the country, as are contemporary Israelis, such as Ram Karmi or the partnership of Bracha and Michael Chyutin. Those Israeli architects who have gained international reputations, such as Safdie and Hecker, have relocated abroad. The reasons for this are unclear.[19] But whether it is Israel's relative youth, its unstable geopolitical situation, the lack of government support for the arts, or the traditional dominance of a collectivist (rather than individualistic) mentality, the country has not generated the same architectural accomplishments as those of Jewish Diaspora. More research may tell us why, but it seems clear that while Israeli architecture can certainly be seen as a subset of Jewish architecture, it is also sui generis.

The New Jewish Architecture: Is It "Good for the Jews"?

However undeniable the achievements of Jewish architects have been in the postwar period, they are not unalloyed. There are certain problematic aspects to the new Jewish architecture that should prevent us from assessing it from a simplistic "contributionist" perspective. Some Jewish architects (like some Christian and Muslim architects) have been criticized for contributing to the "star system" in contemporary architecture, for the exhibitionistic character of their buildings, and for taking commissions from unsavory political regimes. They may also be seen as implicated in what some regard as the increasingly superficial character of American Jewish cultural and religious life. Given the perpetual Jewish interest in the question of whether certain trends are "good for the Jews," it is worth noting some of the ways that new Jewish architectural accomplishments might be less than salutary.

There is no denying that Jewish architects have participated in and benefited from the growing tendency within the western architectural profession to grant celebrity status to its leading representatives. Architects, of course, have long enjoyed international renown, as has been shown in the twentieth century by the careers of Frank Lloyd Wright, Le Corbusier, and Philip Johnson. Yet in recent years the tendency to grant architects star status has increased dramatically. Many have traced this trend to the "Bilbao Effect" sparked by Frank Gehry's Guggenheim Museum. The sensational response to Gehry's masterpiece convinced municipalities, cultural institutions, and commercial developers that eye-catching, iconic architecture could yield tangible economic value, whether by increasing tourism, stimulating consumption, or enhancing corporate brand recognition. Critics have charged, however, that by striving to duplicate the Bilbao Effect, architects have become complicit in the emergence of what Terry Smith has called the new "iconomy" by designing aesthetically ambitious but shallow symbols of global capitalism instead of concentrating on solving more pressing social or environmental problems. Jewish architects have clearly participated in this trend, whether as deconstructivists, postmodern classicists, or modernists. Those who value socially conscious architecture no doubt regard Jewish architects' involvement in the star system as an unfortunate development.[20]

Other critics have charged that the star system, by encouraging the design of iconic buildings, has encouraged an aesthetically misguided tendency toward exhibitionistic sculptural expression. John Silber, in *The Architecture of the Absurd,* and Nikos Salingaros, in *Anti-Architecture and Deconstruction,* have focused their ire on Gehry, Libeskind, and Eisenman for elevating gaudy formalism over more functionally oriented design strategies. They have also objected to these architects' self-promotion, claims to originality, and embrace of abstruse theory. Their criticisms of architectural iconicity have been vigorously challenged, but it is undeniable that Jewish architects have played a role in promoting it. Fortunately, Jewish architects have not been singled out in antisemitic fashion for special criticism (as would surely have taken place in an earlier era). Yet Salingaros's condemnation of Libeskind's design philosophy as underpinned by a "geometry of death" shows how at least some critics have bristled against the practice of seeking inspiration in the Holocaust's legacy.[21]

Jewish architects could also be criticized for accepting commissions from nondemocratic governments. Libeskind recently directed attention to this issue when he proclaimed his own refusal to "work for totalitarian regimes."[22] By contrast, Gehry's willingness to work for the government of Abu Dhabi, Moss's work for the government of Kazakhstan, and even Libeskind's decision to accept a commission from the Chinese government (albeit in the more liberal setting of Hong Kong) show that some Jewish architects have put "getting the job" ahead of principle. To be sure, they are outnumbered by the many non-Jewish architects doing the same thing—for example, Rem Koolhaas and his controversial headquarters for the state-run Chinese television authority, CCTV. But Jewish architects' increased star power has confronted them with new moral and political dilemmas, another sign that their newfound prominence has brought with it unforeseen challenges.

The new prominence of Jewish architects also raises questions about their impact on contemporary Jewish life. In recent years, various observers, such as Leon Wieseltier, have bemoaned the intensifying pace of American Jewish assimilation and argued that, as Jewish identity has become more ethnic and less religious, it has become more superficial. Sociologist Herbert Gans has found that Jews have followed other immigrant groups by embracing a form of "symbolic ethnicity" in which they adhere to symbolic and comparatively easy means of group identification rather than systematically affiliating with any real "functioning groups or networks." American Jewish culture is becoming separated from religious nourishment, according to Stephen Whitfield, a trend threatening its long-term existence. Without a religious component, these observers have noted, Jewish culture has become suffused with vicarious nostalgia. This trend has been especially visible in American Jewish literature, which Irving Howe a generation ago saw as doomed by its reliance upon superficial "immigrant chic," epitomized by the musical *Fiddler on the Roof.* More recent critics have applied

Howe's gloomy ruminations to the work of such contemporary Jewish writers as Gary Shteyngart, Tony Kushner, and Jonathan Safran Foer, arguing that their portrayals of Jewish "otherness" partake of "ethnic shtick" and express an "enervated vision of Jewishness."[23]

One need not agree entirely with these assessments to allow for the possibility that contemporary Jewish architecture may also display signs of superficiality. Much of the Jewish architectural achievement of recent years has been secular. Few celebrated works of Jewish architecture have been synagogues. Indeed, few of the most accomplished American Jewish architects of the last generation have pursued synagogue commissions or brought one to completion.[24] Many, moreover, have emphasized their distance from organized Jewish life. Their strategies of Jewish self-representation are wholly secular, leaving them open to the charge that their work is marred by the same ethnic shtick visible in the work of their literary peers. Gehry's references to his Orthodox grandmother's gefilte fish and his youthful experiences with the Talmud may be seen as rehearsed. The same can be said of Libeskind's recollections of his arrival in America, or Eisenman's, Tigerman's, and Moss's self-representation as alienated Jewish intellectuals. All these architects insist on seeing themselves as embattled outsiders despite their obvious success within the profession. As with the work of American Jewish writers, their embrace of otherness is belied by the assimilated reality of contemporary American Jewish life. As a result, the ways in which these architects have sought to justify their work in Jewish terms might be seen as inauthentic.

To the extent that architecture has gained an increasingly prominent place in Jewish life, moreover, it might be seen as hastening the assimilation process. In the 1950s, Herbert Gans theorized that postwar Jews had begun to express their Jewishness through a form of "objectified" Judaism in which they abandoned traditional practices for "tangible representations . . . to endow what [they have] . . . preserved with concrete reality." Perhaps the most obvious realm where this externalization of Jewishness manifested itself was in architecture. As Edward Shapiro has argued, Jewish knowledge and religiosity declined during the synagogue construction boom of the early postwar decades. Whether architecture caused this decline or was merely correlated with it is open to question. It is possible that the interest in synagogue architecture during these boom years supplanted a more vital focus on Jewish teachings, ethics, and history. Yet, since these trends were already well under way before the building boom (as is shown by the lower rates of synagogue affiliation during the interwar era), postwar synagogues may have temporarily arrested the assimilation that would have been even more severe without them.[25]

It is not just in synagogue architecture, moreover, that the new Jewish culture of exteriority has been visible. It is also apparent in Holocaust museums and Jewish museums. Writing in *Commentary* in 1993, Edward Norden correlated the rush to build Holocaust museums (or what he called "mausoleums") with American Jewish demographic decline. Noting that the "Jews of America are not in good health," Norden pointed to low levels of synagogue affiliation, low birth rates, and rising levels of intermarriage to conclude that there was "something odd about a tribe which successfully moves heaven and earth to . . . commemorate the extermination of a third of its members, while failing in comfortable, safe, prosperous circumstances to reproduce itself." The possibility that external display is masking internal decay is also suggested by the construction of Jewish museums. Ruth Ellen Gruber has observed that, in Europe, Jewish museums have been growing at the same time that

Jewish communities have been disappearing. The situation is less acute in the United States, but the title of Michael Z. Wise's article "Judaism Under Glass: Are Museums the New Synagogues?" reminds us of the possibility that museums are repositories of dead objects removed from their life-giving contexts. It is unclear whether Jews are spending more time in museums than synagogues. But the fact that so much Jewish fundraising and architectural energy have been devoted to creating museums can be seen as evidence of a worrisome museification of Jewish existence. As the skeptical Wieseltier summed it up: "The more museums, the less life."[26]

The reality, however, is less distressing than these critiques would suggest. There is little merit to the charge that the achievements of Jewish architects reflect the increasing superficiality of American Jewish life. The decisions of Eisenman, Gehry, Tigerman, and Libeskind to couch their work in Jewish terms was not motivated by opportunism, trendiness, or ethnic shtick but arose after long periods of personal and professional soul-searching. They were trailblazers, daring to identify as Jews when it was unclear whether doing so would be advantageous. The sources that inspired their self-understanding were also, in the main, rooted in Jewish history and tradition. Gehry's identification with Jewishness may have been nostalgic, but Eisenman's, Tigerman's, and Libeskind's interest in the Holocaust's legacy and in Jewish theological traditions, such as the Kabbalah, displayed all the hallmarks of serious intellectual inquisitiveness. Even though these architects may not be religious or devote attention to designing synagogues, their work's Jewish dimensions deserve to be taken seriously.

The charge that architecture's centrality in Jewish life is complicit in the increase of assimilation is also flawed. Architecture reflects, rather than determines, the realities of Jewish existence. Declining rates of synagogue attendance and increasing rates of intermarriage are realities whose origins are unrelated to architecture. Without Jewish museums, Jews would not necessarily be flocking to synagogues. Prominent museums and their high-priced architecture may draw funds away from other Jewish institutions, but they can help arrest the trends they have been seen as promoting. Indeed, their exhibitions and special programs can counter the erosion of Jewish identity by providing unaffiliated Jews with alternative means of identifying with their Jewishness.[27]

The new Jewish architecture offers more than just relevance to Jews, moreover. Scholars may have abandoned the old "contributionist" discourse and ceased focusing on what the Jews have contributed to civilization. Yet, as Moshe Rosman has argued, they have created a new discourse that focuses on the relevance of the Jewish experience for the multicultural, postmodern world. The response of Jews to modern forms of persecution, their struggle to cope with Diasporic existence, and their effort to balance the temptations of assimilation with the desire to assert ethnic difference can be instructive both to minority groups and the majority societies in which they live. These themes have found expression in recent Jewish architecture, most clearly in the work of Jewish deconstructivists. To the extent that deconstructivism can be seen as a response to the Holocaust, its disruptive forms offer an aesthetic response to the experience of injustice that may inspire other oppressed groups. This has already happened at the National Museum of Australia in Canberra, whose wing dedicated to the history of Australian Aborigines was inspired by the plan of Libeskind's Berlin Jewish Museum. The architecture of Holocaust museums can also show other groups how to thematize their historical experiences of persecution in built form. This, too, has already happened in South Africa's Apartheid Museum in Johannesburg, whose harsh concrete form, evoking incarceration, was inspired by the USHMM's narrative architecture. Finally, in the Federal Republic of Germany, the cooperation of Jews and Christians in building new synagogues shows how architecture may assist reconciliation and provide a model for European Christians and Muslims as they debate the construction of mosques. These examples do not exhaust the relevance of contemporary Jewish architecture, but they show how it relates to current concerns.[28]

The question remains whether the recent surge of Jewish architectural creativity has peaked or will endure. Conventional wisdom holds that once a trend has been identified, it may have already begun to recede. If true, this book represents the beginning of the end for the new Jewish architecture. But other factors may contribute to its fading as well. The Jewish architects who have registered the most notable achievements belong to an older generation. Eisenman, Meier, Safdie, Greenberg, and Stern are all now over seventy years of age, and Gehry, Polshek, and Tigerman are over eighty. Many older architects, of course, have remained productive, Frank Lloyd Wright being the best example. Yet the Jewish architects born before World War II will eventually yield the stage. Architects born in the 1940s, such as Libeskind and Moss, show no signs of losing their creative vigor. And architects born in the 1950s and 1960s, such as Gorlin, Belzberg, and Herz, have long careers ahead of them. Whether their work will continue to display Jewish traits is impossible to predict. To a large degree, that will depend on the Jewish commissions that will emerge in the years to come. In all likelihood, however, there may be fewer in the future than there have been in the recent past. The wave of major Holocaust museum construction is over; the same is probably true of major Jewish museums. By now, most major American cities can boast at least one of these buildings. Synagogues will continue to be built, of course, though it is unlikely that there will again be as many as appeared in the early postwar years. If there are no major occasions to build Jewish institutions, the incentive for Jewish architects to draw on Jewish sources of inspiration may decline. The postwar period may eventually be seen as a uniquely productive but transitory phase.

This is especially possible given the new situation faced by architecture after 9/11. The rise of multiculturalism, postmodernism, and Holocaust consciousness liberated Jewish architects to base their work on Jewish sources of inspiration, but since the attacks of September 11, 2001, these trends have been increasingly questioned. The world has shown growing impatience toward multiculturalism and an increased desire for national unity; it has displayed a diminished tolerance for relativism and an increased desire for certainty; and it has shown a desire to move beyond dwelling on memories of past injustices in order to focus on current concerns.[29] Today, architects have become preoccupied with terrorism, climate change, sustainability, and the crisis of the housing industry. As a result, they may no longer feel that they can take time to reflect on issues of memory and identity.

If true, the topic of Jewishness in architecture may not command attention in the years to come as it has in years gone by. The event that originally led me to affirm the reality of postwar Jewish architectural achievement — Libeskind's victory in the Ground Zero architectural competition of 2003 — may now be seen as the crest of a phenomenon that has since begun to decline. Perhaps it is symbolically fitting that Libeskind has become marginalized from the planning at the World

Trade Center site. His diminished authority suggests that, in the post-9/11 world, lofty rhetorical architectural visions dealing with memory and identity may have lost some of their power.

Yet even if the wave of Jewish architectural productivity has crested, its legacy will remain with us. Jewish architects have had a major impact on postwar western architecture, helping to propel the movements of modernism, postmodernism, and deconstructivism. They have helped produce the very pluralism that defines architecture today. This achievement is appropriate, for it also describes the reality of contemporary Jewish life. There is no single version of Jewishness that has found expression in architectural form. Jewish architecture exists both within the sphere of the secular and the religious; it expresses ongoing tendencies toward assimilation and alienation; it reflects both the nightmares and nostalgia that surround modern Jewish history; and it highlights the divergence between Jewish life in the Diaspora and in Israel. In short, it epitomizes the pluralism of the modern Jewish experience.

These are among the thoughts that now come to mind whenever I drive past the Second Congregational Church in Greenwich. Its architect, Leopold Eidlitz, would have been hard pressed in the mid-nineteenth century to predict the explosion of Jewish architectural creativity that began a century after he arrived in the United States. Most Jewish architects today would be equally surprised to learn that Eidlitz's designs for churches and other secular buildings constitute a milestone in the history of Jewish architecture in America. For me, however, its significance is clear. With Eidlitz began an impressive record of Jewish architectural achievement that continues one hundred and fifty years later. It is a legacy that deserves to continue into the future.

Notes

Introduction

1. Gavriel D. Rosenfeld, "A True Memorial Lies in the Ruins," *Washington Post,* September 23, 2001, B2; Gavriel D. Rosenfeld, "Ground Zero's Future Should Include Present Excavation," *Greenwich Time,* July 17, 2002, A15; Gavriel D. Rosenfeld, "Without Ruins, Mindful of What?" *Washington Post,* November 30, 2003, B5.
2. Edward Wyatt, "Design Chosen for Rebuilding at Ground Zero," *New York Times,* February 27, 2003.
3. Gavriel D. Rosenfeld, "Ground Zero as a Laboratory for Jewish Architecture,'" *Forward,* February 21, 2003, 1.
4. Kalman Bland, *The Artless Jew: Medieval and Modern Affirmations and Denials of the Visual* (Princeton: Princeton University Press, 2001), 40.
5. Ruth Ellen Gruber, *Virtually Jewish: Reinventing Jewish Culture in Europe* (Berkeley: University of California Press, 2002), 27.
6. David Biale, "Preface: Toward a Cultural History of the Jews," in David Biale, ed., *Cultures of the Jews: A New History* (New York: Schocken, 2002), xix–xxi; David Biale, "Introduction," in Biale, *Cultures of the Jews,* 4.
7. On Jewishness, see Simon J. Bronner, "The *Chutzpah* of Jewish Cultural Studies," in Simon J. Bronner, ed., *Jewishness: Expression, Identity, and Representation* (Oxford: Littman Library of Jewish Civilization, 2008), 1–26. Bruce's comment is quoted in Stephen Whitfield, *In Search of American Jewish Culture* (Waltham, Mass.: Brandeis University Press, 1999), 12–13. Norman Podhoretz and Thomas L. Jeffers, ed., *The Norman Podhoretz Reader: A Selection of His Writings from the 1950s Through the 1990s* (New York: Free Press, 2003), 449–56. Yuri Slezkine, *The Jewish Century* (Princeton: Princeton University Press, 2004). Sergio Quinzio and Martina Kempter, *Die jüdischen Wurzeln der Moderne* (Frankfurt: Campus, 1995). Regarding the subjective aspects of "Jewishness," see Vincent Brook, *You Should See Yourself: Jewish Identity in Postmodern American Culture* (New Brunswick, N.J.: Rutgers University Press, 2008).
8. Essentialism is the idea that different social, ethnic, or religious groups display fixed, objectively definable traits that find expression in their cultural behavior and artifacts. Stephen Fuchs, *Against Essentialism: A Theory of Culture and Society* (Cambridge, Mass.: Harvard University Press, 2005). On constructionism, see Peter Berger and Thomas Luckmann, *The Social Construction of Reality: A Treatise in the Sociology of Knowledge* (New York: Doubleday, 1966).
9. Moshe Rosman, *How Jewish Is Jewish History?* (Portland, Ore.: Littman Library of Jewish Civilization, 2007), 112. Cecil Roth, *The Jewish Contribution to Civilization* (Cincinnati: Union of American Hebrew Congregations, 1940).
10. Bland, *Artless Jew,* 26–27.
11. In Europe, the interest in Jewish culture has manifested itself with the embrace of Klezmer music, the creation of Jewish museums, and the gentrification of old Jewish ghetto neighborhoods. In the United States, the growing presence of Jews in popular culture has been visible in television (in shows such as *The O.C., The Simpsons,* and *The Daily Show with Jon Stewart*), music (with the crossover success of Jewish rap stars like Matisyahu), and the fad-

dish embrace of Kabbalah by celebrities like Madonna and Britney Spears.

12. In his book *Freud, Jews, and Other Germans: Masters and Victims in Modernist Culture* (Oxford: Oxford University Press, 1979), Peter Gay rejected the notion that Jews were uniquely skilled cultural innovators by pointing to European antisemites' tendentious use of the idea of Jewish culture (21). Similarly, E. H. Gombrich declared that the "concept of Jewish culture was invented by Hitler and his predecessors." Peter Dittmar, "Gibt es eine jüdische Kultur?" *Die Welt,* October 29, 1998. The trendiness of Jewish culture has been criticized as a superficial substitute for real Jewish intellectual, religious, and communal engagement. See Gabrielle Birkner, "Pop Goes the Hipster Judaism Bubble," *Jewish Week,* December 30, 2005.

13. Karl Schwarz, *Die Juden in der Kunst* (Berlin: Heine-Bund, 1928); Ernst Cohn-Wiener, *Jüdische Kunst: Ihre Geschichte von den Anfängen bis zur Gegenwart* (Berlin: M. Wasservogel, 1929); Franz Landsberger, *A History of Jewish Art* (Cincinnati: Union of American Hebrew Congregations, 1946); Cecil Roth, ed., *Jewish Art: An Illustrated History* (New York: McGraw-Hill, 1961); Gabrielle Sed-Rajna, *Jewish Art* (New York: Abrams, 1997); Helen Rosenau, *A Short History of Jewish Art* (London: J. Clarke, 1948); Clare Moore, *The Visual Dimension: Aspects of Jewish Art* (Boulder: Westview, 1993).

14. Rachel Wischnitzer, *Synagogue Architecture in the United States* (Philadelphia: Jewish Publication Society of America, 1955); Rachel Wischnitzer, *The Architecture of the European Synagogue* (Philadelphia: Jewish Publication Society of America, 1964); Harold Hammer-Schenk, *Synagogen in Deutschland: Geschichte einer Baugattung im 19. und 20. Jahrhundert, (1780 – 1933)* (Hamburg: H. Christians, 1981); Carol Krinsky, *Synagogues of Europe: Architecture, History, Meaning* (Mineola, N.Y.: Dover, 1985); Dominique Jarrassé, *Synagogues: Architecture and Jewish Identity* (Paris: Vilo International, 2001); H. A. Meek, *The Synagogue* (London: Phaidon, 1995); Samuel Gruber, *Synagogues* (New York: Metro, 1999); Samuel Gruber, *American Synagogues: A Century of Architecture and Jewish Community* (New York: Rizzoli, 2003).

15. See Bland, *Artless Jew;* Margaret Olin, *The Nation Without Art: Examining Modern Discourses on Jewish Art* (Lincoln: University of Nebraska Press, 2001); Richard I. Cohen, *Jewish Icons: Art and Society in Modern Europe* (Berkeley: University of California Press, 1998).

16. See Bland, *Artless Jew,* chapters 1 – 2.

17. Schwarz, *Die Juden in der Kunst,* 29; Cohn-Wiener, *Jüdische Kunst,* 31 – 32; the *Jewish Encyclopedia* of 1902 quotation is found in Bland, *Artless Jew,* 30; Abram S. Isaacs, "The Story of the Synagogue," *Architectural Record,* December 1906, 464 – 80.

18. The Graetz quotation is found in Bland, *Artless Jew,* 22; Joseph Carlebach, "Die Architektur der Synagoge," *Jeschurun,* March – April 1928, 111 – 12; Schwarz, *Die Juden in der Kunst,* 203.

19. The Wagner quotation is found in Bland, *Artless Jew,* 27; Adolf Hitler, *Mein Kampf* (Boston: Houghton Mifflin, 1971), 303; the Schultze-Naumburg quotation is found in Peter Adam, *Art of the Third Reich* (New York: Abrams, 1992), 134; the *Völkischer Beobachter* quotation is found in Barbara Miller Lane, *Architecture and Politics in Germany, 1918 – 1945* (Cambridge, Mass.: Harvard University Press, 1968), 162.

20. Bernard Berenson, *Aesthetics and History* (New York: Pantheon, 1948), 179; Aharon Kashtan, "Synagogue Architecture of the Medieval and Pre-Emancipation Periods," in Roth, *Jewish Art,* 253; Percival Goodman, "The Jews in Architecture," in Roth, *Jewish Art,* 721; Krinsky, *Synagogues of Europe,* 71; *Encyclopedia Judaica,* 2nd ed. (New York: Macmillan Reference, 2006), 399; Angeli Sachs and Edward Van Voolen, *Jewish Identity in Contemporary Architecture* (Munich: Prestel, 2004), 21.

21. Max I. Dimont, *Jews, God, and History* (New York: Signet, 2004), 37; Thorleif Boman, *Hebrew Thought Compared with Greek* (London: SCM, 1960), 27.

22. Landsberger, *History of Jewish Art,* 4.

23. Bland, *Artless Jew,* chapter 3; Olin, *Nation Without Art,* chapter 5.

24. Sed-Rajna, *Jewish Art,* 165; Bland, *Artless Jew,* 30 – 31.

25. Martin Heidegger, "Building Dwelling Thinking," in *Poetry, Language, Thought* (New York: Perennial, 2001), 141 – 60.

26. Kashtan, "Synagogue Architecture," 253.

27. "Yibaneh! Jewish Identity in Contemporary Architecture" opened in Amsterdam in 2004 and later traveled to Osnabrück, Warsaw, Berlin, Vienna, Munich, and London. See Sachs and Van Voolen, *Jewish Identity in Contemporary Architecture.* In 2003, a symposium entitled "Die jüdischen Baumeister Berlins" was held in the German capital. "Auf dieses Netzwerk können sie bauen," *Berliner Zeitung,* September 18, 2003. In March 2004, Penn State University hosted the conference "Architecture, Urbanism, and the Jewish Subject." In 2003, Stanford University hosted the conference "Jewish Conceptions and Practices of Space." See the special issue of *Jewish Social Studies* entitled *Jewish Conceptions and Practices of Space* 11, no. 3 (Spring–Summer 2005).

28. See, for example, Herbert Muschamp, "Architecture of Light and Remembrance," *New York Times,* December 15, 1996, Section 2, 1; "Judios de vanguardia: Avant-Garde Jews," *AV Monografias,* January–April 1998, 69–70; David Gissen, "Is There a Jewish Space?" *Thresholds,* Fall 2001, 90–95; David Serlin, "Can a Building Be Jewish?" *Architecture,* July 2004, 23–25; Julia Goldman, "A Foundation," *Jewish Week,* January 6, 2004.

Aaron Betsky, "Building Absence: The Jewish Conspiracy in Architecture," *Archis* 7 (1998): 41–47; Klemens Klemmer, *Jüdische Baumeister in Deutschland: Architektur vor der Shoah* (Stuttgart: Deutsche Verlags-Anstalt, 1998), see esp. 221–23. Mel Alexenberg, *The Future of Art in a Digital Age: From Hellenistic to Hebraic Consciousness* (Bristol, U.K.: Intellect, 2006), esp. 9–25.

29. Fredric Bedoire, *The Jewish Contribution to Modern Architecture, 1830–1930* (Jersey City, N.J.: KTAV, 2004). Klemmer, *Jüdische Baumeister,* 223. See also Franklin Toker, *Fallingwater Rising: Frank Lloyd Wright, E. J. Kaufmann, and America's Most Extraordinary House* (New York: Knopf, 2003). Kathleen James, *Erich Mendelsohn and the Architecture of German Modernism* (Cambridge: Cambridge University Press, 1997); Jencks, *The New Moderns* (New York: Rizzoli, 1990); Renato Rizzi, *Peter Eisenman: Mystisches Nichts* (Basel: Wiese Verlag, 1996).

30. Allan Temko, "Creating a Jewish Sense of Space," *San Francisco Sunday Examiner and Chronicle,* December 8, 1996, 51.

31. Betsky, "Building Absence."

32. This was the claim of David Gissen. Quoted in Goldman, "A Foundation."

33. For a sampling, see Roger Homan, *The Art of the Sublime: Principles of Christian Art and Architecture* (Burlington, Vt.: Ashgate, 2006); Valérie Gonzalez, *Beauty and Islam: Aesthetics In Islamic Art and Architecture* (New York: St. Martin's, 2001); Ran Wei, *Buddhist Buildings* (Vienna: Springer, 2000).

34. Larry Gordon, "As Minorities Thrive, So Do Ethnic Museums," *Los Angeles Times,* May 4, 1998, 1.

35. Michael Cannell, "Cardinal Rules," *Architecture,* July 2000, 60–64, 140–42. Raul A. Barreneche, "A New Museum and Research Center by Polshek and Partners," *Architecture,* July 1999, 85–92. Carol Krinsky, *Contemporary Native American Architecture* (New York: Oxford University Press, 1996).

36. Darell Wayne Fields, *Architecture in Black* (New Brunswick, N.J.: Athlone, 2000); Stephen A. Kliment, "Discovering African Identity in African-American Architecture," *AIA Architect,* August 3, 2007; Nicolai Ouroussoff, "Tracing the Threads That Join America and Africa," *New York Times,* May 4, 2009, C1, C5.

37. Charles Jencks, *The New Paradigm in Architecture: The Language of Post-Modernism* (New Haven: Yale University Press, 2002), 190–91; Charles Jencks, *The Iconic Building* (New York: Rizzoli, 2005), 114–31; Aaron Betsky, *Queer Space: Architecture and Same-Sex Desire* (New York: William Morrow, 1997).

38. Anthony Julius, *Idolizing Pictures: Idolatry, Iconoclasm, and Jewish Art* (New York: Thames and Hudson, 2000), 94.

39. In doing so, I follow William Whyte's holistic approach to determining architectural meaning. William Whyte, "How Do Buildings Mean? Some Issues of Interpretation in the History of Architecture," *History and Theory,* May 2006, 174.

40. As an historian, I naturally favor the New Historicist method of interpretation associated with Stephen Greenblatt over the formalist New Criticism of the mid-twentieth century. I am also sympathetic to some of the views set out by E. D. Hirsch in his book *Validity in Interpretation* (New Haven: Yale University Press, 1967).

41. R. Wolff, "Seid bitte nicht zu nett," *Frankfurter Rundschau,* May 7, 2005.

42. Quoted in Stephen J. Whitfield, "Declarations of Independence: American Jewish Culture in the Twentieth Century," in Biale, *Cultures of the Jews,* 380.

43. David Engel, *Historians of the Jews and the Holocaust* (Palo Alto, Calif.: Stanford University Press, 2009).

44. Andrea Oppenheimer Dean, *Bruno Zevi on Modern Architecture* (New York: Rizzoli, 1983), 163.

45. A partial list of major Jewish writers includes Franz Kafka, Elias Canetti, Isaac Babel, Boris Pasternak, Gertrude Stein, Bernard Malamud, Norman Mailer, and Philip Roth. Prominent poets include Heinrich Heine, Emma Lazarus, Tristan Tzara,

Paul Celan, and Joseph Brodsky. There have been twelve Jewish Nobel Prize winners in literature since 1910. http://www.jewishvirtuallibrary.org/jsource/Judaism/nobels.html. This number represents around 10 percent of the total (the prize has been in existence since 1901). Interestingly, this is about the same percentage of Jews that have won architecture's major prize, the Pritzker Prize. A major difference, however, is the fact that this award has been in existence only since 1979. Since then, three Jews (Gordon Bunshaft, Richard Meier, and Frank Gehry) have won it (another winner, Richard Rogers, is of Jewish descent). The percentage would be much lower had the Pritzker Prize existed as long as the Nobel.

46. Major Jewish composers in Europe include Giacomo Meyerbeer, Felix Mendelssohn-Bartholdy, Jacques Offenbach, Gustav Mahler, Arnold Schönberg, and Kurt Weill, while, in the United States, composers such as Irving Berlin, George Gershwin, Aaron Copland, Richard Rodgers, Oscar Hammerstein II, Leonard Bernstein, Otto Klemperer, and Philip Glass were accomplished in a variety of musical genres, ranging from classical to jazz. The list of accomplished Jewish musicians includes violinists, such as Jascha Heifetz, Pinchas Zuckerman, Isaac Stern, and Yitzhak Perlman, and pianists, such as Vladimir Horowitz, Artur Rubinstein, and Rudolf Serkin. See Artur Holde, *Jews in Music* (New York: Bloch, 1974) and Irene Heskes, *Passport to Jewish Music: Its History, Traditions, and Culture* (Westport, Conn.: Greenwood, 1994).

47. In Europe, actresses such as Sarah Bernhardt and directors such as Max Reinhardt were pioneering figures, while in the United States, Jews contributed mightily to the development of both dramatic theater (especially as playwrights, such as Clifford Odets, George S. Kaufman, and Arthur Miller) and musical theater (whether vaudeville or Broadway). See James Fisher, "Jews in American Drama," in Paul Buhle, ed., *Jews and American Popular Culture*, vol. 2: *Music, Theater, Popular Art, and Literature* (Westport, Conn.: Praeger, 1997), 49–75; Pamela Brown Lavitt, "Vaudeville," in Buhle, 15–35; Andrea Most, "Jews and the Broadway Musical," in Buhle, 37–48. In cinema, Jews helped develop the modern film industry in both Germany and America thanks to the efforts of such directors as Ernst Lubitsch, Fritz Lang, and Billy Wilder, and such Hollywood producers as Louis B. Mayer, Jack Warner, Samuel Goldwyn, and Carl Laemmle. The same is true in the realm of television, where Jewish moguls such as CBS chief William S. Paley and NBC chief Robert Sarnoff dominated the industry in its formative years. Neal Gabler, *An Empire of Their Own: How the Jews Invented Hollywood* (New York: Crown, 1989).

48. Camille Pissarro, Max Liebermann, Chaim Soutine, Marc Chagall, Amedeo Modigliani, Barnett Newman, and Mark Rothko were accomplished as painters, while Alfred Stieglitz, Man Ray (born Emmanuel Radnitsky), Robert Capa (born Andreas Friedmann), and Weegee (born Arthur Fellig) were pioneers in the field of photography.

49. Prior to 1914, the main candidates would be Dankmar Adler and Albert Kahn. I have chosen to exclude them, however, due to the scholarly consensus that their primary contributions were in the realms of engineering and industrial architecture. I do discuss both of them, however, in Chapter 1.

Chapter 1.
From the Wilderness to World War II

1. Stanley Abercrombie, for one, has examined the differences between denotative meaning and connotative meaning in architecture — that is, between the meanings that are inherent in built forms and those that we bestow upon them. Stanley Abercrombie, *Architecture as Art: An Esthetic Analysis* (New York: Van Nostrand Reinhold, 1984), 125–29, 145. Christian Norberg-Schulz, *Meaning in Western Architecture* (New York: Praeger, 1975) shows how the ritual functions of buildings have always determined their deeper significance. See also Robert Harbison, *The Built, the Unbuilt, and the Unbuildable: In Pursuit of Architectural Meaning* (Cambridge, Mass.: MIT Press, 1994).

2. William Whyte, "How Do Buildings Mean? Some Issues of Interpretation in the History of Architecture," *History and Theory*, May 2006, 153–77.

3. On architectural vandalism, see Alexander Demandt, *Vandalismus: Gewalt gegen Kultur* (Berlin: Siedler, 1997). I have explored the connections between architecture and memory in my books *Munich and Memory: Architecture, Monuments, and the Legacy of the Third Reich* (Berkeley: University of California Press, 2000) and (with my coeditor, Paul Jaskot), *Beyond Berlin: Twelve German Cities Confront the Nazi Past* (Ann Arbor: University of Michigan Press, 2008).

4. Jarrassé, *Synagogues*, 11.

5. The two rooms were separated by a curtain (*parokhet*). The first room, known as the "holy place" (*kodesh*), was rectangular in shape and housed an altar of incense along with a lampstand (*menorah*) and a table for the so-called "bread of display" (*Shulhan Lehem Hapanim*); the rear room, known as the "holy of holies" (*kodesh ha-kodashim*), was a perfect square and housed the ark of the covenant and the tablets of the law brought down by Moses from Mount Sinai. The description is found in Exodus 25:1–27:19. David Lieber, ed., *Etz Hayim: Torah and Commentary* (New York: Jewish Publication Society of America, 2001), 485–98. Another Jewish structure defined by impermanence is the *sukkah* (booth), which is traditionally constructed for the holiday of Sukkot. For a brief discussion of its history and present-day relevance for architects, see Samuel Gruber, "A Sukkah Bound for New York," *Forward,* July 2, 2010.

6. The Temple's entrance was at its eastern end. To the west lay an entry vestibule (*ulam*), which connected to a prayer room (*hekhal*), and finally the "holy of holies" (*devir*), a cubic space with the ark of the covenant. The Temple was roughly twice the size of the Tabernacle. Lieber, *Etz Hayim,* 500.

7. Some archaeologists have questioned whether Solomon, like his father, David, ever presided over the kind of extensive empire described in the Bible, citing the absence of physical evidence in Jerusalem from the period. See Israel Finkelstein and Neil Asher Silberman, *The Bible Unearthed: Archaeology's New Vision of Ancient Israel and the Origin of Its Sacred Texts* (New York: Simon and Schuster, 2001), chapter 5.

8. This description is found in Kings 7:13–26. Lieber, *Etz Hayim,* 577–78.

9. The new Temple was ordered built by Zerubabel in approximately 515 BCE. Sed-Rajna, "The Golden Age of the Second Temple: The Splendor of Jerusalem," in Sed-Rajna, *Jewish Art,* 40.

10. The memory of the Temple remained preserved long after its destruction, in coins and in early synagogue frescoes. Sed-Rajna, *Jewish Art,* 15–16.

11. On the origins of the synagogue, see Michael Avi-Yonah, "Synagogue Architecture in the Classical Period," in Roth, *Jewish Art,* 156. The Hebrew terms for house of assembly, prayer, and study are *beit haknesset, beit hatfilah,* and *beit hamidrash*. Jarrassé, *Synagogues,* 13. Salo Baron, *A Social and Religious History of the Jews* (New York: Columbia University Press, 1957), 2: 284. On the Talmud's inattention to synagogue design, see Avram Kampf, *Contemporary Synagogue Art: Developments in the United States, 1945–65* (New York: Union of American Hebrew Congregations, 1966), 22.

12. Kashtan, "Synagogue Architecture," 256; Jarrassé, *Synagogues,* 22.

13. On the Jews' exclusion from guilds, see Franz Landsberger, "From 70 C.E. to the Present," in Peter Blake, ed., *An American Synagogue for Today and Tomorrow* (New York: Union of American Hebrew Congregations, 1954). 29. The Toledo and Regensburg examples appear in Krinsky, *Synagogues of Europe,* 244, 412. On the architectural consequences of Jews' residency restrictions, see Bedoire, *Jewish Contribution to Modern Architecture,* 67, Krinsky, *Synagogues of Europe,* 40–43, and Samuel Gruber, *Synagogues,* 30. On Venetian synagogues, see Kashtan, "Synagogue Architecture," 255, 303; Roberta Curiel and Bernard Dov Cooperman, *The Ghetto of Venice* (London: Tauris Parke, 1990).

14. On subterranean synagogues, see Kashtan, "Synagogue Architecture," 255; Avi-Yonah, "Synagogue Architecture in the Classical Period," 161; Kampf, *Contemporary Synagogue Art,* 87. On Venice, see Curiel and Cooperman, *Ghetto of Venice,* 9. The cross vault example is cited in Kashtan, "Synagogue Architecture," 266. The Worms example is cited in Krinsky, *Synagogues of Europe,* 9.

15. Synagogues at Lublin, Lwów, Zolkiew, and Lancut represented this type. Krinsky, *Synagogues of Europe,* 50–52, 205–11; Kashtan, "Synagogue Architecture," 281–84.

16. For a general survey, see Maria Piechotka and Kazimierz Piechotka, *Wooden Synagogues* (Warsaw: Arkady, 1959). Thomas Hubka, *Resplendent Synagogue: Architecture and Worship in an Eighteenth-Century Polish Community* (Waltham, Mass.: Brandeis University Press, 2003) argues for the role of Christian craftsmen (46–47). The Baron quotation appears in Bland, *Artless Jew,* 46; see also Kashtan, "Synagogue Architecture," 254. The quotation about the Polish vernacular tradition appears in Jarrassé, *Synagogues,* 91.

17. Klemmer, *Jüdische Baumeister,* 46.

18. See Heinrich Hübsch et al., *In What Style Should We Build? The German Debate About Architectural Style,* trans. Wolfgang Hermann (Santa Monica, Calif.: Getty Center for the History of Art and Humanities, 1992).

19. During this period neoclassicism was widely embraced by Jews in synagogue design as a largely nonfigurative, universal style lacking Christian connotations. Helen Rosenau, "German Synagogues in the Early Period of Emancipation," *Leo Baeck Institute Year Book,* vol. 8 (1963): 224. Ulrich Knufinke, "Synagogen des Klassizismus," in Aliza Cohen-Mushlin and Harmen H. Thies, eds., *Synagogen Architektur in Deutschland* (Petersberg, Germany: Michael Imhof Verlag, 2008), 69–78, 151, 163.

20. The speeches given at synagogue dedication ceremonies also evoked the theme of Jewish emancipation. Hammer-Schenck, *Synagogen in Deutschland,* 296, 131, 146.

21. Krinsky, *Synagogues of Europe,* 246–49, 157–59, 180–82; Bedoire, *Jewish Contribution to Modern Architecture,* 116–20. Scott Lerner, "The Narrating Architecture of Emancipation," *Jewish Social Studies* 6, no. 3 (Spring–Summer 2000): 1–8, 26n18. See also Saskia Coenen Snyder's forthcoming volume, *Building a Public Judaism: Monumental Synagogues and Jewish Identity in Northern Europe* (Cambridge, Mass.: Harvard University Press, 2013).

22. While late eighteenth-century synagogues, such as Peter Harrison's Touro Synagogue in Newport, Rhode Island (1763), were built in neoclassical styles, subsequent nineteenth-century synagogues could be neogothic (Henry G. Harrison's Mikve Israel Synagogue in Savannah, Georgia, 1878), Moorish (James Key Wilson's Plum Street Temple in Cincinnati, 1866), and neo-Romanesque (Peter and Francis Herter's Eldridge Street Synagogue on New York's Lower East Side, 1886–87).

23. Olga Bush, "The Architecture of Jewish Identity: The Neo-Islamic Central Synagogue in New York," *Journal of the Society of Architectural Historians,* June 2004, 183.

24. On the *Ostjuden,* see Stephen Aschheim, *Brothers and Strangers: The East European Jew in German and German Jewish Consciousness, 1800–1923* (Madison: University of Wisconsin Press, 1982). The impact of antisemitism on synagogue design, the assertiveness of Jewish architects, and the career of Oppler are discussed in Hammer-Schenk, *Synagogen in Deutschland,* 414, 263, 206, 346.

25. Shulamit Volkov, "The Dynamics of Dissimilation: *Ostjuden* and German Jews," in Jehuda Reinharz and Walter Schatzberg, eds., *The Jewish Response to German Culture: From the Enlightenment to the Second World War* (Hanover, N.H.: University Press of New England, 1985), 192–211. Michael Brenner, *The Renaissance of Jewish Culture in Weimar Germany* (New Haven: Yale University Press, 1996), 22–31. Inka Berz, "Jewish Renaissance — Jewish Modernism," in Emily Bilski, ed., *Berlin Metropolis: Jews and the New Culture, 1890–1918* (Berkeley: University of California Press, 1999), 164–87.

26. See Olin, *Nation Without Art,* esp. chapter 3. For a survey of the quest for a Jewish art, see Gavriel D. Rosenfeld, "Defining 'Jewish Art' in *Ost und West,* 1900–1907: A Study in the Nationalisation of Jewish Culture," *Leo Baeck Institute Yearbook,* 1994, 83–113.

27. The Herzl and Schatz remarks appear in Olin, *Nation Without Art,* 48, 44. Distinguishing between synagogues and churches was demanded by the Berlin engineer, Ernst Hiller, in "Betrachtungen über den modernen Synagogenbau," *Ost und West,* 1906, 31–32. Relocating the bimah was proposed in Felix Feuchtwanger's 1903 article in *Ost und West.* Hammer-Schenck, *Synagogen in Deutschland,* 449. The Augsburg synagogue was praised for its "neo-Jewish" character. Hammer-Schenck, *Synagogen in Deutschland,* 449, 495.

28. Schwarz, *Die Juden in der Kunst,* 212. Lewis Mumford, "Towards a Modern Synagog Architecture," *Menorah,* June 1925, 228. Max Eisler, "Die Synagoge in Sillein," *Menorah,* 1931, 526. Max Eisler, "Die neue Synagoge Amsterdam-Ost," *Menorah,* 1930, 172–73.

29. Other examples include Peter Behrens's domed synagogue in the Slovakian town of Sillein (today Zilina) in 1931 and Richard Neutra's unrealized modernist design for the Vienna-Hietzing synagogue competition in 1924.

30. Mumford, "Towards a Modern Synagog Architecture," 232–34. Max Eisler, "Vom neuen Geist der jüdsichen Baukunst," *Menorah* (1926): 521–22.

31. Rachel Wischnitzer has noted that no new ideas for synagogue design came out of the U.S. in the 1930s. Cited in Jarrassé, *Synagogues,* 214. "Synagogue for Skyscraper Roof," *New York Times,* March 3, 1929.

32. Finkelstein and Silberman, *Bible Unearthed,* chapter 7. The excavated remains of Hasmonean and Herodian palaces and fortresses are discussed in Sed-Rajna, *Jewish Art,* 40–42, 45–49. Landsberger, *History of Jewish Art,* 119.

33. Peter Richardson, *Building Jewish in the Roman East* (Waco, Texas: Baylor University Press, 2004), 337.

34. Vivian B. Mann, "Introduction," *Jewish Texts on the Visual Arts* (Cambridge, U.K.: Cambridge University

Press, 2000), 6.

35. Salo Baron, *A Social and Religious History of the Jews,* 4: 85, 281–82ff; see also Roth, *Jewish Contribution to Civilization,* 158. On the concept of "Jews' houses," see Raphael Isserlin, "Building Jerusalem in the 'Islands of the Sea': The Archaeology of Medieval Anglo-Jewry," in Sharman Kadish, ed., *Building Jerusalem: Jewish Architecture in Britain* (London: Vallentine Mitchell, 1996), 42–45.

36. The building was erected when the political and economic influence of the Prague Jewish community's wealthy leader, Mordecai Marcus Meisel, afforded the community a certain degree of autonomy. Jarrassé, *Synagogues,* 131.

37. The citadel quotation appears in Curiel and Cooperman, *Ghetto of Venice,* 39, 21. The Oppenheim example appears in Bedoire, *Jewish Contribution to Modern Architecture,* 73–74.

38. Mark Zborowski and Elizabeth Herzog, *Life Is with People: The Culture of the Shtetl* (New York: International Universities Press, 1952), 61–62. Thomas Hubka reminds us that Eastern European Jewish poverty was largely a nineteenth-century phenomenon that should not be projected back to earlier, more affluent centuries. Hubka, *Resplendent Synagogue,* 14–15.

39. Adolf Kohut, *Berühmte israelitische Männer und Frauen in der Kulturgeschichte der Menschheit* (Leipzig: Reudnitz, 1901), 326–27. Ita Heinze-Greenberg and Regina Stephan, *Luise und Erich Mendelsohn: Eine Partnerschaft für die Kunst* (Ostfildern-Ruit: Hatje Cantz, 2004), 15. Myra Warhaftig, *Deutsche jüdische Architekten vor und nach 1933 — Das Lexicon: 500 Biographien* (Berlin: Dietrich Reimer, 2005), 19; Bedoire, *Jewish Contribution to Modern Architecture,* 365.

40. The German and Austro-Hungarian examples are cited in Klemmer, *Jüdische Baumeister,* 75–76, 81, 83, 89–92, 100, 241, 281. Edward Jamilly, "Anglo-Jewish Architects, and Architecture in the 18th and 19th Centuries," *Jewish Historical Society of England, Transactions,* 1958, 133–34. Wischnitzer, *Synagogue Architecture in the United States,* 5. Kathryn Holliday, *Leopold Eidlitz: Architecture and Idealism in the Gilded Age* (New York: W. W. Norton, 2008). Also vying for the title of the first American Jewish architect is the German Jewish immigrant Henry Fernbach (1829–1883), who designed the Moorish revival Central Synagogue in Manhattan (1870–72) and various commercial buildings in Manhattan. Schwarz, *Die Juden in der Kunst,* 206. Adler trained as an engineer and is best known for the technical expertise that he provided to Sullivan, who is usually seen as the creative force in the firm. Landsberger, *History of Jewish Art,* 318.

41. The exception to the modest achievements of Jewish historicist architects is probably Alfred Messel, whose Wertheim department store has been hailed by architectural historians, such as Kathleen James, as "perhaps the most admired building . . . since the death of Schinkel in 1841." James, *Erich Mendelsohn and the Architecture of German Modernism,* 111. Other factors behind the modest achievements of Jewish architects include their comparative lack of collective experience in the profession, something that prevented them from possessing the same kinds of mentoring relationships and patronage networks enjoyed by Christian architects. Jewish architects' penchant for conformity is partly explained by Eric Hobsbawm's contention that most Jews tended to work within the national cultural traditions of their homelands as long as emancipation was working. Eric Hobsbawm, "Benefits of Diaspora," *London Review of Books,* October 20, 2005.

42. Scholars have long debated the Jews' role in the development of modernism. Peter Gay and Carl Schorske have rejected the idea that there was a special Jewish contribution to modernism. See Peter Gay, *Weimar Culture: The Outsider as Insider* (New York: Harper and Row, 2001); Gay, *Freud, Jews, and Other Germans;* Carl Schorske, *Fin-de-Siècle Vienna: Politics and Culture* (New York: Knopf, 1980). Later scholars have amended this view. Paul Mendes-Flohr, drawing on Georg Simmel's idea of the stranger, argued that the "outsider" status of Jews in European society led them to express their alienation through intellectual and cultural innovation. Mendes-Flohr, "The Study of the Jewish Intellectual: A Methodological Prolegomenon," in his *Divided Passions: Jewish Intellectuals and the Experience of Modernity* (Detroit: Wayne State University Press, 1991), 23–53. Steven Beller focused on how modern antisemitism contributed to Jewish alienation. Steven Beller, *Vienna and the Jews* (Oxford: Oxford, 1989). Yuri Slezkine shares this view in *Jewish Century.* A related argument holds that Jews became intellectually and culturally productive only as they separated themselves from their religious traditions and engaged with the modern world. See Thorstein Veblen, "The Intellectual

Pre-Eminence of Jews in Modern Europe," *Political Science Quarterly* 34, no. 1 (March 1919): 33–42; Isaac Deutscher, "The Non-Jewish Jew," in Deutscher, *The Non-Jewish Jew and Other Essays* (London: Oxford University Press, 1968). Some scholars claim to have found a specific form of "Jewish Modernism" in turn-of-the-century Europe. See Abigail Gillman, *Viennese Jewish Modernism: Freud, Hofmannsthal, Beer-Hofmann, and Schnitzler* (University Park: Pennsylvania State University Press, 2009) and Scott Spector, "Modernism Without Jews: A Counter-Historical Argument," *Modernism/Modernity*, no. 4 (2006): 615–33. See also Rose-Carol Washton-Long, Matthew Baigell, and Milly Heyd, eds., *Jewish Dimensions in Modern Visual Culture: Antisemitism, Assimilation, Affirmation* (Waltham, Mass.: Brandeis University Press, 2009).

43. This understanding of modernist culture follows the interpretation of Peter Gay. Other notable discussions of modernism include: Matei Calinescu, *Five Faces of Modernity: Modernism, Avant-Garde, Decadence, Kitsch, Postmodernism* (Durham, N.C.: Duke University Press, 1987). Peter Bürger, *The Theory of the Avant-Garde* (Minneapolis: University of Minnesota Press 1984). Andreas Huyssen, *After the Great Divide: Modernism, Mass Culture, Postmodernism* (Bloomington: Indiana University Press, 1986).

44. Jews functioned both as solvents and leavening agents, dissolving established cultural traditions and giving rise to new ones. Ruth Ellen Gruber, *Virtually Jewish*, 41.

45. Manfred Bock, Sigrid Johanisse, Vladimir Stissi, eds., *Michel de Klerk: Architect and Artist of the Amsterdam School, 1884–1923* (Rotterdam: NAI, 1997), 13, 54.

46. El Lissitzky, *Russia: An Architecture for World Revolution* (Cambridge, Mass.: MIT Press, 1970). Lissitzky had a major influence on the Dutch De Stijl movement. Christine Lodder, *Russian Constructivism* (New Haven: Yale University Press, 1983), 248–50. Lissitzky's only completed building was a print shop on Samotechny Lane in Moscow. www.avangard-ru.org/pdf/press/Samoteka_eng.57771.pdf.

47. The Wright quotation appears in Bruno Zevi, *Erich Mendelsohn: The Complete Works* (Basel: Birkhäuser, 1999), 276. Some scholars, such as Kathleen James, shy away from classifying Mendelsohn's work as expressionist, preferring to describe it with the term "dynamic functionalism." James, *Erich Mendelsohn and the Architecture of German Modernism*, 3. The "functionalism with dynamics" quotation appears in Kenneth Frampton, *Modern Architecture: A Critical History* (London: Thames and Hudson, 1992), 120. The size of Mendelsohn's firm is mentioned in James, 96. Reyner Banham, *Theory and Design in the First Machine Age* (Oxford, U.K.: Butterworth-Heinemann, 1994), 168. Mendelsohn's main champion, Bruno Zevi, hailed him as a man "eternally in revolt." Zevi, *Erich Mendelsohn*, 54. Ita Heinze-Greenberg writes that "to this day, scholarly research has tended to neglect Mendelsohn's architecture," a fact that reflects his exclusion "from decisive [architectural] events" in his own lifetime, such as the Weissenhof settlement exhibition of 1927 and the MoMA International Style exhibition of 1932. Heinze-Greenberg, "I often fear the envy of the Gods," in Regina Stephan, ed., *Eric Mendelsohn: Architect, 1887–1953* (New York: Monacelli, 1999), 172.

48. Most German Jewish architects in the early twentieth century belonged to the functionalist camp, according to Myra Warhaftig. Only one of twenty-four members of the Bauhaus Kollegium was a Jew. Only three of twenty-seven members of *Der Ring* were Jews. But 10 percent of the Deutsche Werkbund was Jewish. Warhaftig, *Deutsche jüdische Architekten vor und nach 1933*, 32. Frampton, *Modern Architecture*, 248–49. The Banham remark is cited in Elizabeth A. T. Smith, "R. M. Schindler: An Architecture of Invention and Intuition," in Smith and Michael Darling, eds., *The Architecture of R. M. Schindler* (New York: Museum of Contemporary Art, Los Angeles, 2001), 81. Isabelle Hyman, *Marcel Breuer, Architect: The Career and the Buildings* (New York: Abrams, 2001), 14. On Chareau, see Hasan-Uddin Khan, *International Style: Modernist Architecture from 1925 to 1965* (Cologne: Taschen, 1998), 42, and Nicolai Ouroussoff, "The Best House in Paris," *New York Times*, August 26, 2007. On Josef Frank, see Christopher Long, "The Wayward Heir: Josef Frank's Vienna Years, 1885–1933," in Nina Stritzler-Levine, ed., *Josef Frank, Architect and Designer: An Alternative Vision of the Modern Home* (New Haven: Yale University Press, 1996), 44–61. On Jewish architects in Palestine, see Alona Nitzan-Shiftan, "Contested Zionism—Alternative Modernism: Erich Mendelsohn and the Tel Aviv Chug in Mandate Palestine," *Architectural History* 39 (1996): 147–80.

49. Kahn was also known for his Packard Motor Car Company Building No. 10 (1905) and the original Ford Motor Company Building (1909).

All of Kahn's buildings were built of reinforced concrete and boasted open, glass-enclosed interior spaces without load-bearing walls. Federico Bucci, *Albert Kahn: Architect of Ford* (New York: Princeton Architectural Press, 2002), 24–64. Only Kahn's factories were mentioned in the catalogue to the 1932 MoMA International Style exhibition. Bucci, *Albert Kahn,* 175.

50. Ely Jacques Kahn is less known for any one iconic building than for his overall body of work, such as his high rise at 2 Park Avenue (1928), his office building at 261 Fifth Avenue (1929), and the Bricken Casino Building on Broadway (1931), all of which featured soaring setbacks, highly decorated polychromatic facades, and opulent interior lobbies. Overall, Kahn saw himself as pursuing an American modern style that occupied a middle ground between historicism and functionalism. Jewel Stern and John A. Stuart, *Ely Jacques Kahn, Architect: Beaux-Arts to Modernism in New York* (New York: Norton, 2006), 73, 95.

51. "Baukünstler und Bauten," *C.V.-Zeitung,* July 3, 1931, 337. Max Osborn, "Von Hitzig bis Mendelsohn," *C.V.-Zeitung,* July 3, 1931, 337–38.

52. Breuer declared his desire to withdraw from the Jewish community to the Landesrabbiner of Dessau. Christopher Wilk, *Marcel Breuer: Furniture and Interiors* (New York: Museum of Modern Art, 1981), 15, 187, n2. Neutra's designs for Jewish clients were the main library of the fledgling Hebrew University in Jerusalem in 1923 and two synagogues, the North Shore Temple in Chicago and the Vienna-Hietzing synagogue, in 1924. Thomas S. Hines, *Richard Neutra and the Search for Modern Architecture* (New York: Rizzoli, 2006), 65–66, 68–69. Krinsky, *Synagogues of Europe,* 197–98. On Schindler's bohemian nature, see Stefanos Polyzoides, "Schindler, Lovell, and the Newport Beach House, Los Angeles, 1921–1926," *Oppositions,* no. 18 (1979): 60. Schindler drafted plans for the Homer Emunim Temple and School while working for the Chicago architectural firm of Ottenheimer, Stern, and Reichert. Esther McCoy, *Vienna to Los Angeles: Two Journeys: Letters Between R. M. Schindler and Richard Neutra* (Santa Monica, Calif.: Arts + Architectural Press, 1979), 75. Smith, "R. M. Schindler: An Architecture of Invention and Intuition," 96, 240. On Ely Jacques Kahn's upbringing, see Stern and Stuart, *Ely Jacques Kahn,* 50–51. Fittingly, the Society for Ethical Culture was founded by the German Jewish immigrant (and son of a Reform Jewish rabbi) Felix Adler in 1876. Albert Kahn was born in Germany in 1869 and emigrated to the United States in 1881. Bucci, *Albert Kahn,* 37, 27. He did design a synagogue in 1903, Temple Beth El in Detroit, modeled on the Pantheon in Rome.

53. De Klerk was one of twenty-five children born to Joseph Leman de Klerk, a diamond cutter, who had three marriages. Suzanne Shulof Frank, "Michel de Klerk (1884–1923): An Architect of the Amsterdam School" (Ph.D. diss., Columbia University, 1969), 94–95. Little is known about de Klerk's "Friedmann's emigrants' house," which helped Jews immigrate to British-controlled Palestine before 1914. De Klerk also had planned to visit Palestine with his close friend Erich Mendelsohn, but he died before his departure. Bock, Johanisse, and Stissi, *Michel de Klerk,* 277–79; Ita Heinze-Greenberg, "Around Noon Land in Sight': Travels to Holland, Palestine, the United States, and Russia," in Stephan, *Eric Mendelsohn: Architect,* 59.

54. Lissitzky is well known for the cubist-influenced illustrations in his short Passover-themed book *Had Gadya* (1919). He later went on to do considerable design work for the Soviet regime in the 1920s and 1930s. Victor Margolin, *The Struggle for Utopia: Rodchenko, Lissitzky, Moholy-Nagy, 1917–1946* (Chicago: University of Chicago Press, 1997), esp. 22–42. Lissitzky's functional views on architecture are visible in his discussion of his skyscraper designs for Moscow in "Old Cities — New Buildings," in Lissitzky, *Russia: An Architecture for World Revolution,* 50–56.

55. On Mendelsohn's clients, see James, *Erich Mendelsohn and the Architecture of German Modernism,* 6, 90. On his Jewish projects, see Zevi, *Erich Mendelsohn,* 122–23; Kathleen James, "'Even if the Berlin buildings had been well underway, I would have kept on fighting'": "Small Buildings for the Jewish Communities in Tilsit, Königsberg, and Essen," in Stephan, *Eric Mendelsohn,* 146–51. It is true that Mendelsohn occasionally claimed that Jewish influences had shaped his work, declaring to the German Zionist leader Kurt Blumenfeld, in July 1933, that "I know that the inimitable features of my first constructions are of Jewish origin." Heinze-Greenberg, "Around Noon Land in Sight,'" 60–65. But this remark probably reflected his desire to enhance his Jewish credentials to a major Zionist leader at a time when he was flirting with the idea of relocating his firm to Palestine. Ita Heinze-Greenberg and Regina Stephan, eds., *Erich*

Mendelsohn: Gedankenwelten: Unbekannte Texte zu Architektur, Kulturgeschichte und Politik (Ostfildern-Ruit: Hatje Cantz, 2000), 135.

56. J. Hodin, "The Visual Arts and Judaism," *Art Journal* 23, no. 3 (Spring 1964): 224.

57. Many scholars have pointed out that the word "Jew" never appears in Kafka's fiction. Whitfield, *In Search of American Jewish Culture,* 20. Iris Bruce has shown that Kafka's writings, such as "The Judgment" (1912), "In the Penal Colony" (1914), and *The Trial* (1914), were influenced by the antisemitic events of his era — the Dreyfus Affair (1894 – 1906), the ritual murder trial of Mendel Beilis (1911 – 13), and the Kishinev pogrom (1903 and 1905) — as well as by his growing embrace of cultural Zionism. Iris Bruce, *Kafka and Cultural Zionism: Dates in Palestine* (Madison: University of Wisconsin Press, 2007), esp. chapters 1 and 3.

58. The Dreyfus Affair, according to Ronald Hayman, gave Proust a "temporary boost to the temporary side of his Jewish self-consciousness." At the same time, he was never proud of his half-Jewishness. Ronald Hayman, *Proust: A Biography* (New York: HarperCollins, 1990), 128, 322, 286 – 87. See also Sherban Sidéry, "Israel's Way," in Peter Quennell, ed., *Marcel Proust, 1871 – 1922: A Centennial Volume* (New York: Weidenfeld and Nicolson, 1971), 79 – 105.

59. In 1921 in the Austrian town of Mattsee, Schoenberg was rudely told that the resort he was visiting was closed to Jews; shortly thereafter, in 1923, he had a famous exchange with Wassily Kandinsky about alleged antisemitic pronouncements uttered by members of the Bauhaus. These experiences, plus the rise of the Nazis, eventually prompted him to undo his conversion to Lutheranism (which he had embraced in 1898) and formally rejoin the Jewish faith in 1933. On Schoenberg, see Brenner, *Renaissance of Jewish Culture in Weimar Germany,* 156 – 57. See also Bluma Goldstein, "Schoenberg's Moses und Aron: A Vanishing Biblical Nation," in Charlotte M. Cross and Russell A. Berman, eds., *Political and Religious Ideas in the Works of Arnold Schoenberg* (New York: Garland, 1999), 159 – 92. David Isadore Lieberman, "Schoenberg Rewrites His Will: A Survivor from Warsaw, Op. 46," in Cross and Berman, *Political and Religious Ideas,* 193, 206.

60. Feelings of outsiderness influenced the French impressionist Camille Pissarro, whose origins as a Caribbean-born Jew alienated from his own religious background and led him to embrace a mixture of radical anarchist politics and painterly innovation. Karen Levitov, "Paths to Pissarro," in Karen Levitov and Richard Shiff, *Camille Pissarro: Impressions of City and Country* (New Haven: Yale University Press, 2007), 1 – 13. The same can be said of the German realist and later impressionist painter Max Liebermann, whose sympathetic portrayals of laborers working in communal harmony reflected the longings of an insecure German Jew in the nineteenth-century *Kaiserreich.* See the essays in Barbara Gilbert, *Max Liebermann: From Realism to Impressionism* (Los Angeles: Skirball Cultural Center, 2005). See also Chana Schütz, "Max Lieberman as a 'Jewish' Painter: The Artist's Reception in His Time," in Bilski, *Berlin Metropolis,* 146 – 63. Finally, Russian Jewish painter Chaim Soutine's doubly marginalized status — as an orthodox Jew who violated religious tradition by wanting to paint, and as an Eastern European Jew who was widely perceived as an exotic outsider in interwar Paris — was reflected in his vivid expressionist paintings of bloody carcasses of beef and poultry. See Kenneth Silver, "Where Soutine Belongs: His Art and Critical Reception in Paris Between the Wars," and Norman L. Kleeblatt, "An Expressionist in New York: Soutine's Reception in America at Mid-Century," both in Norman Kleeblatt and Kenneth E. Silver, eds., *An Expressionist in Paris: The Paintings of Chaim Soutine* (Munich: Prestel, 1998), 19 – 40, 41 – 63. On Soutine's Jewishness, see Donald Kuspit, "Jewish Naivete? Soutine's Shudder," in Matthew Baigell and Milly Heyd, eds., *Complex Identities: Jewish Consciousness and Modern Art* (New Brunswick, N.J.: Rutgers University Press, 2001), 87 – 99.

61. Ita Heinze-Mühleib, *Erich Mendelsohn: Bauten und Projekte in Palästina (1934 – 1941)* (Munich: Scaneg, 1986), 21. "Jewish Architects Restricted by Vichy," *New York Times,* September 26, 1942.

62. Klemmer, *Jüdische Baumeister,* 86. See also Bedoire, *Jewish Contribution to Modern Architecture.*

63. William Brustein, *Roots of Hate: Anti-Semitism in Europe Before the Holocaust* (Cambridge: Cambridge University Press, 2003), 192, 201, 205; Slezkine, *The Jewish Century,* 47 – 48.

64. Bedoire, *Jewish Contribution to Modern Architecture,* 172 – 73, 190 – 92, 238 – 47, 308, 360, 357, 132.

65. On Loos, see Beller, *Vienna and the Jews,* 29 – 30. Loos also built the home for the Jewish dadaist Tristan

Tzara in Paris in 1927. Lovell was the "editor of 'Care of the Body' columns" of the *Los Angeles Times*. McCoy, *Vienna to Los Angeles,* 66. Reginald Isaacs, *Gropius: An Illustrated Biography of the Creator of the Bauhaus* (Boston: Little, Brown, 1983), 212–13.

66. Hines, *Richard Neutra and the Search for Modern Architecture,* 96.

67. Toker, *Fallingwater Rising,* 53–58, 12, 69, 286.

Part Two:
After the Holocaust

1. The trees have since been removed, They were cut down in the summer of 2009 to prevent the shedding of needles on the building's roof, which was being damaged by repeated clogs and leaks. Email from Rita Unger, synagogue administrator at KTI, to author, May 24, 2010.

2. Michael Z. Wise, "Deconstructing Philip," *Forward,* October 20, 2006.

Chapter 2.
Adorno's Echoes

1. The use of the term "post-Holocaust" has become increasingly common. See, for example, Berel Lang, *Post-Holocaust: Interpretation, Misinterpretation, and the Claims of History* (Bloomington: Indiana University Press, 2005); Adrian Del Caro and Janet Ward, eds., *German Studies in the Post-Holocaust Age: The Politics of Memory, Identity, and Ethnicity* (Boulder: University Press of Colorado, 2003); Michael Morgan, *Beyond Auschwitz: Post-Holocaust Jewish Thought in America* (Oxford, U.K.: Oxford University Press, 2001).

2. Adorno's famous quotation appeared in his essay "Cultural Criticism and Society," published in 1951. Quoted in Neil Levi and Michael Rothberg, *The Holocaust: Theoretical Readings* (New Brunswick, N.J.: Rutgers University Press, 2003), 281.

3. Susan Gubar, *Poetry After Auschwitz: Remembering What One Never Knew* (Bloomington: Indiana University Press, 2003), 4.

4. In fact, Adorno did not view Auschwitz's cultural legacy as particularly novel, seeing it instead as the final stage of an age-old dialectical struggle between culture and barbarism. He did believe, though, that the Nazi disaster made it impossible after 1945 to ignore the barbaric dynamics within western culture. Gerhard Richter, "Nazism and Negative Dialectics," in Klaus Berghahn and Jost Hermand, eds., *Unmasking Hitler: Cultural Representations of Hitler from the Weimar Republic to the Present* (New York: P. Lang, 2005), 135–37. See also Michael Rothberg, "After Adorno: Culture in the Wake of Catastrophe," *New German Critique,* no. 72 (Autumn 1997): 57–58.

5. In "Meditations on Metaphysics," published in *Negative Dialectics* (1966), Adorno wrote, "Perennial suffering has as much right to expression as the tortured have to scream; hence it may have been wrong to say that after Auschwitz you could no longer write poems." Quoted in Levi and Rothberg, *Holocaust,* 283.

6. Adorno wrote, "The so-called artistic representation of the sheer physical pain of people beaten to the ground by rifle butts contains, however remotely, the power to elicit enjoyment out of it." Cited in "Commitment," Andrew Arato and Eike Gebhardt, eds., *The Essential Frankfurt School Reader,* eds. (New York: Continuum, 1982), 304.

7. Levi and Rothberg, *Holocaust,* 287.

8. Mark Godfrey, *Abstraction and the Holocaust* (New Haven: Yale University Press, 2007), 9–12.

9. Scholars have disagreed particularly about the Holocaust's place in American memory. Some have contended that the Holocaust was ignored until American Jews embraced it for reasons of political and social expediency — the two most important being the defense of Israel's actions in the wake of the Arab-Israeli wars of 1967 and 1973 and the preservation of Jewish group cohesion during a time of increasing assimilation. Peter Novick, *The Holocaust in American Life* (Boston: Houghton Mifflin, 1999); Tim Cole, *Selling the Holocaust, from Auschwitz to Schindler: How History Is Bought, Packaged, and Sold* (New York: Routledge, 1999). Others have pointed to the active discussion of the topic among survivors and its presence in American popular culture. Hasia Diner, *We Remember with Reverence and Love: American Jews and the Myth of Silence After the Holocaust, 1945–62* (New York: New York University Press, 2009). Lawrence Baron, "The Holocaust and American Public Memory, 1945–1960," *Holocaust and Genocide Studies,* Spring 2003, 62–88. David Cesarani, "Introduction," in David Cesarani, ed., *After Eichmann: Collective Memory and the Holocaust since 1961* (Abingdon: Oxon Taylor and Francis, 2004), 1–17.

10. In Western Europe, Germany and France largely avoided confronting the Holocaust until the 1960s, when the Eichmann and Auschwitz trials brought it to the general public's attention, while Austria ignored it until the Waldheim Affair of 1988. Jeffrey Herf, *Divided Memory: The Nazi Past in the Two Germanies* (Cambridge,

Mass.: Harvard University Press, 1997); Henry Rousso, *The Vichy Syndrome* (Cambridge, Mass.: Harvard University Press, 1991). David Art, *The Politics of the Nazi Past in Germany and Austria* (Cambridge, U.K.: Cambridge University Press, 2005). In Eastern Europe, the cold war led communist nations to ignore the Jewish dimensions of the Holocaust entirely. See Tony Judt, "The Past Is Another Country: Myth and Memory in Postwar Europe," *Daedalus*, Fall 1992, 95–100. Israel's political leaders initially downplayed the memory of the Holocaust as detrimental to the Zionist ideological mission but later mobilized it in the 1960s to promote social integration. Tom Segev, *The Seventh Million: The Israelis and the Holocaust* (New York: Hill and Wang, 1993); Idith Zertal, *Israel's Holocaust and the Politics of Nationhood* (Cambridge, U.K.: Cambridge University Press, 2005). For a more skeptical view, see Elhanan Yakira, *Post-Zionism, Post-Holocaust: Three Essays on Denial, Forgetting and the Delegitmation of Israel* (Cambridge, U. K.: Cambridge University Press, 2010).

11. Postwar American Jews' attitudes toward the Holocaust were shaped by feelings of guilt about their wartime inaction on behalf of their European brethren, apprehension about postwar antisemitism, and the desire to integrate into mainstream American society. Hasia Diner, *The Jews of the United States, 1654–2000* (Berkeley: University of California Press, 2006), 208–15, 282. Jews in postwar Europe downplayed the Holocaust in favor of focusing on the monumental challenges of present-day survival. Michael Brenner, *After the Holocaust: Rebuilding Jewish Lives in Postwar Germany* (Princeton, N.J.: Princeton University Press, 1997), 30–45, 67–68. Abraham Peck, "'Our Eyes Have Seen Eternity'": Memory and Self-Identity Among the She'erith Hapletah," *Modern Judaism* 17, no. 1 (1997): 57–74. Maud S. Mandel, *In the Aftermath of Genocide: Armenians and Jews in Twentieth-Century France* (Durham, N.C.: Duke University Press, 2003), chapter 2.

12. Neither in early postwar media reports on the liberation of the concentration camps nor at the later Nuremberg Trials was the Jews' wartime fate represented as different from the fate of other victims. Novick, *Holocaust in American Life*, 64–65.

13. Jonathan Petrie, "The Secular Word, 'Holocaust': Scholarly Myths, History, and Twentieth-Century Meanings," *Journal of Genocide Research* 2, no. 1 (March 2000): 31–63. Zev Garber and Bruce Zuckerman, "Why Do We Call the Holocaust 'The Holocaust?' An Inquiry into the Psychology of Labels," *Modern Judaism,* May 1989, 202–4.

14. Although European and American scholars produced numerous books on Hitler, the Nazi regime, and the Second World War, the most successful of them, such as William Shirer's *The Rise and Fall of the Third Reich,* devoted little attention to the genocide of the Jews. Gavriel D. Rosenfeld, "The Reception of William L. Shirer's *The Rise and Fall of the Third Reich* in the United States and West Germany, 1960–1962," *Journal of Contemporary History,* January 1994, 95–129. Meanwhile, those studies that directly focused on it — by scholars such as Eugen Kogon, Gerald Reitlinger, and Leon Poliakov — attracted minimal notice. Eugen Kogon, *The Theory and Practice of Hell* (New York, 1950); Gerald Reitlinger, *The Final Solution* (London, 1953); Leon Poliakov, *Harvest of Hate* (London, 1956). Raul Hilberg's work initially had trouble finding a publisher: *The Politics of Memory: The Journey of a Holocaust Historian* (Chicago: Ivan R. Dee, 1996), 66.

15. Jean-Paul Sartre's short book *Antisemite and Jew* (1946) indirectly acknowledged the Nazi genocide in examining the roots of anti-Jewish prejudice. Jonathan Judaken, *Jean-Paul Sartre and the Jewish Question: Anti-Antisemitism and the Politics of the French Intellectual* (Lincoln, Neb., 2006). Early postwar theologians such as Martin Buber insisted that "[even in] the time of Hitler . . . there was God." Michael Morgan, *A Holocaust Reader: Responses to the Nazi Extermination* (New York: Oxford University Press, 2001), 14. By contrast, Richard Rubenstein called on Jews to abrogate their covenantal relationship with God and cease believing in him altogether. Morgan, *Beyond Auschwitz,* 70, 65.

16. Levi's famous work *If This Is a Man* (Se questo è un uomo) was initially rejected by the reputable Einaudi Press and ultimately appeared in a very small print run in 1947. Wiesel's memoir *Und di Velt hot geschwign* was published in 1956 in Yiddish by a little-known publisher in Buenos Aires. In 1958, Wiesel published a shortened and refashioned version of his Yiddish memoir in French under the title *La Nuit* (it appeared in English in 1960 as *Night*). Naomi Seidman, "Elie Wiesel and the Scandal of Jewish Rage," *Jewish Social Studies* 3, no. 1 (Fall 1996): 3–4. Levi's book was reprinted with more publicity in 1958 and appeared in English translation as *Survival in*

Auschwitz in 1959. Charlotte Delbo's *None of Us Will Return* was originally written in French in 1946 but not published until 1965, and Jean Améry's *At the Mind's Limits* appeared in 1966. An exception to this trend was Anne Frank's posthumously published wartime diary, which, though not a survivor memoir, was enormously popular when it first appeared in 1952.

17. De-Nur published his autobiographical Hebrew-language novel *Salamandra* in 1946. Jeremy D. Popkin, "Ka-Tzetnik 135633: The Survivor as Pseudonym," *New Literary History*, Spring 2002, 343–55. Tadeusz Borowski's short stories (later collected under the title *This Way for the Gas, Ladies and Gentlemen*) were written in the late 1940s. See also André Schwarz-Bart's mystical novel *The Last of the Just* (1959), Piotr Rawicz's hallucinatory work of fiction *Blood from the Sky* (1961), and Jerzy Kosinski's controversial novel *The Painted Bird* (1965). More realistic treatments of the Holocaust from this time include Leon Uris's quasi-documentary account of the Warsaw Ghetto uprising, *Mila 18* (1961), and Czech Holocaust survivor Arnost Lustig's novel *Prayer for Katarina Horovitzova* (1962).

18. Paul Celan published an early version of his famous poem *Todesfuge* ("Death Fugue") in Romanian in 1947, and he followed it with the more celebrated German-language version in 1952. He most likely wrote the poem in late 1944 or 1945. John Felstiner, *Paul Celan: Poet, Survivor, Jew* (New Haven: Yale University Press, 2001), 26, 45. Sachs's *In den Wohnungen des Todes* (In the Dwellings of Death) appeared in 1946/7. See Susan Gubar, *Poetry After Auschwitz*. Sylvanus's play *Dr. Korczak and the Children* (1957) focused on the famed head of the Warsaw Ghetto orphanage; Hochhuth's controversial play *The Deputy* (1963) addressed the culpability of Pope Pius XII in the Holocaust; Peter Weiss's *Investigation* (1965) tackled the question of German guilt through the lens of the Auschwitz trial in Frankfurt.

19. In 1962, Dmitri Shostakovich composed Symphony No. 13, *Babi Yar*, which memorialized the notorious Nazi murder of Jews in the Ukraine in 1941. In 1965, Mikis Theodorakis composed his *Ballad of Mauthausen*. Before these works, the only notable piece of music was a relatively obscure Arnold Schoenberg oratorio from 1948 inspired by the Warsaw Ghetto uprising. David Isadore Lieberman, "Schoenberg Rewrites His Will: A Survivor from Warsaw, Op. 46," in Cross and Berman, *Political and Religious Ideas*, 216–18, 193–230. Sarah Nathan-Davis, "Music of the Holocaust," in John K. Roth and Elisabeth Maxwell, eds., *Remembering for the Future: The Holocaust in the Age of Genocide*, vol. 3: *Memory* (Houndsmills, U.K.: Palgrave, 2001), 3: 810.

20. Over one hundred Holocaust-related films were produced in more than a dozen countries in the first decade and a half after the war. Lawrence Baron, *Projecting the Holocaust into the Present* (Lanham, Md.: Rowman and Littlefield, 2005), 10, 25. Certain early films, however, such as Alain Resnais's *Night and Fog* (1955), minimized the Jewishness of the Nazi genocide. Later works, by contrast, featured Jewish survivors, concentration camp inmates, and ghetto inhabitants. These included "teleplays" such as Ernest Kinoy's *Walk Down the Hill* (1957) and Rod Serling's *In the Presence of Mine Enemies* (1960). Jeffrey Shandler, *While America Watches: Televising the Holocaust* (New York: Oxford University Press, 1999), chapters 1–3.

21. Chagall's paintings *Resistance, Resurrection,* and *Liberation* (1937–48) were inspired by Jewish suffering in the Holocaust. Newman's "zip" paintings have been interpreted as both hopeful and despairing reactions to the Nazi genocide. Matthew Baigell, "Barnett Newman's Stripe Paintings and Kabbalah: A Jewish Take," *American Art* 8, no. 2 (Spring 1994): 42; Matthew Baigell, *American Artists, Jewish Images* (Syracuse, N.Y.: Syracuse University Press, 2006), chapter 5; Ziva Amishai-Maisels, *Depiction and Interpretation: The Influence of the Holocaust on the Visual Arts* (Oxford: Pergamon, 1993), 57–60, 301–4. Mark Rothko's postwar turn to abstraction has been viewed as representing the artist's embrace of silence as a means of transcending the Holocaust's horrors. Amishai-Maisels, *Depiction and Interpretation*, 262–68. Baigell, *American Artists, Jewish Images*, chapter 4. Morris Louis's "Charred Journal" paintings from 1951 evoked Nazi book burnings. Godfrey, *Abstraction and the Holocaust*, chapter 3. On Hundertwasser, Bak, Giacometti, and Lipschitz, see Amishai-Maisels, *Depiction and Interpretation*, 124–38; 112–13, 198–201. Rapaport designed his famous Warsaw Ghetto Memorial in 1948.

22. Scholars have divided Holocaust literature into works that use a mimetic, naturalistic approach and those that take more fantastic, fabulist, or surrealistic perspectives. See Irving Howe, "Writing and the Holocaust," in Berel Lang, *Writing and the Holocaust* (New York: Holmes and

Meier, 1988), 191. Rosenfeld, *Double Dying,* 71. The desire to break radically with the past was reflected in the decision of individual writers to change their names: Yehiel De-Nur adopted the symbolic nom de plume Ka-Tzetnik 135633 (denoting his concentration camp identity); Paul Ancel changed his Romanian surname to the anagrammatic "Celan"; similarly, Jean Améry changed his surname from Mayer. Segev, *Seventh Million,* 4; Felstiner, *Paul Celan,* 46.

23. Sylvanus embraced the defamiliarizing techniques of Luigi Pirandello by having his play's characters call attention to their role as actors. Robert Skloot, *The Darkness We Carry: The Drama of the Holocaust* (Madison: University of Wisconsin Press, 1988), 95. Hochhuth devised an experimental combination of blank verse and other linguistically innovative strategies to probe the Holocaust's deeper dimensions, especially its theological ones. And Weiss created a hybrid, taking the left-leaning political aims of Bertolt Brecht and Erwin Piscator's Documentary Theatre movement of the 1920s and situating them within a traditional poetic structure. Alvin H. Rosenfeld, *A Double Dying* (Bloomington: Indiana University Press, 1980), 138–41; 154–55.

24. The memorable metaphor "black milk" appears in "Death Fugue," and the neologism "no-one's-rose" appears in the poem "Psalm" (1963). Sachs's observation is quoted in Sander L. Gilman and Jack Zipes, eds. *Yale Companion to Jewish Writing and Thought in German Culture, 1096–1996* (New Haven: Yale University Press, 1997), 693.

25. European films embraced experimental methods more than did American films, which were more commercially minded. Ilan Avisar discusses how Czech Holocaust films—such as Alfred Radok's expressionist *Distant Journey* (1948) and Jan Nemec's *Diamonds of the Night* (1964)—were prone to experimental methods. Ilan Avisar, *Screening the Holocaust: Cinema's Images of the Unimaginable* (Bloomington: Indiana University Press, 1980), chapter 3.

26. Newman destroyed his prewar work and turned to abstraction because he believed that the Holocaust had invalidated previous modes of painting. After seeing photos of Buchenwald and Bergen-Belsen, he proclaimed that "surrealism is dead. . . . No painting can surpass the photographs of German atrocities." Eckhart Gillen, "Night over Germany," in Eckhart Gillen, *German Art from Beckmann to Richter: Images of a Divided Country* (New Haven: Yale University Press, 1997), 70. On Rothko, see Amishai-Maisels, *Depiction and Interpretation,* 262–68. Matthew Baigell, *American Artists, Jewish Images,* chapter 4. Sed-Rajna, *Jewish Art,* 352.

27. Cited in Leland Roth, *Understanding Architecture: Its Elements, History, and Meaning* (Boulder, Colo.: Westview, 1993), 9. Utility, firmness, and beauty are the three Vitruvian goals of architecture.

28. Examples include the London fire of 1666, the Chicago fire of 1871, and Hurricane Katrina in 2005.

29. "Architecture Faces Its H-Hour," *Pencil Points,* June 1945, 57.

30. It is true that abstraction in art has been viewed as compatible with confronting the Holocaust (say, in the work of abstract expressionists). See Godfrey, *Abstraction and the Holocaust.* Yet, while artistic abstraction was highly personal in its articulation, abstraction in modern architecture mostly tended to standardization, uniformity, and anonymity, hardly the traits that signaled a wrestling with recent history.

31. In a 1947 manifesto, several dozen modernists declared that because of Germany's "spiritual breakdown" under the Nazis, the nation's "destroyed [architectural] heritage must not be . . . reconstructed" but should "only emerge for new tasks in a new form." "Ein Aufruf: Grundsätzliche Forderungen," *Baukunst und Werkform,* no. 1 (1947): 29.

32. Rosenfeld, *Munich and Memory,* 55–58.

33. "Homes for Veterans," *Architectural Forum,* July 1945, 8; "Remember to Plan for Safety," *Progressive Architecture—Pencil Points,* October 1945; "From Destruction to Construction," *Architectural Record,* September 1945, 69.

34. Bruno Zevi writes, "modern architecture developed in America without encountering the same formal and stylistic objections as in Europe." Bruno Zevi, *Towards an Organic Architecture* (London: Faber and Faber, 1950), 83.

35. See the discussion of Lachert's proposal in Michael Meng, *Shattered Spaces: Jewish Sites in Germany and Poland After the Holocaust* (Ph.D. diss., University of North Carolina, Chapel Hill, 2008), 124–32. See also Meng, *Shattered Spaces: Encountering Jewish Ruins in Postwar Germany and Poland* (Cambridge, Mass.: Harvard University Press, forthcoming).

36. Quoted in Zevi, *Eric Mendelsohn,* 53.

37. His shift may also have been an exercise in bad faith. By commemorating French suffering, Le Corbusier was able to identify with the victims and efface the fact that, like Mies and Gropius, he had collaborated with fascist governments (in his case, those of Fascist Italy and Vichy France) during the war. Charles Jencks, *Le Corbusier and the Tragic View of Architecture* (Cambridge, Mass.: Harvard University Press, 1973), 130–32.

38. Cited in Koppel Pinson, "Jewish Life in Liberated Germany," *Jewish Social Studies,* 1947, 114n.

39. Abraham Joshua Heschel, *The Sabbath: Its Meaning for Modern Man* (New York: Farrar, Straus and Giroux, 2005), 5, 98, 8.

Chapter 3.
American Synagogue Architecture and the Missing Holocaust

1. I was later told by the synagogue's rabbi, James Prosnit, that I had missed a small Holocaust memorial plaque. But it was not part of Goodman's original design.

2. Rachel Wischnitzer-Bernstein, "The Problem of Synagogue Architecture," *Commentary,* March 1947, 233, 240, 239–41.

3. Ibid., 241.

4. Claire Richter Sherman, "Rachel Wischnitzer: Pioneer Scholar of Jewish Art," *Woman's Art Journal* 1, no. 2 (Autumn 1980–Winter 1981): 42–46.

5. Franz Landsberger, "Expressive of America," *Commentary,* June 1947, 539; Ely Jacques Kahn, "No More Copying," *Commentary,* June 1947, 540; Percival and Paul Goodman, "Tradition from Function," *Commentary,* June 1947, 542.

6. Eric Mendelsohn, "In the Spirit of Our Age," *Commentary,* June 1947, 542.

7. Maurice Eisendrath, "Introduction"; "Contemporary Art in the Synagogue: A Symposium"; Alexander Kline, "The Synagogue in America," all in Blake, *American Synagogue,* xv, 196–97, 43, 45–46.

8. Percival and Paul Goodman, "Modern Artist as Synagogue Builder," *Commentary,* January 1949, 52. Will Herberg, "The Postwar Revival of the Synagogue," *Commentary,* April 1950, 316. Wischnitzer, *Synagogue Architecture in the United States,* 165. Wischnitzer's maiden name was Bernstein; she married Mark Wischnitzer in 1912. Sherman, "Rachel Wischnitzer," 44.

9. Kampf, *Contemporary Synagogue Art,* 27. Henry Stolzman and Daniel Stolzman, *Synagogue Architecture in America: Faith, Spirit, and Identity* (Mulgrave, Victoria, Australia: Woodbridge, 2004), 54. Meredith Clausen, *Spiritual Space: The Religious Architecture of Pietro Belluschi* (Seattle: University of Washington Press, 1992), 16.

10. Atina Grossman, "Trauma, Memory, and Motherhood: Germans and Jewish Displaced Persons in Post-Nazi Germany, 1945–1949," in Richard Bessel and Dirk Schumann, eds., *Life After Death: Approaches to a Cultural and Social History of Europe During the 1940s and 1950s* (Cambridge: Cambridge University Press, 2003), 93–128. Wischnitzer, *Synagogue Architecture in the United States,* 134. The *Commentary* quotations appear in Israel Knox, "Is America Exile or Home?" *Commentary,* November 1946, 401, and Moses Lasky, "A Golden Age," March 1947, *Commentary,* 253, 250.

11. On the factor of suburbanization, see Wischnitzer, *Synagogue Architecture in the United States,* 165; Jarrassé, *Synagogues,* 234–36; Diner, *Jews of the United States,* 282–93.

12. Krinsky, *Synagogues of Europe,* 99. Philip Nobel, "What Design for a Synagogue Spells Jewish?" *New York Times,* December 2, 2001, 34. Samuel Gruber, *American Synagogues,* 85.

13. Jewish affiliation rates are cited in Edward S. Shapiro, *A Time for Healing: American Jewry Since World War II* (Baltimore: Johns Hopkins University Press, 1995), 148. The issue of religious revival is addressed in Will Herberg, "The Postwar Revival of the Synagogue," *Commentary,* April 1950, 315. Nathan Glazer, "The Jewish Revival in America, I," *Commentary,* December 1955, 493–99.

14. Baigell makes this point about early postwar American Jewish artists. Matthew Baigell, *Jewish-American Artists and the Holocaust* (New Brunswick, N.J.: Rutgers University Press, 1997), 18–19.

15. Quoted in Amishai-Maisels, *Depiction and Interpretation,* 311. The quote is from Greenberg's essay "Self-Hatred and Jewish Chauvinism." Godfrey, *Abstraction and the Holocaust,* 16.

16. To be sure, congregations frequently placed memorial plaques marking the Holocaust in their synagogues' interiors. See Diner, *We Remember with Reverence and Love,* 36. Yet this form of commemoration reflected an artistic, not an architectural, response to the Nazi genocide.

17. Scholars differ on the numbers. In 1966, Avram Kampf declared that five hundred synagogues had been built in the United States in the two decades after 1945. Kampf, *Contemporary Synagogue Art,* vii. Janay Jadine Wong cites Arthur Hertzberg's figure of more than one thousand synagogues in the 1950s and 1960s. Janay Jadine Wong, "Synagogue Art of the 1950s: A New Context for Abstraction," *Art Journal,* Winter 1994, 37.

18. Allenstein's Jews made up between

5 and 10 percent of the population. http://ajcarchives.org/AJC_DATA/Files/1921_1922_6_Statistics.pdf. http://en.wikipedia.org/wiki/Olsztyn# Demographics. Zevi, *Eric Mendelsohn,* 83. Ita Heinze-Greenberg, "'We'll leave it to the Schultzes from Naumburg to ignore the Mediterranean as the father of the international art of composition': The Mediterranean Academy Project and Mendelsohn's Emigration," in Stephan, *Eric Mendelsohn,* 182, 184.

19. Zevi, *Eric Mendelsohn,* 84.

20. The 1933 quotation appears in Heinze-Greenberg and Stephan, *Erich Mendelsohn: Gedankenwelten,* 59, 62. Mendeslsohn's work with the U.S. Air Force appears in Mike Davis's book, *Dead Cities and other Tales* (New York, 2002), 66–68. The 1947 and 1951 quotations appear in Heinze-Greenberg, "We'll leave it to the Schultzes from Naumburg," 182.

21. Erich Mendelsohn, "Architecture in a Rebuilt World," in Mendelsohn, *Three Lectures on Architecture* (Berkeley: University of California Press, 1944), 39, 47–48. Oskar Beyer, *Eric Mendelsohn: Letters of an Architect* (New York: Abelard-Schuman, 1967), 95.

22. Mendelsohn's Jewish social hall in Tilsit contained a small synagogue, but it was of minor significance in the overall project. Kathleen James, "'Even if the Berlin buildings had been well underway, I would have kept on fighting': Small Buildings for the Jewish Communities in Tilsit, Königsberg, and Essen," in Stephan, *Erich Mendelsohn,* 146–62.

23. Designs for Jewish houses of worship in Baltimore, Washington D.C., and Dallas were never completed.

24. The synagogue center concept was conceived in the early twentieth century by Rabbi Mordecai Kaplan as a means of getting Jews to participate more actively in Jewish life by expanding the function of the synagogue to include secular activities. Kampf, *Contemporary Synagogue Art,* 23.

25. Hans R. Morgenthaler, "'It will be hard for us to find a home': Projects in the United States," in Stephan, *Erich Mendelsohn,* 255.

26. Zevi, *Eric Mendelsohn,* 77.

27. The 1947 quotation appears in Beyer, 160. The 1946 quotation appears in Mann, *Jewish Texts on the Visual Arts,* 99. The dedication remark is cited in Rosalind Mael Bronsen, *B'nai Amoona: For all Generations* (St. Louis: Congregation B'nai Amoona, 1982), 151.

28. The inscriptions are cited in Zevi, *Eric Mendelsohn,* 406. The 1952 quotations are cited in Michela Robbins, "Eric Mendelsohn Explains Theme for U.S. Memorial to Jews," *New York Times,* May 30, 1952. The memorial's ultimate failure is explained in Rochelle Saidel, *Never Too Late to Remember: The Politics Behind New York City's Holocaust Museum* (New York: Holmes and Meier, 1996), 50–52.

29. Sixty-one separate synagogue designs are listed in the Percival Goodman papers finding aid at Columbia University.

30. Taylor Stoehr, "The Goodman Brothers and *Communitas,*" in Kimberly J. Elman and Angela Giral, eds., *Percival Goodman: Architect, Planner, Teacher, Painter* (New York: Miriam and Ira D. Wallach Art Gallery, Columbia University in the City of New York, 2001), 17–18.

31. "The Reminiscences of Percival and Naomi Goodman," Oral History Office, Columbia University, 1990, 7–8. "To Study Synagogues," *New York Times,* June 22, 1947, 43.

32. Naomi Goodman, "A Memoir," in Elman and Giral, *Percival Goodman,* 165.

33. Stoehr, "The Goodman Brothers and *Communitas,*" 43.

34. In Richard Meier, ed., *Recent American Synagogue Architecture* (New York: Author, 1963), 20.

35. Goodman, "Memoir," 166.

36. Percival Goodman, "The Character of the Modern Synagogue," in Blake, *American Synagogue,* 87. Meier, *Recent American Synagogue Architecture,* 22.

37. Percival Goodman, "The Character of the Modern Synagogue," in Blake, *American Synagogue,* 88.

38. Quoted in Shirley M. Friedman, "Temple in Millburn Example of New Religious Architecture," *Newark Sunday News,* March 23, 1952, 43.

39. The 1947 quotation appears in Paul and Percival Goodman, "Tradition from Function," 543. Percival Goodman, "The Character of the Modern Synagogue," in Blake, *American Synagogue,* 92.

40. Percival Goodman, "Description of Temple Israel, Westport, Connecticut," April 1, 1959, 2. Box 6, Folder: "Temple Israel, Westport, Connecticut." In 1961, he explained that he preferred not to incorporate the Star of David in his synagogue designs because it had been used "by the Nazis as a badge of shame." Gertrude Benson, "Synagogue Designer Explains His Concept of Architecture," *Jewish Exponent,* October 20, 1961. Despite Goodman's aversion to incorporating Jewish symbols in his exteriors, Stars of David appeared in the form of diagonally crisscrossing window mullions in such synagogues as Beth Sholom in Miami, Temple Beth El in Providence, and Beth-El in Springfield, Massachusetts.

41. The closest he came to doing so was in claiming the existence of a Jewish architectural penchant for horizontality, which he cited as a rationale for his low-slung synagogue center complexes. As he put it in 1953, "Our religion, unlike the Christian, is horizontal: all is holy, the temple, the home, the mountain, and the valley. The Christian concept is vertical: from a point on the ground, man aspires to God." In making this claim, Goodman ignored the Talmudic mandate that a synagogue should be the tallest structure in any town where Jews reside. Kimberly J. Elman, "The Quest for Community: Percival Goodman and the Design of the Modern American Synagogue," in Elman and Giral, *Percival Goodman,* 58.

42. Alan Hess, *Googie Redux: Ultramodern Roadside Architecture* (San Francisco: Chronicle, 2004).

43. Evelyn L. Greenberg, "The Tabernacle in the Wilderness: The Mishkan Theme in Percival Goodman's Modern American Synagogues," *Jewish Art* 19/20 (1993/1994): 45–55.

44. The two synagogues were the Hauptsynagoge and the Klaussynagoge. Next to the stones on the brick wall of the sanctuary were the words, "To the heroes and martyrs; the known and the unknown; who died for the sanctifying of the divine name."

45. Letter from Harry Wische (president of B'nai Israel) to Major Hyman (advisor for Jewish affairs), February 10, 1950, Box 7, Folder 27: Max Gruenewald papers, Leo Baeck Center for Jewish History.

46. As he explained, "The Burning bush burned but was never consumed, which reflects the fate of our people." Wong, "Synagogue Art of the 1950s," 37.

47. Percival Goodman papers, Box 32, Folder 6: Millburn Synagogue (n.d.). Goodman invoked biblical passages and praised the construction workers for their labor but never mentioned the Nazi genocide.

48. Letter from Percival Goodman to Maurice Eisendrath, January 25, 1950. Percival Goodman Papers, Box 3: Competitions, Folder 10: American Monument to Six Million Jews, 1949–50.

49. Memorial statement attached to letter from Percival Goodman to A. R. Lerner, November 12, 1949. Percival Goodman Papers, Box 3: Competitions, Folder 10: American Monument to Six Million Jews, 1949–50.

50. On the south side of the memorial wall was engraved, "In memory of six million men, women, and children killed because they were Jews, 1939–1945. Erected by 8,000,000 Jews of America, their kin." Adjacent to these words was a figurative stone sculpture of a "great hand" and dead figures "springing into life, from death." Percival Goodman, "Sculpture—South Wall," n.d. Percival Goodman Papers, Box 3: Competitions, Folder 11: American Monument to Six Million Jews, 1949–50.

51. This resurrectionist discourse found expression in Erwin Sylvanus's play *Korczak and the Children* (which ends with an evocation of Ezekiel's prophecy), in Luise Kaisch's bronze doors at Pietro Belluschi's Temple Brith Kodesh in Rochester, New York (1964), and in Abraham Rattner's painting *Valley of the Dry Bones* (1963). Skloot, *Darkness We Carry,* 98; Kampf, *Contemporary Synagogue Art,* 229; Amishai-Maisels, *Depiction and Interpretation,* 176.

52. Percival Goodman Papers, Box 3: Competitions, Folder 10: American Monument to Six Million Jews, 1949–50. Letter from Percival Goodman to Benjamin Tabachinsky, April 25, 1957; "Typical Letter," n.d. (generic letter drafted by Goodman in response to his critics, probably 1950).

53. Saidel, *Never Too Late to Remember,* 50–51.

54. The Gruber quotation appears in Michael Z. Wise, "America's Most Prolific Synagogue Architect," *Forward,* March 9, 2001. Peter Eisenman, "Percival Goodman," in Elman and Giral, *Percival Goodman,* 141–42.

55. Wischnitzer, *Synagogue Architecture in the United States,* 137–41.

56. See, for example, the description of Percival Goodman's Beth Sholom synagogue in Miami. "Temple Beth Sholom, Miami Beach," *Architectural Record,* December 1953, 128.

57. For images of the Brandeis chapels, see *Architectural Record,* January 1956, 147–53. There were subtle differences in the three chapels' plans, which Abramovitz grounded in the doctrinal differences between the three faiths. The Abramovitz quotation appears in Wischnitzer, *Synagogue Architecture in the United States,* 176. The ecumenical attitude in religious architecture arose partly from the interfaith chapels built for Christian and Jewish servicemen during the Second World War. One of the most celebrated interfaith chapels was Eero Saarinen's chapel on the campus of MIT (1955). The Eisendrath quotation appears in Blake, *American Synagogue,* xiii.

58. Kampf, *Contemporary Synagogue Art;* Samuel Gruber, *American Synagogues;* Jarrassé, *Synagogues,* 227–51.

59. Samuel Gruber, *American Synagogues,* 112–16.

60. This, at least, is the claim of Franz Schulze, *Philip Johnson: Life and Work* (Chicago: University of Chicago Press, 1996), 239. Similar claims are made in Joan Ockman, "The Figurehead: On Monumentality and Nihilism in Philip Johnson's Life and Work," in Emmanuel Petit, ed., *Philip Johnson: The Constancy of Change* (New Haven: Yale University Press, 2009), 88–89; and Kazys Varnelis, *The Philip Johnson Tapes: Interviews with Robert A. M. Stern* (New York: Monacelli, 2008), 113. There is evidence, however, that the KTI design was actually based on Johnson's design for another synagogue, Temple Sholom, in Greenwich (an image of which in Varnelis's book is erroneously labeled a church, despite the presence of two menorahs flanking the *bimah*). See Chapter 3 of this study. To be sure, Johnson's Temple Sholom proposal may itself have been based on the Greenwich church design. Moreover, Johnson claimed that Temple Sholom was based on the "same design" for his own architectural office in New Canaan. Varnelis, *Philip Johnson Tapes*, 114. Either way, the ultimate design for KTI likely had non-Jewish origins.

61. "Church and Monastery for Portsmouth Priory," *Architectural Record,* July 1959, 147–48. Clausen, *Spiritual Space,* 27–29, 81–85, 108–11.

62. Samuel Gruber, *American Synagogues,* 124.

63. Jarrassé, *Synagogues,* 242. Samuel Gruber, *American Synagogues,* 140–45.

64. Cohen's goals are discussed in Brendan Gill, *Many Masks: A Life of Frank Lloyd Wright* (New York: Putnam, 1987), 463. Wright told Cohen that the synagogue's hexagonal floor plan and its sloping sides were meant to depict the "hands of God," enveloping congregants in comfort and security. Harvey Einbinder, *An American Genius: Frank Lloyd Wright* (New York: Philosophical Library, 1986), 356–67; see also Patricia Talbot Davis, *Together They Built a Mountain* (Lititz, Pa.: Sutter House, 1974), 50, 124. Cohen's remark about the "American spirit" is cited in Gill, *Many Masks,* 464; see also "The New Beth Sholom," Promotional Brochure for Beth Sholom (n.d., probably 1954). File: "Writings About Mortimer Cohen," Jewish Theological Seminary. The Steel Cathedral precedent is mentioned in Toker, *Fallingwater Rising,* 161. The synagogue's fame was immediate. It was prominently profiled in "Promised Hosanna," *Time,* May 31, 1954, and "New World Synagogues," *Time,* May 2, 1959. It received landmark status from the U.S. National Parks Service and the Secretary of the Interior in 2007.

65. Schulze, *Philip Johnson,* 104–46, 239. See also Michael Z. Wise, "Deconstructing Philip," *Forward,* October 20, 2006.

66. Schulze, *Philip Johnson,* 238–39.

67. Telephone conversations with Harvey Schiller and Jules Harris (congregants of KTI), November 28, 2007; conversations with Norma Perlstein and Ruth Albert (congregants of Temple Sholom), December 7, 2007. The architect was Ralph Pomerance (1907–95), the brother-in-law of famed historian Barbara Tuchman.

68. Fred Bernstein, "A Redesign Brings a Congregation Closer Together," *New York Times,* February 18, 2007. Telephone conversation with Olga Mack (daughter of Albert and Vera List), December 3, 2007. Telephone conversation with Robert Walker (congregant of KTI), December 10, 2007.

69. On Wright's antisemitism, see Toker, *Fallingwater Rising,* 131, 290. On Wright and Mumford, see Roger Friedland and Harold Zellman, *The Fellowship: The Untold Story of Frank Lloyd Wright and the Taliesin Fellowship* (New York: Regan, 2006), 355, 365; Bruce Brooks Pfeiffer and Robert Wojtowicz, *Frank Lloyd Wright and Lewis Mumford: Thirty Years of Correspondence* (New York: Princeton Architectural Press, 2001), 21–22, 181–82. On Wright and sedition, see Friedland and Zellman, *Fellowship,* 368. On Wright's tactical use of antisemitism, see Friedland and Zellman, *Fellowship,* 257–58, 284–85; Pfeiffer and Wojtowicz, *Wright and Mumford,* 123.

70. Wright stubbornly reminded E. J. Kaufmann in July 1946 that he had begged him "to be one Jew . . . who stood . . . against the Jewish clamor for war." Toker, *Fallingwater Rising,* 292.

71. George M. Goodwin, "Wright's Beth Sholom Synagogue," *American Jewish History,* 86.3 1998, 326–28. Wright had refused commissions for several synagogues earlier in his career, though it is unclear why. Davis, *Together They Built a Mountain,* 4.

72. Bruce Brooks Pfeiffer, *Frank Lloyd Wright: Letters to Clients* (Fresno: Press at California State University, Fresno, 1986), 314.

73. Isaacs, *Gropius,* 54, 81, 175–78, 180, 212–14, 194.

74. According to Samuel Gruber, Oheb Shalom first contacted Leavitt to design the synagogue, but recommended that he enlist "someone with a bigger reputation to . . . help [with] fund raising." Leavitt thereupon contacted Gropius, who contributed the distinc-

tive barrel vaulting to the synagogue's design. http://bersjewishartmonuments.blogspot.com/2009/12/usa-modern-synagogues-of-sheldon.html. Accessed April 14, 2010.

75. Isaacs, *Gropius*, 259–60, 253–54.

76. Samuel Gruber, *American Synagogues*, 129–30.

77. Johnson made this confession to John Cook and Heinrich Klotz in their coedited book *Conversations with Architects* (New York: Praeger, 1973), 36–37.

78. Wischnitzer, *Synagogue Architecture in the United States*, 177, 183. Richard Meier, "Introduction," in Meier, *Recent American Synagogue Architecture*, 7. The press reaction to the exhibition was only lukewarm. See Ada Louise Huxtable, "Architecture: Designs for American Synagogues," *New York Times*, October 5, 1963, 17.

79. Kampf, *Contemporary Synagogue Art*, 28–30, 37.

80. Stolzman and Stolzman, *Synagogue Architecture in America*, 196–202; Christopher Gray, "The Civic Center Synagogue; Contrasting Styles Are Startling on White Street," *New York Times*, December 24, 1989.

81. Gary Tinterow, "Post-World War II Synagogue Architecture," in *Two Hundred Years of American Synagogue Architecture* (Waltham, Mass.: American Jewish Historical Society, 1976), 34.

82. Kampf, *Contemporary Synagogue Art*, 57, 65. One exception identified by Kampf was artist Calvin Albert's lead-alloy ark doors at the Park Avenue Synagogue in New York, which he described as "ripped, burned, and still seething . . . as if they had been just . . . saved from the burning ghetto." Kampf, *Contemporary Synagogue Art*, 208. Other commemorative gestures towards the Holocaust included the display of Jewish liturgical objects salvaged from Nazi-ravaged Europe in synagogue interiors. Diner, *Jews of the United States*, 263.

Chapter 4.
Synagogues in Germany

1. Fewer than two dozen synagogues were erected in the young Federal Republic (and only one in the German Democratic Republic). The only new synagogue erected in the GDR was in Erfurt (1953). Ulrich Knufinke, "Neue Synagogen in Deutschland nach 1945," in Cohen-Mushlin and Thies, *Synagogen Architektur in Deutschland*, 98–99. A new synagogue was established in Dresden in 1950, but it was a renovation of an older mortuary chapel.

2. Salomon Korn, "Synagogenarchitektur in Deutschland nach 1945," in Hans-Peter Schwarz, ed., *Die Architektur der Synagoge* (Frankfurt: Deutsches Architekturmuseum, 1988), 301.

3. The figure of 1,000 synagogues represents two-thirds of the total in 1933. Korn, "Synagogenarchitektur in Deutschland," 309. Germany's Jewish population of just over 500,000 in 1933 totaled 15,000 by the end of the war. A year later, however, 200,000 Jewish displaced persons (DPs) arrived from Eastern Europe and soon created small temporary shuls for themselves in DP camps, private apartments, hospitals, and even air raid shelters. Korn, "Synagogenarchitektur in Deutschland," 292.

4. Whereas some synagogues prior to 1914 had been built to accommodate crowds numbering in the thousands (Berlin itself had more than a dozen), those built after 1945 were designed to hold at most several hundred. Hilmar Hoffmann, "Zum Geleit," in Schwarz, *Die Architektur der Synagoge*, 7.

5. *Synagogen in Berlin: Zur Geschichte einer zerstörten Architektur, Teil 2* (Berlin: Verlag Willmuth Arenhövel, 1983), 113–14.

6. Korn, "Synagogenarchitektur in Deutschland," 307–8.

7. See list of synagogues in Korn, "Synagogenarchitektur in Deutschland," 430–31, footnote 13.

8. Hermann Zvi Guttmann, *Vom Tempel zum Gemeindezentrum: Synagogen im Nachkriegsdeutschland* (Frankfurt: Athenäum, 1989), 13–14.

9. "Ein fast uferloser Optimismus: Offenbachs Synagogen nach 1945," in *Festschrift zum fünfzigjährigen Bestehen der Gesellschaft für christlich-jüdische Zusammenarbeit in Offenbach* (Offenbach, 2000). http://www.dienemann-formstecher.de/fraOffenbach.html.

10. Guttmann, *Vom Tempel zum Gemeindezentrum*, 42–53, 74–81, 82–89, 100–112.

11. Paul Betts, *The Authority of Everyday Objects: A Cultural History of West German Industrial Design* (Berkeley: University of California Press, 2004), chapter 3. André L. Jaumotte, "A Style Was Born: Design During the Fifties: Or the Triumph of Curvilinear Geometry," *Leonardo* 17, no. 3 (1984): 211–12.

12. Alan Hess, "The Origins of McDonald's Golden Arches," *Journal of the Society of Architectural Historians*, no. 1 (1986): 60–67.

13. Guttmann, *Vom Tempel zum Gemeindezentrum*, 11, 61. Primo Levi refers to the Tower of Babel in the context of the Holocaust in his memoir *Survival in Auschwitz* (New York: Collier, 1996), 72–73.

14. Guttmann, *Vom Tempel zum Gemeindezentrum,* 33, 47, 52, 102–03.
15. Ibid., 28, 36–37, 50. Leo Baeck's 1945 sermon also rejected "revenge." *Synagogen in Berlin: Zur Geschichte einer zerstörten Architektur, Teil 2,* 112.
16. Ernst Gottfried Lowenthal, *Die neue Synagoge in Duesseldorf: Zur Einweihung am 7 September 1958* (Düsseldorf, 1958), 30. "Ein fast uferloser Optimismus: Offenbachs Synagogen nach 1945."
17. Guttmann, *Vom Tempel zum Gemeindezentrum,* 54–55.
18. Kathrin Hoffmann-Curtius and Susan Nurmi-Schomers, "Memorials for the Dachau Concentration Camp," *Oxford Art Journal* 21, no. 2 (1998): 40; Young, *Texture of Memory,* 67.
19. Guttmann, *Vom Tempel zum Gemeindezentrum,* 54, 61.
20. Barbara Becker-Jákli, ed., *"Ich habe Köln doch so geliebt": Lebensgeschichten jüdischer Kölnerinnen und Kölner* (Cologne: Emons, 1999), 127.
21. This decision was due to confusion about the legality of his grandfather's marriage, which led the ministry to suspect that his grandfather was not Jewish. Ibid., 139.
22. Becker-Jákli, *"Ich habe Köln doch so geliebt,"* 146, 150; http://gavmayen.de/architekt.htm; Ruth Mader, "'Wir tauschten Pferdemist gegen Steine': Der jüdische Architekt Helmut Goldschmidt und der Wiederaufbau von Mayen," *Mayener Beiträge zur Heimatgeschichte,* no. 10 (2001): 63–79.
23. The smaller buildings were in Koblenz (1950), Wuppertal (1962), and Mönchengladbach (1967).
24. Guttmann's synagogue sat 400 in Düsseldorf, 300 in Hannover, and fewer than 100 in Offenbach. Goldschmidt's synagogue in Münster sat 150, Bonn sat 120, and Dortmund about 200. See Korn, "Synagogenarchitektur in Deutschland."
25. *Synagogengemeinde Zur Weihe der wiederhergestellten Synagoge Roonstrasse und des juedischen Kulturzentrums in Koeln; 20 Sept. 1959 (17 Elul 5719)* (Cologne, 1959), 30–31.
26. Helmut Goldschmidt, "Neubau der Synagoge in Bonn," *Allgemeine Wochenzeitung der Juden in Deutschland,* May 29, 1959, 19.
27. The 1990 quotation appears in Becker-Jákli, *"Ich habe Köln doch so geliebt,"* 144; the 1961 quotations about the Münster synagogue appear in Paul Spiegel, *Festschrift zur Weihe der neuen Synagoge in Muenster/Westf* (Muenster, 1961), 41–42.
28. Becker-Jákli, *"Ich habe Köln doch so geliebt,"* 151–52; *Synagogengemeinde Zur Weihe der wiederhergestellten Synagoge Roonstrasse und des juedischen Kulturzentrums in Koeln,* 7–8.
29. *Synagogengemeinde Zur Weihe der wiederhergestellten Synagoge Roonstrasse und des juedischen Kulturzentrums in Koeln,* 30.
30. Among the damaged synagogues that were demolished or functionally readapted for secular purposes were the Fasanenstrasse synagogue in Berlin, the Steelerstrasse synagogue in Essen, the Goethestrasse synagogue in Offenbach, and the Oberstrasse Temple in Hamburg.
31. Further research on these and other German synagogues is being pursued by the interdisciplinary German-Israeli organization Bet Tfila — Research Unit for Jewish Architecture in Europe. It is cosponsored by the Center for Jewish Art at the Hebrew University of Jerusalem and the Department of Architectural History the Technical University of Braunschweig (Brunswick) http://www.bet-tfila.org/en/pr-n45.htm.
32. *Festschrift zur Einweihung der Synagoge in Stuttgart am 18. Ijar 5712, 13. Mai 1952* (Stuttgart, 1952), 1–2.
33. *Festschrift zur Einweihung der Synagoge in Stuttgart,* 8–10, 22. http://www.alemannia-judaica.de/images/Images%20Bayern/GUGGENHEIMER-STG.pdf.
34. H. G. Sellenthin, *Geschichte der Juden in Berlin und des Gebaeudes Fasanenstrasse 79/80: Festschrift anlaesslich der Einweihung des Juedischen Gemeindehauses* (Berlin, 1959), 56–57.
35. "Neue Synagoge mit Gemeindezentrum Essen," *Der Baumeister,* February, 1961, 101.
36. Sellenthin, *Geschichte der Juden in Berlin,* 125. The architects did participate, however, in determining how the salvaged relics of the Fasanenstrasse synagogue would be incorporated into the final design. Biagia Bongiorno, "Spolien im 20. Jahrhundert: Das Jüdische Gemeindehaus in Berlin," *Das Münster,* no. 1 (2007): 52–56.
37. Sellenthin, *Geschichte der Juden in Berlin,* 122–23, 130, 126.

Chapter 5.
Jewish Architects and Secular Jewish Architecture

1. The building was hailed in 1947 as a "workshop for world peace." "UN Headquarters Progress Report," *Progressive Architecture,* June 1950, 60.
2. Abramovitz was the deputy director of planning; Harrison was the director of planning.
3. Edith Iglauer, "The UN Builds Its Home," *Harper's,* December 1947, 570.
4. Jews also played an important role promoting modern architecture,

whether as historians and critics, such as Sigfried Giedion, Nikolaus Pevsner, and Bruno Zevi, or photographers, such as Julius Shulman and Ezra Stoller.

5. On Elte, see Wischnitzer, *Architecture of the European Synagogue,* 262. On Wiesenthal, see Mary S. Costanza, *The Living Witness: Art in Concentration Camps and Ghettos* (New York: Free Press, 1982), 46–48.

6. Paul Goodman and Percival Goodman, "Jews in Modern Architecture," *Commentary,* July 1957, 29–31.

7. Ibid., 32, 34, 35, 28.

8. Diner, *Jews of the United States,* 209–10.

9. Shapiro, *Time for Healing,* 39.

10. On the origins of modern architecture, see Frampton, *Modern Architecture,* Leonardo Benevolo, *History of Modern Architecture* (Cambridge, Mass.: Harvard University Press, 1992), Henry-Russell Hitchcock, *Architecture: Nineteenth and Twentieth Centuries* (New York: Penguin, 1977), and Sigfried Giedion, *Space, Time and Architecture* (Cambridge, Mass.: Harvard University Press, 1982).

11. Isaac Deutscher, *The Non-Jewish Jew and Other Essays* (London: Oxford University Press, 1968), esp. chapter 1, 25–42.

12. Ezra Mendelsohn has called "universalism . . . a Jewish ideology." Ezra Mendelsohn, "Jewish Universalism: Some Visual Texts and Subtexts," in Jack Kugelmass, ed., *Key Texts in American Jewish Culture* (New Brunswick, N.J.: Rutgers University Press, 2003), 163. The overrepresentation of Jews in groups pursuing universalistic ideologies reflected their embrace of what David Sorkin has called the "ideology of emancipation," the idea that if they embraced secular western learning (known in Germany as *Bildung*), they would be able to assimilate and be granted civil and political equality. Ironically, the Jewish pursuit of *Bildung* enhanced Jewish group cohesion and placed Jews into their own subculture, which impeded their assimilation into European society. See David Sorkin, *The Transformation of German Jewry, 1780–1840* (New York: Oxford University Press, 1987).

13. Herbert J. Gans, "American Jewry: Present and Future," *Commentary,* May 1956, 422–24.

14. Diner, *Jews of the United States,* 116, 209.

15. On Jewish suburbanization and enduring fears of antisemitism, see Shapiro, *Time for Healing,* 195, 28; Diner, *Jews of the United States,* 223, 282. On anticommunist antisemitism, see James Rorty, "The Native Anti-Semite's 'New Look,'" *Commentary,* November 1954, 413–21. David Bernstein, "Jewish Insecurity and American Realities," *Commentary,* February 1948, 119, 120, 126, 127.

16. On Herberg, see Shapiro, *Time for Healing,* 53. On the deemphasis of Jewish particularism, see Diner, *Jews of the United States,* 223–24, 225. Henry Popkin, "The Vanishing Jew of Our Popular Culture," *Commentary,* July 1952, 46. There were no Jewish characters on prime-time television shows between 1954 and 1972. David Zurawik, *The Jews of Prime Time* (Hanover, N.H.: University Press of New England, 2003), 7. See also Leah Garrett, "Just One of the Goys: Salinger's, Miller's, and Malamud's Hidden Jewish Heroes," *AJS Review* 34, no. 2 (November 2010): 171–94.

17. Neutra rarely tackled larger projects, the main exception being his American Embassy in Karachi, Pakistan (1963). On the *Time* cover, see Toker, *Fallingwater Rising,* 336. For an authoritative assessment of Neutra, see Hines, *Richard Neutra and the Search for Modern Architecture,* 210.

18. Richard Neutra, *Life and Shape* (New York: Appleton-Century-Crofts, 1962). There is little doubt that Neutra would have been aware of Viennese antisemitism, given the notoriety of such anti-Jewish rabble rousers as Karl Lueger and Georg Ritter von Schönerer. Neutra mentions Lueger in *Life and Shape*. The quotations from the early 1920s are found in Hines, *Richard Neutra and the Search for Modern Architecture,* 45, 18, 55–56. The November 1922 quotation appears in Dione Neutra, *Richard Neutra, Promise and Fulfilment, 1919–1932: Selections from the Letters and Diaries of Richard and Dione Neutra* (Carbondale: University of Southern Illinois Press, 1986), 73.

19. Hines, *Richard Neutra and the Search for Modern Architecture,* 190–91.

20. Ibid., 194–96.

21. Some critics have claimed that his best buildings were produced with other architects and that his solo efforts were less accomplished. Other critics have declared that his "architecture . . . 'never lived up to'" his furniture." Hyman, *Marcel Breuer, Architect,* 14.

22. From 1932 to 1935, Breuer kept his apartment in Berlin, which he continued to visit, but he divided most of his time between Budapest and Zurich. Wilk, *Marcel Breuer,* 108, 126. Hyman, *Marcel Breuer, Architect,* see chapters 3–4.

23. Breuer worked on one other synagogue project, a 1961 plan for the B'nai Jeshurun congregation in Short Hills, New Jersey, which was never built. He also drew plans for a Jewish hospital in Zagreb, Yugoslavia, in 1930. Hyman, *Marcel Breuer, Architect,* 216, 225. On Breuer's church designs, see Hyman, *Marcel Breuer, Architect,* 219–30. No references to Jewish topics appear either in Marcel Breuer, *Sun and Shadow: The Philosophy of an Architect* (New York: Dodd, Mead, 1955) or Peter Blake, *Marcel Breuer: Architect And Designer* (New York: F. W. Dodge, 1949). The Meier quotations come from author interview with Richard Meier, March 23, 2010. For Gropius's antisemitic attitudes, see Isaacs, *Gropius,* 54, 81, 111. Breuer broke up his partnership with Gropius in 1941. Isaacs, *Gropius,* 247. Regarding Breuer's functionalism, Hyman writes, "to his students, Breuer would not speak about the aesthetics of architecture." Hyman, *Marcel Breuer, Architect,* 100.

24. Carol Krinsky, *Gordon Bunshaft of Skidmore, Owings & Merrill* (Cambridge, Mass.: MIT Press, 1988), 18–20. See Lewis Mumford, "House of Glass," *New Yorker,* August 19, 1952.

25. These included the Union Carbide Corporation headquarters (1960) and the Chase Manhattan Bank (1961).

26. On Bunshaft's religious upbringing, see *Oral History of Gordon Bunshaft: Interviewed by Betty J. Blum* © 1990 and 2000. The Art Institute of Chicago, used with permission, 4, 86. The Krinsky assessment is cited in an email to author from Carol Krinsky, January 26, 2007. For the 1936 quote, see letter from Gordon Bunshaft to the Rotch Traveling Scholarship Office, September 16, 1936. Gordon Bunshaft Papers, Columbia University, Box 1, Folder 16: "Correspondence." On Bunshaft's lack of sensitivity about being Jewish and his war service, see *Oral History of Gordon Bunshaft,* 85–86, 143–46. Bunshaft saw no fighting in the war, being stationed in London for two years and then shifting to Paris after the Germans had already been expelled. Carol Krinsky's exhaustive study of Bunshaft barely mentions the architect's Jewish background. Krinsky, *Gordon Bunshaft,* 2, 252.

27. On Bunshaft's functionalism and opposition to introspection, see Krinsky, *Gordon Bunshaft,* 331, 22. The 1972 quotation appears in David Jacobs, "The Establishment's Architect-Plus," *New York Times Magazine,* July 23, 1972.

28. *Oral History of Gordon Bunshaft,* 20, 230, 86.

29. In his unpublished autobiography, Kahn laconically wrote: "My father . . . came to the United States from Austria . . . [and my] mother was born in New York . . . of French lineage." Ely Jacques Kahn Autobiography (unpublished manuscript), "New Chapter III," 1. Avery Archive, Columbia University. On Kahn's experiences with anti-Jewish prejudice and his relationship with Mendelsohn, see Stern and Stuart, *Ely Jacques Kahn,* 48, 203. For the Holocaust memorial, Kahn had the minor responsibility of designing the foundation for Davidson's figurative sculpture. Saidel, *Never Too Late to Remember,* 48–49. Kahn's wife's anti-Zionism is cited in Stern and Stuart, *Ely Jacques Kahn,* 200.

30. Schindler was not recognized by the architectural establishment until the early 1970s. He was excluded from the 1932 MoMA exhibition on the International Style, which he resented. David Gebhard, *An Exhibition of the Architecture of R. M. Schindler* (Los Angeles: University of California, Santa Barbara, Art Gallery, 1967), 32–33. Judith Sheine, *R. M. Schindler* (Barcelona, 1998), 8–9. Kurt G. Helfrich, "Contextualizing 'Space Architecture': What the Schindler Archive Reveals," in Elizabeth A. T. Smith and Michael Darling, eds., *The Architecture of R. M. Schindler* (New York: Abrams, 2001), 163.

31. Smith and Darling, *Architecture of R. M. Schindler,* 96–97. Schindler married Pauline Gibling in 1919.

32. He had long been drawn to the United States, thanks to the recommendations of his mentor Adolf Loos, who had lived there in 1893–96, and his father, who had worked in New York City for ten months in 1880 and 1881. Richard Guy Wilson, "Schindler's Metaphysics: Space, the Machine, and Modernism," in Smith and Darling, *Architecture of R. M. Schindler,* 127.

33. Goldberg's father was also born in Chicago, while his grandfather had emigrated from Germany in the mid-nineteenth century. *Oral History of Bertrand Goldberg, interviewed by Betty J. Blum* © 1992, The Art Institute of Chicago, used with permission, 248–49. The 2001 edition is a revised version of the original 1992 interview.

34. Ibid., 18, 33, 35–36.

35. Ibid., 131–32. Lori Hanna Boyer, "Bertrand Goldberg and the Legacy of 1945," http://www.bertrandgoldberg.org/resources/bg_legacy.html.

36. Lapidus's other notable works include the Americana of New York Hotel (1962), which was the tallest concrete building in the world at the time of completion. Lapidus discusses his idiosyncratic forms in Morris Lapidus, *Too Much Is Never Enough* (New York: Rizzoli, 1996), 99. On critics' hostility to Lapidus, see "Lapidus Cuts Loose," *Architecture,* February 1997, 41. The Johnson quotation appears in Alice T. Friedman, "The Luxury of Lapidus: Glamour, Class, and Architecture in Miami Beach," *Harvard Design Magazine,* no. 11 (Summer 2000): 8.

37. Lapidus, *Too Much Is Never Enough,* 60.

38. Morris Lapidus, *Architecture: A Profession and a Business* (New York: Reinhold, 1967).

39. Lapidus designed the Shaare Zion Congregation in Brooklyn, New York (1954), the Hewlett-East Rockaway Jewish Centre (1950–54) on Long Island, Temple Beth-El in Saint Petersburg, Florida (1960), Temple Beth T'filoh in Pikesville, Maryland (1965), and Temple Judea in Coral Gables, Florida (1964). See Morris Lapidus, *Architect of the American Dream* (Basel, Switzerland: Birkhäuser Verlag, 1992), 222. The school building was the Hebrew Academy in Miami Beach (1960). Cook and Klotz, *Conversations with Architects,* 153, 176.

40. Friedman, "Luxury of Lapidus," 5–7. Huxtable, who herself is Jewish, summed up Lapidus's overall work as "uninspired superschlock."

41. Morris Lapidus, *An Architecture of Joy* (Miami: Seemann, 1979), 129, 214.

42. Another example is Eric Mendelsohn, who, before his death in 1953, designed the Maimonides Hospital in San Francisco (1948–50) and the Atomic Energy Commission Laboratory Building at the University of California at Berkeley (1952–53), in addition to several private homes in the Bay Area. None of these buildings exhibited any identifiable Jewish traits.

43. This assessment can be found in John Harwood and Janet Parks, *The Troubled Search: The Work of Max Abramovitz* (New York: Miriam and Ira D. Wallach Art Gallery, Columbia University, 2004), 34, 7. For a detailed discussion of Abramovitz's technological breakthroughs, see 46–63.

44. Abramovitz's family arrived in the United States in 1903, five years before he was born. *Max Abramovitz Oral Memoir,* interview by Jayne Hilary Bruns (New York, 1975), 12–14, 59, 69. Max Abramovitz Architectural Records and Papers Collection; Avery Archive, Columbia University: *Oral History Interview with Max Abramovitz,* interview by Sharon Zane. New York Oral History Project, Lincoln Center for the Performing Arts (New York, 1990), 267.

45. *Oral History Interview with Max Abramovitz,* 68–69, 18; *Max Abramovitz Oral Memoir,* 18, 29.

46. Max Abramovitz, "Trends in Synagogue Design," *Bulletin of the American Institute of Architects,* May 1948, 19–20. Max Abramovitz Papers, Published Material; Articles by Abramovitz, 1997.001.

47. Max Abramovitz, "Synagogues," typed draft dated March 3, 1947, 25. Max Abramovitz Papers, Published Material; Articles by Abramovitz, 1997.001.

48. On Abramovitz's army service, see *Oral History Interview with Max Abramovitz,* 75. On his exposure to antisemitism, see *Max Abramovitz Oral Memoir,* 159. On his entering class in architecture school and his sense of Jewishness, see *Max Abramovitz Oral Memoir,* 61, 14. Abramovitz's ability to live in a mixed world reflected the fact that "Chicago was not as Jewish conscious as New York." *Max Abramovitz Oral Memoir,* 13.

49. "Student Religious Center Based on Synagogue," *Architectural Record,* June 1948, 139–40.

50. He pursued other Jewish projects as well, including his Beth Zion synagogue in Buffalo, New York (1967); the Library of the American Jewish Historical Society in Waltham, Massachusetts (1960); the new home for the Hebrew Union College-Jewish Institute of Religion near the campus of New York University in 1979; and the West Point Jewish Chapel on the grounds of the U.S. Military Academy (1964–84). Harwood and Parks, *Troubled Search,* 138–39. Max Abramovitz Papers, Box 2 1997.004, Folder 64. In all these projects, Abramovitz felt little inclination to articulate Jewishness in architectural form.

51. *Max Abramovitz Oral Memoir,* 71–73. On the relevance of Jewishness to his work, Abramovitz noted, "I personally have . . . always been ready to contribute my services . . . as a Jew, but I haven't made a fetish of it" (162).

Chapter 6.
Toward a More Jewish Modernism

1. Laurie Kerr, "An Early Kahn Gem Restored," *Wall Street Journal,* February 13, 2007. The renovation was undertaken by James Stewart Polshek's firm, Polshek Partnership (recently renamed Ennead Architects).

2. Susan Braudy, "The Architectural Metaphysic of Louis Kahn," *New York Times Magazine,* November 15, 1970, 77.

3. Robert McCarter, *Louis I. Kahn* (London: Phaidon, 2005), 8.

4. See Khan, *International Style.*

5. According to David Brownlee, Kahn "must be assigned a role in the historicist tendency of recent decades." David Brownlee, Review of Sarah Williams Goldhagen, *Louis Kahn's Situated Modernism,* in *Journal of the Society of Architectural Historians* 61,

no. 2 (June 2002): 240.

6. He furthermore abandoned the modernist open plan in favor of plans that emphasized distinct spaces (which he referred to as "served" and "servant" spaces). David Brownlee and David G. De Long, *Louis I. Kahn: In the Realm of Architecture* (New York: NY Universe, 1991), 58–59.

7. Vincent Scully, "Louis I. Kahn and the Ruins of Rome," in Vincent Scully, *Modern Architecture and Other Essays* (Princeton: Princeton University Press, 2003), 311–17.

8. Sarah Williams Goldhagen, *Louis Kahn's Situated Modernism* (New Haven: Yale University Press, 2001), 13.

9. In reference to his Ahmedabad Institute of Management, Kahn asked: "Why hide the beauty of open brickwork? I asked the brick what it wanted and it said I want to be an arch, so I gave it an arch." Brownlee and De Long, *Louis I. Kahn*, 371.

10. Vincent Scully, "Introduction," in Brownlee and De Long, *Louis I. Kahn*, 13. McCarter, *Louis I. Kahn*, 8.

11. Heinrich Klotz, *The History of Postmodern Architecture* (Boston: MIT Press, 1988), 111. David Brownlee writes: "By reconnecting architecture with the fundamentals of history, he . . . awakened an entire generation of architects who followed." Brownlee and De Long, *Louis I. Kahn*, 71.

12. Scholars who stress Kahn's mystical and Jewish influences include John Lobell, *Between Silence and Light: Spirit in the Architecture of Louis I. Kahn* (Boulder, Colo.: Shambhala, 1979); Robert Coombs, "Light and Silence: The Religious Architecture of Louis Kahn," *Architectural Association Quarterly,* October 1981, 26–36; Joseph Burton, "Notes from Volume Zero: Louis Kahn and the Language of God," *Perspecta* 20 (1983): 69–70; Alexander Gorlin, "Biblical Imagery in the Work of Louis I. Kahn," *A + U,* May 1985, 83–92; Richard Saul Wurman, *What Will Be Has Always Been: The Words of Louis I. Kahn* (New York: Access, 1990); Alexandra Tyng, *Beginnings: Louis I. Kahn's Philosophy of Architecture* (New York: Wiley, 1984). Scholars who emphasize Kahn's practical side include Goldhagen, *Louis I. Kahn's Situated Modernism,* 91–92; Susan G. Solomon, *Louis I. Kahn's Trenton Jewish Community Center* (New York: Princeton Architectural Press, 2000). See also Solomon's dissertation, "Secular and Spiritual Humanism: Louis I. Kahn's Work for the Jewish Community in the 1950s and 1960s" (Ph.D. diss., University of Pennsylvania, 1997). Michael Lewis agrees, noting that while "religious qualities are often ascribed to Kahn's late architecture, . . . its religious spirit was by no means specifically Jewish" but rather "ecumenical." Lewis, "What Louis Kahn Built," *Commentary,* March 1992, 41–42.

13. Kahn invoked religion in discussing projects that involved assembly. Assembly, Kahn noted, had a "religious atmosphere"; "A house of legislation," he declared, "is a religious place." Brownlee and De Long, *Louis I. Kahn,* 82.

14. Until recently, most biographies of Kahn listed his birthplace as the Estonian town of Arensburg (today Kuressaare) on the island of Ösel (today Saaremaa). Carter Wiseman, however, contends that Kahn was born on the Estonian mainland in the town of Pernau (today Pärnu). Carter Wiseman, *Louis I. Kahn: Beyond Time and Style: A Life in Architecture* (New York: W. W. Norton, 2007), 13. Kahn and his immediate family did live in Arensburg for a time, however, as did other relatives. On Kahn's Jewish upbringing, see Solomon, *Louis I. Kahn's Trenton Jewish Community Center,* 1; Goldhagen, *Louis I. Kahn's Situated Modernism,* 91–92; Wiseman, *Louis I. Kahn,* 20. In 1950, the Kahn family sent a Christmas carol composed by their daughter Sue Ann that included the line "Jesus Christ our living king is born." Louis Kahn papers, University of Pennsylvania. 30.11.A.60.20.

15. On the mysticism of Kahn's mother and grandfather, see Burton, "Notes from Volume Zero," 75–76. Wiseman points out that Bertha's last name was Mendelowitsch. Wiseman, *Louis I. Kahn,* 13. Susan Solomon writes that "Kahn had neither a mystical outlook nor a firm grounding in Jewish texts, education, or practice." Solomon, *Louis I. Kahn's Trenton Jewish Community Center,* 1.

16. On Kahn's frequent moves and being called "scarface," see Anne Griswold Tyng, ed., *Louis Kahn to Anne Tyng: The Rome Letters, 1953–1954* (New York: Rizzoli, 1997), 14. Kahn's scarlet fever is mentioned in Brownlee and De Long, *Louis I. Kahn,* 20. The quotations by Safdie and Nathaniel Kahn appear in the film *My Architect.* Kahn's gregariousness is cited in Goldhagen, *Louis Kahn's Situated Modernism,* 3–4.

17. On the antisemitism faced by Kahn, see Goldhagen, *Louis Kahn's Situated Modernism,* 13. The Huff quotation appears in Wiseman, *Louis I. Kahn,* 58. In the film, *My Architect,* the architect and editor of Kahn's writings, Richard Saul Wurman, noted: "Blood was important in Philadelphia and . . . Lou's blood had a yellow armband." Michael Lewis adds that Jewish architects like Kahn found that "the great institutional patronage of the city was closed to them" due to the "inward-looking" orientation of its blue-blooded elite. Michael Lewis, "Kahn's Graphic Modernism," in Eugene J. Johnson and Michael J. Lewis, *Drawn from the Source: The Travel Sketches of Louis I. Kahn* (Cambridge, Mass.: MIT Press, 1996), 6–7. The Kahn and Howe episode appears in Peter Blake, *No Place Like Utopia* (New York: Knopf, 1993), 36. On the American Academy, see Fikret Yegül's *Gentlemen of Instinct and Breeding: Architecture at the American Academy in Rome, 1894–1940* (New York: Oxford University Press, 1991), which shows how the Academy regularly denied positions to Jews and women prior to World War II (21, 34, 36); see also Solomon, *Secular and Spiritual Humanism*, 22. On the other hand, Kahn was admitted to the Architectural Society, which had previously refused Jewish applicants. Wiseman, *Louis I. Kahn*, 26. The second Wurman quotation appears in *My Architect*.

18. On Kahn's 1928 visit, see McCarter, *Louis I. Kahn*, 25. On this trip, Kahn felt a close family bond, recalling in 1973 that when he visited relatives near Riga and "saw my people. . . . , I was very much moved by it." Wurman, *What Will Be Has Always Been*, 225. Kahn probably did not discuss the war frequently with his parents, who moved from the East Coast to California in the late 1930s and thereafter kept in contact mostly through letters. Wiseman, *Louis I. Kahn*, 47.

19. Brownlee and De Long, *Louis I. Kahn*, 42–43. Goldhagen, *Louis I. Kahn's Situated Modernism*, 26–27.

20. Solomon, *Louis I. Kahn's Trenton Jewish Community Center*, 5–12; Goldhagen, *Louis Kahn's Situated Modernism*, 14.

21. On Kahn's desire for monumentality, see Brownlee and De Long, *Louis I. Kahn*, 42. The 1953 quotation is cited in Solomon, *Louis I. Kahn's Trenton Jewish Community Center*, 22. Kahn's "techno-organicist" phase is discussed in Goldhagen, *Louis Kahn's Situated Modernism*, chapter 3.

22. The importance of Rome for Kahn is emphasized by Vincent Scully. See, for example, Scully's introduction to Brownlee and De Long, *Louis I. Kahn*, 12–14. The significance of Roman ruins is stressed by Brownlee (50). Joseph Burton has written that "it is with the discovery of the pyramid hieroglyphic . . . that the birth of Kahn's mature architectural creativity . . . began." Burton, "Notes from Volume Zero," 79. Kahn incorporated pyramidal forms into the Yale Art Gallery's hollow coffered tetrahedral ceiling and the Trenton Bath House's roofs (1956). The McCarter quotation appears on page 59.

23. On Kahn's 1949 trip, see Solomon, *Louis I. Kahn's Trenton Jewish Community Center*, 13. Kahn's view of Israel as a "new state" is cited in Solomon, *Secular and Spiritual Humanism*, 73, 74–80. Solomon's long quotation appears in *Louis I. Kahn's Trenton Jewish Community Center*, 17–19. Scully's observation about Kahn and Egypt is cited in Vincent Scully, "A Virtual Landmark," *Progressive Architecture*, September 1993. Kahn's "Zionist impulse" is mentioned in Solomon, *Louis I. Kahn's Trenton Jewish Community Center*, 28. Kahn referred to the immigrants arriving in Israel as "refugees." Undated draft of report: "Recommended Planning and Building Program." Louis I. Kahn Papers, 30.11.A.35.30.

24. Goldhagen, *Louis Kahn's Situated Modernism*, 105. Solomon, *Louis I. Kahn's Trenton Jewish Community Center*, 3. Brownlee, Review of Goldhagen, 239. As Kahn fondly recalled: "I discovered myself after designing that little concrete block bathhouse in Trenton." Solomon, *Louis I. Kahn's Trenton Jewish Community Center*, 137.

25. Brownlee and De Long, *Louis I. Kahn*, 63. "Avant-Garde Anachronist," *Time*, June 10, 1966.

26. Other Jewish projects never got beyond the early discussion stage with clients. These included a new library for the Jewish Theological Seminary and new buildings for Gratz College in Philadelphia. Letter from Louis Finkelstein to Louis Kahn, September 8, 1965. Louis I. Kahn Papers, 30.II.A.70.2. For Kahn's interest in the Gratz College project, see 30.II.A.64.35. On Kahn's failure to realize many of his designs, see McCarter, *Louis I. Kahn*, 391. Kahn's disdain for Wright's synagogue is evident in his remark that one should not design "an architecture school representing an Ionic column or a synagogue representing Mt. Sinai." Goldhagen, *Louis Kahn's Situated Modernism*, 152. The Kahn quotation about God is cited in Wurman, *What Will Be Has Always Been*, 16.

27. Solomon, *Secular and Spiritual Humanism*, 306–7; Brownlee and De Long, *Louis I. Kahn*, 401; McCarter, *Louis I. Kahn*, 405.

28. On Kahn's views of light, see Brownlee and De Long, *Louis I. Kahn*, 126–29. Kahn's views of silence and light grew out of his neo-Platonic distinction, which he made in 1960, between "form" and "design"—the former referring to the ideal structure, the latter to the method of producing it. Lobell, *Between Silence and Light,* 20.

29. Lobell, *Between Silence and Light,* 22.

30. Solomon, *Secular and Spiritual Humanism,* 300, 316–18.

31. In Kahn's papers, there is an April 28, 1961, issue of *Israel Digest,* which provided extensive coverage of the Eichmann trial. Kahn Papers, 30.11.A. 35.29. The fact that Kahn also kept clippings about Israel's difficult geopolitical situation from the same period supports the notion that he saw links between the Nazi past and Israel's present. Kahn kept many issues of the newsletters *Israel Digest* and *Near East Report.* See Louis I. Kahn Papers, 30.11.A.64.35. Among the Holocaust books read by Kahn were John Hersey's novel *The Wall,* Alexander Donat's study *Holocaust Kingdom,* and various issues of *Yad Vashem Studies.* Louis I. Kahn Papers. Kahn's desire for the memorial to promote healing is discussed in Solomon, *Secular and Spiritual Humanism,* 334, 341–42, 366.

32. Undated rough draft of essay, "The Memorial to Commemorate the Six Million Jewish Martyrs." A second draft of the same essay, "The Memorial to Commemorate the Six Million Jewish Martyrs," is dated May 3, 1968. Louis I. Kahn Papers, 30.II.A.36.6.

33. On the significance of immigration, see Solomon, *Secular and Spiritual Humanism,* 309. Kahn's remark about "dematerialization" is cited in McCarter, *Louis I. Kahn,* 405. The Solomon quotation is found in *Secular and Spiritual Humanism,* 362.

34. Ada Louis Huxtable, "Plan for Jewish Martyrs' Monument Here Unveiled," *New York Times,* October 17, 1968, 47. Solomon, *Secular and Spiritual Humanism,* 348, 352, 355, 370, 375, 376.

35. Kahn produced an earlier unrealized design for another synagogue, Adath Jeshurun synagogue in Philadelphia (1954–55). It was only marginally related to sources of Jewish influence, however, being mostly shaped by Kahn's interest in new building technologies, such as space frames. Solomon, *Secular and Spiritual Humanism,* 141–52.

36. For the most complete discussion of Mikveh Israel, see Susan G. Solomon, *Louis I. Kahn's Jewish Architecture: Mikveh Israel and the Midcentury American Synagogue* (Waltham, Mass.: Brandeis University Press, 2009), which expands upon Solomon's research in *Secular and Spiritual Humanism.* The Kahn quotation appears in Brownlee and De Long, *Louis I. Kahn,* 364. The Huxtable assessment appears in *New York Times,* October 5, 1963.

37. On Strickland and the sukkah, see Solomon, *Secular and Spiritual Humanism,* 263–65, 274–90. The Kahn quotation appears in Brownlee and De Long, *Louis I. Kahn,* 364. On the influence of Albi, see Eugene Johnson, "A Drawing of the Cathedral of Albi by Louis I. Kahn," *Gesta* 25, no. 1, Essays in Honor of Whitney Snow Stoddard (1986): 159–65; Paul Goldberger, "A Spiritual Quest Realized But Not in Stone," *New York Times,* October 13, 1996, 44.

38. Kieffer was the first scholar to identify the connection between Kahn's design and the sephirothic tree, describing in his self-published volume *Louis Kahn and the Ritual of Architecture* (1981) how a one-time employee in Kahn's office, Victor Rivera, noted the similarity of the Mikveh Israel plan to the cover image on the 1963 edition of Gershom Scholem's book *Zohar: The Book of Splendor* (New York: Schocken, 1963). See also Jeffry Kieffer, "A Reading of Louis Kahn's Salk Institute Laboratories," *A + U,* April 1993, 3–17. The image was a reproduction of the early modern text *Portae Lucis* by the sixteenth-century German Jewish convert to Christianity and professor of philosophy at the University of Pavia, Paulus Ricius (also known as Paolo Riccio). http://www.jewishencyclopedia.com/view.jsp?artid=273&letter=R&search=riccio.

In his most recent book, *Readings from the Architecture of Louis I. Kahn* (2001), 89, 111–12, Kieffer notes that he shared his information with Joseph Burton, then a Ph.D. candidate at Penn, who went on to examine the connection in his article "Notes from Volume Zero." See also Brownlee and De Long, *Louis I. Kahn,* 80, 92; Gorlin, "Biblical Imagery in the Work of Louis I. Kahn," 86.

39. Kent Larson, *Louis I. Kahn: Unbuilt Masterworks* (New York: Monacelli, 2000), 93.

40. On Jewish American painters' response to the Holocaust, see Ori Z. Soltes, *Fixing the World: Jewish American Painters in the Twentieth Century* (Waltham, Mass.: Brandeis University Press, 2002), 61–78, 117; Mark Godfrey, *Abstraction and the Holocaust.* Godfrey argues that Newman's synagogue design was created in 1951 and later unearthed for the synagogue architecture exhibition of 1963. Mark Godfrey, "Barnett Newman's Stations of the Cross," in Melissa Ho, ed., *Reconsidering Barnett Newman* (Philadelphia: Philadelphia Museum of Art, 2005), 63; Baigell, "Barnett Newman's Stripe Paintings and Kabbalah." For a discussion of Newman's views of the Kabbalah, see Thomas B. Hess, *Barnett Newman* (New York: Museum of Modern Art, 1971), 109–13. Hess argues that Newman was inspired by the same drawing of the sephirothic tree from the book *Portae Lucis* that inspired Kahn's Mikveh Israel design. Newman's Kabbalistic titles include *Moment* (1946), *Black Fire* (1963), and *White Fire* (1968). Newman also produced a sculpture, entitled *Zim Zum*, in 1969, featuring a series of eight-foot-high steel plates assembled in accordion-like fashion along the lines of his original synagogue plan. Nan Rosenthal, "The Sculpture of Barnett Newman," in Ho, *Reconsidering Barnett Newman*, 128–29.

41. Larson, *Louis I. Kahn*, 121.

42. Solomon, *Secular and Spiritual Humanism*, 318–19, 325, 329.

43. This was the phrase used in the introduction written by Stephen Kayser in Piechotka and Piechotka, *Wooden Synagogues*, 5.

44. Temple Beth-El's website is: http://www.bethelnw.org/about_temple/history.php?page=146. On Kahn's remarks at the dedication, see "Louis I. Kahn Remarks at Inauguration of New Temple Beth El, May Fifth, 1972," in scrapbook of articles on Temple Beth El, at Temple Beth El, Chappaqua, New York. On the creation of the memorial, see Gary Kriss, "Remembrances," *New York Times*, September 22, 1985, WC3. Solomon's claim about retroactivity is found in *Secular and Spiritual Humanism*, 399–401. The 1976 reference is found in the *Dispatch* (White Plains, New York), which described the synagogue as "modeled after the extinct wooden synagogues of Eastern Europe, particularly Poland." July 31, 1976. Located in scrapbook of articles on Temple Beth El, at Temple Beth El. A subsequent rabbi at the synagogue, Chaim Stern, emphasized the synagogue's links to the Holocaust in a letter to the editor to the *New York Times*, "A Monument to Modesty," October 27, 1996.

45. McCarter, *Louis I. Kahn*, 413. Kahn made his second trip to Israel in 1958 and later drafted plans for a new town called Besor. Solomon, *Secular and Spiritual Humanism*, chapter 4. The Israeli architect Ram Karmi was initially invited to submit a design but instead recommended Kahn.

46. On Kahn's research for the project, see Tamara Sue Morgenstern, "Origins, Meaning, and Memory in Louis I. Kahn's Hurva Synagogue Proposal" (master's thesis, University of California, Los Angeles, 1999), 43–49. The Kahn quotation is in Larson, *Louis I. Kahn*, 129.

47. These influences are all discussed in Larson, *Louis I. Kahn*, 135–39, and Morgenstern, "Origins, Meaning, and Memory," 43–49, 63–64, 35–38. See also Luis Mariano Akerman, "The Evocative Character of Louis Kahn's Hurva Synagogue Project, 1967–1974," in Bianca Kuhnel, ed., *The Real and Ideal Jerusalem in Jewish, Christian and Islamic Art: Studies in Honor of Bezalel Narkiss on the Occasion of His Seventieth Birthday* (Jerusalem: Jerusalem Center for Jewish Art, 1998), 245–53.

48. Morgenstern, "Origins, Meaning, and Memory," 55–57. Akerman, "Evocative Character of Louis Kahn's Hurva Synagogue Project," 252.

49. On Kahn's views of the beauty of ruins, see Brownlee and De Long, *Louis I. Kahn*, 70; see also Christopher Woodward, *In Ruins* (New York: Pantheon, 2002). The Scully quotation is found in Vincent Scully, "Foreword," in Larson, *Louis I. Kahn*, 9. Regarding the Hurva's political aspects, Jerusalem's Mayor Teddy Kollek told Kahn that it was problematic to "have a building of major importance which 'competes' with the Mosque and the Holy Sepulcher, and . . . the Western Wall of the Temple." Larson, *Louis I. Kahn*, 151. The Hurva has since been rebuilt; see Gavriel Rosenfeld, "A New Ruin Rising: The Hurva Synagogue's Latest Incarnation,'" *Forward*, November 9, 2007, B1.

Part III:
Jewish Architecture in the Postmodern Era

1. Stanley Tigerman, *Versus: An American Architect's Alternatives* (New York: Rizzoli, 1982), 28, 145.

Chapter 7.
Postmodernism, Post-Holocaust Culture, and Architectural Discourse

1. Samuel Moyn has written that the "development of post-Holocaust culture is coming to be understood as a transition between two regimes of memory. An initial period of repression gave way, after twenty years or more, to one of obsession." Moyn, "Two Regimes of Memory," *American Historical Review* 103, no. 4 (October 1998): 1182–86.

2. On the origins of postmodernity, see Jean-François Lyotard, *The Postmodern Condition: A Report on Knowledge* (Minneapolis: University of Minnesota Press, 1979). See also Jürgen Habermas, "Modernity—An Incomplete Project," in Hal Foster, ed.,

Postmodern Culture (London: Pluto, 1985), 3 – 15, and Habermas, "Modernity vs. Postmodernity," *New German Critique,* 1981, 2 – 14. See also Zygmunt Baumann, *Modernity and Ambivalence* (Oxford: Polity, 1991); David Harvey, *The Condition of Postmodernity* (Cambridge, Mass.: Blackwell, 1990), esp. part 2; Frederic Jameson, "Postmodernism or the Cultural Logic of Late Capitalism," *New Left Review,* July – August 1984, 52 – 92. On the left-wing origins of postmodernism, see Perry Anderson, *The Origins of Postmodernity* (London: Verso, 1998), chapter 2.

3. See Foucault's classic study *Madness and Civilization: A History of Insanity in the Age of Reason* (New York: Vintage, 1988). On Derrida, see Terry Eagleton, *Literary Theory: An Introduction* (Minneapolis: University of Minnesota Press, 1996), 127 – 34.

4. The modern notion of artistic autonomy dates back to Théophile Gautier's idea of "art for art's sake" (*l'art pour l'art*) in his 1834 novel *Mademoiselle de Maupin*. Donald Drew Egbert, *Social Radicalism and the Arts* (New York: Knopf, 1970), 153. The idea of aesthetic purity is found in Clement Greenberg's famous 1939 essay "Avant-Garde and Kitsch." Painting's pursuit of purity via purging is discussed in Steven Connor, *Postmodernist Culture: An Introduction to Theories of the Contemporary* (Oxford: Basil Blackwell, 1991), 83. Modern architecture's pursuit of purity diverged from the larger modernist movement's aversion to usefulness, as modern architects wanted form to follow function. The "great divide" between high and low culture is discussed in Huyssen, *After the Great Divide*. That some modernists resisted the elitist divide is shown by the efforts of the so-called avant-garde. Bürger, *Theory of the Avant-Garde*.

5. On pastiche, see Charles Jencks, *What Is Post-Modernism?* (London: Academy, 1996), 18; Linda Hutcheon, *A Poetics of Postmodernism: History, Theory, Fiction* (New York: Routledge, 1988), 5. On blurring cultural boundaries, see Connor, *Postmodernist Culture,* 153 – 54, 98 – 99.

6. The result was that modernist buildings were chronically subjected to misinterpretation. A famous example of modernism's inarticulateness was the fact that many visitors to the campus of the Illinois Institute of Technology, for example, could not distinguish between Ludwig Mies van der Rohe's chapel and the boiler house. Charles Jencks, *The Language of Post-Modern Architecture* (London: Academy, 1991), 28 – 29.

7. Nan Ellin, *Postmodern Urbanism* (Cambridge, Mass.: Blackwell, 1996), 1 – 6, 104 – 18. The return to history was related to the postmodern return to place. Harvey, *Condition of Postmodernity,* 272 – 83, 292. Among the dynamic trends that preceded postmodernism was the sculptural New Brutalist movement and the pop/utopian work of the British group Archigram.

8. Architectural historians in the 1980s struggled to define the movement. Diane Ghirardo termed it "theoretical postmodernism" and contrasted it to the "stylistic postmodernism" of Robert Stern, Michael Graves, and others. Ghirardo, "Past or Post Modern in Architectural Fashion," *Journal of Architectural Education,* no. 4 (1986): 2. For his part, Robert Stern referred to it as "schismatic postmodernism." Robert A. M. Stern, "The Doubles of Post-Modern," *Harvard Architecture Review,* Spring 1980, 83. Charles Jencks referred to it as "neo-Modernism." Jencks, *New Moderns*. Others used the term "neo-constructivists." Mary McLeod, "Architecture and Politics in the Reagan Era: From Postmodernism to Deconstructivism," *Assemblage,* February 1989, 24.

9. Ghirardo, "Past or Post Modern in Architectural Fashion," 4 – 5.

10. Most Jews appreciated how they had benefited politically from the Enlightenment ideals of freedom and equality (even as many realized that the demands of Enlightenment reason had forced them to sacrifice many of their religious traditions). David Biale, Michael Galchinsky, and Susannah Heschel, "Introduction," in Biale, Galchinsky, and Heschel, eds., *Insider/Outsider: American Jews and Multiculturalism* (Berkeley: University of California Press, 1998), 4 – 6.

11. On American Jews' growing affluence and security, see Shapiro, *Time for Healing,* 155, chapter 2. Alan Dershowitz, *Chutzpah* (New York: Little Brown & Co 1991), 7, 19.

12. Shapiro, *Time for Healing,* 151 – 52. Interest in the shtetl reflected the fact that Jews — unlike other ethnic groups in America — could not gaze back nostalgically to a single country of origin. Hana Wirth-Nesher, "Language as Homeland in Jewish-American Literature," in Biale et al., *Insider/Outsider,* 219.

13. Steven T. Rosenthal, *Irreconcilable Differences? The Waning of the American Jewish Love Affair with Israel* (Hanover, N.H.: University Press of New England, 2001). Roth's 1993 novel *Operation Shylock* featured a character, "Philip Roth," who urged Jews to leave Israel and return to Europe.

Kitaj's *First Diaspora Manifesto* (1989) affirmed the Diaspora as the foundation for contemporary Jewish art. See Sander L. Gilman, "R. B. Kitaj's 'Good Bad' Diasporism and the Body in American Jewish Art," in Steven Feinstein, ed., *Absence/Presence: Critical Essays on the Artistic Memory of the Holocaust* (Syracuse: Syracuse University Press, 2005), 167–93. See also Adam Shatz, "In Praise of Diasporism, or, Three Cheers for Irving Berlin," *Nation,* April 9, 2004. The construction of the National Yiddish Book Center and the publication of popular books on Yiddish, such as Michael Wex, *Born to Kvetch: Yiddish Language and Culture in All of Its Moods* (New York: St. Martin's, 2006), illustrated this trend, as did the success of such musical groups as the Klezmatics and Brave Old World.

14. In music, 2 Live Jews, Matisyahu, Hip Hop Hoodios, and Yidcore merged rap, reggae, salsa, and punk with Jewish melodies and lyrics. Zurawik, *The Jews of Prime Time,* chapters 4, 6, 7. http://jewishjournal.com/home/preview.php?id=13369. Expressions of Jewishness were also visible in high culture. Jewish artists followed in the multicultural footsteps of other ethnic groups by thematizing issues of Jewish identity (especially stereotypical ones) in their work, as was demonstrated by the major 1996 exhibition *Too Jewish?* at the Jewish Museum, New York. Norman Kleeblatt, ed., *Too Jewish? Challenging Traditional Identities* (New Brunswick, N.J.: Rutgers University Press, 1996). See also *New Jews.* Meanwhile, a "new wave" of young Jewish novelists, including Allegra Goodman, Michael Chabon, Jonathan Safran Foer, and Gary Shteyngart, made Jewish topics central to their literary narratives. Morris Dickstein, "Ghost Stories: The New Wave of Jewish Writing," *Tikkun,* November–December 1997, 33–37.

15. See www.heebmagazine.com. Julia Goldman, "High Gloss: After a Year in Print, Heeb Is Looking To Be More Than a Magazine ," *Jewish Week,* February 21, 2003, 43; Anthony Weiss, "VH-1 Goes Jewish," *Forward,* December 16, 2005, 2.

16. Alvin H. Rosenfeld, "The Americanization of the Holocaust," in Alvin H. Rosenfeld, ed., *Thinking About the Holocaust: After Half a Century* (Bloomington: Indiana University Press, 1997), 119–50. For a broader view, see Daniel Levy and Natan Sznaider's book, *The Holocaust and Memory in the Global Age* (Philadelphia: Temple University Press, 2006).

17. Gesine Schwan, *Politik und Schuld: Die zerstörerische Macht des Schweigens* (Frankfurt: Fischer, 1997). Nick Thomas, *Protest Movements in 1960s West Germany: A Social History of Dissent and Democracy* (Oxford: Berg, 2003).

18. In Germany, the interest of leftists in probing the economic roots of what they broadly defined as fascism led them to ignore the subjects of antisemitism and the Holocaust; the political right, meanwhile, ignored them in favor of focusing on its official postwar stance of philosemitism. Hans Kundnani, *Utopia or Auschwitz: Germany's 1968 Generation and the Holocaust* (New York: Columbia University Press, 2009). Y. Michal Bodemann, *In den Wogen der Erinnerung* (Berlin: Deutscher Taschenbuch Verlag, 2002). In France, the general trend was not to differentiate the Jewish experience from that of other Frenchmen and women during the Second World War. This began to change in the late 1960s following the Treblinka Affair. Samuel Moyn, *The Treblinka Affair* (Waltham, Mass.: Brandeis University Press, 2005).

19. The scholarship, literature, and films produced by American Jews on the Holocaust — especially the NBC docudrama *Holocaust* — played an important role in reminding ordinary Germans about the Nazi genocide. Shlomo Shafir, "Constantly Disturbing the German Conscience: The Impact of American Jewry," in Dan Michman, ed., *Remembering the Holocaust in Germany, 1945–2000* (New York: Lang, 2002), 121–41. Pierre Vidal-Naquet, *Assassins of Memory: Essays on the Denial of the Holocaust* (New York: Columbia University Press, 1992).

20. Geoffrey H. Hartmann, ed., *Bitburg in Moral and Political Perspective* (Bloomington: Indiana University Press, 1986). Charles Maier, *The Unmasterable Past: History, Holocaust, and German National Identity* (Cambridge, Mass.: Harvard University Press, 1988); Henry Rousso, *Vichy Syndrome.*

21. The Hitler Wave was sparked by Albert Speer's 1969 bestselling memoir, *Inside the Third Reich* (New York: Macmillan, 1970), and was followed by Werner Maser's *Hitler: Legend, Myth and Reality* (New York: Harper and Row, 1974) and Joachim Fest's *Hitler* (New York: Jovanovich, 1974), among others. The fascination with fascist imagery was visible in films, such as Luchino Visconti's *The Damned* (1969), Liliana Cavani's *The Night Porter* (1973), and Hans-Jürgen Syberberg's *Hitler: Ein Film aus Deutschland* (1977); in novels, such as George Steiner's *The Portage to San Cristobal of A. H.* (1982); in works of art, such as German painter Anselm Kiefer's early 1970s series of photographs and paintings portraying Hitler salutes; and in the music of popular rock acts like David Bowie, Kiss, and Pink Floyd. See Saul Friedlander, *Reflections of Nazism: An Essay on Kitsch and Death* (New York: Harper and Row, 1982) and Alvin H. Rosenfeld, *Imagining Hitler* (Bloomington: Indiana University Press, 1985). Lisa Saltzman, *Anselm Kiefer and Art After Auschwitz* (Cambridge, U.K.: Cambridge University Press, 1999).

22. By the 1970s, two competing "intentionalist" and "functionalist" schools of thought on the Holocaust's origins had emerged. Soon thereafter, academic debates about the Holocaust entered the mainstream, with the Historians' Debate of 1986–87 and the controversy over Daniel Goldhagen's *Hitler's Willing Executioners,* a decade later, testifying to the general public's increasing interest in Holocaust scholarship.

23. Feldman hinted that his percussion piece "The King of Denmark" (1964) and his arrangement "Rothko Chapel" (1971) were inspired by the events of the Holocaust. Alex Ross, "American Sublime: Morton Feldman's Mysterious Musical Landscapes," *New Yorker,* June 19, 2006. Steve Reich wrote the composition "Different Trains" in 1988 to illustrate the differences between train travel in the United States and Nazi-occupied Europe. Nathan-Davis, "Music of the Holocaust," 811. The Holocaust also influenced popular rock bands, such as Rush, whose 1984 song "Red Sector A" was inspired by lead singer Geddy Lee's desire to honor his mother, a survivor of Bergen-Belsen. Scott Benarde, "How the Holocaust Rocked Rush Front Man Geddy Lee," *Jewish News Weekly of Northern California,* June 25, 2004. George Tabori's Holocaust-related plays from this period include *My Mother's Courage* (1979) and *Jubilee* (1983); R. B. Kitaj dealt with aspects of Jewish suffering under the Nazis in such works as *If Not, Not* (1975–76), *The Jew* (1976–79), and *The Jewish School (Drawing of a Golem)* (1980). In these works Kitaj explicitly tried to create an appropriate "post-Auschwitz" form of "Jewish art." Amishai-Maisels, *Depiction and Interpretation,* 318–23. Kitaj published his *First Diaspora Manifesto* in 1989. Memorials were built in American cities such as New York (1982 and 1985), San Francisco (1984), Los Angeles (1991), and Boston (1995), as well as in cities throughout the Federal Republic of Germany. Young, *Texture of Memory.*

24. Dora Apel, *Memory Effects: The Holocaust and the Art of Secondary Witnessing* (New Brunswick, N.J.: Rutgers University Press, 2002), 6–7.

25. Robert Eaglestone, *The Holocaust and the Postmodern* (Oxford: Oxford University Press, 2005), 251; Alan Milchman and Alan Rosenberg, eds., *Postmodernism and the Holocaust* (Amsterdam: Rodopi, 1998). Jean-François Lyotard's book on the incompatibility of language games, *Le Differend* (1983), was partly inspired by his reflections on Holocaust denial. Lyotard, *The Differend: Phrases in Dispute* (Minneapolis: University of Minnesota Press, 1988). Allan Stoekl, "Blanchot, Violence, and the Disaster," in Lawrence D. Kritzman, ed., *Auschwitz and After: Race, Culture, and the "Jewish Question" in France* (New York, 1995), 133–48. Maurice Blanchot's book *The Writing of the Disaster* (1980) pointed to the Holocaust as proving both the impossibility (and necessity) of writing. Derrida's assault on the western metaphysical philosophical tradition was expressed in idiosyncratic conceptual terms — "cinders," "traces," "shadows," "absence," "deportation," "diaspora" — that reflected the Holocaust's impact on his thinking. For a broader discussion, see David Michael Levin, "Cinders, Traces, Shadows on the Page: The Holocaust in Derrida's writing," in Milchman and Rosenberg, *Postmodernism and the Holocaust,* 265–86.

26. Bauman and Aly argued that the Holocaust's origins lay in the modern bureaucratic drive toward social engineering, capitalist exploitation, and revolutionary modernization. Götz Aly and Susanna Heim, *Vordenker der Vernichtung* (Hamburg: Hoffmann und Campe, 1991), Zygmunt Baumann, *Modernity and the Holocaust* (Ithaca, N.Y.: Cornell University Press, 1989). White claimed that the Holocaust's magnitude required new modes of historical narration to adequately represent the event. See Hayden White, "Historical Emplotment and the Problem of Truth," in Saul Friedlander, ed., *Probing the Limits of Representation: Nazism and the "Final Solution"* (Cambridge, Mass.: Harvard University Press, 1992), 50–52.

27. Barbara Foley, "Fact, Fiction, Fascism: Testimony and Mimesis in Holocaust Narratives," *Comparative Literature,* Autumn 1982, 354–58. Sue Vice, *Holocaust Fiction* (London: Routledge, 2000).

28. Lanzmann's film was partly inspired by the issues of representation raised by the NBC docudrama *Holocaust,* which was criticized by intellectuals as a soap opera that aestheticized the concentration camp universe and reduced it to a commodity.

29. The postmodern return to figuration was visible in many of Kiefer's works, such as *Margarethe* (1981) and *Sulamith* (1983), both of which played off Paul Celan's famous poem "Death Fugue." Saltzman, *Anselm Kiefer and Art after Auschwitz,* 58, 29–32. The postmodern blurring of original and copy was visible in Audrey Flack's 1975 painting *World War II (Vanitas),* which featured a rendition of Margaret Bourke-White's famous photo of concentration camp inmates at Buchenwald; feminist theory informed Judy Chicago's multimedia "Holocaust Project" (1993), which controversially interpreted the Nazi genocide as an extreme example of male domination. Baigell, *Jewish-American Artists and the Holocaust,* 95–96; Rosenfeld, "Americanization of the Holocaust," 131–34.

30. For example, Jochen and Esther Gerz's "Monument Against Fascism" in Hamburg-Harburg was a steel pillar that was gradually lowered into the ground after its original installation in 1986 until it completely disappeared in 1993. James Young, *At Memory's Edge: After-Images of the Holocaust in Contemporary Art and Architecture* (New Haven: Yale University Press, 2000).

31. Gavriel D. Rosenfeld, "The Architects' Debate: Architectural Discourse and the Memory of Nazism in the Federal Republic of Germany, 1977–1997," in Geulie Ne'eman Arad, ed., *Passing into History: Nazism and the Holocaust Beyond Memory,* special issue of *History and Memory,* no. 1/2 (Fall 1997): 193.

32. Already in the early 1970s Charles Jencks and Philip Johnson had highlighted these connections. See Jencks, *Modern Movements in Architecture* (Garden City, N.Y.: Anchor, 1973); for Johnson's remarks, see John W. Cook and Heinrich Klotz, *Conversations with Architects* (New York: Praeger, 1973), 37–38.

33. Rosenfeld, "Architects' Debate," 200.

34. Leon Krier, "Eine Architektur der Sehnsucht," reprinted in *Bauwelt,* no. 28/29 (1987): 1037, 1043.

35. Krier, "Eine Architektur der Sehnsucht," 1041, 1045. Krier, in the words of Peter Neitzke, wished to "eliminate the memory of the *underside* of the . . . splendor that survives in the photographs of . . . [Speer's architectural] monuments. Neitzke, "Wollustige Beklemmung—hinreißende Bilder," *Bauwelt,* no. 28/29 (1987): 1049.

36. Dean, *Bruno Zevi on Modern Architecture,* 114, 98, 105.

37. *Towards an Organic Architecture* was first published in Italian and appeared in English in 1950. See esp. 96, 105–12. The 1967 speech is cited in Dean, *Bruno Zevi,* 150–51. Zevi cited Gropius's monumental American Embassy in Athens (1959–61) and Mies's austere Seagram Building in New York as prime examples of this trend, and singled out Max Abramovitz and Wallace Harrison's complex of buildings at Lincoln Center in New York as the "biggest scandal of recent years." Zevi's criticism of the "classicizing trend" is found in Dean, 55. The 1967 quotation is found in Dean, 149. The idea that modernism was reverting to classicism is discussed in Zevi, *The Modern Language of Architecture* (1967), 51.

38. Dean, *Bruno Zevi,* 156–57.

39. Ibid., 157, 161.

40. Ibid., 164–65.

41. Ibid., 164.

42. Ibid., 163–65.

43. Ibid, 60. Zevi's lack of Jewish education is shown by his negative reply to Cecil Roth's invitation to contribute a chapter on contemporary Jewish architects to *Jewish Art: An Illustrated History;* he wrote, "I do not know enough to write such a chapter." Letter from Bruno Zevi to Cecil Roth, November 6, 1954, in Percival Goodman papers, Box 31, Folder 19: MS-Religion. The quotation from the Association for Organic Architecture is found in Dean, *Bruno Zevi,* 17–22, 39. The 1945 quotation is found in Zevi, *Towards an Organic Architecture,* 144. The 1979 quotation is found in Dean, *Bruno Zevi,* 89, while the final quotation is found at 60.

44. Dean, *Bruno Zevi,* 89, 40, 90, 116. Zevi directed his ire at the postmodernism revival of Beaux-Arts classicism—epitomized by Philip Johnson's "grotesque atrocity," the AT&T building in New York City. He described Rossi's modernized classicism as an "architecture of death" that stood for "authoritarian formalism, [and] suicide."

45. Ibid., 91.

46. Ibid., 160.

47. Ibid., 92.

48. Ibid., 94.

Chapter 8.
The Deconstructivists

1. Mark Wigley, "Deconstructivist Architecture," in Philip Johnson and Mark Wigley, eds., *Deconstructivist Architecture* (Boston: Little, Brown, 1988), 10–11.

2. The term "deconstructivism" was coined by the architecture critic Joseph Giovannini. See Giovannini, "Breaking All the Rules," *New York Times Magazine,* June 12, 1988.

3. Indeed, an aesthetics of instability was present in western architecture in the 1970s, before the influence of deconstruction had even been felt, in such designs as those by James Wines's firm SITE, including the BEST supermarket chain in the 1970s and an entry in the Frankfurt Museum of Modern Art competition (1983). Wines, *De-Architecture* (New York: Rizzoli, 1987), 152–59, 144–52.

4. Gehry asserted: "I am not a deconstructivist! That term really drives me crazy." "Frank Gehry: The American Center in Paris," *The New Modern Aesthetic* (London: Academy, 1990), 74.

5. Philip Johnson emphatically asserted that "deconstructivist architecture is not a new style." Wigley, "Deconstructivist Architecture," 7.

6. Deconstructivism's pessimism was echoed by its antihumanism. See Jencks, *New Moderns,* 17. The Tschumi remark is cited in Joseph Giovannini, "The Limit of Chaos Tempts a New School of Architects," *New York Times,* February 4, 1988, C1. Herbert Muschamp first used the term "parabuilding" in his article "One Way to Get Taller in a City of Giants," *New York Times,* May 16, 1999, B2. The Wigley quotation is found in Wigley, "Deconstructivist Architecture," 18.

7. Anthony Vidler, "Deconstruction Boom," *Artforum International,* December 2003, 33.

8. This oversight was especially true at the time of the MoMA exhibition. The most important exception was Charles Jencks, who alluded to the prominence of Jews within what he called the "Neo-Modernist" movement. See Jencks, "The Resurrection and Death of the New Moderns," in *New Modern Aesthetic,* 23, 31. Somewhat later, Aaron Betsky took note of this as well in his article "Building Absence: The Jewish Conspiracy in Architecture," *Archis,* no. 7 (1998): 41–47. More recently, Karyn Ball has explored the existence of a "Jewish" style of memorial design known as "deconstructive minimalism." Ball, *Disciplining the Holocaust* (Albany: SUNY Press, 2008), 89.

9. That said, these architects exhibited many of the same traits as their Jewish deconstructivist colleagues. Hadid, Koolhaas, Tschumi, and the firm of Coop Himmelb(l)au were all outsiders to the mainstream architectural profession; they also exhibited a penchant for theorizing over building, an interest in art and sculpture, and what Bruno Zevi would call a "Hebraic" tendency toward ebullient expressionism rather than sober rationalism or traditional classicism. The Iraqi-born British citizen Hadid has been seen as expressing "personal history as a cultural and political exile" in her dynamically expressive architecture. Herbert Muschamp, "Women of Steel," *New York Times Magazine,* March 28, 2004, 63.

10. See Philip Johnson's remarks about Eisenman and Gehry in *Peter Eisenman and Frank Gehry* (New York: Rizzoli, 1991), 3–4. Bruno Zevi in 1992 called Eisenman, Gehry, and Libeskind the three "most significant Jewish architects in the world today." "Interview with the Editor of L'Architettura, Prof. Bruno Zevi," *Architecture of Israel Quarterly,* August 1992, 49.

11. Eisenman was a driving force behind MoMA's "Deconstructivist Architecture" exhibition and lent the movement much of its conceptual integrity. Schulze, *Philip Johnson,* 398. Originally, Eisenman wanted the show to be called "Violated Perfection" or "Deconstruction," but he was overruled by museum officials. Jencks, *New Moderns,* 222.

12. Rizzi, *Peter Eisenman: Mystisches Nichts;* Jencks, *New Moderns,* 250.

13. The Whites gained visibility in an exhibition at the Museum of Modern Art in 1969, followed up by the book *Five Architects* (New York: Oxford University Press, 1975), written in 1972.

14. Klotz, *History of Postmodern Architecture,* 211.

15. Kenneth Frampton, "Eisenman Revisited: Running Interference," in Arie Graafland, ed., *Peter Eisenman: Recent Projects* (Amsterdam: Nijmegen, 1989), 50. Diane Ghirardo, *Architecture After Modernism* (London: Thames and Hudson, 1996), 34.

16. Houses IV and V were unbuilt. Cynthia Davidson, ed., *Tracing Eisenman: Peter Eisenman, Complete Works* (New York: Thames and Hudson, 2006), 396.

17. In *The Order of Things: An Archaeology of Human Sciences* (New York: Random House, 1994), Foucault described how modern scientific fields of inquiry decentered humankind by illuminating the existence of impersonal and structural forces that determined existence. Peter Eisenman, "Editorial: Post-Functionalism," *Oppositions,* Fall 1976, n.p.

18. For a survey of Eisenman's architectural transition at this time, see Thomas Patin, "From Deep Structure to an Architecture in Suspense: Peter Eisenman, Structuralism, and Deconstruction," *Journal of Architectural Education,* November 1993, 88–100.

19. Eisenman, "Editorial: Post-Functionalism."

20. Eisenman's paternal grandfather came to the United States in the 1880s.

His American-born father "was a lefty . . . up until the 1938 Moscow trials. . . . He was anti-religion and we never went to synagogue." Author interviews with Peter Eisenman, December 5, 2006, and March 14, 2007. "The Peter Principles," *Architecture,* November 1998, 92. Niklas Maak, "Im Stelengang," *FAZ,* August 16, 2003, 31. Simon Houpt, "Building a Different View of Memory," *Toronto Globe and Mail,* February 7, 2001.

21. Jencks, *New Moderns,* 209 – 11; author interviews with Peter Eisenman, December 5, 2006, and March 14, 2007.

22. Author interviews with Peter Eisenman, December 5, 2006, and March 14, 2007.

23. Ibid. Allan Temko, "Creating a Jewish Sense of Space," *San Francisco Sunday Examiner and Chronicle,* December 8, 1996, 51.

24. Eisenman's remarks to Krier appear in "Interview: Leon Krier and Peter Eisenman," *Skyline,* February 1983, 14. The 1985 quotation is cited in Janet Abrams, "(Mis)Reading Between the Lines," *Blueprint,* February 1985, 16 – 17. Eisenman's remark to Derrida is found in Jeffrey Kipnis, ed., *Chora L Works* (New York: Monacelli, 1997), 7 – 8. Eisenman noted, "There were no graven images in the temple, and . . . the Hebrew language contains no present tense of the verb 'to be' — only 'was' and 'will be.' Thus Hebraic thought deals more with absence than presence. . . . [It] might [therefore] be interesting to . . . construct a relationship between Hebraic and architectural thought."

25. Eisenman's shift in intellectual interests is described in "Interview: Peter Eisenman," *Transition,* April – July 1984, 37. Eisenman's interests in Steiner and Adorno are found in author interview with Peter Eisenman, December 5, 2006. References to Hiroshima reflected the intensifying fears of nuclear war between the United States and Soviet Union in the early 1980s following the Soviet invasion of Afghanistan and the crisis over the stationing of Pershing missiles in West Germany. Culturally, these fears were illustrated by the primetime airing of the television film *The Day After* in 1983.

26. Eisenman has denied any connection, noting that he and Zevi never agreed on architectural matters. Author interview with Peter Eisenman, December 5, 2006. Eisenman's invocation of Zevi's idea of Hebraic architecture in 1985, however, suggests otherwise.

27. Peter Eisenman, "Behind the Mirror: On the Writings of Philip Johnson," *Oppositions,* Fall 1977, 12. These remarks were reprinted in Philip Johnson, *Writings: Philip Johnson* (New York: Oxford University Press, 1979), 22 – 23.

28. Peter Eisenman, "The House of the Dead as the City of Survival," in *Aldo Rossi in America, 1976 to 1979* (New York: Institute for Architecture and Urban Studies, 1979), 5, 15. Eisenman further used Holocaust imagery to describe Rossi's Elementary School at Fagano Olona, where he described the library as the "antechamber of the death camps and the light fixtures . . . as gas jets" (13).

29. The 1977 remark appears in Eisenman, "Behind the Mirror," 12. The "mythos" quotation is cited in "Interview: Peter Eisenman," 37. The final quotation is found in Peter Eisenman, "The Futility of Objects: Decomposition and the Process of Difference," *Harvard Architectural Review,* Winter 1984, 65.

30. The first three quotations in this paragraph are found in Eisenman, "Futility of Objects," 65 – 66. The 1983 remark is found in "Interview: Leon Krier and Peter Eisenman," 12. The 1982 remark is found in "Interview: Robert Venturi and Peter Eisenman," *Skyline,* July 1982, 14.

31. The quotation about a "centerless world" is found in "Interview with Peter Eisenman," *Yale Seminars in Architecture* (New Haven, 1982), 2: 79. The "vector" quotation is in Peter Eisenman, "Misreading," in *Houses of Cards* (New York: Oxford University Press, 1987), 172. The remark about anthropocentrism is cited in Eisenman, "Futility of Objects," 66.

32. The "third way" remark is found in Eisenman, "Futility of Objects," 67. The quotations about a "transgressive" architecture that is "not-classical" are found in "Futility of Objects," 66, and Peter Eisenman, "The End of the Classical: The End of the Beginning, the End of the End," in K. Michael Hays, *Architecture Theory Since 1968* (Cambridge, Mass.: MIT Press, 1998), 531. The quotation about not symbolizing function is cited in Peter Eisenman, "Post-El Cards: A Reply to Jacques Derrida," *Assemblage,* no. 12 (August 1990): 16. The quotations about not symbolizing "enclosure" or "shelter," as well as about "dislocating architecture," are in Peter Eisenman, "Blue Line Text," *Architectural Design,* August 1988, 7 – 8. The remarks about "instabilities" and "presence and absence" are in Eisenman, "Misreading," 185. As Eisenman noted to Jacques Derrida, "I am preoccupied with absence. . . . because architecture . . . is dominated by presence." Eisen-

man, "Post-El Cards," 15. The quotation about "traces" is in Eisenman, "End of the Classical," 533, 537, n22.

33. Eisenman's remarks about the L-shape and psychoanalysis are found in Jencks, *New Moderns,* 229–30, 210. Mark Taylor, *Disfiguring: Art, Architecture, Religion* (Chicago: University of Chicago Press, 1992), 265–67. Renato Rizzi offers a Kabbalistic interpretation of the El-shape, calling it a "contracted cube" resembling God's withdrawal from the world into himself (Rizzi, *Peter Eisenman,* 68).

34. Artificial excavation was influenced by Rossi's belief that buildings preserve collective memory and Derrida's concepts of the trace and the palimpsest. Eisenman first employed artificial excavation in his Canareggio Town Square project in Venice (1978). His site-specific orientation is highlighted on his firm's website, which declares that "Eisenman Architects' unique approach to design projects is to consider the layers of physical and cultural archaeologies at each site, not just the obvious . . . programs of a building." See the link "Firm Profile" at http://www.eisenmanarchitects.com.

35. Peter Eisenman and Jacquelin Robertson, Koch-Friedrichstrasse, Block 5, *Architectural Design,* no. 1/2 (1983): 91. Other architects recognized the project's connection to the Nazi era. Stanley Tigerman, for instance, praised Eisenman's design "for showing the rupture of 1945, the Holocaust." "Interview with Stanley Tigerman," *Transition,* April–July 1984, 26.

36. Quoted in "Peter Eisenman, Wexner Center for the Visual Arts," *Architectural Design,* no. 3/4 (1988): 63.

37. "Interview: Peter Eisenman," 42.

38. Indeed, the patron of the project himself, Gottfried Reinhardt—the son of the famed theater director—likened the design to a "symbol of Kristallnacht." *Bauwelt,* no. 4 (1993): 129.

39. Eisenman's early synagogue design depicts a tall, hexagonal sanctuary flanking a rectangular school building and an adjoining courtyard. Author interview with Peter Eisenman, March 14, 2007. On Eisenman's menorah (which was accompanied by a post-structuralist description focusing on the theme of absence and presence), see *Nerot Mitzvah: Contemporary Ideas for Light in Jewish Ritual* (Jerusalem: Israel Museum, 1986), 62. Significantly, the exhibition had a strong link to the Holocaust. As Erica Jesselson, one of the exhibition's main financial supporters, noted, Hitler's destruction of Judaica in the Holocaust—an event in which "most of our beautiful belongings were melted down"—provided the impetus to "recreate lost belongings" by finding new "ways to create and strive for excellence in design." Eisenman's comments about the San Francisco project are cited in Temko, "Creating a Jewish Sense of Space," 35, 50, and Lesley Pearl, "Museum Should Open Jewish Life to Masses," *Jewish Bulletin of Northern California,* June 14, 1996, 3. The 1996 remarks are in project position paper, by Peter Eisenman, addressed to the Committee for the Jewish Museum of San Francisco, January 7, 1996, author's possession.

40. Natalie Weinstein, "Daring Architect Will Draw Up Jewish Museum Plans," *Jewish Bulletin of Northern California,* May 8, 1998.

41. Peter Eisenman, "Project Dedicated to the Jewish Victims of the Nazi Regime in Austria, 1938–45, Vienna," *ANY,* no. 15 (1996): 58–61.

42. Quoted in "Ein Ort, nichts," *Frankfurter Rundschau,* May 10, 2005; Peter Davey, "Field of Memory," *Architectural Review,* July 2005, 80; Philip Gessler and Jörn Kabisch, "Jetzt übernimmt das Denkmal," *TAZ,* August 16, 2003.

43. Quoted in Peter Eisenman, "The Silence of Excess," in *Holocaust Memorial Berlin: Eisenman Architects* (Baden: Lars Müller, 2005), n.p.; "Das Eisenman-Revier," *TAZ,* August 10, 2002, 27; "Eisenman Interview II," *FAZ,* February 1, 2001; Gessler and Kabisch, "Jetzt übernimmt das Denkmal."

44. Eisenman, "Silence of Excess."

45. "Fragezeichen statt eines Schlusspunkts," *SZ,* May 10, 2005. For a general discussion of the controversy, see Bil Niven, *Facing the Nazi Past: United Germany and the Legacy of the Third Reich* (New York: Routledge, 2003), 194–233.

46. Benjamin Forgey, "A Stark Forest of Remembrance," *Washington Post,* December 18, 2005, N1. "Feld ohne Eigenschaften," *Der Spiegel,* no. 19 (2005): 34–38. Gerhard Matzig, "Eine Form der Möglichkeit," *SZ,* May 9, 2005. Gustav Seibt, "Aller Stelen," *SZ,* December 14, 2004.

47. Most commentators mistakenly depicted Eisenman as having little connection to the Holocaust in his previous architectural projects. See, for example, David Dudley, "The Eisenman Principle," *Cornell Alumni Magazine Online* 108, no. 1 (July–August 2005). Astrid Schmeing, "Eisenman's Design for the Berlin Holocaust Memorial—A Modern Statement?" *Architectural Design,* October 2000, 61–65. Even scholarly treatments of the memorial overlooked its roots in Eisenman's thought from the 1970s and 1980s. See, for example, Young, *At Memory's Edge,* 184–223, and Godfrey, *Abstraction and the Holocaust,* 239–65.

48. "Warnung vor der Vernunft," Interview with Peter Eisenman, *Aufbau,* Issue 15, 1999. http://aufbauonline.com/1999/issue15/pages15/titel15.html. Accessed January 2003. "Das Denkmal soll seelische Schwelbrände auslösen," *FAZ,* August 17, 2003.

49. The quotation about Jews living in the Diaspora appears in author interview with Peter Eisenman, December 5, 2006. All other quotations are found in "Warnung vor der Vernunft." In this interview, Eisenman said of the Holocaust's non-Jewish victims that the Nazis "were against the Gypsies, homosexuals, against all who were 'other.' For this reason I tried to symbolically show that this 'otherness' included more than just Jews." It is notable that Eisenman did not use the word "Jew" in his description of the memorial project. See Andrew Benjamin, ed., *Blurred Zones: Investigations of the Interstitial. Eisenman Architects, 1988–1998* (New York: Monacelli, 2003), 314.

50. Peter Eisenman, *Giuseppe Terragni: Transformations, Decompositions, Critiques* (New York: Monacelli, 2003). Cynthia Davidson, *Eisenman/Krier: Two Ideologies* (New York: Monacelli, 2004). See the discussion of Eisenman and Johnson in Schulze, *Philip Johnson,* 371–78.

51. Diane Ghirardo, "Eisenman's Bogus Avant-Garde," *Progressive Architecture,* November 1994. Another critical attack was by Kazys Varnelis, "'We Cannot Not Know History': Philip Johnson's Politics and Cynical Survival," *Journal of Architectural Education* 49, no. 2 (1995): 100. See also Ghirardo's response in the May 1995 issue of *Progressive Architecture,* 12–15.

52. Instead, Eisenman organized a larger discussion on the relationship between politics and architectural form. See "Eisenman (and Company)," *Progressive Architecture,* February 1995, 88–91.

53. Robert Locke, "Peter Eisenman: 'Liberal Views Have Never Built Anything of Value,'" Archinect, July 27, 2004. www.archinect.com.

54. Author interview with Peter Eisenman, December 5, 2006.

55. Accounts of the incident include Peter Eisenman, "Memorial to the Murdered Jews of Europe," *The Leo Baeck Memorial Lecture* (New York: Leo Baeck, 2006), 7–8; Marlies Emmerich, "Jüdische Gemeinde: Mahnmal ist ein 'Horror,'" *Berliner Zeitung,* March 8, 2004.

56. Author interview with Peter Eisenman, December 5, 2006.

57. Daniel Libeskind, *Breaking Ground: Adventures in Life and Architecture* (New York: Riverhead, 2004), 111–12, 117.

58. Ibid., 202, 34, 8–9, 34–35.

59. Libeskind's nonsectarian self-definition is found in "Daniel Libeskind: An Architectural Design Interview," *Architectural Design,* no. 7 (1990): 15. The quotations about homelessness are found in Aaron Betsky, "Berlin's New Cutting Edge," *Metropolitan Home,* December 1990, 61. The remarks about Chasidic Jews, wandering Jews, and the "Jewish dimension" to Libeskind's life are all found in Julia Goldman, "The Architecture of Hope," *Jewish Week,* December 27, 2002. Libeskind's observations about frequent moves and being "pigeonholed" are found in Libeskind, *Breaking Ground,* 7, 134. Libeskind's statement about "being a Jewish architect" and having a "Jewish sensibility" are found in "Rebuilding the World," *Jerusalem Report,* January 18, 1999, 46–47, and author interview with Daniel Libeskind, July 15, 2008.

60. The collages and machines are featured in Daniel Libeskind, *Between Zero and Infinity* (New York: Rizzoli, 1981); Libeskind, *Countersign* (London: Rizzoli, 1991), 48–49; Libeskind, *Architecture 1* (Milan, 1988). The quotation from "End Space" is in Libeskind, "End Space," in *Between Zero and Infinity,* 81. The remarks about architecture's demise appeared in his essays "Upside Down X" and "The Pilgrimage of Absolute Architecture," in *Countersign,* 9, 38.

61. The drawings' lack of perspective is pointed out in "Libeskind's Practice of Laughter: An Introduction by Stanley Allen," *Assemblage* 12 (1990): 22–23. Eisenman's remarks are found in Peter Eisenman, "Representation of the Limit," in Libeskind, *Countersign,* 120. The quotation about "deconstructive constructions" is in Dalibor Veseley, "The Drama of the Endgame," in Libeskind, *Between Zero and Infinity,* 105.

62. Quoted in Libeskind, *Countersign,* 110.

63. Ibid. Libeskind's later linking of the phrase "ordered disorder" to Albert Speer in his 1987 Berlin City Edge proposal further suggests that he had the Nazi legacy in mind when he produced his *Chamber Works.*

64. Quotations are from author interview with Daniel Libeskind, July 15, 2008. Krier's controversial essay "An Architecture of Desire" was published in the same year as *Chamber Works,* 1983. Daniel Libeskind, "Peter Eisenman and the Myth of Futility," *Harvard Architectural Review* 3 (Winter

1984): 63.

65. His being in Germany, Libeskind notes, "certainly mobilized my ideas" in ways that never would have happened "had I stayed in New York." Author interview with Daniel Libeskind, July 15, 2008.

66. Wigley, *Deconstructivist Architecture,* 34.

67. Jencks, *New Moderns,* 269.

68. Libeskind, *Countersign,* 65.

69. For a discussion, see Karen Till, *The New Berlin: Politics, Memory, Place* (Minneapolis: University of Minnesota Press, 2005), chapter 3.

70. The Berlin Museum's zigzag line derived from Libeskind's 1988 design "Line of Fire." Kurt W. Forster, "Monstrum Mirabile et Audax," in Kristin Feireiss, ed., *Daniel Libeskind, Erweiterung des Berlin Museums mit Abteilung Jüdisches Museum; Extension to the Berlin Museum with Jewish Museum Department* (Berlin: Wiley-VCH, 1992), 20, 67. The other justifications for the plan are cited in Libeskind, *Breaking Ground,* 91–94. In case jury members overlooked Libeskind's plan's links to the Holocaust, the architect picked the unsubtle number 6,000,001 to identify his proposal. Libeskind, *Breaking Ground,* 94.

71. The quotations about Enlightenment, reason, modernity, and society's backbone are cited in Feireiss, *Daniel Libeskind,* 63, 67, 29. The remark about the false sense of security is in Betsky, "Berlin's New Cutting Edge," 61. The remark about fragmentation is in Libeskind, "Between the Lines," 49.

72. The remark about "eradicated memory" is found in Feireiss, *Daniel Libeskind,* 67. The rest of the quotations are located in Libeskind, *Breaking Ground,* 79–80, 136, 134, 141–46. http://www.dhm.de/lemo/html/ biografien/EichmannAdolf/index.html. Accessed November 12, 2007.

73. The quotation about Berlin's reactionary tendencies is cited in Daniel Libeskind, "Letter from Berlin," *ANY,* May–June 1994, 48–49. Broadly, see Paul B. Jaskot, "Reunification, Daniel Libeskind's Jewish Museum in Berlin, and the Specter of a Resurgent Nazi Present," in Sabine Hake and Philip Broadbent, eds., *Berlin: Divided City, 1949–89* (New York: Berghahn, 2010).

74. Since 2001, visitors have been able to walk on top of an installation of 10,000 iron plates bearing screaming faces, entitled "Fallen Leaves," by the Israeli artist Menashe Kadishman.

75. Martin Filler, "Into the Void," *New Republic,* October 1, 2001, 27.

76. On the initial response to the museum, see Steven Erlanger, "A Memory-Strewn Celebration of Germany's Jews," *New York Times,* September 10, 2001, A8. For positive reviews, see "The Presence of Absence: Libeskind Builds," *Architecture,* September 1998; "Provocative Encounter: Libeskind's Jewish Museum," *Architectural Record,* January 1999. Filler, "Into the Void," 26, 29. Herbert Muschamp, "The New Berlin—Building on the Rubble of History," *New York Times,* April 11, 1999. Nicolai Ouroussoff, "The Pain and Hope Live On," *Los Angeles Times,* August 29, 1999, 6.

77. For criticism of the exhibition, see Amos Elon, "A German Requiem," *New York Review of Books,* November 15, 2001, 40–43; Henryk M. Broder, "'Es ist vergeblich," *Der Spiegel,* no. 39 (2001): 264–66. For criticism of the edifice, see Ruth Franklin, "Mr. Memory," *New Republic,* February 7, 2005, 30. For post–Ground Zero comments, see Michael J. Lewis, "Into the Void with Daniel Libeskind," *Commentary,* May 2003, 42; Michael Kimmelman, "Shattered Shapes: Architect's Rhetoric of Suffering," *New York Times,* April 14, 2004, E1.

78. Libeskind won the competition for this building in 1995, six years after he entered the Berlin Jewish Museum competition. Felix Nussbaum was a native of Osnabrück and fled Germany after the rise of the Nazis, eventually settling in Belgium, where he spent the war years hiding from the Germans and painting haunting, surrealistic self-portraits. In 1944 he was discovered and deported to Auschwitz, where he was murdered. Alan Riding, "Reviled in Life, Embraced in Death," *New York Times,* August 12, 1998, B1.

79. Daniel Libeskind, *The Space of Encounter* (New York: Thames and Hudson, 2001), 92. Originally, the museum was supposed to penetrate the neoclassical edifice. See the original plan, as reproduced in Lilli Thurn und Taxis's article "Potz Blitz," *Baumeister,* September 1995.

80. Sachsenhausen was built in 1936 outside of Berlin in the state of Brandenburg as the central administrative control center for the Nazi concentration camp system. After 1945 it fell under the control of East German authorities, who used it as training grounds for the army. In 1961 a small section of the site was turned into a memorial, but the rest remained undeveloped. The descriptions of Libeskind's plan appear in Libeskind, *Space of Encounter,* 90–91. Oranienburg's political leaders ultimately rejected their original plan to build a housing development on the site and brought back Libeskind in 1997 to refine his earlier plan, but resistance from Brandenburg historic preservationists brought about its defeat. Instead, a new museum complex by the German firm HG Merz was commissioned and completed in 2005. Daniel Libeskind, *Radix-Matrix* (Munich: Prestel, 1997), 102. Mary Williams Walsh, "A Grand Design for Nazi Camp," *Los Angeles Times,* January 17, 1998, 1. Christian Welzbacher, "Kopfschuettelnde Denkmalpflege," *Frankfurter Allgemeine Zeitung,* March 21, 2001, 71.

81. The StoneBreath plan is described in Libeskind, *Space of Encounter,* 160. Libeskind's explanation involving the complex axial relationships between the Reichstag, the Brandenburg Gate, and the Goethe Monument was more convoluted than the comparatively straightforward description of his other projects.

82. Libeskind's quotation is found in *Space of Encounter,* 96. The remark about the antiredemptory quality of Libeskind's work is found in Young, *At Memory's Edge,* 180–82.

83. The flying beam reference is in Libeskind, *Radix-Matrix,* 18. The quotation about the "hope incision" is located in "Oranienburg — Urbanisierung eines ehemaligen asernengeländes," *Bauwelt,* no. 14/15 (1993): 704. The Felix Nussbaum museum remarks are in Libeskind, *Radix-Matrix,* 56; Libeskind, *Space of Encounter,* 92. The E. T. A. Hoffmann garden was composed of forty-nine tilted columns, each twenty feet high and spaced three feet apart, filled with earth and planted with trees. Forty-eight of the columns were filled with earth from Berlin, "signifying the birth of the State of Israel in 1948," while a single column was filled with earth from Jerusalem, signifying the city of Berlin. Libeskind, *Space of Encounter,* 26.

84. Weinstein, "Daring Architect Will Draw Up Jewish Museum Plans."

85. The Duisburg project is described in Libeskind, *Space of Encounter,* 19–20. Libeskind first used the Aleph in the form of his "Aleph Wing" in his 1988 sculpture and included it in his 1991 Potsdamer Platz proposal. Libeskind, *Countersign,* 140.

86. The building's facade was to be clad with slate tiles displaying a Star of David pattern. The plan was titled "DarknessFireVoice" and represented the "rebirth of the community in Dresden from its darkest assimilation into the Shoah and into a hopeful future." Libeskind, *Space of Encounter,* 60–62.

87. http://www.daniel-libeskind.com/projects/show-all/contemporary-jewish-museum. Accessed November 30, 2007. Contemporary Jewish Museum press release: "Symbolism in the Building," n.d.

88. On the museum as a parabuilding, see Herbert Muschamp, "Museum Unveils Libeskind's Design," *New York Times,* February 23, 2000, E1. Nicolai Ouroussoff, "Conflict and Harmony Together in One Design," *Los Angeles Times,* April 2, 2000, 65. James E. Young, "Daniel Libeskind's New Jewish Architecture," in Connie Wolf, ed., *Daniel Libeskind and the Contemporary Jewish Museum: New Jewish Architecture from Berlin to San Francisco* (New York: Rizzoli, 2008), 58. The Libeskind quotations are found in Weinstein, "Daring Architect Will Draw Up Jewish Museum Plan," and Jesse Hamlin, "Jewish Museum Coming to Life," *San Francisco Chronicle,* February 23, 2000. Libeskind intended the PaRDeS wall, as it was called, to embody the museum's philosophy of "embracing multiple interpretations and layers of meaning through its artistic and educational programs." See "Symbolism in the Building." The word "pardes" also refers to a form of biblical exegesis. Libeskind's belief that the museum should be Jewish is found in Andy Altman-Ohr, "Striking New Museum Reaches for 'Other Side of Midnight,'" *Jewish News Weekly of Northern California,* February 25, 2000.

89. On the museum as a "Talmudic text," see Daniel Libeskind, "Mitzvah — The Danish Jewish Museum, Copenhagen." http://www.danskjoediskmuseum.dk/dokument/mitzvah_english.pdf. Accessed December 3, 2007. On the museum's slanted wooden design, see Libeskind, *Breaking Ground,* 124, and http://www.jewmus.dk/arkitektur.asp.

90. The notion that Libeskind could design only Jewish spaces is raised in Ouroussoff, "Conflict and Harmony." The Berlin proposal is mentioned in Libeskind, *Space of Encounter,* 142–43. The Manchester museum is discussed in Jencks, *New Paradigm in Architecture,* 249; Libeskind says that he came up with the idea by throwing a teapot out of a window and reassembling the largest shards. Libeskind, *Breaking Ground,* 231; Libeskind, *Space of Encounter,* 62–63.

91. The planning for Ground Zero has been the subject of intense scholarly analysis. Philip Nobel, *Sixteen Acres: Architecture and the Outrageous Struggle for the Future of Ground Zero* (New York: Metropolitan, 2004); Paul Goldberger, *Up from Zero: Politics, Architecture, and the Rebuilding of New York* (New York: Random House, 2004). For a discussion of Libeskind's competitors, see Martin Filler, "Back

to Babel," *New Republic,* February 3, 2003, 23 – 27. The Libeskind quotations are cited in *Breaking Ground,* 29, 31.
92. Libeskind's quotations are found in *Breaking Ground,* 43, 47. Architect Eli Attia subsequently cast doubt on Libeskind's claims about the wedge of light. Edward Wyatt, "Shadows to Fall, Literally, over 9/11 'Wedge of Light,'" *New York Times,* May 1, 2003.
93. Libeskind, *Breaking Ground,* 12 – 13.
94. See *Counterpoint: Daniel Libeskind. In Coversation with Paul Goldberger* (New York: Monacelli, 2008).
95. See Nicolai Ouroussoff, "A Razor-Sharp Profile Cuts into a Mile-High Cityscape," *New York Times,* October 12, 2006, E1; David Littlejohn, "It Works Despite Libeskind's Best Efforts," *Wall Street Journal,* February 15, 2007, D7; Michael J. Lewis, "Into the Void with Daniel Libeskind," *Commentary,* May 2003, 42.
96. This was Lisa Rochon's critique of the ROM, which she assailed as an "oppressive" structure that "raged at the world." Lisa Rochon, "Crystal Scatters No Light," *Globe and Mail* (Toronto), June 2, 2007. Edward Rothstein noted that the destabilized features of Libeskind's Contemporary Jewish Museum in San Francisco clashed with its upbeat message. "Museum's Vision: West Coast Paradise," *New York Times,* June 9, 2008, E6. For other critiques, see Ulrike Knöfel, "Den Schmerz verspielt," *Der Spiegel,* no. 27 (2002): 156 – 57; "Dekoration des Banalen," *Die Welt,* January 22, 2001.
97. Robin Pogrebin, "The Incredible Shrinking Daniel Libeskind," *New York Times,* June 20, 2004.
98. Suzanne Stephens, "The Bilbao Effect," *Architectural Record,* May 1999.

99. On the general response to the Gehry House, see Rosemarie Haag Bletter, "Frank Gehry's Spatial Reconstructions," in *The Architecture of Frank Gehry* (New York: Rizzoli, 1986), 11 – 25. The remark about the house representing "a *de-construction* kind of gesture" is in Suzanne Stephens, "Out of the Rage for Order," *Progressive Architecture,* March 1980, 82. Gehry's remark about playing with disaster is in Peter Arnell and Ted Bickford, eds., *Frank Gehry: Buildings and Projects* (New York: Rizzoli, 1985), 134. Frampton's remark is cited in Bletter, 46. Gehry's designs for the Wagner House (1978) and Familian House were similarly unstable. Bletter, 52 – 57. Francesco Dal Co and Kurt W. Forster, eds., *Frank O. Gehry: The Complete Works* (New York: Monacelli, 1998), 168 – 71, 178 – 79.
100. Pilar Viladas, "The 1980s," in *Architecture of Frank Gehry,* 159. Architecture critics have never coined an adequate term to describe this design approach. Some have referred to Gehry's preference for designing "room buildings." Adele Freedman, "The Next Wave: Frank Gehry's Views on his Work," *Progressive Architecture,* October 1986. Others have referred to "house cities." Germano Celant, "Reflections on Frank Gehry," in Arnell and Bickford, *Frank Gehry,* 6. Mildred Friedman has referred to Gehry's "objects-in-a-landscape" and his "village concept." Mildred Friedman, "Architecture in Motion," in Jean-Louis Cohen et al., eds., *Frank Gehry, Architect* (New York: Solomon R. Guggenheim Foundation, 2001), 291 – 92.
101. Witold Rybczynski, "Some Guy Just Wrapped It," *Times Literary Supplement,* April 9, 1999, 4.

102. Gehry's relationship with artists is discussed in Thomas S. Hines, "Heavy Metal: The Education of F. O. G.," in *Architecture of Frank Gehry,* 11 – 24, 19, and Francesco Dal Co, "The World Turned Upside-Down: The Tortoise Flies and the Hare Threatens the Lion," in Dal Co and Forster, *Frank O. Gehry,* 42. The 1986 quotation is found in Bletter, 25. The Morandi citation is in Cristina Bechtler, ed., *Frank O. Gehry and Kurt W. Forster* (Ostfildern-Ruit: Cantz, 1999), 25 – 26.
103. The 1999 quotation appears in Robert Ivy, "Frank Gehry: Plain Talk with a Master." *Architectural Record,* May 1999. Gehry's use of unconventional materials is described in Joseph Giovannini, "Edges, Easy and Experimental," in *Architecture of Frank Gehry,* 63 – 64. The epigraph is found in *Architecture of Frank Gehry,* 1.
104. Hines, "Heavy Metal," 11 – 24. Jencks sees Gehry's design method as deriving from the same roots as Eisenman's. See also Alexenberg, *Future of Art in a Digital Age.*
105. On Gehry's family background, see Gillian MacKay, "Frank Gehry: The Early Years," *Frank Gehry: Toronto* (Toronto: Art Gallery of Toronto, 2006), 10 – 13, and 16 for the quotation about thinking "Jewish." On Gehry's Jewish upbringing, see Hines, "Heavy Metal," 11; Martin Knelman, "Native Son Gehry Recalls Boyhood," *Toronto Star,* January 26, 2004; MacKay, 12. The remark about Gehry's "golden hands" is from the film *Sketches of Frank Gehry* (2005). The remarks about the Talmud and Torah are found in Lisa Rochon, "Growing Up Canadian: An Interview with Frank Gehry," in Rochon, *Up North: Where Canada's Architecture Meets the Land* (Toronto: Key Porter, 2005), 91, and

"Häuser zum Abheben," Hanno Rauterberg interview with Frank Gehry, *Die Zeit,* July 3, 2003.

106. Quoted in Rochon, "Growing Up Canadian," 88–91.

107. On Gehry's alienation from Judaism, see Rochon, "Growing Up Canadian," 91. Deborah Solomon, "Towering Vision," *New York Times Magazine,* May 1, 2003, 11. "Häuser zum Abheben." On Gehry's views on building a church or mosque, see Steve Cohen, "The Insider," *Philadelphia City Paper.Net,* November 29, 2006, http://www.citypaper.net/articles/2006/11/30/The-Insider. Accessed November 11, 2007. "Ich würde eine Moschee bauen," *Der Standard* (Austria), September 24, 2007. http://derstandard.at/3040601. Accessed June 9, 2010.

108. Regarding his politics, Gehry observes, "I have this socialistic or liberal attitude about people and politics. I think of the starving kids and that do-gooder stuff." Cited in "'No, I'm an Architect': Frank Gehry and Peter Arnell: A Conversation," in Arnell and Bickford, *Frank Gehry,* xiv. The remark about saving the world is cited in Charles Jencks, ed., *Frank O. Gehry: Individual Imagination and Cultural Conservatism* (London: Academy, 1995), 40. The quotation about social housing is found in Mildred S. Friedman, ed., *Gehry Talks: Architecture + Process* (London: Thames and Hudson, 2003), 172. The quotation about being a Jewish liberal is from Paul Goldberger, "The Masterpieces They Call Home," *New York Times Magazine,* March 12, 1995, 44.

109. On Gehry's grandfather, see MacKay, "Frank Gehry: The Early Years," 10, 17. Gehry's move to Timmins is discussed in Rochon, "Growing Up Canadian," 88. Gehry getting beaten up is discussed in Richard Lacayo, "The Frank Gehry Experience," *Time,* June 18, 2000; Martin Knelman, "Native Son Gehry Recalls Boyhood," *Toronto Star,* January 26, 2004. In 2004, Gehry described one of his tormentors: "There was this Polish kid — Poland was incredibly antisemitic and still is — so he was probably a product of the crap his parents fed him. So he beat me up." Rochon, "Growing Up Canadian," 88. The quotation about the restaurant is found in Rochon, "Is Gehry in the Building?" Gehry recalls being aware of the threat facing Jews in Europe in the 1930s, recalling how "scared" he was after hearing "Hitler speeches on the radio." Barbara Isenberg, *Conversations with Frank Gehry* (New York: Knopf, 2009), 251. In the Holocaust, Gehry lost between "thirty-three or thirty-four" family members (14).

110. On Gehry's name change, see Hines, "Heavy Metal," 12. Michaela Cordes, "Playdate with Frank O. Gehry," *GG (Global Guide: Lifestyle, People, and Real Estate),* June–August 2007, 53.

111. The Air Force episode is cited in Isenberg, *Conversations with Frank Gehry,* 30. The USC professor episode is mentioned in *Sketches of Frank Gehry.* Gehry names the instructor as Bill Schoenfeld. Bechtler, *Frank O. Gehry and Kurt W. Forster,* 54. The fraternity example is cited in Calvin Tomkins, "The Maverick," *New Yorker,* July 7, 1997, 41. Gehry's desire to spare his children antisemitism is cited in Hanno Rauterberg, "Der grosse Architainer," *Die Zeit,* June 13, 2001, 40. The 2004 quotation is found in "Frank Gehry: Form over Function," Morning Edition, NPR, March 10, 2003. http://www.npr.org/templates/story/story.php?storyId=1187549. Accessed October 24, 2007. The Goldbergs example is mentioned in "Frank Gehry: Form over Function."On Gehry changing his name, see Hines, "Heavy Metal," 16–17. The final quotation is found in "Frank Gehry: Form over Function."

112. The street fighter example is mentioned in Adele Freedman, "The Next Wave: Frank Gehry's Views on his Work," *Progressive Architecture,* October 1986, 97. Gehry remarked: "I get my inspiration from the streets.... I'm more of a street fighter than a ... scholar." On Gehry's rough childhood, see Lisa Rochon, "Is Gehry in the Building?" *Globe and Mail,* January 29, 2004, R1. The episode of Gehry beating up his classmate is discussed in Rochon, "Growing Up Canadian," 83. On Gehry playing hockey and boxing, see Beatriz Colomina, "The House That Built Gehry," in Cohen, *Frank Gehry, Architect,* 304.

113. On Gehry's psychoanalysis, see Jencks, "Deconstruction: The Pleasure of Absence," *Architectural Design* 58, no. 3–4 (1988): 18, and Hines, "Heavy Metal," 19. The Wexler quotation is from *Sketches of Frank Gehry.* On Gehry quitting commercial work, see Colomina, "House That Built Gehry," 306, 317; Forster, "Architectural Choreography," in Dal Co and Forster, *Frank O. Gehry,* 36. The quotation about the cliff is from *Sketches of Frank Gehry.*

114. Michael Sorkin, "Frozen Light," in Friedman, *Gehry Talks,* 35. Adele Freedman, "Fish and Flying Cubes Lead Gehry's Assault," *Globe and Mail,* March 18, 1982.

115. Interview with Frank O. Gehry — Part One. Filmed on January 22, 2002. http://www.netropolitan.org/gehry/gehryint.html. Accessed November

8, 2007. In 2003, he cited the fact that he "grew up with the Talmud" and the Golden Rule to explain why his buildings tried to adapt to the surrounding environment. "Häuser zum Abheben." In 1992 he said, "Designing a chair is a Talmudic question." Friedman, "Architecture in Motion," 298, 299 n12. Gehry further invokes the Talmud in Cordes, "Playdate with Frank O. Gehry," 49.

116. In the early 1980s, Gehry discussed many details of his biography without referring to his Jewish background. In 1980 he explained his installation for a Los Angeles County Museum of Art exhibition, "The Avant-Garde in Russia, 1910–1930," by referring to his "Polish-Russian background" (as opposed to his Eastern European Jewish background). Arnell and Bickford, *Frank Gehry*, 178. In 1982, moreover, Gehry mentioned the USC professor who discouraged him from pursuing a career in architecture without interpreting it as antisemitic (as he did in the film *Sketches of Frank Gehry*). Freedman, "Fish and Flying Cubes Lead Gehry's Assault."

117. Martin Filler, "The Spirit of '76," *New Republic*, July 9 and 16, 2001, 33. Herbert Muschamp, "The Miracle in Bilbao," *New York Times Magazine*, September 7, 1997, 82. Kurt W. Forster, "Architectural Choreography," 10–12. Jencks, *New Moderns*, 194. The view that Gehry's fish was a mere "folly" has also been expressed. "Conspicuous Consumption: Follies for Sale," *Progressive Architecture*, December 1983, 23. Jencks suspects that the fish is little more than a "convenient symbol" for branding and marketing his work. Isenberg, *Conversations with Frank Gehry*, 129; Jencks, *New Moderns*, 194.

118. On the Smith house, see Giovannini, "Edges, Easy and Experimental," 76, and Coosje van Bruggen, "Leaps into the Unknown," in *Architecture of Frank Gehry*, 144. On Gehry's bridge project with Serra, see Mildred Friedman, "Fast Food," in *Architecture of Frank Gehry*, 97, 100–101; see also Gehry's design for a fish sculpture in 1981, Dal Co and Forster, *Frank O. Gehry*, 224; Arnell and Bickford, *Frank Gehry*, 230–31. On Gehry's fish lamps, see Dal Co and Forster, 278, 255; Giovannini, 77; Bruggen, 155.

119. On Gehry's critique of postmodernism, see Adele Freedman, "By Design, Gehry Still Swimming Against the Tide," *Globe and Mail*, August 23, 1986, D13. The quotation about going back three hundred million years to fish is in "Frank Gehry: Form over Function." Gehry's remark to Jencks is found in Charles Jencks, *Architecture Today* (New York, 1988), 250–51. On Gehry's fish as a critique of classicism, see Dal Co and Forster, *Frank O. Gehry*, 326. On the fish as a symbol of man's displacement, see Dal Co and Forster, 55. The 1984 quotation appears in "'No, I'm an Architect': Frank Gehry and Peter Arnell: A Conversation," xvii.

120. Links between fish and Jewishness were most recently confirmed by an exhibition of Gehry's fish lamps at the Jewish Museum of New York in fall 2010.

121. Before 1984, Gehry discussed the fish without connecting it to his Jewish upbringing. See, for example, Freedman, "Fish and Flying Cubes Lead Gehry's Assault." In 1983, Gehry related the story of the carp and the bathtub, even mentioning gefilte fish, without clarifying its Jewish dimensions. Joe Morgenstern, "Obsession of an Architect with Fish on a Grand Scale," *Los Angeles Herald-Examiner*, March 4, 1983, A3. In 1988, Gehry designed a literal representation of his childhood memory at the Toronto office of Chiat/Day, where he suspended a lead fish inside a porcelain bathtub. Dal Co and Forster, *Frank O. Gehry*, 384. On Gehry's relationship with his grandmother, see Hines, "Heavy Metal," 12. On the symbolism of fish as unrealized potential, see Sorkin, "Frozen Light," 37.

122. Jencks, *New Moderns*, 194; Knelman, "Native Son Gehry Recalls Boyhood."

123. On early works including snakes, see Bruggen, "Leaps into the Unknown," 132, Giovannini, "Edges, Easy and Experimental," 78–81. Gehry has noted that he was inspired by the appearance of snakes in the work of his friend Richard Serra. Gehry's remark about snakes and fear is in Arnell and Bickford, *Frank Gehry*, 268. That Gehry connected fish and snakes is further revealed in one of his drawings featuring the line, "1 fish = ? snakes." *Frank O. Gehry, Design Museum Vitra* (Berlin: Aedes, 1989), 10.

124. Arnell and Bickford, *Frank Gehry*, 268.

125. On the fish in Florence, see Giovannini, "Edges, Easy and Experimental," 80–81, 101; Dal Co and Forster, *Frank O. Gehry*, 302. The quotation about kitsch is on 326. The Minneapolis, Venice, and Barcelona examples are discussed in Friedman, *Gehry Talks*, 44; Dal Co and Forster, 333–38. The quotation about movement is found in Friedman, 49. The quotation about language is in "Frank Gehry: Form over Function."

126. Forster, "Architectural Choreography," 31. It was an associate in Gehry's firm, Jim Glymph, who located the CATIA program and established it

as the new system for translating Gehry's designs into three dimensions.
127. Friedman, *Gehry Talks,* 16–18.
128. Martin Filler, "Ghosts in the House," *New York Review of Books,* October 21, 1999, 13.
129. One of Gehry's main critics has been John Silber in his book, *Architecture of the Absurd: How "Genius" Disfigured a Practical Art* (New York: Quantuck Lane, 2007). The fact that Gehry designed a line of jewelry for the Tiffany chain angered others who felt doing so belied his purported commitment to social causes. On the T-shirts, see the website: http://www.fuckyoga.com/cart.php?target=product&product_id=756&category_id=94. The *Time* example appears in Richard Lacayo, "Frank Gehry," *Time Magazine,* April 26, 2004.
130. Quoted in Zevi, *Erich Mendelsohn,* 422.
131. "Out of the Rage for Order," *Progressive Architecture,* March 1980, 82. The Prague comment was by Josef Pesch and originally published in *Kunst und Kultur* 4.5 (June–August 1997): 14–17. http://lava.ds.arch.tue.nl/gallery/praha/tgehryen.html. Accessed December 3, 2007.
132. "Häuser zum Abheben." More recently Gehry remarked, "The world doesn't let you forget you're Jewish. . . . Certainly Hitler proved that." Isenberg, *Conversations with Frank Gehry,* 31.
133. All quotations, except that from 1997 interview, are found in Cordes, "Playdate with Frank O. Gehry," 53. "Revisiting the LA 12: Interview with Frank Gehry Santa Monica, May 9, 1997." http://www.volume5.com/ghery12/revisiting_the_la_12_frank_ge1.html. Accessed December 1, 2007.
134. Dal Co and Forster, *Frank O. Gehry,* 526–31. In Gehry's defense, the building restrictions imposed by city authorities at the Pariser Platz made any radical architectural gesture nearly impossible. That said, the architect undermined the restriction's spirit by including an enormous, expressive horse-head-shaped conference room and a giant fish-shaped skylight in the building's interior.
135. The 1995 quotation is in Friedman, *Gehry Talks,* 248; see also Patrick Barton, "Man will hier das 19. Jahrhundert wieder aufbauen," *SZ,* July 3, 2001, 9. The 1999 quotation is found in Ronald L. Nagel, "Frank O. Gehry: Sculptor and Architect for the Twenty-First Century," *Einstein Quarterly Journal of Biology and Medicine* (2002) 19, 42. The 1997 quotation is cited in "Revisiting the LA 12." The 2001 quotation is cited in Patrick Barton, "Man will hier das 19. Jahrhundert wieder aufbauen," *SZ,* July 3, 2001, 9.
136. Michal Zadara, "A World Remembered," *Jerusalem Report,* May 6, 2002, 42. Melissa Radler, "Poland Plans Warsaw Museum on Polish Jewish History," *Jerusalem Post,* January 11, 2002, 6A. Rob Eshman, "A World Destroyed, To Be Displayed," *Jewish Journal,* September 27, 2002, 25. The Polish foreign minister said that the museum aimed to show both the "light and dark sides" of Polish-Jewish relations as a means of "abolish[ing] harmful stereotypes." Ruth E. Gruber, "Warsaw's Museum Will Document 1,000 Year History of Poland's Jews." http://www.ujc.org/page.html?ArticleID=33795. Accessed December 3, 2007.
137. For the institution's mission, see its website at: http://www.wiesenthal.com/site/pp.asp?c=lsKWLbPJLnF&b=4441257. In an interview, Gehry described his emotional reaction to the Western Wall when he first visited the city in the late 1970s. Arlynn Nellhaus, "Letter from Jerusalem: Tolerating Frank Gehry," December 7, 2002. www.the-idler.com/IDLER-C2/12–7.html. Accessed December 20, 2002. The Gehry quote is in Samuel G. Freedman, "Frank Gehry's Mideast Peace Plan," *New York Times,* August 1, 2004, AR1. Daniel Belasco, "Go Fish," *Jewish Week,* June 29, 2001, 1.
138. The Gehry quotation is cited in "Ich würde eine Moschee bauen," *Der Standard* (Austria), September 24, 2007. The Webb quotation is in Daniel Belasco, "Go Fish," *Jewish Week,* June 29, 2001, 1.
139. See Michael Sorkin, "Critique," *Architectural Record,* June 2004, 117, and the reply by Marvin Hier, *Architectural Record,* August 2004, 67. Tom Tugend, "Wiesenthal's Project in Jerusalem on Hold Amid Dispute," *Jewish Journal,* February 24, 2006. See also the long and politicized discussion of Gehry's role in the project in *Critical Inquiry,* no. 3 (Spring 2010).
140. Paul Goldberger, "A House Slipcovered in Metal," *New York Times,* May 17, 1979, C6. The critic Adele Freedman also wrote of Gehry's work: "Out of the ugly, the beautiful" ("Fish and Flying Cubes Lead Gehry's Assault").

Chapter 9.
Jewish Architects Between Alienation and Assimilation

1. *Stanley Tigerman: Buildings and Projects, 1966–1989* (New York: Rizzoli, 1989), 20–23, 52–55. *Oral History of Stanley Tigerman: Interviewed by Betty J. Blum* © 2003, The Art Institute of Chicago, used with permission, 89.

2. *Oral History of Stanley Tigerman,* iv, 237, 229. Tigerman, *Versus,* 30.

3. The quotation about cultural phenomena is in Tigerman, *Versus,* 42, 120. For a survey of these buildings, see *Versus,* chapters 6 – 7. See also *Oral History of Stanley Tigerman,* 112.

4. On cleaving buildings, see *Oral History of Stanley Tigerman,* 116; Tigerman, *Versus,* 145, 155, 158 – 60.

5. Tigerman, *Versus,* 130.

6. Ibid., 114. In a 1982 interview he explained his turn to religious values in his architecture, noting: "I was about forty-five when I got my shit together and suddenly realized that I was in trouble. . . . The subject of death . . . deeply affected me and I began to think about things." "JAE/Interview: Stanley Tigerman" (with Peter C. Papademetriou), *JAE* 36, no. 1 (Autumn 1982): 43.

7. On Tigerman's grandfather, see *Oral History of Stanley Tigerman,* 23. See also Author interview with Stanley Tigerman, April 22, 2008. Tigerman dedicated one of his books, *The Architecture of Exile,* to his grandfather. *Oral History of Stanley Tigerman,* 231.

8. On Tigerman's mother, see *Oral History of Stanley Tigerman,* 5. The 1985 quotation is found in Barbaralee Diamonstein, *American Architecture Now II* (New York: Rizzoli, 1985), 223. Even after Tigerman received his diploma from Yale, his mother did not grasp the significance of his achievement. As he recalled in 2008: "She said, 'Now you can make money.' In other words, she never understood." Author interview with Stanley Tigerman, April 22, 2008. This interview also contains Tigerman's self-assessment as a Jew.

9. On Tigerman's knowledge of the Holocaust, see videotape of Stanley Tigerman talk at the Yale University conference, "Constructing the Ineffable: Contemporary Sacred Architecture," Session 1, October 26, 2007, Sterling Library. On antisemitism in the architectural profession, see *Oral History of Stanley Tigerman,* 82. See also 79 – 81. On hostility in Tigerman's architecture, see author interview with Stanley Tigerman, April 22, 2008.

10. Tigerman discusses *Versus* in *Oral History of Stanley Tigerman,* 117. The quotations about Tigerman's "faulty" work and the Jewish mother are cited in Tigerman, *Versus,* 9–11. The interview quotation is found in "JAE/Interview: Stanley Tigerman," 41. The quotation about simultaneity is in *Versus,* 9.

11. The quotation about "idealist objectivity" is found in Tigerman, *Versus,* 161. This chapter's title, "Post-Modernism Is a Jewish Movement," was originally supposed to be the title for the entire book; Diamonstein, *American Architecture Now II,* 224. The reference to the "unsynthesized dialectic" is in *Versus,* 147, 11.

12. Tigerman, *Versus,* 163 – 64.

13. Tigerman invoked the Holocaust in 1979 in his explanation of his Pensacola II Apartment Project in Chicago, entitled "Optimism and Skepticism and the Linear City, 1979." In it he described the modernist rebellion against nineteenth-century historicism and opaquely referred to the modernist hatred of the "Auschwitz of the Aristocracy" — a phrase seemingly meant to indict classical Beaux-Arts training. Quoted in *Versus,* 29. Tigerman, *The Architecture of Exile* (New York: Rizzoli, 1988).

14. Tigerman, *Architecture of Exile,* 139, 154.

15. The quotation about two world wars is found in Tigerman, *Architecture of Exile,* 154. The quotation about the human race is located in Stanley Tigerman, "Construction, (De)Construction, (Re)Construction: Architectural Antinomies and a (Re)newed Beginning," *Architectural Design,* no. 1/2 (1989): 77. The reference to America in the 1960s is in Tigerman, *Versus,* 151, 10. The reference to Vietnam appears in "Interview with Stanley Tigerman," *Transition,* April – July 1984, 25. Tigerman noted: "What Vietnam was to America [in the world of politics] . . . Venturi was to architecture. Each dealt a terminal blow to simplistic thought and [brought] poignancy into American life and American architecture." *Versus,* 28. The 1989 quotation is found in *Stanley Tigerman: Buildings and Projects, 1966 – 1989,* 12.

16. For the German projects, see *Stanley Tigerman: Buildings and Projects, 1966 – 1989,* 180, 178. In the Tegel building, Tigerman used yellow, red, and black to evoke the colors of the German flag. See also "A House Divided," *Architectural Record,* July 1989, 88. The 2008 quotation is from author interview with Stanley Tigerman, April 22, 2008.

17. *Stanley Tigerman: Buildings and Projects, 1966 – 1989,* 226 – 29.

18. Aaron Betsky, "On Tigerman," *Progressive Architecture,* December 1983, 92. The remarks to Betty Blum appear in *Oral History of Stanley Tigerman,* 117, 122. Tigerman explained that even though *Versus* was published in 1982, "it was written in the seventies." On assigning meaning to architecture, Tigerman added, "Now, you can say,

'Well, therefore you're investing it with your Jewishness as both an afterthought and as a rationale, in a way.' Perhaps that's true." On the gap between Tigerman's buildings and rhetoric, see Paul Goldberger, "Building Against the Grain," *New York Times*, August 8, 1982. Tigerman's classically inspired buildings included his neoclassical Hard Rock Cafe in Chicago (1984–85) and his neohistoricist design for a Mediterranean villa in Florida (1986–89). *Stanley Tigerman: Buildings and Projects, 1966–1989*, 158–61, 166; "Architecture: Stanley Tigerman," *Architectural Digest*, February 1989, 149.

19. Jayne Merkel, "Architecture of Dislocation: The L.A. School," *Art in America*, February 1, 1994. Anthony Vidler, "The Baroque Effect," in *Eric Owen Moss: Buildings and Projects 2* (New York: Rizzoli, 1996), 6.

20. Moss has long been grouped with other L.A.-based architects, such as Frank Gehry, Thom Mayne, Michael Rotondi, and Frank Israel, as part of the Los Angeles School. Merkel, "Architecture of Dislocation."

21. Paola Giaconia, *Eric Owen Moss: The Uncertainty of Doing* (Milan: Skira, 2006), 22.

22. Vidler, "Baroque Effect," 10. The 1991 quotation appears in *Eric Owen Moss: Buildings and Projects* 11. The 1996 quotation appears in *Eric Owen Moss: Buildings and Projects 2*, 12. The 2002 quotation appears in an interview with Leon Whiteson, 2002: http://www.netropolitan.org/moss/mossint.html; *Eric Owen Moss: Buildings and Projects 3* (New York: Rizzoli, 2002), 217.

23. The remark about the perpetual fight is cited in *Eric Owen Moss: Buildings and Projects*, 12. The other quotations appear in "James Steele Interviews Eric Owen Moss," in *Eric Owen Moss* (New York: Academy, 1993), 10–13. Moss further revealed his interest in the writings of Paul de Man and affirmed that "deconstruction is an affirmation of a stage of not knowing."

24. Eric Owen Moss, *Gnostic Architecture* (New York, 1999), 1.3, 1.4, 5.9.

25. Moss studied with Tigerman when the latter was a guest professor at UC Berkeley. Giaconia, *Eric Owen Moss*, 42.

26. Moss's family background (and associated quotations) can be found in author interview with Eric Owen Moss, April 12, 2008. Morton Moss dropped out of Columbia in the 1930s and went to Los Angeles to become a writer. "My dad was a self-taught man," Moss notes. "He was out there in the bookstores trying to figure out what the fuck was going on." The elder Moss's main works are *In Sight of the Invisible* (Independence, Mo.: International University Press, 1987) and *Soliloquies of Constantine* (London: Janus, 1998). On the Petal House, see *Eric Owen Moss: Buildings and Projects*, 36; Peter Cook, "Enigmatic Flower," *Progressive Architecture*, June 1984, 105. The quotation about believing is cited in Mack Scogin, "Foreword," in *Eric Owen Moss: The Box* (Princeton, N.J.: Princeton Architectural Press, 1996), 9.

27. Author interview with Eric Owen Moss, April 12, 2008.

28. Ibid., May 8, 2008.

29. Moss Herbert, *Holy Holocaust: The Two-Millennia Christian Wasting of the Jews* (London: Janus, 1998). The afterword to the book is dated 1983, though it was only published fifteen years later. Herbert's views of religion may be summed up by the book's concluding lines: "How odd of God/to charge the Jews/two thousand years/of Christian dues" (a play on British journalist William Norman Ewer's couplet "How odd of God/To choose the Jews"). Eric Owen Moss says his father's poem was viewed as "poison" in the early 1980s. Moss's quotations appear in author interview with Moss, April 12, 2008.

30. On the project, see *Eric Owen Moss: Buildings and Projects 3*, 251. The "plaza of ecumenicism" was to stand in dialogue with the neighboring Catholic church and Mexican Museum. It is unclear whether Moss's reference to a public stair along a curving interior wall in the museum was meant to allude to Mauthausen's notorious stone stairway. The remarks about Kafka and light are found in *Eric Owen Moss: Buildings and Projects 3*, 253, 254, 256.

31. Charles Gandee, "Gathering Moss," *Architectural Record*, July 1985, 34; Moore, "Complexity and Contradiction," 42.

32. Patricia Leigh Brown, "Architecture's Young Old Fogies," *New York Times*, February 9, 1995. Paul Goldberger, "Back to the Past," *New Republic*, November 27, 1995, 44. On the Richard H. Driehaus Prize, see http://driehausprize.nd.edu/greenberg.shtml.

33. On Greenberg's views of New Haven, see Allan Greenberg, *The Architecture of Democracy: American Architecture and the Legacy of the Revolution* (New York: Rizzoli, 2006), 14, 20. The quotation about architecture as a personal style is in Allan Greenberg, "Why Classical Architecture Is Modern," *Architecture*, November 1994.

34. Greenberg, *Architecture of Democracy*, 21–22.

35. Cesar Pelli, ed., *Yale School of Architecture Seminar Papers* (New Haven, 1982), 2: 151–52.

36. For a review of Greenberg's Manchester building, see David Cast, "Good, Ordinary, Classical, Modern," *Progressive Architecture,* October 1981, 80. Greenberg's other university buildings included McGlothlin Street Hall at the College of William and Mary (1989–95) and the Humanities Building at Rice University in Houston (1997–2000).

37. The 1994 quotation is cited in "Interview with Allan Greenberg," *American Enterprise Institute for Public Policy,* March–April 1997, 54. Allan Greenberg, "The Architecture of Democracy," in Andreas Papadakis and Harriet Watson, eds., *New Classicism: Omnibus Volume* (New York: Rizzoli, 1990), 69.

38. The quotation about "blood, tribe, or land" is in Greenberg, "Why Classical Architecture Is Modern," 59. Greenberg's other observations are found in Greenberg, *Architecture of Democracy,* 43, 127, 103–10, and Greenberg, "Architecture of Democracy," 72.

39. Greenberg, *Architecture of Democracy,* 10, 20.

40. Greenberg confirms that his Jewish background was "certainly . . . a factor" in his decision to leave South Africa. Author interview with Allan Greenberg, September 16, 2008. Of the roughly 120,000 Jews who lived in South Africa in the early 1970s, some 40,000 emigrated between 1970 and 1992. http://www.jewishvirtuallibrary.org/jsource/vjw/South_Africa.html.

41. On Greenberg's experiences with antisemitism, see author interview with Allan Greenberg, September 16, 2008. Greenberg produced plans for an unrealized synagogue restoration for Washington, D.C.'s Kesher Israel congregation in 2001–3. He has gone on record, moreover, saying that he would like to design a synagogue.

42. Greenberg attributes his Jewish knowledge to the influence of his Orthodox wife. Author interview with Allan Greenberg, September 16, 2008. On the Puritans, see Greenberg, *Architecture of Democracy,* 72–74, and "Classical Training: A Conversation with Allan Greenberg," *Forward,* February 24, 2006, 13. This article also includes Greenberg's reference about being a "good Jew." The quotation about the architectural implications of Jewishness is found in author interview with Allan Greenberg.

43. The 2008 quotation is from author interview with Allan Greenberg, September 16, 2008. Greenberg, *Architecture of Democracy,* 142–49. Greenberg, "Architecture of Democracy," 72.

44. Robert Taylor, *The Word in Stone: The Role of Architecture in the National Socialist Ideology* (Berkeley: University of California Press, 1974); Adam, *Art of the Third Reich;* see Frederic Spotts, *Hitler and the Power of Aesthetics* (New York: Overlook, 2004).

45. Author interview with Allan Greenberg, September 16, 2008.

46. The project, entitled "Proposed Holocaust Memorial," is described in *Allan Greenberg: Selected Works* (London: Academy, 1995), 124–25.

47. For the observation about Rieff, see author interview with Allan Greenberg, September 16, 2008. Michael Sorkin said the memorial's architecture was "so tendentious and specific that its appropriateness as collective expression must . . . be called into question." Sorkin, *Exquisite Corpse* (New York: Verso, 1991), 224. On Greenberg's inclusion of the Ten Commandments, see Allan Greenberg, "Genesis of the Holocaust Memorial," *ICA Currents,* no. 18 (November 1984): 1–2. Greenberg added that the memorial would remind people that their sacrifice had "led to the creation of the State of Israel by which Jews regained their Promised Land." On the memorial's conical form, see *Allan Greenberg: Selected Works* (London: Academy, 1995), 124–25. The memorial also bore a strong resemblance to the World War I Monument to the Missing at Thiepval, France, by Sir Edwin Lutyens, the architect of British imperialism. George Hersey, "Allan Greenberg and the Classical Game," *Architectural Record,* October 1985, 161. Regarding the memorial's failure to be built, Greenberg was able to secure a meeting with Howard Squadron, chairman of the Conference of Presidents of Major American Jewish Organizations, but he "refused to look at anything" Greenberg presented and insisted that the Holocaust was best commemorated by bringing American political officials to Yad Vashem in Israel. Author interview with Allan Greenberg.

48. Elisabeth Bumiller, "From Architectural Showman to Yale Dean," *New York Times,* September 23, 1998.

49. The quotation about modernist boxes appears in Robert A. M. Stern, *Pride of Place: Building the American Dream* (Boston: Houghton Mifflin, 1986), 2. The Wiseman Residence was influenced by Robert Venturi's house for his mother (known as the Vanna Venturi House, 1962). Vincent Scully, "The Star in Stern: Sightings and Orientation," in Robert A. M. Stern, *Robert Stern* (London: Academy, 1981), 9. Examples of Stern's ironic work include his Gramercy Park Apartment (1979) and Best Products Showroom (1979). Peter Arnell and Ted Bickford, eds., *Robert A. M. Stern, 1965–1980: Toward a Modern Architecture After Modernism* (New York: Rizzoli, 1981), 150, 174, 136. The Shingle-Style homes are surveyed in "The Residential Works of Robert A. M. Stern," *A + U,* July 1982. The remarks about abandoning modernism and his work being schizophrenic are in Robert A. M. Stern, "Introduction: Modern Traditionalism, Robert A. M. Stern," in Robert A. M. Stern and Luis F. Rueda, eds., *Buildings and Projects, 1981–1985: Robert A. M. Stern* (New York: Rizzoli, 1986), 7.

50. Robert Stern, "Stompin' at the Savoye," *Architectural Forum,* May 1973, 48. The quotation about the tyranny of the present is found in Robert A. M. Stern, "What the Classical Can Do for the Modern," in Papadakis and Watson, *New Classicism,* 31. The quotation about postmodernism's main principles is in the "Postscript" section of Robert A. M. Stern, *New Directions in American Architecture* (New York: Braziller, 1977). Stern, "Introduction: Modern Traditionalism," 7. The quotation about going backward is in Robert A. M. Stern, "On Style, Classicism, and Pedagogy," *Precis* 5 (1984): 20.

51. The quotations about language and narrativity are in Stern, "On Style, Classicism, and Pedagogy," 19. The remark about hybridization is in Robert A. M. Stern, "Beginnings," *Residential Works of Robert A. M. Stern, A + U,* July 1982, 15. On architecture's storytelling role, see Arnell and Bickford, *Robert A. M. Stern,* 12. The comment about architectural culture is in Stern, "Beginnings," 15.

52. Elizabeth Kraft, ed., *Robert A. M. Stern: Buildings and Projects, 1987–1992* (New York: Rizzoli, 1992), 146–55, 210–19, 224–25, 240–41. "Stern to Design Bush Presidential Library," *Architectural Record,* August 29, 2007.

53. Author interview with Robert A. M. Stern, May 22, 2008.

54. The quotation about America is in Robert A. M. Stern, "The Postmodern Continuum," in William J. Lillyman, Marilyn F. Moriarty, and David J. Neuman, eds., *Critical Architecture and Contemporary Culture* (Oxford, U.K.: Oxford University Press, 1994), 62. Tigerman's quotation appears in *Oral History of Stanley Tigerman,* 115. Sorkin's remarks are found in Sorkin, *Exquisite Corpse,* 164, 184. The Our Crowd reference was to Stephen Birmingham, *Our Crowd: The Great Jewish Families of New York* (New York: Harper and Row, 1967).

55. Stern and Rueda, ed., *Buildings and Projects, 1981–1985,* 211, 229–30; Kraft, *Robert A. M. Stern,* 118–19, 312–13.

56. Stern does not recall his family discussing the Holocaust either during or after the war. Author interview with Robert A. M. Stern, May 22, 2008. The quotation about memory is found in Arnell and Bickford, *Robert A. M. Stern,* 12.

57. Stern, *Pride of Place,* 3, 9, 285.

58. The four quotations are found in the following: Robert A. M. Stern with Raymond W. Gastil, *Modern Classicism* (New York: Rizzoli, 1988), 44; Stern, "What the Classical Can Do for the Modern," 31–32; Stern, "Introduction: Modern Traditionalism," 6; Robert A. M. Stern, "The Doubles of Post-Modern," *Harvard Architecture Review,* Spring 1980, 87.

59. The comment about hermeticism is in Robert A. M. Stern, "Doubles of Post-Modern," 83. The reference to headlines is in Stern, "What the Classical Can Do for the Modern," 32. The quotation about enduring art is in Stern, "Introduction: Modern Traditionalism," 6.

60. The 1986 quotation is in "Introduction: Modern Traditionalism," 6. The comment about affirmation is in Robert A. M. Stern, "Introduction," in Peter Morris Dixon, *Robert A. M. Stern: Buildings and Projects, 1999–2003* (New York: Monacelli, 2003), 9. The references to a usable past and to humanistic values are in Stern, *Pride of Place,* 9. The reference to a stronghold for humanism is in Stern, "Introduction," in Dixon, *Robert A. M. Stern,* 9. The quotation about the tortured soul is in Stern, "Post-Modern Continuum," 61–62.

61. The 2008 quotation is from author interview with Robert A. M. Stern, May 22, 2008. Stern first visited Germany in 1977. On the Tegel design, see Kraft, *Robert A. M. Stern,* 94–95. The Tacheles building, originally built as the Friedrichstrassen-Passage, was later owned by the Wertheim family and the Jewish-owned company AEG. It was taken over by the Nazis prior to World War II. After 1990, the building was transformed into the bohemian artist colony known as "Tacheles" (yiddish for "straight talk"). http://super.tacheles.de/cms/. Duany Plater Zyberk has planned to incorporate the ruin into its commercial buildings at the site, thereby reducing its evocative character. On the Hohenzollern Palace, see Rainer Haubrich, "New York braucht man nicht neu zu erfinden," *Die Welt,* April 25, 2001, 31. In declaring that "Berlin's tragedy was not the wartime destruction but the demolitions that occurred thereafter in both east and west," Stern echoed the arguments of German historic preservationists, whose contention that postwar modernism was more destructive to Germany's built environment than World War II bombing raids elided Germany's responsibility for starting the war in the first place. See Rosenfeld, *Munich and Memory,* chapters 5–6. A similar sentiment was expressed in Stern's call after 9/11 to rebuild the World Trade Center towers. "To Rebuild or Not," *New York Times Magazine,* September 23, 2001, 81.

62. On commemoration controversies at the Börneplatz, see Georg Heuberger, *Stationen des Vergessens: Der Börneplatz-Konflikt* (Frankfurt am Main: Jüdisches Museum, 1992), 154. Stern was invited to participate in the competition. Author interview with Robert A. M. Stern, May 22, 2008. Kraft, *Robert A. M. Stern,* 58–59.

63. The project is surveyed in Robert A. M. Stern, "On Being Modern and Traditional," *A + U,* May 1988, esp. 105, 140–41. See also "Berlin Academy of Science Competition and Controversy," *Progressive Architecture,* June 1988, 29.

64. "Why Is Richard Meier's Getty Center So Disappointing?" *Progressive Architecture,* February 1992, 103.

65. Joseph Rykwert, "Introduction," Richard Meier, *Richard Meier, Architect: 1964–1984* (New York, 1984), 11.

66. The quotation about spatial richness is in Richard Meier, Royal Gold Medal Address, 1988, RIBA, October 25, 1988, in *Richard Meier: Buildings and Projects, 1979–1989* (London: Academy, 1990), 212. The remark about timeless ideas is found in "Richard Meier on the Spirit of Architecture," *Architectural Digest,* June 1981, 156, 164. On neomodernism, see Jencks's discussion of Meier in *New Moderns.*

67. Abigail Pogrebin, *Stars of David: Prominent Jews Talk About Being Jewish* (New York: Broadway, 2007), 263.

68. Meier's great-grandparents emigrated from Frankfurt, Germany, in the mid-nineteenth century and settled in New Jersey. Richard Meier, *Building the Getty* (Berkeley: University of California Press, 1999), 6. Pogrebin, *Stars of David,* 264.

69. Regarding the synagogue exhibition, Meier's friendship with the curator of the Jewish Museum, Alan Solomon (with whom he studied at Cornell), helped him land the job. Meier's stint working for the firm of Davis, Brody, and Wisniewski, which designed the acclaimed Sons of Israel synagogue in Lakewood, New Jersey (1963), may have influenced his interest in synagogue design. He also worked on Marcel Breuer's unrealized B'nai Jeshurun synagogue. Meier, *Building the Getty* 9. Rochelle Furstenberg, "Dreaming in White (and Beige)," *Jerusalem Report,* August 3, 1998, 42–43; Tom Tugend, "First Impressions," *Jewish Journal,* December 19, 1997, 13. Meier's remarks about being concerned about the Nazis as a child and the unimportance of anti-semitism in his career appear in author interview with Richard Meier, March 23, 2010. The teenage dating episode is recounted in Pogrebin, *Stars of David,* 264.

70. The five quotations are found in Meier, Royal Gold Medal Address, 214; Jencks, in *Richard Meier: Buildings and Projects, 1979–1989,* 31. Charles Jencks, "Richard Meier Interviews, 1980–1988," in *Richard Meier: Buildings and Projects, 1979–1989* (London: Academy Editions, 1990), 28; Volker Fischer, *Richard Meier: Der Architekt als Designer und Künstler: The Architect as Designer and Artist* (Fellbach: Edition Axel Menges, 2003), 11. "Richard Meier: On Defining Architecture," in *Richard Meier, Building for Art: Bauen für die Kunst* (Basel, 1990), 30.

71. The 1984 remark appears in Rykwert, "Introduction," 9. The 1990 remark appears in "Richard Meier: On Defining Architecture," in *Richard Meier, Building for Art: Bauen für die Kunst* (Basel: Birkhäuser Verlag, 1990), 30. The quotation about architecture being joyful is in Jencks, in *Richard Meier: Buildings and Projects, 1979–1989,* 32. The 2010 quotation is in author interview with Richard Meier, March 23, 2010.

72. The 1985 quotation is in Fischer, *Richard Meier,* 13. The remark about wounds is quoted in Jencks, *New Moderns,* 254. Manfred Sack, "'What I am striving for is presence, not illusion.' Richard Meier's dialogue with Gothic in Ulm," in Manfred Sack, *Richard Meier: Stadthaus Ulm* (Stuttgart: Edition Axel Menges, 1994), 15. The remark about reconciliation appears in author interview with Richard Meier, March 23, 2010.

73. The remarks about religious space, Jewish identity, and promoting understanding are all found in Pogrebin, *Stars of David,* 262. Meier noted that the three concentric shells represented the Holy Trinity, while the reflecting pool symbolized the baptismal ritual. *Richard Meier: Architect 1992/1999* (New York: Rizzoli, 1999), 407. The Zevi quotation is found in Herbert Muschamp, "Architecture of Light and Remembrance," *New York Times,* December 15, 1996, 44. The remark about a new Christianity is in Bruno Zevi, *L'Architecttura,* no. 7 (1996): 67. Meier's claim to be extremely proud is in "Q & A with Richard Meier," *ArchNewsNow,* October 23, 2003. http://wirednewyork.com/forum/showthread.php?t=4168.

Chapter 10.
Holocaust Museums

1. In 2007, the museum was renamed the Holocaust Memorial Center Zekelman Family Campus following a $10 million gift by industrialist Alan Zekelman and his brothers Barry and Clayton. http://www.wzzm13.com/news/news_article.aspx?storyid=68773.
2. For a list, see http://www.science.co.il/holocaust-museums.asp.
3. See, for example, Harold Marcuse, *Legacies of Dachau: The Uses and Abuses of a Concentration Camp, 1933–2001* (Cambridge: Cambridge University Press, 2001).
4. The most dramatic was Austrian architect Günter Domenig's deconstructivist documentation center at Nuremberg's Reich Party Rally Grounds (1998–2001), which symbolically grappled with the Nazi past by dramatically puncturing Ludwig and Franz Ruff's monumental Congress Hall (1935–45). By contrast, the Bergen-Belsen center, designed by KSP Engel and Zimmermann; the Dachau center, designed by Florian Nagler Architekten; and the new documentation center housing Berlin's Topography of Terror exhibition, designed by Ursula Wilms, are all comparatively restrained and minimalist in their architecture, in sharp contrast to their burdened surroundings.
5. In Norway, a Holocaust museum opened in 2005 in Villa Grande, the former wartime residence of Nazi collaborator Vidkun Quisling. On the Norwegian Center for Studies of Holocaust and Religious Minorities, see http://www.hlsenteret.no/English. A hybrid solution was pursued in Hungary, where the Holocaust Memorial Center opened in a new building that was added to Lipot Baumhorn's early twentieth-century Pava Synagogue (which in 1944–45 was used as an internment camp for Jews). For the Budapest museum, see http://www.hdke.hu/index.php. In Rome, a brand-new building housing Italy's new Holocaust museum, designed by Luca Zevi (the son of Bruno Zevi) and Giorgio Tamburini, is planned on the grounds of Mussolini's Villa Torlonia. "Ein Monolith gegen das Vergessen," *Die Zeit,* January 27, 2011.
6. Cole, *Selling the Holocaust,* chapter 6; Oren Baruch Stier, *Committed to Memory: Cultural Mediations of the Holocaust* (Amherst: University of Massachusetts Press, 2003), chapter 4. Dan Stone, "Memory, Memorials, and Museums," in Dan Stone, ed., *The Historiography of the Holocaust* (Houndsmills, U.K.: Basingstoke, 2004), 508–32. Jeffrey Shandler, "Heritage and Holocaust on Display: New York City's Museum of Jewish Heritage—A Living Memorial to the Holocaust," *Public Historian* 21, no. 1 (Winter 1999): 73–86. Anson Rabinbach, "Holocaust Memorialization in America Since Bitburg," in Geulie Ne'eman Arad, ed., *Passing into History: Nazism and the Holocaust Beyond Memory,* special issue of *History and Memory,* no. 1/2 (Fall 1997): 226–55; Omer Bartov, "Chambers of Horror: Holocaust Museums in Israel and the United States," *Israel Studies* 2, no. 2: 66–87. Jon Wiener, "The Other Holocaust Museum," *Tikkun,* May 1995, 22–23, 82–84.
7. Yosef Lishinsky, "Yad Vashem as Art," *Ariel,* 1983, 15–16.
8. The remark about the gal-ed appears in Young, *Texture of Memory,* 253. The reference to unchanging eternity appears in Lishinsky, "Yad Vashem as Art," 17–18. The memorial's interior was empty except for the names of twenty-two concentration camps etched into the mosaic flagstone floor (beneath which lay ashes of murdered Jews) and an eternal flame.
9. Paul Goldberger discussed these matters in "A Memorial Evokes Unspeakable Events with Dignity," *New York Times,* April 20, 1989, H36.
10. On the history of the museum, see Edward Linenthal, *Preserving Memory: The Struggle to Create America's Holocaust Museum* (New York: Viking, 1995). President's Commission on the Holocaust, *Report to the President* (Washington D. C., 1979), 9.
11. The Wiesel and Hilberg comments appear in Linenthal, *Preserving Memory,* 61, 74, 292. The desire for a new building was reported in "'Somebody Had to Tell the Story,'" *Washington Post,* April 18, 1993, A29.
12. For this phase of the museum's creation, see Linenthal, *Preserving Memory,* 75–79. On the resemblance of Kaufman's design to fascist architecture, see Adrian Dannatt, *United States Holocaust Memorial Museum: James Ingo Freed* (London, 1996), 4; Irvin Molotsky, "Washington Talk: Commission of Fine Arts; Arbiters of Monumental Taste," *New York Times*, July 8, 1987.
13. "The United States Holocaust Memorial Museum," *A + U,* November 1993, 91. Freed recalled hiding with

his father during the days of violence by riding city streetcars and evading attention by reading antisemitic newspapers. Benjamin Forgey, "James Freed and the Building Blocks of the Past," *Washington Post,* April 18, 1993, G5.

14. *Oral History of James Ingo Freed: Interviewed by Betty J. Blum,* © 2000, The Art Institute of Chicago, used with permission, 108. Linenthal, *Preserving Memory,* 85 – 86.

15. The first quotation is in Forgey, "James Freed," G5, and Linenthal, *Preserving Memory,* 88. The second quotation is in "Contemplation and Commemoration," *Forward,* October 3, 1997. The third quotation is in Jashajahu Weinberg and Rina Elieli, *The Holocaust Museum in Washington* (New York: Rizzoli, 1995), 25.

16. "United States Holocaust Memorial Museum," *A + U,* November 1993, 92 – 93. "The Architecture and Art of the United States Holocaust Memorial Museum" (Museum Brochure from USHMM), 1.

17. Ken Johnson, "Art and Memory," *Art in America,* November 1993. "United States Holocaust Memorial Museum," *A + U,* November 1993, 93. Linda Friedlander, *How to Remember? Designing the United States Holocaust Memorial Museum* (South Hadley, Mass.: Mount Holyoke College Art Museum, 1997), 11

18. "Memorial to Atrocity," *Progressive Architecture,* February 1993, 65.

19. Friedlander, *How to Remember,* 11.

20. The references to the steel plate and to an architecture of sensibility are in "Memorial to Atrocity," 67. The comment about slits is in Linenthal, *Preserving Memory,* 103.

21. Herbert Muschamp, "Shaping a Monument to Memory," *New York Times,* April 11, 1993, H1. Mildred Schmertz, "In Remembrance," *Architecture,* July 1993, 61. Joan Branham, "Mapping Tragedy in the U.S. Holocaust Memorial Museum," *Architectural Design,* October 2000, 56. The Hilberg remark appears in Linenthal, *Preserving Memory,* 108.

22. One critic who saw the museum as too restrained was Ziva Freiman, who said she felt nearly "unscathed" after visiting the museum; see her essay "Memory Too Politic," *Progressive Architecture,* October 1995, 62 – 64. See also David Cohn, "Kann Architektur erzählen?" *Deutsche Bauzeitung,* June 1993, 156 – 57. The reference to the museum as troubling is in Benjamin Forgey, "A Miraculous Monument to Catastrophe," *Washington Post,* April 18, 1993, G1.

23. *Oral History of James Ingo Freed,* 107, 118.

24. Saidel, *Never Too Late to Remember,* 107.

25. Ibid., 135 – 40.

26. The Gill quotation and Cuomo's plans for the site are found in Saidel, *Never Too Late to Remember,* 127, 141 – 45. Raymond Sokolov, "Rm. to Let. Landmark Bldg. 77,000 Sq. Ft.," *Wall Street Journal,* October 3, 1984, 1. "What to Do With the Custom House," *New York Times,* August 11, 1984, 22.

27. Saidel, *Never Too Late to Remember,* 150.

28. On Polshek's family background, see Susan Gray and Paul Goldberger, *Architects on Architects* (New York, 2001), 143, in which Polshek described his family as "nonobservant" and his father as a "politically progressive anti-Zionist." Polshek designed a Holocaust memorial garden at the Brotherhood Synagogue (which he restored) near Gramercy Park in New York. "Synagogue's Garden of Remembrance," *New York Times,* May 3, 1982, B2. The Polshek quotation is found in *James Stewart Polshek, Context and Responsibility: Buildings and Projects, 1957 – 1987* (New York: Rizzoli, 1988), 54.

29. The Polshek quotation is found in *James Stewart Polshek: Context and Responsibility,* 55. For a discussion of the design, see Joseph Giovannini, "Museum's Design Based on Promising Concept," *New York Times,* September 5, 1986, B4.

30. Saidel, *Never Too Late to Remember,* 158, 226.

31. On the stock market crash, see ibid., chapter 11. The Treblinka Tower reference is in ibid., 160 – 61. The *Forward* reference is in ibid., 232 – 34. See also Diana Jean Schemo, "New York Is Still Waiting for Its Own Holocaust Museum," *New York Times,* December 12, 1993, 46. The reference to the best possible museum is in Saidel, *Never Too Late to Remember,* 160.

32. On Roche's Jewish museum, see Paul Goldberger, "An Addition That Leaves Well Enough Alone," *New York Times,* June 5, 1988, 35. Herbert Muschamp, "Jewish Museum Renovation: A Celebration of Gothic Style," *New York Times,* June 11, 1993. The Roche quotation is in Karrie Jacobs, "Never Forget," *New York Magazine,* September 8, 1997, 119.

33. "Profile: Kevin Roche, Museum Architect," *A Living Memorial to the Holocaust: Museum of Jewish Heritage* 11, no. 1 (March 1997): 7.

34. For a review of the museum, see Michael Kimmelman, "In the Faces of the Living, Honor for the Dead," *New York Times,* September 12, 1997, B1. For evidence of the design changes to the museum, see the photograph of the 1994 model in Saidel, *Never Too*

Late to Remember. Herbert Muschamp, "Museum Tells a Tale of Resilience: Tuned to the Key of Life," *New York Times,* September 15, 1997, 1.

35. Ellen Trachtenberg et al., eds., *Ten Years: Remembrance, Education* (Houston: Holocaust Museum Houston, 2005), 9, 15 – 25.

36. Bob Tutt, "Survivors Remember on the Opening Day of Holocaust Museum Houston," *Houston Chronicle,* March 3, 1996.

37. Reed Kroloff, "Dark Remembrance," *Architecture,* November 1996, 117. Sachs and Van Voolen, *Jewish Identity in Contemporary Architecture,* 59. Patricia Johnson, "Where Art Confronts Evil," *Houston Chronicle,* May 26, 1996, 11.

38. Trachtenberg, *Ten Years,* 18, 19, 15, 71. Kroloff, "Dark Remembrance," 114. http://register.hmh.org/article.asp?id=164. The Los Angeles Museum of Tolerance averages 350,000 annual visitors, while the USHMM averages around two million. Cole, *Selling the Holocaust,* 246.

39. Rabbi Charles H. Rosenzveig was inspired by a visit to Yad Vashem in 1958 to undertake a similar project in the Detroit area. He began collecting oral histories of survivors in the early 1970s. Mary E. Kremposky, "Witnessing the Darkness; Uncovering the Light," *CAM Magazine,* Fall 2004, 2 – 3.

40. The reference to a shtetl is found in *Holocaust Memorial Center Newsletter,* Spring 1999. http://www.holocaustcenter.org/index.php?option=com_content&task=view&id=420. The remarks about ideas and hideousness are found in Joel Kurth, "Memorial Sparks Outrage," *Detroit News,* November 7, 2003, and *Holocaust Memorial Center Newsletter,* Fall 1999. http://www.holocaustcenter.org/index.php?option=com_content&task=view&id=415. See also Jeffrey Zaslow, "Should a Museum Look as Disturbing as What It Portrays?" *Wall Street Journal,* October 8, 2003, A1, A16. The Neumann quotations are found in "Controversial Holocaust Museum, Evocative of Concentration Camp, Opens in Michigan," *Architectural Record,* April 21, 2004. http://archrecord.construction.com/news/daily/archives/040421holocaust.asp; and also *Holocaust Memorial Center Newsletter,* Fall 1999.

41. See the "About" tab on the museum's website: http://www.holocaustcenter.org.

42. For a discussion of the museum's iconography, see Zaslow, "Should a Museum Look as Disturbing as What It Portrays?" A1, A16 and Krempsoky, "Witnessing the Darkness," 4. The museum's interior also echoed its exterior symbolism, culminating in a darkened, cramped space called the abyss that was illuminated only by the light from documentary newsreels exposing the camp carnage at the moment of liberation.

43. "Shock Value; Organizers of Museum Modeled on Concentration Camp See Worth in the Raw Truth," *Grand Rapids Press,* December 21, 2003, A27; Zaslow, "Should a Museum Look as Disturbing as What It Portrays?" A16.

44. The quotations are found in Zaslow; "Shock Value," A16, A27. The Neumann quotation is in "Controversial Holocaust Museum." On the museum receiving an award, see http://www.aiami.com/aiami_design_awards/design_awards_2004/honor_awards_04_home.htm.

45. On the museum's history, see "Holocaust Museum Opens in Skokie," *Chicago Tribune,* June 3, 1985, 4. Tigerman insisted that opposition to the museum reflected "straight virulent antisemitism, period." Author interview with Stanley Tigerman, April 22, 2008. Gila Wertheimer, "Some Skokie Residents Remain Upset After Trustees 'Kick Out' a Holocaust Museum, While Others Argue: Not in My Back Yard," *Chicago Jewish Star,* February 21, 2002, 1. Ed Finkel, "Holocaust Museum Site in Skokie Dedicated," *Chicago Tribune,* September 12, 2003, 4.

46. Author interview with Stanley Tigerman, April 22, 2008.

47. Ibid. See also the museum's website: http://www.ilholocaustmuseum.org.

48. Craig Barner, "Understanding the Unthinkable," *Midwest Construction,* October 2007.

49. Videotape of Stanley Tigerman talk at the Yale University conference, "Constructing the Ineffable: Contemporary Sacred Architecture," Session 1, October 26, 2007. Sterling Library. See also Stanley Tigerman, "The Tribe Versus the City-State: An Architectural Conundrum for the Jewish Project," *Images* 2 (2008): 156 – 65.

50. Author interview with Stanley Tigerman, April 22, 2008. On critics' views, see Blair Kamin, "In Skokie, a New Holocaust Museum Opens, at Once Moving and Flawed," *Chicago Tribune,* April 18, 2009, and Barbara Vitello, "Architect Instills Sense of Poignancy in Design," *Chicago Daily Herald,* April 17, 2009.

51. The center's mission is described at http://www.wiesenthal.com. On the museum's origins, see Young, *Texture of Memory,* 305 – 6. On Hier, see Sheldon Teitelbaum, "The Unorthodox Rabbi," *Los Angeles Times Mag-*

azine, July 15, 1990, 6–11, 36.

52. Edward Norden, "Yes and No to the Holocaust Museums," *Commentary,* August 1993, 23.

53. Allison Lawlor, "Architect Made His Mark in California," *Globe and Mail,* March 17, 2004. Gabe Gonda, "Maxwell Starkman, 82: Architect Grew Up Hungry," *Globe and Mail,* January 6, 2004.

54. On planning for the USHMM, see Joseph Giovannini, "Design for the U.S. Holocaust Museum Is Ready," *New York Times,* May 21, 1987, C26. Norden, "Yes and No to the Holocaust Museums," 23.

55. The reference to Middle Eastern architecture is in "Bearing Witness in Bricks and Steel," *Architectural Record,* April 1988, 65. The MOT's setback cubic forms resembled those of Starkman's Sony Plaza building in Culver City (1988).

56. The museum's popularity (it draws 350,000 visitors a year) proves that attention-grabbing architecture is no precondition for a museum's success.

57. On whether Los Angeles needs two museums, see Rebecca Spence, "L.A.'s First Holocaust Museum to Expand," *Forward,* November 30, 2007, A6. On the museum's origins and visitor numbers, see Young, *Texture of Memory,* 304.

58. Tom Tugend, "L.A. Holocaust Museum Wanders as It Tries to Remain in Business," *Jewish Telegraphic Agency,* June 2, 2004. "Budget Cuts Imperil Nation's First Shoah Museum," *Forward,* May 17, 2002, 4.

59. Belzberg's first quotation is found at: http://www.belzbergarchitects.com. His second remark is found in Jonah Lowenfeld, "A New Jewish Museum Pushes Toward the Future," *Jewish Journal,* August 31, 2010.

60. Author interview with Hagy Belzberg, October 5, 2008.

61. Christopher Hawthorne, "Sleek, and Yet Oddly Bashful; the L.A. Museum of the Holocaust Takes an Overly Deferential Approach," *Los Angeles Times,* October 28, 2010; Guy Horton, "The Indicator: Wind Swept Dune," *Arch Daily*, October 29, 2010. http://www.archdaily.com/85852/the-indicator-wind-swept-dune/#more-85852. See also Sam Lubell, "Belzberg Architects Delivers a Dose of Raw Emotional Impact at Poignant New Home for LA Institution," *Architect's Newspaper*, October 14, 2010. http://www.archpaper.com/e-board_rev.asp?News_ID=4910.

62. "Larry Wasser, 1946–2003: The Man and the Museum," *St. Petersburg Times,* June 29, 2003. David Olinger, "Holocaust Museum Plans Move to City," *St. Petersburg Times,* April 19, 1997, 3B.

63. Waveny Ann Moore, "Building on an Idea," *St. Petersburg Times,* February 15, 1998, 2X; Waveny Ann Moore, "Harsh Angles by Design," *St. Petersburg Times,* February 15, 1998, 3X.

64. Author conversation with HDEC executive vice president Rositta Kenigsberg, July 14, 2010. "Holocaust Relived at Center's New Home," *Miami Herald,* April 28, 2006. Plans for the building exist but do not yet provide a sense of its exterior. See http://www.hdec.org.

65. Elli Wohlgelernter, "Interactive Remembrance," *Jerusalem Post,* April 16, 1993.

66. Wendy Kohn, ed., *Moshe Safdie* (London: Academy, 1996), 59–71, 75–80, 99–105, 285–301, 263–75. Safdie's essay is discussed in Witold Rybczynski, "Northern Lights," in Kohn, 32. Peter G. Rowe, "Trajectories, Traces, and Tropes," in Kohn, 29. Safdie declared, "Over the years I have undergone many changes but . . . I have remained a critical modernist." "Closing a Circle—Interview with Architect Moshe Safdie," *Architecture in Israel Quarterly,* no. 54.

67. The quotation about imbalance is in Larissa MacFarquhar, "Truth in Architecture," *New Yorker,* January 20, 2003. Moshe Safdie, "The Medium and Language of Architecture," in Kohn, *Moshe Safdie,* 13. See also Corinna Da Fonseca Wollheim, "Sacred Ground, Sullied Ground," *New York Sun,* May 10, 2005, 13.

68. On Safdie's identity, see Michael Wise, "The Many Facades of Moshe Safdie," *Forward,* April 19, 1996; Yad Vashem, *Moshe Safdie—The Architecture of Memory* (Baden, Switzerland: Lars Müller, 2006), 92. The reference to business as usual is found in the entry: "3 March 2005: New Holocaust History Museum to Open at Yad Vashem," at: http://www1.yad-vashem.org. The reference to annals of civilization is found in Yad Vashem, *Moshe Safdie—The Architecture of Memory,* 95.

69. For photos of Safdie's Yad Vashem work, see Moshe Safdie, *Moshe Safdie II* (Mulgrave, Australia: Images, 2009), 74–99.

70. The Shalev quotation is in Barbara Horwitz Bennett, "For the Six Million," *Building Design and Construction,* April 2005, 34. Laura King, "Depth and Despair," *Los Angeles Times,* March 27, 2005, E37. Yad Vashem, *Moshe Safdie—The Architecture of Memory,* 23.

71. The reference to an earthquake is found in Yad Vashem, *Moshe Safdie—The Architecture of Memory,* 97, as is the discussion of the interior's triangular shape (21), the reference to the horn (23), and the mention of Jews prevailing (99). Safdie conceived of the concrete bands as "huge fingers of two huge hands, extending farther out over the valley," but this plan was rejected after certain Yad Vashem officials saw them as "too figurative" and "too . . . fascist." Steven Erlanger, "Israel Dares to Recast a Story Set in Stone," *New York Times,* February 13, 2005, section 2, 16. At the end of the exhibition is the Hall of Names, which Safdie designed in the form of a cone, displaying hundreds of photographs of Holocaust victims. It is suspended over an inverted cone excavated into the rock below. Filled with groundwater, the excavated cone reflects the photos suspended above "in memory of those whose names will never be known."

72. Olga Tarnopolsky, "Jerusalem; Yad Vashem," *Forward,* April 29, 2005, 13. Esther Zandberg and Zvi Elhyani, "Stealing the Shoah," *Blueprint,* May 2005, 42 – 46.

73. Author interview with Allan Greenberg, September 16, 2008.

74. The Hertzberg quotation is cited in Novick, *The Holocaust in American Life,* 199. The idea that it is not synagogues but prayers that make holy space is mentioned in Jarrassé, *Synagogues,* 19.

75. Freiman, "Memory Too Politic," 68.

76. Russel Miller, "Israel's Abusement Park," *Forward,* April 1, 1994, 9.

77. Tova Reich, *My Holocaust* (New York: HarperCollins, 2007). Gary Shteyngart, *Absurdistan* (New York: Random House, 2006), 269 – 70.

78. For the Dallas museum, slated to be designed by Corgan Associates, see http://www.dallasholocaustmemorialcenter.org.

Chapter 11.
Jewish Architecture Between Nightmare, Nostalgia, and Normalcy

1. See, for example, Wolfram Selig, *Synagogen und jüdische Friedhöfe in München* (Munich: Aries, 1988); Israel Schwierz, St*einerne Zeugnisse jüdischen Lebens in Bayern: Eine Dokumentation* (Munich: Bayerische Landeszentrale für Politische Bildungsarbeit, 1988); Thea Altaras, *Synagogen in Hessen — Was geschah seit 1945?* (Königstein im Taunus: Langewiesche, 1990); Karl Heinz Krüger, "'Wer ein Haus baut, will bleiben," *Der Spiegel,* October 31, 1988, 109 – 20.

2. Korn, "Synagogenarchitektur in Deutschland," 308.

3. Willi Jasper, "Der Bruch als Symbol," *Die Zeit,* no. 49 (1999). See the essays in Salomon Korn, *Geteilte Erinnerung: Beiträge zur 'deutsch-jüdischen' Gegenwart* (Berlin: Philo, 2001).

4. The references to fractures and the memorial tablet appear in Korn, "Synagogenarchitektur in Deutschland," 307. The quotation about architectural metaphors is in Korn, *Geteilte Erinnerung,* 33. See also Korn's description of the project in "Jewish Community Center Frankfurt am Main" (Frankfurt, 1988). See also Susanne Schönborn, "The New Börneplatz Memorial and the Nazi Past in Frankfurt am Main," in Rosenfeld and Jaskot, *Beyond Berlin,* 273 – 94; for Korn's stance on the issue, see Salomon Korn, "Börneplatz Frankfurt," *Der Architekt,* April 1988, 258 – 63.

5. The reference to the bend is in Korn, "Synagogenarchitektur in Deutschland," 307. The remark about spiritual provincialism appears in Korn, *Geteilte Erinnerung,* 73 – 75, and the house reference on 71.

6. Korn, "Synagogenarchitektur in Deutschland," 308.

7. Jeffrey Peck, *Being Jewish in the New Germany* (New Brunswick, N.J.: Rutgers University Press, 2006).

8. The population of Jews in Germany today is estimated to be over 200,000. The difference between affiliated and unaffiliated Jews often has to do with whether they are halakhically Jewish. Many recent immigrants have only a vague sense of themselves as Jews. Peck, *Being Jewish,* chapter 3. According to the Statistiches Bundesamt Deutschland, the number of Jews was officially 108,000 in 2005. An estimated 190,000 Jews have arrived in Germany since 1989; http://www.dw-world.de/dw/article/0,2144,1789258,00.html. Ludger Heid, "Ein geöffnetes Buch in Stein," *SZ,* November 29, 1996; Dagmar Allund and David Wessel, "New Synagogues for Germany," *Wall Street Journal,* June 21, 2000, B1; Michael Wise, "Germany's New Synagogues," *Architecture,* October 2001, 66; Till-R. Stoldt, "Das Symbolik der Synagoge," *Die Welt,* December 8, 2002, 11.

9. The figure of 30 is cited in "In welchem Stil sollen wir bauen?" *FAZ,* May 18, 1995. Stiftung Baukultur Rheinland-Pfalz, ed., *Gebauter Aufbruch: Neue Synagogen in Deutschland* (Regensburg: Schnell and Steiner, 2010). New synagogues were built in Aachen, Bad Kreuznach, Bamberg, Berlin, Bielefeld, Bochum, Braunschweig, Chemnitz, Dresden, Duisburg, Gelsenkirchen, Hannover, Heidelberg, Kassel, Krefeld, Lörrach, Mainz, Munich, Offenbach, Schwerin, Wuppertal-Barmen, and Würzburg. http://www.zentralratdjuden.de/de/topic/387.html. Existing synagogues were renovated in other cities, such as

Magdeburg, Floss (Bavaria), and Kitzingen (Bavaria). Currently, other synagogues are being planned in Speyer and Potsdam.

10. Aalund and Wessel, "New Synagogues for Germany."

11. Korn, "Synagogenarchitektur in Deutschland," 318.

12. Ibid., 306. Susanne Klingenstein, "Ellipsen jenseits der Angst," *FAZ,* July 7, 2000. Krüger, "'Wer ein Haus baut, will bleiben,'" 120.

13. *Die Bürgerschaft gibt der Jüdischen Gemeinde eine Synagoge zurück: Einweihung der Synagoge in Darmstadt, 9. November 1988, Ansprachen* (Darmstadt, 1989), 24–28.

14. The Metzger and Fränkel quotations are in *"Die Bürgerschaft gibt der Jüdischen Gemeinde eine Synagoge zurück,* 5, 12. The Korn quotation is in Korn, "Synagogenarchitektur in Deutschland," 307. The reference to the "Wall of Suffering" appears in Renate Stahlheber, "In der Reinheit klaren Denkens," *Kunst und Kirche,* no. 4 (1996): 263–65.

15. The 2001 quotation is in B. J. Almond, "Built to Heal," *Rice News* 11, no. 5 (September 20, 2001); see also Howie Movshovitz, "Synagogues as Symbols," *Denver Post,* March 15, 1997, E10. The 2002 remark is in Dankwart Guratzsch, "Die Sehnsucht nach dem Spirituellen," *Die Welt,* May 29, 2002. Jacoby's opposition to synagogues as Holocaust memorials appears in Movshovitz, E10. The Wittgenstein reference is in Aalund and Wessel, "New Synagogues for Germany." Jacoby's respect for elderly congregants is mentioned in Movshovitz, E10, and Almond.

16. The exhibition is discussed in Almond, "Built to Heal." The remark about a second chance is in Alfred Jacoby, "Synagogenbau in Deutschland nach 1945," in Esther Haß et al., eds., *Synagogen in Kassel* (Marburg, 2002), 87.

17. The Speyer synagogue was not entirely new, as it was an adaptive reuse of an abandoned church. Lisa Borgemeister, "Junger Pfälzer," *Jüdische Allgemeine,* June 26, 2008, 19. Jacoby also produced unrealized designs for synagogues in Duisburg, Dresden, Mainz, and Munich. The fabric reference appears in Haß et al., *Synagogen in Kassel,* 87. Memorials to the Holocaust were present in front of the Aachen synagogue. See Wolfgang Krücken and Alexander Lohe, *Mahnmal und Gedenkstätte an der Aachener Synagoge* (Aachen: Shaker Verlag, 2001).

18. Movshovitz, "Synagogues as Symbols."

19. On the Offenbach synagogue, see Alfred Jacoby, *In einem neuen Geiste: Synagogen von Alfred Jacoby* (Frankfurt, 2002), 32. "Ein Edelstein in würdevoller Fassung," *Das Münster,* March 1999, 255–56. The quotation by Schreiter is in Allund and Wessel, "New Synagogues for Germany," B1. The Jacoby quotation is in Ann Gerhart, "Synagogues of Today Are Facing Tomorrow," *Houston Chronicle,* December 2000, 8.

20. This pattern also explains the interest of German architects in the virtual reconstruction of synagogues destroyed on Kristallnacht. See the impressive effort by the Technical University of Darmstadt professors Marc Grellert and Manfred Koob to use CAD technology to create reconstructed versions of destroyed German synagogues. *Synagogues in Germany: A Virtual Reconstruction* (Basel: Birkhäuser, 2004).

21. The local desire to rebuild the synagogue is mentioned in Hanno Rauterberg, "Unverbrüchlich anders," *Die Zeit,* no. 46 (2001). The quotation about destruction is found in Kieran Long, "Out of the Ashes," *World Architecture,* March 2002.

22. The plan is described in Wandel, Hoefer, Lorch, und Hirsch, "Geschichte und Baukonzeption der Neuen Synagoge Dresden," in Adolf Diamant, *Denkschrift zur Einweihung der Neuen Synagoge und des Gemeindehauses zu Dresden am 9. November, 2001* (Dresden, 2001), 19. The glass shards in the synagogue's courtyard had to be removed within a year of being installed, as they became stuck in visitors' shoes and damaged the floor of the community center. The shards were replaced with barely discernible metal rails embedded in the gravel.

23. The reference to Christian precedents is in "'Im Spannungsfeld zwischen Rekonstruktion und DDR-Moderne': Interview mit Architekt Nikolaus Hirsch," *Kunst und Kirche,* no. 4 (2001): 237. On the Temple and Tabernacle, see Karen Glaser, "Tribute Wrong," *Building Design,* February 8, 2002. The references to Judaism are in David Cohn, "A Complex and Tragic History Informs Wandel Hoefer Lorch + Hirsch's Poetic Design for the New Dresden Synagogue," *Architectural Record,* June 2002, 105. See also Neue Synagoge Schalom Dresden: Ein modernes jüdisches Gotteshaus am Rande der Altstadt— doch mitten unter uns; http://www.das-neue-dresden.de/synagoge.html.

24. Kieran Long, "Out of the Ashes," *World Architecture,* March 2002. Hanno Rauterberg, "Unverbrüchlich

anders," *Die Zeit,* no. 46 (2001).
25. Adolf Diamant, *Denkschrift zur Einweihung der Neuen Synagoge und des Gemeindehauses zu Dresden am 9. November, 2001* (Dresden, 2001), 33.
26. On the architects, see http://www.japan-architect.co.jp/english/2maga/au/Architects/w/WandelHoeferLorchHirsch.html. On the firm's memorials, see "Gedenkstätte Neuer Börneplatz," *Bauwelt,* no. 26 (1996): 1504–5; Johannes Heesch and Ulrike Braun, *Orte Erinnern: Spuren des NS-Terrors in Berlin: Ein Wegweiser* (Berlin: Nicolai, 2003), 177–81. On the Hinzert memorial, see http://www.politische-bildung-rlp.de/fileadmin/download/Hinzert-e.pdf. Hanno Rauterberg, "Unverbrüchlich anders," *Die Zeit,* no. 46 (2001).
27. Local comments about the building are found in author conversation with Eli Bar-Chen, June 28, 2009. On the building's assertiveness, see Wolfgang Jean Stock, "Ein Haus der Begegnung: A House of Meeting," in Jutta Fleckenstein and Bernhard Purin, eds., *Jüdisches Museum München: Jewish Museum Munich* (Munich: Prestel Verlag, 2007), 79–89.
28. Dieter Bartetzko, "Der Hinterhof ist überstanden," *FAZ,* November 10, 2006, 39.
29. Till-R. Stoldt, "Das Symbolik der Synagoge," *Die Welt,* December 8, 2002, 11.
30. See the Gemeindeblatt of the Evangelische Kirchengemeinde Bulmke, *Horizonte,* Winter 2003. Accessed 2004. Photo at: http://architektur-wuppertal.de/cms/front_content.php?id cat=3&idart=207.
31. Stoldt, "Das Symbolik der Synagoge."
32. http://www.zvihecker.com/index_entry.html. Wolfgang Pehnt, "Ein altes Buch mit neuen Seiten," *Kunst und Kirche,* no. 4 (2001): 240–42.
33. The Hecker quotation is in Reed Kroloff, "Out of the Ashes," *Architecture,* November 1999, 100. http://www.zvihecker.com/index_entry.html.
34. See Jencks, *Language of Post-Modern Architecture,* 85–87.
35. The school's spiraling form was borrowed from an earlier design for the Ramat Hasharon Civic Centre complex in Tel-Aviv (1986/95). "The Sunflower Berlin," *A + U,* August 1992, 22. "Jewish Optimism: Zvi Hecker's Heinz Galinski School in Berlin," *Archis,* no. 4 (1997): 9–15. For descriptions of the other projects, see www.zvihecker.com.
36. The quotation about Jewish and Christian coexistence is found in Andreas Rossmann, "Fünf Finger sind keine Faust," *FAZ* 24 (June 1999): 49. Kroloff, "Out of the Ashes," 100.
37. "Licht der Diaspora," in *Gebauter Aufbruch,* 54, 57. Manuel Herz, "Meor Hagolah: Licht der Diaspora," *Kunst und Kirche,* no. 4 (2001): 249. "Neubau der Synagoge in Mainz," www.jgmainz.de/synagoge.htm. http://www.arcspace.com/architects/manuel_herz/. Annette Westhoff, "Der Kölner Architekt Manuel Herz entwarf die neue Synagoge in Mainz," *Welt am Sonntag* 3 (November 2002).
38. The reference to the realm of the ordinary appears in Herz, "Meor Hagolah," 249. The quotation about the Nazis as coauthors is in *Gebauter Aufbruch,* 58.
39. Herz describes his family background as follows: "My mother's father fled Germany in the mid-thirties, going to … Palestine. My father's family fled Sweden to South America. They returned to Germany because of cultural roots and a feeling of belonging to Europe." Email from Manuel Herz to author, May 30, 2008. The 2001 remark is found in "Gespräch mit Manuel Herz, Köln," *Kunst und Kirche,* no. 4 (2001): 254.
40. The reference to visibility appears in Annette Westhoff, "Der Kölner Architekt Manuel Herz entwarf die neue Synagoge in Mainz," *Welt am Sonntag* 3 (November 2002). The remark about a Jewish conception of space is found in Manuel Herz, "Neubau der Synagoge in Mainz," www.jgmainz.de/synagoge.htm. Herz was especially interested in how the idea of the eruv, as discussed in the Talmud, distinguished between private and public space in the Jewish tradition. Email from Manuel Herz to author, May 30, 2008. The reference to the absurd is mentioned in "Gespräch mit Manuel Herz, Köln," 254–55. The reference to eliciting attention is in Herz, "Meor Hagolah," 251.
41. On the project's financial difficulties, see Dieter Bartetzko, "Segen im Bau," *FAZ,* December 7, 2000. The Russian project was for the International Lubavitch Center. "Jewish Community Center, Smolensk," *A 10: New European Architecture,* no. 6 (November–December 2005). The 2008 remark appeared in "Mainz erhält eine neue Synagoge," *Frankfurter Rundschau,* February 22, 2008; Roman Hollenstein, "Sebstbewusste Monumente," http://www.magazine-deutschland.de/magazin/IS-Synagoge_5–07.php. Dieter Bartetzko, "Am Ende Siegt das Wort: Neue Synagoge in Mainz," *Frankfurter Allgemeine Zeitung,* September 3, 2010. "Neue Synagoge in Mainz eingeweiht," *Frankfurter Rundschau,* September 3, 2010.
42. "Auf der grünen Wiese," *Jüdische Allgemeine,* October 22, 2009, 11.

43. Richard Chaim Schneider, "Wer braucht eigentlich eine Synagoge?" *SZ*, March 29, 2001. Manuel Herz, "Institutionalized Experiment: The Politics of 'Jewish Architecture' in Germany." *Jewish Social Studies*, Spring–Summer 2005, 63.

44. On the Dresden synagogue, see Susanne Vees-Gulani, "The Politics of New Beginnings: The Continued Exclusion of the Nazi Past in Dresden's Cityscape," in Rosenfeld and Jaskot, *Beyond Berlin*, 38–39. On the Munich bomb plot, see "Szenerie des Grauens," *FAZ*, September 13, 2003. Herz, "Institutionalized Experiment," 64.

45. This was the assessment of Chil Aronson, "Wooden Synagogues of Poland," *Menorah Journal*, Autumn 1937, 326.

46. Piechotka and Piechotka, *Wooden Synagogues*; Alfred Werner, "A Jewish and Unique Art," *Commentary*, July 1960, 90.

47. Richard Meier, "Introduction," *Recent American Synagogue Architecture*, 7. Gruber notes that Davis, Brody, and Wisniewski consulted the Piechotkas' book. Gruber, *American Synagogues*, 160. The rabbi at Sons of Israel commented that the synagogue's form represented a "translation of the lines of the 16th-Century Eastern European synagogue into contemporary architecture." "An Old Tradition," *P/A*, March 1965, 140.

48. The Kayser quotation appears in Piechotka and Piechotka, *Wooden Synagogues*, 5–6. The Oppenheimer remark is in "Temple Sholom," *P/A*, March 1966, 151.

49. Sokolov, "Rm. to Let." Percival Goodman, "Building Type Haunted by History," *Architecture*, January 1986, 75.

50. Alastair Gordon, *Romantic Modernist: The Life and Work of Norman Jaffe, Architect* (New York, 2005), 204.

51. Paul Goldberger, "Norman Jaffe's Grand Design," *Jewish Center of the Hamptons Newsletter*, December 1999. Norman Jaffe Papers, Columbia University, Folder: "Gates of the Grove Synagogue, Published Papers." The Jaffe quotation is found in untitled document labeled "Entrance." Norman Jaffe Papers, Folder: "Gates of the Grove Synagogue: Ten Paths."

52. The Goodman quotation appears in Suzanne Slesin, "Currents; Fusion in a Synagogue," *New York Times*, July 20, 1995. The reference to the Piechotkas' book is in Steve Lipman, "A Shteibel in New England," *Jewish Week*, August 4, 1995, 28.

53. The "neo-shtetl" reference is in William Zimmer, "Art Takes a Prominent Spot in Chester's New Synagogue," *New York Times*, December 9, 2001. Stolzman and Stolzman, *Synagogue Architecture in America*, 240–43. The Hamburg reference appears in Samuel Gruber, "At Syracuse University: Undulating Walls Commemorate Vanishing Barriers," *Forward*, December 10, 2004.

54. The quotation about historical memory is cited in Elizabeth Mehren, "A Real Mensch," *Los Angeles Times*, July 28, 1997, E2. On Moore's building philosophy, see Sandee Brawarsky, "Unearthing a 'Jewish Atlantis,'" *Jewish Week*, June 20, 1997; Jeri Zeder, "Book Center Turns New Page," *Forward*, August 10, 2007, A12. In 2007, plans were announced for a new education wing in the same neo-shtetl style. See also Michael Arnold, "A Yiddishe Home," *Jerusalem Post International Edition*, August 2, 1997, 19. Lansky called it "European shtetl."

55. The Lansky quotation is in Elizabeth Mehren, "A Real Mensch," *Los Angeles Times*, July 28, 1997, E2. The reference to the USHMM is in Arnold, "A Yiddishe Home," 19. The remark about a guilty building is in "Interview with Allen Moore," *The Book Peddler (Der Pakn Treger)*, Summer 1994, 30. The fundraising letter was entitled "Dear Friend" and issued by the National Yiddish Book Center, n.d.

56. *The National Yiddish Book Center: Dedication of the Harry and Jeanette Weinberg Building, Sunday, June 15, 1997; Remarks by Aaron Lansky* (Amherst, Mass.: National Yiddish Book Center, 1997), 3–4, 6–7, 12.

57. The reference to neurosis is found in E. J. Kessler, "Replica of Wooden Synagogue Planned in Calif.," *Forward*, September 10, 1999, 23. On fundraising problems, see June Bell, "Wooden Synagogue Project Abandoned," *Forward*, March 21, 2003, 3. See also www.zabludow.com.

58. Ruth R. Wisse discusses the identification of left-leaning Jews with Yiddish. Ruth R. Wisse, "Yiddish: Past, Present, Imperfect," *Commentary*, November 1997, 38. See also Jeffrey Shandler, "Imagining Yiddishland," *History and Memory*, Spring–Summer 2003, 123–149.

59. On the North Shore synagogue, see Charles K. Gandee, "North Shore Congregation Israel," *Architectural Record*, June 1983, 106; Samuel Gruber, *American Synagogues*, 180–83; "North Shore Congregation Israel," *A + U*, May 1987, 37. On the Belluschi synagogue, see Clausen, *Spiritual Space*, 174–77; *P/A*, June 1990, 122. On Oseh Shalom and Temple Micah, see Benjamin Forgey, "Where God Is in the Details," *Washington Post*, September 16, 1995; Ira Rifkin, "The Synagogue as Statement," *Baltimore Jewish*

Times, January 24, 1992, 15. D1. http://www.templemicah.org/aboutus/ourbuilding/index.html#exterior. Tigerman, *Buildings and Projects,* 216–17. The project was never realized because of objections from neighboring homeowners, who sued the lodge's original owners. Tigerman attributes the defeat to antisemitism. Author interview with Stanley Tigerman, April 22, 2008.

60. The Pittsburgh Jewish center's vertical stair tower was meant to serve as a "beacon, guiding students at night." http://www.rdarch.com/image/4_inst_hillel_s04b.jpg. On the Jewish Center at Williams College, see "Honor Award — New Construction," *Journal of the Interfaith Forum on Religion, Art, and Architecture,* Winter 1991–92, 13. On the Ramaz School, see "A New-Fashioned Schoolhouse," *Architectural Record,* October 1981, 90–93. See also www.jamesrossant.com. On buildings incorporating a sukkah, see www.msafdie.com; "Joseph Slifka Center for Jewish Life," *Architectural Record,* July 1998, 96–101; Wolf, *Daniel Libeskind and the Contemporary Jewish Museum,* 101.

61. Jody Myers, *Kabbalah and the Spiritual Quest: The Kabbalah Centre in America* (Westport, Conn.: Praeger, 2007).

62. Gordon, *Romantic Modernist,* 20, 132, 186, 197, 203.

63. On the bent columns, see Andrea Oppenheimer Dean, "The Beauty of Holiness," *Architecture,* December 1989, 69. Jaffe added that the bent forms recalled Jewish "davening." Quoted in the text of *Interfaith Forum on Religion, Art, and Architecture, 1988 Award of Merit.* Norman Jaffe Papers, Folder: Published Papers: *Journal of the Interfaith Forum.* Jaffe's quotation about light is found in Jaffe, "Redefining the Classic," *Faith and Form: Journal of the Interfaith Forum on Religion, Art, and Architecture,* Spring 1992, 15. Jaffe's remark about the tree is found in Dean, "Beauty of Holiness," 69. The forest comment appears in Jaffe's unpublished manuscript "Ten Arks of the Temple," 15. Norman Jaffe Papers, Folder: "Gates of the Grove Synagogue: Ten Paths."

64. The Jaffe quotations are found in Gordon, *Romantic Modernist,* 144, 205. For reviews of the building, see Dean, "Beauty of Holiness," 69. See also Carol Krinsky, "Gates of the Grove Synagogue: A New Space Encloses the Past, Present, and Future," *Faith and Form,* Winter 1989–90, 45–47. "A Gateway to Prayer," *Architectural Record,* January 1990, 125–27.

65. On Gorlin's design for Libeskind, see Christopher Hawthorne, "The Architect's Architect," *New York Magazine,* April 12, 2004, 32–39. On Gorlin's background, see author interview with Alexander Gorlin, April 8, 2008; Email from Alexander Gorlin to author, May 30, 2008. For Gorlin's Temple project, see Tigerman, *Architecture of Exile,* 177. For a general survey of Gorlin's work, see Alexander Gorlin, *Alexander Gorlin Buildings and Projects* (New York: Rizzoli, 1997).

66. Gorlin, "Biblical Imagery in the Work of Louis I. Kahn," 83–92. Alexander Gorlin, "Architecture and Kabbalah," *Faith and Form,* no. 2 (2008).

67. Author interview with Alexander Gorlin, April 8, 2008. See also printed description, "North Shore Synagogue, Kings Point." Undated document courtesy of Alexander Gorlin Architects.

68. http://www.gorlinarchitects.com/index_content.htm.

69. Email from Alexander Gorlin to author, May 30, 2008. Gorlin writes: "My interest in Kabbalah derives in part from the Holocaust."

70. For a survey of Jewish museums, see Grace Cohen Grossman, *Jewish Museums of the World* (Westport, Conn.: Hugh Lauter Levin, 2003).

71. The reference to strengthening understanding appears in Jan Breslauer, "Skirball's Vision for All Visitors," *Los Angeles Times,* April 20, 1996, 1 http://www.skirball.org/index.php?option=com_content&task=view&id=16.

72. On the use of Jerusalem stone in the museum, see Michael Z. Wise, "The Many Facades of Moshe Safdie: From Columbus Circle to Rabin's Tomb," *Forward,* April 19, 1996, 9. Safdie also originally planned to include a giant smokestack, evoking a concentration camp crematorium, at the center of the Skirball exhibit. Email from Sharon Gillerman to author, July 15, 2008. For the first Herscher quotation, see "Jewish History Museum Opening in Los Angeles," *New York Times,* April 21, 1996. The second Herscher quotation is in Diane Haithman, "Take the 405 to Utopia," *Los Angeles Times,* November 19, 1995, 3.

73. The first two quotations by Safdie are found in Karen D. Stein, "City on a Hill," *Architectural Record,* August 1996, 96. The third Safdie quotation appears in Tom Tugend, "Hillside Heritage," *Jerusalem Post,* April 5, 1996, 9. The fourth Safdie quotation appears in Suzanne Muchnic, "Joyful Forum for Jewish Tradition Building," *Los Angeles Times,* February 21, 1991, 1. The fifth Safdie quotation appears in Herbert Muschamp, "Architecture of Light and Remembrance," *New York Times,* December 15, 1996, section 2, 44. On the Spanish colonial influence of Safdie's design, see Michael Webb, "Expulsion into Paradise," *Metropolis,* July – August 1996, 73, 84. See also Leon Whiteson, "Monument to Identity," *Los Angeles Times,* February 21, 1991, 1.

74. Karen D. Stein, "City on a Hill," *Architectural Record,* August 1996, 96. Muschamp, "Architecture of Light and Remembrance," section 2, 1. The expectation that architecture should express identity also held true for other ethnically related buildings, which explains Nicolai Ouroussoff's disappointment that the Japanese American National Museum in Los Angeles was silent about the "painful history of the Japanese American experience." Nicolai Ouroussoff, "A New Landmark That Could Have Been Much More," *Los Angeles Times,* January 21, 1999, 12.

75. For the first Sulkin quotation, see http://www.spertus.edu/aboutspertus/building/glassfacade.php. The second Sulkin quotation is found in Sharon Cohen, "A Museum of Great Reflection," *Hadassah Magazine,* April 2008, 64.

76. Sulkin's remarks about glass are found in Cohen, "Museum of Great Reflection," 62. The remark about *yehi or* is found in Gilla Wertheimer, "Spertus Steps Up," *Chicago Jewish Star,* November 30 – December 6, 2007, 1. The comment about the Jewish educational tradition is found in Thomas Mullaney, "Creative Visions But for Many Millions Less," *New York Times,* March 12, 2008, 12. Sulkin recalled expressing his initial concern to the architects that their original design was not "Jewish" and convinced them to try to lend it a more distinctively Jewish character. The Krueck and Sexton remarks are found at http://www.ksarch.com. The firm further described the building as a "signature architectural statement about the nature of Jewish culture and learning." The first Kamin quotation is in Blair Kamin, "Like a Cut Diamond," *Architectural Record,* May 1, 2008, 194. The second is in Blair Kamin, "Blades of Glass," *Chicago Tribune,* November 25, 2007.

77. The quotation about educating Jews and non-Jews alike is found at: http://www.nmajh.org/future_nmajh/index.htm. Joseph Dennis Kelly, "Jewish-American Museum Rising in Philly," *Architectural Record,* January 22, 2008. Jon Hurdle, "Alongside the History of the Nation, the Story of Jewish Immigrants," *New York Times,* January 12, 2008.

78. http://www.nmajh.org/future_nmajh/images/Museum_exterior_day.jpg. http://www.nmajh.org/future_nmajh/press_releases/11_11_2002_four_renowned_consultants.html.

79. Kelly, "Jewish-American Museum Rising in Philly." Jon Hurdle, "Alongside the History of the Nation." The Fleischer reference is cited in Gavriel D. Rosenfeld, "When Is a Glass Box Not Just a Glass Box?" *Forward,* July 16, 2010, 13, 15.

80. One of the more critical reviews was Inga Saffron, "Building and Message at Odds," *Philadelphia Inquirer,* November 14, 2010. For a selection of reviews, see "NMAJH in the News" on the museum's webpage: http://www.nmajh.org/photogallery.aspx. See also "Four Architects, Sittin' Around Talkin,'" PlanPhilly, November 16, 2010. http://planphilly.com/four-architects-sittin-around-talkin.

81. Libeskind's rationale for the building contained no references to Jewish themes; it merely asserted that the Center would "provide facilities which will enable its central concept: using the arts and humanities to build community." Email from Alex Rabe at Studio Daniel Libeskind, June 2, 2010. Plans for the center are on hold due to insufficient funds.

Conclusion

1. Slezkine, *Jewish Century,* 24 – 35; for a discussion of how kinship ties worked in the early film industry, see Dennis B. Klein, "The Movies: Notes on the Ethnic Origins of an American Obsession," in Buhle, *Jews and American Popular Culture,* 1 – 12.

2. Melvin L. Mitchell, *The Crisis of the African-American Architect: Conflicting Cultures of Architecture and (Black) Power* (New York: Writers Advantage, 2003), 82 – 83.

3. For a discussion of Muschamp's role, see Michael Lewis, "Architecture (Bling!)," *Commentary,* October 2004, 71 – 75.

4. Fred A. Bernstein, "It's a Bird. It's a Helmet. It's an Eyelid," *New York Times,* October 26, 2003, section 2, 1, 30. To be sure, other Jewish architects continue to crave anonymity. Calatrava's Catalonian colleague, the postmodern architect Ricardo Bofill, is also of Jewish descent, while the Pritzker-winning British architect Richard Rogers is of Italian Jewish background. Neither architect has related to his Jewish heritage in any meaningful way in his work, and so neither is discussed in this study.

5. Betsky, "Building Absence," 43.

6. Amiram Harlap's book *New Israeli Architecture* (Rutherford, N.J.: Fairleigh Dickinson University Press, 1982) was the last major survey. There have been numerous academic studies that have explored Zionist and Israeli notions of architecture and urban space, but there have not been any comprehensive surveys of Israeli architecture since the state's founding in 1948. The best source for learning about Israeli architectural trends is the *Architecture of Israel Quarterly* (*AI*).

7. Author interview with Peter Eisenman, December 5, 2006.

8. Deborah Dash Moore and S. Ilan Troen, eds., *Divergent Jewish Cultures: Israel and America* (New Haven: Yale University Press, 2001).

9. The reference to flimsy homes is in Adolf Friedmann, "Jüdische Kunst in Palästina," *Palästina*, no. 2 (1908): 17–19. See Harlap, *New Israeli Architecture*, 41–42, on Israeli architecture in the early 1900s. On the ugliness of Tel Aviv, see the remarks of Marvin Lowenthal and Ludwig Lewisohn in the *Menorah Journal* in 1925. Quoted in Barbara Mann, *A Place in History: Modernism, Tel Aviv, and the Creation of Jewish Urban Space* (Palo Alto, Calif.: Stanford University Press, 2006), 156. The examples of "oriental" architecture are discussed in Diana Dolev, "Architectural Orientalism in the Hebrew University—the Patrick Geddes and Frank Mears Master-Plan," *Assaph, Studies in Art History* (1998). See also Harlap, *New Israeli Architecture*, 43; Myra Warhaftig, "Alex Baerwald," *Bauwelt*, no. 32 (1990): 1562–64. On the Palm House, see Harlap, 45. See also Sir Banister Fletcher, *A History of Architecture, Twentieth Edition* (London: Architectural Press, 2001), 1457. Barsky apparently wrote on his building "Copyright—all rights reserved—Jewish Style." The Ratner quotation is in S. Ilan Troen, *Imagining Zion: Dreams, Designs, and Realities in a Century of Jewish Settlement* (New Haven: Yale University Press, 2003) 147–48.

10. On the Engel House, see Harlap, *New Israeli Architecture*, 46. On Tel Aviv more broadly, see Michael D. Levin, *White City: International Style Architecture in Israel* (Tel Aviv: Tel Aviv Museum, 1984); Mann, *Place in History*. See also: http://www.whitecity.co.il/english/index.htm. For the Weltsch remark, see Sigal Davidi Kunda and Robert Oxman, "The Flight of the Camel: The Levant Fair of 1934 and the Creation of a Situated Modernism," in Haim Yacobi, ed., *Constructing a Sense of Place: Architecture and the Zionist Discourse* (Aldershot, U.K.: Ashgate, 2004), 64. For the Ratner quotation, see Silvina Sosnovsky, *Yohanan Ratner: The Man, the Architect, and His Work* (Haifa: Architectural Heritage Research Center, 1992), 27E. On Mendelsohn, see Alona Nitzan-Shiftan, "Contested Zionism—Alternative Modernism: Erich Mendelsohn and the Tel Aviv Chug in Mandate Palestine," *Architectural History* 39 (1996): 161–73. Regarding the abandonment of vernacular visions, Mann notes how modernism became defined as Jewish because traditional architecture was deemed to be Arab. Mann, *Place in History*, 163.

11. On the frustration about the lack of an Israeli national style, see Yohanan Ratner, "Will Israel Have a National Style of Architecture?" in Sosnovsky, *Yohanan Ratner*, 35; Harlap, *New Israeli Architecture*, 48–49. Samuel Mozes, "Contemporary Design in Israel," *Architectural Record,* November 1952, 382; see also Harlap, 51. Gershon Canaan agreed, writing in 1951 that "a true national architecture is still in its infancy in modern Israel." Gershon Canaan, *Rebuilding the Land of Israel* (New York: Architectural Book Pub. Co., 1951), 4. On the history and reception of the Knesset, see Susan Hattis Rolef, "The Knesset Building in Giv'at Ram: Planning and Construction," *Cathedra,* October 2003. http://www.knesset.gov.il/building/architecture/eng/article1_eng.htm. Michael D. Levin, "The Second Generation of Israeli Architects," *Journal of Jewish Art,* 1980, 70–78.

12. "The Israel Supreme Court Building," *A + U,* November 1993, 62–65; David Kroyanker, "The New Design Code of Jerusalem: The Fashion of Quoting," *AI,* April 1995, 4–5. "A Long Hall for Jerusalem," *World Architecture,* April 1997, 54. For a critical deconstruction of the Zionist narratives embedded within the Supreme Court building, see Haim Yacobi, "Form Follows Metaphors," *Journal of Architecture,* Summer 2004, 219–39. Lane Flint, "The Search for an Israeli Architectural Identity," *Architect and Builder,* January 1979, 18–21. The headline "Is There an Israeli Style?" was on the cover of the October 1999 issue of *Blueprint,* which featured the article "Non-Style Wars," by David Bass.

13. The reencounter with Arab architecture is discussed in Ami Ran's essay "Encounters: The Vernacular Paradox of Israeli Architecture," *AI,* Spring 1998, 17. The embrace of Mediterranean traditions is mentioned in Alona Nitzan-Shiftan, "The Israeli 'Place' in East Jerusalem: How Israeli Architects Appropriated the Palestinian Aesthetic After the '67 War," *Jerusalem Quarterly,* Summer 2006, 22–25. The Hadid project is discussed in Esther Zandberg, "A Jump Start for Palestinian Architecture," *Haaretz,* December 21, 2006. In light of ongoing Israeli-Palestinian tensions, some Israelis have called for abandoning regionally inspired architecture in favor of the more "authentically" Israeli Bauhaus style. Nitzan-Shiftan, "The Israeli 'Place' in East Jerusalem," 25 – 26.

14. On the Great Synagogue, see Eric Schechter, "Rising from the Ashes," *Jerusalem Report,* May 22, 2000, 28. The synagogue seats 6,000. Gavriel D. Rosenfeld, "A New Ruin Rising: The Hurva Synagogue's Latest Incarnation," *Forward,* November 9, 2007, B1. Lisa Keys, "Repackaging the Old World as a Tourist Attraction," *Forward,* June 6, 2003, 2. http://www.shtetlfoundation.org. Jeffrey Shandler, "The Shtetl Subjunctive: Yaffa Eliach's Living History Museum," in Benjamin Nathans and Gabriella Safran, eds., *Culture Front: Representing Jews in Eastern Europe* (Philadelphia: University of Pennsylvania Press, 2008), 288 – 306.

15. These buildings are discussed in the Fall 1999 issue of *AI.*

16. An exception to this trend is Ram Karmi's Yad Layeled Museum dedicated to children killed in the Holocaust, which was built at Kibbutz Lohamei Hagetaot in 1995. Its circular, tiered form, which descends into the ground, was meant to evoke a whirlpool from which there is no escape. For a discussion, see Yael Padan, "Re-Placing Memory," 257 – 61.

17. For a survey of the debate, see Nicolai Ourossoff, "A Line in the Sand," *New York Times,* January 1, 2006, section 2, 1, 30. See also Eyal Weizman, *Hollow Land: Israel's Architecture of Occupation* (London: Verso, 2007); Rafi Segal, David Tartakover, and Eyal Weizman, eds., *A Civilian Occupation: The Politics of Israeli Architecture* (London: Verso, 2003). Meron Benvenisti, *City of Stone: The Hidden History of Jerusalem* (Berkeley: University of California Press, 1998) and *Sacred Landscape: The Buried History of the Holy Land Since 1948* (Berkeley: University of California Press, 2000). Michael Z. Wise, "Re-Modernizing Tel Aviv," *Travel + Leisure,* August 2005. On the Palmach museum, see David Bass, "Ground Force," *Blueprint,* October 1999, 35 – 37.

18. Michael and Bracha Chyutin, *Architecture and Utopia: The Israeli Experiment* (Aldershot, U.K.: Ashgate, 2007).

19. Some observers contend that the creative impulses of Diaspora Jewish life have somehow gone stale in the Jewish nation-state. Anna Isakova, "The State of Our Arts," *Jerusalem Report,* March 29, 1999, 54. See also Eric Hobsbawm, "Benefits of Diaspora."

20. On the Bilbao Effect, see Witold Rybczynski, "The Bilbao Effect," *Atlantic Monthly,* September 2002. On the iconomy, see Terry Smith, *The Architecture of Aftermath* (Chicago: University of Chicago Press, 2006), 7 – 25. Philip Nobel describes the rise of the term "starchitects" as a phenomenon of the post-9/11 world. Philip Nobel, "Anti-Starchitecture Chic," Metropolismag.com. Posted June 20, 2007. Many more non-Jews can be viewed as starchitects, of course, such as Rem Koolhaas, Zaha Hadid, Jean Nouvel, and Norman Foster, among others. Not only deconstructivism, but also revivalist postmodernism can be seen as guilty of abandoning socially conscious architectural design. See, for example, Paul Goldberger, "80s Design: Wallowing in Opulence and Luxury," *New York Times,* November 13, 1988.

21. Silber, *Architecture of the Absurd.* Silber was especially irked by the cost overruns and leaks that plagued Gehry's Stata Center at MIT. Nikos Salingaros, *Anti-Architecture and Deconstruction* (Solingen: Umbau-Verlag, 2007). Salingaros calls deconstructivism "destructive," "arrogant," and a "cult" that commits "aggression on our senses" by striving to "generate physical anxiety and discomfort" (35, 71). For another critique, see James Gardner, "The Conformity of Rebellion," *New York Sun,* June 1, 2006, 15. For a response to such critiques, see Nicolai Ourossoff, "Let the 'Starchitects' Work All the Angles," *New York Times,* December 16, 2007, 1, 4; Mark Lamster, "The Big Buildup," *Los Angeles Times Book Review,* R2. See also Jencks, *Iconic Building.* Occasionally, antisemitic condemnations of Jewish architects' recent work have surfaced. See http://www.stormfront.org/forum/showthread.php?t=124392. The reference to a "geometry of death" appears in Salingaros, *Anti-Architecture and Deconstruction,* 56.

22. Robin Pogrebin, "I'm the Designer; My Client's the Autocrat," *New York Times,* June 22, 2008, 1, 25.

23. The reference to Wieseltier appears in Pogrebin, *Stars of David,* 156. Herbert Gans, "Symbolic Ethnicity: The Future of Ethnic Groups and Culture in America," *Ethnic and Racial Studies,* no. 1 (January 1979): 8, 12. Gans saw the hallmark of this symbolic ethnicity as "nostalgic allegiance to the culture of the immigrant generation" (9). Whitfield writes that "only religion can form the inspiration core of a viable and meaningful Jewish culture." Whitfield, *In Search of Jewish Culture,* 224. For a discussion of Howe, who claimed that the authentic immigrant experiences that inspired such writers as Abraham Cahan and Henry Roth in the early twentieth century were no longer relevant to younger writers in an era of rapid assimilation, see Adam Rovner, "So Easily Assimilated: The New Immigrant Chic," *AJS Review,* November 23, 2007, 324. Rovner's contention runs counter to the positive assessment of recent American Jewish fiction by Donald Weber, "Permutations of New-World Experiences Rejuvenate Jewish-American Literature," *Chronicle of Higher Education,* September 17, 2004.

24. This holds true for modernists, postmodernists, and deconstructivists. Gehry, Greenberg, Moss, and Meier have never designed a new synagogue. Libeskind, Eisenman, and Tigerman have designed a handful but have never completed one. Only Stern has succeeded in doing so.

25. Gans, "American Jewry: Present and Future," 427–28. For Gans, first generation Jews did not "require the presence of physical objects in order to live [their] . . . culture." Shapiro, *Time for Healing,* 149, 163.

26. Norden, "Yes and No to Holocaust Museums," 32. Ruth Ellen Gruber, *Virtually Jewish,* 127. Michael Wise, "Judaism Under Glass: Are Museums the New Synagogues?" *Forward,* March 18, 1994, 1. This essay also contains the Wieseltier quotation.

27. This argument is implicitly supported by Steven M. Cohen and Ari Kelman's sociological study of the interests of unaffiliated Jews, whom they describe as increasingly interested in nontraditional opportunities for Jewish identification. Quoted in Gabriel Sanders, "They're Building It, But Will They Come?" *Forward,* November 23, 2007, B4.

28. Rosman, *How Jewish Is Jewish History?* 121–30. The National Museum of Australia was built in 2001 in Canberra, by the firm of Ashton Raggatt McDougall (ARM). Jencks, *New Paradigm in Architecture,* 198–203. The developers of South Africa's Apartheid Museum, Solly and Abe Krok, were inspired by the USHMM and brought their team of architects, led by Sidney Abramowitch, to visit before settling on a final design. Chris McGreal, "'We Have Children Who Don't Believe Apartheid Happened,'" *Guardian,* December 12, 2001. See also http://www.stainbank.co.za/images/Founding2of2.pdf.

29. For more on these trends, see Gavriel Rosenfeld, "A Looming Crash or a Soft Landing: Forecasting the Future of the 'Memory Industry,'" *Journal of Modern History,* March 2009, 122–58.

Acknowledgments

As a building nears completion, its construction crew typically holds a topping-out ceremony. The same is true of books. After writers have finished their conclusions and doublechecked their footnotes, they gratefully turn their attention to acknowledging the many people who helped bring their book into existence. I feel very fortunate to be able to partake in this tradition and wish to extend sincere thanks to a great many individuals and institutions. Without their help, my book would not have been built at all.

I first want to thank the many architects who generously made time in their busy schedules to discuss their work with me. Whether sitting down with them in their offices, talking to them over the phone, or exchanging views over email, I was privileged to be able to interact with the very subjects of my study. I am extremely grateful to Hagy Belzberg, Peter Eisenman, Alexander Gorlin, Allan Greenberg, Manuel Herz, Salomon Korn, Daniel Libeskind, Richard Meier, Eric Owen Moss, Robert A. M. Stern, and Stanley Tigerman for patiently answering my questions and showing interest in my research. I would also like to thank the many individuals at their firms who provided me with supporting materials: Thierry Debaille and Alex Rabe at Studio Daniel Libeskind; Ryan Deemer and Vanessa Jauregui at Eric Owen Moss Architects; Brock DeSmit at Belzberg Architects; Peter Dixon at Robert A. M. Stern Architects; Cynthia Davidson and Mathew Ford at Eisenman Architects; Mara Pederson Wilhelm at Tigerman McCurry Architects; Patricia Price at Allan Greenberg Architects; Monika Finger at Architekturbüro Jacoby; Anne Atherley at the National Yiddish Book Center; and Cathy Chase at Kevin Roche John Dinkeloo and Associates. I especially appreciate their willingness to send me scans of buildings, models, and project descriptions. Special thanks, finally, go to Harold DiVito at Tigerman McCurry Architects for providing me with a guided tour of the new Illinois Holocaust Museum and Education Center while it was still under construction.

I am also grateful to Fairfield University for granting me a sabbatical leave during the 2007–8 academic year, which freed me from teaching and enabled me to complete the bulk of my writing. Special thanks go to my department chair, David McFadden, for steadfastly supporting my research proposals, and to Jesus Escobar and Philip Eliasoph in the department of art history for many years of lunchtime architectural discussions. I would also like to extend my appreciation to Ellen Umansky for inviting me to speak about my work in front of her Lunch and Learn students. I owe a special debt of gratitude to John Cayer, the director of Fairfield's DiMenna-Nyselius Library's interlibrary loan office, for ordering me many hard-to-find books and articles. And I am extremely grateful to Dean Robbin D. Crabtree of the College of Arts and Sciences for providing grant money to assist in the book's publication.

Thanks are also due many academic colleagues and friends who provided me with assistance as my book took shape. I am particularly grateful to Carol Krinsky for her extremely careful reading of my first draft, her suggestions for tightening my argument, and her wise but witty corrections of scattered factual errors. I would also like to thank my father, Alvin Rosenfeld, for his perceptive comments on the manuscript from its earliest drafts to its final version. Over the years I have presented portions of my research in different academic settings. I would like to thank the Association for Jewish Studies and the Lessons and Legacies organization for allowing me to speak at their annual and biannual conferences. I am also grateful to the scholars who helped me organize conference panels at which I spoke: Matthew Baigell, Asher Biemann, Matthew Girson, Tal Gozani, Paul Jaskot, Michael Meng, James Young, and Carol Zemel. Further thanks go to Michael Brenner and Eugene Sheppard, who invited me on separate occasions to speak about my work at Brandeis University; David Gissen, who welcomed me to Penn State University; Jonathan Zatlin, who brought me to speak at Harvard University; Alon Confino, who hosted me at the University of Virginia; and Hava Tirosh-Samuelson, who brought me to Arizona State University. I am also grateful to the many scholars who fielded questions and provided valuable feedback as I conducted my research. Thanks go to Betty Blum, David Brownlee, Jan Otakar Fischer, Sharon Gillerman, George M. Goodwin, Grace Cohen Grossman, Samuel Gruber, Thomas Hines, Kathleen James-Chakraborty, Franz Schulze, Susan G. Solomon, Franklin Toker, and Kazys Varnelis. I also appreciate the willingness of Meredith Bzdak, Jesse Cohen, Kent Larson, Marcial Lavina, Jay Nachman, Joshua Nowicki, Marcela Ramos, Alice Roegholt, Avra Shapiro, Sarah Sherman, Chuck Smith, Andrea Wandel, and Isabel von Wendorff to send me copies of photos and articles. Finally, Eli Bar-Chen, Dani Eshet, Josh Goode, Ethan Kleinberg, Adam Rubin, Eugene Sheppard, and Birgit Woldt deserve thanks for years of intellectual exchange.

My sincere gratitude also goes to the individuals and institutions that assisted in the process of editing and producing my book. I would like to thank the anonymous reviewers of Yale University Press for their helpful recommendations. Special thanks go my editor, Michelle Komie, for her many thoughtful editorial suggestions, all of which helped bring my much wordier manuscript to a more manageable size. I am also extremely grateful to Heidi Downey, Sarah Henry, and Mary Mayer — all at Yale Press as well — for their invaluable help in finalizing the book's text and images. Finally, of inestimable help were the Littauer Foundation and the Alisa and Peter Savitz Foundation, both of which generously provided financial assistance that enabled the inclusion of multiple color and black-and-white photographs in the text.

I would also like to extend my appreciation to the clergy and congregants of several synagogues that I visited in the course of my research. I am grateful to Rabbi Jaymee Alpert of Kneses Tifereth Israel in Port Chester, New York, for showing me around its famous modernist sanctuary and for putting me in touch with congregants Jules Harris, Harvey Schiller, and Robert Walker, as well as synagogue administrator Rita Unger, all of whom cordially shared their recollections about the building's history. I would also like to thank Rabbi Josh Davidson at Temple Beth-El in Chappaqua, New York, for walking me through Louis I. Kahn's only realized synagogue and allowing me to look at the congregation's scrapbook of its construction history. Rabbi Mitchell Hurvitz of Temple Sholom in Greenwich, Connecticut, together with congregants Norma Perlstein and Ruth Albert, were similarly helpful in answering questions about the synagogue's history. Thanks also go to Rabbi James Prosnit of Temple B'nai Israel in Bridgeport, Connecticut, for inviting me to speak and showing me the synagogue. I am also grateful to the staff of the new synagogue in Dresden for granting me a quick look at the synagogue's interior without having made prior arrangements. Finally, thanks go to Olga Mack for sharing her recollections about her parents, Albert and Vera List.

In writing this book, I conducted research at a variety of institutions that I would like to acknowledge. Special thanks go to Janet Parks, Julie Tozer, Annemarie van Henneberg, and Jason Escalante at Columbia University's Avery Architecture Library and to Bill Whitaker at the Louis I. Kahn Archive at the University of Pennsylvania. I am also grateful to the personnel at the Jewish Theological Seminary, the Center for Jewish History, the architecture library at Yale University, the University of California at Los Angeles, the Getty Center Research Institute, and the Syracuse University Special Collections Research Center, all of whom were helpful in providing access to various materials.

Finally, I owe a great deal of thanks to my family. I have long been inspired by the example of my cousin-in-law, Barry Gittelson, an accomplished architect in Los Angeles, who has always been eager to chat with me about architectural history and join me on driving trips to significant architectural sites. My book has profited immeasurably from his influence. I would also like to thank my wife, Erika Banks, who long ago became accustomed to being dragged on architectural pilgrimages while on family vacations and who no longer bothers to point out the disproportionate presence of buildings in family photo albums. I am grateful for her indulgence, her companionship, and her love. My children, Julia and Benjamin, also deserve thanks for patiently listening to countless impromptu tutorials on how to recognize different architectural styles ("Look kids, another streamline moderne building!"). I am unendingly grateful for the joy that they bring to my life. Finally, I would like to thank my parents, Alvin and Erna Rosenfeld, who for years have faithfully sent me news clippings about architecture from newspapers and magazines, each of which symbolizes their enduring involvement in my intellectual development. I dedicate this book to all of my family, whose dependability and support are stronger than any building.

Index

Numbers in *italics* indicate images.

Aachen synagogue (Jacoby), 304
Aaron of Lincoln, 26
Abercrombie, Stanley, 360n1
Abramovitz, Max, 68, *69*, 75, *76*, 93, 95, 97, 110–13, 282
Absurdistan (Shteyngart), 293
Academy of Sciences headquarters, proposal for (Berlin; Stern), 250
Adenauer, Konrad, 83, 87
Adjaye, David, 7
Adler, Dankmar, 28
Adorno, Theodor, ix, 46, 155, 164, 176, 216, 260, 262
Aesthetics and History (Berenson), 5
African Americans, architecture of, 7
Albert Speer: Architecture, 1932–1942 (Krier), 151, 152
Alcoa Corporation headquarters (Pittsburgh; Abramovitz), 110, *111*
Aldrophe, Alfred-Philibert, 22
alienation: architects of, 220–34; rooted in mindset of assimilation, 228
allusive modernism, 310
Altes Museum (Berlin; Schinkel), 150
Altneuschul (Prague), *14*, 15, 18
Aly, Götz, 149
American Academy of Rome, 118
Americana Hotel (Miami Beach; Lapidus), 110
American Council for Judaism, 105
American embassy, Angola (L. I. Kahn), 132
American Jewish identity, postwar crisis of, 97–98
American Memorial to Six Million Jews of Europe, proposal for (Mendelsohn), 61–62
American Synagogue for Today and Tomorrow, An (Blake, ed.), 55
Amsterdam School, 29
. . . and the Bush Was Not Consumed (Ferber), 66
aniconism, 3, 4, 5

Animal Crackers House (Tigerman), 221
Animation Studios, Walt Disney Corporation (Burbank, CA; Stern), 245, 293, *294*
Anshei Israel (Tucson; Moore), 68
Anti-Architecture and Deconstruction (Salingaros), 351
antisemitism: Bunshaft's awareness of, 104; causing Jews to question embrace of architectural particularism, 22; decline in, 147; effect of, on E. J. Kahn, 104–5; Eisenman's experiences with, 163–64; Gehry's experiences with, 204–6, 208; Gropius's, 73–74; Johnson's, 72, 73; L. I. Kahn's experiences with, 118; limiting Jewishness of architects' output, 35; Neutra's experiences with, 98–99; in postwar United States, 97–98; proponents of, citing absence of Jewish architectural style, 4–5; reversing trend toward assimilation, 56; Tigerman's experiences with, 223; waning of, in American society, 95; Wright's, 73
Apartheid Museum (Johannesburg), 354
Appelbaum, Ralph, 273, 275
architects. *See* Jewish architects; star system, for architects
Architects' Collaborative, 68–70
Architects' Debate, 150–52, 184, 188
architectural history, field of, 8
architectural meaning, 15–16
Architectural Record, 4, 68
architecture: architectural meaning in, 15–16; collaborative nature of, 35; dialectical tension in, 232; European Jews entering the field of, 21; Hebraic, 153–54; as least individualistic of the arts, 48; liberation of, from classical rules, 153; as most conservative and public of the arts, 344; not confronting the Holocaust, 47–51; optimistic nature of, 34–35;

organic, 152–53; postmodernism's effect on, 145; reflecting realities of Jewish existence, 353; response to, 7; skepticism about, following the Holocaust, 50–51; transitioning from historicism to modernism, 49; unique features of, as branch of modernist movement, 34–35. *See also* religious architecture
Architecture of the Absurd, The (Silber), 351
Architecture of Democracy, The (Greenberg), 238, 239, 240
Architecture of Exile, The (Tigerman), 225
Architecture of Kabbalah, The (Gorlin), 327
architecture parlante, 260, 268, 310
Architecture: A Profession and a Business (Lapidus), 109
Aronoff Center, University of Cincinnati (Eisenman), 172
artificial excavation, 168–72, 174, 306
Ascent at Roebling's Bridge (Covington, KY; Libeskind), 198
Ascher, Felix, 24
assimilation: architects of, 234–50; ideal of, coming under attack, 147
Association for Organic Architecture, 154
Astor Plaza Building (New York; E. J. Kahn), 104
Atheneum (New Harmony, IN; Meier), 252
atrocity, architecture's proper response to, 260, 262
AT&T (Sony) Building (Johnson), 145, *146*
Augsburg, Landauer's synagogue in, 23
authorial intention, 7
autonomy, artistic, 144
Avery Fisher Hall (Philharmonic Hall), Lincoln Center (New York; Abramovitz), 111

Baeck, Leo, 80

Baerwald, Alex, 345
Baigell, Matthew, 129
Baltimore Hebrew Congregation (Goodman), 64
Banham, Reyner, 31
Bank of England (Soane), 323
Barmen Declaration, 309–10
Baron, Salo, 18, 19, 26
Barsky, Joseph, 345
Basevi, George, 28
Bat Yam city hall (Hecker), 312
Bauhaus, antisemitism of members of, 366n59
Bauman, Zygmunt, 149
Bedoire, Fredric, 6, 28
Beebe Residence (Montauk, NY; Stern), 243
Beeby, Thomas, 220
Beehive (Culver City, CA; Moss), 229
Behrens, Peter, 37
Beinecke Rare Books and Manuscript Library, Yale University (New Haven, CT; Bunshaft), 102
Belluschi, Pietro, 68, 70, 71, 323
Below, Bernhard, *86, 87*
Belzberg, Hagy, 284–86
Belzberg Architects, 283–85
Belz World Center (Jerusalem; Blatt), 348
Benjacob, Nick, 286
Benjamin, Walter, 164
ben Judah, Gershom, 313
Berenson, Bernard, 5
Bergen-Belsen, documentation center at, 259
Bergische Synagoge (Wuppertal-Barmen; Goedeking and Schmidt), 309–10, *311*
Berkeley Street office building (Boston; Stern), 245
Berlin: documentation center at, 259; future architectural form of, 152
Berlin City Edge, 192–93
Berlin Holocaust memorial, competition for, 192

Berlin Jewish Community Center (Knoblauch and Heise), 89–91, 298
Berlin Jewish Museum (Libeskind), 179, 186–90, *336*, 337
Berlin Museumsinsel, design for (Gehry), 213
Berlin Wall, 185
Berlin Wall Project design (Tigerman), 226–27
Bernstein, David, 97
Best Buy store (Bloomington, IN), 342, *343*
Beth Shalom (Munich), 316
Beth Sholom (Elkins Park, PA; Wright), 68, 70–71, 72, 73, 75, 123
Beth Sholom (Miami; Goodman), 64, *65*
Beth Sholom Rodfe Zedek (Chester, CT; Lloyd), 320
Beth Zion (Buffalo, NY; Abramovitz), 75, *76*
Betsky, Aaron, 227, 342
Between Zero and Infinity (Libeskind), 182
Biale, David, 2
Biden, Joseph, 335
Bilbao Effect, 350–51
binoculars, Chiat/Day Building (Venice, CA; Oldenburg), *212*
Bitburg Affair, 187, 297
Black Form: Dedicated to the Missing Jews (LeWitt), 320
Blake, Peter, 55
Blanchot, Maurice, 164
Bland, Kalman, 5
Blatt, Yitzhak, 348
Blum, Betty, 227–28
B'nai Amoona Synagogue and Community Center (St. Louis; Mendelsohn), 60–61
Bofill, Ricardo, 145, 412n4
Boman, Thorleif, 5, 7, 153, 154, 164, 224
Booth, Laurence, 220
Börneplatz memorial (Frankfurt; WHLH), 308
Brandeis, Louis, 333

422   Index

Brandeis University: chapels at (Abramovitz), 68, *69*, 71, 112–13; master plan for (Abramovitz), 111
Branham, Joan, 268
Braverman and Helperin, 68
Brazil (dir. Gilliam), 145
Breaking Ground (Libeskind), 196, 198
Breger, William N., 75
Bremen synagogue (Gerle), 88
Breuer, Marcel, 31, 33, 43, 74, 93, 94, 95, 97, 100–105
Bronfman, Samuel, 338
Brunner, Arnold, 95
Buber, Martin, 22
Bunshaft, Gordon, 43, 45, 93, 95, 97, 102–4, 105, 108, 112, 160, 203, 282
Burton, Joseph, 117, 128
Bush (George W.) Presidential Library (Dallas; Stern), 245

CAD (computer-aided design), 210, 212
Calatrava, Santiago, 341
Capen, Judith, 323
Cardinal, Douglas Joseph, 7
Carlebach, Joseph, 4
Carter, Jimmy, 262
Casa del Fascio (Como; Terragni), 177
Casting Center Walt Disney World (Lake Buena Vista, FL; Stern), 245
Castle Clinton (Castle Garden), 126
Cathedral of St. Cecile (Albi, France), 128
CATIA software, 210
CCTV headquarters (China; Koolhaas), 351
Celan, Paul, 47, 196
Celebration (FL), 245
Center for the Visual Arts (Toledo; Gehry), 210
Central Europe, development of Jewish architecture in, 21
Central Intelligence Agency headquarters (Langley, VA; Abramovitz), 110

Central Synagogue (New York; Fernbach), 22
Central Union of German Citizens of the Jewish Faith, 32–33
Chagall, Marc, 34
Chamber Works (Libeskind), 183, 184
Chapel of Notre Dame du Haut (Ronchamp, France; Le Corbusier), 50
Chareau, Pierre, 31–32, 94
Charles, Prince of Wales, 145
Chermayeff, Serge, 39
Chernikov, Yakov, 158
Chiat/Day Building (Venice, CA; Gehry), 212
Chiat (Jay) offices, fish torso conference room (Venice; Gehry), 209
Chicago Seven, 220–21
Childs, David, 197
Chutzpah (Dershowitz), 147
Chyutin, Bracha, 349, 350
Chyutin, Michael, 349, 350
City of Culture of Galicia (Santiago de Compostela, Spain; Eisenman), 283
City Edge proposal (Berlin; Libeskind), 185
City Hall, San Jose (CA; Meier), 252
Civic Center Synagogue (New York; Breger), 75
Clarke, Brian, 303
classicism: embrace of, 235; return to, 244–45
Clausen, Meredith, 56
Cleveland Trust Company skyscraper (Cleveland; Breuer), 100
Clinton (William J.) Presidential Center (Little Rock, AR; Polshek), 270
Cohen, Dennis, 39
Cohen, Mortimer J., 70, 73
Cohen, Stuart, 220
Cohn-Wiener, Ernst, 3
Columbia University School of Architecture, 109
Comcast Center skyscraper (Philadelphia; Stern), 245
Commentary, 54–56

concentration camp iconography, 258, 260, 266, 274–77, 285, 290, 293
Congregation Ahavath Israel (Philadelphia; L. I. Kahn), 119, *120*
Congregation Beth Israel (Berkeley, CA), 322
Congregation B'nai Israel (Bridgeport, CT; Goodman), *52*, 53, 64
Congregation B'nai Israel (Millburn, NJ; Goodman), 65
Congregation Shaarey Zedek (Southfield, MI; Goodman), 64–65, 75
Congregation Shaare Zion synagogue social hall (Brooklyn, NY; Stern), 247
Congregation Sons of Israel (Lakewood, NJ; Davis, Brody, and Wisniewski), 318
Congregation Sons of Israel (Woodmere, NY; Nathan), 68
Connecticut State Library and Supreme Court, West Wing Addition (Hartford; Greenberg), 236
constructivism, 158
Contemporary Arts Center (Cincinnati; Hadid), 159
Contemporary Jewish Museum of San Francisco (Libeskind), *156*, 157, 159, 194–95, 342, *343*
Contemporary Synagogue Art (Kampf), 75
Coop Himmelb(l)au, 157
counter-monuments, 149
Crisis of the African-American Architect, The (Mitchell), 338
Crown Hall building, IIT (Mies), 221
Cuomo, Mario, 269
C.V.-Zeitung, 33

Dachau, documentation center at, 259
Dachau Memorial Chapel (Guttmann), 83–84
Daisy House (Tigerman), 221, *222*
Danish Jewish Museum (Copenhagen; Libeskind), 195

Danziger Studio and Residence (Los Angeles, Gehry), 199
Darmstadt synagogue (Jacoby), 301–3, 305
Davidson, Jo, 105
Davis, Brody, and Wisniewski, 318
Davis, Ron, 202
Davis studio (Malibu; Gehry), 199
decomposition, as new form of architecture, 166–67
deconstruction, 158
deconstructivism, 141, 147, 217; abandoning optimistic faith in progress, 158; as aesthetic response to injustice, 353–54; connecting to modernist ideal of constant innovation, 159; as Jewish movement, 159–60; Nazi past used to legitimize, 248; origins of, 157–58; response to, of Israeli and Jewish Diaspora architects, 349; spread of, 342; translating postmodern skepticism into architectural form, 159; at Yad Vashem, 289–90
"Deconstructivist Architecture" (MoMA, 1988), 157–58, 159
Degussa, 178
De Klerk, Michel, 29, *30,* 31, 33
Denver Art Museum (Libeskind), 198
Derrida, Jacques, 144, 149, 164
Dershowitz, Alan, 147
De Stijl synagogue (Amsterdam-Zuid; Elte), 24
destruction, architectural response to, 48
Destruction of the European Jews (Hilberg), 46
Deutscher, Isaac, 96
dialectical lyric, 232
Dialectic of Enlightenment (Adorno and Horkheimer), 155
Diamond, Jack, 347
Diaspora: architecture resulting from, 349–50; culture of, growing interest in, 322; as reason for lack of Jewish architecture, 4, 5; rendering Jews as outsiders, 177, 280, 299, 338, 344–45
Dimont, Max, 5
Dinkeloo, John, 271
dissimilation, 22–23
Dix, Otto, 34
Dohány Street synagogue (Budapest; Förster), 22
D.O.M. Corporate Headquarters, design for (Germany; Tigerman), 222
domes, in synagogue design, 23, 24, 60
Dortmund synagogue (Goldschmidt), 85, 86
Douglas House (Harbor Springs, MI; Meier), 251
Dresden, buildings of, 296
Dresden Military History Museum, addition to (Libeskind), 198
Dresden synagogue (Libeskind), 193, 194
Dresden synagogue (Semper), 21, 302, 306
Duisburg Jewish community center and synagogue complex (Hecker), 310–13
Duisburg synagogue (Libeskind), 193–94
Düsseldorf synagogue (Guttmann), 81, 83
dynamism, penchant for, 7
DZ Bank headquarters (Berlin; Gehry), 214, 215

Eastern Europe, synagogues in, 19
Eco, Umberto, 145
Edelman, A. M., 24, *25*
Eden Roc hotel (Miami Beach; Lapidus), 108
Edgemar Development commercial complex (Santa Monica; Gehry), 201, 212
Eidlitz, Leopold, vi, 28, 95, 355
Eiffel, Gustav, 34
Eigen Haard housing association (Amsterdam; Klerk), 29, 94
Einstein tower (Potsdam; Mendelsohn), 31
Eisendrath, Maurice N., 68
Eisenman, Peter, 6, 8, 67, 140, 141, 157, 159–79, 182, 194, 196, 206, 208, 209, 217, 283; assailing classicism and modernism, 166; calling for new form of architecture, 166–67; career of, Gehry's career similar to, 202; criticized for his success, 211; criticized for politically indeterminate stance, 177; distinguishing between Jews and Israelis, 177, 344; early career of, 160–61; evolving Jewishness of, 177; fierce critic of postmodernism, 207; Gehry's work similar to, 201; growing interest of, in the Holocaust, 164–66; Holocaust memorials, designs for, 174–77; Jewish identity of, heightened sense of, 162–64; Jewishness of his architecture, 160; Libeskind's criticism of, about Auschwitz's architectural legacy, 184; nihilistic strategy of, 248; opposed to moralism, 178–79; post-Holocaust architecture of, 167–79; preoccupied with formalism, 161–62; private houses designed by, 161, 167; reflecting on the Jewish religion, 172–74; responding to Libeskind's *Micromegas,* 182; self-portrayal of, 352; theme of rupture in works of, 170–72, *173;* theoretical approach of, to architecture, 178; work of, distinguished from Libeskind's, 179–80
Eisler, Max, 24
Elhanani, Arieh, 261
Eliot, T. S., 34
Ellis Island, 126
Elte, Harry, 24, 94
Emanu-El Synagogue and Community Center (Grand Rapids, MI; Mendelsohn), 60
Emery Roth and Sons, 45

Encyclopedia Judaica, 5
Engel, David, 8
Engel House (Tel Aviv; Rechter), 345–46
Enlightenment, 147, 151, 155, 176. *See also* Holocaust, as byproduct of Enlightenment rationality
Enlightenment project, 143
Ennead Architects, 332–35
Erskine, Ralph, 312
Essen, Körner's synagogue in, 23
Essen synagogue (Knoblauch and Heise), 89
essentialism, 7, 357n8
Europe, Jewish wealth in (19th–early 20th c.), 37
Exhibition House, Museum of Modern Art (New York; Breuer), 100
expressionism, 29
exteriority, new Jewish culture of, 352–53
Ezekiel, Moses Jacob, 334–35

Fallingwater (Wright), *38, 39,* 154
Famous Israelite Men and Women . . . (Kohut), 27
Farm House (Greenwich, CT; Greenberg), 237
Fasanenstrasse synagogue (Berlin; Hessel), 23, 79, 89–91
fascist architecture, 177
Federation of German Architects, 36
Felix Nussbaum-Haus (Osnabrück, Germany; Libeskind), 190–92, 193
Ferber, Herbert, 66
Fergusson, James, 132
Fernbach, Henry, 22, 363n40
Fiddler on the Roof, 351
15 Central Park West (New York; Stern), 245
Fifth Avenue Synagogue (New York; Goodman), 64
Filler, Martin, 190, 197
Fishdance Restaurant, fish sculpture (Kobe, Japan; Gehry), 208, 209, *210*
fish forms, in Gehry's work, 206–11

fish lamp (Gehry), 207, 209
Five Polytechnic Institutes (Bangladesh; Tigerman), 220
Fleischer, Joseph, 334
Fleischer, Max, 28
Florence fashion house, fish sculpture at (Gehry), 209
Florida Holocaust Museum (St. Petersburg; Nick Benjacob and Associates), 280, 286
Foer, Jonathan Safran, 352
Fontainebleau hotel (Miami Beach; Lapidus), 108, *109*
Ford, Henry, 35
Ford Foundation Building (New York; Kevin Roche John Dinkeloo and Associates), 271
Ford Motor Company, Kahn's buildings for, 32
Förster, Ludwig von, 22
Foster, Norman, 196
Foucault, Michel, 144, 162
Foucault's Pendulum (Eco), 145
Frampton, Kenneth, 31, 201
Frank, Josef, 32, 94
Fränkel, Josef, 303
Frankfurt Jewish old age home, synagogue for (Guttmann), 81
Frank Gehry: The Complete Works, 202
Freed, James Ingo, 126, 220, 263–68, 270, 271–72
Freedman, Adele, 206
Freedom Tower (Libeskind), 1, 196–97
Freiman, Ziva, 293, 404n22
Freud, Sigmund, 96
Friedlander, Saul, 149
Friedman, Alexander, 348
Friedman, Alice T., 110
Friedmann, Robert, 24

Gad, Dora, 347
Galinski, Heinz, 89
Gallagher and Associates, 287
Gans, Herbert, 97, 351, 352
Gary Group office building (Culver City, CA; Moss), 229, *230*

Gates of the Grove synagogue (East Hampton, NY; Jaffe), 319–20, 324–25
Gaylord, Harry, 205
Gaylord, Hartley, 205
Gehry, Anita, 205, 206
Gehry, Berta, 206
Gehry, Frank, 140, 141, 157, 158, 159–60, 350–51; changing his name, 205; concerned with social justice, 204; criticized for his success, 211; deconstructivist turn in career of, 202; early work of, 199–201; fading interest of, in religion, 203–4; fierce critic of postmodernism, 207; fish forms in work of, 206–11; fragmentation strategy of, 201; importance to, of working in Israel, 216; influences on, 202; Jewish aspects of work of, 202; Jewish identity of, 202–6; nontheoretical bent of, 202; praising Libeskind's Jewish Museum, 213–14; as reluctant representative of deconstructivism, 198–99; residence of, 159; returning to his Jewish background, 206; self-image of, 205–6; self-portrayal of, 352; uncomfortable working in Germany, 214; upbringing of, 203; use of CAD, 210–11; using irony to express Jewishness, 199; working for government of Abu Dhabi, 351; work of, sharing similar origins as Eisenman and Libeskind, 199; works of, linked to the Holocaust, 211–16
Gehry House (Santa Monica; Gehry), 200–201, 209, 213, 217
Gemarker Kirche (Wuppertal-Barmen), 309, *311*
General Motors world headquarters (Detroit; Kahn), *32*
Gerle, Karl, 88
German Architecture Museum (Frankfurt; Ungers), 250
German Jews: searching for truly

Jewish architectural form, 22–23; synagogue architecture of, 21–22
Germany: architects from, confronting the Holocaust, 305–10; early postwar, synagogue architecture in, 78–92; Gehry uncomfortable working in, 214; historical amnesia of, 187–88; increasing Jewish population of, 300; Jewish architecture in, 297–300; Jewish/Christian cooperation on synagogues in, 354; reconstruction strategy for, 49; right-wing extremism in, present political threat of, 316–17; synagogues in, since reunification, 300–310
Gestapo Headquarters (Cologne), 258
Getty Center (Los Angeles; Meier), 251, 252, *253*, 256
Ghirardo, Diane, 177
Giacometti, Alberto, 183
Gilbert, Cass, 269
Gilbert, C. P. H., 271
Gill, Brendan, 269
Gilliam, Terry, 145
Glass House (New Canaan, CT; Johnson), 165
Glazer, Nathan, 57
Gnostic Architecture (Moss), 230–32
Godfrey, Mark, 129
Goedeking and Schmidt, 309–10, *311*
Goff, Bruce, 312
Gold, Michael, 96
Goldberg, Bertrand, 106–8, 112, 282
Goldberger, Paul, 216–17, 235, 319–20, 335
Goldman, Leopold, 36, 37
Goldschmidt, Helmut, 80, 84–87, 91, 301
Goldwyn (Frances Howard) Regional Branch Library (Hollywood; Gehry), 201
Goodman, M. Louis, 320
Goodman, Naomi, 63
Goodman, Paul, 55, 56, 63, 94–95
Goodman, Percival, 5, *52*, 53, 55, 56, 72, 77, 80, 82, 94–95, 101, 112, 124, 129, 135, 319; committed to Jewish architectural projects, 63; design differences between memorials and buildings, 67; disinterest of, in imbuing synagogues with Jewish symbolism, 64; early life and career of, 62–63; early postwar synagogues of, displaying few discernible Jewish traits, 58; effect on, of the Holocaust, 63; emphasizing consolation and reconciliation in Holocaust memorial, 66; modernist architectural principles of, 63–64; most prolific designer of postwar American synagogues, 62; participating in New York City Holocaust memorial competition (1949), 66–67; religious architecture of, epitomizing assimilationist mindset, 68; synagogue designs of, rarely alluding to the Holocaust, 62, 63–66; synagogues of, lacking signature style, 64
"googie" architecture, 64, *65*
Gore Hall, University of Delaware (Newark; Greenberg), 237
Gorlin, Alexander, 326–28
Graetz, Heinrich, 4
Graves, Michael, 160, 166, 245
Great Synagogue (France; Aldrophe), 22
Great Synagogue of Jerusalem (Friedman), 348
Greco, Charles, 24
Greenberg, Allan, 140, 141, 219, 244, 257; as architect of assimilation, 234–42; classical designs of, 235–36; growing up in apartheid South Africa, 238–39; Jewishness of, and its effect on his work, 239–40; promoting classicism as humanistic and democratic form of architecture, 238; refraining from confronting the Holocaust's legacy, 240; training and early career of, 235–36

Greenberg, Clement, 58
Gringauz, Samuel, 50–51
Gropius, Walter, 5, 39, 49, 68, *70*, 72, 73–74, 100, 101, 116, 151–53, 198, 247
Grosse Halle (Berlin; Speer), 240
Ground Zero: competition for, 190; master plan for, 196–98; redeveloping, 1
Gruber, Ruth Ellen, 352–53
Gruber, Samuel, 3, 57, 67
Gruen, Victor, 202
Gruenewald, Max, 65–66
Guardiola House (Eisenman), *167*
Guggenheim, Siegfried, 82–83
Guggenheim, Solomon, 73
Guggenheimer, Ernst, 88–90
Guggenheim Museum (Bilbao; Gehry), 159, 199, 210–11, 350–51
Guttmann, Hermann Zvi, 80–84, 86, 91, 301
Gwathmey, Charles, 160, 196

Habermas, Jürgen, 143
Habitat mass housing scheme, Montreal World Expo of 1967 (Safdie), 288
Hadid, Zaha, 157, 159, 339, 348
Hamburg synagogue (May and Wrongel), 87–88
Hammer-Schenk, Harold, 3
Hammond, Beeby, and Babka, 322–23
Hannover Jewish cemetery reception hall (Guttmann), 81, 82
Hannover synagogue, (Guttmann), 81, 83
Harrison, Wallace K., 93, 110
Haus der Deutschen Kunst (Munich; Troost), *42*
Hebraic architecture, 153–54
Hebraism, as source of architectural creativity, 153–54
Hebrew alphabet, as source of architectural motifs, 174, 180, 194–95, 296, 310–11, 313, 324, 340

Hebrew Thought Compared with Greek (Boman), 5, 153, 154
Hebrew Union College (Safdie), 347
Hecht, Ben, 96
Hecker, Zvi, 301, 310–13, 316, 349
Heidegger, Martin, 5
Heidelberg synagogue (Jacoby), 304–5
Heidereutergasse synagogue (Berlin), 18–19
Heinz-Galinski School (Berlin; Hecker), 312
Heise, Heinz, 78, *79*, 89–90
Hejduk, John, 160
Helmsley Building (New York), 45
Herberg, Will, 56, 98
Herscher, Uri, 329–30
Hertzberg, Arthur, 292
Herz, Manuel, 301, 310, 313–17
Herzl, Theodor, 23
Herzliyah Gymnasium (Tel Aviv; Barsky), 345
Herzog, Elizabeth, 27
Heschel, Abraham Joshua, 51, 153
Hessel, Ehrenfried, 23, 78
Het Schip (Amsterdam; De Klerk), 29, *30*
Hetzelt, Friedrich, 250
Hier, Marvin, 281, 282–83
High Museum of Art (Atlanta; Meier), 252
Hilberg, Raul, 46, 263
Hillel building, Harvard-Radcliffe (Safdie), 323
Hillel Houses (Abramovitz), 112
Hillel Jewish University Center (near University of Pittsburgh; Rothschild Doyno Architects), 323
Hines, Thomas S., 98, 202
Hinzert concentration camp, memorial site at (near Trier; WHLH), 308
Hiram of Tyre, 17
Hirsch, Nikolaus, 308
Hirshhorn Museum (Washington, DC; Bunshaft), 102

Historians' Debate, 151–52, 187, 297
historicism, 21, 24, 25
history, returning to, with postmodernism, 144, 145–47
History of Architecture (Fergusson), 132
Hitchcock, Henry-Russell, 31
Hitler, Adolf, 4, 42, 240–41
Hitler Wave, 149, 385–86n21
Hitzig, Georg Friedrich Heinrich, 28
Hochhuth, Rolf, 47
Hoefer, Andreas, 308
Hoefer, Rena Wandel, 308
Hoffman, Josef, 24
Hoffman garden (Berlin; Libeskind), 193
Hohenzollern Palace (Berlin), reconstruction of, 249
Holl, Steven, 196
Holocaust: absence of references to, in early postwar synagogues, 53; affirmative response to, 56, 126; architectural discourse and, in the postmodern era, 150–55; architectural response to, ix; architecture not confronting, 47–51; artistic works based on, 368–70nn16–26; as byproduct of Enlightenment rationality, 173, 187, 303; Eisenman's growing interest in, 164–66; Gehry's work linked to, 211–16; German architects confronting, in synagogue design, 305–10; history of, field of, 8–9; iconography from, 83–84 (*see also* concentration camp iconography); influencing synagogue architecture in early postwar Germany, 78; Jewish dimensions of, ignored in Eastern Europe, 368n?; legacy of, in architecture, 152, 341–44; L. I. Kahn's approach to, 115–16; limited importance of, for Moss, 233–34; little impact of, on postwar secular Jewish architecture, 93; memory of, periodizing, 342–44; origins of, 386nn22–

26; place of, in American memory, 367n9; in popular culture, 385n19, 386n23; postwar treatment of, by American and European Jews, 368nn11–12, 14–15; postwar western architecture's failure to confront, 45; providing backdrop for understanding Jewish architecture after 1945, 43; providing grounds to renounce architecture, 50–51; rarely invoked in early postwar discussions on synagogue design, 55–56; role of, in discrediting antisemitism in U.S. society, 74; shaping design of recent synagogues, 141; shaping western culture, 342; status of, in western memory, 46; studies of and reflection on, 46–47; viewing, from a redemptive perspective, 56; writings and artwork dealing with, 47
Holocaust consciousness, rise of, 141, 148–50
Holocaust Documentation and Education Center (Hollywood, FL), 280, 287
Holocaust Education Center (Houston), 273
Holocaust Memorial Center of Michigan (Farmington Hills; Neumann Smith and Associates), 258, *259, 275–77, 293, 294*
Holocaust Memorial Council, 263
Holocaust Memorial Foundation of Illinois, 277
Holocaust memorials, 123–27; Eisenman's designs for, 174–77; proposal for, in Frankfurt (Stern), 249–50; proposal for, in New York (Greenberg), 241–42
Holocaust Museum Houston (Ralph Appelbaum Associates with Mucasey), 273–75
Holocaust museums, 141; architecture of, future of, 292–93; differences in, between Europe and the U.S.,

258–60; emergence of, 260–62; lessons of, 354; as new architectural genre, 258, 341–42; rush to build, 352
Holy Holocaust (Morton Moss), 233
hope, in Libeskind's work, 192–93
horizontal skyscrapers (Lissitzky), *30*
Horkheimer, Max, 155
Hot Dog House (Tigerman), 229
House VI (Cornwall, CT; Eisenman), *161*
housing, mass production of, 34
Howe, George, 118
Howe, Irving, 351–52
Huckleberry House (New Canaan, CT; Greenberg), 237
Huff, William, 118
humanism, death of, 165
Hurva synagogue (Jerusalem; L. I. Kahn), 126, 131–34, 348
Huxtable, Ada Louise, 110, 126, 128, 212
hybridity, in postmodernism, 144–45

IBA Apartment Building (Berlin; Eisenman), 168–69
IBA Apartment Houses (Berlin; Tigerman and Stern), *218*, 219, 226, 227, 248–49
iconomy, 351
identity politics, 147
Illinois Holocaust Museum and Education Center (Skokie; Tigerman), 228, 277–80
Illinois Regional Library for the Blind and the Physically Handicapped (Chicago; Tigerman), 220, *221*
immigrant chic, 351
Imperial War Museum of the North (Manchester, England; Libeskind), 196
instability: aura of, in Gehry's works, 212–13; theme of, in Moss's work, 228–32
Institute for Architecture and Urban Studies (IAUS), 161

International Style, 25, 29, 31, 33, 93, 345–46; breaking the hold of, on western architecture, 116–17; functionalism of, 152; in Israel's architecture, 154; in the Middle East, 121
Irwin, Robert, 202
Israel: architecture in, 344–50; importance to Gehry, of working in, 216
Israel Housing Survey Committee, 121
Israel Museum (Mansfeld and Gad), 347
Israel Supreme Court building (Karmi and Karmi-Melamede), 347

Jacken, Werner, 309–10
Jacob Javits Convention Center (New York; Freed), 264
Jacoby, Alfred, 300–305, 308, 316
Jaffe, Norman, 319–20, 324–25
Jaluzot, Jules, 37
James, Kathleen, 6
Janson (Ellen) Residence (Los Angeles; Schindler), 105
Jarrassé, Dominique, 3
Jefferson, Thomas, 238
Jencks, Charles, 6, 160, 202, 207, 208
Jerusalem City Hall (Diamond), 347
Jessie Street Pacific Gas and Electric Power substation (San Francisco), *156*, 157, 174, 194
Jewish architects: absent from elite ranks of modernist movement, 35–36; accomplishments of, compared with Jews in other cultural realms, 9; conformist mindset of, 28, 363n41; differing from other Jewish modernist artists, 34; early postwar synagogues and, 58–68; impact of, on contemporary Jewish life, 351–53; in interwar period, 31–33; losing ability to work in pre–World War II Europe, 36; not following the time concept, 154; as overachievers, 9; possessing weak sense of Jewish identity, 33–34; postwar success of, 93, 94–95, 338–40; reluctant to be identified as "Jewish architects," 8; rise of, and secular Jewish architecture, 25–36; turning to expressionism, 310–17; work of, not achieving major significance (late 1800s–early 1900s), 28
Jewish architecture: absence of, 4; achievements of, 337–41; ancient secular, 25–26; assessing, in the postwar period, 9–11; controversy surrounding, 1–2; defining, viii–ix; diversity of, 15, 16, 340; future of, 354; hastening the assimilation process, 352; Holocaust museums as branch of, debate regarding, 292; Jewishness of, 1, 7–8, 15–16, 141, 339–41; memory of the Holocaust and, 341–44; non-Jewish, 328–35; problem of, 3–6; questioning its benefit for the Jewish people, 350–51; religious, early postwar discussion about, 54–58; revival of religious symbolism, in, 322–28; studying, methodological reflections on, 6–9; superficiality of, 352; surging creativity in, 6
Jewish-Catholic relations, 256
Jewish Center, Williams College (Williamstown, MA; Herbert S. Newman and Partners), 323
Jewish Community Center (Berlin; Knoblauch and Heise), 78, *79*
Jewish Community Center (New Haven, CT; L. I. Kahn), 119
Jewish Community Center of Frankfurt (Korn), 298–99
Jewish Community Centers, 119
Jewish culture, 359–60nn45–49; increasing manifestations of, 357–58n11; problem of, 2–3; trendiness of, 358n12
Jewish Encyclopedia, 4
Jewish history, field of, 8

428 Index

"Jewish Identity in Contemporary Architecture," 6
Jewish Museum (Berlin; Libeskind), 159, 323–24
Jewish Museum (New York; Roche), 63, 271
Jewish museums, building of, masking Jews' internal decay, 352–53
Jewish Museum of San Francisco (Eisenman), 172–74, *175*, 315; design for (Moss), 234
Jewish mysticism, 117
Jewishness: affirmative expressions of, 148; architects' identification with, 353; architectural expressions of, disinterest in, 68; in architecture, 15–16; as category of cultural analysis, 2–3; Eisenman's notion of, 177; Gehry identifying with, 204, 206–7, 213; growing sense of, in traditional Jewish buildings, 296; inhibiting the expression of, 18; lacking in synagogue design, eventually seen as deficiency, 75–76; of L. I. Kahn, 117; of modernist synagogues, 68–74; positive sense of, in Libeskind's work, 193–94; of secular Jewish architecture, 95–98; Stern deemphasizing, 246; traits of, attempting to identify, 7; viewed as a liability, 98
Jewish Town Hall (Prague; Roder), 26
Jews: American, asserting themselves, 147–48; as archetypal outsiders, 29; committed to assimilation, 4; denying their identity, 27–28; embracing symbolic ethnicity, 351–52; entering the architectural profession, 21, 27; increasing prominence of, in western architecture, 1; Israeli, identity of, 344–45; non-Jewish, 96–112; as people without art, 3–4; postmodernism's implications for, 147–48; as prototypical modern/postmodern outsiders, 7–8; second-generation, 97; solidarity of, 338; undistinguished as architects, during the biblical era, 25–26; viewing multiculturalism with suspicion, 147; wealth of, in Europe, 37
"Jews in Modern Architecture: After a Late Start" (Goodman and Goodman), 94–95
John D. O'Bryant African-American Institute (Lee), 7
John Paul II, 256
Johnson, Philip, viii, *42*, 43, 49, 66, 68, *69*, 71–74, 108, 116, 123, 145, 154, 157, 165, 177
Joyce, James, 34
Jubilee Church (La Chiesa di Dio Padre Misericordioso—Rome; Meier), 252, 256
Judaism, elevating time over space, 51
Jüdisches Gemeindehaus (Berlin), 78
Julius, Anthony, 7

Kabbalah, 125, 128–29, 132, 160, 279, 324–28
Kafka, Franz, 34, 96
Kahn, Albert, 32, 33, 35
Kahn, Alphonse, 37
Kahn, Beatrice, 105
Kahn, Bertha Mendelsohn, 117
Kahn, Ely Jacques, 32, 33, 45, 55, 104–5, 364–65n50
Kahn, Esther, 117
Kahn, Louis I., 43, 72, 95, 97, 155, 180–81, 200, 216, 236, 279, 318, 320; ancient architecture's influence on, 121; becoming interested in Nazi past, 125–26; experiencing anti-semitism, 118; forward-looking stance of, 119; identity of, as rootless Jewish outsider, 118; as influence on Kabbalah-informed architecture, 324, 325, 327–28; laying groundwork for architectural embrace of Judaism, 115–16; lending mystical aura to architecture, 116–17; mysticism of, 117; personifying classical qualities of immigrant Jewish experience, 118; postwar work of, shaped by Jewish influences, 119–20; on silence and light, 124–25; style of, 116; synagogues of, 123, 127–34; techno-organicist phase of, 120; travel to Israel, influence of, 121; turning to the past, 120–23; viewed as most important 20th-century Jewish architect, 116; wedded to modernist beliefs, 135; Yale Art Gallery as turning point in success of, 115
Kahn, Nathaniel, 116, 118
Kalamazoo revitalization plan (Gehry), 207
Kallis (Maurice) Residence and Studio (Los Angeles; Schindler), 105
Kamin, Blair, 332
Kampf, Avram, 56, 75, 76
Karmi, Dov, 350
Karmi, Ram, 121, 347, 350, 414n16
Karmi-Melamede, Ada, 347
Karnak, temple of, 132
Kashtan, Aharon, 5
Kassel synagogue (Jacoby), 304
Kastner, Alfred, 119
Katsav, Moshe, 310
Kauffmann, Richard, 32
Kaufman, Karl, 263
Kaufmann, Edgar J., 38, 39, 73, 99
Kaufmann Desert House (Palm Springs; Neutra), 98, *99*
Kayser, Stephen, 318
Kevin Roche John Dinkeloo and Associates, 271
"kidney table" (*Nierentisch*) aesthetic, 81
Kieffer, Jeffry, 128, 327
Kimbell Art Museum (Fort Worth, TX; L. I. Kahn), 122, 123
Kitaj, R. B., 164
Klarwein, Joseph, 347
Klemmer, Klemens, 6
Klerk, Michel de, 94
Kline, Alexander, 55
Klutznick, Philip, 119

Kneses Tifereth Israel (Port Chester, NY; Johnson), viii, 42–43, 68, *69*, 72–73, 75
Knesset (Tel Aviv; Klarwein), 347
Knights of Columbus Tower (New Haven, CT; Kevin Roche John Dinkeloo and Associates), 271
Knoblauch, Charlotte, 309
Knoblauch, Dieter, 78, *79*, 89–90
Knoblauch, Eduard, *20*, 21
Koch, Ed, 268
Kohl, Helmut, 187
Kohut, Adolf, 27
Kol Israel Synagogue (Brooklyn, NY; Stern), 247
Kollegienhaus (Berlin), 188, *189*
Kollek, Teddy, 253
König, Carl, 28
Koolhaas, Rem, 157, 159, 351
Korn, Salomon, 78, 80, 298–300, 301, 303
Körner, Edmund, 23
Kornhäusel, Josef, 21
Kosher Kitchen for a Jewish American Princess (Tigerman), 222
Kosinski, Jerzy, 47
Kramer, Piet, 29
Kreis, Wilhelm, 242
Krier, Leon, 145, 151–52, 164, 177, 178, 184, 240
Krier, Rob, 185
Krinksy, Carol, 3, 5, 57, 102, 319
Kristallnacht, 65–66, 78, 79, 83, 88, 134, 194, 263, 296, 297–98, 306, 314, 334
Kroll, Lucien, 312
Krueck and Sexton, 330–32
KTI. *See* Kneses Tifereth Israel
Kushner, Tony, 322, 352

Lachert, Bohdan, 49–50
Lampugnani, Vittorio Magnano, 151
Landauer, Fritz, 23, 24, *25*, 94
Landsberger, Franz, 3, 5, 55
Lang House (Washington, CT; Stern), 243

Lansky, Aaron, 320–22
Lapidus, Morris, 93, 95, 97, 108–10, 202, 203
Larson, Kent, 133
Lassaw, Ibram, 43
Last of the Just, The (Schwarz-Bart), 241
Law Faculty Building, College of Administration (Rishon LeZion; Rechter and Rechter), 349
Leavitt, Sheldon, 74
Leavitt Associates, 68–70
Le Corbusier, 34, 37, *50*, 116, 151, 161, 240
Lee, David, 7
Leitl, Alfons, 88
Lescaze, William, 118
Levant Fair (1934), 346
Lever House office building (New York; Bunshaft), 45, 102, *103*, 104, 120
Levine, Sherrie, 145
Levy, Benjamin, 39
LeWitt, Sol, 320
Libeskind, Daniel, x, 1, 140, 141, *156*, 157, 159–60, 174, 206, 209, 217, 290, 323–24; accepting commission from Chinese government, 351; apartment for (Gorlin), 326; career of, Gehry's career similar to, 202; changing stature of, 197–98; criticism of, 211, 306; criticizing postmodernism and modernism, 183–84; deconstructivist sensibility of, 182–83; defeated in competitions for Holocaust-related projects, 192; dissatisfaction of, with architecture, 182–83; early career of, 181–82; fierce critic of postmodernism, 207; Herz and, 314–15; Holocaust-related buildings of, 186–93; hope as element of his architectural work, 192–93; Jewish identity of, 180–81; Jewish meanings in designs of, 193–96; marginalized from planning at the World Trade Center site, 354–55; proposed design for Boston's new Jewish museum, 335; self-portrayal of, 352; striving for confrontation with nearby buildings, 188–90, 194; striving to develop distinctly Jewish form of architectural expression, 193; viewing Holocaust from a postmodern perspective, 187; writings of, increasingly invoking the Holocaust, 182–86
Liebermann, Max, 34, 366n60
Life Is with People (Zborowski and Herzog), 27
Life and Shape (Neutra), 98
Lindenstrasse synagogue (Berlin; Hecker, Ullman, and Weizman), 312
Lishinsky, Yosef, 260–61
Lissitzky, El, 29–31, 33
List, Albert and Vera, 72–73
Lloyd, Steven L., 320
Loebenberg, Walter, 286
Loos, Adolf, *36*, 37
Looshaus (Vienna; Loos), *36*
Lorch, Wolfgang, 308
Los Angeles Martyrs Museum, Jewish Federation building, 283
Los Angeles Museum of the Holocaust (Belzberg Architects), 280, 283–86
Louis, Morris, 47
Lovell, Philip, 37–39
Lovell Beach House (Neutra), 31, 37–39
Lovell Health House (Los Angeles; Neutra), 31, *32*, 37–39, 99Loyola University Law School (Gehry), 201
L-shape, in Eisenman's work, 167
Lutyens, Edwin, 236
LVMH Tower (New York; Portzamparc), 331
Lyndon Baines Johnson Presidential Library and Museum (Austin, TX; Bunshaft), 102
Lyotard, Jean-François, 143, 149, 164

Mahler, Alma, 73–74

Maimonides, Moses, 225
Mainz Synagogue and Jewish Community Center (Herz), 313–14
Malevich, Kazimir, 158
Mamilla residential developments (Jerusalem; Safdie), 288, 347
Manchester courthouse (Connecticut; Greenberg), 237
mannerism, 152, 153
Mansfeld, Alfred, 347
Marina City complex (Chicago; Goldberg), 106, *107*
Marx, Karl, 96
Mashantucket Pequot Museum (Polshek), 7
May, Franz, 87–88
McCarter, Robert, 121
Meek, H. A., 3
Meier, Richard, 75, 101, 102, 140, 141, 160, 196, 220, 250–57, 318; considering himself an insider, 254; designs of, moving beyond Corbusian revival, 252; displaying little interest in the Holocaust, 253–54; fundamental architectural concerns of, 254; German commissions of, 254–56; Jewish identity of, privatized, 253; pursuing strict version of modernism, 250–52; whiteness in work of, 254; works of, showing no signs of Jewish influence, 252–53
Memorial to the Murdered Jews of Europe (Berlin; Eisenman), 174–77; design for (Hecker), 312
Memorial to the Six Million Jewish Martyrs (New York; L. I. Kahn), 123–27, 128, 134
memory, architecture of, 145, 178, 186, 188
"Memory Foundations" (Libeskind), x, 1, 196–97
memory studies, 8, 9
Mendelsohn, Abraham, 117
Mendelsohn, Eric/Erich, 27, 31, 33–34, 36, 39, 55, 77, 80, 82, 93, 94, 95, 100, 101, 104, 116, 124, 129, 135, 153–54; believing memory has little place in architecture, 60; believing that Jewish architects should provide consolation, 60; early postwar synagogues of, displaying few discernible Jewish traits, 58; giving his synagogue designs some Jewish symbolism, 60; life of, 59; looking optimistically ahead, 59–60; making little effort to acknowledge the Holocaust in his postwar work, 59–60; nursing resentments against Germans, 59; proposal for American Holocaust memorial, 61–62; trying to create semitic brand of architecture, 346; winning New York City Holocaust memorial competition (1949), 66
Mendelsohn, Louise, 100
Messel, Alfred, 28, 33, 363n41
Mestrovic, Ivan, 61
metanarratives, 158; opposition to, 144; skepticism toward, 149; suspicion of, 264
Metivier, Jean Baptiste, 21
MetLife Building (New York; Emery Roth and Sons), 45
Metropolitan Museum of Art (New York): additions to (Kevin Roche John Dinkeloo and Associates), 271; Lehman Wing (Roche), 273
Metzger, Günther, 303
Miami Beach, Lapidus's hotels in, 108, 110
Micromegas (Libeskind), 182, 183
Mies van der Rohe, Ludwig, 37, *44*, 45, 49, 108, 110, 116, 151, 152–53, 198, 338; as cultural ambassador, 247; influence of, 220–21
Mikveh Israel (Philadelphia; L. I. Kahn), 127–29, 132, 134
Miralles, Enric, 283
Mitchell, Melvin, 338
Moccatta, David, 28
modern architecture, evoking rootlessness of Jewish culture, 5
modernism: ahistorical principles of, balancing with remembrance, 80; American Jews' embrace of, in synagogue design, 57; "dumb box" of, exploding, 201, 202; effect of, on early postwar synagogue architecture, 53–57; fascist leanings of, 154; forward-looking character of, in architecture, 34–35; ignoring local influences, 145; inarticulateness of, 384n6; increasing achievements for Jewish architects in, 29–30; Jewish architects' embracing of, 97; Jews' role in developing, 363–64n42; leading to man's diminution, 162; linked with political and economic conditions, 247; losing credibility, 144; optimism of, 58; path to, in postwar German synagogue architecture, 79–80; postmodernism's effect on, 144–45; rejecting historicism, 24; severing postwar Jewish architecture from the Jewish past, 77; shunning expressions of particularism, 96; success of, in Israel, 345–46; themes of, 34
modernity, project of, 143
modern period, Jewish architectural patronage during, 36–39
Modern Traditionalism, 244
Moholy-Nagy, László, 74
Mole Antonelliana synagogue (Turin), 22
monumentality, 119
Moore, Allen, 320–21
Moore, Cecil, 68
Moore, Charles, 145, 185, 245
Moore House (Ojai; Neutra), 98
Morandi, Giorgio, 202
Moses, Robert, 66–67
Moss, Eric Owen, 140, 141, 219, 228–34, 257; absence of Jewish themes in work of, 228; as architect of alienation, 228–34; assimilated identity of, 233–34; background

Index **431**

of, 232–33; deconstructivist bent of, 228; resisting conventional forms of Jewish identity, 233; self-portrayal of, 352; working for Kazakhstan government, 351
Moss, Morton, 232–33
Mount Zion Synagogue and Community Center (St. Paul, MN; Mendelsohn), 60
Mucasey, Mark, 273
multiculturalism, 147–48
Mumford, Lewis, 24, 73
Münster synagogue (Goldschmidt), 85, 86–87
Muschamp, Herbert, 158, 190, 197, 268, 273, 330
Museum for African Art (Stern), 7
Museum of Contemporary Art (Barcelona; Meier), 252
Museum of Cultural History (Osnabrück, Germany), 190–92
Museum of Decorative Arts (Frankfurt; Meier), 252, 255
Museum of the History of Polish Jews (Warsaw; Gehry), 216
Museum of Jewish Heritage — A Living Memorial to the Holocaust (New York; Roche), 268–73
Museum of Tolerance (Los Angeles; Starkman and Associates), 280, 281–86
My Architect (dir. Nathaniel Kahn), 116, 118
My Holocaust (Reich), 293

Nagle, James, 220
Nathan, Fritz, 68, 94
National Assembly Building (Dhaka, Bangladesh; L. I. Kahn), 122, 123, 128, 132
National Jewish Welfare Board, Building Bureau, 119
National Museum of African American History and Culture, 7
National Museum of the American Indian (Cardinal), 7

National Museum for American Jewish History (Philadelphia; Ennead Architects), 332–35
National Museum of Australia (Canberra), 353–54
National Yiddish Book Center (Amherst, MA), 320–22
Nationale-Nederlanden Office Building (Prague; Gehry), 213, *215*
Native Americans, architecture of, 6–7
Nazi period, modernist memory of, postmodernists challenging, 151
Nazis, architectural philosophy of, 240
neoclassicism, 151, 235
neo-shtetl design, 320
Nerot Mitzvah: Contemporary Ideas for Light in Jewish Ritual, 172
Neue Staatsgalerie (Stuttgart; Stirling), 142, *143,* 146, 150
Neue Zollhoff commercial development (Düsseldorf; Gehry), 210
Neufeld, S. J., 89
Neumann, Kenneth, 276, 277
Neumann/Smith and Associates, 275–77
Neutra, Dione, 100
Neutra, Josephine, 100
Neutra, Richard, 31, *32,* 33, 43, 73, 93, 95, 97–101, 102, 104, 105, 108, 160
New Brutalism, 75, 261
New Center for Arts and Culture, design for (Boston; Libeskind), 335
Newman, Barnett, 47, 129, 279
Newman (Herbert S.) and Partners, 323
Newseum (Washington, DC; Polshek), 270
New Synagogue, Dresden (Wandel Hoefer Lorch and Hirsch), 296, *297,* 305–8, 310
New York Art Commission, 62
New York City Holocaust memorial competition (1949), 66–67, 72
New York Five, 160–61, 220, 244
Nick Benjacob and Associates, 286

Nobel, Philip, 57
nondemocratic governments, architects accepting work from, 351
non-Jewish Jews, 96–112, 204
Norden, Edward, 282, 352
Norman Rockwell Museum (Stockbridge, MA; Stern), 245
North Shore Congregation (Kings Point, NY; Gorlin), 326–28
North Shore Congregation Synagogue (Yamasaki; Chicago), 68, 70
North Shore Synagogue sanctuary and social hall (Glencoe, IL; Hammond, Beeby, and Babka), 322–23
Norton Simon Gallery and Guest House (Malibu, CA; Gehry), 212
nostalgia, 170–71, 188, 302, 322
Nouvel, Jean, 331
Nunotani headquarters (Tokyo; Eisenman), 172, *173*
Nuremberg, documentation center at, 259
Nussbaum, Felix, 190

Obersalzberg mountain retreat (Berchtesgaden), 259
Oberstrasse Temple (Hamburg; Ascher and Friedmann), 24
objective truth, challenge to, 144
Offenbach synagogue (Guttmann), 80–82
Offenbach synagogue (Jacoby), 304
Ohel Jakob synagogue (Munich; WHLH), 308–9, 310, 316
Oldenburg, Claes, 202, *212*
Olin, Margaret, 5
100 Park Avenue (New York; E. J. Kahn), 104
O'Neill Hay Barn (San Juan Capistrano; Gehry), 199
Oppenheimer, Brady, and Lehrecke, 318
Oppenheimer, Herbert, 318, 320
Oppler, Edwin, 22
Oradour-sur-Glane, ruins of, *48*

Oranienburgerstrasse synagogue (Knoblauch; Berlin), *20,* 21
organic architecture, 152–54
Or Shalom, proposal for (Chicago; Tigerman), 323
Osborn, Max, 33
Oseh Shalom (Laurel, MD; Price), 323
Ottostrasse synagogue (Goldschmidt), 85
Ouroussoff, Nicolai, 190, 194

Palestine, Jewish architects in, 344–45; Jewish villages in, 345; Jews of, developing no architectural style, 18; new style in, 346
Palestinian Art and Culture museum (Umm al-Fahm), 348
Palmach History Museum (Tel Aviv; Hecker), 349
Palm House (Tel Aviv; Tabatchnik), 345
parabolic forms, 81–82
parabuildings, 158–59, 228–29
Paramount Laundry building (Culver City, CA; Moss), 229
Park Synagogue (Cleveland; Mendelsohn), *60*
particularism, 21, 22; discouraged, in modern architecture, 35; expressions of, modernism shunning, 96
pastiche, 144
patronage, architectural, 36–39, 94, 338
Pattison, Harriet, 118
Paul, Bruno, 219, 248–49
Paxton, Joseph, 34
Pei, I. M., 263
Pensacola Place II apartment tower (Chicago; Tigerman), *138–39,* 140
Pereire, Emil, 37
Pereire, Isaac, 37
Perkins Eastman, vi
persecution, reflected in Jews' secular buildings, 27
Petal House (Moss), 228, 233
Philadelphia, antisemitism in, 118

Phillips Exeter Academy Library (Exeter, NH; L. I. Kahn), 122
Piacentini, Marcello, 152
Piazza d'Italia (New Orleans; Moore), 145
Piechotka, Kazimierz, 130, 317–18, 319, 320
Piechotka, Maria, 130, 317–18, 319, 320
Pissarro, Camille, 34, 366n60
Plan Voisin (Paris; Le Corbusier), 240
Plauen, synagogue in (Landauer), 24, *25*
Point West Place (Framingham, MA; Stern), *244,* 245
Polish wooden synagogue architecture, 20, 130–31, 317–22
Polshek, James Stewart, 7, 140, 270–71, 332–35
Popkin, Henry, 98
Portae Lucis (Riccio), *128*
Portsmouth Abbey church (Portsmouth, RI; Belluschi), 70
Portzamparc, Christian de, 331
post-functionalism, 162
post-Holocaust culture, 142, 148–50
post-Holocaust era, significance of, 45–46
postmodernism: advent of, effect on Jewish architecture, 140–41; architectural, 145–46; blurring cultural boundaries, 149; criticism of, 207; Eisenman's impressions of, 165–66; fascist leanings of, 154; implications of, for Jewish cultural and social life, 147–48; Lapidus's work anticipating, 108; rise of, 142–47; L. I. Kahn as father of, 117; talmudic thought compared to, 140; Tigerman's move to, 140
postmodernists, implicating modern architecture in the Holocaust, 151
post-structuralism, 143, 144, 155, 158, 164, 166, 172, 178, 207–8, 226, 230, 232
Potsdamer Platz (Berlin): Master Plan proposal (Meier), 255; proposal for reconstruction of (Libeskind), 196
Poundbury (UK), 145
President's Commission on the Holocaust, 262–63
Price, Travis, 323
Pride of Place (PBS), 246
Princeton University, Center for Jewish Life (Princeton, NJ; Stern), 247
"Prison, The" (Gehry), 208, 209
Pritzker Prize, 360n45
Prix, Wolf, 233
Progressive Architecture, 68
Protestant, Catholic, Jew (Herberg), 98
Proust, Marcel, 34
psychoanalysis, 163, 167, 206, 217, 222
Public Library and Federal Government Headquarters (Vancouver; Safdie), 288

Ramaz School (New York; Rossant), 323
Rapaport, Nathan, 123, 216
Rathenau, Emil, 37
Ratner, Yohanan, 345, 346
Rau, Johannes, 310
Rauterberg, Hanno, 308, 213
Rawicz, Piotr, 47
Raymond Hilliard Houses (Chicago; Goldberg), 106
Rebecca's Restaurant fixtures (Venice, CA; Gehry), 207
rebuilding, 47–48
"Recent American Synagogue Architecture" (Jewish Museum, New York), 75, 128, 129, 253
reception theory, 7
Rechter, Amnon, 349
Rechter, Yacov, 347, 349
Rechter, Zeev, 32, 345–46, 350
"Recollecting Forward" (Moss), 234
Redstone, Louis Gordon, 68
reductionism, 7
Regensburg, synagogue of, 18
Reich, Tova, 293

Reich Main Security Office (Berlin), 258–59
Reinhardt (Max) House (Berlin; Eisenman), 172, *173*
religious architecture, Jewish, pre-Holocaust, 16–25
Religious Liberty (Ezekiel), 334–35
Residence and Office Building, Quartier am Tacheles (Berlin; Stern), 249
Riccio, Paolo, 128
Richards (Alfred Newton) Medical Research Building, Univ. of Pennsylvania (L. I. Kahn), 122, 123
Richardson, Peter, 25
Richmond Riverside Development (Surrey, UK; Terry), 145
Rieff, Philip, 242
Rizzi, Renato, 6, 160
Roche, Kevin, 271–73
Roder, Pancratius, *26*
Rogers, Richard, 412n4
Roonstrasse synagogue (Cologne; Below, Schreiterer, Goldsmith), *86,* 87
Rose Center for Earth and Space, Museum of Natural History (New York; Polshek), 270
Rosenberg, Harold, 2, 8
Rosenblatt, Arthur, 263
Rosenzveig, Charles H., 275, 277, 405n39
Rosman, Moshe, 353
Rossant, James, 323
Rossi, Aldo, 145, 154, 165, 303
Roth, Cecil, 3
Roth and Moore, 323
Rothko, Mark, 47, 129
Rothschild, Lionel de, 37
Rothschild Doyno Architects, 323
Royal Ontario Museum (Toronto; Libeskind), 198
ruins: L. I. Kahn's evocation of, 132–34; wrapping around buildings, 132
rupture, 174; defining synagogue architecture in early postwar Germany, 79; as element of Libeskind's works, 192
Ruscha, Ed, 202
Rybczynski, Witold, 202
Rykwert, Joseph, 252

Sabbath, The (Heschel), 51
Sachar, Abraham, 112–13
Sachs, Nelly, 47
Sachsenhausen concentration camp, redesign of, 192, 193
Safdie, Moshe, 118, 140, 284, 287–92, 323, *328,* 329–30, 347
Salingaros, Nikos, 351
Salk Institute for Biological Studies (La Jolla, CA; L. I. Kahn), 122, 128, 132
Saltzman, Murray, 125, 129–30
Saltzman House (East Hampton, NY; Meier), 251
Samitaur office building (Culver City, CA; Moss), 229, *231*
Sans Souci hotel (Miami Beach; Lapidus), 108
Santa Monica Place shopping mall (Gehry), 199
Schatz, Boris, 23
Schindler, Rudolf, 31, 33, 73, 95, 105–6
Schinkel, Karl Friedrich, 150
schismatic postmodernism, 147
Schmertz, Mildred, 268
Schnabel Residence (Brentwood, CA; Gehry), 212
Schneider, Richard Chaim, 316
Schoenberg, Arnold, 34
Scholem, Gershom, 128, 327
Schönberg, Arnold, 96
Schossberger, Henryk, 37
Schreiter, Johannes, 304–5
Schreiterer, Wilhelm Emil, *86,* 87
Schultze-Naumburg, Paul, 4, 150
Schwarz, Karl, 3, 4, 24
Schwarz-Bart, André, 241
Scottish Parliament complex (Edinburgh; Miralles), 283
Scully, Vincent, 117, 121, 134
Scuola Grande Tedesca (Venice), 18, *19*
Scuola Spagnola (Venice), 18
Seagram Building (New York; Mies van der Rohe), *44,* 45, 104, 338
Seattle Public Library (Koolhaas), 159
Second Commandment, 3, 5, 9, 325
Second Congregational Church (Greenwich, CT; Eidlitz), vi, *vii*
Second Temple, 17
secular Jewish architecture: Jewishness of, 95–98; and rise of Jewish architects, 25–36
Sed-Rajna, Gabrielle, 3
Seitenstettengasse Synagogue (Vienna; Kornhäusel), 21
Semper, Gottfried, 21, 296, 302
Sephardic Study Center design (Brooklyn, NY; Stern), 247
sephirot, 128–29
September 11, 2001, architecture after, 354–55
Serra, Richard, 174, 202, 207
708 House (Los Angeles; Moss), 228, *229*
Sha'are Orah, 128
Shahn, Ben, 96
Shaker Village Visitors Center, design for (Pleasant Hill, KY; Tigerman), 222
Shalev, Avner, 290
Shapiro, Edward, 352
Sharon, Arieh, 32, 121, 350
Sharon, Eldar, 347
shtetl: interest in, 384n12; life in, architectural consequences of, 27
Shtetl, The—The Living History Museum of the Jewish World (Rishon LeZion), 348–49
Shteyngart, Gary, 293, 352
Siemens Headquarters (Munich; Meier), 255
Silber, John, 351
Silverstein, Larry, 197
Simon Wiesenthal Center's Beit Hashoah—Museum of Tolerance

(Los Angeles; Starkman and Associates), 280, 281–83
Singer, I. J., 96
Skidmore, Owings, and Merrill, 102, 104
Skirball Cultural Center (Los Angeles; Safdie), 284, 288, *328*, 329–30
Slifka Student Center, Yale University (Roth and Moore), 323
Smith, Frederick, 228
Smith, Laurie Samitaur, 228
Smith, Norris Kelly, 154
Smith, Terry, 351
Smith house, proposal for (Los Angeles; Gehry), 207
Smith House (Darien, CT; Meier), 251
snakes, in Gehry's designs, 208–9
Soane, John, 28
Society for Ethical Culture, 365n52
Solomon, Alan, 402n69
Solomon, Susan, 117, 121, 122, 125, 126, 131
Soltes, Ori, 129
SOM. *See* Skidmore, Owings, and Merrill
Sony Pictures Plaza (Culver City, CA; Starkman and Associates), 282
Sorkin, Michael, 206, 242, 246, 271
South Africa, 238–39, 241, 354
South Florida Holocaust Museum (Hollywood, FL; Gallagher and Associates), 287
Soutine, Chaim, 34, 96, 203, 366n60
Soyer, Raphael, 96
space, devaluing, 51
Speer, Albert, 151, 152, 177, 184, 185–86, 240–41
Speer, Albert, Jr., 178, 179
Speiser, Joseph, 72–73
Spertus Institute of Jewish Studies (Chicago; Krueck and Sexton), 330–32
Spiegel, Paul, 176
Spinoza, Baruch, 96
Spiral Apartment House (Ramat Gan; Hecker), 312

Squadron, Howard, 400n47
stability, penchant for, 7
Stadthaus (Exhibition and Assembly Building—Ulm, Germany; Meier), 252, 254–56
Starkman, Maxwell, 281
Starkman and Associates, 281–82
star system, for architects (starchitecture), 11, 350–51
Stata (Ray and Maria) Center, MIT (Cambridge, MA; Gehry), 212, *213*
Statue of Liberty, 126
Steel Cathedral (New York; Wright), 71
Stein, Karen, 330
Stein, Michael, 37, 39
Steiner, George, 51, 164
Steiner, Hugo, 37
Steiner, Lilly, 37, 39
Steiner Haus (Loos), 37
Stern, Fritz, 304
Stern, Robert A. M., 7, 140, 141, 166, 185, 219, 234–35, 242–50, 257, 293; advocating a return to classicism, 244–45; on architecture providing refuge from problems, 248; assimilationist approach of, 246; avoiding the Holocaust's legacy, 248–50; career of, 242–43; criticizing use of the Nazi past to legitimize deconstructivism, 248; defending classicism over against modernism, 247–48, 250; embracing the American architectural tradition, 246; embracing tradition, 243–44; proposal for Holocaust memorial, 250; taking on Jewish commissions, 246–47; work of, displaying few Jewish influences, 245–46
Stewart, Martha, home of (Greenberg), 237
Stiassny, Wilhelm, 28
Stimmann, Hans, 188
Stirling, James, 142, 145, 150
Stolzman, Daniel, 56
Stolzman, Henry, 56

StoneBreath (Libeskind), 192
Strickland, William, 128
structuralism, 143, 144, 161, 162, 178
Stuttgart synagogue (Guggenheimer), 88–89
suburbanization, 57
Sulkin, Howard A., 331–32
Sullivan, Louis, 28
Summit Jewish Center, design for (New Jersey; Gorlin), 327
Sunset Media Tower (Hollywood; Starkman and Associates), 282
suspension bridge, proposal for (Gehry), 207
Sylvanus, Erwin, 47
"A Symbolic Museum for a Painting That Will Never Go There," plan for (Guernica, Spain; Tigerman), 222
symmetry, 154
synagogue center, 60
Synagogue of El Transito (Toledo), 18
synagogues, 18, 24; American Jews' embrace of modern architecture for, 53–57; architects accepting commission for, to enhance their reputations, 72; becoming Judaism's primary physical locus, 18; critically celebrated, designed by non-Jews, 68–69; in early postwar years, 53, 58–68, 75–76, 78–92; four-pillared stone, 19; increased construction of, after World War II, 56–57; internal configuration of, 23–24; invisibility of, 21; Jewish form of, 53; Kabbalah and, 324–28; of L. I. Kahn, 123, 127–34; modernist, Jewishness of, 68–74; Moorish style of, campaign against, 22; optimistic design predictions for, ignoring the Holocaust, 55–56; postwar, averse to historical reference, 58; subterranean character of, 18–19; wooden, 19, *20*. *See also* Polish wooden synagogue architecture

Index **435**

Tabatchnik, Y. C., 345
Tabernacle, 16, *17*, 25
Talmud, 18, 174, 195, 206, 225, 296, 313, 340
Tampa Bay Holocaust Memorial Museum and Educational Center, 286
Taylor, Mark, 167
Team Disneyland Administration Building (Anaheim, CA; Gehry), 212
Technion (Haifa; Baerwald), 345
Tel Aviv: architecture of, 345–46; "White City" of, 32
Temple (Herod's), 17–18
Temple (Solomon's), 16–17, 132, 225, 227, 280
Temple Beth El (Akron; Braverman and Helperin), 68
Temple Beth El (Bloomfield Hills, MI; Yamasaki), 75
Temple Beth-El (Chappaqua, NY; L. I. Kahn), 125, 126, 129–31, 134, 318
Temple Beth El (Flint, MI; Redstone), 68
Temple Beth El (Gary, IN; Goodman), 64
Temple Beth El (Providence, RI; Goodman), 64
Temple Beth El (Rochester, NY; Goodman), 64
Temple Beth-El (Springfield, MA; Goodman), 64
Temple Beth-El, addition to (Chappaqua, NY; Gorlin), 327
Temple Beth-Israel (Portland, OR; Whitehouse), 323
Temple B'rith Kodesh (Rochester, NY; Belluschi), 68, 70
Temple Israel (Greenfield, MA; Goodman), 320
Temple Micah (Washington, DC; Capen and Weinstein), 323
Temple Oheb Shalom (Baltimore; Gropius), 68, *70*, 72, 73–74
Temple Shalom (Norwalk, CT; Oppenheimer, Brady, and Lehrecke), 318
Temple Sholom (Greenwich, CT; Perkins Eastman), vi–viii, 72–73

Temple Sinai, proposed addition for (Gorlin), 327
Temple Tifereth Israel (Cleveland; Greco), 24
temporariness, as feature of construction, 27
Terragni, Giuseppe, 151, 161, 177, 178
Terry, Quinlan, 145
Theater of the Palace of Abraxas (Paris; Bofill), 145
Theatre (Givatayim; Chyutin and Chyutin), 349
theoretical postmodernism, 147
THINK, 196
Tigerman, Stanley, *138–39*, 140, 203, 219, 232, 249, 257, 323; ambivalent about his Jewish identity, 222–23; as architect of alienation, 220–28; deconstructivist impulses of, 221–22; designing Illinois Holocaust Museum, 278–80; eclecticism of, related to Jewishness, 220, 223–24; increasingly referring to Jewish themes, 222–23; mentioning the Holocaust in his writings, 225–26; opposing Platonic tradition, 224; political outlook of, 220; postmodernist turn of, 221; recommending Aristotelian approach, 224–25; self-portrayal of, 352; on Stern, 246; thematizing the Nazi past, 226–27
tikkun olam, 125, 129, 196, 279
time, role of, in Hebraism, 153–54
Tinterow, Gary, 75–76
Tischler (Adolph) Residence (Los Angeles; Schindler), 105
Toker, Franklin, 6
Towards an Organic Architecture (Zevi), 152, 154
Track 17 memorial (Berlin; WHLH), 308
Tremaine House (Montecito; Neutra), 98
Trenton Bath House (Trenton, NJ; L. I. Kahn), 121–22
Trier synagogue (Leitl), 88

Troost, Paul Ludwig, *42*
Tschumi, Bernard, 157, 158
Tugendhat, Fritz, 37
Tugendhat House (Mies), 37
"Two Hundred Years of American Synagogue Architecture" (Brandeis University), 75–76
Tyng, Anne, 118

Ullman, Micha, 312
Umbrella Building (Culver City, CA; Moss), 229, *231*
UNESCO headquarters (Paris; Breuer), 100
Ungers, Oswald Mathias (O.M.), 85, 145, 250
Union Dime Building (New York; E. J. Kahn), 104
United Architects, 196
United Hebrew Congregation (St. Louis; Belluschi), 323
United Nations headquarters (New York; Abramovitz), *92*, 93
United States: architecture in, during the early postwar period, 49; home of postwar Jewish architectural renaissance, 95; Jewish community in, social ambitions following World War II, 57–58; openness of, to immigrants, 95; rupture in, 226; synagogue construction in, pre-Holocaust, 22
United States Custom House (New York), 269
United States Holocaust Memorial Museum (Washington, DC; Freed), 126, 258, 262–68, 320
universalism: Jews' attraction to, 377n12; pursuit of, 97
Universal Pictures Building (New York; E. J. Kahn), 104, *105*
U.S. State Department, interior remodeling of offices (Washington, DC; Greenberg), 237
U.S. Steel headquarters (Pittsburgh; Abramovitz), 110, 111

Venturi, Robert, 145, 166, 243, 244, 245, 339
Versus: An American Architect's Alternatives (Tigerman), 224–26
verticality, associated with Jewishness, 27
victimization, culture of, 148
Vidler, Anthony, 229
Vienna Holocaust memorial (Eisenman), 174, *175*
Vienna School of Architecture, 32
Vila Olimpica (Barcelona; Gehry), 209, *210*
Villa Schlikker (Osnabrück, Germany), *191,* 192
Villa Stein (Corbusier), 37
Ville Radieuse (Le Corbusier), 236
Vitra International Design Museum (Weil-am-Rhein, Germany; Gehry), 210
voids, as element of Libeskind's works, 186–92
volume zero, 132
Vom Tempel zum Gemeindezentrum (Guttmann), 80, 82
Vontz Center for Molecular Studies, University of Cincinnati (Gehry), 212

Wagner, Richard, 4
Walker Art Center, fish house (Minneapolis; Gehry), 209
Walt Disney Concert Hall (Los Angeles; Gehry), 211
Wandel, Andrea, 308
Warhaftig, Myra, 27–28
Warhol, Andy, 145
"Warning Column" (Berlin Jewish Community Center; Knoblauch and Heise), 90–91
Washington, D.C., Commission of Fine Arts, 263
Webb, Craig, 216
"Wedge of Light" (Libeskind), 196–97
Weese, Ben, 220

Weinstein, Robert, 323
Weisman (Frederick R.) Art and Teaching Museum (Minneapolis; Gehry), 210
Weiss, Peter, 47
Weizman, Eyal, 312
Weltsch, Willie, 346
Werfel, Franz, 74
Werner, Alfred, 317–18
Wertheim department store (Messel), *28*
Westchester Reform Temple (Scarsdale, NY; Breuer), 101
Westenrieder Strasse synagogue (Munich; Metivier), 21
Western Europe, synagogues in, 18–19
Western Wall, 17, *19*
Wexler, Milton, 206
Wexner Center for the Visual Arts (Columbus, OH; Eisenman), 159, 170–71, 176
"What Wall?" warehouse renovation (Culver City, CA; Moss), 229
White, Hayden, 149
Whitehouse, Brookman, 323
Whiteread, Rachel, 174
Whites, the, 160–61
Whitfield, Stephen, 351
Whitney Museum of American Art (New York; Breuer), 100, *101*
WHLH (Wandel Hoefer Lorch and Hirsch), 296, *297,* 301, 305–9, 316
Whyte, William, 15
Wiesel, Elie, 51, 263, 292, 322
Wieseltier, Leon, 351, 353
Wiesenthal, Simon, 94
Wiesenthal (Simon) Center for Human Dignity—Museum of Tolerance Jerusalem (Gehry), 216
Wigley, Mark, 157, 159
Wilshire Boulevard Temple (Los Angeles; Edelman), 24, *25*
Winton Guest House (Wayzata, MN; Gehry), 201
Wischnitzer(-Bernstein), Rachel, 3, 54–55, 56, 75

Wise, Michael Z., 353
Wiseman Residence (Montauk, NY; Stern), 243
Wittgenstein, Ludwig, 303
Wolpa synagogue (Poland), *20*
Wooden Synagogues (Piechotka and Piechotka), 130, 131, 317–18, 319, 320
Woodlawn Gardens Apartment Complex (Chicago; Tigerman), 220
World Savings and Loan Association (West Hollywood; Gehry), 212
World Trade Center, slurry wall of, 196, *197*
Worms, synagogue of, 19
Wosk residence (Beverly Hills; Gehry), 201
Wright, Frank Lloyd, 31, *38, 39,* 68, 70–71, 72, 73, 95, 106, 123, 152, 154
Wrongel, Karl-Heinz, 87–88
Wu (Gordon) Hall, Princeton University (Princeton, NJ; Venturi), 145
Wulff, Christian, 316
Wurman, Richard Saul, 118
Würzburg synagogue (Guttmann), 81

Yad Layeled Museum (Kibbutz Lohamei Hagetaot; Karmi), 414n16
Yad Vashem Holocaust Martyrs' and Heroes' Remembrance Authority (Jerusalem), 260–61, 287–92
Yale University Art Gallery extension (New Haven, CT; L. I. Kahn), *114,* 115, 120
Yamasaki, Minoru, 68, 70, 75
Yeshivat Porat Yosef (Jerusalem; Safdie), 288
Young, James, 194

Zborowski, Mark, 27
Zevi, Bruno, 9, 50, 60, 141, 152–55, 164, 224, 256
zimzum, 125, 129, 279, 326, 327
Zionists, cultural, 23

Index **437**

Illustration Credits

The photographers and the sources of visual material other than the owners indicated in the captions are as follows. Every effort has been made to supply complete and correct credits; if there are errors or omissions, please contact Yale University Press so that corrections can be made in any subsequent edition.

Michael Arad & Peter Walker, courtesy of Studio Daniel Libeskind: 93; The Architectural Archives, University of Pennsylvania, Marshall D. Meyers Collection: 58; Avery Architectural and Fine Arts Archive, Columbia University: 31–34, 159, 163; Belzberg Architects: 140; Peter Berger, from Wikimedia Commons: 125; Bitter Bredt Fotografie, courtesy of Studio Daniel Libeskind: 88–90, 92; Burts, from Wikimedia Commons: 151; James Byrum, from Flickr: 7; Barbara Brady Conn, courtesy of the National Yiddish Book Center: 160; Deror avi, from Wikimedia Commons: 8; Francisco Diez, from Wikimedia Commons: 102; Dick Frank Studio: 74; Ebyabe, from Wikimedia Commons: 141; Eisenman Architects: 73, 75, 80–82; Eric Owen Moss Architects: 111; Esto Images, courtesy of Holocaust Museum Houston: 135; Farewell Mills Gatsch Architects, LLC: 59; The Getty Research Institute, Research Library, Special Collections and Visual Resources: 36; ©Jeff Goldberg/Esto: 78, 167 (courtesy of National Museum of American Jewish History); Alexander Gorlin: 65, 164; Allan Greenberg: 113, 115, 116; ©Geoffrey Gross, *Tomorrow's Houses: New England Modernism* (Rizzoli, 2011): 122; Gryffindor, from Wikimedia Commons: 21; Zvi Hecker: 154, 155; ©Manuel Herz Architects: 156, 157; Hoyasmeg, from Wikimedia Commons: 173; HNK Architectural Photography, Inc., courtesy of Tigerman McCurry Architects: 69; Timothy Hursley: 118, 165 (courtesy of the Skirball Center); Il conte di Luna, from Flickr: 103; J. Paul Getty Trust. Used with permission. Julius Shulman Photography Archive, Research Library at the Getty Research Institute (2004.R.10): 19, 49; Alfred Jacoby: 41, 148, 149; The Jewish Museum, New York/Art Resource, NY: 97; Jlord, from Wikimedia Commons: 27; Bert K, from Flickr: 54; Karla Kaulfuss, from Wikimedia Commons: 166; Kevin Roche John Dinkeloo and Associates LLC: 134; Ulrich Knufinke: 46, 147, 153; Kent Larson: 68; Library of Congress: 20, 171; Louis I. Kahn Collection, University of Pennsylvania and the Pennsylvania Historical and Museum Commission: 61 (George Pohl), 62–64, 67 (George Pohl); Magister, from Wikimedia Commons: 174; Museum Het Schip, Amsterdam: 16; Museum of Tolerance: 139; Till Niermann, from Wikimedia Commons: 99; Josh Nowicki: 136, 144; D. G. Olshavsky/ARTOG, courtesy of Eisenman Architects: 77; Paparutzi, from Flickr: 123; Dave Parker, from Wikimedia Commons: 127; Martin Pauer, from Wikimedia Commons: 14; Rabendeviaregia, from Flickr: 126; Raulbot, from Wikimedia Commons: 114; Riina, from Wikimedia Commons: 100; Paul Rocheleau: 37, 39; Gavriel D. Rosenfeld: 1, 2, 12, 18, 22–25, 28, 35, 38, 40, 43, 47, 50–53, 56, 57, 66, 70, 76, 83, 94–97, 101, 105, 109, 110, 112, 119, 124, 128, 130–133, 138, 146, 152, 158, 161, 162, 168, 169; Bernt Rostad, from Flickr: 10; Rüdiger Wölk, from Wikimedia Commons: 44; Seth Rubin, 4; Hans Peter Schaefer, from Wikimedia Commons: 45; Stefan Schulze, from Wikimedia Commons: 48; David Seide, Defined Space, courtesy of Tigerman McCurry Architects: 137; David Shankbone, from Wikimedia Commons: 71; Shigeo Ogawa/Shinkenchiku, courtesy of Eisenman Architects: 79; 663highland, from Wikimedia Commons: 98; Souravdas, from Flickr: 60; Stu Spivack, from Wikimedia Commons: 29; Robert A. M. Stern: 117, 120, 121; Ştudio Daniel Libeskind: 3, 72, 84, 85–87, 91, 170; Syracuse University Library Special Collections Research Center: 55; Avishai Teicher, from Wikimedia Commons: 175; Tigerman McCurry Architects: 104, 106–108; TwoWings, from Wikimedia Commons: 26; USHMM Photo Archives: 129; Andrea Wandel: 150; Xurble, from Flickr: 145; Yad Vashem: 142, 143; YIVO Institute for Jewish Research: 9, 30.